About This Book

The *Sams Teach Yourself* series from Sams Publishing is designed to carefully instruct readers at the beginning level of its individual topics with step-by-step examples and easy-to-follow instructions. Some topics, of course, are more complex than others and imply some requisite knowledge or experience. This book, *Sams Teach Yourself PL/SQL in 21 Days*, is aimed particularly at readers who have either some knowledge of Oracle (such as power users or database designers) or some knowledge of programming (such as non-Oracle, SQL programmers or nondatabase, C++ programmers, and so on). The goal of this book is to instruct readers how to use Oracle's proprietary extension of the Structured Query Language (SQL) to take full advantage of PL/SQL's specifically designed capabilities for interacting with data in the Oracle environment.

With the recent release of Oracle8, Oracle programmers are in increasing demand, both for new and updated systems. Understanding and using PL/SQL is at the heart of programming for any Oracle system, and this book gives you a strong, solid start in creating scripts that improve the efficiency of adding, modifying, retrieving, and generally working with data—in single, multiple-user, and online database systems.

In *Sams Teach Yourself PL/SQL in 21 Days*, you'll find out the basis of PL/SQL in SQL; how to build programs and scripts—block by block; many new features of Oracle8 for PL/SQL; how to package queries for efficiency; how to use specific responses from the database (or *events*) to create messages for alerting purposes; how to incorporate PL/SQL into a Java program, and much more. By the time you finish your three-week course, you will know the structure, definition, and theory of the components of PL/SQL, such as statements and loops, and how they work together. You also will have on hand complete, reusable scripts to adapt for your own real-world programming needs.

Sams
Teach
Yourself
PL/SQL™

in 21 Days

Sams Teach Yourself
PL/SQL™
in 21 Days

Tom Luers
Timothy Atwood
Jonathan Gennick

SAMS
PUBLISHING

201 West 103rd Street
Indianapolis, Indiana 46290

To my wife Cathy, and children Jon, Sarah, and Matthew
—Tom Luers

To my wife, Michelle
—Tim Atwood

To my daughter Jenny who lost her father for three months while he worked on this book. I love you, and let's schedule a "Daddy Day" soon.
—Jonathan Gennick

Copyright © 1997 by Sams Publishing
FIRST EDITION

International Standard Book Number: 0-672-31123-2

Library of Congress Catalog Card Number: 97-66672

2000   99   4   3

Interpretation of the printing code: The rightmost double-digit number is the year of the book's printing; the rightmost single digit, the number of the book's printing. For example, a printing code of 97-1 shows that the first printing of the book occurred in 1997.

Composed in AGaramond and MCPdigital by Macmillan Computer Publishing

Printed in the United States of America

Trademarks

President   Richard K. Swadley
Publisher and Director of Acquisitions   Jordan Gold
Director of Product Development   Dean Miller
Executive Editor   Rosemarie Graham
Managing Editor   Jodi Jensen
Indexing Manager   Johnna L. VanHoose
Director of Marketing   Kelli S. Spencer
Product Marketing Manager   Wendy Gilbride
Marketing Coordinator   Linda B. Beckwith

Acquisitions Editor
Elaine Brush

Development Editor
Marla Reece

Software Development Specialist
John Warriner

Production Editor
Dana Rhodes Lesh

Copy Editor
Margaret Berson

Indexer
Christine Nelsen

Technical Reviewer
Jeff Shockley

Editorial Coordinators
Mandie Rowell
Katie Wise

Technical Edit Coordinator
Lorraine E. Schaffer

Resource Coordinators
Charlotte Clapp
Deborah Frisby

Editorial Assistants
Carol Ackerman
Andi Richter
Rhonda Tinch-Mize

Cover Designer
Tim Amrhein

Cover Illustration
Eric Lindley

Cover Production
Aren Howell

Book Designer
Gary Adair

Copy Writer
David Reichwein

Production Team Supervisors
Brad Chinn
Andrew Stone

Production
Michael Henry
Tim Osborn
Gene Redding
Ian Smith

Overview

Contents

5 Using Functions, IF Statements, and Loops   **101**

Acknowledgments

I wish to thank my lovely wife, Cathy, and my great kids, Jon, Sarah, and Matt. Without their support, patience, and dedication, this project would not have been possible. I also wish to acknowledge the LSO sports organization and KI for providing many hours of fun for my family while they left me alone to work on this book.

—*Tom Luers*

I would like to thank Elaine Brush, Dana Rhodes Lesh, Marla Reece, and everyone else at Sams who worked hard to bring this book to print. Also thanks to my coauthors, Jonathan Gennick and Tom Luers, for their hard work and contributions.

I would also like to thank my wife who was my inspiration, my children Rebecca and Andrew, and my parents, Ken and Geri, for their support. Thanks to Dianne Warren for accommodating me while working on this book. I would like to thank my cat Dutchess, who kept me company the many times I saw the sunrise while working on this book. Finally, I would like to thank my good friends Glenn Koniewicz, Tom Dunk, and Greg Hodgson who still wonder if I even exist.

—*Tim Atwood*

Many people have put a lot of effort into making this a quality book. You can read their names on the copyright page, and they all have my heartfelt thanks. I would particularly like to thank Elaine Brush for convincing me to work on this book and Marla Reece for her always encouraging comments about my writing.

—*Jonathan Gennick*

About the Authors

Tom Luers

Tom Luers is a senior consultant with a leading international information technology consulting firm. Over the past 14 years, he has worked with clients and business partners in Europe, North America, and Asia. Tom specializes in Oracle technologies and implementing IT solutions to meet manufacturing and engineering business needs. He is also the author of Sams Publishing's *Essential Oracle7*.

Timothy Atwood

Timothy Atwood, a degreed professional in business administration and computer science, currently works as both a consultant and an instructor for Devry Institute of Technology. He has worked in database development, local and wide area networking, Web development, and UNIX/PC programming for various companies, ranging in size from small to Fortune 50. Throughout his 16 years in the field, Tim has used his auditing and business skills as well as his computer expertise to save his clients several million dollars, with the implementation of efficient automation primarily using Oracle.

Jonathan Gennick

Jonathan Gennick is a professional software developer with over 12 years experience using a variety of platforms and technologies. Since 1990, Jonathan has focused on relational database technology, and he has extensive experience with Oracle and Oracle Rdb. Jonathan is currently employed as a senior technology consultant for KPMG Peat Marwick, where he continues to be involved in projects using Oracle, Sybase, and other relational database technologies.

You can reach him by e-mail at `gennick@worldnet.att.net`.

Tell Us What You Think!

As the reader of this book, *you* are our most important critic and commentator. We value your opinion and want to know what we're doing right, what we could do better, what areas you'd like to see us publish in, and any other words of wisdom you're willing to pass our way.

As the Executive Editor for the Database team at Macmillan Computer Publishing, I welcome your comments. You can fax, e-mail, or write me directly to let me know what you did or didn't like about this book[md]as well as what we can do to make our books stronger.

Please note that I cannot help you with technical problems related to the topic of this book, and that due to the high volume of mail I receive, I might not be able to reply to every message.

When you write, please be sure to include this book's title and author as well as your name and phone or fax number. I will carefully review your comments and share them with the author and editors who worked on the book.

Fax: 317-817-7070

E-mail: cs_db@mcp.com

Mail: Bryan Gambrel
            Executive Editor
            Macmillan Computer Publishing
            201 West 103rd Street
            Indianapolis, IN 46290 USA

Introduction

Welcome to *Sams Teach Yourself PL/SQL in 21 Days*. Your purchasing this book indicates that you have an interest in learning the PL/SQL language. PL/SQL is Oracle's relational database procedural programming language. It allows you to develop powerful and complex programs to access and manipulate data in the Oracle database. We have attempted to include as many examples of PL/SQL code as possible to illustrate PL/SQL features.

This book is organized to teach you the major components of Oracle's procedural language in 21 days, a chapter per day. Each chapter covers a specific topic in PL/SQL and should take approximately 3-5 hours to complete. Of course, this time depends on your own pace. This book introduces you to concepts and practical applications of them in your PL/SQL programs. As the authors of this book, we strongly encourage you to practice what you read. Go ahead and type in the listings in your local Oracle database and experience PL/SQL for yourself. Better yet, copy them from the CD-ROM at the end of the book. You will gain a much deeper understanding of PL/SQL by practicing as you go along. Feel free to experiment on your own with any concepts presented, as this will reinforce what you learn.

We have made several assumptions about you, the reader. We have assumed that you are familiar, though not a guru, with SQL and the Oracle database. Specifically, we feel you should have a working knowledge of how SQL works. Additionally, you should have some knowledge about Oracle database objects such as tables and other schema objects. If needed, you might want to read *Teach Yourself SQL in 21 Days* prior to reading this book. We have also assumed that you want to learn some practical applications of PL/SQL and not just the syntax of the language. As such, we have incorporated examples and notes to meet this goal.

What This Book Is About

The beginning of this book lays the foundation on which you will build PL/SQL programs. We discuss the development environment for writing PL/SQL as well as the fundamental structures of PL/SQL. In the first week, you will discover the building blocks of PL/SQL, such as expressions, looping constructs, and built-in functions. After this foundation is built, in the second week, we will move directly into teaching you more advanced PL/SQL. Week 2 teaches you how to build PL/SQL programs with procedures, packages, error-handling routines, composite database structures, triggers, and cursor processing. Finally, the third week covers recursion, dynamic SQL, and transaction processing. When you complete this book, you will be able to develop your own PL/SQL programs. You will have the knowledge to store these programs in the database and execute them.

Many of the chapters build on earlier ones. As the book progresses from chapter to chapter, the topics covered will be drilled down in more detail and complexity. So it is advisable to start at the beginning and work through all 21 days. If you are already familiar with PL/SQL, you can go to the chapters that are of specific interest to you.

You should be aware of the version of your own system in regards to the code that is used here. Although Oracle8 has been released and included in the development of this book, most of the code here is backward compatible with earlier versions of Oracle. We also mention new objects and features of Oracle8 so that those of you who have already upgraded can take advantage of these enhancements.

Is This Book for Me?

This book is developed for the beginning-to-intermediate programmer. Certainly, as a resource, this book is going to be beneficial to the more experienced developer as well. The details covered in this book will allow the novice to get up to speed quickly and start developing PL/SQL applications immediately.

Conventions Used in This Book

This book uses the following typeface conventions:

- ☐ New terms are introduced by the New Term icon **NEW TERM** and appear in *italic*.
- ☐ All code in the listings appears in monospace.

  The Input icon **INPUT** and Output icon **OUTPUT** also identify the nature of the code.

  The combination Input/Output icon **INPUT/OUTPUT** is used with code listings that have both input and output. In these listings, the code that you type in (input) appears in **boldface monospace**, and the output appears in standard monospace without bold.

- ☐ Many code-related terms within the text also appear in monospace.
- ☐ Placeholders in code appear in *italic monospace*.
- ☐ When a line of code is too long to fit on one line of this book, it is broken at a convenient place and continued to the next line. A code continuation character (➥) precedes the continuation of a line of code. (You should type a line of code that has this character as one long line without breaking it.)

☐ Paragraphs that begin with the Analysis icon **ANALYSIS** explain the preceding code example.

☐ The syntax icon identifies syntax statements.

SYNTAX

Special design features enhance the text material:

☐ Notes

☐ Tips

☐ Warnings

☐ Do/Don'ts

NOTE

Notes explain interesting or important points that can help you understand SQL concepts and techniques.

TIP

Tips are little pieces of information that help you in real-world situations. Tips often offer shortcuts or information to make a task easier or faster.

WARNING

Warnings provide information about detrimental performance issues or dangerous errors. Pay careful attention to Warnings.

Do   **Don't**

Do use this concise list for quick reminders on important points.

Don't forget to refer back to these boxes as a quick resource after you've finished the book.

WEEK 1

At a Glance

Get ready! You are about to embark on a three-week journey to learn Oracle's PL/SQL programming language. PL/SQL is at the core of several Oracle products, including Developer/2000 and the Oracle database itself. During the first week, you will cover the basics of the PL/SQL language. During the second week, you will learn some of the more advanced features, and you will also learn how to use PL/SQL in conjunction with the database. Week 2 also explores some of Oracle8's new object-oriented features. The third week takes you into the world of Oracle's built-in packages.

Where You Are Going

Day 1 starts the week off with an introduction to PL/SQL, a discussion of how it relates to other Oracle products, and an example of a stored function written in PL/SQL. Day 2 discusses selecting a development tool and reviews some of the choices available to you in this area. On Days 3 and 4, you will move on to learn the basics of the PL/SQL language. You will learn about the datatypes available to you in PL/SQL and what they can be used for; how to write PL/SQL expressions; and about the block structure used to write PL/SQL code and what that means to you as a developer. Days 5 and 6 teach you about the various control structures, such as loops and IF statements, that are available. The week finishes with Day 7 and a discussion of PL/SQL's built-in functions. Day 7 discusses the major categories of functions that are available, gives you some tips for experimenting with them, and provides examples showing how you can use the more commonly used functions. Good luck and have fun!

Week 1

Day 1

Learning the Basics of PL/SQL

by Jonathan Gennick

Congratulations on your decision to read this book, *Sams Teach Yourself PL/SQL in 21 Days*! If you are new to the Oracle environment, this book will help you quickly learn and master Oracle's built-in procedural language. Knowledge of PL/SQL (Procedural Language/Structured Query Language) is becoming a fundamental necessity no matter which of Oracle's many products you use.

Today, on your first day, you will accomplish these tasks:

- ☐ Learn what PL/SQL is and why you should master it
- ☐ Learn how PL/SQL relates to other Oracle products
- ☐ Learn what resources you need to finish this book
- ☐ Write your first PL/SQL function

Over the remaining 20 days, you'll delve ever deeper into the power and capabilities of this language and learn how to leverage its power in your applications regardless of whether you are doing client/server programming with Oracle's tools (such as Developer/2000), using other front-end tools (such as PowerBuilder), or simply need to write some batch jobs that run on the server.

What Is PL/SQL?

PL/SQL is a procedural language that Oracle developed as an extension to standard SQL in order to provide a way to execute procedural logic on the database.

NEW TERM If you have worked with relational databases in the past, you are no doubt familiar with SQL, which stands for *Structured Query Language*. SQL itself is a powerful declarative language. It is *declarative* in the sense that you describe the results that you want but not how they are obtained. This is good because you can insulate your applications from the specifics of how the data is physically stored. A competent SQL programmer can also push a great deal of processing work back to the server level through the creative use of SQL.

There are limits, though, to what you can accomplish with a single declarative query. The real world is seldom as neat and clean as we would like it to be. Developers often find themselves needing to execute several queries in succession and process the specific results of one query before going on to the next. This leads to two problems in a client/server environment:

- ☐ The procedural logic, that is, the definition of the process, resides on client machines.
- ☐ The need to look at the data from one query and use it as the basis for the next query results in an increased amount of network traffic.

Why are these problems? The procedural logic on client machines can quickly become out of sync if the software is upgraded. It can also be implemented incorrectly, resulting in a loss of database integrity. The need to pull down large amounts of intermediate data to a client results in a long wait for the end users who must sit there staring at the hourglass while the data is transferred to their machines. The cumulative effects of a number of clients pulling large amounts of data across the network add to the slowdown and further decrease performance.

PL/SQL provides a mechanism for developers to add a procedural component at the server level. It has been enhanced to the point where developers now have access to all the features of a full-featured procedural language at the server level. It also forms the basis for programming in Oracle's continually evolving set of client/server development tools, most notably Developer/2000.

Why Learn PL/SQL?

If you are developing with Oracle products, such as Developer/2000, Oracle Forms, or Oracle Reports, the answer to this question is simple. You need to know PL/SQL because those products use PL/SQL for any procedural code. But what if you don't develop with Oracle's products? What if all you use is Oracle's database engine? Is PL/SQL of any use to you? Absolutely, it is!

Regardless of the front-end tool that you are using, you can use PL/SQL to perform processing on the server rather than the client. You can use PL/SQL to encapsulate business rules and other complicated logic. It provides for modularity and abstraction. You can use it in database triggers to code complex constraints, which enforce database integrity; to log changes; and to replicate data. It can also be used with stored procedures and functions to provide enhanced database security. Finally, it provides you with a level of platform independence. Oracle is implemented on many hardware platforms, but PL/SQL is the same on all of them. It makes no difference whether you are running Personal Oracle on a laptop or Oracle7 Workgroup Server on Windows NT.

Regardless of what development tools you use, if you are developing in an Oracle environment, your knowledge of PL/SQL and your ability to apply it will give you a competitive advantage against those who do not. With PL/SQL you have the power to make your applications more robust, more efficient, and more secure.

SQL, SQL*Plus, PL/SQL: What's the Difference?

This question has bedeviled many people new to Oracle. There are several products with the letters "SQL" in the title, and these three, SQL*Plus, SQL, and PL/SQL, are often used together. Because of this, it's easy to become confused as to which product is doing the work and where the work is being done. This section briefly describes each of these three products.

SQL

SQL stands for Structured Query Language. This has become the lingua franca of database access languages. It has been adopted by the International Standards Organization (ISO) and has also been adopted by the American National Standards Institute (ANSI). When you code statements such as SELECT, INSERT, UPDATE, and DELETE, SQL is the language you are using. It is a declarative language and is always executed on the database server. Often you will find yourself coding SQL statements in a development tool, such as PowerBuilder or Visual Basic, but at runtime those statements are sent to the server for execution.

PL/SQL

PL/SQL is Oracle's *Procedural Language* extension to SQL. It, too, usually runs on the database server, but some Oracle products such as Developer/2000 also contain a PL/SQL engine that resides on the client. Thus, you can run your PL/SQL code on either the client or the server depending on which is more appropriate for the task at hand. Unlike SQL, PL/SQL is *procedural*, not declarative. This means that your code specifies exactly how things get done. As in SQL, however, you need some way to send your PL/SQL code up to the server for execution. PL/SQL also enables you to embed SQL statements within its procedural code. This tight-knit relationship between PL/SQL and SQL is the cause for some of the confusion between the products.

SQL*Plus

SQL*Plus is an interactive program that allows you to type in and execute SQL statements. It also enables you to type in and execute PL/SQL code and is one of the most common front ends used to develop and create stored PL/SQL procedures and functions.

What happens when you run SQL*Plus and type in a SQL statement? Where does the processing take place? What exactly does SQL*Plus do, and what does the database do? If you are in a Windows environment and you have a database server somewhere on the network, the following things happen:

1. SQL*Plus transmits your SQL query over the network to the database server.
2. SQL*Plus waits for a reply from the database server.
3. The database server executes the query and transmits the results back to SQL*Plus.
4. SQL*Plus displays the query results on your computer screen.

Even if you're not running in a networked Windows environment, the same things happen. The only difference might be that the database server and SQL*Plus are running on the same physical machine. This would be true, for example, if you were running Personal Oracle on a single PC.

PL/SQL is executed in much the same manner. Type a PL/SQL block into SQL*Plus, and it is transmitted to the database server for execution. If there are any SQL statements in the PL/SQL code, they are sent to the server's SQL engine for execution, and the results are returned back to the PL/SQL program.

The important thing is that SQL*Plus does not execute your SQL queries. SQL*Plus also does not execute your PL/SQL code. SQL*Plus simply serves as your window into the Oracle database, which is where the real action takes place. Figure 1.1 illustrates this relationship.

Figure 1.1.

Relationship of SQL*Plus, PL/SQL, and Oracle.

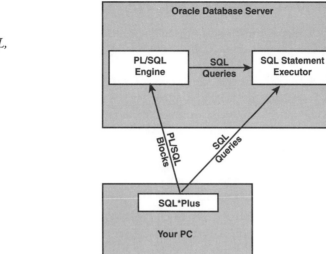

Several other tools besides SQL*Plus can serve as your window to the database. SQL*DBA and its recent replacement, Server Manager, also enable you to execute SQL queries and PL/SQL code. Oracle has a product named Procedure Builder, which is specifically designed for use in the creation and debugging of PL/SQL procedures and functions. In addition, there is a growing list of tools from other vendors that are designed to help developers create SQL queries and stored database procedures.

SQL*Plus is used for most of the examples in this book because of its almost universal availability to developers. It is perhaps still the most widely used tool to develop, test, and create PL/SQL stored procedures and SQL queries.

NOTE

These tools are currently available for the development of server procedures and functions using PL/SQL:

☐ *SQL-Programmer* by Sylvain Faust, Inc.
  Web address: www.sfi-software.com

☐ *SQL-Station* by Platinum Technology, Inc.
  Web address: www.platinum.com

☐ *SQL-Navigator* by TechnoSolutions Corp.
  Web address: www.technosolutions.com

What You Need to Finish This Book

In order to try the examples and complete the exercises in this book, you will need access to

☐ An Oracle7 or later database

☐ SQL*Plus

NOTE

Most of the exercises in this book have been designed to run equally well under both Oracle7 and Oracle8. However, Oracle8 does include several new features that are not found in Oracle7. In particular, you will need Oracle8 in order to run the exercises in Day 13, "Using Oracle8 Objects for Object-Oriented Programming."

You can also use a front-end tool other than SQL*Plus to run the exercises. If you do that, the screen shots won't match because they were done using SQL*Plus, but other than that the listings should run as shown.

If you do not currently have access to an Oracle database, you can obtain a 60-day evaluation version of Personal Oracle from Oracle Corporation. You'll find details on how to obtain this later in this chapter in the section "How to Obtain Personal Oracle."

You will need these database privileges:

☐ CREATE PROCEDURE

☐ CREATE SEQUENCE

☐ CREATE SESSION

☐ CREATE TABLE

☐ CREATE TRIGGER

☐ CREATE VIEW

☐ CREATE TYPE (necessary for Oracle8)

The following Oracle-supplied packages should be available:

☐ DBMS_OUTPUT

☐ DBMS_SQL

☐ UTL_FILE

☐ DBMS_PIPE

☐ DBMS_ALERT

Your database administrator can help you verify that these packages are available to you. Of the preceding packages, the DBMS_OUTPUT is the most essential and is used throughout most of the exercises and examples to display results. The other packages are discussed only in specific chapters.

WARNING

I recommend that you do not use a production database and that you create the sample tables in a schema that is not shared with other users. If you are using Personal Oracle on your own PC, you won't have a problem with this. If you are using an employer's facilities, you might want to discuss use of the database with your employer's database administrator, or DBA, as they are often called. There is nothing inherently dangerous in any of the exercises or examples, but there is always the risk that a coding mistake, such as an infinite loop, might tie up CPU or I/O resources. It's always good etiquette to minimize the potential impact of your mistakes on other developers and end users.

How to Obtain Personal Oracle

Oracle Corporation currently offers a 60-day trial version of Personal Oracle, which is a version of Oracle designed for use by a single user on a desktop PC. If you have a fast Internet connection, you can download it from Oracle's Web site at the following address:

www.oracle.com

If you prefer, you can also order it on CD-ROM from the Oracle Store. Phone 1-800-ORACLE1 for more information.

Getting Started with PL/SQL

By now you should have a basic understanding of what PL/SQL is and how it relates to other Oracle products. You should have access to an Oracle database environment either at work or at home. During the rest of this chapter, you will learn some of the basics of PL/SQL, and you will write your first Oracle stored function.

PL/SQL Is Block Structured

NEW TERM PL/SQL is referred to as a *block structured* language. A PL/SQL block is a syntactical unit that might contain program code, variable declarations, error handlers, procedures, functions, and even other PL/SQL blocks.

The Syntax for a PL/SQL Block

```
DECLARE
    variable_declarations
BEGIN
    program_code
END;
```

In this syntax, `variable_declarations` are any variables that you might want to define. Cursor definitions and nested PL/SQL procedures and functions are also defined here. `program_code` refers to the PL/SQL statements that make up the block.

The declaration section of the PL/SQL block is optional, although in practice it is unusual not to have any declarations at all.

NOTE

> When you're defining PL/SQL functions and procedures, the keyword DECLARE is not used. When defining a function, the function specification, or function header as it is sometimes called, begins the block. Similarly, procedure specifications begin procedure blocks. Function and procedure blocks are covered in more detail on Day 3, "Writing Declarations and Blocks."

NEW TERM Any variable declarations must immediately follow DECLARE and come before BEGIN. The BEGIN and END keywords delimit the procedural portion of the block. This is where the code goes. The semicolon at the end is the PL/SQL statement *terminator*, and signifies the end of the block.

TIP

> Omitting the semicolon at the end of a block is a common oversight. Remember to include it and you will save yourself lots of aggravation.

Blocks such as the one shown in the syntax "The Syntax for a PL/SQL Block" form the basis for all PL/SQL programming. An Oracle stored procedure consists of one PL/SQL block. An Oracle stored function consists of one PL/SQL block. An Oracle database trigger consists of one PL/SQL block. It is not possible to execute PL/SQL code except as part of a block.

PL/SQL blocks can be *nested*. One block can contain another block as in the following example:

```
DECLARE
    variable declarations go here
BEGIN
    some program code
```

```
BEGIN
  code in a nested block
END;
  more program code
END;
```

Nesting blocks is often done for error-handling purposes. You will read more about error handling on Day 8, "Procedures, Packages, Errors, and Exceptions."

Compiling and Executing a Simple Block

Are you ready to try writing your first PL/SQL code? Good. Remember that for this and all other examples in this book, you will be using SQL*Plus to send the PL/SQL code to the Oracle database for execution.

NOTE

If you are using Personal Oracle, you must first start your Oracle database by running the Start Database program from the Personal Oracle7 program group.

1. Begin by running SQL*Plus and connecting to your Oracle database. Your initial SQL*Plus screen should look like the one shown in Figure 1.2.

Figure 1.2.

*Initial SQL*Plus screen.*

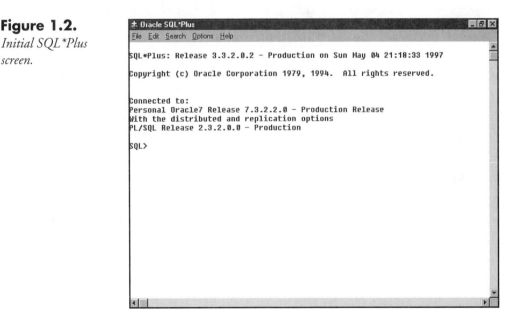

2. Next, type in the following lines of code from Listing 1.1 exactly as shown. Notice the slash at the end. It must be typed in as well, exactly as shown.

 Listing 1.1. Your first PL/SQL block.

```
DECLARE
  x        INTEGER;
BEGIN
  x := 65400;
END;
/
```

 NOTE

The slash at the end tells SQL*Plus that you are done typing PL/SQL code. SQL*Plus will then transmit that code to the Oracle database for execution. The slash has meaning to SQL*Plus only, not to PL/SQL.

TIP

The slash character must be typed on a line by itself; otherwise, it will be sent to the database and generate an error message. It must also be the first character on the line.

After you type the slash, SQL*Plus transmits your code to Oracle for execution. After your code executes, your SQL*Plus screen should look like Figure 1.3.

The code you just executed was probably not very exciting, possibly because there was no output. PL/SQL does have some limited output facilities, and next you will learn how to produce some simple screen output.

What About Some Output?

When it was originally designed, PL/SQL had no output facilities at all. Remember that PL/SQL is not a standalone language. It is almost always used in conjunction with some other program or tool that handles the input, output, and other user interaction.

Oracle now includes the DBMS_OUTPUT package with PL/SQL, which provides you with some limited output capabilities. You will learn more about packages during Day 8, but for now it's enough to know that you can use the dbms_output.put_line procedure as shown in Listing 1.2.

Figure 1.3.

SQL*Plus screen after executing a PL/SQL block.

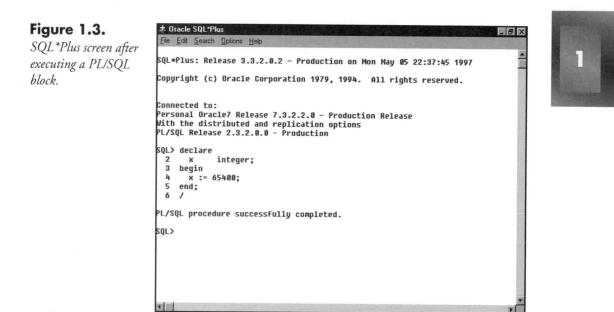

Listing 1.2. PL/SQL block showing the use of the `dbms_output.put_line` procedure.

```
DECLARE
  x      INTEGER;
BEGIN
  x := 65400;
  dbms_output.put_line('The variable  X = ');
  dbms_output.put_line(x);
END;
/
```

The `dbms_output.put_line()` procedure takes exactly one argument and generates a line of text as output from the database server. In order for you to see that line of text, you must tell SQL*Plus to display it. This is done with the SQL*Plus command:

`SQL> SET SERVEROUTPUT ON`

1. Type the preceding command now. It needs to be executed only once per session, so you won't need to reissue it unless you exit SQL*Plus and get back in again.

2. Next, type in the PL/SQL code from Listing 1.2. The resulting output from SQL*Plus should look like that shown in Figure 1.4.

OUTPUT

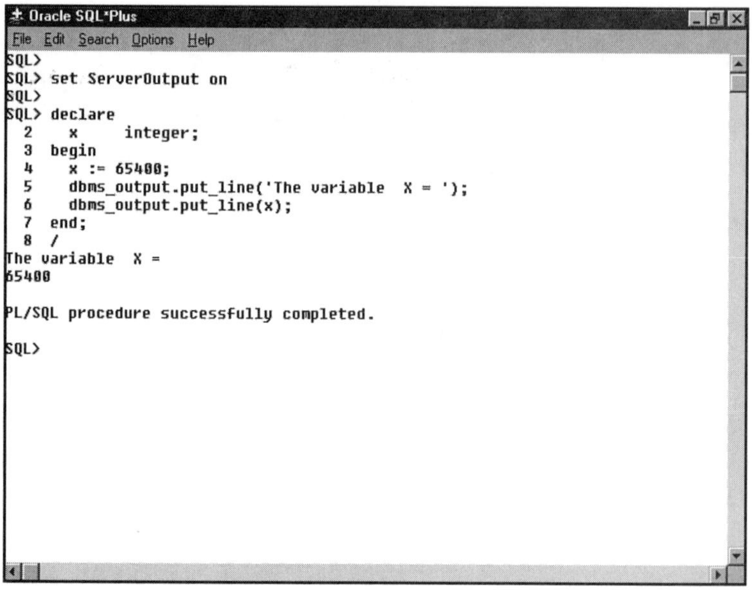

Figure 1.4.

Producing output
with dbms_
output.put_line().

```
± Oracle SQL*Plus                                          _ 8 X
File  Edit  Search  Options  Help
SQL>
SQL> set ServerOutput on
SQL>
SQL> declare
  2    x       integer;
  3  begin
  4    x := 65400;
  5    dbms_output.put_line('The variable  X = ');
  6    dbms_output.put_line(x);
  7  end;
  8  /
The variable  X =
65400

PL/SQL procedure successfully completed.

SQL>
```

NOTE

It is SQL*Plus that prints the server output on the screen for you to see. You must remember to execute the SET SERVEROUTPUT ON command, or you won't see any output. You also can use the SET SERVEROUTPUT OFF command to turn off output when you don't want to see it.

Alternatives to Retyping

Until now you have been retyping each PL/SQL block as you tried it. No doubt, if you made a mistake, you had to type the code all over again. It is possible to place your PL/SQL code in files, and depending on your personal preferences and just what you are trying to do, there are three basic ways to go about this:

☐ Cut and paste from Notepad.

☐ Execute a text file using the SQL*Plus @ command.

☐ Use the SQL*Plus EDIT command.

The first method involves running Windows Notepad, typing your PL/SQL code (or SQL queries) into it, and then copying and pasting from Notepad into SQL*Plus to execute the desired code. This method is ideal for experimenting with short snippets of PL/SQL code and SQL queries. You can keep several related items in the same text file where you can easily call them up when you want to work on them.

The second method makes use of a SQL*Plus command to execute a file. For example, if you have a text file named `test.sql` with the code from Listing 1.2, you could execute that file by typing this command:

```
SQL> @c:\a\test
```

The resulting SQL*Plus screen output would look like Figure 1.5.

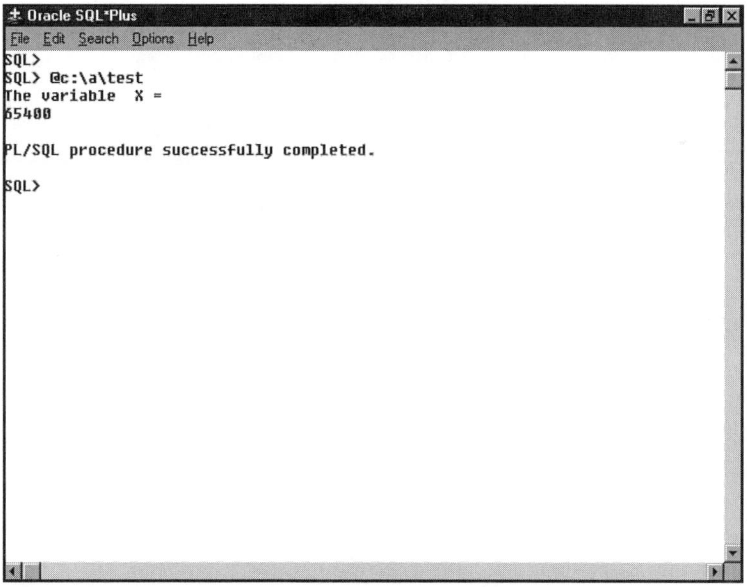

Figure 1.5.

Executing a PL/SQL block from a file.

```
Oracle SQL*Plus
File Edit Search Options Help
SQL>
SQL> @c:\a\test
The variable  X =
65400

PL/SQL procedure successfully completed.

SQL>
```

NOTE

When you're executing a file, the default file extension is usually `.SQL`, unless you have changed it. SQL*Plus looks for the file first in the default directory and then follows a search path that you can define. How you define this path is operating system–specific and outside the scope of this book. For details, you should consult the *SQL*Plus User's Guide* and also your operating system documentation.

Executing commands from a file like this is most useful in cases where you are re-creating a stored procedure, function, or database trigger and you have the definition already stored in its own text file.

The third option involves using the SQL*Plus EDIT command to invoke your system's text editor. Under Windows, this will again be Notepad unless you have specifically defined a different editor. When you issue the EDIT command, SQL*Plus will launch Notepad and automatically place in it the text of the most recently executed PL/SQL or SQL command. See Figure 1.6 for an example of this.

Figure 1.6.

*Using the SQL*Plus* EDIT *command.*

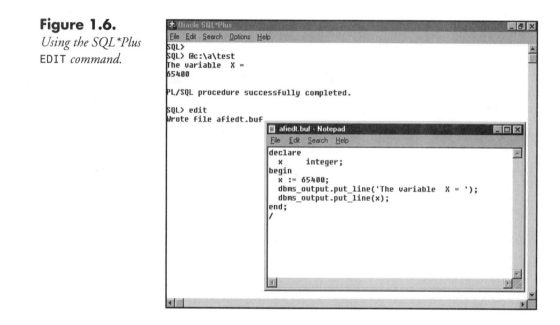

After you've brought up Notepad, you can edit the PL/SQL block to your satisfaction and then exit from Notepad, being sure to save the file. When you save your file, SQL*Plus will not immediately reexecute it. It is merely placed in an internal buffer. You must use the / command, by typing / on a line by itself, in order to execute the code you just edited.

Using the EDIT command works well as long as you keep a couple of important things in mind. The entire file must be executable, so unlike the first method, you cannot keep scraps of PL/SQL lying around in the file for later reference. Another thing to keep in mind is that SQL*Plus remembers only the most recent SQL command or PL/SQL block.

WARNING

For this reason, do not allow the SQL*Plus buffer to contain your only copy of a long procedure. It's too easy to enter a SQL command without thinking and wipe out the much longer PL/SQL procedure that you have been developing.

Which of these three methods you choose to use is up to you, and depends in part on your personal preferences. You are likely to find the first method, copying and pasting between Notepad and SQL*Plus, most useful during the first few chapters of this book. As you write ever larger PL/SQL functions and procedures, you will find yourself gravitating toward keeping each in its own file.

Writing Your First Function

Perhaps one of the most useful things you can do with your knowledge of PL/SQL is to use it to write stored functions and stored procedures. Encapsulating the code you wrote earlier into a stored function enables you to compile it once and store it in the database for future use. Then the next time you want to run that PL/SQL block, all you need to do is invoke the function. Using SQL*Plus, type in the input code shown in bold in Listing 1.3, which will create a PL/SQL function to return the value that was output by Listing 1.2.

**INPUT/
OUTPUT** **Listing 1.3. The SS_THRESH function.**

```
1: CREATE OR REPLACE FUNCTION ss_thresh
2: RETURN NUMBER AS
3:   x      NUMBER(9,2);
4: BEGIN
5:   x := 65400;
6:   RETURN x;
7: END;
8: /
9: Function created
```

ANALYSIS Compare the code in Listing 1.3 to that in Listing 1.2. Notice that the keyword DECLARE has been replaced in lines 1 and 2 by the words CREATE OR REPLACE FUNCTION ss_thresh RETURN NUMBER AS. This will be explained further on Day 3. Also notice that the calls to dbms_output.put_line() have been replaced by the RETURN command (line 6), which returns the value of the variable x to the caller. The only output from Listing 1.3 is a confirmation that the function has been successfully created, which is shown in line 9. Figure 1.7 shows how your SQL*Plus screen will look after creating the SS_THRESH function.

OUTPUT

Figure 1.7.
Creating the
SS_THRESH *function.*

Notice that Oracle has created the function. SQL*Plus indicates this by displaying the words
`Function created.`

Finding Compilation Errors

You probably were able to type in the code from Listing 1.3 and create the SS_THRESH function
with no errors. However, that might not have been the case. To show you how to deal with
an error, Listing 1.4 contains the same code as Listing 1.3, but with one small error.

**INPUT/
OUTPUT**   **Listing 1.4. The SS_THRESH function with an error.**

```
1: CREATE OR REPLACE FUNCTION ss_thresh
2: RETURN NUMBER AS
3:   x       NUMBER(9,2);
4: BEGIN
5:   x = 65400;
6:   RETURN x;
7: END;
8: /
9: Warning: Function created with compilation errors.
```

Unlike most compilers, which will display a listing of errors found in source code, Oracle stores any errors it finds in a database table named USER_ERRORS. If you want to see the specific details, and you probably do, then you need to retrieve the error listing yourself. Use the SQL*Plus command SHOW ERRORS, as shown in Listing 1.5, to do this.

INPUT/OUTPUT

Listing 1.5. The SHOW ERRORS command.

```
1: SHOW ERRORS
2: Errors for FUNCTION SS_THRESH:
3:
4: LINE/COL ERROR
5: -------- ----------------------------------------------------------------
6: 5/5      PLS-00103: Encountered the symbol "=" when expecting one of the
7:          following:
8:          := . ( @ % ;
9:          The symbol ":= was inserted before "=" to continue.
```

ANALYSIS   As you can see, the error listing has two columns of output. The first column contains the line number where the error occurred and also the character position within that line. The second column contains the specific error message. In this example, the error occurred in line 5 at the fifth character position. The error message tells you that Oracle encountered an equal sign when it was really expecting something else. That "something else," in this case, is the assignment operator, represented by :=.

Figure 1.8 shows the SQL*Plus screen as it would look after executing Listings 1.4 and 1.5.

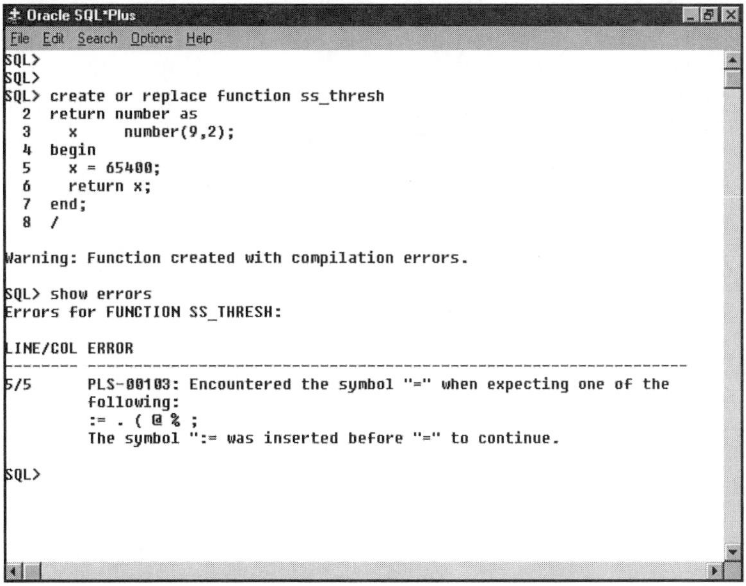

Figure 1.8.

Error listing for
SS_THRESH.

TIP

Typing = instead of := is a common mistake to make, especially if you also program in other languages that really do use = for assignment.

Displaying the Function's Return Value

Now that you have written and compiled the function, it's time to execute it and see the results. The easiest way to do this using SQL*Plus is to issue the following SQL command:

```
SELECT SS_THRESH FROM DUAL;
```

NOTE

The SS_THRESH function does not have any parameters, so be sure not to add any parentheses when you call it. In other words, don't use SS_THRESH() because Oracle will return an error.

The table DUAL is a special Oracle table that always exists, always has exactly one row, and always has exactly one column. It's the perfect table to use when experimenting with functions.

After executing the preceding SELECT command, your SQL*Plus screen should look something like that shown in Figure 1.9.

Figure 1.9.

Executing the
SS_THRESH *function.*

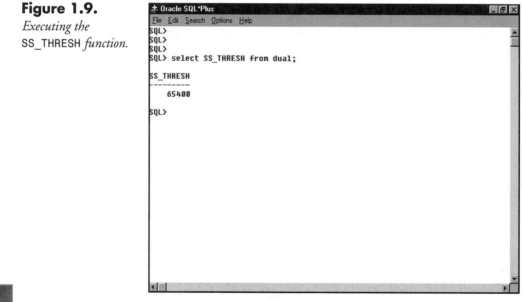

Can Even This Simple Function Be Useful?

The SS_THRESH function is a very simple function, and you might rightly wonder if something so absurdly simple can be useful. The value this function returns happens to represent the Social Security Contribution and Benefit Base. This value changes from year to year. If you were a programmer working on a payroll system and needed to write several queries using this value, you could use a function like this to *encapsulate* this information. One of the benefits of this approach is that your queries become more self-documenting. It's a bit easier to remember six months later what you meant when you see

```
SELECT * FROM employee_table
 WHERE emp_salary > SS_THRESH;
```

than if you had simply hard-coded the value

```
SELECT * FROM employee_table
 WHERE emp_salary > 65400;
```

Summary

In this chapter you learned a little about PL/SQL, what it is, and why it is used. You know that PL/SQL is Oracle's procedural language extension to SQL, and that you can use it to write procedures and functions that execute on the server.

This chapter also explains the relationship between PL/SQL, SQL, and SQL*Plus. This should give you a good grasp of how PL/SQL fits into the larger Oracle picture.

Finally, you wrote your first PL/SQL stored function, which should give you a good feel for the mechanics of programming with PL/SQL.

Q&A

Q Where does PL/SQL code execution take place?

A Usually, execution takes place at the server level. For the examples in this book, that will always be the case. Some Oracle products, such as Oracle Forms and Developer/2000, also have the capability to execute PL/SQL blocks locally on the client machine.

Q Can I write a complete application with PL/SQL?

A Generally speaking you cannot, at least not as most people envision an application. For an end-user application, you would still need a tool, such as PowerBuilder or Developer/2000, in order to design screens and generate reports.

Q I executed some PL/SQL code which used `dbms_output.put_line()` to print some data, but I didn't see anything. How come?

A You probably forgot to enable the server output option. Use this SQL*Plus command:

```
SET SERVEROUTPUT ON
```

If you forget that, your PL/SQL output goes to oblivion.

Workshop

Use the following workshop to test your comprehension of this chapter and put what you've learned into practice. You'll find the answers to the quiz and exercises in Appendix A, "Answers."

Quiz

1. What tells SQL*Plus to send your PL/SQL code to the Oracle database for execution?
2. What is the fundamental basis of all PL/SQL code?
3. List an advantage of pushing program logic up to the server level.
4. Name three Oracle products that use PL/SQL.
5. What command tells SQL*Plus to display PL/SQL output?
6. Name at least two options for managing your PL/SQL source code.

Exercises

1. If you didn't encounter any errors when compiling your first function, try putting some in on purpose. Then try out the SHOW ERRORS command.
2. Try each of the three ways mentioned in the chapter for managing your source code. Become familiar with the SQL*Plus EDIT command. Try using the @ command or the START command to execute your PL/SQL code from a text file.

Day 2

Selecting a
Development Tool

by Tom Luers

Oracle's PL/SQL can be used with a variety of development tools including:

- [ ] SQL*Plus
- [ ] Developer/2000 Forms
- [ ] Developer/2000 Reports
- [ ] Developer/2000 Graphs
- [ ] Enterprise Manager
- [ ] Oracle Call Interfaces
- [ ] Oracle Precompiler
- [ ] Oracle Data Browser

This chapter focuses primarily on the SQL*Plus development tool because you will find that to be the most useful in most cases. Later in the chapter, a few of the other development tools are described briefly. For additional information on Oracle and obtaining its products, you can visit Oracle's Web site at www.oracle.com.

SQL*Plus

In this book, most of the examples and exercises will be executed through SQL*Plus. This chapter covers the most useful SQL*Plus commands that will serve you best while working with PL/SQL.

SQL*Plus is an Oracle product that provides an open window into the Oracle database. It gives developers and end users the ability to interact directly with the database. SQL*Plus has a command-line interpreter so that users can directly submit SQL and SQL*Plus commands and PL/SQL blocks.

SQL commands and PL/SQL blocks are submitted in SQL*Plus to query, manipulate, or delete data in the Oracle databases. In fact, using SQL*Plus is the most common method of interacting with the Oracle database.

There are different groups of SQL*Plus commands that control or manipulate different aspects of your interaction with Oracle. For example, you use environment commands to set the line and page size. Likewise, you can use formatting commands to format the data returned from the database. Additionally, through SQL*Plus you can do all of the following:

- Manage every aspect of the database
- Enter, edit, retrieve, and run SQL statements and PL/SQL blocks
- Create well-polished, formatted reports
- Display column definitions for any table
- Access and copy data between databases
- Send messages to and accept responses from an end user
- Generate SQL and SQL*Plus code dynamically

Environment Commands

The SQL*Plus environment commands define the system parameters within which you work. You use the set and show commands to control these parameters. The set command has an extensive number of options that control the interaction of the user's terminal with other SQL commands. The show command displays the current setting of the various parameters that have been established by the set command.

The Syntax for the `set` Command

SYNTAX

The general syntax of the `set` command is

```
set parameter value
```

where *parameter* represents the system variable that is to be defined, and *value* is the state or value that you want the system variable to be set to.

The following sections go into detail on the various specific SQL*Plus parameters.

Session Commands

These parameters establish the general look and feel of your SQL*Plus session. You establish the parameter values with the `set` command. The following are the options to use with the session commands:

- [ ] `feedback` *n*—Defines the number of records returned by a query where the query selects at least *n* records. The default value is 6.

- [ ] `feedback on/off`—Determines whether the feedback display is on or off. The default is on.

- [ ] `pause msg`—Displays a message after scrolling through one screen full of output when running reports. At the time the message displays, the user responds by pressing the Enter key. There is no default value.

- [ ] `pause on/off`—Determines whether the pause feature is on or off. The default value is on.

- [ ] `pagesize` *n*—Sets the number of lines per page to *n*. The default value is 14.

- [ ] `linesize` *n*—Sets the number of characters per line to *n*. The default value is 80.

- [ ] `heading on/off`—Determines whether column headings are displayed. The default is on.

- [ ] `space` *n*—Sets the number of spaces between columns. The maximum value is 10. The default value is zero.

- [ ] `echo on/off`—Determines whether each command in a text file is displayed on the screen as it is being executed. The default is off.

- [ ] `verify on/off`—Determines whether each command in a SQL statement is displayed before and after SQL*Plus substitution parameters are replaced by actual values. The default value is on.

Listing 2.1 highlights a few of these parameters.

INPUT/OUTPUT **Listing 2.1. Setting system parameters for SQL*Plus.**

```
set pagesize 6
set pause 'Press <return> to continue...'
set pause on
SELECT city_name from city_index
city_name
---------
charlotte
chicago
clarion
davidson
donaldston
dover

Press <return> to continue...
```

Display Controls for Headers and Footers

The following set of parameters controls the header and footer formats of the output reports:

- [ ] ttitle—Defines the header text. By default, this command centers the header. Insert a vertical line in the text to split the header across several lines.

- [ ] ttitle off—Turns the header off.

- [ ] btitle—Defines the footer text. By default this command centers the footer.

- [ ] btitle off—Turns the footer off.

All parameter settings remain in effect until explicitly changed or the SQL*Plus session ends. Therefore, it is always a good idea to clear the header and footer after each report. The SQL*Plus commands in Listing 2.2 will place a header and footer in the output report.

INPUT/OUTPUT **Listing 2.2. Creating a header and footer.**

```
set pagesize 22
set linesize 60
set feedback off
ttitle 'Monthly Sales¦for June'
btitle 'Confidential'

SELECT sales_region, sales_totals from master_sales
WHERE sales_month = '06'

Monthly Sales
For June
```

```
SALES_REGION       SALES_TOTALS
------------       ------------

North East         99204
South East         72900
Mid West           921892
Plains             69916
South West         98421
West               1027653
North West         87367

Confidential


ttitle off
btitle off
```

Display Controls for Columns

The column parameters enable you to change the headings and formats of the report columns and are as follows:

- ☐ column *column_name*—Displays the current setting for the specified column.
- ☐ column—Displays the settings for all columns.
- ☐ column *column_name* clear—Clears all settings for the specified column.
- ☐ clear columns—Clears the settings for all columns.

All parameter settings remain in effect until explicitly changed or the SQL*Plus session ends. Therefore, it is always a good idea to clear the column parameters after each report. Listing 2.3 is similar to Listing 2.2 except that column headers are specified.

INPUT/OUTPUT **Listing 2.3. Defining column headers.**

```
set pagesize 22
set linesize 60
set feedback off
ttitle 'Monthly Sales¦for June'
btitle 'Confidential'
column sales_region heading 'Sales Region' format A15
column sales_totals heading 'Total Sales' format $99,999,999

SELECT sales_region, sales_totals from master_sales
WHERE sales_month = '06'

Monthly Sales
For June
```

continues

Listing 2.3. continued

```
Sales Region      Total Sales
-----------       -----------

North East        $99,204.00
South East        $72,900.00
Mid West          $921,892.00
Plains            $69,916.00
South West        $98,421.00
West              $1,027,653.00
North West        $87,367.00

Confidential


column sales_region clear
column sales_total clear
ttitle off
btitle off
```

In Listing 2.3, the format clause was used to control the positions of certain punctuation marks as well as output character suppression. Use the following formats to meet your requirements:

- 9—Represents a single zero suppression digit.
- ,—Represents the position of a comma.
- .—Represents the position of a period.
- $—Represents a floating dollar sign.
- A*n*—Defines a display width of *n* for character and date columns.

Bind Variables

Bind variables are variables created outside PL/SQL but referenced within a PL/SQL block. In this chapter, you define bind variables as variables that are created in SQL*Plus. These variables can then be referenced in a PL/SQL program as if they were declared variables in the PL/SQL program. Bind variables are necessary because variables declared in PL/SQL programs are not accessible to SQL*Plus. Bind variables are used frequently to manage subprogram return codes.

To create a bind variable, use the variable command.

The Syntax for the variable Command

The syntax is

```
variable variable_name type
```

where *variable name* is the name of the bind variable that you want to create, and *type* is the datatype for the variable.

To reference the bind variable in a PL/SQL subprogram, precede the bind variable with a colon (:). For example, the following statement references the bind variable `sales_total` by assigning the value of zero to it in a PL/SQL program:

```
:sales_total :=0
```

To display the value of the `sales_total` bind variable, use the SQL*Plus `print` command, which is

```
print sales_total
```

Substitution Variables

A *substitution variable* is a user-defined variable name that is preceded by an ampersand (&). SQL*Plus treats the substitution variable as though it were the value of the substitution variable, rather than the variable itself. You can use substitution variables anywhere in SQL and SQL*Plus commands, except as the first command entered during a SQL*Plus session. If you do not supply a value for the substitution variable, SQL*Plus will prompt you for a value.

In the following examples, the variable `sort1` is defined as `position` and the variable `table1` is defined as `master_parts`. The first example uses substitution variables:

```
break on &sort1
SELECT * from &table1
ORDER BY &sort 1 asc
```

The next example uses the values of the substitution variables:

```
break on position
SELECT * from master_parts
ORDER BY position asc
```

Both of the preceding examples produce the same results.

The following system variables affect substitution variables:

- ☐ `set scan`—Turns substitution on and off.
- ☐ `set define`—Defines the substitution character. By default it is the ampersand (&).
- ☐ `set escape`—Defines the escape character that you would use before the substitution character. This character instructs SQL*Plus to treat the substitution character as an ordinary character.
- ☐ `set verify on`—Defines whether each line of the command file is listed before and after substitution.
- ☐ `set concat`—Defines the concatenation character. By default it is the period (.).

The following example uses the concatenation character. SQL*Plus will automatically query the user for the value of `sales` because it is not previously defined:

```
SQL> SELECT * from master_parts
WHERE parts_codes = '&c_parts.001'
```

```
Enter value for c_parts: 21345
```

This will be interpreted as:

```
SQL> SELECT * from master_sales
WHERE sales_region = '21345001'
```

Now look at a realistic example where the ORDER BY clause is used with the substitution variable. Notice in Listing 2.4 that SQL*Plus queries the user for input to every substitution variable.

Listing 2.4. ORDER BY **clause with substitution variables.**

```
SQL> SELECT * from master_personnel
SQL> WHERE job = '&c_job'
SQL> ORDER BY &c_job

Enter value for c_job: teacher
old SELECT * from master_personnel
old WHERE job = '&c_type'
new SELECT * from master_personnel
new WHERE job = 'teacher'


Enter value for c_job: teacher
old ORDER BY &c_job
new ORDER BY 'teacher'
```

Note from Listing 2.4 that you had to enter in the value for the substitution variable &c_job twice. SQL*Plus will prompt you for every substitution variable. You can avoid being prompted repeatedly for the same values by using the double ampersand (&&). This directs SQL*Plus to automatically define the substitution variable with && as equal to the substitution variable with one ampersand (&). This way, you can recode the preceding statement to avoid the reprompting as follows:

```
SELECT * from master_personnel
WHERE job = '&c_job'
ORDER BY &&c_job
```

Building a Simple Break Report

A *break report* is a report in which duplicate values are suppressed in the specified column. Additionally, in the break report, a line will be skipped every time a value changes in the break column. The following is the normal (non-break) output from the master_sales table:

```
Monthly Sales
For June


    sales_region          sales_totals
    -----------           -----------
    North East            55100
    North East            43104
    North East            1004
    South East            72900
    Mid West              811460
    Mid West              110432
    Plains                69916
    North West            31012
    North West            21101
    North West            5243
    North West            30011

    Confidential
```

Listing 2.5 contains the SQL*Plus commands that will be issued to create a break report.

Listing 2.5. Break report.

```
set pagesize 22
set linesize 60
set feedback off
ttitle 'Monthly Sales¦for June'
btitle 'Confidential'
column sales_region heading 'Sales Region' format A15
column sales_totals heading 'Total Sales' format $99,999,999
break on sales_region skip 1

SELECT sales_region, sales_totals from master_sales
WHERE sales_month = '06'

Monthly Sales
For June


Sales Region      Total Sales
-----------       -----------
North East        $55,100
                  $43,104
                  $1,004

South East        $72,900

Mid West          $811,460
                  $110,432

Plains            $69,916
```

continues

Listing 2.5. continued

```
North West              $31,012
                        $21,101
                        $5,243
                        $30,011

Confidential
```

Summary Computations

After you have your report broken into subunits with the `break` command, you can perform additional operations on the rows within each subset. You do this with the `compute` command. There are eight summary functions that you can use in a break report.

The Syntax for the `compute` Command

The syntax is

```
compute function of compute_column on break_column
```

where *function* represents one of the functions listed in the following bulleted list, *compute_column* is the column or expression you want to use in the computation, and *break_column* is the event that SQL*Plus will use as a break.

The eight functions to be used with the `compute` function are as follows:

- [ ] `sum`—Computes the sum of the values in the column.
- [ ] `count`—Counts the number of non-null values in the column.
- [ ] `num`—Counts the number of rows in the column.
- [ ] `min`—Computes the minimum value in the column.
- [ ] `max`—Computes the maximum value in the column.
- [ ] `avg`—Computes the average of the values in the column.
- [ ] `std`—Computes the standard deviation of the values in the column.
- [ ] `var`—Computes the variance of the values in the column.

Continuing with the example used in the earlier listings, the `compute` command with the `sum` function is added to display the total sales for each region in Listing 2.6.

INPUT/OUTPUT **Listing 2.6.** compute **command using the** sum **function.**

```
set pagesize 22
set linesize 60
set feedback off
ttitle 'Monthly Sales for June'
btitle 'Confidential'
column sales_region heading 'Sales Region' format A15
column sales_totals heading 'Total Sales' format $99,999,999
break on sales_region skip 1
compute sum of sales_totals on sales_region

SELECT sales_region, sales_totals from master_sales
WHERE sales_month = '06'

Monthly Sales
For June


Sales Region        Total Sales
- - - - - - - - - - -    - - - - - - - - - - -
North East          $55,100
                    $43,104
                    $1,004
************        - - - - - - -
sum                 $99,204

South East          $72,900
************        - - - - - - -
sum                 $72,900

Mid West            $811,460
                    $110,432
************        - - - - - - -
sum                 $921,892

Plains              $69,916
************        - - - - - - -
sum                 $69,916

North West          $31,012
                    $21,101
                    $5,243
                    $30,011
************        - - - - - - -
sum                 $87,357

Confidential
```

To calculate the grand total for a column, use the report clause with the break and compute commands. In Listing 2.7, the ORDER BY command is included in this example to order the output in ascending order.

Listing 2.7. Report with ORDER BY command.

```
set pagesize 22
set linesize 60
set feedback off
ttitle 'Monthly Sales¦for June'
btitle 'Confidential'
column sales_region heading 'Sales Region' format A15
column sales_totals heading 'Total Sales' format $99,999,999
break on sales_region skip 1 on report
compute sum of sales_totals on sales_region on report

SELECT sales_region, sales_totals from master_sales
WHERE sales_month = '06'
ORDER BY sales_region, sales_totals

Monthly Sales
For June


Sales Region          Total Sales
------------          ------------
Mid West              $111,460
                      $810,432
************          --------
sum                   $921,892

North East            $55,100
                      $43,104
                      $1,004
************          -------
sum                   $99,204

North West            $31,012
                      $31,101
                      $20,243
                      $5,011
************          -------
sum                   $87,357

Plains                $69,916
************          -------
sum                   $69,916

South East            $72,900
************          -------
sum                   $72,900


sum                   $1,251,269

Confidential
```

Developer/2000 Tools (Forms, Reports, and Graphs)

The previous section covers SQL*Plus extensively because this will be your most commonly used development tool. This section shows you an example in which PL/SQL is used with Oracle's Developer/2000 Forms.

Listing 2.8 contains a PL/SQL procedure being used inside an Oracle Forms Program Unit. PL/SQL is quite powerful when used within any of the Oracle development tools.

Listing 2.8. PL/SQL procedure within Oracle Forms.

```
 1: PROCEDURE CREATE_INITIALS IS
 2: BEGIN
 3: IF :FIRST_NAME IS NOT NULL AND :LAST_NAME IS NOT NULL THEN
 4:    IF :SYSTEM.RECORD_STATUS = 'INSERT' THEN
 5:      :GLOBAL.TEMP_PERSON_KEY := 0;
 6:    ELSE
 7:      :GLOBAL.TEMP_PERSON_KEY := :PERSON.PERSON_KEY;
 8:    END IF;
 9:    DECLARE
10:      TEMP_INITIALS   CHAR(3);
11:      TEMP2_INITIALS  CHAR(5);
12:      TEMP3_INITIALS  CHAR(5);
13:    BEGIN
14:      TEMP_INITIALS := SUBSTR(:FIRST_NAME,1,1)||SUBSTR(:MIDDLE_NAME,1,1)||
15:               SUBSTR(:LAST_NAME,1,1);
16:      :GLOBAL.TEMP_INITIALS := TEMP_INITIALS;
17: BREAK;
18:      SELECT INITIALS INTO TEMP2_INITIALS FROM PERSONS
19:        WHERE SUBSTR(INITIALS,1,3) = TEMP_INITIALS AND
20:          PERSON_KEY_2 = :GLOBAL.TEMP_PERSON_KEY;
21:        :GLOBAL.TE_INITIALS := TEMP2_INITIALS;
22: BREAK;
23:        BEGIN
24:          SELECT INITIALS INTO TEMP3_INITIALS FROM employee
25:          WHERE INITIALS = TEMP2_INITIALS;
26:          :GLOBAL.TEMP_3 := TEMP3_INITIALS;
27:          :INITIALS := TEMP_INITIALS||
28:            TO_CHAR(TO_NUMBER(NVL(SUBSTR(TEMP3_INITIALS,4,2),0))+1);
29:        END;
30:    EXCEPTION
31:      WHEN NO_DATA_FOUND THEN
32:        :GLOBAL.TEMP_INIT_NULL := -1;
33:        :INITIALS := TEMP_INITIALS;
34:      WHEN TOO_MANY_ROWS THEN
35:
36:      BEGIN
37:        SELECT MAX(INITIALS) INTO TEMP3_INITIALS FROM employee
38:        WHERE SUBSTR(INITIALS,1,3) = TEMP_INITIALS;
```

continues

Listing 2.8. continued

```
39:        :GLOBAL.TEMP_3A := TEMP3_INITIALS;
40:
41:        :INITIALS := TEMP_INITIALS||
42:          TO_CHAR(TO_NUMBER(NVL(SUBSTR(TEMP3_INITIALS,4,2),0))+1);
43:      EXCEPTION
44:        WHEN OTHERS THEN
45:          NULL;
46:      END;
47:    END;
48:  ELSE
49:    :INITIALS := NULL;
50:  END IF;
51: END;
```

Oracle Precompiler

The final development tool to cover is the Oracle Precompiler. The Oracle Precompiler allows you to embed Oracle code inside a non-Oracle program such as C so that you can take advantage of the power of PL/SQL within your program. In the following example, the source code for a partial C program is shown, which includes the use of a PL/SQL cursor (see Day 10, "Manipulating Data with Cursors, DELETE, and UPDATE," and Day 12, "Using Cursors for Complex Processing," for additional information on cursors):

```
...
exec sql DECLARE emp_names cursor for
SELECT emp_name from emp
WHERE pay_type = 'S';

exec sql open emp_names;
...
```

Summary

Oracle offers many development tools in which you can use PL/SQL.

SQL*Plus is an Oracle product that provides an open window into the Oracle database. It gives developers and end users the ability to interact directly with the database.

Q&A

Q **Why do I need a development tool for PL/SQL?**

A SQL*Plus and other development tools such as Oracle Forms provide you a means to interactively use PL/SQL blocks directly with the database. You could write PL/SQL in your preferred text editor and compile the blocks that call them by some other means. By using some of the development tools, however, not only can you interact with the database, but you can also use PL/SQL within these other tools.

Q **Is there a difference in the PL/SQL code and syntax from one development tool to another?**

A No. PL/SQL prescribes only one syntax. No matter when, where, or how you are using PL/SQL, it always follows the same coding rules.

Q **Are the development tools mentioned in this chapter only for use with PL/SQL?**

A No. SQL*Plus and the other development tools might use, for example, SQL as well as PL/SQL.

Workshop

The following workshop will test your knowledge of the development tools available for use with PL/SQL. The quiz answers and exercise solution can be found in Appendix A, "Answers."

Quiz

1. Name several PL/SQL development tools.
2. What is a bind variable?
3. What is a substitution variable?

Exercise

Write a simple piece of code outline that uses substitution variables and bind variables.

Week 1

Day 3

Writing Declarations and Blocks

by Jonathan Gennick

The *block* is the fundamental unit of PL/SQL programming. Blocks contain both program code and variable declarations. Understanding the various datatypes available to you when declaring variables is crucial when programming in any language, and PL/SQL is no exception. It's also important to understand PL/SQL's block structure, its use, and its impact on the scope of variable declarations. Today you are going to learn more about:

- ☐ PL/SQL datatypes
- ☐ PL/SQL blocks
- ☐ Scoping rules

Datatypes

PL/SQL provides a number of datatypes for your use, as shown in Table 3.1.

Table 3.1. PL/SQL datatypes.

Datatype	Usage
VARCHAR2	Variable-length character strings
CHAR	Fixed-length character strings
NUMBER	Fixed or floating-point numbers
BINARY_INTEGER	Integer values
PLS_INTEGER	New in version 2.3; used for fast integer computations
DATE	Date/Time values
BOOLEAN	true/false values

These datatypes can be used for creating simple scalar variables, or they can be combined into structures such as records or PL/SQL tables. You will learn more about records and tables during Day 9, "Using SQL: INSERT, SELECT, Advanced Declarations, and Tables."

NEW TERM A *scalar variable* is a variable that is not made up of some combination of other variables. Scalar variables don't have internal components that you can manipulate individually. They are often used to build up more complex datatypes such as records and arrays.

You might notice that some of the datatype names match those used by Oracle for defining database columns. In most cases the definitions are the same for both the database and PL/SQL, but there are a few differences. These differences are noted when discussing each particular datatype.

NEW TERM PL/SQL also provides *subtypes* of some datatypes. A subtype represents a special case of a datatype, usually representing a narrower range of values than the parent type. For example, POSITIVE is a subtype of BINARY_INTEGER that holds only positive values. In some cases the subtypes exist only to provide alternative names for compatibility with the SQL standard or other popular database brands on the market.

Variable Naming Rules

Before you go on to learn about each of the datatypes in detail, you should first consider some basic rules and conventions for naming variables. Oracle has some simple rules for variable naming. Variable names can be composed of letters, dollar

3

signs, underscores, and number signs. No other characters can be used. A variable name must start with a letter, after which any combination of the allowed characters can be used. The maximum length for a variable name is 30 characters. Variable names, like those of keywords and other identifiers, are not case sensitive.

In addition to the preceding rules, it is often helpful to follow some sort of naming convention for variables and to make their names as descriptive as possible. For example, although `empyersal` is a legal variable name, your code might be easier to read if you used `emp_yearly_salary`. Another option, which uses capital letters to highlight each word in order to dispense with the underscores, is `EmpYearlySalary`. Many programmers also capitalize language keywords in order to more easily distinguish them from variable, function, and procedure names.

The naming rules for variables also apply to function and procedure names. The importance of a consistent naming convention for all identifiers is discussed in more detail on Day 14, "Debugging Your Code and Preventing Errors."

3

In the next few subsections, you'll learn about each of the PL/SQL datatypes. You'll learn the type of data that each one holds, what the range of possible values is, and any subtypes that are defined for it.

VARCHAR2

The `VARCHAR2` datatype is used to hold variable-length character string data. It typically uses 1 byte per character and has a maximum length of 32767 bytes.

The Syntax for the `VARCHAR2` Datatype

```
variable_name VARCHAR2(size);
```

In this syntax, `variable_name` is whatever name you want to give to the variable, and `size` is the maximum length, in bytes, of the string.

Here are some examples:

```
employee_name VARCHAR2(32);
employee_comments VARCHAR2(10000);
```

NOTE

Even though PL/SQL allows a maximum of 32767 bytes for a `VARCHAR2` variable, the Oracle database does not. The Oracle database itself only allows `VARCHAR2` columns to be a maximum of 4000 bytes long. You can use longer strings in PL/SQL, but 4000 is the limit if you want to store the string in the database. Prior to version 8, the limit was 2000 characters.

Referring to the example declaration of `employee_name`, here are some sample assignment statements showing values that could be assigned to this variable:

```
employee_name := 'Jenny Gennick';
employee_name := 'Jonathan Gennick';
```

VARCHAR2 Subtypes

Oracle has two subtypes defined for VARCHAR2, which are

- [ ] VARCHAR
- [ ] STRING

These subtypes exist for compatibility with other database brands and also with the SQL standard. Both have the exact same meaning as VARCHAR2. However, Oracle currently recommends against using the VARCHAR datatype because its definition is expected to change as the SQL standards evolve.

CHAR

The CHAR datatype is used to hold fixed-length character string data. Unlike VARCHAR2 strings, a CHAR string always contains the maximum number of characters. Strings shorter than the maximum length are padded with spaces. Like VARCHAR2, the CHAR datatype typically uses 1 byte per character and has a maximum length of 32767 bytes.

The Syntax for the CHAR Datatype

variable_name CHAR*(size)*;

In this syntax, *variable_name* is whatever you want to call the variable, and *size* is the size, in bytes, of the string.

Here are some examples:

```
employee_name CHAR(32);
employee_comments CHAR(10000);
```

NOTE

> The Oracle database only allows CHAR columns to be 2000 bytes long, 255 if you are using Oracle7. Even though PL/SQL allows a maximum of 32767 bytes for a CHAR variable, 2000 (or 255 with Oracle7) is the limit if you want to store the string in the database.

Referring to the example declaration of `employee_name`, here are some sample assignment statements showing values that could be assigned to this variable:

```
employee_name := 'Jenny Gennick';
employee_name := 'Jeff Gennick';
```

Because CHAR variables are fixed length and the preceding strings are each less than 32 characters long, they will be right-padded with spaces. Thus the actual values in employee_name would be

```
'Jenny Gennick                   '
```

and

```
'Jeff Gennick                    '
```

This point is important to remember, especially when doing string comparisons, because the trailing spaces count as part of the string. Try typing in and executing the input code shown in Listing 3.1.

Note

Before executing the code shown in Listing 3.1 and most of the other listings in this chapter, make sure that you have first executed the following command at least once during the session:

```
SET SERVEROUTPUT ON
```

If you omit this command, SQL*Plus won't display the output generated by the calls to DBMS_OUTPUT.PUT_LINE. You need to execute this command only once each time you start SQL*Plus. For listings in which this is important, a comment is included at the beginning to remind you.

3

INPUT/ OUTPUT **Listing 3.1. Comparison of CHAR with VARCHAR2.**

```
 1: --Remember to execute: SET SERVEROUTPUT ON
 2: SET ECHO ON
 3: DECLARE
 4:    employee_name_c CHAR(32);
 5:    employee_name_v VARCHAR2(32);
 6: BEGIN
 7:    --Assign the same value to each string.
 8:    employee_name_c := 'Jenny Gennick';
 9:    employee_name_v := 'Jenny Gennick';
10:
11:    --Test the strings for equality.
12:    IF employee_name_c = employee_name_v THEN
13:      DBMS_OUTPUT.PUT_LINE('The names are the same');
14:    ELSE
15:      DBMS_OUTPUT.PUT_LINE('The names are NOT the same');
16:    END IF;
17: END;
18: /
19: The names are NOT the same
20:
21: PL/SQL procedure successfully completed.
```

ANALYSIS What happened here? The same value was assigned to both strings, yet they did not test as being equal. This occurred because the CHAR string contains a number of trailing spaces, whereas the VARCHAR2 string does not.

 TIP When comparing CHAR strings against VARCHAR2 strings, use the rtrim function to eliminate trailing spaces, as in the following example:

```
IF rtrim(employee_name_c) = employee_name_v THEN...
```

The rtrim function is one you will learn more about on Day 7, "Using Oracle's Built-in Functions."

CHAR **Subtypes**

Oracle has one subtype defined for the CHAR datatype, and it is called CHARACTER. It has exactly the same meaning as CHAR.

NUMBER

The NUMBER datatype is used for declaring both fixed-point and floating-point numbers. It can be used to represent numbers in the range 1.0E-123 through 9.99E125, and it allows for up to 38 decimal digits of precision. It is very commonly used and is a bit more complicated than the character datatypes discussed earlier.

 The Syntax for the NUMBER **Datatype**

```
variable_name NUMBER [(precision[,scale])]
```

In this syntax, *variable_name* is whatever name you want to give this variable. *precision* specifies the number of decimal digits used to represent the value internally. The range is 1 to 38, and the default is 38. *scale* indicates where the decimal point is and where rounding occurs. The range is -84 to 127, and the default is zero.

Here are some examples:

```
dollar_amount NUMBER (5,2);
no_cents NUMBER (3);
big_floating NUMBER;
shares_traded NUMBER (5,-2);
microns NUMBER (1,6)
```

The easiest way to understand precision and scale is to think of precision as telling you how many digits are used to represent the number. Then the scale tells you where the decimal point is.

The dollar_amount variable, defined in the preceding example as NUMBER(5,2), would then be precise to five digits, two of which would be to the right of the decimal. All amounts would be rounded to the nearest hundredth. It could store values such as 123.45, -999.99, and so on. Assigning it a value of 123.456 would result in the value being rounded off to 123.46.

> Trying to assign any number a value greater than its precision, for example, assigning dollar_amount a value of 1000, will result in an error.

The no_cents variable, defined in the preceding example as NUMBER(3), would take the default scale of zero. Thus it could store no digits to the right of the decimal, and all values will be rounded to the nearest whole number. Assigning it a value of -123.45 would result in it being rounded off to -123.

The big_floating variable, defined only as NUMBER, has no precision and scale specified in its declaration. Use this to define a floating-point value.

The shares_traded variable is interesting because the example declared it with a negative scale, that is, as NUMBER(5,-2). It stores five digits of precision, but all values are in hundreds. It could store values ranging from 0 to 9,999,900, but all values would be rounded to the nearest hundred. Assign it a value of 100, and it will store 100. Assign it a value of 327, and it will be rounded off to 300. Why use a variable like this? It saves a bit of space and allows you to use the 38 digits to represent some very large numbers without making excessive demands on memory. For a real-world example, take a look at the stock market listings in almost any newspaper, and you will see that the number of shares traded is usually reported in blocks of 100.

The microns variable is also a bit unusual because the example specified a scale that is larger than the precision. This is perfectly legitimate and is really the reverse of what was done with shares_traded. It will store values of one millionth, two millionths, and so on up to nine millionths. All values will be rounded to the nearest millionth, so if you assigned it a value of 0.00000016, you would get 0.0000002. Because the precision is only one, trying to assign a value of 0.000001 would result in an error. 0.000001 is 10 millionths, which in this case requires two digits of precision to store.

The NUMBER datatype is the only numeric datatype that is available both at the database level and in PL/SQL. It is stored using a hardware-independent representation and manipulated using hardware-independent code. Oracle guarantees portability of this datatype across the various platforms supported by Oracle.

NUMBER **Subtypes**

Oracle has defined several subtypes of NUMBER. Most of these have exactly the same meaning as, and can be used interchangeably with, the keyword NUMBER. Table 3.2 shows a complete list of NUMBER subtypes and describes their use.

Table 3.2. Subtypes of the NUMBER datatype.

Subtype	Usage
DECIMAL	Same as NUMBER.
DEC	Same as DECIMAL.
DOUBLE PRECISION	Same as NUMBER.
NUMERIC	Same as NUMBER.
REAL	Same as NUMBER.
INTEGER	Equivalent to NUMBER(38).
INT	Same as INTEGER.
SMALLINT	Same as NUMBER(38).
FLOAT	Same as NUMBER.
FLOAT(*prec*)	Same as NUMBER(*prec*), but the precision is expressed in terms of binary bits, not decimal digits. Binary precision can range from 1 through 126.

Subtypes of NUMBER are not considered to be constraining. The same underlying datatype is used, and subject to the precision and scale you specify, all the subtypes can store the same range of values. Strange as it may seem, even an integer can be defined to hold noninteger, decimal values. Take a look at Listing 3.2, which shows all the NUMBER subtypes being used to declare identical variables.

INPUT/OUTPUT **Listing 3.2. Identical declarations using NUMBER subtypes.**

```
 1: --Remember to execute: SET SERVEROUTPUT ON
 2: DECLARE
 3:    --all these declarations are identical.
 4:    num_dec    DECIMAL(5,2);
 5:    num_int    INTEGER(5,2);
 6:    num_dbl    DOUBLE PRECISION(5,2);
 7:    num_num    NUMERIC(5,2);
 8:    num_real   REAL(5,2);
 9:    num_sint   SMALLINT(5,2);
10:
11:    --decimal precision / 0.30103 = binary precision,
12:    --so 5/.30103 = 16.6. Round it up to 17.
13:    num_flt    FLOAT(17);
14:
15: BEGIN
16:    --Assign the same value to each variable, and make it one
17:    --that needs to be rounded.
18:    num_dec := 123.456;
19:    num_int := 123.456;
20:    num_dbl := 123.456;
```

3

```
21:     num_num := 123.456;
22:     num_real := 123.456;
23:     num_sint := 123.456;
24:     num_flt := 123.456;
25:
26:     --Now display each value to demonstrate that they are all the same.
27:     DBMS_OUTPUT.PUT_LINE(num_dec);
28:     DBMS_OUTPUT.PUT_LINE(num_int);
29:     DBMS_OUTPUT.PUT_LINE(num_dbl);
30:     DBMS_OUTPUT.PUT_LINE(num_num);
31:     DBMS_OUTPUT.PUT_LINE(num_real);
32:     DBMS_OUTPUT.PUT_LINE(num_sint);
33:     DBMS_OUTPUT.PUT_LINE(num_flt);
34: END;
35: /
36: 123.46
37: 123.46
38: 123.46
39: 123.46
40: 123.46
41: 123.46
42: 123.456
43:
44: PL/SQL procedure successfully completed.
```

ANALYSIS Notice that even the variables defined as INTEGER and SMALLINT still can hold noninteger values. The underlying datatype allows it, and the use of INTEGER(5,2) in the declaration overrides the integer subtype definition of NUMBER(38).

Notice also that the last value printed was 123.456. Why was this not rounded? Because that value came from the variable declared as FLOAT(17). Variables of subtype FLOAT store floating-point values, so rounding might not occur. There is no exact correspondence between binary and decimal precision either. Seventeen bits is slightly more than enough to hold any value that a NUMBER(5,2) variable could hold.

TIP Please don't take advantage of the fact that you can declare an INTEGER variable with a precision and scale, for example INTEGER(5,2), and assign a value to it. Knowing that this can be done is interesting, but actually doing it will be confusing to other programmers.

BINARY_INTEGER

The BINARY_INTEGER datatype is used for declaring signed integer variables. Compared to the NUMBER datatype, BINARY_INTEGER variables are stored in binary format, which takes less space. Calculations on binary integers can also run slightly faster because the values are already in a binary format.

SYNTAX

The Syntax for the BINARY_INTEGER Datatype

variable_name BINARY_INTEGER;

In this syntax, *variable_name* is whatever you want to name the variable.

Here is a sample declaration:

my_integer BINARY_INTEGER;

A BINARY_INTEGER variable can store any integer value in the range -2,147,483,647 through 2,147,483,647.

TIP

> If you are running PL/SQL version 2.3 or later, you have access to the new PLS_INTEGER datatype, which is optimized for fast calculations. For new applications I recommend using it instead of BINARY_INTEGER.

BINARY_INTEGER Subtypes

Oracle has defined five subtypes for the BINARY_INTEGER datatype, as explained in Table 3.3.

Table 3.3. Subtypes of BINARY_INTEGER.

Subtype	Usage
POSITIVE	Allows only positive integers to be stored, up to the maximum of 2,147,483,647. Zero is not considered a positive number, and so is not an allowed value.
NATURAL	Allows only natural numbers to be stored, which includes zero. Allowed values are 0, 1, 2, 3, and so on up to the maximum of 2,147,483,647.
POSITIVEn	Like POSITIVE but cannot be null.
NATURALn	Like NATURAL but cannot be null.
SIGNTYPE	Restricts a variable to only the values -1, 0, and 1. Oracle's built-in sign() function returns values in this range depending on whether its argument is negative, zero, or positive. (New for Oracle8.)

Unlike the subtypes defined for NUMBER, these subtypes are constraining. There is no way, for example, to define a POSITIVE in such a way as to still allow negative values.

Why would you want to use these subtypes? One reason might be for purposes of documentation. A subtype might be more descriptive of the type of data you intend to store in a variable, which can help prevent mistakes by other programmers who later work on the code. Another reason might be for error detection. If the code is later modified to assign the wrong type of value to a variable, a VALUE_ERROR exception will be generated, alerting the programmer to the mistake. Listing 3.3 shows an example of this.

Listing 3.3. An attempt to assign a negative value to a POSITIVE variable.

```
 1: --Remember to execute: SET SERVEROUTPUT ON
 2: DECLARE
 3:    age    POSITIVE;
 4:
 5:    current_year   NATURAL;      --a year of 00 is valid.
 6:    current_month POSITIVE;
 7:    current_day    POSITIVE;
 8:
 9:    birth_year     NATURAL;      --a year of 00 is valid.
10:    birth_month    POSITIVE;
11:    birth_day      POSITIVE;
12:
13:    birth_date     DATE := TO_DATE('11-15-1961','mm-dd-yyyy');
14:    current_date   DATE;
15: BEGIN
16:    --Set the current date.  Normally we would do "current_date := sysdate",
17:    --but LET'S pretend it's the year 2000.
18:    current_date := TO_DATE ('12-1-2000','mm-dd-yyyy');
19:
20:    --Show the effect of trying to set a negative age.
21:    --Pretend it's the year 2000 and we forgot to convert this code.
22:    --Note that only the two digit year is retrieved.
23:    current_year := TO_NUMBER(TO_CHAR(current_date,'yy'));
24:    current_month := TO_NUMBER(TO_CHAR(current_date,'mm'));
25:    current_day := TO_NUMBER(TO_CHAR(current_date,'dd'));
26:
27:    --Oops! Only two digits allowed for birth year.
28:    birth_year := TO_NUMBER(TO_CHAR(birth_date,'yy'));
29:    birth_month := TO_NUMBER(TO_CHAR(birth_date,'mm'));
30:    birth_day := TO_NUMBER(TO_CHAR(birth_date,'dd'));
31:
32:    --Now make the actual computation.
33:    IF current_month > birth_month THEN
34:      age := current_year - birth_year;
35:    ELSIF (current_month = birth_month) and (current_day >= birth_day) THEN
36:      age := current_year - birth_year;
37:    ELSE
38:      age := current_year - birth_year - 1;
39:    END IF;
40: END;
41: /
42: DECLARE
43: *
44: ERROR at line 1:
45: ORA-06502: PL/SQL: numeric or value error
46: ORA-06512: at line 25
```

Had the variable age been declared as a BINARY_INTEGER, it would have been assigned a negative value and the result of the "Year 2000" error might show up in a manner far removed from the problem code. Because of the use of the subtype POSITIVE, you know instantly when an error occurs.

PLS_INTEGER

The PLS_INTEGER datatype is new in release 2.3 of PL/SQL and is used for declaring signed integer variables. Like the BINARY_INTEGER datatype, it also stores values in the range -2,147,483,647 through 2,147,483,647. How is it different from a BINARY_INTEGER then? The PLS_INTEGER datatype uses the native machine instructions for performing computations. Thus PLS_INTEGER calculations are much faster than BINARY_INTEGER calculations, which use library functions to perform arithmetic.

The Syntax for the PLS_INTEGER Datatype

```
variable_name PLS_INTEGER;
```

In this syntax, *variable_name* is whatever name you want to give to the variable.

Here is a sample declaration:

```
my_integer PLS_INTEGER;
```

> **NOTE**
>
> Oracle recommends use of the PLS_INTEGER datatype over the BINARY_INTEGER datatype in all new applications.

DATE

The DATE datatype is used to store date and time values. A better name might perhaps be DATETIME because the time component is always there whether you use it or not. The range for date variables is from 1 Jan 4712 BC through 31 Dec 4712 AD. If you do not specify a time when assigning a value to a variable of type DATE, it will default to midnight (12:00:00 a.m.).

The Syntax for the DATE Datatype

```
variable_name DATE;
```

In this syntax, *variable_name* is the name that you want to give the variable.

Here are some examples:

```
hire_date DATE;
emp_birthdate DATE;
```

TIP Be careful when comparing dates. The time value can trip you up. Values in a database that are intended to contain only dates sometimes mistakenly have a time value stored with them, and this can cause comparisons for equality to fail. To be safe, if you really don't care about the time of day, you can use the TRUNC() function. For example, instead of

```
IF hire_date = fire_date THEN...
```

use

```
IF TRUNC(hire_date) = TRUNC(fire_date) THEN...
```

Use of the TRUNC() function will truncate any time value so that you are truly comparing only dates. This function will be discussed in more detail on Day 7.

BOOLEAN

The BOOLEAN datatype is used to store true/false values. Its range is only the two values, true and false.

SYNTAX

The Syntax for the BOOLEAN Datatype

variable_name BOOLEAN;

In this syntax, *variable_name* is the name that you want to give this variable.

Here are some examples:

```
hired_fired_same_day BOOLEAN;
birthday_is_today BOOLEAN;
print_this_record BOOLEAN;
```

Boolean variables are often used as flag variables, and are also used to store the results of logical calculations. For example, if you needed to know if an employee's birthday was today, you could write this code:

```
birthday_is_today := (emp_birthdate = trunc(sysdate))
```

Then you could reference birthday_is_today anywhere in your code where you need to know this information. You would not have to recompare each time.

TIP

Using boolean variables to store the results of comparisons can be a powerful construct. If you code a comparison only once, you can go back and change the calculation later without having to find and change several occurrences in your program. It can also add to readability. With a variable named `birthday_is_today`, you know why the comparison was made.

LONG

The LONG datatype in PL/SQL is just like VARCHAR2 except that it can store a maximum of 32760 bytes instead of 32767, which is actually 7 bytes less than the VARCHAR2 type. For this reason you should usually use VARCHAR2 instead.

The Syntax for the LONG Datatype

```
variable_name LONG(size);
```

In this syntax, `variable_name` is the name that you want to give this variable, and `size` is the size, in bytes, of the variable. This must be a number between 1 and 32760.

Here are some sample declarations:

```
emp_comment LONG(32760);
work_history LONG(10000);
```

NOTE

The PL/SQL LONG differs from the database version of a LONG in that a LONG database column can store 2 gigabytes of data, whereas the PL/SQL version can store only 32760 bytes.

RAW

The RAW datatype is used to store strings of byte-oriented data. The difference between a RAW and a VARCHAR2 string is that Oracle does no character set translation on raw data. Thus if you are retrieving raw data from an Oracle server using ASCII to a machine using the EBCDIC character set, no translation would be done.

The Syntax for the RAW Datatype

```
variable_name RAW(size);
```

In this syntax, `variable_name` is the name you want to give the variable, and `size` is the size, in bytes, of the variable. This must be a number between 1 and 32767.

Here are some sample declarations:

```
sound_bytes RAW(32767);
some_data RAW(255);
```

Like VARCHAR2, the maximum length of a RAW variable is 32767 bytes.

NOTE

The database version of RAW allows only 2000 bytes, 255 prior to Oracle8.

LONG RAW

The LONG RAW datatype is just like RAW except that the maximum length is 32760 bytes. That's not a misprint. In PL/SQL the maximum length of a LONG RAW really is 7 bytes less than the maximum length of a RAW.

The Syntax for the LONG RAW Datatype

variable_name LONG RAW(*size*);

In this syntax, *variable_name* is the name you want to give this variable, and *size* is the size, in bytes, of the variable. This must be a number between 1 and 32760.

Here are some examples:

```
sound_byte LONG RAW(20000);
a_picture LONG RAW(30000);
```

As with a RAW, no character set conversion is performed.

NOTE

The database version of LONG RAW allows up to 2 gigabytes of data.

ROWID

ROWID is a special datatype that enables you to store Oracle's internal key for database records.

The Syntax for the ROWID Datatype

variable_name ROWID;

In this syntax, *variable_name* is the name that you want to give the variable.

Here is an example:

```
employee_row_id ROWID;
```

Each row in an Oracle table has a unique internal key associated with it. This key can be useful if you are planning to access the same record multiple times. For example, you might use a cursor to retrieve a number of rows, including the ROWID for each row, and then use that ROWID in a DELETE statement to delete some of the rows. Using the ROWID results in better performance because it tells Oracle exactly where to find the record so no index searches or table scans are necessary.

MSLABEL

The MSLABEL datatype is used with *Trusted Oracle*, which is a version of Oracle designed for use in high security environments such as those dealing with classified data.

The Syntax for the MSLABEL Datatype

```
variable_name MSLABEL;
```

In this syntax, `variable_name` is the name you want to give this variable.

Here is an example:

```
binary_label MSLABEL;
```

In a Trusted Oracle system, this datatype is used to store binary operating system labels. Standard Oracle allows the datatype to be declared, but only null values can be assigned to it.

Block Structure

On Day 1, "Learning the Basics of PL/SQL," you saw that the fundamental programming structure in PL/SQL is referred to as a block. In order to master PL/SQL, it is essential to understand the block structure, to understand the various types of blocks, and to understand how blocks are used. In the rest of this chapter, you will learn about anonymous blocks, trigger blocks, function blocks, and procedure blocks. You will also learn that blocks can be nested and what the implications are in terms of scoping.

Anonymous Blocks

NEW TERM   An *anonymous block* is one that is unnamed and that does not form the body of a procedure, function, or trigger. Remember the examples and exercises from Day 1? They were all anonymous blocks.

Anonymous blocks can be used inline as part of a SQL*Plus script, and can also be nested inside procedure and function blocks for purposes of error handling.

The Syntax for PL/SQL Anonymous Blocks

```
[DECLARE
  variable_declarations]
BEGIN
  program_code
[EXCEPTION
  error_handling_code]
END;
```

In this syntax, *variable_declarations* is where you declare your variables. *program_code* is where you write your PL/SQL program statements. *error_handling_code* is an optional section to which control branches in the event of an error.

As you can see, the keyword DECLARE is used to begin the block. Any variable declarations must follow this and precede the next keyword, which is BEGIN.

The keyword BEGIN signifies the beginning of the procedural section of the block. The program code goes here.

The keyword EXCEPTION begins the portion of the block that contains exception-handling code. The exception-handling portion of a block is optional, and you might not always use it. If the exception-handling portion is present, any runtime error or exception will cause program control to branch to this part of the block. The word *exception* is used to connote something that is outside the normal flow of events. It is used rather than *error* because an exception does not always imply that something is wrong. For example, issuing a SELECT statement and not getting any data back might be an exception to what you would normally expect, but it does not necessarily mean that an error occurred.

Listing 3.4 shows an example of an anonymous block. Note especially the declaration used for the hundreds_counter variable.

INPUT/ OUTPUT **Listing 3.4. An example of an anonymous block.**

```
 1: --Count up by hundreds until we get an error.
 2: DECLARE
 3:   --Note that with a scale of -2 this variable can only
 4:   --hold values like 100,200,300... up to 900.
 5:   hundreds_counter  NUMBER(1,-2);
 6: BEGIN
 7:   hundreds_counter := 100;
 8:   LOOP
 9:     DBMS_OUTPUT.PUT_LINE(hundreds_counter);
10:     hundreds_counter := hundreds_counter + 100;
11:   END LOOP;
12: EXCEPTION
13: WHEN OTHERS THEN
14:   DBMS_OUTPUT.PUT_LINE('That is as high as you can go.');
15: END;
```

continues

Listing 3.4. continued

```
16: /
17:
18: 100
19: 200
20: 300
21: 400
22: 500
23: 600
24: 700
25: 800
26: 900
27: That is as high as you can go.
```

ANALYSIS Take a look at Listing 3.4. A counter variable named hundreds_counter is declared in line 5. Because it is defined with a precision of one, it is only using one digit to represent the value. The scale of -2 tells you that you are using that one digit to represent hundreds. Lines 8 through 11 contain a loop that prints the value of the counter and then increments it by one hundred. Because the counter's precision is only one digit and the two zeros are assumed, the program can only count up to 900. When you try to go past 900 to 1000, the variable won't be able to hold the value and an exception will be triggered.

Look at the output from Listing 3.4. You can see that the code indeed works as described. It successfully counted up to 900, and when the variable was incremented to 1000, an exception was generated that displayed a message before execution ended.

Function and Procedure Blocks

PL/SQL allows you to define functions and procedures. These are similar to functions and procedures defined in any other language, and they are always defined as one PL/SQL block.

The Syntax for Defining a Function

```
FUNCTION name [( argument_list )] RETURN datatype {IS,AS}
  variable_declarations
BEGIN
  program_code
[EXCEPTION
  error_handling_code]
END;
```

In this syntax, the placeholders are as follows:

- [ ] name—The name you want to give the function.

- [ ] argument_list—A list of input and/or output parameters for the function.

- [ ] datatype—The datatype of the function's return value.

☐ *variable_declarations*—Where you declare any variables that are local to the function.

☐ *program_code*—Where you write the PL/SQL statements that make up the function.

☐ *error_handling_code*—Where you write any error-handling code.

Notice that the keyword DECLARE has been replaced by the function header, which names the function, describes the parameters, and indicates the return type. Except for this, the function block looks just like the declarations for the anonymous blocks that you have seen so far.

You will learn more about functions on Day 5, "Using Functions, IF Statements, and Loops." Listing 3.5 shows an example of a function.

INPUT   **Listing 3.5. A function block.**

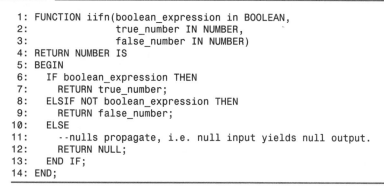

```
 1: FUNCTION iifn(boolean_expression in BOOLEAN,
 2:               true_number IN NUMBER,
 3:               false_number IN NUMBER)
 4: RETURN NUMBER IS
 5: BEGIN
 6:   IF boolean_expression THEN
 7:     RETURN true_number;
 8:   ELSIF NOT boolean_expression THEN
 9:     RETURN false_number;
10:   ELSE
11:     --nulls propagate, i.e. null input yields null output.
12:     RETURN NULL;
13:   END IF;
14: END;
```

ANALYSIS   To execute the function shown in Listing 3.5, you need to declare it and execute from within a PL/SQL block. The section "Nesting Functions and Procedures," later in this chapter, shows how this is done.

The declaration for a procedure is almost identical to that of a function.

The Syntax for Declaring a Procedure

```
PROCEDURE name [( argument_list )] {IS,AS}
  variable_declarations
BEGIN
  program_code
[EXCEPTION
  error_handling_code]
END;
```

In this syntax, the placeholders are as follows:

☐ *name*—The name you want to give the procedure.

☐ *argument_list*—A list of input and/or output parameters for the procedure.

- [ ] *variable_declarations*—Where you declare any variables that are local to the procedure.
- [ ] *program_code*—Where you write the PL/SQL statements that make up the procedure.
- [ ] *error_handling_code*—Where you write any error-handling code.

As you can see, the procedure declaration resembles a function declaration except that there is no return datatype and the keyword PROCEDURE is used instead of FUNCTION. Listing 3.6 shows an example of a procedure.

INPUT   **Listing 3.6. A procedure block.**

```
1:  PROCEDURE swapn (num_one IN OUT NUMBER, num_two IN OUT NUMBER) IS
2:      temp_num    NUMBER;
3:    BEGIN
4:      temp_num := num_one;
5:      num_one := num_two;
6:      num_two := temp_num ;
7:    END;
```

ANALYSIS   You will see how this function is executed later in this chapter in the section titled "Nesting Functions and Procedures."

Procedures and functions are both useful constructs that promote modularity, allow you to hide complexity, and facilitate reuse of code. During Day 7, you will read about many of the built-in functions provided by Oracle, and on Day 5, you will learn more about creating your own functions.

Trigger Blocks

PL/SQL can also be used to write database triggers. Triggers are used to define code that is executed when certain actions or events occur. At the database level, triggers can be defined for events such as inserting a record into a table, deleting a record, and updating a record.

The following syntax for creating a database trigger is much more complex than that for a function or a procedure. Don't try and understand it all now. Triggers are discussed in more detail on Day 11, "Writing Database Triggers."

The Syntax for Creating a Database Trigger

```
CREATE [OR REPLACE] TRIGGER trigger_name
  {BEFORE|AFTER} verb_list ON table_name
  [[REFERENCING correlation_names] FOR EACH ROW [WHEN (condition)]]
DECLARE
  declarations
BEGIN
  pl/sql_code
END;
```

In this syntax, the placeholders are as follows:

- [ ] *trigger_name*—The name you want to give the trigger.
- [ ] *verb_list*—The SQL verbs that fire the trigger.
- [ ] *table_name*—The table on which the trigger is defined.
- [ ] *correlation_names*—Allows you to specify correlation names other than the default of OLD and NEW.
- [ ] *condition*—An optional condition placed on the execution of the trigger.
- [ ] *declarations*—Consists of any variable, record, or cursor declarations needed by this PL/SQL block.
- [ ] *pl/sql_code*—The PL/SQL code that gets executed when the trigger fires.

As you can see, even though the specification for a trigger is much more complex than that of a procedure or a function, the basic PL/SQL block structure is still present. The first three lines of the declaration tell Oracle the type of trigger, the table it is associated with, and when it should be fired. The remainder is simply the PL/SQL block that executes when the trigger fires.

Listing 3.7 shows a database trigger that sets the primary key of a new record being inserted into the database table my_table.

INPUT **Listing 3.7. Trigger that sets a primary key.**

```
 1: CREATE OR REPLACE TRIGGER my_table_set_key
 2:         BEFORE INSERT ON my_table
 3:         REFERENCING NEW AS n
 4:         FOR EACH ROW
 5: DECLARE
 6:   new_key INTEGER;
 7: BEGIN
 8:   SELECT key_for_table.NEXTVAL INTO new_key FROM DUAL;
 9:   :n.fld_pk := new_key;
10: END;
```

Again, don't worry if you don't understand triggers completely right now. Day 11 contains a complete discussion of their benefits and how to use them.

Nested Blocks

PL/SQL blocks can be nested, one inside the other. This is often done for purposes of error handling, and also for purposes of modularity. Listing 3.8 shows a nested anonymous block.

INPUT/OUTPUT **Listing 3.8. A nested anonymous block.**

```
 1: --Be sure to execute: SET SERVEROUTPUT ON
 2: --before executing this PL/SQL block.
 3: --This is an example of nested anonymous blocks.
 4: DECLARE
 5:   error_flag  BOOLEAN := false;  --true if an error occurs while counting.
 6:
 7: BEGIN
 8:   DBMS_OUTPUT.PUT_LINE('We are going to count from 100 to 1000.');
 9:
10:   --Execute the nested block to do the actual counting.
11:   --Any errors will be trapped within this block.
12:   DECLARE
13:     hundreds_counter  NUMBER(1,-2);
14:   BEGIN
15:     hundreds_counter := 100;
16:     LOOP
17:       DBMS_OUTPUT.PUT_LINE(hundreds_counter);
18:       hundreds_counter := hundreds_counter + 100;
19:       IF hundreds_counter > 1000 THEN
20:         EXIT;
21:       END IF;
22:     END LOOP;
23:   EXCEPTION
24:   WHEN OTHERS THEN
25:     --set the error flag if we can't finish counting.
26:     error_flag := true;
27:   END;
28:
29:   --We are done. Were we successful?
30:   IF error_flag THEN
31:     DBMS_OUTPUT.PUT_LINE('Sorry, I cannot count that high.');
32:   ELSE
33:     DBMS_OUTPUT.PUT_LINE('Done.');
34:   END IF;
35: END;
36: /
37:  We are going to count from 100 to 1000.
38: 100
39: 200
40: 300
41: 400
42: 500
43: 600
44: 700
45: 800
46: 900
47: Sorry, I cannot count that high.
48:
49: PL/SQL procedure successfully completed.
```

ANALYSIS The exception handler on the inner block, lines 23 through 26, sets the error_flag variable to true if any error occurs while counting. This allows the outer block to detect the error and display an appropriate message.

Nesting Functions and Procedures

Functions and procedures can be declared and executed from within other PL/SQL blocks. Remember the iifn function shown in Listing 3.5? That function takes three arguments: one boolean and two numbers. It functions as an inline IF statement. If the first argument is true, the first number is returned. If the first argument is false, the second number is returned. You can see how the function works by writing a simple PL/SQL block to declare and execute it, as shown in Listing 3.9.

INPUT/OUTPUT

Listing 3.9. Executing the iifn function.

```
1: --This is a pl/sql wrapper that exercises the
2: --function shown in Listing 3.5.
3: --Be sure to execute: SET SERVEROUTPUT ON
4: --
5: DECLARE
6: temp   NUMBER;
7:
8:   FUNCTION iifn(boolean_expression IN BOOLEAN,
9:                 true_number IN NUMBER,
10:                 false_number IN NUMBER)
11:   RETURN NUMBER IS
12:   BEGIN
13:     IF boolean_expression THEN
14:       RETURN true_number;
15:     ELSIF NOT boolean_expression THEN
16:       RETURN false_number;
17:     ELSE
18:       --nulls propagate, i.e. null input yields null output.
19:       RETURN NULL;
20:     END IF;
21:   END;
22: BEGIN
23:   DBMS_OUTPUT.PUT_LINE(iifn(2 > 1,1,0));
24:   DBMS_OUTPUT.PUT_LINE(iifn(2 > 3,1,0));
25:   --
26:   --The next few lines verify that a null input yields a null output.
27:   temp := iifn(null,1,0);
28:   IF temp IS NULL THEN
29:     DBMS_OUTPUT.PUT_LINE('NULL');
30:   ELSE
31:     DBMS_OUTPUT.PUT_LINE(temp);
32:   END IF;
33: END;
34: /
35: 1
36: 0
37: NULL
38:
39: PL/SQL procedure successfully completed.
```

ANALYSIS Line 5 begins a PL/SQL anonymous block. The iifn function is declared within the scope of this outer block (see lines 8 through 21). The keyword BEGIN in line 22 marks the start of the procedural section of the outer block. Because the iifn function is declared within the outer block, it can also be called from the procedural section of the outer block.

Line 23 calls the iifn function with a boolean expression that evaluates as true. It then prints the value returned, which in this case is the second argument.

Line 24 calls the iifn function with a boolean expression that evaluates as false, so the third argument is returned.

Finally, in lines 26–32, a null expression is passed to the function. A null input should result in a null output, and you can see that the function properly handles this case by returning a null value.

A procedure can be nested in the same manner as a function. Listing 3.10 shows a simple PL/SQL block illustrating the use of the swapn procedure you saw earlier in Listing 3.6.

INPUT/ OUTPUT **Listing 3.10. Executing the swapn procedure.**

```
 1: --Demonstration of a nested procedure block.
 2: --Be sure you have executed: SET SERVEROUTPUT ON
 3: --This is a PL/SQL wrapper that executes the
 4: --procedure shown in Listing 3.6.
 5: DECLARE
 6:    first_number     NUMBER;
 7:    second_number    NUMBER;
 8:
 9:    PROCEDURE swapn (num_one IN OUT NUMBER, num_two IN OUT NUMBER) IS
10:       temp_num     NUMBER;
11:    BEGIN
12:       temp_num := num_one;
13:       num_one := num_two;
14:       num_two := temp_num ;
15:    END;
16:
17: BEGIN
18:    --Set some initial values and display them.
19:    first_number := 10;
20:    second_number := 20;
21:    DBMS_OUTPUT.PUT_LINE('First Number = ' || TO_CHAR (first_number));
22:    DBMS_OUTPUT.PUT_LINE('Second Number = ' || TO_CHAR (second_number));
23:
24:    --Swap the values
25:    DBMS_OUTPUT.PUT_LINE('Swapping the two values now.');
26:    swapn(first_number, second_number);
27:
28:    --Display the results
29:    DBMS_OUTPUT.PUT_LINE('First Number = ' || to_CHAR (first_number));
30:    DBMS_OUTPUT.PUT_LINE('Second Number = ' || to_CHAR (second_number));
31: END;
32: /
33: First Number = 10
```

```
34: Second Number = 20
35: Swapping the two values now.
36: First Number = 20
37: Second Number = 10
38:
39: PL/SQL procedure successfully completed.
```

ANALYSIS The swapn procedure simply swaps two numeric values. You can see in lines 12 through 14 that it does just that, using the temp_num variable to hold the value of num_one until it can be assigned to num_two, after num_two has been assigned to num_one.

Scope Rules

With any language, and PL/SQL is no exception, it is important to have an understanding of the *scope* of the various variables, procedures, and functions that you declare. *Scope* means the range of code within which a given identifier can be referenced.

In PL/SQL the general rule is: An identifier (that is, variable name, procedure name, function name) can be referenced only by code executing inside the block in which the identifier was declared. This includes code inside any nested blocks, procedures, or functions.

Take a look at the code in Listing 3.11, which has been carefully constructed to illustrate this point.

**INPUT/
OUTPUT** **Listing 3.11. Illustrates the scope of various identifiers.**

```
 1: --Be sure to execute: SET SERVEROUTPUT ON
 2:
 3: DECLARE
 4:   a_name   VARCHAR2(30) := 'Jeff Gennick';
 5:
 6: PROCEDURE name_print IS
 7: BEGIN
 8:   DBMS_OUTPUT.PUT_LINE(a_name);
 9: END;
10:
11: BEGIN
12:   DBMS_OUTPUT.PUT_LINE(a_name);
13:
14:   DECLARE
15:     b_name   VARCHAR2(30) := 'Jenny Gennick';
16:   BEGIN
17:       DBMS_OUTPUT.PUT_LINE('Inside nested block');
18:       DBMS_OUTPUT.PUT_LINE(a_name);
19:       DBMS_OUTPUT.PUT_LINE(b_name);
20:       name_print;
21:   END;
22:
```

continues

Listing 3.11. continued

```
23:    DBMS_OUTPUT.PUT_LINE('Back in the main block');
24:
25:    --But we cannot compile the following line because b_name
26:    --is not defined in this block.
27:    --DBMS_OUTPUT.PUT_LINE(b_name);
28:
29:    --Our procedure, however, can access the value of a_name.
30:    name_print;
31: END;
32: /
33: Jeff Gennick
34: Inside nested block
35: Jeff Gennick
36: Jenny Gennick
37: Jeff Gennick
38: Back in the main block
39: Jeff Gennick
```

ANALYSIS   The code shown in Listing 3.11 consists of two nested anonymous blocks and one procedure definition. The outermost block begins at line 3 and ends on line 31. A nested anonymous block begins on line 14 and ends on line 21. Lines 6 through 9 define the name_print procedure.

The variable a_name is declared in the outermost block (see line 4), thus any nested block, procedure, or function has access to it. To demonstrate this, the outer block displays the value of a_name in line 12, the nested block displays the value of a_name in line 18, and in line 30 of the outer block, the nested procedure name_print is called to also print the value of a_name. The name_print procedure, because it is defined within the outer block, has access to all other identifiers declared at that same level.

The variable b_name is declared in the inner block (see line 15) and can only be referenced within that block. If you were to uncomment line 27 and try to execute the code shown in the listing, you would receive an error because b_name would not be recognized.

Summary

In this chapter you learned about the many datatypes that are available to you when programming in PL/SQL. You learned about the several nuances and variations of the NUMBER datatype, which are important to understand as you continue to work with PL/SQL.

This chapter also discusses the PL/SQL block structure in detail and illustrates several different types of blocks, that is, functions, procedures, triggers, and anonymous blocks.

No discussion of PL/SQL blocks is complete without addressing the issue of scope. You should now feel comfortable that when you declare an identifier, whether it be a variable, function, or procedure, you fully understand from where it can be referenced.

Q&A

Q Why shouldn't I use the VARCHAR datatype?

A Oracle warns against it because the definition of that datatype might be changed in the near future, and any change might have adverse ramifications on your code. Use VARCHAR2 instead.

Q What is a subtype?

A A subtype allows you to declare variables of a particular datatype that hold only a subset of the possible values that are normally handled by that datatype.

Q What is the difference between the BINARY_INTEGER type and the PLS_INTEGER type?

A Both use binary representations to store values. However, operations on PLS_INTEGERS use native machine instructions, whereas operations on BINARY_INTEGERS use internal library functions, which are slower.

Q What is the difference between a function and a procedure?

A A function returns a value and can be used in an expression. A procedure does not return a value and cannot be used in an expression.

Workshop

Use the following workshop to test your comprehension of this chapter and put what you've learned into practice. You'll find the answers to the quiz and exercises in Appendix A, "Answers."

Quiz

1. What are three benefits of using functions and procedures?
2. What values can a variable declared as NUMBER(6,2) hold? What will be the maximum value?
3. What values can a variable declared as NUMBER(2,2) hold? Where will rounding occur?
4. What is the maximum length of a VARCHAR2 variable in PL/SQL? In the Oracle database?

5. What can you do to ignore the time portion of a DATE variable?

6. When comparing a VARCHAR2 and a CHAR variable, how can you eliminate any trailing spaces?

Exercises

1. Try writing an anonymous block that declares a variable and displays its value. Then add a nested block that declares a variable of the same name and displays its value. What happens and why?

2. Write a function that computes a person's age in years. Hint: To get started on this, look at Listing 3.3.

Day 4

Writing PL/SQL Expressions

by Jonathan Gennick

Today's lesson is about expressions. Expressions enable you to manipulate data inside your PL/SQL routines. They combine values and operators and are used to perform calculations and compare data. Without expressions, you would get precious little done.

PL/SQL Basics: Operators, Expressions, and Conversion

NEW TERM PL/SQL expressions are composed of *operands* and *operators*. *Operands* represent values. An operand is often a variable, but can also be a literal, a constant, or a function call. *Operators* specify actions, such as addition, multiplication, and so on, which can be performed using one or two operands. Here is a typical expression:

```
total_wages := hourly_rate * hours_worked
```

The three variables, `total_wages`, `hourly_rate`, and `hours_worked`, are all examples of operands. The `*` is the multiplication operator, and the `:=` is the assignment operator.

Yesterday you learned about datatypes and variable declarations. Today you will read about the operators you can use to manipulate those variables. You'll see how to build simple expressions, such as the one just shown that multiplies two numbers together. You'll see how to build much more complex expressions that consist of function calls, operations using variables, and relational comparisons. You'll also learn how to control the order in which an expression is evaluated.

Expressions often contain operands of multiple datatypes. It's not unusual, for example, to want to subtract a number of years from a date. In cases like this, you must first convert the values being operated on to a compatible datatype. Only then can the necessary calculation be performed. In many cases, when the conversion is obvious, PL/SQL will handle this for you. You'll learn how and when PL/SQL does this. You'll also learn how you can explicitly specify the conversion, when you should do it, and why.

Operators

Operators are the glue that hold expressions together. A very simple expression could consist of just one variable or value, but to accomplish anything useful, you need more than that. Operators enable you to take one or two values and perform an operation that uses those values and returns a result. The operation could be as simple as adding two numbers together and returning the total, or it could be a complex logical expression used in an `IF` statement. PL/SQL operators can be divided into the following categories:

- ☐ Arithmetic operators
- ☐ Comparison operators
- ☐ Logical operators
- ☐ String operators

NEW TERM PL/SQL operators are either *unary* or *binary*. Most are binary operators, which means that they act on two values. An example is the addition operator, which adds two numbers together. A few, such as the negation operator, are unary. Unary operators only operate on one value.

Each of these types of operators are described in the following sections. There is nothing unusual about the operators in PL/SQL, and if you have any other programming experience, you will see that the operators and the order of evaluation are not much different than for any other language.

Arithmetic Operators

Arithmetic operators are used for mathematical computations, such as addition and subtraction. Table 4.1 shows the arithmetic functions supported by PL/SQL.

Table 4.1. Arithmetic operators.

Operator	Example	Usage
**	10**5	The exponentiation operator. It raises one number to the power of another. In the example shown, it raises 10 to the fifth power, resulting in a value of 100,000.
*	2*3	The multiplication operator. The example shown, 2 times 3, results in a value of 6.
/	6/2	The division operator. In the example, 6 divided by 2, the result would be 3.
+	2+2	The addition operator, which is used to add two values together. The example evaluates to 4.
-	4-2	The subtraction operator, which is used to subtract one number from another. The example subtracts 2 from 4 resulting in a value of 2.
-	-5	The negation operator. Used by itself, the minus sign negates the operand. The expression shown evaluates to a negative 5.
+	+5	Used by itself, the plus sign is the identity operator. It complements the negation operator, and the result of the expression is simply the value of the operand. In the example shown, the result is 5.

Addition, Subtraction, Multiplication, and Division

The basic four arithmetic operators, addition, subtraction, multiplication, and division, probably need no further explanation. Listing 4.1 shows some sample expressions, and the output shows their resulting values.

NOTE

Before executing the code shown in Listing 4.1 and most other listings in this chapter, make sure that you have first executed the following command at least once during the session:

`SET SERVEROUTPUT ON`

If you omit this command, SQL*Plus won't display the output generated by the calls to DBMS_OUTPUT.PUT_LINE. You only need execute this command once each time you start SQL*Plus. For listings in which this is important, a comment is included at the beginning to remind you.

INPUT **Listing 4.1. The basic four arithmetic operators in action.**

```
1: --The basic arithmetic operators in action.
2: --Remember to execute: SET SERVEROUTPUT ON
3: BEGIN
4:   DBMS_OUTPUT.PUT_LINE(4 * 2);   --multiplication
5:   DBMS_OUTPUT.PUT_LINE(24 / 3);  --division
6:   DBMS_OUTPUT.PUT_LINE(4 + 4);   --addition
7:   DBMS_OUTPUT.PUT_LINE(16 - 8);  --subtraction
8: END;
9: /
```

OUTPUT
```
8
8
8
8
PL/SQL procedure successfully completed.
```

ANALYSIS As you can see, the DBMS_OUTPUT.PUT_LINE procedure was used to display the values of four simple expressions, all of which evaluated to eight.

Exponentiation

Exponentiation, or raising a number to a power, is simply the act of multiplying a number by itself a specified number of times. Table 4.2 shows a few examples of exponentiation together with equivalent expressions using multiplication and the resulting values.

Table 4.2. Examples of exponentiation.

Example	Equivalent to	Result
10**5	10*10*10*10*10	100,000
2**3	2*2*2	8
6**2	6*6	36

Negation and Identity

You are familiar with negation, in its simplest form, when you use it to write a negative value such as -242.24. One way to look at it would be to say that the - preceding the number indicates that the value is negative. Another way to look at this is that you wrote a positive number, in other words 242.24, and applied the negation operator to it, thus yielding a negative value. Take the latter approach, and you will quickly realize that the target of the negation operator could just as well be a variable or an expression.

The identity operator, represented by the plus sign, doesn't do much at all. It's the opposite of the negation operator and simply returns the value of its operand.

Listing 4.2 shows some examples of how you can use these two operators.

INPUT   **Listing 4.2. The negation and identity operators in action.**

```
 1: --The negation and identity operators in action.
 2: --Remember to execute: SET SERVEROUTPUT ON
 3: DECLARE
 4:    x    NUMBER;
 5: BEGIN
 6:    DBMS_OUTPUT.PUT_LINE(-242.24);
 7:    --You can also negate a variable.
 8:    x := 5;
 9:    DBMS_OUTPUT.PUT_LINE(-x);
10:    --Negating a negative number yields a positive value.
11:    x := -5;
12:    DBMS_OUTPUT.PUT_LINE(-x);
13:    --The identity operator simply returns the value of its operand.
14:    DBMS_OUTPUT.PUT_LINE(+10);
15:    DBMS_OUTPUT.PUT_LINE(+x);
16: END;
17: /
```

OUTPUT
```
-242.24
-5
5
10
-5
PL/SQL procedure successfully completed.
```

ANALYSIS   In line 6, the negation operator is used to simply write a negative number. In lines 7 through 9, the negation operator is used to negate the value of a variable. In line 12, it is used again, but this time the variable contains a negative number to start with, so the resulting value is positive. The remaining lines show the identity operator returning the operand's value unchanged.

Comparison Operators

Comparison operators are used to compare one value or expression to another. You can use them in your code to ask questions such as "Are these two values equal?" and then make decisions based on the result. Table 4.3 lists all the comparison operators supported by PL/SQL.

Table 4.3. Comparison operators.

Operator	Example	Usage
=	IF A = B THEN	The equality operator. This compares two values to see if they are identical.
<>	IF A <> B THEN	The inequality operator. This compares two values to see if they are *not* identical.
!=	IF A != B THEN	Another inequality operator, synonymous with <>.
~=	IF A ~= B THEN	Another inequality operator, synonymous with <>.
<	IF A < B THEN	The less than operator. Checks to see if one value is less than another.
>	IF A > B THEN	The greater than operator. Checks to see if one value is greater than another.
<=	IF A <= B THEN	The less than or equal to operator. Checks to see if one value is less than or equal to another.
>=	IF A >= B THEN	The greater than or equal to operator. Checks to see if one value is greater than or equal to another.
LIKE	IF A LIKE B THEN	The pattern-matching operator. Checks to see if a character string matches a specified pattern.
BETWEEN	IF A BETWEEN B AND C THEN	Checks to see if a value lies within a specified range of values.
IN	IF A IN (B,C,D) THEN	Checks to see if a value lies within a specified list of values.
IS NULL	IF A IS NULL THEN	Checks to see if a value is null.

NEW TERM The first eight operators shown in Table 4.3 are referred to as *relational operators*. These operators are very common and are present in almost any programming language.

All comparison operators return a boolean result. They either represent a true statement or they do not. This true/false, or boolean, result can be used in a branching statement such as an IF...THEN statement, or it can be assigned to a boolean variable for later reference.

With the exception of the LIKE operator, you can use all comparison operators with any of the *scalar* datatypes discussed on Day 3, "Writing Declarations and Blocks." The LIKE operator is only valid for character strings.

The Relational Operators: =, <>, !=, ~=, <, >, <=, >=

Like the basic arithmetic operators, the relational operators are commonly used in almost every programming language, and there is probably no need to elaborate much on the explanations in Table 4.3.

The relational operators test values for equality, inequality, and to see if one value is less than or greater than another. You can use these operators to compare two values belonging to any of the scalar datatypes. Table 4.4 gives some sample true and false expressions.

Table 4.4. Relational operator examples.

True Expressions	False Expressions
5 = 5	5 = 3
'Jonathan' = 'Jonathan'	'Jonathan ' = 'Jonathan'
5 != 3	5 <> 5
'Jonathan ' ~= 'Jonathan'	'Jonathan' ~= 'Jonathan'
10 < 200	10.1 < 10.05
'Jeff' < 'Jenny'	'jeff' < 'Jeff'
TO_DATE('15-Nov-61' < '15-Nov-97')	TO_DATE('1-Jan-97' < '1-Jan-96')
10.1 <= 10.1	10 <= 20
'A' <= 'B'	'B' <= 'A'
TO_DATE('1-Jan-97') <= TO_DATE('1-Jan-97)	TO_DATE('15-Nov-61') <= TO_DATE('15-Nov-60')

You should be aware of some considerations when comparing dates and character strings. Oracle dates contain a time component, and it's important to remember that when comparing two dates for equality. String comparisons are case-sensitive, are dependent on the character set being used, and are affected by the underlying datatype. Comparing two values as CHAR strings might yield different results than the same values compared as VARCHAR2 strings. These issues are discussed later in this chapter in the section "Use of Comparison Operators with Strings."

LIKE

LIKE is PL/SQL's pattern-matching operator and is used to compare a character string against a pattern. It's especially useful for performing wildcard searches when you need to retrieve data from the database and you aren't exactly sure of the spelling of your search criteria. Unlike the other comparison operators, LIKE can only be used with character strings.

The Syntax for LIKE

```
string_variable LIKE pattern
```

In this syntax, *string_variable* represents any character string variable, whether VARCHAR2, CHAR, LONG, and so on. *pattern* represents a pattern. This can also be a string variable, or it can be a string literal.

The LIKE operator checks to see if the contents of *string_variable* match the pattern definition. If the string matches the pattern, a result of true is returned; otherwise, the expression evaluates to false.

NEW TERM Two *wildcard* characters are defined for use with LIKE, the percent sign (%) and the underscore (_). The percent sign matches any number of characters in a string, and the underscore matches exactly one. For example, the pattern 'New %' will match 'New York', 'New Jersey', 'New Buffalo', and any other string beginning with the word 'New '. Another example is the pattern '___day'. It is looking for a six-letter word ending with the letters 'day', and would match 'Monday', 'Friday', and 'Sunday'. It would not match 'Tuesday', 'Wednesday', 'Thursday', or 'Saturday' because those names have more than three letters preceding 'day'.

Listing 4.3 shows a short function that makes use of the LIKE operator to return the area code from a phone number. Figure 4.1 shows how the function works.

INPUT ### Listing 4.3. A function using the LIKE operator to return a phone number's area code.

```
 1: CREATE OR REPLACE FUNCTION area_code (phone_number IN VARCHAR2)
 2: RETURN VARCHAR2 AS
 3: BEGIN
 4:   IF phone_number LIKE '___-___-____' THEN
 5:     --we have a phone number with an area code.
 6:     RETURN SUBSTR(phone_number,1,3);
 7:   ELSE
 8:     --there is no area code
 9:     RETURN 'none';
10:   END IF;
11: END;
12: /
```

Function created.
SQL>

 The preceding code simply creates a stored function. Type it into SQL*Plus exactly as it is shown. The LIKE operator is used in line 4 to see if the phone number matches the standard XXX-XXX-XXXX format, which would indicate that an area code is part of the number. Figure 4.1 demonstrates the use of this area_code function.

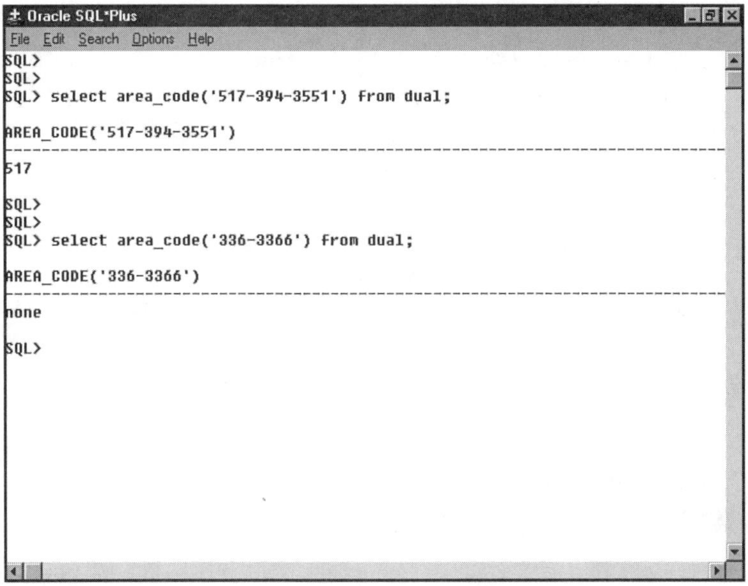

Figure 4.1.

The area_code
function in action.

BETWEEN

The BETWEEN operator tests to see if a value falls within a given range of values.

The Syntax for BETWEEN

the_value [NOT] BETWEEN *low_end* AND *high_end*

In this syntax, *the_value* is the value you are testing, *low_end* represents the low end of the range, and *high_end* represents the high end of the range.

A result of true is returned if the value in question is greater than or equal to the low end of the range and less than or equal to the high end of the range.

You might have already guessed that the BETWEEN operator is somewhat redundant. You could easily replace any expression using BETWEEN with one that used <= and >=. The equivalent expression would look like this:

(*the_value* >= *low_end*) AND (*the_value* <= *high_end*)

Table 4.5 shows some expressions using BETWEEN and the equivalent expressions using <= and >=.

Table 4.5. Expressions using the BETWEEN operator.

Expression	Result	Equivalent Expression
5 BETWEEN -5 AND 5	true	(5 >= -5) AND (5 <= 5)
4 BETWEEN 0 AND 3	false	(4 >= 0) AND (4 <= 3)
4 BETWEEN 3 AND 5	true	(4 >= 3) AND (4 <= 5)
4 NOT BETWEEN 3 AND 4	false	(4 >= 3) AND (4 <= 4)

TIP

Even though the BETWEEN operator is redundant, using it can add clarity to your code, making it more readable.

IN

The IN operator checks to see if a value is contained in a specified list of values. A true result is returned if the value is contained in the list; otherwise, the expression evaluates to false.

The Syntax for IN

```
the_value [NOT] IN (value1, value2, value3,...)
```

In this syntax, *the_value* is the value you are testing, and *value1*, *value2*, *value3*,... represents a list of comma-delimited values.

A result of true is returned if the value in question matches one of the values in the list.

Table 4.6 shows some examples of the IN operator in use.

Table 4.6. Expressions using the IN operator.

Expression	Result
3 IN (0,1,2,3,4,5,6,7,8,9)	true
'Sun' IN ('Mon','Tue','Wed','Thu','Fri')	false
'Sun' IN ('Sat','Sun')	true
3 NOT IN (0,1,2,3,4,5,6,7,8,9)	false

Listing 4.4 shows a short sample of code that uses the IN operator to see if a holiday will result in a three-day weekend.

INPUT **Listing 4.4. The IN operator used to test for long weekends.**

```
 1: --Remember to execute: SET SERVEROUTPUT ON
 2: DECLARE
 3:    test_date      DATE;
 4:    day_of_week    VARCHAR2(3);
 5:    years_ahead    INTEGER;
 6: BEGIN
 7:    --Assign a date value to test_date.
 8:    --Let's use Independence Day.
 9:    test_date := TO_DATE('4-Jul-1997','dd-mon-yyyy');
10:    --Now let's look ahead ten years and see how many
11:    --three day July 4 weekends we can expect.
12:    FOR years_ahead IN 1..10 LOOP
13:      --get the name for the day of the week.
14:      day_of_week := TO_CHAR(test_date,'Dy');
15:      --most employers give an extra day if July 4 falls on a weekend.
16:      IF day_of_week IN ('Mon','Fri','Sat','Sun') THEN
17:        DBMS_OUTPUT.PUT_LINE(TO_CHAR(test_date,'dd-Mon-yyyy')
18:                             || '   A long weekend!');
19:      ELSE
20:        DBMS_OUTPUT.PUT_LINE(TO_CHAR(test_date,'dd-Mon-yyyy')
21:                             || ' Not a long weekend.');
22:      END IF;
23:      --advance one year (12 months)
24:      test_date := ADD_MONTHS(test_date,12);
25:    END LOOP; --for each year
26: END;
27: /
```

OUTPUT
```
04-Jul-1997    A long weekend!
04-Jul-1998    A long weekend!
04-Jul-1999    A long weekend!
04-Jul-2000 Not a long weekend.
04-Jul-2001 Not a long weekend.
04-Jul-2002 Not a long weekend.
04-Jul-2003    A long weekend!
04-Jul-2004    A long weekend!
04-Jul-2005    A long weekend!
04-Jul-2006 Not a long weekend.
PL/SQL procedure successfully completed.
```

ANALYSIS The preceding code checks the date for Independence Day over a 10-year period, and tells you whether or not it will result in a long weekend. Line 9 is where the starting date of 4 July 1997 is set. A FOR loop is used in lines 12 through 25 to check the July 4 day for a 10-year period. In line 14, the TO_CHAR function is used to retrieve the day of the week on which July 4 falls during the year in question. Line 16 uses the IN operator to test for a long weekend. The obvious cases to check for are when Independence Day falls on a Monday or a Friday, resulting in a three-day weekend. The test in line 16 also includes Saturday and Sunday because many employers still give employees a day off, resulting in a three-day weekend. Line 24 uses PL/SQL's ADD_MONTHS function to advance the date twelve months, which is one year. You will read more about ADD_MONTHS on Day 7, "Using Oracle's Built-in Functions." It is also covered in Appendix B, "Oracle Functions Reference."

IS NULL

The IS NULL operator is used to test a variable for the absence of a value. Variables that have no value are referred to as being *null* and are most commonly encountered when retrieving data from a database. Variables you declare in a PL/SQL block are also initially null, or have no value, and remain null until your code specifically assigns a value to them.

The Syntax for IS NULL

the_value IS [NOT] NULL

In this syntax, *the_value* is a variable, or another expression, that you are testing.

If the value you are testing is null, then the IS NULL operator returns true. You can also reverse the test by using IS NOT NULL, in which case true is returned if the variable or expression in question contains a value.

Listing 4.5 shows an example of using the IS NULL operator to demonstrate that a variable has no value until one is specifically assigned.

INPUT **Listing 4.5. The IS NULL operator in action.**

```
 1: --Remember to execute: SET SERVEROUTPUT ON
 2: DECLARE
 3:   test  INTEGER;
 4: BEGIN
 5:   --The variable TEST is currently null because
 6:   --a value hasn't been assigned to it yet.
 7:   IF test IS NULL THEN
 8:     DBMS_OUTPUT.PUT_LINE('The variable TEST is null.');
 9:   END IF;
10:   --Assign a value to TEST and display it.
11:   test := 1;
12:   DBMS_OUTPUT.PUT_LINE('TEST = ' ¦¦ TO_CHAR(test));
13:   --Test is no longer null because a value has been assigned to it.
14:   IF test IS NOT NULL THEN
15:     DBMS_OUTPUT.PUT_LINE('The variable TEST is NOT null.');
16:   END IF;
17: END;
18: /
```

OUTPUT
```
The variable TEST is null.
TEST = 1
The variable TEST is NOT null.
PL/SQL procedure successfully completed.
```

ANALYSIS The variable test is declared in line 3. Initially it has no value and is considered to be null. The IS NULL operator is used in line 7 to check for this. Because no value has yet been assigned, the comparison evaluates to true and the message is printed. In line 11, a value is assigned to the variable test, and it is no longer considered to be null. The IS NOT NULL test in line 14 proves this.

TIP It is extremely important to understand the effects of null values on expressions, especially comparison expressions. The rule about comparison expressions being either true or false flies right out the window when nulls are introduced into the equation, and nulls are often encountered when retrieving data from databases. Be sure to read the section entitled "Null Values in Expressions," later in this chapter.

Logical Operators

PL/SQL implements three logical operators: AND, OR, and NOT. The NOT operator is typically used to negate the result of a comparison expression, whereas the AND and OR operators are typically used to link together multiple comparisons.

NOT

Use the NOT operator when you are interested in the case in which a comparison is not true.

The Syntax for the NOT Operator

NOT *boolean_expression*

In this syntax, *boolean_expression* can be any expression resulting in a boolean, or true/false, value. This is often a comparison expression such as (a = b), but can also be a variable of the BOOLEAN datatype.

Applying the NOT operator to an expression causes the expression to evaluate to the opposite of what it normally would. For example, the following expression evaluates to true:

(8 = 8)

Applying the NOT operator to that same expression results in a value of false being returned, for example:

NOT (8 = 8)

It is possible to write the preceding expression without using the NOT operator. For example, the two expressions shown next are equivalent:

NOT (8 = 8)
(8 <> 8)

In a simple case like the preceding example, using the second expression will probably result in clearer code. With more complex expressions, that decision becomes a judgment call. Sometimes it is easier to define the case you aren't interested in and then negate it.

AND

The AND operator is used to join two comparison expressions when you are interested in testing whether both expressions are true. It can also be used for the same purpose with two boolean variables—to check and see if both are equal to true.

The Syntax for the AND **Operator**

SYNTAX

boolean_expression AND *boolean_expression*

In this syntax, *boolean_expression* can be any expression resulting in a boolean, or true/false, value. This is often a comparison expression such as (a = b), but can also be a variable of the BOOLEAN datatype.

The AND operator returns a value of true if both expressions each evaluate to true; otherwise, a value of false is returned. Use AND when you need to test several conditions and execute some code only when they are all true. Table 4.7 shows some sample expressions using the AND operator.

Table 4.7. Expressions using the AND operator.

Expression	Result
(5 = 5) AND (4 < 100) AND (2 >= 2)	true
(5 = 4) AND (5 = 5)	false
'Mon' IN ('Sun','Sat') AND (2 = 2)	false

OR

The OR operator is used to join two comparison expressions when you are interested in testing whether at least one of them is true. It can also be used with two boolean variables to see whether at least one is set to true.

The Syntax for the OR **Operator**

SYNTAX

boolean_expression OR *boolean_expression*

In this syntax, *boolean_expression* can be any expression resulting in a boolean, or true/false, value. This is often a comparison expression such as (a = b), but can also be a variable of the BOOLEAN datatype.

The OR operator returns a value of true if any one of the expressions evaluates to true. A value of false is returned only if both the expressions evaluate to false. Table 4.8 shows some sample expressions using the OR operator.

Table 4.8. Expressions using the OR operator.

Expression	Result
(5 <> 5) OR (4 >= 100) OR (2 < 2)	false
(5 = 4) OR (5 = 5)	true
'Mon' IN ('Sun','Sat') OR (2 = 2)	true

String Operators

PL/SQL has two operators specifically designed to operate only on character string data. These are the LIKE operator and the concatenation (¦¦) operator. The LIKE operator is a comparison operator used for pattern matching and was described earlier in the section titled "Comparison Operators," so only the concatenation operator is described here.

The Syntax for the Concatenation Operator

SYNTAX

string_1 ¦¦ *string_2*

In this syntax, *string_1* and *string_2* are both character strings and can be string constants, string variables, or string expressions. The concatenation operator returns a result consisting of all the characters in *string_1* followed by all the characters in *string_2*.

Listing 4.6 shows several ways in which you can use the concatenation operator.

INPUT **Listing 4.6. Use of the concatenation operator.**

```
 1: --Remember to execute: SET SERVEROUTPUT ON
 2: DECLARE
 3:    a      VARCHAR2(30);
 4:    b      VARCHAR2(30);
 5:    c      VARCHAR2(30);
 6: BEGIN
 7:    --Concatenate several string constants.
 8:    c := 'Jack' ¦¦ ' AND ' ¦¦ 'Jill';
 9:    DBMS_OUTPUT.PUT_LINE(c);
10:    --Concatenate both string variables and constants.
11:    a := 'went up';
12:    b := 'the hill';
13:    DBMS_OUTPUT.PUT_LINE(a ¦¦ ' ' ¦¦ b ¦¦ ',');
14:    --Concatenate two string variables.
15:    a := 'to fetch a ';
16:    b := 'pail of water.';
17:    c := a ¦¦ b;
18:    DBMS_OUTPUT.PUT_LINE(c);
19: END;
20: /
```

4

OUTPUT
```
Jack and Jill
went up the hill,
to fetch a pail of water.
PL/SQL procedure successfully completed.
```

ANALYSIS The preceding code shows the concatenation operator used in several different ways. Notice that you do not always have to assign the result directly to a string variable. For example, in line 13, the concatenation operator is used to create a string expression that is passed as input to the PUT_LINE procedure.

Use of Comparison Operators with Strings

You can use any of the PL/SQL comparison operators to compare one character string to another. Strings can be compared for equality, for inequality, to see if one string is less than another, to see if one string matches a given pattern, and so on. When using character strings in comparison expressions, the result depends on several things:

- ☐ Character set
- ☐ Datatype
- ☐ Case (upper versus lower)

The Effect of Character Set on String Comparisons

When comparing two strings to see if one is less than another or greater than another, the result depends on the sort order of the underlying character set being used. In the typical ASCII environment, all lowercase letters are actually greater than all uppercase letters, digits are less than all letters, and the other characters fall in various places depending on their corresponding ASCII codes. However, if you were working in an EBCDIC environment, you would find that all the digits were greater than the letters and all lowercase letters are less than all uppercase letters, so be careful.

The Datatype's Effect on String Comparisons

NEW TERM The underlying datatype has an effect when comparing two string variables or when comparing a string variable with a constant. Remember that variables of the CHAR datatype are fixed length and padded with spaces. Variables of the VARCHAR2 datatype are variable length and are not automatically padded with spaces. When comparing two CHAR datatypes, Oracle uses *blank-padded comparison semantics*. This means that Oracle conceptually adds enough trailing spaces to the shorter string to make it equal in length to the longer string and then does the comparison. Trailing spaces alone will not result in any differences being found between two springs. Oracle also does the same thing when comparing two string constants. However, when one of the values in a comparison is a variable-length string,

Oracle uses *non-padded comparison semantics*. The use of *non-padded comparison semantics* means that Oracle does not pad either of the values with spaces, and any trailing spaces will affect the result. Listing 4.7 shows several string comparisons that illustrate this point.

INPUT   **Listing 4.7. Demonstration of string comparison semantics.**

```
 1: --Remember to execute: SET SERVEROUTPUT ON
 2: DECLARE
 3:   fixed_length_10  CHAR(10);
 4:   fixed_length_20  CHAR(20);
 5:   var_length_10    VARCHAR2(10);
 6:   var_length_20    VARCHAR2(20);
 7: BEGIN
 8:   --Constants are compared using blank-padded comparison semantics,
 9:   --so the trailing spaces won't affect the result.
10:   IF 'Jonathan' = 'Jonathan            ' THEN
11:     DBMS_OUTPUT.PUT_LINE
12:      ('Constant: ''jonathan'' = ''Jonathan            ''');
13:   END IF;
14:   --Fixed length strings are also compared with blank-padded
15:   --comparison semantic, so the fact that one is longer doesn't matter.
16:   fixed_length_10 := 'Donna';
17:   fixed_length_20 := 'Donna';
18:   IF fixed_length_20 = fixed_length_10 THEN
19:     DBMS_OUTPUT.PUT_LINE('Char: ''' || fixed_length_10 || ''' =
                             ➡''' || fixed_length_20 || '''');
20:   END IF;
21:   --Comparison of a fixed length string and a literal also
22:   --results in the use of blank-padded comparison semantics.
23:   IF fixed_length_10 = 'Donna' THEN
24:     DBMS_OUTPUT.PUT_LINE('Char and constant: '''
25:       || fixed_length_10 || ''' = ''' || 'Donna' || '''');
26:   END IF;
27:   --But compare a variable length string
28:   --against a fixed length, and the
29:   --trailing spaces do matter.
30:   var_length_10 := 'Donna';
31:   IF fixed_length_10 = var_length_10 THEN
32:     DBMS_OUTPUT.PUT_LINE('Char and Varchar2: '''
33:       || fixed_length_10 || ''' = '''
34:       || var_length_10 || '''');
35:   ELSE
36:     DBMS_OUTPUT.PUT_LINE('Char and Varchar2: '''
37:       || fixed_length_10 || ''' NOT = '''
38:       || var_length_10 || '''');
39:   END IF;
40:   --The maximum lengths of varchar2 strings do not matter,
41:   --only the assigned values.
42:   var_length_10 := 'Donna';
43:   var_length_20 := 'Donna';
44:   IF var_length_20 = var_length_10 THEN
45:     DBMS_OUTPUT.PUT_LINE('Both Varchar2: '''
```

continues

Listing 4.7. continued

```
46:        || var_length_20 || ''' = '''
47:        || var_length_10 || '''');
48:    ELSE
49:      DBMS_OUTPUT.PUT_LINE('Both Varchar2: '''
50:        || var_length_20 || ''' NOT = '''
51:        || var_length_10 || '''');
52:    END IF;
53: END;
54: /
```

```
Constant: 'jonathan' = 'Jonathan          '
Char: 'Donna     ' = 'Donna             '
Char and constant: 'Donna     ' = 'Donna'
Char and Varchar2: 'Donna     ' NOT = 'Donna'
Both Varchar2: 'Donna' = 'Donna'
PL/SQL procedure successfully completed.
```

You can see from the output that the first three comparisons in Listing 4.7 use blank-padded comparison semantics. The strings being compared are considered to be equal even though the number of trailing spaces differs in each case. The fourth comparison however, compares a VARCHAR2 variable against a CHAR variable. Because one of the strings in question is variable length, the trailing spaces count, and the two strings are not considered to be equal.

The Effect of Case on String Comparisons

PL/SQL string comparisons are always case sensitive. The obvious ramification of this is that a lowercase string such as 'aaa' is not considered equal to its uppercase equivalent of 'AAA'. But case also makes a difference when comparing two strings to see which is greater. In an ASCII environment, the letter 'A' will be less than the letter 'B'. However, the letter 'a' will not only be greater than 'B'; it will be greater than 'Z'.

> **TIP**
>
> If you need to perform case-insensitive string comparisons, use PL/SQL's built-in UPPER() function, for example:
>
> ```
> IF UPPER('a') < UPPER('B') THEN...
> ```
>
> You can use the LOWER() function in the same manner.

Use of Comparison Operators with Dates

Date comparison works pretty much as you might expect and has fewer complexities than string comparisons do. Earlier dates are considered to be "less than" later dates, and it follows that more recent dates are "greater than" earlier dates. The only complication arises from the fact that PL/SQL date variables also contain a time component. Listing 4.8 illustrates this and one potential problem to be aware of when comparing date values against each other.

INPUT **Listing 4.8. Date comparison example.**

```
 1: --Remember to execute: SET SERVEROUTPUT ON
 2: DECLARE
 3:   payment_due_date  DATE;
 4: BEGIN
 5:   --In real life the payment_due date might be read from
 6:   --a database or calculated based on information from a database.
 7:   payment_due_date := TO_DATE('1-Jun-1997','dd-mon-yyyy');
 8:   --Display the current date and the payment date.
 9:   DBMS_OUTPUT.PUT_LINE('Today is ' ¦¦ TO_CHAR(SYSDATE,'dd-Mon-yyyy'));
10:   DBMS_OUTPUT.PUT_LINE('Payment is due on '
11:     ¦¦ TO_CHAR(payment_due_date,'dd-Mon-yyyy'));
12:   IF payment_due_date = SYSDATE THEN
13:     DBMS_OUTPUT.PUT_LINE('Payment is due today.');
14:   ELSE
15:     DBMS_OUTPUT.PUT_LINE('Payment can wait a while.');
16:   END IF;
17:   --In reality, the time does not matter when speaking of a due date.
18:   IF TRUNC(payment_due_date) = TRUNC(SYSDATE) THEN
19:     DBMS_OUTPUT.PUT_LINE('Wrong! Payment is due today!');
20:   ELSE
21:     DBMS_OUTPUT.PUT_LINE('Wrong! Payment can wait a while.');
22:   END IF;
23: END;
24: /
```

OUTPUT
```
Today is 01-Jun-1997
Payment is due on 01-Jun-1997
Payment can wait a while.
Wrong! Payment is due today!
PL/SQL procedure successfully completed.
```

ANALYSIS Today's date and the payment due date both match, yet the IF statement in line 12 failed to detect this. Why? Because SYSDATE is a function that returns the current date and time, with the time resolved down to the second. The payment_due_date variable will contain a time of midnight because none was specified in the assignment statement in line 7. So the only time line 12 would function correctly would be for one second at midnight at the beginning of 1-Jun-1997. In line 18, the TRUNC function is used to truncate the time values from the two dates, resulting in a comparison that works as desired in this case.

Having the time as part of a date variable is not necessarily a bad thing. It's just something you need to be aware of, especially when comparing dates with each other.

Expressions

When you combine values and operators to produce a result, you have an expression. You have already learned about the various datatypes available in PL/SQL, and you have just read about PL/SQL's extensive collection of operators. In addition, in order to use expressions effectively in your code, you also need to understand

- ☐ Operator precedence
- ☐ Use of parentheses
- ☐ Types of expressions
- ☐ The effects of null values in an expression
- ☐ Conversion between datatypes

Understanding the effects of a null value on an expression is particularly important, especially when you move into retrieving data from a database. The remainder of this chapter discusses each of these items in detail.

Expressions Defined

Simply put, an expression is some combination of variables, operators, literals, and functions that returns a single value. Operators are the glue that hold an expression together and are almost always present. The other elements might not all be present in every expression.

In its very simplest form, an expression might simply consist of a literal value, a variable name, or a function call. The first few entries in Table 4.9 are examples of this type of expression. More typical expressions involve two values and an operator, the operator defining the action to be taken and the result to be returned. Complex expressions can be built up by stringing several simple expressions together with various operators and function calls. Finally, the unary operators can be applied to any expression or value.

Table 4.9. Sample expressions.

Expression	Comments
1000	Evaluates to one thousand
some_variable_name	Evaluates to the contents of the variable
SYSDATE	An Oracle function that returns the current date
1000 + 2000	A typical expression using a binary operator
-1000	An expression using a unary operator
10 * 20 + 30 / 2	Two expressions joined together

Expression	Comments
`LENGTH('Lansing ' ¦¦ 'MI')`	A function call evaluating a sub-expression that is itself an expression
`1-5**2<=10*4-20`	Two expressions, each containing sub-expressions, joined together

Take a look at the last example in Table 4.9. The comment notes that it is actually two expressions joined together, but which two? What value should Oracle return for this expression? The answer to both these questions can be found in the rules governing operator precedence.

Operator Precedence

When evaluating an expression consisting of different values, datatypes, and operators, Oracle follows a specific set of rules that determine which operations are done first. Each operator has an assigned precedence. Operators with a higher precedence are evaluated first. Operators of the same precedence level are evaluated from left to right. Table 4.10 shows these precedence levels for each of the various operators.

Table 4.10. Operator precedence.

Precedence	Operators	Operation
First	`**`, `NOT`	Exponentiation and logical negation
Second	`+`, `-`	Arithmetic identity and negation (+ and - used as unary operators)
Third	`*`, `/`	Multiplication and division
Fourth	`+`, `-`, `¦¦`	Addition, subtraction, and string concatenation
Fifth	`=`, `<>`, `!=`, `~=`, `<`, `>`, `<=`, `>=`, `LIKE`, `BETWEEN`, `IN`, `IS NULL`	Comparison
Sixth	`AND`	Logical conjunction
Seventh	`OR`	Logical inclusion

Take another look at the expression referred to in the previous section. The following list shows the steps Oracle would take to evaluate it:

1. `1-5**2<=10*4-20`

2. `1-25<=10*4-20`

3. `1-25<=40-20`

4. `-24<=20`

5. `true`

You can control the order in which Oracle evaluates an expression by using parentheses. Oracle will evaluate any part of an expression in parentheses first. If parentheses are nested, Oracle will always evaluate the innermost expression first and then move outwards. Here is what happens to the preceding expression if you add some parentheses:

1. `(1-5)**2<=10*(4-20)`

2. `(-4)**2<=10*(-16)`

3. `16<=-160`

4. `false`

 TIP

> Use parentheses in complex expressions, even when they are not strictly necessary, in order to make the intended order of evaluation clear to other programmers.

Types of Expressions

One way of classifying expressions is by the datatype of the resulting value. Using this scheme, expressions can be classified as one of these types:

☐ Arithmetic or numeric

☐ Boolean

☐ String

☐ Date

Any expression returning a numeric value is referred to as an arithmetic expression, or sometimes as a numeric expression.

A boolean expression is any expression that returns a `true` or `false` value. Comparison expressions are really special cases of this type, but they are not the only way to get a `true`/`false` value. A boolean variable—or several boolean variables linked together with the logical operators `AND`, `OR`, and `NOT`—will also return a boolean result.

String expressions are those that return character strings as results, and date expressions are those that result in a datetime value.

Generally speaking, you can use an expression of the appropriate datatype anywhere in your PL/SQL code where a value is required. The exception to this would be in function and procedure calls that modify their arguments.

Null Values in Expressions

Until now, the discussion has ignored the effect of nulls in expressions. This was done in order to concentrate on the normal function of each of the operators and also because nulls pretty much have the same effect regardless of the operation being done.

What is a null? The term is best understood as referring to an "unknown value." Any variable or expression is considered null when the value of that variable or expression is unknown. This situation can occur if you declare a variable and use it in an expression without first assigning a value. Because the variable has no assigned value, the result of the expression can't be known. More commonly, nulls are encountered when reading data from a database. Oracle, like any other relational database, does not force you to store a value for each column in a table. When no specific value is stored, the contents of that column are considered "unknown," and the column is referred to as being null.

NEW TERM The effects of nulls are particularly insidious when writing boolean expressions, such as the WHERE clause in a SQL SELECT statement. SQL uses what is called *three-valued logic*. Three-valued logic says that the result of a boolean expression can be either true, false, or NULL. Many a programmer has felt the sting of an IF statement gone awry because of an unexpected null value, and some consider three-valued logic to be more of a three-pronged pitchfork prodding them in the behind. The code in Listing 4.9 shows why nulls can cause so much grief.

INPUT **Listing 4.9. Effects of nulls on boolean expressions.**

```
 1: --Remember to execute; SET SERVEROUTPUT ON
 2: DECLARE
 3:    a      INTEGER;
 4:    b      BOOLEAN;
 5:    n      INTEGER;        --this will be our null value.
 6: BEGIN
 7:    --Assign a value to the variable A, but leave N null.
 8:    a := 2;
 9:    --Note that the test for A=N fails.
10:    IF a = n THEN
11:      DBMS_OUTPUT.PUT_LINE('a = n is true');
12:    ELSE
13:      DBMS_OUTPUT.PUT_LINE('a = n is not true');
14:    END IF;
15:    --But also note that the test for a <> n fails.
16:    IF a <> n THEN
17:      DBMS_OUTPUT.PUT_LINE('a <> n is true');
18:    ELSE
19:      DBMS_OUTPUT.PUT_LINE('a <> n is not true');
20:    END IF;
21:    --Here is an expression that many people first
22:    --expect to always be true.
23:    IF (a = n) OR (a <> n) THEN
```

continues

Listing 4.9. continued

```
24:        DBMS_OUTPUT.PUT_LINE('(a = n) or (a <> n) is true');
25:    ELSE
26:        DBMS_OUTPUT.PUT_LINE('(a = n) or (a <> n) is not true');
27:    END IF;
28:    --TRUE and NULL = NULL
29:    IF (a = 2) AND (a <> n) THEN
30:        DBMS_OUTPUT.PUT_LINE('TRUE and NULL = TRUE');
31:    ELSE
32:        DBMS_OUTPUT.PUT_LINE('TRUE and NULL = NULL');
33:    END IF;
34:    --TRUE or NULL = TRUE
35:    IF (a = 2) OR (a <> n) THEN
36:        DBMS_OUTPUT.PUT_LINE('TRUE or NULL = TRUE');
37:    ELSE
38:        DBMS_OUTPUT.PUT_LINE('TRUE or NULL = NULL');
39:    END IF;
40:    --NOT NULL = NULL
41:    IF (NOT (a = n)) IS NULL THEN
42:        DBMS_OUTPUT.PUT_LINE('NOT NULL = NULL');
43:    END IF;
44:    --TIP: try this if you want a null value to be
45:     --considered "not equal".
46:    --Be careful though, if BOTH A and N are NULL
47:    --NVL will still return TRUE.
48:    IF NVL((a <> n),true) THEN
49:        DBMS_OUTPUT.PUT_LINE('The values are not equal.');
50:    ELSE
51:        DBMS_OUTPUT.PUT_LINE('The values are equal.');
52:    END IF;
53:    --TIP: a three-valued IF construct.
54:    b := (a <> n);
55:    IF b THEN
56:        DBMS_OUTPUT.PUT_LINE('a <> n is TRUE');
57:    ELSIF NOT b THEN
58:        DBMS_OUTPUT.PUT_LINE('a <> n is FALSE');
59:    ELSE
60:        DBMS_OUTPUT.PUT_LINE('a <> n is NULL');
61:    END IF;
62: END;
63: /
```

OUTPUT

```
a = n is not true
a <> n is not true
(a = n) or (a <> n) is not true
TRUE and NULL = NULL
TRUE or NULL = TRUE
NOT NULL = NULL
The values are not equal.
a <> n is NULL
PL/SQL procedure successfully completed.
```

ANALYSIS Listing 4.9 is a somewhat contrived example, but it illustrates very well the effects of nulls on comparison expressions. Take a close look at what is going on here. The first IF statement in line 10 tests for a = n. As you might expect, this is not true, but it is important to understand that it is not false either. The second IF statement in line 16 proves this. The test there is for a <> n, the exact opposite of the previous comparison, and it also is not true. Line 23 shows an extreme case, an expression which many people at first glance would expect to always be true. However, because the value of n is unknown, the truth of this expression is also unknown and it evaluates to NULL.

There are three basic things to remember when dealing with nulls:

☐ How nulls propagate in expressions

☐ How the logical operators AND, OR, and NOT handle nulls

☐ How the IF statement deals with nulls

In an expression, null values propagate. For the most part, any arithmetic, date, string, or boolean expression containing even one null value will also evaluate to NULL. There are some exceptions to this rule, which are described shortly.

The logical operators AND, OR, and NOT are often used to link together comparison expressions. Table 4.11 shows how these operators function in expressions with null values.

Table 4.11. Three-valued logic truth table.

Operator	Expression	Result
AND	TRUE AND TRUE	TRUE
	TRUE AND FALSE	FALSE
	TRUE AND NULL	NULL
	FALSE AND NULL	FALSE
	NULL AND NULL	NULL
OR	TRUE OR TRUE	TRUE
	TRUE OR FALSE	TRUE
	TRUE OR NULL	TRUE
	FALSE OR NULL	FALSE
	NULL OR NULL	NULL
NOT	NOT TRUE	FALSE
	NOT FALSE	TRUE
	NOT NULL	NULL

Lines 28 through 43 in Listing 4.9 contain some IF statements that demonstrate how each of the logical operators operate on null values.

The IF statement is the fundamental decision-making structure of PL/SQL. Give it a boolean expression, and it evaluates that expression and makes a decision as to which piece of code to execute. However, boolean expressions can have three values: true, false, and NULL. An IF statement has only two parts: the code to be executed when an expression is true and the code to be executed when it isn't. There is a mismatch here, and it's very important to keep in mind that the ELSE portion will be executed when the result of an expression is unknown, or, in other words, when the expression is null.

 TIP   Lines 53 through 61 of Listing 4.9 show a way to construct an IF statement that has separate execution paths for true, false, and NULL.

There are some exceptions to the general rule that nulls propagate in expressions. Null character strings are sometimes handled as if they were zero-length strings, and PL/SQL does have some functions and operators that have been specifically designed to help you work with nulls.

You can concatenate strings, even if one is null, and get the results you would expect. This is because the concatenation operator simply ignores any null strings. However, if all the strings are null, then the result will be null. Also bear in mind that PL/SQL treats a zero-length VARCHAR2 string as a null value.

You can use the IS NULL operator to see whether or not a particular variable or expression is null. It allows your code to detect and act on null values. You saw an example of this earlier in Listing 4.5. The IS NULL operator returns only a true or false value, never a NULL.

 WARNING   Always use the IS NULL operator when checking for null values. Do not use the equality or inequality operators to compare a variable to NULL. You can code a statement such as IF some_var = NULL, but you won't get the results you might expect. Use IF some_var IS NULL instead.

The built-in NVL function allows you to specify an alternate value to be used when its argument is null. Lines 44 through 52 of Listing 4.9 show an interesting use of this function to account for the possibility of the variable n being null. Appendix B describes this useful function.

The built-in DECODE function actually treats NULL as a specific value instead of an unknown value. It might seem contradictory, but it's useful. DECODE is also described in Appendix B.

Do	Don't

Do initialize all your variables in order to eliminate the possibility of null values.

Do use NVL where feasible when retrieving values from that database in order to replace null values with an acceptable alternative.

Don't forget to think through the possible implications of null values in every expression you write, especially the boolean, including comparison, expressions.

Datatype Conversions

Sometimes you need to convert a value of one datatype to another. This is frequently true with dates and numbers, which are often converted to and from character strings. For example, you might want to display a date, so you must first convert it to a character string of the desired format. There are two ways of approaching the issue of conversion. One is to rely on Oracle to implicitly convert datatypes, which it will do automatically when it makes sense. The second and more preferred method is to code your conversions explicitly.

Implicit Conversion

NEW TERM   When you mix different datatypes in an expression, Oracle will convert them for you when it makes sense to do so. This is referred to as *implicit conversion*. Listing 4.10 shows several examples of implicit conversion.

INPUT   **Listing 4.10. Implicit conversion examples.**

```
 1: --Remember to execute: SET SERVEROUTPUT ON
 2: DECLARE
 3:    d1      DATE;
 4:    cd1     VARCHAR2(10);
 5:    cd2     VARCHAR2(10);
 6:    n1      NUMBER;
 7:    cn1     VARCHAR2(10);
 8:    cn2     VARCHAR2(10);
 9: BEGIN
10:    --Assign a value to this string which represents a date.
11:    cd1 := '15-Nov-61';
12:    --Now assign the string to a date variable.
13:    --The conversion is implicit.
14:    d1 := cd1;
15:    --Now assign that date variable to another string.
16:     --Again the conversion
17:    --is implicit, but this time the conversion is
18:     --from a date to a string.
19:    cd2 := d1;
```

continues

Listing 4.10. continued

```
20:    --Display the two character strings to show that they are the same.
21:    DBMS_OUTPUT.PUT_LINE('CD1 = ' || cd1);
22:    DBMS_OUTPUT.PUT_LINE('CD2 = ' || cd2);
23:    --Repeat the same example as above, but with numbers.
24:    cn1 := '995';
25:    n1 := cn1 + .99 ;
26:    cn2 := n1;
27:    DBMS_OUTPUT.PUT_LINE('CN1 = ' || cn1);
28:    DBMS_OUTPUT.PUT_LINE('CN2 = ' || cn2);
29: END;
30: /
```

OUTPUT
```
CD1 = 15-Nov-61
CD2 = 15-NOV-61
CN1 = 995
CN2 = 995.99
PL/SQL procedure successfully completed.
```

ANALYSIS The code in Listing 4.10 illustrates some common implicit conversions. The first assignment, in line 11, causes no conversion at all because a string is assigned to a string variable. The assignment statement in line 14, however, does represent an implicit conversion because it must convert the string representation of the date to Oracle's internal format before it can assign the value to d1. In line 19, that date is again converted back to a string format. Lines 23 through 28 repeat the same process, but this time with a number.

Implicit conversions are convenient, but beware. In relying on them, you are relying on Oracle's built-in assumptions and on default settings you might not even be aware of, and which might change from one release to another. The format of a date leads to some good examples. Did you know that Oracle's default date format varies depending on the language setting? That it can also be installation-dependent? And that it can vary between a client PC executing a Developer/2000 script and a database server? In fact, the date format can even be changed for the duration of a particular session. Figure 4.2 illustrates this by showing the same PL/SQL code succeeding once and then failing after the date format has been changed.

For the reasons just listed, it is often safer to code conversions explicitly. Explicit conversions also better document your code by making it clear to other programmers exactly what is happening.

Explicit Conversion

Oracle has several built-in functions that are designed to convert information from one datatype to another. These are shown in Table 4.12.

4

Figure 4.2.

The default date format is changed.

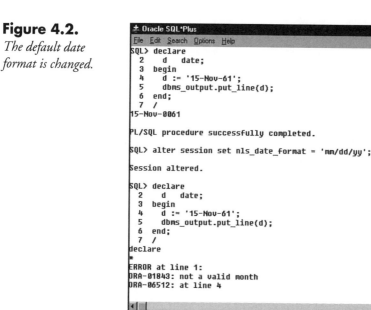

```
± Oracle SQL*Plus
File  Edit  Search  Options  Help
SQL> declare
  2    d    date;
  3  begin
  4    d := '15-Nov-61';
  5    dbms_output.put_line(d);
  6  end;
  7  /
15-Nov-0061

PL/SQL procedure successfully completed.

SQL> alter session set nls_date_format = 'mm/dd/yy';

Session altered.

SQL> declare
  2    d    date;
  3  begin
  4    d := '15-Nov-61';
  5    dbms_output.put_line(d);
  6  end;
  7  /
declare
*
ERROR at line 1:
ORA-01843: not a valid month
ORA-06512: at line 4
```

Table 4.12. Conversion functions.

Function	Purpose
TO_DATE	Converts a character string to a date
TO_NUMBER	Converts a character string to a number
TO_CHAR	Converts either a number or a date to a character string

Each of these functions takes three arguments: the value to be converted, a format string specifying how that conversion is to take place, and optionally a string containing language-specific parameters. These functions are described in detail on Day 7, but Listing 4.11 gives some common examples of how you can use them.

INPUT **Listing 4.11. Examples of the conversion functions.**

```
 1: --Remember to execute: SET SERVEROUTPUT ON
 2: DECLARE
 3:    d1    DATE;
 4:    d2    DATE;
 5:    d3    DATE;
 6:    d4    DATE;
 7:    n1    NUMBER;
 8:    n2    NUMBER;
 9:    n3    NUMBER;
```

continues

Listing 4.11. continued

```
10:  BEGIN
11:    --Here are some common date formats which you might encounter.
12:    d1 := TO_DATE('1/1/02','mm/dd/yy');
13:    d2 := TO_DATE('1-1-1998','mm-dd-yyyy');
14:    d3 := TO_DATE('Jan 1, 2000','mon dd, yyyy');
15:    --Year 2000 problems? Note the effect of using rr instead of yy.
16:    d4 := TO_DATE('1/1/02','mm/dd/rr');
17:    DBMS_OUTPUT.PUT_LINE('d1 = ' || TO_CHAR(d1,'dd-Mon-yyyy'));
18:    DBMS_OUTPUT.PUT_LINE('d2 = ' || TO_CHAR(d2,'mm/dd/yyyy'));
19:    DBMS_OUTPUT.PUT_LINE('d3 = ' || TO_CHAR(d3,'Day, Month dd, yyyy'));
20:    DBMS_OUTPUT.PUT_LINE('d4 = ' || TO_CHAR(d4,'Dy, Mon dd, yyyy'));
21:    --Here are some examples of numeric conversions.
22:    n1 := TO_NUMBER ('123.99','999D99');
23:    n2 := TO_NUMBER ('$1,235.95','$9G999D99');
24:    DBMS_OUTPUT.PUT_LINE('n1 = ' || TO_CHAR(n1,'999D99'));
25:    DBMS_OUTPUT.PUT_LINE('n2 = ' || TO_CHAR(n2,'$9G999D99'));
26: END;
27: /
```

OUTPUT
```
d1 = 01-Jan-1902
d2 = 01/01/1998
d3 = Saturday , January   01, 2000
d4 = Tue, Jan 01, 2002
n1 =   123.99
n2 =   $1,235.95
PL/SQL procedure successfully completed.
```

ANALYSIS   Lines 12 through 16 show the TO_DATE function being used to convert some common date formats to date variables. Lines 17 through 20 display these dates and show some more formatting possibilities. Lines 22 through 25 show some examples of conversions between numeric and character datatypes.

Summary

Today you have learned about writing PL/SQL expressions. You have read descriptions of each of the PL/SQL operators, and have seen examples of these operators in action. You have also seen how to write complex expressions and how the rules of operator precedence govern Oracle's evaluation of these expressions. Remember that you can use parentheses when you need to exercise control over a calculation. Most important to remember are the effects of null, or unknown, values on expressions. This is a particularly important subject to keep in mind when writing comparisons for use with IF statements. Mastering this one area will save you countless grief as you write code in the future.

Q&A

Q Why does the expression TRUE AND NULL evaluate to NULL, but the expression TRUE OR NULL evaluates to true?

A This is a good question. To understand the answer, it might help to think in terms of null being an unknown value. The AND operator requires that *both* its operands be true in order to return a true result. If one of the operands is unknown, then you can't be sure that if it were known it would be true, so AND must evaluate to null in this case. Things are different, however, for the expression TRUE OR NULL. The OR operator only requires one of its operands to be true in order to return a true result. In the case of TRUE OR NULL, you do know that one operand is true. Whether the other operand is true or false or unknown doesn't matter at this point because you have one that you know is true, and one is all you need.

Q Does the IN operator let me do anything that I couldn't do otherwise?

A No, not really, but it does make your code more readable and easier to maintain. The expression x IN (1,3,4,10,30,30,40,100) is equivalent to x=1 OR x=3 OR x=4 OR x=10 OR x=30 OR x=40 OR x=100, but you will probably find the first version a bit easier to read and understand.

Q You said that a statement such as IF X = NULL THEN... would not work as expected, and that IF X IS NULL THEN... should be used instead. Why?

A The first expression will never be true. It will always evaluate to NULL because one of the operands is null and it can never be known if two values are equal when one of the values is unknown. The second expression uses the IS NULL operator, which is designed to check for nulls. It specifically checks to see if the value of X is unknown and evaluates to true if that is the case.

Q When I am comparing strings, especially when comparing a CHAR string to a VARCHAR2 string, is there a convenient way to tell PL/SQL to ignore any trailing spaces in the CHAR string?

A Yes, use the built-in RTRIM function, for example: IF RTRIM(char_string) = varchar2_string then...

Q I'm comparing two dates and only want to know if they are in the same year. Can I use the TRUNC function to accomplish this?

A Yes. By default, the TRUNC function truncates the time portion of a date, but the optional second argument enables you to specify a different point of truncation. To compare only the years, you can write: IF TRUNC(date_1,'yyyy') = TRUNC(date_2,'yyyy') THEN...

4

Q Sometimes you capitalize your date format strings. Why?

A When converting a date to a character string for display purposes, capitalizing parts of the format string controls whether or not that part of the date is capitalized. Suppose that it is currently the month of January. The expression `TO_CHAR(SYSDATE,'mon')` would result in a value of `'jan'`, the expression `TO_CHAR(SYSDATE,'Mon')` would result in a value of `'Jan'`, and the expression `TO_CHAR(SYSDATE,'MON')` would result in a value of `'JAN'`.

Workshop

Use the following workshop to test your comprehension of this chapter and put what you've learned into practice. You'll find the answers to the quiz and exercise in Appendix A, "Answers."

Quiz

1. What is the difference between a unary operator and a binary operator?
2. What are the results of each of the following expressions?

   a. `(5-4)-(3-1)`

   b. `4*2**3-2`

   c. `4*2**(3-2)`

   d. `4=4 AND 5=6 OR 3=3`
3. Using the `NOT` operator, write equivalent expressions for each of the following:

   a. `A <> B`

   b. `A < B`

   c. `(A <= B) AND (B <= C)`
4. Match the patterns and strings shown following. Hint: Not every string or pattern has a match, and one pattern matches more than one string.

   `'123-45-6789'` `'___-__-____'`

   `'Boom'` `'John%'`

   `'Johnson'` `'_oo_'`

   `'517-555-1212'`

   `'Broom'`

   `'Jonson'`

   `'Johnston'`
5. When does PL/SQL not pad strings with spaces, in order to make them of equal length, when doing comparisons?

Exercise

Write a function to compute wages based on an hourly rate and the number of hours worked. Have it use a minimum wage of $5 per hour if the rate is unknown. Have it also use the minimum wage if the rate is too low.

4

Week 1

Day 5

Using Functions, IF Statements, and Loops

by Timothy Atwood

Functions, IF statements, and loops are simple yet powerful features of PL/SQL. Today's lesson covers the following topics:

- ☐ Functions
- ☐ The NULL statement
- ☐ The IF statement
- ☐ Nested IFs
- ☐ The ELSIF statement
- ☐ FOR loops

PL/SQL Functions

As you saw in Day 1, "Learning the Basics of PL/SQL," functions are very similar to PL/SQL procedures except for the following differences:

☐ Functions return a value.

☐ Functions are used as part of an expression.

Why should you write functions? There are many reasons. The main reason is to reduce the total lines of coding and take a modular approach to writing code. You could retype in each PL/SQL block the same repetitive lines of code, or you could write a function. What if all those blocks of code had to be changed for one small reason? Just trying to find and change all these would make a COBOL programmer shudder when contemplating all the year 2000 changes! With functions, you would simply make the change in one location. Keep in mind that if the parameters to be passed to the function have changed, you still will have some editing to do within the PL/SQL blocks.

Even if you do not write your own functions, don't forget that Oracle provides you with a vast array of powerful built-in functions. However, if you do not get the opportunity to write your own functions, you will be missing out on a very powerful feature of PL/SQL.

In Day 1, you created a function called SS_THRESH, which is shown in Listing 5.1. This function simply returned a value formatted as a number with nine total digits, two of which are allocated to the decimal place. Your values would range from -9999999.99 to 9999999.99.

INPUT   **Listing 5.1. The SS_THRESH function.**

```
CREATE OR REPLACE FUNCTION ss_thresh
RETURN NUMBER AS
   x      NUMBER(9,2);
BEGIN
   x := 65400;
   RETURN x;
END;
/
```

The Syntax for Declaring a Function

A function is declared as follows:

```
FUNCTION function_name [(parameters {IN|OUT|IN OUT})]
      RETURN return_datatype
IS|AS
      <declaration statements>
BEGIN
      <executable statements>
[EXCEPTION]
      <exception handler statements>
END function_name;
```

In this syntax, the statements and parameters are as follows:

☐ *function_name*—The function name follows the keyword FUNCTION and follows the standard naming convention, which is covered on Day 3, "Writing Declarations and Blocks."

☐ *parameters*—Functions allow for the passing in and out of parameters. This is optional as denoted by the brackets [ ]. The SS_THRESH function does not require parameters.

☐ RETURN—This is the type of data returned. You can have more than one RETURN statement in a function, but only one will be executed. One RETURN statement is required even if you return nothing or ignore what is returned.

☐ IS¦AS—These parameters allow you to set up variables local to the function. These variables can hold values passed from the parameters or hold values assigned in the function. The variables can't be seen outside of the function.

☐ BEGIN—This statement starts the execution of statements pertinent to the function.

☐ EXCEPTION—Again, this statement is optional, but allows you to handle the PL/SQL block properly when an error occurs. If you do not address this up front, then when an error occurs, control will be passed back to the PL/SQL block with the original values instead of the values that should have been returned.

☐ END—This statement denotes the end of the function. The function name must follow the END statement or errors will result.

Listing 5.2 shows an example of a full function.

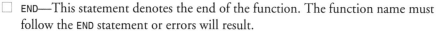

INPUT   **Listing 5.2. The emptype function.**

```
CREATE OR REPLACE FUNCTION emptype (paytype CHAR)
    RETURN VARCHAR2 IS
BEGIN
    IF paytype = 'H' THEN
        RETURN 'Hourly';
    ELSIF paytype = 'S' THEN
        RETURN 'Salaried';
    ELSIF paytype = 'E' THEN
        RETURN 'Executive';
    ELSE
        RETURN 'Invalid Type';
    END IF;
EXCEPTION
    WHEN OTHERS THEN
        RETURN 'Error Encountered';
END emptype;
/
```

5

The function in Listing 5.2 is titled emptype. It uses parameters passed from a procedure called paytype of type CHAR. The function returns a value of type VARCHAR2, which will be Hourly, Salaried, Executive, Invalid Type, or Error Encountered. When you begin the function's statements, you use IF...ELSIF to determine text to return. IF statements are covered later in the chapter in the section "The IF Statement." If an exception occurs, the function stops processing and returns the value Error Encountered. The function is then terminated by calling the END statement followed by the function name.

Defining Formal Parameters

Parameters are a key feature of PL/SQL. A parameter is a value that you can pass from a block of statements to a function. The function then performs calculations, checks, and so on, and might or might not return a value based upon the conditions in the function. This concept is similar to functions in other third-generation languages such as C. Make sure that you code your functions to accept parameters that can be used from other areas of your PL/SQL code.

The Syntax for Defining a Parameter

SYNTAX

```
parameter_name [MODE] parameter_type [:= value ¦ DEFAULT value]
```

In this syntax, parameter_name is the name you assign to the parameter, and parameter_type is the variable type you assign.

The simplest parameter can be coded as

```
(p_squared NUMBER)
```

p_squared is the parameter_name, and NUMBER is the parameter_type.

But what if you want to accept a parameter from a table, and you do not want to hard-code a parameter type because it might change in the future? You can simply add a %TYPE after the parameter, and the %TYPE will pick up the field type from the table. For instance, the following line sets the parameter p_emptype to the field definition of pay_type in the table employee:

```
(p_emptype employee.pay_type%TYPE)
```

This is a common method when referencing tables and is highly recommended. There is much less rework if the type in the database changes from CHAR to VARCHAR2 than if you hard-code the type in the function and then go back and change the function, too. You can see how good functions and good coding can reduce the effort required to develop an application!

MODE

The optional MODE statement gives you complete control over your incoming parameters. Table 5.1 lists the three types of modes along with how the MODE statement operates.

5

Table 5.1. Types of modes.

MODE	Handling of Parameter	Description
IN	Read-only	When you specify IN, you are stating that the parameter is read-only and completely protected from being changed.
OUT	Write-only	When you specify OUT, you are ignoring any parameters passed from the calling statement, and assigning values to this parameter from within the function; therefore, it is write-only.
IN OUT	Read or write	This gives you full control over the parameter. You will read in the parameter as passed, and if you like, you can change the value of the parameter from within the function, and upon exit the values are assigned to the values written inside the function. This method allows you to return more than one value.

The following includes some examples of the *MODE* statement:

```
FUNCTION addemployee(
    p_hiredate_in IN DATE,
    p_employeeID_out OUT NUMBER,
    p_hourlyrate_in_out IN OUT NUMBER,
    p_empname_in_out IN OUT varchar2)
```

In addemployee, you would not be able to change the hire date because it would be read-only. You would assign an employee ID in the function and write it out to this parameter. You can change the hourly rate if the initial rate was too low, and you could change the employee name if the employee gets married before being added to your database.

Assigning Values to Parameters

Sometimes you might want to assign values to parameters either by using := or DEFAULT. When using a default value, if no parameter is passed, the DEFAULT assignment is used within the function. If a value is passed, that value is used. The following has an example of assignment with both DEFAULT and :=:

```
p_emptype CHAR DEFAULT 'H'
p_hourlyrate NUMBER := 4.25 --minimum wage
```

Return Types

In a function, you must declare a return datatype. The return datatype can be any datatype allowed by Oracle, such as

☐ CHAR

☐ VARCHAR2

5

☐ NUMBER

☐ INTEGER

☐ DATE

☐ BOOLEAN (true/false values)

☐ TABLE

☐ RECORD

As you see, you have complete flexibility in the way you process and return data from the function to the PL/SQL statements.

Exception Handling

As you saw in Listing 5.2, you coded the EXCEPTION statement. Again, this statement tells Oracle what to do if some error occurs while processing the function or procedure.

The Syntax for Exceptions

```
EXCEPTION
     WHEN OTHERS THEN
          <statements>
```

In this syntax, *statements* is one or more statements that will be processed when the exception occurs.

You could always code a NULL statement if no action is to be taken. This would help clarify your intent in the PL/SQL code to let others know you have thought of all conditions. NULL statements are covered later in this chapter in the section "The NULL Statement."

Creating a Stored Function

A stored function is a function saved to the database that can be called by any PL/SQL code. The only difference between a function and a stored function is the addition of the CREATE [OR REPLACE] keywords before the keyword FUNCTION. Refer to "The Syntax for Declaring a Function" earlier in this chapter for an explanation of the parameters.

The Syntax for Creating a Stored Function

```
CREATE [OR REPLACE]FUNCTION function_name [(parameters {IN¦OUT¦IN OUT})]
     RETURN return_datatype
IS¦AS
     <declaration statements>
BEGIN
     <executable statements>
[EXCEPTION]
     <exception handler statements>
END function_name;
```

You are now going to write your first stored function in PL/SQL. You will create a function that simply returns the shortened value of pi (3.14) and calls the function mypi.

The first line you will need is to identify the stored function:

```
CREATE OR REPLACE FUNCTION mypi
```

Notice that you did not have to put parentheses after the function name mypi because you do not need to pass parameters to the function. If you were calculating the diameter of a circle, you would then pass the value of the radius.

The next line requires the return type. In this case you are returning a NUMBER. The next line entered would be

```
RETURN NUMBER IS
```

You now need to start the body of your function by typing the keyword BEGIN:

```
BEGIN
```

Because you are not performing anything in this function except to return a value, you will code a NULL statement, which is discussed later in this chapter in the section "The NULL Statement," and the RETURN statement to pass the value of pi.

```
NULL;
RETURN 3.14;
```

You can now end the function by typing the keyword END followed by the function name:

```
END mypi;
```

Listing 5.3 contains the entire function that you should have just entered. Review the listing to make sure you have typed the lines in correctly.

INPUT   **Listing 5.3. The mypi function.**

```
CREATE OR REPLACE FUNCTION mypi
    RETURN NUMBER IS
BEGIN
    NULL;
    RETURN 3.14;
END mypi; --end of mypi function
```

OUTPUT   When you type / to execute the code, you should see the following Oracle output:

```
PL/SQL procedure successfully completed.
```

You can now call the function mypi from any PL/SQL statements.

To prove that the process worked, you can write a miniprocedure to see the value of pi. Enter the code in Listing 5.4 and type / to execute the PL/SQL block.

NOTE

> Before you continue, make sure that you have entered SET
> SERVEROUTPUT ON at the SQL*Plus prompt. This allows you to see
> output to the screen as the PL/SQL code executes.

INPUT **Listing 5.4. Verifying the `mypi` function.**

```
BEGIN
    DBMS_OUTPUT.PUT_LINE('value of pi is ' ¦¦ mypi);
END;
/
```

By using the SET SERVEROUTPUT ON statement with the DBMS_OUTPUT.PUT_LINE, you can send variables to the console (screen). Your output should have been

OUTPUT `value of pi is 3.14`

Finding Errors

In Day 1, you learned how to use the EDIT command directly from Oracle. Instead of entering the code line by line, you can now practice using the EDIT command. For learning how to debug compilation errors, I am going to make extensive use of the built-in editor. If you haven't done so already, you are going to enter the mypi function into the editor, with planned errors.

To start the process, simply type EDIT mypi and press Enter. Because the SQL code does not exist, Oracle will prompt you to create a new file. Go ahead and click Yes. When the edit screen appears, enter the code exactly as it appears in Listing 5.5.

INPUT **Listing 5.5. A poorly written function.**

```
CREATE OR REPLACE FUNCTION mypi
    RETIRN NUMBER IS
BEGIN
    NULL;
    RETURN 3.14
END
```

After you have entered the function, click File and then Exit, and when it asks you if you want to save changes, click Yes. You are now ready to execute this poorly written function.

 5

Type the command GET mypi and press Enter. The function will be loaded to your buffer and listed on the screen. Type / to execute this function. You should now see the following error message:

```
Warning: Function created with compilation errors.
```

Where do you go from here? Simply type SHOW ERRORS and press Enter. Your screen should contain the same errors as the following output:

```
LINE/COL ERROR
-------- --------------------------------------------------------------------
2/5      PLS-00103: Encountered the symbol "RETIRN" when expecting one of
         the following:
         ( return compress compiled wrapped
         The symbol "return was inserted before "RETIRN" to continue.

6/1      PLS-00103: Encountered the symbol "END" when expecting one of
         the following:
         * & = - + ; < / > in mod not rem an exponent (**)
         <> or != or ~= >= <= <> and or like between is null is not ¦¦
```

What does this tell you? You could look up Oracle help, but the error code PLS-00103 will only state that there is a syntax error when parsing the PL/SQL code. However, you can go immediately to the line and column in question.

Go back and edit mypi by typing EDIT mypi and pressing Enter. Now go to row 2, column 5. The error is at the keyword RETURN. You can see that it expected a RETURN statement but could not find any. Go ahead and make the correction.

Now go to column 6, line 1. The error message states that it encountered the END statement before finding required punctuation. When looking for errors, start working your way from the error to the top of the code. In line 6 you should see that the required ; is missing! Go ahead and make that correction, save the function, and exit.

TIP

After you type the last END; statement, make sure that you press the Enter key to insert a blank line when using the built-in editor. If you do not do this, even if you've added the semicolon, you will receive the same compiler error because Oracle does not recognize the semicolon in the last END statement.

Type GET mypi and press Enter. You always have to reload the code back into the buffer after it has been changed. Now execute the PL/SQL code to create the function by typing / and pressing Enter. If the function was successfully created, you should see the words:

```
Function created.
```

The NULL Statement

The NULL statement is simply a statement that does nothing. Its format is simply

```
NULL;
```

Why Use the NULL Statement?

There are many reasons to use the NULL statement. One reason is to improve readability, especially if you have a block of code that does absolutely nothing. Another good reason is to use it as a placeholder. As you saw in the mypi function, you used the NULL statement to indicate that the function had no procedures, but simply returned a value.

How to Call a Function from PL/SQL With or Without Parameters

You can call a function from PL/SQL in many ways. If there are no parameters to pass, you can simply call the function without the parentheses as you did in verifying the mypi function.

The second way is to pass actual values, using commas as placeholders for parameters that you do not want to pass (in this case DEFAULT would become the new value of the parameter). Go ahead and create the stored function squareme from Listing 5.6 to create the squared function. This function simply multiplies the number by itself.

INPUT   **Listing 5.6. The stored function squareme.**

```
CREATE OR REPLACE FUNCTION squareme(thenum number)
     RETURN NUMBER IS
BEGIN
     RETURN thenum * thenum;
END squareme;
```

After you have entered the function, go ahead and execute. You can now troubleshoot if there are any errors by typing the SQL command SHOW ERRORS at the SQL*Plus prompt.

You are now ready to enter a block of PL/SQL code to see actual output and the passing of parameters. Go ahead and enter and then execute the code in Listing 5.7.

INPUT   **Listing 5.7. Passing parameters to squareme.**

```
BEGIN
     DBMS_OUTPUT.PUT_LINE('9 squared is ' || squareme(9) );
END;
```

OUTPUT Your output should be

```
9 squared is 81
```

One last word on passing values to a function. Values can either be constants or variables. Remember, if no parameters are passed, make sure that you have a DEFAULT or that your code prohibits passing parameters to a function.

PL/SQL Statements

The two statements covered today are the IF statement and the FOR loop. These statements help you to control the execution of PL/SQL blocks. Tomorrow's lesson covers additional statements and loops.

The IF Statement

The IF statement allows you to evaluate one or more conditions. Some examples of IF statements are

☐ IF the salary is over $500,000 per year, grant the officer $2,000 in stock options.

☐ IF the pay_type equals Salaried, then the total hours paid is equal to 40.

☐ If the pay_rate is between $9.00 to $10.00 and the pay_type is Hourly, then the pay grade is level 9.

The Syntax for the IF Statement

The format of a simple IF statement is as follows:

SYNTAX

```
IF <some_condition_evaluates_to_true>
THEN
<perform_statements>
END IF;
```

In this syntax, the first parameter *some_condition_evaluates_to_true* is the BOOLEAN condition you want to check. If the BOOLEAN condition evaluates to true, then the parameter *perform_statements* executes, which contains one or more statements.

Suppose you wanted to calculate for an hourly employee how many hours of overtime he worked during the week. Go ahead and type the IF statement from Listing 5.8.

INPUT **Listing 5.8. Calculating overtime hours with IF.**

```
set echo on
DECLARE
   v_HoursWorked Number := 50 ; --Number of hours worked by hourly employee
   v_OverTime Number := 0 ; --Storage of Overtime Hours
BEGIN
   IF v_HoursWorked > 40 THEN
```

continues

5

Listing 5.8. continued

```
    v_OverTime := v_HoursWorked - 40;
        DBMS_OUTPUT.PUT_LINE('Hours overtime worked = ' ¦¦ v_OverTime);
  END IF;
END;
/
```

By previously typing SET SERVEROUTPUT ON, you are telling Oracle to run the DBMS_OUTPUT package, which aids in the debugging process by allowing you to display output to the screen. This, combined with the DBMS_OUTPUT.PUT_LINE statement, shows you the calculated values of the variable v_OverTime.

OUTPUT   Your output should be

```
Hours overtime worked = 10
```

You have set up two variables—V_HoursWorked and v_OverTime—to store the actual number of hours worked and the calculated number of overtime hours. These two variables are defined as a NUMBER to allow calculations on these values:

```
v_HoursWorked NUMBER := 50 ; --Number of hours worked by hourly employee
v_OverTime NUMBER := 0 ; --Storage of Overtime Hours
```

PL/SQL then starts evaluating the IF statement. Because you initialized v_HoursWorked to a value of 50 and 50 is greater than 40, and the IF statement is evaluated to true. Because the condition is true, you will process all statements under the THEN keyword.

```
IF v_HoursWorked > 40 THEN
```

You can now calculate the hours of overtime by simply subtracting 40 from v_HoursWorked. You can then display the output to the screen using the DBMS_OUTPUT.PUT_LINE command.

```
v_OverTime := v_HoursWorked - 40;
        DBMS_OUTPUT.PUT_LINE('Hours overtime worked = ' ¦¦ v_OverTime);
```

Finally, the ending / tells Oracle to execute the statements entered.

The IF...THEN...ELSE Statement

In the preceding example, you did not care what the results were if the hours were under 40 because you were only trying to determine the total hours of overtime worked. However, what if you did not initialize v_OverTime to a value of zero? The IF...THEN...ELSE statement allows you to process a series of statements under ELSE if the condition is false.

The Syntax for the IF...THEN...ELSE Statement

SYNTAX

```
IF <some_condition_evaluates_to_true>
THEN
<perform_statements_condition_true>
    ELSE
<perform_statements_condition_false>
END IF;
```

In this syntax, the first parameter, *some_condition_evaluates_to_true*, tests a BOOLEAN condition that you provide. If the condition is *true*, the second parameter, *perform_statements_condition_true*, executes. If the condition is *false*, the parameter *perform_statements_condition_false* executes.

You can now alter your original IF statement to reflect what to do if the condition is *false* (see Listing 5.9).

TIP

> Adding the ELSE statement is good programming practice not only to make sure that you know what will happen for all possible conditions, but also to make your logic easy to follow and understand for another Oracle programmer.

INPUT **Listing 5.9. Adding ELSE to the IF block.**

```
set echo on
DECLARE
  v_HoursWorked Number := 50 ; --Number of hours worked by hourly employee
  v_OverTime Number ; --Storage of Overtime Hours
BEGIN
  IF v_HoursWorked > 40 THEN
    v_OverTime := v_HoursWorked - 40;
      DBMS_OUTPUT.PUT_LINE('Hours overtime worked = ' ¦¦ v_OverTime);
    ELSE
        v_OverTime := 0;
  END IF;
END;
/
```

Again, the only change was to remove the initialization of variables in the declaration area and to set the value of v_OverTime to zero if there was no overtime under the ELSE statement.

NOTE

> You still could have initialized v_OverTime to a value of zero in the declaration section, and under the ELSE statement made good use of the NULL statement as discussed earlier in this chapter.

5

Nested IF Statements

By nesting IF statements, you can check for many complex conditions before executing a series of statements. This allows you to defer executing inner IF statements unless the outer IF conditions apply.

TIP

In order to improve processing time and decrease costly CPU time, always make sure the outermost loop is the loop that will narrow down your search criteria the most, so that you do not have to execute statements in the inner loops. For instance, if you were querying a database of employees who were mainly hourly, but only a few worked overtime, your outermost condition should look for total hours worked over 40, and the next condition would check to make sure the employee was hourly, not salaried. This would produce a lot less checking because you would easily filter the population of employees to a small group by the time you hit the next condition instead of the other way around!

The Syntax for Nested IF Statements

SYNTAX

```
IF <condition1 evaluates to true>
THEN
    IF <condition2 evaluates to true>
    THEN
        <perform statements>
    ELSE <both conditions have been evaluated to false>
        IF <condition3 evaluates to true>
        THEN
            <perform statements>
        ELSE
            <perform statements>
        END IF;
    END IF;
END IF;
```

Did you notice that even on the ELSE statements you can keep on adding IF statements? As you can see, it is possible to continue to nest loops for as long as you need, but nesting too much will most likely cause you grief in the debugging stage. Imagine just four levels of IF statements and trying to go through all the possible conditions to make sure that you produce the desired outcome.

In the overtime example, you will first determine how many people worked over 40 hours. If the employee is hourly, overtime hours are calculated. If the employee paytype is set to 'S', then the employee is salaried with no overtime. If the employee paytype is set to 'E', then the employee is executive management who gets no overtime (but lots of options!). See the code in Listing 5.10.

5

INPUT **Listing 5.10. Using nested IF statements.**

```
DECLARE
  v_HoursWorked Number := 80 ; --Number of hours worked by hourly employee
  v_OverTime Number := 0 ; --Storage of Overtime Hours
  v_PayType char(1) := 'E'; --Classification of employee, E, S, or H

BEGIN
IF v_HoursWorked > 40 THEN
    IF v_PayType = 'H' THEN
        v_OverTime := v_HoursWorked - 40;
        DBMS_OUTPUT.PUT_LINE('Hours overtime worked = ' || v_OverTime);
    ELSE
        IF v_PayType = 'S' THEN
            DBMS_OUTPUT.PUT_LINE('Employee is Salaried');
        ELSE
            DBMS_OUTPUT.PUT_LINE('Employee is Executive Management');
        END IF;
    END IF;
END IF;
END;
/
```

In Listing 5.10, the first IF statement evaluates to true. Notice that because most employees do not work over 40 hours, you would have to avoid all the inner logic! The second statement evaluates to false because the paytype is set to 'E' for executive management. Control passes to the ELSE statement where another IF statement is evaluated. Again, the condition is evaluated to false because the value of paytype is set to 'E'. The final ELSE statement then defaults to executive management as there are only three types of workers.

NOTE

Instead of nested IF statements, consider the use of boolean AND. For instance, you could easily have changed the preceding code to

```
IF v_HoursWorked > 40 AND
        v_PayType =l 'H' THEN
```

In addition, this example of nested IF statements is a poor programming choice. What happens if another classification of paytype is added? This would be better suited to reading data from a form or creating a user-defined function to handle these situations.

TIP

If you do use logical AND, because Oracle evaluates from left to right, make sure that the first condition checked narrows down the population as extensively as possible!

Using IF...ELSIF

In all the examples so far, you were coding IF statements in an AND environment. You might often want to check a value against a series of conditions, which have distinct boundaries. In a third-generation language, you would think of this as a CASE statement, or in boolean logic, you would be separating the conditions with a logical OR.

The Syntax for IF...ELSIF

```
IF <condition1_evaluates_to_true>
THEN
     <perform_statements>
ELSIF <condition2_evaluates_to_true>
THEN
     <perform_statements>
ELSIF <condition3_evaluates_to_true>
THEN
     <perform_statements>
...
ELSE <this is always optional as the default value>
     <perform_statements>
END IF;
```

In this syntax, the IF...ELSIF statement acts like a logical OR statement. The first parameter, *condition1_evaluates_to_true*, is a BOOLEAN condition. If it evaluates to true, then one or more statements are executed at the *perform_statements* parameter. You will keep adding as many ELSIF statements as required for all the conditions. You will notice that only one END IF statement is required, unlike the other IF...THEN...ELSE statements. Also note that the ELSE statement is optional, and it acts as a default value if none of the other values are true.

 TIP When utilizing ELSIF, do not allow for any overlapping of values to evaluate because you will not get the desired result. If you were checking for grades, you would not want to check for values of between 70 and 80 for a C and then check for values of 80 to 90 for a B. The person who received an 80 percent would be upset at a grade of C instead of the letter grade she deserved of B!

Listing 5.11 is an example of using ELSIF to determine the grade letter for a student. You have several approaches. One would be to check a range using BETWEEN; another method would be to use the > or < for evaluation, and finally, you could use a default letter 'E' or have it as part of the conditional criteria. To ensure no overlapping, the following example will use the < sign, and to practice a default, use the letter 'E' for failure.

5

INPUT **Listing 5.11. Using IF...ELSIF to determine a grade.**

```
DECLARE
v_Score Number := 85; --Percentage
v_LetterGrade Char(1);
BEGIN
IF v_Score >= 90 THEN
     v_LetterGrade := 'A';
ELSIF v_Score >= 80 THEN
     v_LetterGrade := 'B';
ELSIF v_Score >= 70 THEN
     v_LetterGrade := 'C';
ELSIF v_Score >= 60 THEN
     v_LetterGrade := 'D';
ELSE
     v_LetterGrade := 'E';
END IF;
     DBMS_OUTPUT.PUT_LINE('Your Letter Grade is: ' ¦¦ v_LetterGrade);
END;
/
```

OUTPUT When you execute the code from Listing 5.11, your output will be

```
Your Letter Grade is B
```

Remember, IF...ELSIF will continue through all cases until the first evaluates to true, and then the rest of the statements are ignored. Had you started out with v_Score >= 60, 85 would have evaluated to true and the student would have received a v_LetterGrade of 'D'.

Nested IF Versus ELSIF

You could think of nested IF statements as performing a logical AND whereas ELSIF would be performing a logical OR. The nice feature about using ELSIF instead of nested IFs is that it is much easier to follow the logic in the ELSIF statement because you can easily identify which statements will occur under which logical conditions.

The Formatting of IF Statements

Although there are no specific rules set in stone on placement of IF...THEN...ELSIF, and so forth, there are some general rules, which will help make your code more readable and easy to follow. See Listing 5.12 for an example of proper formatting.

☐ When using multiple IF statements, indent the next IF statement five spaces inward. See line 2 of Listing 5.12 for an example of this.

☐ Always match the END IF in the same column in which the IF statement occurs. See line 11 of Listing 5.12 for an example of this.

☐ It is helpful to put comments after the END IF statement, especially when nesting IFs to state the ending of a condition. I would abbreviate and use the -- for comments instead of multiple lines of /* ... */. See line 12 of Listing 5.12.

5

☐ Always indent the blocks of statements five spaces inward from the IF statement. See line 3 of Listing 5.12.

☐ If any conditions or statements "wrap" around, meaning they are too big for one line, simply indent an additional five spaces on the next line. See line 5 of Listing 5.12.

☐ Always match ELSE underneath the IF statement associated with ELSE. See line 6 of Listing 5.12.

Listing 5.12. Formatting IF statements.

```
 1: IF v_HoursWorked > 40 THEN
 2:     IF v_PayType = 'H' THEN
 3:         v_OverTime := v_HoursWorked - 40;
 4:         DBMS_OUTPUT.PUT_LINE('The many Hours which have been worked
 5:             overtime= ' ¦¦ v_OverTime);
 6:     ELSE
 7:         IF v_PayType = 'S' THEN
 8:             DBMS_OUTPUT.PUT_LINE('Employee is Salaried');
 9:         ELSE
10:             DBMS_OUTPUT.PUT_LINE('Employee is Executive Management');
11:         END IF;
12:     END IF; -- End check for PayType = H
13: END IF;
14: END;
15: /
```

Avoiding Common Mistakes When Using IF

You can avoid some of the more common pitfalls when using IF statements by keeping this list in mind.

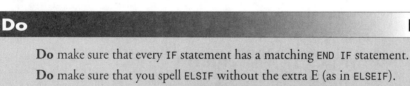

Do   **Don't**

Do make sure that every IF statement has a matching END IF statement.

Do make sure that you spell ELSIF without the extra E (as in ELSEIF).

Do make sure that you place a space between the END IF statement instead of either no space or a dash.

Don't make nested loops too complex. Complexity will make it harder to follow and debug if problems or changes occur. Evaluate your logic and see if a function might accomplish the same task.

Don't forget your punctuation. You do need semicolons after END IF and after each of the statements, but not after the keyword THEN.

Looping Statements

This section discusses one form of looping by using the FOR statement. Looping allows you to execute a block of code repeatedly until some condition occurs. Day 15, "Exploring Advanced Topics," demonstrates a similar use with recursion; however, recursion calls the same function repeatedly until some condition occurs.

The Syntax for FOR Loops

SYNTAX

```
FOR loop_index IN [REVERSE] low_value..high_value LOOP
     Statements to execute
END LOOP;
```

The `loop_index` is defined by Oracle as a local variable of type INTEGER. REVERSE allows you to execute the loop in reverse order. The `low_value..high_value` is the range to execute the loop. These can be constants, or they can be variables. The line must be terminated with LOOP with no semicolon at the end of this line. You can list the statements to be executed until the LOOP is evaluated to `false`.

NOTE

> You can use the EXIT statement to terminate a loop prematurely based upon some boolean condition; however, this practice should be avoided because the purpose of the FOR loop is to execute from beginning to end of the predetermined range. Day 6, "Implementing Loops and GOTOs," discusses the EXIT statement.

Go ahead and enter and then execute the code in Listing 5.13 for your first FOR loop.

INPUT **Listing 5.13. Your first FOR loop.**

```
set echo on
BEGIN
     FOR v_loopcounter IN 1..5 LOOP
          DBMS_OUTPUT.PUT_LINE('Loop counter is ' || v_loopcounter);
     END LOOP;
END;
/
```

OUTPUT   When you execute the preceding loop, your output should be

```
Loop counter is 1
Loop counter is 2
Loop counter is 3
Loop counter is 4
Loop counter is 5
```

5

You can now start to get a little more complex by nesting FOR loops. When you nest FOR loops, the outer loop is executed once, then the inner loop is executed for as many times as the range indicates, and then control is returned to the outer loop until its range expires. Go ahead and type in and then execute the loop from Listing 5.14.

INPUT **Listing 5.14. Nesting FOR loops.**

```
BEGIN
     FOR v_outerloopcounter IN 1..2 LOOP
          FOR v_innerloopcounter IN 1..4 LOOP
               DBMS_OUTPUT.PUT_LINE('Outer Loop counter is ' ||
                    v_outerloopcounter ||
                        ' Inner Loop counter is ' || v_innerloopcounter);
          END LOOP;
     END LOOP;
END;
/
```

OUTPUT When you execute the preceding code, your output will look like

```
Outer Loop counter is 1 Inner Loop counter is 1
Outer Loop counter is 1 Inner Loop counter is 2
Outer Loop counter is 1 Inner Loop counter is 3
Outer Loop counter is 1 Inner Loop counter is 4
Outer Loop counter is 2 Inner Loop counter is 1
Outer Loop counter is 2 Inner Loop counter is 2
Outer Loop counter is 2 Inner Loop counter is 3
Outer Loop counter is 2 Inner Loop counter is 4
```

Again, the order of nested loops is important depending upon what you are trying to accomplish.

Reversing the Loop

By adding the keyword REVERSE after IN, you tell Oracle to process the loop in reverse. You still must list the range from low to high values, otherwise the loop will not execute. The test of REVERSE also demonstrates using variables instead of fixed constants as shown in Listing 5.15.

INPUT **Listing 5.15. Reversing the loop.**

```
DECLARE
     v_Start Integer := 1;
BEGIN
     FOR v_loopcounter IN REVERSE v_Start..5 LOOP
          DBMS_OUTPUT.PUT_LINE('Loop counter is ' || v_loopcounter);
     END LOOP;
END;
/
```

OUTPUT Your output should appear as follows:

```
Loop counter is 5
Loop counter is 4
Loop counter is 3
Loop counter is 2
Loop counter is 1
```

TIP

> The example in Listing 5.15 has the starting counter as a variable, but it is always good practice to make all the LOOP parameters into variables as well. Following this guideline makes it easier to understand your code and make changes, including assigning dynamic values to the LOOP parameters.

Different Incrementing Through a Loop

As you can see, Oracle provides no option to step through a loop with an increment other than one. You can write loops that will execute with a different increment by executing statements only if a certain condition is true. The example from Listing 5.16 demonstrates how to increment by a value of 2.

INPUT **Listing 5.16. Changing the loop increment.**

```
BEGIN
    FOR v_loopcounter IN 1..6 LOOP
        IF MOD(v_loopcounter,2) = 0 THEN
            DBMS_OUTPUT.PUT_LINE('Loop counter is ' || v_loopcounter);
        END IF; -- End execution of statements for even counter
    END LOOP;
END;
/
```

OUTPUT After the loop has executed, your output should appear as

```
Loop counter is 2
Loop counter is 4
Loop counter is 6
```

This is just one of many ways in which you could increment a loop. The MOD function in this case simply tests to make sure that the number is divisible evenly by a value of 2. You could easily change this to 3, 5, or whatever you want to increment. To decrement, simply add the keyword REVERSE.

Final Programming Tips on Loops

Just like IF statements, FOR loop syntax must be coded properly. Some common pitfalls are as follows:

- ☐ Not putting a space between END LOOP;.
- ☐ Forgetting semicolons after the END LOOP;.
- ☐ Entering the counter from high to low when using REVERSE or setting the range from high to low and forgetting to use REVERSE.
- ☐ Setting variables in a loop so the lower boundary has a value greater than the upper boundary.
- ☐ Variables for the boundaries winding up with NULL values.
- ☐ When nesting loops, make sure that the statements follow the intended logic. (When in doubt, use the DBMS_OUTPUT package, which is discussed on Day 18, "Writing to Files and the Display.")

Summary

You accomplished a lot in Day 5! First, you took a closer look at how to create your own functions. Just the reduction of code and ease of use are two major reasons to write functions. If you work in a corporate environment and must share code, creating functions is a must.

NULL statements are simply that. They do nothing, but act as a placeholder.

IF statements can take many forms. IF statements are always evaluated from left to right (unless overridden by parentheses), and if one of the conditions becomes false, then the whole statement is invalid. This is important to know because the largest room for error is not syntax, but rather the logical errors, which are much harder to debug. Formatting the IF statement blocks is important not only from a coding perspective, but also from a readability perspective. Regular IF and nested IF statements operate like AND; whereas IF...ELSIF statements act like an OR, which allows you to create the equivalent of CASE statements as long as none of the conditions overlap!

Finally, loops allow you to repeat a series of PL/SQL code either until a condition is met, or you break out of the loop using EXIT. It is important to know the order of execution of the loops to reduce logic errors. You also saw a neat trick on how to increment loops by values other than one, an option which is not provided by Oracle.

Q&A

Q Does Oracle allow you to create your own functions?

A Yes! This is what makes Oracle so powerful. It allows you to reduce the amount of PL/SQL coding.

Q Can you call functions from any PL/SQL code?

A Yes, but this is only a recent development to include stored functions as part of the Oracle product.

Q Is there any reason to use the NULL statement?

A The NULL statement acts as a placeholder to make your code more readable. It is also used when no action is required.

Q What is the difference between nested IFs and IF...ELSIF?

A Nested IFs allow you to do logical AND checking. In addition, you do not always have to execute nested IF statements further in the block if the first IF statement evaluates to false. IF...ELSIF blocks allow you to check through a series of mutually exclusive choices.

Q What is the order of execution of nested loops?

A The outer loop executes first. The inner loop then executes in full from low to high values before it returns control to the outer loop. All looping ends when the outer loop has been completed or an EXIT statement has occurred.

Workshop

You can now review your knowledge of functions and conditional branching starting with a quick quiz, followed by some challenging exercises. The answers to both can be found in Appendix A, "Answers."

Quiz

1. What parts of the function are required for coding?
2. If a function takes parameters, is it always necessary to pass these parameters from the calling statement?
3. If an error occurs and you haven't coded an EXCEPTION statement, what is returned from the function?
4. Is there a way to return more than one value from a function?

5. If you code an IF...ELSE statement, and you do not have any conditions to execute if the statement is false, how would you code the ELSE statement?

6. What are some of the common pitfalls in coding IF statements?

7. How can I determine what is wrong with my code when it compiles?

8. When coding a loop in reverse, how must the beginning and ending values be coded?

Exercises

1. Rewrite the Grade example from Listing 5.11 as a stored function that passes the parameter of the score and returns a value of a grade letter.

2. Rewrite the Grade example from Listing 5.11 and use between for the ranges. Make sure that there is no overlapping of ranges.

3. Write a loop that increments by a value of 3 and then multiplies a counter by the returned value of the function mypi. The range should be from 1 to 9. Output the values with DBMS_OUTPUT. Make sure that you have entered SET SERVEROUTPUT ON to see the output.

4. Write a loop to calculate a factorial. For example, 6! is 6 * 5 * 4 * 3 * 2 * 1. Allow the high boundary to be a variable that can change. Use an initial value of 3 for testing.

5

Day **6**

Implementing Loops
and GOTOs

by Timothy Atwood

Day 5, "Using Functions, IF Statements, and Loops," demonstrates ways to change the order of execution with PL/SQL. Today's lesson covers several additional methods of changing the order of execution. Today's material covers the following topics:

- ☐ Statement labels
- ☐ The GOTO statement
- ☐ The WHILE loop
- ☐ The simple LOOP
- ☐ Emulating a REPEAT...UNTIL loop

Labels and the GOTO **Statement**

The GOTO statement allows for unconditional branching to a statement label. You will first learn about statement labels, which are required before you can even use the GOTO statement.

Statement Labels

Statement labels are identifiers of a block of code, similar to a function, but they are not actual PL/SQL statements. These labels can be accessed directly by the GOTO statement. In addition, these labels can be accessed by loops, which are covered in the section "The EXIT and EXIT WHEN Statements." The format of the label is

```
<<label_name>>
```

You will notice two things immediately about the label:

- ☐ The label is surrounded by double brackets << >>.
- ☐ The label must not have a semicolon after the label name.

The label name does not contain a semicolon because it is not a PL/SQL statement, but rather an identifier of a block of PL/SQL code.

 TIP

> You must have at least one statement after the label or an error will result. Labels can't take the place of required statements. If your intention is to execute the code with a label, you should evaluate your code and choose an alternative method such as using a function.

The GOTO **Statement**

The GOTO statement enables you to immediately transfer control to another labeled PL/SQL block without the need for conditional checking. As soon as the GOTO statement is encountered, all control is then transferred to the code underneath the matching *label_name*.

 SYNTAX

The Syntax for the GOTO **Statement**

```
GOTO label_name;
```

label_name is the matching *label_name* that must be contained within the same PL/SQL block of code.

Scoping Rules for the GOTO **Statement**

The GOTO destination must be in the same block, at the same level as or higher than the GOTO statement itself. This means that the label must be within the same scope as the GOTO statement itself. Conditions that would cause Oracle to not compile the PL/SQL code include

☐ Jumping into a lower level block

☐ Jumping into a loop

☐ Jumping into an IF statement

☐ Using GOTO to jump from one part of an IF statement to another

☐ Jumping from an exception handler back to a current block of PL/SQL code

The error message you'll encounter if you do not follow the proper coding of GOTO statements and their labels is

```
PLS-00375:  illegal GOTO statement; this GOTO cannot branch to label
```

Again, if you want a more global approach, stored functions would be one appropriate method.

Jumping into a Lower Level Block

You can't jump from an outer block of PL/SQL code back to an inner block of PL/SQL code. Listing 6.1 is an example of an illegal GOTO call.

WARNING

The following listing and the next few after it are for illustration purposes only. Due to the errors they generate, you might not want to enter and execute them. However, if you do enter and execute these listings, they will not destroy anything, and they might help you to troubleshoot errors in your coding in the future because you can see what errors these listings generate.

INPUT **Listing 6.1. Illegal GOTO call to an inner block.**

```
 1: DECLARE
 2:      v_Emergency_Warning VARCHAR2(50);
 3:      v_Status NUMBER = 0;
 4: BEGIN
 5:      GOTO Emergency_Check;
 6:      BEGIN
 7:          <<Emergency_Check>>
 8:              IF v_Status = 1 THEN
 9:                  PANIC();
10:              END IF;
11:      END;
12: END;
```

In the code in Listing 6.1, you see the first block of PL/SQL code as noted by the BEGIN statement. The block then calls the PL/SQL GOTO statement, which then attempts to transfer control to the <<Emergency Check>> label. Because the label is within a separate block of PL/SQL code as noted by the BEGIN statement, it is out of the required scope of the GOTO statement. If, instead of the keyword BEGIN, there was an <<Emergency_Check>> label within the first block, everything would have compiled and executed properly (barring errors in the logic of the code).

Jumping into a Loop

The scope of the loop is not complete until the entire range of the loop has completed. Therefore, attempting to jump into the middle of the loop is illegal. Listing 6.2 shows an attempt to make an illegal call into a FOR loop.

WARNING

The following listing is another that is for illustration purposes only because it generates several errors. You might or might not want to enter and execute this listing, depending on whether you want to see what kinds of errors it generates.

INPUT **Listing 6.2. Illegal GOTO call to a loop.**

```
1: BEGIN
2: GOTO insideloop;
3:      FOR v_loopcounter IN 1..5 LOOP
4:          <<insideloop>>
5:              DBMS_OUTPUT.PUT_LINE('Loop counter is ' || v_loopcounter);
6:      END LOOP;
7: END;
```

As you can see, although the loop and the GOTO statement are within the same block of PL/SQL code, Oracle would not know how to handle the jump inside the loop. The obvious question would be: What is the value of the loop counter? Because there is no answer, any attempt to implement this logic would result in a compile error.

Jumping into an IF Statement

Another illegal attempt to use the GOTO statement would be to jump inside an IF statement. Listing 6.3 provides an example of another illegal call.

WARNING

The following listing is another that is for illustration purposes only because it generates several errors. You might or might not want to enter and execute this listing, depending on whether you want to see what kinds of errors it generates.

INPUT **Listing 6.3. Illegal GOTO call inside an IF statement.**

```
 1: DECLARE
 2:       v_Emergency_Warning VARCHAR2(50);
 3:       v_Status NUMBER = 0;
 4:       v_ReactorStatus VARCHAR2(10);
 5: BEGIN
 6:       GOTO Emergency_Check;
 7:       IF v_ReactorStatus = 'Very Hot' THEN
 8:             <<Emergency_Check>>
 9:                   PANIC();
10:       END IF;
11:  END;
```

From the GOTO call in Listing 6.3, if this block of PL/SQL code were allowed to actually execute, it would never check to see if v_ReactorStatus = 'Very Hot'. There might not even be an emergency because v_ReactorStatus could have a value of 'Cool'. Because the value is never evaluated, the program always goes into crisis mode. Fortunately, this improper use of GOTO is not allowed!

Jumping from One Part of an IF Statement to Another

Although you can call a label from an IF statement, it is illegal for the jump to go from the IF clause to the THEN clause. Listing 6.4 is yet another example of not being within the same scope as the GOTO.

WARNING

The following listing is another that is for illustration purposes only because it generates several errors. You might or might not want to enter and execute this listing, depending on whether you want to see what kinds of errors it generates.

6

Listing 6.4. Illegal `GOTO` call from one clause of an `IF` statement to another clause.

`INPUT`

```
 1: DECLARE
 2:     v_Emergency_Warning VARCHAR2(50);
 3:     v_Status NUMBER = 0;
 4:     v_ReactorStatus VARCHAR2(10);
 5: BEGIN
 6:     IF v_ReactorStatus = 'Very Hot' THEN
 7:         GOTO Emergency_Check;
 8:     ELSE
 9:         <<Emergency_Check>>
10:             PANIC();
11:     END IF;
12: END;
```

As Listing 6.4 suggests, the program is jumping from an evaluation of the `IF` statement as true to executing code as if the entire statement were false. This is a definite misuse of the `GOTO` statement, and the code in this case probably does not require a `GOTO` statement.

From Listing 6.5, it should be apparent that you can't raise an error and then go back to the original block of code where the error was generated from the exception handler.

WARNING

The following listing is another that is for illustration purposes only because it generates several errors. You might or might not want to enter and execute this listing, depending on whether you want to see what kinds of errors it generates.

`INPUT` **Listing 6.5. Illegal `GOTO` call from an exception handler.**

```
 1: DECLARE
 2:     v_Emergency_Warning VARCHAR2(50);
 3:     v_Status NUMBER = 0;
 4:     v_ReactorStatus VARCHAR2(10);
 5: BEGIN
 6:     <<Emergency_Check>>
 7:         PANIC();
 8: EXCEPTION
 9:     WHEN e_TOOHOT THEN
10:         GOTO Emergency_Check;
11: END;
```

An Example of the GOTO Statement in Action

So far, you have seen conditions that exceed the scope of the GOTO statement. Now, here's an example of a legitimate block of PL/SQL code. See Listing 6.6 for a proper GOTO.

INPUT **Listing 6.6. Example of a proper GOTO statement.**

```
 1: DECLARE
 2:      v_Status NUMBER := 1;
 3: BEGIN
 4:      IF v_Status = 1 THEN
 5:          GOTO mybranch;
 6:      ELSE
 7:          v_Status := 1;
 8:      END IF;
 9: <<mybranch>>
10:      NULL;
11: END;
```

In the GOTO example from Listing 6.6, the program checks the value of v_Status. If the value is equal to 1, then the program goes immediately to the block <<mybranch>>; if the value is false, the program changes the value of v_Status to equal 1.

Why Use the GOTO Statement?

As with any procedural language, the use of GOTO statements is highly discouraged. As you saw from the listings earlier in the chapter, GOTO statements are very easy to code improperly. In almost all cases, your code can and should be written to avoid the unnecessary use of GOTO. There are several reasons not to use the GOTO statement:

- [ ] It is very easy to make logic errors when using GOTO.
- [ ] It is very easy to make coding errors even when you are trying to make the process work.
- [ ] If you use multiple GOTO statements, your code will jump all over the place out of sequence, which is known as spaghetti code. Using multiple GOTOs not only causes longer execution times, but also leads to confusion when you try to review your code and make changes.
- [ ] Almost all cases in which you would use the GOTO statement can be written with other Oracle constructs.

Perhaps the only use of GOTO statements is to immediately stop all other execution of statements and branch to a section of code to handle an emergency situation.

WHILE **Loops**

The WHILE loop enables you to evaluate a condition before a sequence of statements would be executed. In fact, if the condition is false, the code would never be executed. This is different from the FOR loop where you must execute the loop at least once.

The Syntax for the WHILE **Loop**

The syntax of the WHILE loop is

```
WHILE <condition is true> LOOP
      <statements>
END LOOP;
```

The WHILE loop requires the keywords LOOP and END LOOP in order to designate the statements to execute.

NOTE

> WHILE loops are invaluable because the program does not have to ever execute the code within the LOOP parameters. This is one fact I can never stress enough!

Examples of WHILE **Loops**

All these WHILE loops are meant to be entered and executed so that you can get some experience coding WHILE loops.

NOTE

> When you first sign on to the database, it is a good idea to create a login script. Or you can make a habit of typing and executing the statement SET SERVEROUTPUT ON. When you learn about the DBMS_OUTPUT package on Day 18, "Writing to Files and the Display," using this statement will allow you to see the actual output as the PL/SQL code executes to make PL/SQL easier to understand.

You can enter the loops directly or use the EDIT command to save a file, which can be executed at any time. Listing 6.7 demonstrates how the conditions for a WHILE loop can cause the loop to never execute.

Listing 6.7. Example of a WHILE loop that never executes.

```
1: DECLARE
2:      v_Calc NUMBER := 0;
3: BEGIN
4:      WHILE v_Calc >= 10 LOOP
5:          v_Calc := v_Calc + 1;
6:          DBMS_OUTPUT.PUT_LINE('The value of v_Calc is ' || v_Calc);
7:      END LOOP;
8: END;
9: /
```

In Listing 6.7, the condition is never evaluated to true. The condition v_Calc >= 10 from line 4 is never true because v_Calc is initialized at line 2 to a value of 0, which is less, not greater than 10. When Listing 6.7 is executed, no output is sent to the screen.

Listing 6.8 shows the corrected version of this WHILE loop.

Listing 6.8. Corrected WHILE loop that executes.

```
1: DECLARE
2:      v_Calc NUMBER := 0;
3: BEGIN
4:      WHILE v_Calc <= 10 LOOP
5:          v_Calc := v_Calc + 1;
6:          DBMS_OUTPUT.PUT_LINE('The value of v_Calc is ' || v_Calc);
7:      END LOOP;
8: END;
9: /
The value of v_Calc is 1
The value of v_Calc is 2
The value of v_Calc is 3
The value of v_Calc is 4
The value of v_Calc is 5
The value of v_Calc is 6
The value of v_Calc is 7
The value of v_Calc is 8
The value of v_Calc is 9
The value of v_Calc is 10
The value of v_Calc is 11
```

To make the WHILE loop execute, I simply changed the >= to <= in line 4. The loop executes at least once because v_Calc <= 10.

It is important to understand that the loop continues to execute until v_Calc <= 10. This can potentially be a source of logic error flaws if the intent was to enter the loop until v_Calc had a value of 10 and not 11.

When debugging loops in general, it is a good idea to use Oracle's DBMS_OUTPUT package to track the flow of the logic. It is a great help when testing all possible outcomes to make sure that the logic portion is working properly. A full discussion of this package occurs on Day 18.

Listing 6.9 illustrates how to step through a WHILE loop in increments other than one.

INPUT **Listing 6.9. Stepping through a WHILE loop.**

```
 1: DECLARE
 2:     v_Radius NUMBER := 2;
 3: BEGIN
 4:     WHILE v_Radius <=10 LOOP
 5:         DBMS_OUTPUT.PUT_LINE('The Area is ' ||
 6:             mypi * v_Radius * v_Radius);
 7:         v_Radius := v_Radius + 2 ; -- Calculates Area for Even Radius
 8:     END LOOP;
 9: END;
10: /
```

On Day 5, you created a method to trick Oracle into stepping through a FOR loop. The WHILE loop gives you more flexibility in looping, whether you are stepping through a loop, or even executing a loop! Listing 6.9 demonstrates stepping through the loop. This sequence increments v_Radius by a value of 2 from line 7 until it is equal to 10 from the condition specified in line 4. The following segment shows the output of this practice loop:

OUTPUT
```
The Area is 12.56
The Area is 50.24
The Area is 113.04
The Area is 200.96
The Area is 314
```

NOTE  Did you even need the <= boolean operators? You could easily have set the condition to exit if v_Radius != 12. You could have then incremented, decremented, or had fun doing both with the value of v_Radius.

The next WHILE loop will be contained in a function. In addition, this will allow you to review functions from Day 5. If you run into any problems, it doesn't hurt to go back and review the prior chapter. Go ahead and create the stored function in Listing 6.10.

INPUT **Listing 6.10. The WHILE loop as part of a function.**

```
 1: CREATE OR REPLACE FUNCTION dontcountsp(p_pass_string VARCHAR2)
 2:      RETURN NUMBER IS
 3:              v_MYCOUNTER INTEGER := 1;
 4:              v_COUNTNOSP NUMBER := 0;
 5: BEGIN
 6:      WHILE v_MYCOUNTER <= LENGTH(p_PASS_STRING) LOOP
 7:          IF SUBSTR(p_PASS_STRING,v_MYCOUNTER,1) != ' ' THEN
 8:                  v_COUNTNOSP := v_COUNTNOSP + 1;
 9:          ELSE
10:                  NULL;
11:          END IF;
12:          v_MYCOUNTER := v_MYCOUNTER + 1;
13:      END LOOP;
14:      RETURN v_COUNTNOSP ;
15: END dontcountsp;
16: /
```

ANALYSIS You have just created a function called dontcountsp in Listing 6.10, which will count all characters *except* spaces from a variable-length string up to 20 characters long. The function is passed a string from p_PASS_STRING called from the procedure. The return type in line 14 is simply a number telling you how many characters are actually contained in the string.

Of the two variables, v_MYCOUNTER holds the positional location for the current location in the string. V_COUNTNOSP holds the total count of characters that are not spaces.

The program finally enters the WHILE loop. The loop will continue to execute as long as v_MYCOUNTER is less than the total LENGTH of the string. In the body of the loop, the program checks each character, beginning at position one all the way to the length of the string, and checks for the value of a space, defined by ' '. If there is no space, the program increments v_COUNTNOSP by 1 because the value was not a space. If the value is a space, the program does nothing, as indicated by the NULL statement. The placeholder in the string v_MYCOUNTER is then incremented by 1, and the loop continues to execute until it reaches the end of the string. To see the function in action, go ahead and type the procedure in Listing 6.11 and then execute it.

INPUT **Listing 6.11. Executing the WHILE loop function.**

```
1: DECLARE
2:      v_MYTEXT VARCHAR2(20) := 'THIS IS A TEST';
3: BEGIN
4:      DBMS_OUTPUT.PUT_LINE('Total count is ' ¦¦ dontcountsp(v_MYTEXT));
5: END;
6: /
```

The code in Listing 6.11 simply creates a variable called v_MYTEXT and assigns it a value of 'THIS IS A TEST' in line 2. It then outputs to the console (screen) the total count of characters not including spaces in line 4.

 NOTE

> Both the SUBSTR() function and the LENGTH() function will be covered on Day 7, "Using Oracle's Built-in Functions."

The EXIT and EXIT WHEN **Statements**

The EXIT and EXIT WHEN statements enable you to escape out of the control of a loop. The format of the EXIT loop is

```
EXIT;
```

To terminate a loop, simply follow your condition with the EXIT statement. This is common when using IF statements.

The Syntax for the EXIT WHEN **Loop**

 The syntax of the EXIT WHEN loop is

```
EXIT WHEN <condition is true>;
```

The EXIT WHEN statement enables you to specify the condition required to exit the execution of the loop. In this case, no IF statement is required.

 TIP

> Always try to use the EXIT WHEN statement. It requires much less coding on your part, and it is easier to follow. The only reason you would use nested IF statements is for fine-tuning Oracle to speed up the process.

Examples Using EXIT **and** EXIT WHEN

In this chapter, you created a WHILE loop that incremented by a value of 2 to calculate the area of a circle. You will change this code so that the program exits when the value of the radius is 10 after you have calculated the area. Enter and execute the code in Listing 6.12.

Listing 6.12. Using EXIT with a WHILE loop.

```
 1: DECLARE
 2:     v_Radius NUMBER := 2;
 3: BEGIN
 4:     WHILE TRUE LOOP
 5:         DBMS_OUTPUT.PUT_LINE('The Area is ' ||
 6:             mypi * v_Radius * v_Radius);
 7:         IF v_Radius = 10 THEN
 8:             EXIT;
 9:         END IF;
10:         v_Radius := v_Radius + 2 ; -- Calculates Area for Even Radius
11:     END LOOP;
12: END;
13: /
```

You will notice that the output is the same as the WHILE loop output from Listing 6.9.

NOTE

> It's important to make sure that the statements are in the correct order for the proper logic to be performed. If you had switched the DBMS_OUTPUT statement and the IF statement around, the DBMS_OUTPUT statement would only produce four values instead of five because the loop would exit before the area is printed to the screen. If you were writing records to a table, you could easily see how incorrect data can be written to a table. Test with the DBMS_OUTPUT package as described in Day 18.

Switching the output statements with the IF statement from Listing 6.12, which would alter your output, is illustrated in the following block of code:

```
IF v_Radius = 10 THEN
    EXIT;
END IF;
DBMS_OUTPUT.PUT_LINE('The Area is ' || mypi * v_Radius * v_Radius);
```

Logic errors cause the most problems in any coding situation and can be very difficult to resolve! Next, you will see how to code EXIT WHEN instead of EXIT in Listing 6.13 to achieve the same results.

INPUT   **Listing 6.13. Using EXIT WHEN with a WHILE loop.**

```
 1: DECLARE
 2:     v_Radius NUMBER := 2;
 3: BEGIN
 4:     WHILE TRUE LOOP
 5:         DBMS_OUTPUT.PUT_LINE('The Area is ' ||
 6:                 mypi * v_Radius * v_Radius);
 7:         EXIT WHEN v_RADIUS = 10;
 8:         v_Radius := v_Radius + 2 ; -- Calculates Area for Even Radius
 9:     END LOOP;
10: END;
11: /
```

ANALYSIS   Listing 6.13 performs the same function as Listing 6.12, but uses the EXIT WHEN statement on one line, instead of the multiple lines of IF...THEN...EXIT statements from Listing 6.12. This version is much easier to read and understand.

If you can exit from a WHILE loop, you should be able to exit from a FOR loop. The code from Listing 6.14 will perform the same function as the code from Listings 6.9, 6.12, and 6.13 to calculate the area of a circle, but this time using a FOR loop.

INPUT   **Listing 6.14. Using EXIT with a FOR loop.**

```
 1: BEGIN
 2:     FOR v_loopcounter IN 1..20 LOOP
 3:         IF MOD(v_loopcounter,2) = 0 THEN
 4:             DBMS_OUTPUT.PUT_LINE('The AREA of the circle is ' ||
 5:                     v_loopcounter*v_loopcounter * mypi);
 6:         END IF; -- End execution of statements for even counter
 7:         IF v_loopcounter = 10 THEN
 8:             EXIT;
 9:         END IF;
10:     END LOOP;
11: END;
12: /
```

ANALYSIS   The loop terminates after the area has been calculated for a radius of 10 from line 7. Notice that the IF condition from line 7 fully terminates the loop prematurely before the loop can increment to a value of 20.

If you exit out of a loop in the middle of the function, what happens? To see the outcome, first enter the code in Listing 6.15 to create the function called exitfunc.

INPUT Listing 6.15. Impact of EXIT in a function.

```
 1: CREATE OR REPLACE FUNCTION exitfunc(p_pass_string VARCHAR2)
 2:     RETURN NUMBER IS
 3:         v_MYCOUNTER INTEGER := 1;
 4:         v_COUNTNOSP NUMBER := 0;
 5: BEGIN
 6:     WHILE v_MYCOUNTER <= LENGTH(p_PASS_STRING) LOOP
 7:         IF SUBSTR(p_PASS_STRING,v_MYCOUNTER,1) != ' ' THEN
 8:             v_COUNTNOSP := v_COUNTNOSP + 1;
 9:         ELSE
10:             NULL;
11:         END IF;
12:         v_MYCOUNTER := v_MYCOUNTER + 1;
13:         EXIT WHEN SUBSTR(p_PASS_STRING,v_MYCOUNTER,1) = ' ';
14:     END LOOP;
15:     RETURN v_COUNTNOSP ;
16: END exitfunc;
17: /
```

ANALYSIS You will notice the addition of only one statement that tells the program to exit the loop if it encounters a space. Now, to test and execute the function, enter the code from Listing 6.16.

INPUT Listing 6.16. Executing EXIT within a function.

```
1: DECLARE
2:     v_MYTEXT VARCHAR2(20) := 'THIS IS A TEST';
3: BEGIN
4:     DBMS_OUTPUT.PUT_LINE('Total count is ' || exitfunc(v_MYTEXT));
5: END;
6: /
```

OUTPUT The output when executed should be

```
Total count is 4
```

The effect of breaking out of a loop in the function is that it will still return the value of the variable when the EXIT statement has been executed. Instead of counting all of the characters in the line, it stops when it hits the first space and properly returns the value of 4 for the word 'Test'.

TIP

If you do use the EXIT or EXIT WHEN statement in a loop, make sure to always initialize the parameters. This way, some value will always return if the loop never executes.

Using Labels and EXIT Statements with Loops

You can use labels within loops to identify a loop. When you're nesting loops, labels help to document the coding.

The Syntax for Using Labels with Loops

```
<<label_name1>>
LOOP (FOR, WHILE, LOOP)
    <<label_name2>>
    LOOP (FOR, WHILE, LOOP)
        ...
    END LOOP <<label_name2>>
END LOOP <<label_name1>>
```

You will use the example of nested FOR loops from Day 5 (Listing 5.14) and modify it with label names, as shown in Listing 6.17.

INPUT **Listing 6.17. Using labels with loops.**

```
 1: BEGIN
 2:     <<outerloop>>
 3:     FOR v_outerloopcounter IN 1..2 LOOP
 4:         <<innerloop>>
 5:         FOR v_innerloopcounter IN 1..4 LOOP
 6:             DBMS_OUTPUT.PUT_LINE('Outer Loop counter is ' ¦¦
 7:                 v_outerloopcounter ¦¦
 8:                 ' Inner Loop counter is ' ¦¦ v_innerloopcounter);
 9:         END LOOP innerloop;
10:     END LOOP outerloop;
11: END;
12: /
```

ANALYSIS The only difference between Listing 5.14 in Day 5 and Listing 6.17 is the use of the label names outerloop and innerloop. Otherwise there is no difference in execution, output, and so on, but it is much easier to follow the logic.

You can even change the order of execution of a loop by using the EXIT and EXIT WHEN statements, as seen in Listing 6.18.

INPUT **Listing 6.18. Changing labeled loop execution with EXIT statements.**

```
 1: BEGIN
 2:     <<outerloop>>
 3:     FOR v_outerloopcounter IN 1..2 LOOP
 4:         <<innerloop>>
 5:         FOR v_innerloopcounter IN 1..4 LOOP
 6:             DBMS_OUTPUT.PUT_LINE('Outer Loop counter is '
 7:                 ¦¦ v_outerloopcounter ¦¦
```

```
 8:                              ' Inner Loop counter is ' || v_innerloopcounter);
 9:                       EXIT outerloop WHEN v_innerloopcounter = 3;
10:              END LOOP innerloop;
11:        END LOOP outerloop;
12: END;
13: /
```

OUTPUT   When you run the code shown in Listing 6.18, you should see the following output:

```
Outer Loop counter is 1 Inner Loop counter is 1
Outer Loop counter is 1 Inner Loop counter is 2
Outer Loop counter is 1 Inner Loop counter is 3
```

The EXIT WHEN statement directs the program to exit the outer loop when the inner loop reaches a value of 3. Notice that this completely aborts the execution of both loops.

Simple LOOPs

The final loop to discuss today is the simple LOOP.

The Syntax for a Simple LOOP

The syntax of the simple LOOP is

```
LOOP
  <statements>
END LOOP;
```

If you do not have an EXIT or EXIT WHEN statement located in the loop, you will have an infinite loop.

> **TIP**
>
> When using EXIT or EXIT WHEN, always try to place these commands either at the beginning of the LOOP block or at the end of the LOOP block. This way, you can avoid many logic errors.

Sample Simple LOOPs

> **WARNING**
>
> The following is an example of an infinite loop. You will probably *not* want to execute this example. As you can see, the loop will never end, and the loop will never do anything!

6

```
BEGIN
     LOOP
            NULL;
     END LOOP;
END;
/
```

You can now properly exit out of a loop by simply adding the word EXIT after the NULL statement. Go ahead and execute the code in Listing 6.19.

INPUT **Listing 6.19. Using EXIT with a simple LOOP.**

```
1: BEGIN
2:      LOOP
3:              NULL;
4:              EXIT;
5:      END LOOP;
6: END;
```

Creating a REPEAT...UNTIL Loop

Oracle does not have a built-in REPEAT <statements> UNTIL <condition is true> loop. However, you can simulate this by using the simple LOOP and the EXIT or EXIT WHEN statements.

The Syntax for a Simulated REPEAT...UNTIL Loop

```
LOOP
  <statements>
     IF <condition is true>
          EXIT;
     END IF;
END LOOP;
```

Alternatively, you could use the preferable method of

```
LOOP
  <statements>
     EXIT WHEN <condition is true>;
END LOOP;
```

 TIP Always try to use the EXIT WHEN statement. It requires much less coding on your part, and it is easier to follow. The only reason you would use nested IF statements is for fine-tuning Oracle to speed up the process.

An Example of a Simulated REPEAT...UNTIL Loop

Go ahead and enter the code in Listing 6.20. You will still be calculating the area of a circle as you did in Listings 6.9, 6.12, 6.13, and 6.14, but this time you will use a simulated REPEAT...UNTIL loop.

INPUT   **Listing 6.20. Demonstrating a REPEAT...UNTIL loop.**

```
 1: DECLARE
 2:     v_Radius NUMBER := 2;
 3: BEGIN
 4:     LOOP
 5:         DBMS_OUTPUT.PUT_LINE('The Area is '
 6:              || v_RADIUS*v_RADIUS * mypi);
 7:         v_Radius := v_Radius + 2;
 8:         EXIT WHEN v_Radius > 10;
 9:     END LOOP;
10: END;
```

ANALYSIS   Notice that the code in Listing 6.20 creates the same five output lines computing the area of the circle that were produced by Listing 6.12. This simulated REPEAT...UNTIL loop simply starts the loop, outputs the area of the loop to the screen, increments the radius, and then exits when the radius is greater than 10. This allows you to use the values 2, 4, 6, 8, and 10 as in the other examples.

What Loop Should I Use?

All of these loop options can get confusing! As you saw in the examples, you can take the FOR, WHILE, and LOOP statements to create the same output. However, Table 6.1 shows some general guidelines for when to use what type of loop.

Table 6.1. When to use which loop.

Loop	When to Use
FOR	Always use the FOR loop if you know specifically how many times the loop should execute. If you have to code an EXIT or EXIT WHEN statement in a FOR loop, you might want to reconsider your coding and go with a different loop or different approach.
WHILE	Use this if you might never even want to execute the loop one time. Although you could duplicate this in a FOR loop using EXIT or EXIT WHEN, this is best left for the WHILE loop. The WHILE loop is the most commonly used loop because it provides the most flexibility.

continues

6

Table 6.1. continued

Loop	When to Use
LOOP	The simple LOOP can be used if you want to create a REPEAT <statements> UNTIL <condition is true> type of loop. This simple LOOP is perfect for performing this task.

Loop Guidelines

Some loop guidelines you should follow are shown in the following Do/Don't box.

Do	Don't

Do make sure when you are using a LOOP with an EXIT or EXIT WHEN statement that the condition will be met at least once; otherwise, you'll have an infinite loop.

Don't ever create an infinite loop.

Do always try to use label names with loops. This makes the coding much easier to follow; plus it gives you flexibility.

Do make sure when you're using label names that the label name follows the END LOOP statement.

Do code label names that are used with the GOTO statement to the far left; otherwise, Oracle does not see the label name.

Do try to use EXIT WHEN instead of EXIT. EXIT WHEN is much easier to follow and requires less coding.

Do refer to Table 6.1 for some general guidelines if you don't know which loop to use.

Do make sure that you have proper punctuation in your loops.

Do choose which type of loop to use with increments. You can handle any type of increment with any loop. Refer to the examples in Day 5 and in this lesson.

Don't use a RETURN statement from within a loop when using loops in a function. Although it might work, this is poor programming practice that could have some unwanted results and is the improper termination of a loop.

Do, when using FOR loops, make variables out of the lower and upper boundaries if either of the boundaries can potentially change in the future. You can assign these on-the-fly in your coding. In reality you will most likely not have a fixed boundary, so you should do this automatically!

6

Style Tips for Loops

Two last things I want to mention on loops are the use of label names and proper indentation. Always use loop names if creating any type of nested loop or when nesting FOR loops to make the index counter more meaningful.

Proper spacing should include aligning the END LOOP with the LOOP statement, and the usual indent of five spaces for statements within the loop. Listing 6.21 contains an example in which the spacing is proper, but the loop itself would appear confusing by not following these tips. After Listing 6.21, you will see the same example but with a better style of coding in Listings 6.22 and 6.23.

INPUT   **Listing 6.21. A confusing FOR loop.**

```
 1: BEGIN
 2:      FOR I = 1995 to 1997
 3:      LOOP
 4:          FOR J = 1 to 31
 5:          LOOP
 6:              FOR K = 1 to 12
 7:              LOOP
 8:                  <statements>
 9:              END LOOP;
10:          END LOOP;
11:      END LOOP;
12: END;
```

A programmer might take an initial look at the code in Listing 6.21 and say "Huh?" A better approach is shown in Listing 6.22.

INPUT   **Listing 6.22. Making the FOR loop more meaningful.**

```
 1: BEGIN
 2:      FOR year = 1995 to 1997
 3:      LOOP
 4:          FOR day = 1 to 31
 5:          LOOP
 6:              FOR month = 1 to 12
 7:              LOOP
 8:                  <statements>
 9:              END LOOP; --end month
10:          END LOOP; --end day
11:      END LOOP; --end year
12: END;
```

6

ANALYSIS As you can see, not only does this example clarify the counters, but it also clarifies the END LOOP statements. You can further clarify the loop by adding label names as seen in Listing 6.23.

INPUT **Listing 6.23. Further clarifying the FOR loop.**

```
 1: BEGIN
 2:     <<year_loop>>
 3:     FOR year = v_START_YEAR to v_END_YEAR
 4:     LOOP
 5:         <<day_loop>>
 6:         FOR day = 1 to v_last_day_of_month
 7:         LOOP
 8:             <<month_loop>>
 9:             FOR month = 1 to 12
10:             LOOP
11:                 <statements>
12:                 END LOOP month_loop;
13:             END LOOP day_loop;
14:         END LOOP year_loop;
15: END;
```

ANALYSIS Again, the code in Listing 6.23 is the ideal way to code this nested FOR loop. The label names are concise and easy to follow. In addition, I changed the outer boundary of the day loop to a variable called v_last_day_of_month. Because this value is truly a variable, you should code it as such. I also made the beginning and ending years a variable because the analysis period could change some time down the road!

Summary

Congratulations on completing another day! You learned how to branch by using the GOTO statement followed by the appropriate label name. You also learned that the label name must appear in the same block and within the same scope as the GOTO statement.

This day continued with more ways to loop PL/SQL code. You started off with the WHILE loop, which allows you to not even execute the loop once because it checks for a condition first. This concept is very important and should be retained, because the other loops must execute once (unless you use EXIT or EXIT WHEN statements at the beginning of the other loop types, which is probably not the best way to code the loop). You continued with learning ways to exit loops and ways to change the execution of nested loops by using the EXIT or EXIT WHEN statements in conjunction with label names. You then learned about the simple LOOP and how to create a REPEAT...UNTIL loop. Finally, to clear up the loop options, you reviewed the loop types and the best time to use which loop.

Q&A

Q **What is the scope of the label called by the GOTO statement?**

A The *label_name* must be within the same PL/SQL block of code that was called by the corresponding GOTO statement.

Q **How many times must the WHILE loop execute?**

A Depending upon the condition, the WHILE loop might never have to execute. This is one of the great features of this type of loop.

Q **What is the syntax and purpose of the EXIT statement?**

A The EXIT statement is simply coded as EXIT. It gives you a means to abort out of a loop without executing the loop in its entirety.

Q **Can you exit out of loops contained in a function and still return a value?**

A Yes. However, the returned value is the value assigned to the variable at the time the EXIT statement has been called.

Q **Can you change the execution order of nested loops with EXIT or EXIT WHEN?**

A Yes. You can abort both loops with the use of EXIT and EXIT WHEN if you use label names with loops.

Q **What statement must be present in a simple LOOP or it will become an infinite loop?**

A The EXIT or EXIT WHEN statement is required. Although these statements are not part of the syntax, not using them will make a loop infinite, which you should try to avoid at all costs.

Workshop

Use the following workshop to review and practice the GOTO statement, WHILE loops, and the simple LOOP statement. The answers to the quiz and exercises can be found in Appendix A, "Answers."

Quiz

1. True or False: The label name must be within the same PL/SQL block of code as the GOTO statement calling the label name.

2. When should GOTO be used?

3. WHILE loops must end with a(n) _____ statement.

4. Can you potentially write a WHILE loop that never ends?

5. What statement(s) allow you to abort the processing of a loop?

6. In order to change execution of nested loops, you can use the EXIT and EXIT WHEN statement in conjunction with _____.

7. Must you have EXIT or EXIT WHEN as part of a simple LOOP?

8. Does Oracle have a REPEAT...UNTIL loop?

9. In a simple LOOP, where is the best location for the EXIT or EXIT WHEN statements to appear?

Exercises

1. Create an example using GOTO that checks some variable for a value of 10 and then branches off to a NULL statement.

2. Create a WHILE loop to calculate a factorial. For example, 6! is 6 * 5 * 4 * 3 * 2 * 1. Use an initial value of 4! for testing. Make sure to issue the command SET SERVEROUTPUT ON and use DBMS_OUTPUT.

3. Create the same factorial calculation as Exercise 2, but use a simple LOOP statement instead.

Day 7

Using Oracle's Built-in Functions

by Timothy Atwood

Day 5, "Using Functions, IF Statements, and Loops," demonstrates how to create functions, both within the code and stored. However, Oracle already comes complete with hundreds of excellent functions. With so many of these functions, it is unlikely that even the best Oracle guru will have them all memorized. Today's lesson covers the most frequently used functions. I highly recommend that you review Appendix B, "Oracle Functions Reference," and keep it near you while you work. Appendix B contains a complete listing of Oracle functions, their purpose, and their syntax.

TIP

The best way to learn a programming language, whether it is a third-generation language or a database management language, is to always initially review all the commands and functions, their syntax, and their usage. Any time you need to use any of these, you can then refer to this chapter for the syntax and definition. Otherwise, you might miss some very powerful features, never knowing that they even exist. This methodology also helps you to easily understand and learn competing vendor's products and makes you a more valuable programmer.

SQL Functions Versus PL/SQL Functions

As with any database, you can use SQL within PL/SQL to take advantage of all the features of PL/SQL. Almost all the functions will work within PL/SQL except those functions that operate on rows such as MAX, MIN, or any other "grouping/summary" type functions, as well as special functions like DECODE and DUMP.

The Major Categories of Functions

Tables 7.1 through 7.6 summarize Oracle's functions within the category types character functions, number functions, date functions, conversion functions, group functions, and miscellaneous functions.

Table 7.1. Character functions.

Function Name	Function Description
ASCII	Returns the ASCII code of the character.
CHR	Returns a character when given its ASCII value.
CONCAT	Joins (concatenates) two strings together (same as using the ¦¦ operator, which you might have noticed on Day 5 and Day 6, "Implementing Loops and GOTOs").
INITCAP	Returns a string in which the first letter in each word is capitalized and all remaining characters are converted to lowercase. Does not affect any nonalphabetic characters.
INSTR	Returns the location of a string within another string.
INSTRB	Returns the location of a string within another string, but returns the value in bytes for a single-byte character system.

Function Name	Function Description
LENGTH	Returns the length of a character string, including pads. Returns NULL if the value is NULL.
LENGTHB	Returns the length of a character string in bytes, except that the return value is in bytes for single-byte character sets.
LOWER	Returns the entire character string to lowercase. Does not affect any nonalphabetic characters.
LPAD	Pads a string on the left side with any string specified.
LTRIM	Trims character string on the left side with any character string specified.
NLS_INITCAP	Same as the INITCAP function except that it can use a different sort method as specified by NLSSORT.
NLS_LOWER	Same as the LOWER function except that it can use a different sort method as specified by NLSSORT.
NLS_UPPER	Same as the UPPER function except that it can use a different sort method as specified by NLSSORT.
NLSSORT	Changes the method of sorting the characters. Must be specified before any NLS function; otherwise, the default sort will be used.
REPLACE	Replaces every occurrence of one string with another string.
RPAD	Pads a string on the right side with any string specified.
RTRIM	Trims character string on the right side with any character string specified.
SOUNDEX	Returns the phonetic representation of a string. Useful for words that are spelled differently but sound alike.
SUBSTR	Returns a portion of a string from within a string.
SUBSTRB	Same as SUBSTR except the parameters are expressed in bytes instead of characters to handle single-byte character systems.
TRANSLATE	Same as REPLACE except operates at a character-level basis instead of a string-level basis.
UPPER	Returns the entire character string to uppercase. Does not affect any nonalphabetic characters.

7

Table 7.2. Number functions.

Function Name	Function Description
ABS	Returns the absolute value of a number.
ACOS	Returns the arc (inverse) cosine of a number, expressed in radians.
ASIN	Returns the arc (inverse) sine of a number, expressed in radians.
ATAN	Returns the arc (inverse) tangent of a number (x), expressed in radians.
ATAN2	Returns the arc (inverse) tangent of a number (y/x), expressed in radians.
CEIL	Returns the value representing the smallest integer, which is greater than or equal to a specified number.
COS	Returns the cosine of a number, expressed in radians.
COSH	Returns the hyperbolic cosine of a number, expressed in radians.
EXP	Returns the exponentiation of e raised to the power of some number, where $e = 2.7182818...$
FLOOR	Returns the value representing the largest integer, which is greater than or equal to a specified number.
LN	Returns the natural logarithm of some number x.
LOG	Returns the logarithm of some base x of some number y.
MOD	Returns the remainder of some number x divided by some number y.
POWER	Returns some number x to the power of some number y.
ROUND	Returns x rounded to y places.
SIGN	Determines if a number is negative, zero, or positive by the following rules: If x is negative, returns a value of -1. If x is zero, returns zero. If x is positive, returns a value of 1.
SIN	Returns the sine of some number x in radians.
SINH	Returns the hyperbolic sine of some number x in radians.
SQRT	Returns the square root of some number x. The value of x can't be an imaginary number—x must never be negative!
TAN	Returns the tangent of some number x in radians.
TANH	Returns the hyperbolic tangent of some number x in radians.
TRUNC	Returns some number x, truncated to y places. Does not round, just cuts off at the location specified.

Table 7.3. Date functions.

Function Name	Function Description
ADD_MONTHS	Adds one month to the date specified. It does not add 30 or 31 days, but simply adds one to the month. If the resulting month has fewer days, it will return the last day of that month instead.
LAST_DAY	Returns the last day of the given month. A very useful function, especially for programming in accounting departments.
MONTHS_BETWEEN	Computes the months between two dates. Returns an integer if both dates are the last days of the month; otherwise, it returns the fractional portion of a 31-day month.
NEW_TIME	Returns the time/day value from a time zone specified by the user.
NEXT_DAY	Returns the date of the first day of the week specified in a string after the beginning date.
ROUND	Gives you full flexibility to round to the nearest date parameter of your choice, such as month, year, century, and so on.
SYSDATE	Simply returns the system date and time in type DATE format.
TRUNC	Truncates up to the specified date parameter, such as day, month, and so on.

Table 7.4. Conversion functions.

Function Name	Function Description
CHARTOROWID	Converts CHAR or VARCHAR2 from the external format provided by Oracle to its internal binary format.
CONVERT	Converts from one character set to another character set.
HEXTORAW	Converts hex string values to internal raw values.
RAWTOHEX	Converts internal raw values to an external hex string.
ROWIDTOCHAR	Converts the ROW ID into its external 18-character string representation.
TO_CHAR	Converts DATES, MLSLABELS, and NUMBERS to a VARCHAR2 string.
TO_DATE	Converts a CHAR or VARCHAR2 string into a DATE value.
TO_LABEL	Converts a CHAR or VARCHAR2 string into an MLSLABEL.

continues

7

Table 7.4. continued

Function Name	Function Description
TO_MULTI_BYTE	Converts any single-byte string of characters into a multibyte string.
TO_NUMBER	Converts a CHAR or VARCHAR2 string into a NUMBER value.
TO_SINGLE_BYTE	Converts any multibyte string of characters into a single-byte string.

Table 7.5. Grouping functions.

Function Name	Function Description
AVG	Average of a column of values
COUNT	Total count of rows returned in a query
GLC	Greatest lower bound of an MLSLABEL
LUB	Least upper bound of an MLSLABEL
MAX	Returns the largest value of a row in a column from a query
MIN	Returns the smallest value of a row in a column from a query
STDDEV	Returns the standard deviation of a selected column in a query
SUM	Returns the SUM of a selected column in a query
VARIANCE	Returns the statistical VARIANCE of a selected column in a query

Table 7.6. Miscellaneous functions.

Function Name	Function Description
BFILENAME	Similar to C language. Returns a pointer, which is referred to as a *locator* in Oracle, to the associated physical LOB binary file where the file is stored.
DECODE	Acts like nested IF...THEN...ELSE statement from a list of values.
DUMP	Provides a dump of values in a string VARCHAR2 to see the representation in many different formats.
EMPTY_BLOB	Used to initialize a BLOB variable or column that will contain no data.
EMPTY_CLOB	Used to initialize a CLOB variable or column that will contain no data.

Function Name	Function Description
GREATEST	Takes a list of values or expressions and returns the largest evaluated value.
GREATEST_LB	Takes a list of MLSLABELS and returns the greatest lower bound.
LEAST	Takes a list of values or expressions and returns the smallest evaluated value.
LEAST_LB	Takes a list of MLSLABELS and returns the least lower bound.
NLS_CHARSET_ID	Returns the NLS character set ID number associated with the NLS character set name.
NLS_CHARSET_NAME	Returns the NLS character set name associated with the ID passed to the function.
NVL	Selects the first non-null value from a list of values or expressions.
SQLCODE	Returns an error code based upon the current error.
SQLERRM	Returns the error message associated with the Oracle error code.
UID	Returns the USER ID assigned to the user in Oracle.
USER	Returns the name of the current user in a VARCHAR2 string.
USERENV	Returns information about your current working environment.
VSIZE	Returns the number of bytes in some value.

Experimenting with Functions

The best way to understand functions in Oracle is to test all of them out with your own data. However, the easiest way is to use SQL*Plus and the SQL command SELECT FUNCTION(*arguments, column_headings*) from DUAL to test these functions. The examples in today's lesson use this method.

NOTE

What is DUAL and why would you select from DUAL? The DUAL table is simply a standard Oracle table, which is used as a dummy table to evaluate a condition to true. When you are testing your functions while selecting from DUAL, the table allows you to return one result. Use DUAL only when data itself is irrelevant.

7

Conversion Functions

Some of the most important and widely used functions are the conversion functions. These functions allow you to convert from one datatype to another datatype. This section discusses two major types of conversions: going from a CHAR or VARCHAR2 datatype to either a NUMBER or a DATE, or converting from a DATE or a NUMBER datatype to a VARCHAR2.

Using TO_DATE

The TO_DATE function converts a character string (CHAR or VARCHAR2) as denoted by the apostrophe (') surrounding the character string to an actual DATE value.

The Syntax for the TO_DATE Function

TO_DATE(character string, format, NLS_DATE_LANGUAGE)

The *format* parameter is optional, and if it is not used, the default DATE format will apply, which is DD-MMM-YY. The format must be the representation of the character date you are supplying to convert.

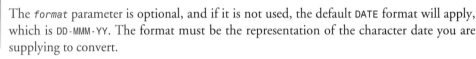

TIP   Always make sure that you specify the proper format for the date you are supplying; otherwise, you will get to know the Oracle error messages very well. For instance, if you forgot to use the format option and passed '061167', Oracle would return an error message stating that the month is invalid. Considering that the default format is DD-MMM-YY, it's easy to see that the day would be 06, but the month would not be proper at 116.

The TO_DATE function has some limitations:

☐ You can pass no more than 220 characters into the function for conversion.

☐ You are limited to the format masks listed in Table 7.7.

☐ You can't mix and match formats such as specifying 24-hour time and also requesting AM/PM because you want either 24-hour time or 12-hour time.

☐ You can't specify the same element twice in the conversion such as YYYY-MM-MMM-DD. The MM-MMM are duplicate elements. The function will have problems attempting to decode the intent and will always cause an error.

Refer to Table 7.7 for the available format masks you can pass when using the TO_DATE function.

Table 7.7. Date format elements.

Format Element	Description
BC, B.C.	BC indicator, which can be used with or without the periods.
AD, A.D.	AD indicator, which can be used with or without the periods.
CC, SCC	Century code. Returns negative value if using BC with SCC format.
SYYYY, YYYY	Four-digit year. Returns negative value if using BC with SYYYY format.
IYYY	Four-digit ISO year.
Y,YYY	Four-digit year with a comma inserted.
YYY, YY, Y	The last three, two, or one digits of the year. The default is the current century.
IYY, IY, I	The last three, two, or one digits of the ISO year. The default is the current century.
YEAR, SYEAR	Returns the year spelled out. SYEAR returns a negative value if using BC dates.
RR	Last two digits of year in prior or future centuries.
Q	Quarter of the year, values 1 to 4.
MM	The month number from 01 to 12, Jan=01, Feb=02, and so on.
MONTH	The month name always allocated to nine characters, right-padded with blanks.
MON	The month name abbreviated to three characters.
RM	Roman numeral representation of the month, values I to XII.
WW	The week in the year, values 1 to 53.
IW	The ISO week in the year, values 1 to 52 or 1 to 53.
W	The week in the month, values 1 to 5. Week 1 begins on the first day of the month.
D	The day of the week, values 1 to 7.
DD	The day of the month, values 1 to 31.
DDD	The day of the year, values 1 to 366.
DAY	The name of the day spelled out, always occupying nine characters, right space padded.
DY	Abbreviated name of the day to two characters.

continues

7

Table 7.7. continued

Format Element	Description
J	Julian day counted since January 1, 4712 BC.
HH, HH12	The hour of the day, values 1 to 12.
HH24	The hour of the day, values 0 to 23.
MI	The minute of the hour, values 0 to 59.
SS	The second of the minute, values 0 to 59.
SSSS	How many seconds past midnight, values 0 to 86399 (60 minutes/hr * 60 seconds/minute * 24 hours = 86400 seconds).
AM, A.M.	The ante meridiem indicator for morning, with or without the periods.
PM, P.M.	The post meridiem indicator for evening, with or without the periods.
Punctuation	All punctuation passed through to a maximum of 220 characters.
Text	All text passed through to a maximum of 220 characters.
TH	Suffix to convert numbers to ordinal format, so 1 would be 1st, 2 would be 2nd, and so on. Always returns value in English language only.
SP	Converts a number to its spelled format so 109 becomes one hundred nine. Always returns value in English language only.
SPTH	Spells out numbers converted to ordinal format, so 1 would be FIRST, 2 would be SECOND, and so on. Always returns value in English language only.
FX	Uses exact pattern matching between data element and the format.
FM	Fill Mode: Toggles suppression of blanks in output from conversion.

Finally, the last part of the TO_DATE function is NLS_DATE_LANGUAGE. For all you network gurus, this is simply the language you want returned, such as English, Spanish, and so on. Remember, certain functions will only return values in the English language, such as SPTH, SP, and so forth.

Just to confuse you even further, take a look at the syntax of the TO_DATE function using Julian days. Again, this is the number of days that have elapsed since January 1, 4712 BC.

SYNTAX

TO_DATE(*number*, *format*, *NLS_Params*)

The syntax is not much different than the previous syntax for normal character-based dates, except that you are now passing to the function a number value that represents the Julian days.

As you can see, this simple function can be formatted in many different ways. The best way is to go ahead and type in all the following listings to see your output. These examples use SQL*Plus as a quick method for testing, but these could easily be used in your PL/SQL code except where specified as SQL only. Go ahead and enter and execute Listings 7.1 and 7.2.

INPUT

Listing 7.1. Converting number representation to DATE format.

```
SELECT TO_DATE('061167','MMDDYY') "Birthday" from DUAL;
```

OUTPUT

The output will appear as

```
Birthday
--------
11-JUN-67
```

INPUT   ### Listing 7.2. Converting spelled date to DATE format.

```
SELECT TO_DATE('January 15','MONTH DD') "Sample" from DUAL;
```

OUTPUT

Your output should appear similar to the following:

```
Sample
--------
15-JAN-97
```

ANALYSIS

Notice that even though the example did not specify the century or the year, it takes the default system century and year.

What are some of the possible errors that you can encounter with TO_DATE? What if you leave off the mask, or incorrectly specify the mask? Listing 7.3 reflects a sample error.

INPUT   ### Listing 7.3. Errors with TO_DATE.

```
SELECT TO_DATE('061167') "Error" from DUAL;
```

7

OUTPUT You should get the error message

```
ERROR:
ORA-01843: not a valid month


no rows selected
```

Because you did not apply a mask, the standard date mask was applied from the format DD-MON-YY. Because 06 is a valid day, Oracle had no problems with handling of the day. However, when the program arrives at the month, the default date used the three-letter abbreviation for the month. The value 116 is not a valid abbreviation for a month. Listing 7.4 shows an instance when the default date can be used.

INPUT **Listing 7.4. Proper use of default format mask.**

```
SELECT TO_DATE('06-Jan-67') "Correct" from DUAL;
```

OUTPUT The output will appear as

```
Correct
--------
06-JAN-67
```

As you can see, making sure that you pass the format mask in the same manner as the character string is highly important!

The next example demonstrates using TO_DATE as part of PL/SQL code for practice. Enter the code in Listing 7.5.

NOTE Before you continue, make sure that at the SQL*Plus prompt you have entered SET SERVEROUTPUT ON. This allows you to see output to the screen as the PL/SQL code executes.

INPUT **Listing 7.5. Using TO_DATE within PL/SQL.**

```
1: DECLARE
2:      v_Convert_Date DATE;
3: BEGIN
4:      v_Convert_Date := TO_DATE('061167','MMDDYY');
5:      DBMS_OUTPUT.PUT_LINE('The converted date is: ' || v_Convert_Date);
6: END;
7: /
```

OUTPUT All the PL/SQL code does is to create a variable of type DATE in line 2 and assign it to the converted character date in line 4. The output should be

```
The converted date is: 11-JUN-67

PL/SQL procedure successfully completed.
```

How many people know a foreign language? How do you convert to the Oracle built-in DATE from another language? Remember to use the NLS_DATE_LANGUAGE parameter to specify the language. Listing 7.6 is an example of converting a German date to an Oracle DATE.

INPUT ## Listing 7.6. Converting German date to DATE format.

```
SELECT TO_DATE('februar-23','MONTH-DD','NLS_DATE_LANGUAGE=german')
    "Converted" from DUAL;
```

OUTPUT The output will appear in the default Oracle format as

```
Converted
---------
23-FEB-97
```

Finally, how about some calculations on that date just returned? Listing 7.7 reflects adding 10 days to the converted date.

INPUT ## Listing 7.7. Performing calculations on a converted date.

```
1: DECLARE
2:      v_Convert_Date DATE;
3: BEGIN
4:      v_Convert_Date := TO_DATE('061167','MMDDYY') + 10;
5:      DBMS_OUTPUT.PUT_LINE('The converted date is: ' ¦¦ v_Convert_Date);
6: END;
7: /
```

OUTPUT Your output should appear as follows:

```
The converted date is: 21-JUN-67

PL/SQL procedure successfully completed.
```

You have taken a converted date of 06/11/67 and added 10 days in line 4, which brings you to the proper result of 21-JUN-67!

You should now be starting to get a grasp on how Oracle converts characters to dates. Experiment with some of the other formats in the rest of this section.

Using TO_CHAR for Dates

If you can turn character strings into dates, you should be able to reverse this process. Oracle provides you with the answer by using the TO_CHAR function.

The Syntax for the TO_CHAR Function

```
TO_CHAR(date, format, NLS_Params)
```

Remember to refer to Table 7.7 for allowable mask formats. The best way to demonstrate TO_CHAR is through many examples, especially with format varieties. The first example will take the current system date and time from the SYSDATE function and format it to a spelled-out date in Listing 7.8.

NOTE	Some of these listings allow you to enter the code directly at the SQL*Plus prompt, or you can enter it directly into the editor. If you use the editor, do not use the ending semicolon for the one line SQL listings. If you are entering at the prompt, the semicolon performs the SQL statement, similar to using a / to execute the code.

INPUT   **Listing 7.8. Converting DATE to spelled-out character format.**

```
SELECT TO_CHAR(SYSDATE,'MONTH DDTH YYYY') "Today" from DUAL;
```

OUTPUT   Your output should appear as follows:

```
Today
-------------------
JUNE       03RD 1997
```

How about using this as a PL/SQL procedure and going back to the good old days of BC? Listing 7.9 shows another example of using TO_CHAR with converting and formatting dates.

INPUT   **Listing 7.9. Converting DATE to spelled-out character format.**

```
1: DECLARE
2:     v_Convert_Date DATE := TO_DATE('06112067BC','MMDDYYYYBC');
3:     v_Hold_Date VARCHAR2(100);
4: BEGIN
5:     v_Hold_Date := TO_CHAR(v_Convert_Date,'MMDDSYYYY');
6:     DBMS_OUTPUT.PUT_LINE('The converted date is: ' ¦¦ v_Hold_Date);
7: END;
8: /
```

ANALYSIS There are several items to make note of here. First, in order to assign a date to a DATE value, you need to convert a character date to a DATE datatype by using the TO_DATE function, as shown in line 2. If you simply tried to enter or assign a date such as in the following example, you would generate an error:

```
v_Convert_Date DATE := 11-JUN-67;
```

The second item to notice is how Oracle displays dates for BC. When you run the code from Listing 7.9, your output will appear as follows:

OUTPUT
```
The converted date is: 0611-2067

PL/SQL procedure successfully completed.
```

As you can see, a negative sign before the year value represents BC.

Finally, you can have some fun with using another language for your output. Enter and execute the code in Listing 7.10 for an example of German output.

INPUT ### Listing 7.10. Converting DATE to another language.

```
SELECT TO_CHAR(SYSDATE,'MONTH DD YY','NLS_DATE_LANGUAGE=german')
       "German Date" from DUAL;
```

OUTPUT Your output should appear as

```
German Date
- - - - - - - - - - - - - - - -
JUNI     04 97
```

NOTE Make sure when you are displaying your output that you specify such mask formats as Month or MONTH, because the output will display in the same case-sensitive format of either all uppercase, all lowercase, or proper case (that is, JUNE, june, or June).

Using TO_NUMBER

The TO_NUMBER function is very similar to the TO_DATE function. This function converts a character string of type CHAR or VARCHAR2 into a number. As with TO_DATE, the format mask is very important for a proper conversion.

The Syntax for the TO_NUMBER Function

TO_NUMBER(*character_string*, *format*, *NLS_Params*)

There are many reasons to convert from a character to a number value. For instance, you decide to store data of type VARCHAR2 for the age when hired. Suppose you want to perform some calculations on the age to determine retirement income and information. Simply use the TO_NUMBER function to change to a NUMBER datatype and then perform the calculation. It's more efficient to store numbers in the CHAR or VARCHAR2 format because most systems will store as a single byte instead of two bytes with a NUMBER datatype, and you would not perform calculations very often on this data.

TIP If you are using a field to perform calculations on frequently, never store it as a VARCHAR2 or CHAR because the process to convert to a number will really slow down the system, and other end users will not be too happy!

See Table 7.8 for the available format masks you can pass when using the TO_NUMBER function.

Table 7.8. Number format elements.

Format Element	Sample(s)	Description
9	9999	Each nine is considered a significant digit. Any leading zeros are treated as blanks.
0	09999 or 99990	By adding the 0 as a prefix or suffix to the number, all leading or trailing zeros are treated and displayed as zeros instead of drawing a blank (pun intended). Think of this display type as NUMERIC values, such as 00109.
$	$9999	Prefix of currency symbol printed in the first position.
B	B9999	Returns any portion of the integer as blanks if the integer is 0. This will override the leading zeros by using a 0 for the format.
MI	9999MI	Automatically adds a space at the end to hold either a minus sign if the value is negative, or to hold a placeholder space if the value is positive.

Format Element	Sample(s)	Description
S	S9999 or 9999S	Displays a leading or trailing sign of + if the value is positive, and a leading or trailing sign of - if the value is negative.
PR	9999PR	If the value is negative, angle brackets <> are placed around the number; otherwise, placeholder spaces are used if the number is positive.
D	99D99	Decimal point location. The nines on both sides reflect the maximum number of digits allowed.
G	9G999G999	Specifies a group separator such as a comma.
C	C99	Returns ISO currency symbol in the specified position.
L	L9999	Specifies the location of the local currency symbol (such as $).
,	9,999,999	Places a comma in specified position, regardless of the group separator.
.	99.99	Specifies the location of the decimal point, regardless of the decimal separator.
V	999V99	Returns the number multiplied to the $10n$ power, where n is the number of nines after the V.
EEEE	9.99EEEE	Returns the value in scientific notation.
RM, rm	RM, rm	Returns the value as upper- or lowercase Roman numerals.
FM	FM9,999.99	Fill Mode: Removes leading and trailing blanks.

After the format mask are several possible NLS parameters:

- ☐ NLS_NUMERIC_CHARACTERS—Specifies characters to use for group separators and the decimal point.

- ☐ NLS_CURRENCY—Specifies the local currency.

- ☐ NLS_ISO_CURRENCY—Character(s) to represent the ISO currency symbol.

In the examples in this section, you can practice some of these conversions. First, you'll perform a simple character-to-number conversion. Go ahead and execute the code in Listing 7.11.

7

Listing 7.11. Converting a character to an integer value.

```
 1: DECLARE
 2:     v_Convert_Number VARCHAR2(20) := '1997';
 3:     v_Hold_Number NUMBER ;
 4: BEGIN
 5:     v_Hold_Number := TO_Number(v_Convert_Number,'9999');
 6:     DBMS_OUTPUT.PUT_LINE('The converted number is: ' || v_Hold_Number);
 7:     DBMS_OUTPUT.PUT_LINE('The converted number plus 10 is: ' ||
 8:                          (v_Hold_Number+10));
 9: END;
10: /
```

OUTPUT After executing the PL/SQL block, your output should be

```
The converted number is: 1997
The converted number plus 10 is: 2007
```

ANALYSIS This block of code simply converted a character integer with a value of 1997, converted it to a number in line 6, and then additionally performed a mathematical calculation to add 10 to the integer in line 7. Without the TO_NUMBER function, you would not be able to perform any type of calculations on characters.

You will often need to convert a field in a table from one datatype to another. For instance, a real estate company uses Oracle to track its listings. Unfortunately, the house prices were declared as a type VARCHAR2(20). The format entered was always the currency symbol ($) followed by the price, offset in commas. The range of prices can be from $.01 to $999,999,999.99. You could write a function to update a column added to the table, change the datatype, and delete the extra column no longer needed. For now, you only need to calculate your commission for some property you had just sold. The going commission rate for agents in the area is 6%. Listing 7.12 shows the conversion of VARCHAR2 to NUMBER and then calculates your commission.

INPUT **Listing 7.12. Converting a character formatted as currency to an integer value.**

```
 1: DECLARE
 2:     v_Convert_Number VARCHAR2(20) := '$119,252.75';
 3:     v_Hold_Number NUMBER ;
 4: BEGIN
 5:     v_Hold_Number := TO_Number(v_Convert_Number,'$999,999,999.99');
 6:     DBMS_OUTPUT.PUT_LINE('The converted number is: ' || v_Hold_Number);
 7:     DBMS_OUTPUT.PUT_LINE('Your commission at 6% is: ' ||
 8:                          (v_Hold_Number*.06));
 9: END;
10: /
```

OUTPUT When you execute this code, your output appears as

```
The converted number is: 119252.75
Your commission at 6% is: 7155.165
```

ANALYSIS This PL/SQL block has an unusually long format mask. When you convert a number, the format mask must be equal to or greater than the length of the number of characters to convert. Remember, the largest value could be $999,999,999.99, so you should create the format for the largest possible value as demonstrated in line 5. But what happens if you break this rule? Go ahead and enter and then execute the code in Listing 7.13.

INPUT ## Listing 7.13. Errors with the format mask.

```
 1: DECLARE
 2:     v_Convert_Number VARCHAR2(20) := '$119,252.75';
 3:     v_Hold_Number NUMBER ;
 4: BEGIN
 5:     v_Hold_Number := TO_Number(v_Convert_Number,'$99,999.99');
 6:     DBMS_OUTPUT.PUT_LINE('The converted number is: ' || v_Hold_Number);
 7:     DBMS_OUTPUT.PUT_LINE('Your commission at 6% is: ' ||
 8:                          (v_Hold_Number*.06));
 9: END;
10: /
```

OUTPUT Immediately upon execution of this code, you will receive the following errors:

```
ORA-06502: Message 6502 not found;  product=RDBMS73; facility=ORA
ORA-06512: Message 6512 not found;  product=RDBMS73; facility=ORA
; arguments: ["SYS.STANDARD", ] [720]
ORA-06512: Message 6512 not found;  product=RDBMS73; facility=ORA
; arguments: [] [5]
```

How do you handle these errors? Simply execute the program Oracle Messages and Codes. Then click on Find and enter the first code, which is ORA-06502. The help you will receive from Oracle is

```
ORA-06502  PL/SQL: numeric or value error

Cause:    An arithmetic, numeric, string, conversion, or constraint error
 occurred. For example, this error occurs if an attempt is made to assign
 the value NULL to a variable declared NOT NULL, or if an attempt is made
 to assign an integer larger than 99 to a variable declared NUMBER(2).
Action:  Change the data, how it is manipulated, or how it is declared so
 that values do not violate constraints.

Copyright (C) 1995, Oracle Corporation
```

You're probably wondering, What does all that error code mean? Next, when you get help on the second error message, you will see

7

```
ORA-06512  at str line num
```

```
Cause:  This is usually the last of a message stack and indicates where
 a problem occurred in the PL/SQL code.
Action:  Fix the problem causing the exception or write an exception
 handler for this condition. It may be necessary to contact the
 application or database administrator.
```

```
Copyright (C) 1995, Oracle Corporation
```

 NOTE

> When you look up error messages, make sure that you type the code in the same exact manner as displayed. For example, do not type in ORA-06502 as ORA-6502 because Oracle will never find the match for the error in the help file.

When Oracle compiles, it looks for all possible errors. The first error message indicates that the number assigned to the variable is too large for the mask. Remember, Oracle has no clue as to your intent. In the case of the error messages, you could have made an incorrect declaration, or according to the second error message, you did not create a large enough mask for the function TO_NUMBER.

The last example is a store, which stored all the sales percentages as a VARCHAR2(4) field in the format 33.33. You will need to convert these numbers to their decimal equivalent. Run through the code in Listing 7.14.

Listing 7.14. Converting VARCHAR2 percentage data to a
INPUT decimal equivalent.

```
 1: DECLARE
 2:     v_Convert_Number VARCHAR2(20) := '33.33';
 3:     v_Hold_Number NUMBER ;
 4: BEGIN
 5:     v_Hold_Number := TO_Number(v_Convert_Number,'999.999999');
 6:     DBMS_OUTPUT.PUT_LINE('The converted number is: ' ¦¦ v_Hold_Number);
 7:     DBMS_OUTPUT.PUT_LINE('Your decimal equivalent is: ' ¦¦
 8:                     (v_Hold_Number/100));
 9: END;
10: /
```

OUTPUT When you execute the code in Listing 7.14, your output should appear as

```
The converted number is: 33.33
Your decimal equivalent is: .3333
```

The PL/SQL code in Listing 7.14 is simply a repeat, except that you now divide the converted number by 100 with the statement in lines 7 and 8 to arrive at the decimal point.

Always use the TO_NUMBER function if you need to convert characters to numbers for computations or for changing datatypes. The next section explains the inverse function TO_CHAR.

Using TO_CHAR for Numbers

Once again, if you can change characters to numbers, you should also be able to change numbers to characters by using the function TO_CHAR.

TO_CHAR(*number*, *format*, *NLS_Params*)

The format mask and the NLS parameters are identical to the TO_NUMBER function. You can review the format masks in Table 7.8. The NLS parameters again are

☐ NLS_NUMERIC_CHARACTERS—Specifies characters to use for group separators and the decimal point.

☐ NLS_CURRENCY—Specifies the local currency.

☐ NLS_ISO_CURRENCY—Character(s) to represent the ISO currency symbol.

You can now make some decent format attempts for numbers in a column. You will print out an employee ID number with leading zeros and a total length of 10 characters. Go ahead and try the PL/SQL code in Listing 7.15.

INPUT

Listing 7.15. Converting number to character formatted as a numeric string.

```
1: DECLARE
2:     v_Convert_Number NUMBER := 90210;
3:     v_Hold_Char VARCHAR2(21) ;
4: BEGIN
5:     v_Hold_Char := TO_CHAR(v_Convert_Number,'0000000000');
6:     DBMS_OUTPUT.PUT_LINE('The employee ID is: ' ¦¦ v_Hold_Char);
7: END;
8: /
```

OUTPUT   After executing the PL/SQL code block, your output should appear as

```
The employee ID is:  0000090210
```

You were able to take a five-digit number, or any NUMBER with a value of 10 digits as specified by the mask in line 5, and pad the number to the left with zeros. The number 90210 becomes 0000090210 because you use 0s for the format mask, which means that zeros should be output instead of blanks.

7

You can now look at some other types of NUMBER formatting. Suppose you are asked to do some work for engineers or scientists. They require you to express the results in scientific notation. This is simply the number converted to however many significant digits to the *m*th power of 10. The number 1000 would be 1.00E+03 because you would shift the decimal point to the left three places. You can practice this in Listing 7.16.

INPUT **Listing 7.16. Expressing your work in scientific notation.**

```
1: DECLARE
2:     v_Convert_Number NUMBER := 90210;
3:     v_Hold_Char VARCHAR2(21) ;
4: BEGIN
5:     v_Hold_Char := TO_CHAR(v_Convert_Number,'9.99EEEE');
6:     DBMS_OUTPUT.PUT_LINE('The Scientific Notation is: ' ¦¦ v_Hold_Char);
7: END;
8: /
```

OUTPUT   Your output would appear as

```
The Scientific Notation is: 9.02E+04
```

Again, 90210 would allow you to shift the decimal point to the left four spaces. Because you are taking only two significant digits after the decimal point, the result is 9.02E+04. Go ahead and practice formatting numbers. When you are finished, you can continue with performing calculations on dates!

DATE **Functions**

Oracle provides several built-in date functions to perform many complex date calculations. Oracle holds the true system DATE in the format DD-MM-YYYY to handle all dates from January 1, 4712 BC to December 31, 4712 AD. By that time you will be working with Oracle version 5000! In addition, Oracle holds the true system TIME in the format HH-MM-SS in 24-hour military format.

SYSDATE

The SYSDATE function returns the current date and time in the Oracle server. Note the distinction that it is the *server* and not the *client's* date and time that is being returned. The format for the SYSDATE function is

SYSDATE

That's it! Not only can you get the system DATE and TIME from Oracle, but also you can format it in any way possible, and you can perform calculations on the system DATE and TIME. Refer to Table 7.7 for possible formats. You can now begin with the standard output from using SYSDATE from Listing 7.17.

INPUT   **Listing 7.17. Default output of SYSDATE.**

```
SELECT SYSDATE from DUAL;
```

OUTPUT   Your output should appear similar to

```
SYSDATE
--------
01-JUN-97
```

Don't forget that SYSDATE is not a variable but a function that retrieves the date and time from the server. You can add the TO_CHAR function to format the system date and time to something you are more familiar with, as shown in Listing 7.18.

INPUT   **Listing 7.18. Combining TO_CHAR to format SYSDATE.**

```
SELECT TO_CHAR(SYSDATE,'MM/DD/YYYY HH:MM:SS AM')
       "Today's Date and Time" from DUAL;
```

OUTPUT   A similar output should look like

```
Today's Date and Time
-----------------------------
06/01/1997 11:06:21 PM
```

As you can see from the time, the standard programming time of all hours of the night still exists! In the rest of this section, you can practice some of the other built-in DATE functions.

The TRUNC Function

The TRUNC function is useful for returning a truncated DATE or TIME to a specified mask. For instance, you can truncate to the nearest day, month, quarter, century, and so on. The main use of TRUNC is to simply eliminate the time from the SYSDATE by setting all time values for all dates to 12:00 a.m.

The Syntax for the TRUNC Function

```
TRUNC(date_passed,truncate mask)
```

In order to understand the TRUNC function, see Table 7.9, which provides a list of possible values to use with the TRUNC and ROUND functions.

Table 7.9. Masks used with the ROUND and TRUNC functions.

Mask Options	Description
CC, SCC	Rounds or truncates to the century
YYYY, SYYYY, YEAR, SYEAR, YYY, YY, Y	Truncates to the year, or rounds up to the next year after July 1st
IYYY, IYY, IY, I	ISO year
Q	Truncates to the quarter or rounds up to the nearest quarter on or after the sixteenth day of the second month of the quarter
MM, MON, MONTH, RM	Truncates the month or rounds up to the next month on or after the sixteenth day
DD, DDD, J	Truncates or rounds to the day
WW	Same day of the week as the first day of the year
IW	Same day of the week as the first day of the ISO year
W	Same day of the week as the first day of the month
Day, Dy, D	Truncates or rounds to the first day of the week
HH24, HH12, HH	Truncates to the hour, or rounds up to the next hour on or after 30 minutes
MI	Truncates to the minute or rounds up on or after 30 seconds

Now that you have seen all the possible masking options, try out how the TRUNC function operates by testing it with different examples. You will first truncate the time from the system date. Remember, you will still see the time displayed, but if you use TRUNC on all dates, the time will always be 12:00 a.m. instead of the time the date was assigned; therefore, all dates can be calculated properly regardless of time. Go ahead and execute the SQL code in Listing 7.19.

INPUT **Listing 7.19. Removing the time from SYSDATE.**

```
1: SELECT TO_CHAR(TRUNC(SYSDATE),'MM/DD/YYYY HH:MM:SS AM')
2:     "Today's Date and Time"
3:      from DUAL;
```

OUTPUT   Your output will appear similar to

```
Today's Date and Time
---------------------
06/01/1997 12:00:00 AM
```

Notice that the time element will still be displayed, but if you were to subtract two truncated dates with the same time, you would get an even number of days. One more observation is that the default for TRUNC would be the same as a format mask of DD, which simply eliminates the need to worry about the time in your calculations.

You can test the TRUNC function by truncating the SYSDATE to the nearest quarter by executing the code in Listing 7.20.

INPUT **Listing 7.20. Truncating to the quarter.**

```
1: SELECT TO_CHAR(TRUNC(SYSDATE,'Q'),'MM/DD/YYYY HH:MM:SS AM')
2:     "Today's Date and Time"
3:  from DUAL
```

OUTPUT Assuming today's date was 06/01/97, you would get the following output:

```
Today's Date and Time
---------------------
04/01/1997 12:00:00 AM
```

This result makes sense because June is in the second quarter, and the quarter ranges from 04/01/97 to 06/30/97. Truncating to the quarter gives the beginning date for the applicable quarter. You'll get the opportunity to test this function in the exercises at the end of the chapter.

The ADD_MONTHS Function

The ADD_MONTHS function adds or subtracts months from a date. Because this function is *overloaded*, which means that you can pass different datatypes to the same function or change the order of the parameters, you can specify the parameters in any order.

The Syntax for the ADD_MONTHS Function

SYNTAX

Therefore, the syntax can be expressed in two ways:

ADD_MONTHS(*date_passed*,*months_to_add*)

or

ADD_MONTHS(*months_to_add*,*date_passed*)

If *months_to_add* is positive, it will add months into the future. If the *months_to_add* number is negative, it will subtract months from *date_passed*. You can specify *months_to_add* as a fraction, but Oracle completely ignores the fraction. You can go down to the day level by using other Oracle functions. Another caution is that Oracle will return the same day in the resulting calculation except if the last day in one month is the 31st (for example, March 31st)

and the resulting month does not have as many days (for example, April 30th would be the answer to adding one month). The following three examples in Listing 7.21 will provide the same result.

INPUT   **Listing 7.21. Adding two months to SYSDATE.**

```
1: SELECT ADD_MONTHS(SYSDATE,2) from DUAL;
2: SELECT ADD_MONTHS(2,SYSDATE) from DUAL;
3: SELECT ADD_MONTHS(SYSDATE,2.654) from DUAL;
```

OUTPUT   All of these (assuming the date is 06/02/97) will produce the following output:

```
ADD_MONTH
---------
02-AUG-97
```

You can see what happens for the last day of the month by adding one month to March 31st, as shown in Listing 7.22.

INPUT   **Listing 7.22. Adding one month to SYSDATE.**

```
SELECT ADD_MONTHS(TO_DATE('31-MAR-97'),1) from DUAL;
```

OUTPUT   This example will output

```
ADD_MONTH
---------
30-APR-97
```

Again, Oracle could not output April 31st because no such date exists.

The NEXT_DAY Function

The NEXT_DAY function returns the next date in the week for the day of the week specified after the input date. The time returned is the time specified by the input date when called.

The Syntax for the NEXT_DAY Function

```
NEXT_DAY(input_date_passed,day_name)
```

The NEXT_DAY function provides lots of possibilities. You could calculate anything from the first Monday of every month to each payday in a calendar year. You'll start off by testing the NEXT_DAY function on the SYSDATE function to find the next Monday. Assume the SYSDATE is June 3rd, 1997. Your own results will differ when you execute the code in Listing 7.23.

INPUT

Listing 7.23. Finding the first Monday after the current date and time.

```
1: SELECT TO_CHAR(NEXT_DAY(SYSDATE,'Monday'),'MM/DD/YYYY HH:MM:SS AM')
2:     "Next_Day"
3:   from DUAL;
```

OUTPUT

The result returned for the SYSDATE of June 3rd, 1997 is

```
Next_Day
--------------------
06/09/1997 07:06:38 AM
```

ANALYSIS

The first Monday after the date is June 9th, 1997. Because you are using the SYSDATE, the corresponding time value will be returned when the function is called.

You can find the first Monday for August, 1997 by executing the code in Listing 7.24.

INPUT

Listing 7.24. Finding the first Monday in the month of August.

```
1: SELECT TO_CHAR(NEXT_DAY('01-AUG-97','Monday'),'MM/DD/YYYY HH:MM:SS AM')
2:     "Next_Day"
3:   from DUAL;
```

OUTPUT

Your output will be

```
Next_Day
--------------------
08/04/1997 12:00:00 AM
```

ANALYSIS

Although the first Monday in August *is* 08/04/97, is there a logic problem here? If you repeat the example, but use a month in which Monday is the first day of the month, what happens? Execute the code in Listing 7.25.

INPUT

Listing 7.25. Finding the first Monday in the month of September.

```
1: SELECT TO_CHAR(NEXT_DAY('01-SEP-97','Monday'),'MM/DD/YYYY HH:MM:SS AM')
2:     "Next_Day"
3:   from DUAL;
```

OUTPUT

Your output will be

```
Next_Day
--------------------
09/08/1997 12:00:00 AM
```

7

ANALYSIS The result is definitely not what you had in mind! The NEXT_DAY function returns the next day of the day specified. If the day of the week specified matches the input date, it will add one week to the input date. If you want to calculate the first occurrence of any day in the month, always use the end date of the previous month. Review the proper code in Listing 7.26.

INPUT ### Listing 7.26. The proper method to find the first Monday in a given month.

```
1: SELECT TO_CHAR(NEXT_DAY('31-AUG-97','Monday'),'MM/DD/YYYY HH:MM:SS AM')
2:      "Next_Day"
3:   from DUAL;
```

OUTPUT Your output will be

```
Next_Day
--------------------
09/01/1997 12:00:00 AM
```

You finally have the proper logic for what you intended to find originally!

The LAST_DAY Function

This function provides the last day of the given month. A very useful purpose would be to determine how many days are left in the given month.

The Syntax for the LAST_DAY Function

LAST_DAY(*input_date_passed*)

You will compute the last day in the month for when summer officially starts from 1997. Go ahead and execute the code in Listing 7.27.

INPUT ### Listing 7.27. Finding the last day of the month starting summer.

```
1: SELECT TO_CHAR(LAST_DAY('30-JUN-97'),'MM/DD/YYYY HH:MM:SS AM') "Last_Day"
2:   from DUAL;
```

OUTPUT Your output will be

```
Last_Day
--------------------
06/30/1997 12:06:00 AM
```

I purposefully used the last day of the month to illustrate an important fact. Unlike NEXT_DAY, which will add one week if the day of the week specified is the same as the input date, the LAST_DAY function will always return the last day of the month even if the input date is the same.

You can take this one step further and see how many days of summer exist in the month of June by subtracting the last day of the month by the start date of summer. Execute Listing 7.28 to see the result.

INPUT

Listing 7.28. Calculating the number of days of summer in June.

```
1: SELECT LAST_DAY('20-JUN-97') "Last_Day",
2:        LAST_DAY('20-JUN-97') - TO_DATE('20-JUN-97') "Days_Summer"
3:     from DUAL;
```

OUTPUT

Your output will be

```
Last_Day  Days_Summer
--------- -----------
30-JUN-97          10
```

The MONTHS_BETWEEN Function

This function returns the number of months between two given dates. If the day is the same in both months, you will get an integer value returned. If the day is different, you will get a fractional result based upon a 31-day month. If the second date is prior to the first date, the result will be negative.

The Syntax for the MONTHS_BETWEEN Function

MONTHS_BETWEEN(*input_date1*,*input_date2*)

You can see all the possible returned values by executing the code in Listing 7.29.

INPUT

Listing 7.29. Experimenting with MONTHS_BETWEEN.

```
1: SELECT MONTHS_BETWEEN('25-DEC-97','02-JUN-97') "Fractional",
2:        MONTHS_BETWEEN('02-FEB-97','02-JUN-97') "Integer"
3:     from DUAL;
```

OUTPUT

Your output will be

```
Fractional  Integer
----------  -------
 6.7419355       -4
```

7

TIP

Who cares about seeing the fractional part of a 31-day month? To convert the fraction to days, simply multiply the TRUNC value of the fractional part by 31 to convert to days. If you want to display the month, use TRUNC on this value.

The NEW_TIME Function

Have you ever wondered what time it was in Germany? Would the phone call be waking the person up in the middle of the night? The NEW_TIME function enables you to find out the time in the time zones listed in Table 7.10 by simply passing the date and time of the first zone, and specifying the second zone.

The Syntax for the NEW_TIME Function

NEW_TIME(*input_date and time,time_zone1,time_zone2*)

What are the valid time zones? See Table 7.10.

Table 7.10. Time zones.

Time Zone Abbreviation Passed	Time Zone Description
AST	Atlantic Standard Time
ADT	Atlantic Daylight Saving Time
BST	Bering Standard Time
BDT	Bering Daylight Saving Time
CST	Central Standard Time
CDT	Central Daylight Saving Time
EST	Eastern Standard Time
EDT	Eastern Daylight Saving Time
GMT	Greenwich Mean Time (Date Line!)
HST	Alaska-Hawaii Standard Time
HDT	Alaska-Hawaii Daylight Saving Time
MST	Mountain Standard Time
MDT	Mountain Daylight Saving Time
NST	Newfoundland Standard Time
PST	Pacific Standard Time

7

Time Zone Abbreviation Passed	Time Zone Description
PDT	Pacific Daylight Saving Time
YST	Yukon Standard Time
YDT	Yukon Daylight Saving Time

You can compute the date and time difference between Chicago and Los Angeles by specifying Central Daylight Time to Pacific Daylight Time. Enter and execute the code in Listing 7.30.

INPUT **Listing 7.30. Time change from Chicago to Los Angeles.**

```
1: SELECT TO_CHAR(NEW_TIME(TO_DATE('060297 01:00:00 AM',
2:          'MMDDYY HH:MI:SS AM'),
3:          'CDT','PDT'), 'DD-MON-YY HH:MI:SS AM') "Central to Pacific"
4:     from DUAL;
```

TIP

Remember, minutes are expressed as MI, not MM. This is a common mistake!

OUTPUT Your output will be

```
Central to Pacific
--------------------
01-JUN-97 11:00:00 PM
```

ANALYSIS Because there is a two-hour time difference, you not only see the revised time, but the revised date as well. I guess you truly can go back in time!

TIP

In a database that traverses time zones, you might want to store the time and date for all entries in one standardized time zone, along with the time zone abbreviation from the original time zone. This will save you a lot of time and coding when designing the database.

7

The ROUND Function

ROUND is very similar to the TRUNC function. In fact, it uses the same format mask as TRUNC did in Table 7.9. This function enables you to round up or down based upon the format mask. The default mask when specifying a DATE value is DD. Some useful purposes for this are

- ☐ Rounding to the nearest minute for billing cellular-based calls
- ☐ Rounding to closest month to determine a pay period

The Syntax for the ROUND Function

SYNTAX

ROUND(*input_date and time or number,rounding_specification*)

You can practice rounding to the nearest minute to charge people who use cellular phones by entering the code in Listing 7.31.

INPUT   **Listing 7.31. Rounding to the nearest minute.**

```
1: SELECT TO_CHAR(ROUND(TO_DATE('060297 01:00:35 AM',
2:            'MMDDYY HH:MI:SS AM'),
3:            'MI'), 'DD-MON-YY HH:MI:SS AM') "Rounded to nearest Minute"
4:      from DUAL;
```

OUTPUT   Your output will be

```
Rounded to nearest Minute
-------------------------
02-JUN-97 01:01:00 AM  10
```

ANALYSIS   Because the seconds were 30 or greater, this example rounded to the next minute at 1:01 from 1:00. Had the number of seconds been 22, the return value would be 1:00. You should test this on your own.

Summary

Today, you discovered only a fraction of Oracle's powerful built-in function. Today's lesson stressed the importance of converting data and working with dates. I highly recommend that you refer to Appendix B to review the rest of the functions. A final huge tip: Punctuation is very important!

Q&A

Q Are all functions available from within PL/SQL?

A No. There are several functions that can be used in SQL only. Refer to Appendix B.

Q Must I use Oracle's built-in functions?

A No. You could always create your own similar functions, but when speed is of the essence, why reinvent the wheel? Use the built-in functions whenever possible.

Q What date does the Julian system start counting from?

A January 1, 4712 BC.

Q When using TO_DATE, is the format mask important?

A Not just a little bit important, very important and required! Without the proper format mask, you will most certainly get an Oracle error message.

Q How long should the number format mask be?

A At least equal to or greater than the length of the largest value.

Q What function allows you to perform mathematical computations on character strings?

A TO_NUMBER converts the character strings to numbers so that you can perform any mathematical calculations you want.

Q From what machine does the SYSDATE date and time originate?

A If you are using Personal Oracle, the system date and time come from the PC's internal clock. If you are in a client/server environment, the system date and time are pulled from the server.

Workshop

Use the following workshop to test your ability to understand and use several of Oracle's built-in functions. The answers to the quiz and exercises can be found in Appendix A, "Answers."

Quiz

1. True or False: All functions are accessible from within PL/SQL.

2. What function would I use to combine two strings together?

3. What function would convert '11/28/97' to an Oracle DATE?

4. In a VARCHAR2 string, each string can be a variable length. What function would you use to determine the length so that you can search through the entire string?

5. How do you get rid of padded spaces to the right of a string in Oracle?

6. To determine the remainder, you would use the _____ function.

7. To determine how many months a customer is delinquent, you can use the _____ function.

8. The TRUNC and ROUND functions can be used with what datatypes?

Exercises

1. Create a PL/SQL block that reads in the month of a date and displays the month in a Roman numeral format. Use a date of 06/11/67. This will allow you to practice the TO_CHAR function. When printing the Roman numeral equivalent, use LTRIM to remove spaces padded to the left of the Roman numeral. If you are really ambitious, on your own you could create the same RM type function by using IF...THEN...ELSE statements for practice from Day 5. Remember, practice helps to solidify your knowledge through repetition and understanding.

2. Use the TRUNC function on the SYSDATE to round to the nearest century.

3. Use CONCAT to link two strings together. Repeat the same line by using ¦¦ instead of CONCAT.

4. Calculate the number of days between 01/01/97 to 03/31/97. Remember to use the TRUNC function to eliminate the TIME dependency.

5. Convert the CHARACTER string '06/11/67' to a date, and subtract from 06/11/97 to see how old your author is (and holding).

6. Calculate how many months are between 05/15/97 to 08/22/97.

7. Round the SYSDATE to the nearest century.

8. Calculate the time in Newfoundland from Central Standard Time from 02/22/97, 05:00 a.m.

9. From Listing 7.22, subtract one month and explain the answer.

10. Calculate the number of days until Christmas from the last day of the month of today's date! (We don't get paid until the end of the month!)

WEEK

1

1

2

3

4

5

6

7

In Review

Here you are at the end of Week 1. By now you should have a good grasp of the basics of PL/SQL. On the first day, you read about the relationship of PL/SQL to other Oracle products, and you also saw your first example of a short, but still useful, PL/SQL function. On the second day, you had a chance to learn about some of the choices you have in terms of a development environment. Day 3 covers the various PL/SQL datatypes and gives examples of how they are used. During the following day, Day 4, you went over PL/SQL expressions and operators. You learned how operator precedence affects an expression's order of evaluation and how you can control that by using parentheses. You learned about three-valued logic and the effect of null values on an expression's evaluation, and you learned how data is converted from one type to another. Days 5 and 6 cover the PL/SQL statements that control program flow and execution. These include IF statements, FOR loops, and WHILE loops. The week concluded with Day 7 and a discussion of the many powerful, built-in functions that Oracle provides as part of PL/SQL.

WEEK 2

8

9

10

11

12

13

14

At a Glance

Congratulations! You completed Week 1 and are now ready to take on Week 2. During Week 1, you learned many of the building blocks and core features of PL/SQL.

Where You Are Going

During Week 2 you will take some of the features you learned in Week 1 and learn more complex methods of using them. In this second week, you will begin to integrate your PL/SQL code with the Oracle database as well as begin to store your code inside the database. You will create some sample tables and then use your PL/SQL code to manipulate data in these tables. By the end of the week, you will know how to perform multiple row queries and process the rows one at a time, all within PL/SQL. On Day 13, you will be introduced to the new Oracle8 database objects. Additionally, in Week 2, you will learn how to code your programs to anticipate and handle many different runtime errors that can occur in your PL/SQL code.

Great job in completing Week 1! Now continue with Week 2, starting with Day 8.

Day 8

Procedures, Packages, Errors, and Exceptions

by Tom Luers

Procedures and packages enable you to organize your code into logical groups for easier maintenance and implementation. Likewise, these groups have built-in error trapping to prevent the code from abnormally stopping during processing.

Procedures

A *procedure* is a logically grouped set of SQL and PL/SQL statements that perform a specific task. It's a miniature self-contained program. A *stored procedure* is a procedure that has been compiled and stored inside the database. At this point, the procedure is a *schema* (specific database) object.

Procedures have several parts. The declarative part contains declarations of types, cursors, constants, variables, exceptions, and nested subprograms. Procedures can be declared in PL/SQL blocks, packages, and other procedures. The executable part contains statements that control execution and manipulate data. Occasionally, the procedure will contain an exception-handling part to deal with exceptions raised during execution. Procedures can be defined and executed by using any Oracle tool that supports PL/SQL, like SQL*Plus.

Why Use Procedures?

Procedures are created to solve a specific problem or task. PL/SQL procedures offer the following advantages:

☐ In PL/SQL, you can tailor your procedure to suit your specific requirements.

☐ These procedures are modular; that is, they let you break a program down into manageable, well-defined units.

☐ Because procedures are stored in the database, they are reusable. Once validated, procedures can be used over and over without recompiling or distributing them over the network.

☐ Procedures improve database security. You can restrict database access by allowing them to access data only through stored procedures.

☐ Procedures improve memory by taking advantage of shared memory resources.

Procedures Versus Functions

Procedures and functions are PL/SQL subprograms that are stored in the database. The significant difference between the two is simply the types of output the two objects generate. A function returns a single value, whereas a procedure is used to perform complicated processing when you want a substantial amount of information back.

Creating Procedures

The CREATE PROCEDURE command creates a procedure.

The Syntax for the CREATE PROCEDURE Command

```
CREATE OR REPLACE PROCEDURE procedure_name
(arguments)
AS
 [pl/sql body code]
```

8

In this syntax, the keywords and parameters are as follows:

☐ OR REPLACE—This keyword is optional, but I strongly suggest you always use it. This keyword will re-create the procedure if it already exists. You can use this keyword to change an existing procedure without having to drop and re-create the procedure.

☐ *procedure_name*—The name you assign to the procedure being created.

☐ *arguments*—The arguments in the procedure, which can be the following:

  ☐ in—This parameter specifies that you must pass a value to the subprogram being called. The in parameter might not be assigned a value because it acts like a constant. The actual value that corresponds to the parameter can be a constant, literal, initialized variable, or expression.

  ☐ out—Specifies that the procedure returns a value to the calling program. This parameter acts like an uninitialized parameter; therefore, its value cannot be assigned to another variable. The actual value that corresponds to the parameter must be a variable. It cannot be a literal, constant, or expression. Within your subprogram, the out parameter must be assigned a value.

  ☐ inout—Specifies that you must pass a value to the procedure and that the procedure returns a value to its calling environment after execution.

☐ *pl/sql body code*—The logic of the procedure.

The code shown in Listing 8.1 creates a simple stored procedure. This procedure accepts two arguments, the part_id and the qty.

INPUT Listing 8.1. Creating a stored procedure.

```
CREATE OR REPLACE PROCEDURE parts (part_id number, qty number)

AS BEGIN
UPDATE journal
set journal.qty = journal.qty + qty
WHERE journal_id = part_id
END;
```

Normally, procedures are created as standalone schema objects. However, you can create a procedure as part of a package; this topic is discussed later in this chapter in the section titled "Packages."

The RETURN Statement

The RETURN statement causes a subprogram to immediately complete its execution and return to the calling program. Execution in the calling program resumes with the statement following the procedure call.

In procedures, the RETURN statement cannot contain an expression. Its sole purpose is to return control to the calling program before the end of the procedure is reached.

Procedure Dependencies

One of the inherent features of Oracle is that it will check the database to make sure that the operations of a procedure, function, or package are possible based on the objects the user has access to. For example, if you have a procedure that requires access to several tables and views, Oracle will check during compilation time to see whether those tables and views are present and available to the user. The procedure is said to be *dependent* on these tables and views.

WARNING

Oracle will automatically recompile all dependent objects when you explicitly recompile the parent object. This automatic recompilation of dependent objects happens when the dependent object is called. Therefore, you should not recompile a parent module in a production system. This will cause all dependent objects to recompile and consequently can cause a performance issue for your production system.

Discovering Dependencies

You can discover object dependencies in several different ways. You can examine the procedure or function code and determine which database objects it depends on. Also, you can talk with the DBA and examine the schema to identify dependencies. Finally, you can run the Oracle utldtree.sql script. This script will generate a temp table and a view that lets you see the objects that are dependent on a given object. This script will only generate a listing for those objects to which you have access.

Recompiling a Stored Procedure

To explicitly recompile a stored procedure, issue the ALTER PROCEDURE command. This command must only be used on standalone stored procedures and not on procedures that are part of the package.

Recompiling a procedure does not change the procedure's declaration or definition. You must use the CREATE PROCEDURE with the OR REPLACE clause to do these. If Oracle successfully recompiles a procedure, then the procedure becomes a valid procedure that can be executed without runtime compilation. If compilation fails, the procedure becomes invalid and must be debugged.

You can use the ALTER PROCEDURE command to explicitly recompile a procedure that is invalid. After a procedure is compiled, it does not need to be recompiled implicitly during runtime processes. This leads to reduced overhead and elimination of runtime compilation errors.

You can produce debugging information from within a application by issuing the PUT or PUT_LINE commands. These commands place the debugging information into a buffer that was created by the DBMS_OUTPUT package. To display the contents of the buffer, simply type the SET SERVEROUTPUT ON command at the SQL*Plus prompt.

The code in Listing 8.2 illustrates the PUT_LINE command line that you can include inside your procedure.

INPUT **Listing 8.2. PUT_LINE command within a procedure.**

```
CREATE PROCEDURE parts (part_id number, qty number)
AS BEGIN
UPDATE journal;
PUT_LINE ('Original Qty =' ¦¦ journal.qty);        -- debug Line
set journal.qty = journal.qty + qty
WHERE journal_id = part_id;
PUT_LINE ('New Qty =' ¦¦ journal.qty);             -- debug Line
```

The following statements are issued at the SQL*Plus command line to execute the parts procedure and to display the debugging information:

```
SQL> set server on
SQL> execute user_01.parts
```

The following are the results of these statements being executed. This information is generated from the dba_output buffer area:

```
Original Qty = 100
New Qty = 200
Original Qty = 200
New Qty = 325
... and so on
```

Re-creating and Modifying Procedures

A valid, standalone procedure cannot be altered; it must be either replaced with a new definition or dropped and re-created. For example, you cannot just slightly alter one of the PL/SQL statements in the procedure. Instead, you must re-create the procedure with the modification.

When replacing a procedure, you must include the OR REPLACE clause in the CREATE PROCEDURE statement. The OR REPLACE clause is used to replace an older version of a procedure with a newer version of the procedure. This replacement keeps all grants in place; therefore, you will not have to re-create the grants. However, if you drop the procedure and re-create it, the grants are dropped and consequently will have to be rebuilt. If you attempt a CREATE PROCEDURE command for a procedure that already exists, Oracle will generate an error message.

Listing 8.3 re-creates the procedure named `parts`.

INPUT **Listing 8.3. Re-creating a procedure.**

```
CREATE OR REPLACE PROCEDURE parts
(part_id number, qty number)
AS BEGIN
UPDATE journal
set journal.qty = (journal.qty*.05) + qty
WHERE journal_id = part_id
END;
```

Invoking Stored Procedures

Procedures can be invoked from many different environments including SQL*Plus and Oracle Forms. Also, procedures can be invoked from within another procedure or trigger.

For example, the procedure `parts_sum` can be called from with another procedure or trigger with the following statement:

```
...                             -- other PL/SQL block code
...
parts_sum(qty, wip_nbr);    -- calls parts_sum procedure
...
```

Another example where the same procedure is executed from within SQL*Plus is the following:

```
SQL> execute parts_sum(qty, wip_nbr);
```

The following example shows a procedure being called from within a precompiler program:

```
exec sql execute
BEGIN
parts_sum(qty, :wip_nbr)
END
END-exec
```

Parameters

Procedures use *parameters* (variables or expressions) to pass information. When a parameter is being passed to a procedure, it is known as an *actual parameter*. Parameters declared internal to a procedure are known as *internal* or *formal* parameters.

The actual parameter and its corresponding formal parameter must belong to compatible datatypes. For example, PL/SQL cannot convert an actual parameter with a datatype of DATE to a formal parameter with a datatype of LONG. In this case, Oracle would return an error message. This compatibility issue also applies to the return values.

8

Parameter Definitions

When you invoke a procedure, you must pass it a value for each of the procedure's parameters. If you pass values to the parameter, they are positional and must appear in the same order as they appear in the procedure declaration. If you pass argument names, then they can appear in any order. You can have a combination of values and names in the argument values. If this is the case, the values identified in order must precede the argument names.

Listing Stored Procedure Information

Oracle provides several data dictionary views that provide information about procedures that are currently stored in your schema:

- [ ] `all_errors`—A list of current errors on all objects accessible to the user
- [ ] `all_source`—Text source of all stored objects accessible to the user
- [ ] `user_objects`—A list of all the objects the current user has access to
- [ ] `dba_errors`—Current errors on all stored objects in the database
- [ ] `dba_object_size`—All PL/SQL objects in the database
- [ ] `dba_source`—Text source of all stored objects in the database
- [ ] `user_errors`—Current errors on all a user's stored objects
- [ ] `user_source`—Text source of all stored objects belonging to the user
- [ ] `user_object_size`—User's PL/SQL objects

The code in Listing 8.4 queries the `user_errors` view to obtain information about the current errors on a procedure owned by `user_01`.

INPUT/ OUTPUT   **Listing 8.4. Viewing errors in the database.**

```
SELECT LINE, TYPE, NAME, TEXT from user_errors

LINE  TYPE   NAME    TEXT
----  ----   ------  ----------------------------------
  4   PROC   PST_QTY  PL/SQL-00387: into variable cannot be a database object
                      PL/SQL: SQL statement ignored
```

Additionally, you can select from the user_objects table and interrogate which objects are invalid and need to be recompiled. The following piece of code will produce the object names and their types for those database objects that need to be evaluated for recompilation:

```
SELECT object_name, object_type
from user_objects
WHERE status = 'INVALID';
```

Dropping a Stored Procedure

Issue the SQL statement DROP procedure to drop a procedure object. The following statement drops the procedure parts_qty:

```
DROP PROCEDURE parts_qty;
```

Overloading

Oracle permits you to call the same procedure name in a package but with different arguments. This is known as *overloading*. This technique is very useful, especially when you want to execute the same procedure several times but with arguments that have different datatypes. One example of using procedure overload is with the package DBMS_OUTPUT. In this package, the PUT_LINE procedure is called numerous times to produce output lines of different datatypes.

The following example illustrates the definition of two overloaded local procedures:

```
DECLARE
PROCEDURE compute_sales (begin_date in date) RETURN boolean
is
BEGIN
RETURN begin_date > :start_date;
END;

PROCEDURE compute_sales (sales_in in date) RETURN boolean
is
BEGIN
RETURN sales_in > :sales_target;
END;
```

When the PL/SQL engine encounters a call to compute_sales, the compiler executes the module in the body that has the correct and matching module header.

Recursion

A *recursive procedure* is a procedure that calls itself. Each recursive call creates a new instance of any object declared in the procedure, including parameters, variables, cursors, and exceptions. Also, new instances of SQL statements are created at each level in the recursive procedure.

With recursive logic, the procedure must be able to terminate itself at some predefined point or else the recursion would last forever. This point of termination is defined in a *terminating condition*. The following example uses a conditional statement to terminate the recursive cycle:

```
FUNCTION inv_calc
BEGIN
IF qty = > :max_qty THEN -- terminating condition;
RETURN 1;
ELSE
```

```
RETURN qty * inv_calc (qty * :part_qty); -- recursive call
...
END IF
END inv_calc;
```

Be careful with recursion and where you place the recursive call. If you place the recursive call inside a cursor FOR loop or between OPEN and CLOSE statements, a cursor is opened at each call. This can open enough cursors to violate the maximum allowable open cursors permitted by the OPEN_CURSOR initialization parameter.

Packages

A *package* is an encapsulated collection of related schema objects. These objects can include procedures, functions, variables, constants, cursors, and exceptions. A package is compiled and then stored in the database's data dictionary as a schema object.

The packages contain stored subprograms, or standalone programs, which are called the package's *subprograms*. These subprograms can be called from another stored program, triggers, precompiler programs, or any of the interactive Oracle programs like SQL*Plus. Unlike the stored subprograms, the package itself cannot be called, passed parameters to, or nested.

A package usually has two components to it, a specification and a body. The specification declares the types, variables, constants, exceptions, cursors, and subprograms that are available for use. The body fully defines cursors, functions, and procedures and so implements the specification.

Why Use Packages?

Packages offer the following advantages:

☐ Packages enable you to organize your application development more efficiently into modules. Each package is easily understood, and the interfaces between packages are simple, clear, and well-defined.

☐ Packages allow you to grant privileges more efficiently.

☐ The package's public variables and cursors persist for the duration of the session. Therefore, all cursors and procedures that execute in this environment can share them.

☐ Packages enable you to perform overloading on procedures and functions.

☐ Packages improve performance by loading multiple objects into memory at once. Therefore, subsequent calls to related subprograms in the package require no I/O.

☐ Packages promote code reuse through the use of libraries that contain stored procedures and functions, thereby eliminating redundant coding.

Package Helpful Hints

The following helpful hints can make your use of Oracle packages more successful.

Do	Don't

Do keep packages simple and general to promote their reuse in future applications.

Don't write packages that replicate existing Oracle functionality.

Do design your package body after you design the application. Place only those objects that you want visible to all users in the package specification.

Don't place too many items in the package specification, specifically those that need compiling. Changes to a package body do not require Oracle to recompile dependent procedures. However, changes to the specification of a package require Oracle to recompile every stored subprogram that references the package.

Package Specification

The package specification contains public declarations of the name of the package and the names and datatypes of any arguments. This declaration is local to your database and global to the package. This means that the declared objects in your package are accessible from anywhere in the package. Therefore, all the information your application needs to execute a stored subprogram is contained in the package specification.

The following is an example of a package declaration. In this example, the specification declares a function and a procedure:

```
CREATE PACKAGE inv_pck_spec as

FUNCTION inv_count(qty number, part_nbr varchar2(15))
RETURN number;

PROCEDURE inv_adjust(qty number);

END inv_pck_spec;
```

Sometimes a specification only declares variables, constants, and exceptions, and therefore, a package body is not necessary. The following example is a package specification for a package that does not have a package body:

```
CREATE PACKAGE inv_costings is

type inv_rec is record
(part_name varchar2(30),
part_price number,
part_cost number);
```

8

```
price number;
qty   number;
no_cost exception;
cost_or exception;
```

The Package Body

The body of a package contains the definition of the public objects you declared in the specification. The body also contains other object declarations that are private to the package. The objects declared privately in the package body are not accessible to other objects outside the package. Unlike the package specification, the declaration portion of the package body can contain subprogram bodies.

NOTE   Remember that if the specification declares only constants and variables, the package body is not necessary.

After the package is written, applications can reference its types, call its subprograms, use its cursor, or raise its exceptions. After the package is created, it is stored in the database for all to use.

Creating Packages

The first step to creating a package is to create its specification. The specification publicly declares the schema objects that are continued in the body of the package.

To create a specification, issue the CREATE PROCEDURE command:

```
CREATE OR REPLACE PACKAGE inv_pck_spec as

FUNCTION inv_count(qty integer, part_nbr varchar2(15))
RETURN integer;

PROCEDURE inv_adjust(qty integer);

END inv_pck_spec;
```

Note that the OR REPLACE clause was used. This clause re-creates the package specification without losing any grants that already exist.

After the specification is created, you create the body of the package. The body of a package is a collection of schema objects that was declared in the specification. These objects, or package subprograms, are accessible outside the package only if their specifications are included in the package specification.

In addition to the object definitions for the declaration, the package body can also contain private declarations. These private objects are for the internal workings of the package and are local in scope. External objects cannot reference or call internal declarations to another package.

If you perform any initialization in the package body, it is executed once when the package is initially referenced.

The following is an example of the body of the package that was specified in the previous example's specification:

```
CREATE OR REPLACE PACKAGE BODY inv_control is

FUNCTION inv_count
(qty integer,
part_nbr varchar2(15))
RETURN integer is ;
new_qty integer;
BEGIN
new_qty:= qty*6
INSERT into mst_inv values
(new_qty,part_nbr);
RETURN(new_qty);
END inv_count;

PROCEDURE inv_adjust(qty integer);
BEGIN
DELETE from user_01.mst_inv
WHERE inv_qty<10000;
END;

BEGIN   -- package initialization begins here
INSERT into inv_audit values
(SYSDATE, user);
END inv_control;
```

The final part of the procedure body in the preceding example is the package initialization. By definition, this runs only once when the procedure is referenced the first time.

Calling Package Subprograms

When a package is invoked, Oracle performs three steps to execute it:

- ☐ Verify user access—Confirms that the user has the execute system privilege grant for the subprogram.

- ☐ Verify procedure validity—Checks with the data dictionary to determine whether the subprogram is valid or not. If the object is invalid, it is automatically recompiled before being executed.

- ☐ Execute—The package subprogram is executed.

To reference the package's subprograms and objects, you must use *dot* notation.

The Syntax for Dot Notation

package_name.type_name
package_name.object_name
package_name.subprogram_name

In this syntax, *package_name* is the name of the declared package. *type_name* is the name of the type that you define, such as record. *object_name* is the name of the constant or variable you declare. *subprogram_name* is the name of the procedure or function contained in the package body.

To reference the variable `max_balance` in the package named inventory, the referencing statement would be

```
DECLARE
max_balance number;
BEGIN
...
IF inventory.max_balance < curr_balance THEN
...
END IF
```

When Oracle executes a package subprogram, an implicit savepoint will be created. If the subprogram fails with an unhandled exception, before returning to the host environment, Oracle will roll back to the savepoint, thereby undoing any changes made by the package subprogram.

Recompiling Packages

To recompile a package, use the `ALTER PACKAGE` command with the `compile` keyword. This explicit recompilation eliminates the need for any implicit runtime recompilation and prevents any associated runtime compilation errors and performance overhead. It is common to explicitly recompile a package after modifications to the package.

Recompiling a package recompiles all objects defined within the package. Recompiling does not change the definition of the package or any of its objects.

The following examples recompile just the body of a package. The second statement recompiles the entire package including the body and specification:

```
ALTER PACKAGE inventory_pkg compile body
```

```
ALTER PACKAGE inventory_pkg compile package
```

All packages can be recompiled by using the Oracle utility dbms_utility:

```
execute dbms_utility.compile_all
```

Private Versus Public Package Objects

Within the body of a package, you are permitted to define subprograms, cursors, and private declarations for types and objects. For objects that are declared inside the package body, you are restricted to use within that package. Therefore, PL/SQL code outside the package cannot reference any of the variables that were privately declared within the package.

Any items declared inside the package specification are visible outside the package. This enables PL/SQL code outside the package to reference objects from within the package. These objects declared in the package specification are called *public*.

Variables, Cursors, and Constant Persistence

Variables, cursors, and constants can change their value over time and have a specific life span. This life duration can vary depending on where the declaration is located. For standalone procedures, variables, cursors, and constants persist only for the duration of the procedure call and are lost when the procedure execution terminates.

If the variable, constant, or cursor was declared in a package specification or body, their values persist for the duration of the user's session. The values are lost when the current user's session terminates or the package is recompiled.

Package State

A package is always either valid or invalid. A package is considered valid if none of its source code or objects it references have been dropped, replaced, or altered since the package specification was last recompiled.

The package is considered invalid if its source code or any object that it references has been dropped, altered, or replaced since the package specification was last recompiled. When a package becomes invalid, Oracle will also make invalid any object that references the package.

Package Dependency

During the recompiling of a package, Oracle invalidates all dependent objects. These objects include standalone or package subprograms that call or reference objects declared in the recompiled specification. If another user's program calls or references a dependent object before it is recompiled, Oracle automatically recompiles it at runtime.

During package recompilation, Oracle makes a determination whether objects on which the package body depends are valid. If any of these objects are invalid, Oracle will recompile them before recompiling the package body. If recompilation is successful, then the package body becomes valid. If any errors are detected, the appropriate error messages are generated and the package body remains invalid.

Trapping Errors and Exceptions

Sometimes the Oracle server or the user's application causes an error to occur during runtime processing. Such errors can arise from hardware or network failures, application logic errors, data integrity errors, and many other sources. These errors are known as *exceptions*; that is, these unwanted events are exceptions to the normal processing that is expected.

Typically, when an error occurs, processing of the PL/SQL block terminates immediately. Hence, your application stops processing and the task at hand goes unfinished. Oracle enables you to be prepared for these errors and write logic in your programs to handle them gracefully and allow processing to carry on as you have designed it. This logic written to manage errors is known as *exception-handling code*. With Oracle exception handling, when an error is detected, control is passed to the exception-handling portion of your program, and then processing completes normally. Handling errors also provides valuable information for debugging applications and for better "bulletproofing" the application against future errors.

Without a means to handle exceptions, a program must check for execution errors after each statement, as the following example shows:

```
SELECT....
IF error-- check for error associated with SELECT statement
THEN....
INSERT ....
IF error-- check for error associated with INSERT statement
THEN...
UPDATE....
IF error-- check for error associated with UPDATE statement
THEN...
```

As you can see, this increases the processing overhead because you have to explicitly check for errors after each statement. There is always a risk that you might overlook a statement and fail to check for errors, thereby leaving open the potential for an abnormal termination to your application.

With exception handling incorporated into your application, the same statement would be transformed to look like

```
BEGIN
SELECT....
INSERT....
UPDATE....
exception
-- check for and process errors here
END
```

This way of handling errors removes all the added processing required to explicitly handle errors. Also, the readability of the program is improved.

Exception-Handling Structures

In PL/SQL, the user can anticipate and trap for certain runtime errors. Exceptions can be internally defined by Oracle or the user.

There are three types of exceptions:

- ☐ Predefined Oracle errors
- ☐ Undefined Oracle errors
- ☐ User-defined errors

Predefined Oracle Errors

To build the exception-handler portion of your program, start the block of code with the keyword exception followed by the when clause. The following is the typical syntax of an exception-handling PL/SQL block.

The Syntax for the exception Command

SYNTAX

```
exception
when exception_1 THEN
statements
when exception_2 THEN
statements
...
```

In this syntax, exception_1 and exception_2 are the names of the predefined exceptions. statements is the PL/SQL code that will be executed if the exception name is satisfied.

The Oracle server defines several errors with standard names. Although every Oracle error has a number, the errors must be referenced by name. PL/SQL has predefined some common Oracle errors and exceptions. Some of these predefined exception names are

- ☐ no_data_found—Single row SELECT returned no data.
- ☐ too_many_rows—Single row SELECT returned more than one row.
- ☐ invalid_cursor—Illegal cursor operation was attempted.
- ☐ value_error—Arithmetic, conversion, truncation, or constraint error occurred.
- ☐ invalid_number—Conversion of a number to a character string failed.
- ☐ zero_divide—Attempted to divide by zero.
- ☐ dup_val_on_index—Attempted to insert a duplicate value into a column that has a unique index.
- ☐ cursor_already_open—Attempted to open a cursor that was previously opened.
- ☐ not_logged_on—A database call was made without being logged into Oracle.
- ☐ transaction_backed_out—Usually raised when a remote portion of a transaction is rolled back.
- ☐ login_denied—Login to Oracle failed because of invalid username and password.
- ☐ program_error—Raised if PL/SQL encounters an internal problem.
- ☐ storage_error—Raised if PL/SQL runs out of memory or if memory is corrupted.
- ☐ timeout_on_resource—Timeout occurred while Oracle was waiting for a resource.
- ☐ value_error—Arithmetic, conversion, truncation, or constraint error occurred.
- ☐ others—This is a catchall. If the error was not trapped in the previous exception traps, the error will be trapped by this statement.

Oracle declares predefined exceptions globally in the package standard. Therefore, you do not need to declare them yourself.

The following example illustrates a PL/SQL exception-handling block:

```
...
SELECT * from employees
WHERE name like 'Bluekers%';
...
exception               -- Exception block beginning
when no_data_found      -- first exception trap
CREATE_employee ('new','Bluekers';
COMMIT;
when others THEN        -- second exception trap
ROLLBACK;
COMMIT;
END                     -- end of exception handling
```

Undefined Oracle Errors

As you saw in the earlier example of exception-handling blocks, the others exception was used as a catchall exception handler. others is normally used when the exact nature of the exception isn't important, when the exception is unnamed, or even when it's unpredictable.

A different way to handle an error that is unnamed is with the pragma exception_init compiler directive. This directive simply transfers information to the compiler. The pragma tells the compiler to associate an exception name with an Oracle error number. In this way, you can refer to any internal exception by name and write a specific handler for it.

The declaration of the pragma exception_init must appear in the declarative portion of the PL/SQL block, packages, or subprogram. The following is the syntax for this declaration:

```
pragma exception_init (exception_name, error_number);
```

The exception name is a previously declared execution. The pragma declaration must appear somewhere after the exception declaration. The following example shows the exception and pragma declarations and the exception-handling block for the exception:

```
insufficient_funds  exception;
pragma exception_init (insufficient_funds, -2019);
BEGIN
...
exception
when insufficient_funds THEN
ROLLBACK;
END;
```

User-Defined Errors

Users can explicitly raise an exception with the RAISE command. The raise exceptions procedure should only be used when Oracle does not raise its own exception or when processing is undesirable or impossible to complete.

Steps for trapping a user-defined error include the following:

1. Declare the name for the user exception within the declaration section of the block.

2. Raise the exception explicitly within the executable portion of the block using the RAISE command.

3. Reference the declared exception with an error-handling routine.

The following example illustrates the use of the user-defined exception:

```
DECLARE
invalid_pay_type        exception;              -- user-defined exception
pay_type_code varchar2(2);
BEGIN
...
IF pay_type_code not in ('H','S') THEN  -- error trap
RAISE invalid_pay_type;                       -- raise user-defined exception
END IF;
exception                               -- handle user-defined exception
when invalid_pay_type THEN
ROLLBACK;
END
```

Exceptions can be raised in declarations when declarations and initializations are done incorrectly. When this happens, the exception handler must reside in the enclosing block. This is called *exception propagation*, which is discussed in more detail later in this chapter in the section titled "Propagate Exceptions."

SQLCODE and SQLERRM

In the exception-handling part of your program, use the functions SQLCODE and SQLERRM to obtain information about the most recent error that has occurred. This is especially useful when the exception is trapped with the when others clause. The when others clause is used to trap unanticipated or unknown exceptions.

The SQLCODE function returns the error code for the exception. SQLERRM returns the corresponding error message. The following are the valid values from the SQLCODE function:

☐ 0—Indicates that no exception has been raised.

☐ 1—Indicates that a user-defined exception has been raised.

☐ +1403—Indicates that a no_data_found exception has been raised.

☐ -###—The remaining negative values correspond to the actual error codes as defined in the *Oracle Server Messages and Codes* manual.

The following example traps and records the error code and message of the offending exception and stores it in a table for access at a later time:

```
DECLARE
error_code   number;
error_msg    varchar2(250);
BEGIN
...
```

```
exception
...
when others THEN
error_code := SQLCODE;
error_msg := SQLERRM;
INSERT into user_exceptions_table (error_message)
values (to_char(error_code) || ': ' || error_msg)
COMMIT;
END;
```

You can now perform a SELECT on the user_exceptions_table to view the exception error code and message.

You cannot use SQLCODE and SQLERRM directly in a SQL statement. Instead, you must assign their values to local variables and then use these variables in the SQL statement.

If PL/SQL cannot find an exception handler for an error, it turns the exception over to the host environment for handling.

Continue Processing After an Exception

Exception handlers let you handle errors that normally would be fatal to your application. But exception handlers as described so far in this chapter create a logic processing problem. Look at the following PL/SQL block:

```
DECLARE
invalid_fam_code        exception;              -- user-defined exception
part_fam_code varchar2(2);
BEGIN
...
IF part_fam_code not in ('AU','UC','BG') THEN   -- error trap
RAISE invalid_fam_code;                         -- raise user-defined exception
END IF;
INSERT....
UPDATE....
....
exception                       -- handle user-defined exception
when invalid_fam_code THEN
ROLLBACK;
END
```

When the invalid_fam_code exception occurs, process control is transferred to the handler. The INSERT and UPDATE commands are never executed in this scenario. This could pose a problem for your application. To get around the problem of code being bypassed due to exceptions, embed the exception handler in its own sub-block, as shown in the following example:

```
DECLARE
invalid_fam_code        exception;                  -- user-defined exception
part_fam_code varchar2(2);
BEGIN
...
BEGIN                                               -- sub-block begin
IF part_fam_code not in ('AU','UC','BG') THEN   -- error trap
exception                               -- handle user-defined exception
```

```
when invalid_fam_code THEN
ROLLBACK;
END IF;
END;                                    -- sub-block end
INSERT...
UPDATE...
...
END;
```

In this example, the exception `invalid_fam_code` is handled locally in its own sub-block. This arrangement allows the INSERT, UPDATE, and any other following statements to be executed.

Retry After an Exception

Sometimes you'll want to retry a transaction after some exception. For example, say you are creating new identification numbers for new parts coming out of the factory. You make an attempt to create a new part number and receive a message stating that that particular part number already exists. What would you do? Normally, you create a different part number and retry the task. The following example uses this same scenario. You would not want to cease transaction processing when you get a duplicate part number message. Fortunately, you know enough about the causes of the problem to add corrective logic to your program.

```
DECLARE
max_count       integer;
part_number     integer := 1;
BEGIN
SELECT count(*) into max_count from new_parts
LOOP  FOR I in 1..max_count loop
BEGIN                               -- create a sub-block
savepoint top_loop;                 -- establish rollback point
part_number :=part_number+1;        -- create new part number
INSERT into inventory value (part_number);
COMMIT;
EXIT;
exception
when dup_val_on_index THEN
part_number :=part_number+1;     -- create a newer part number
ROLLBACK to top_loop;            -- force us to top of loop
END;                            -- end sub-block
END LOOP;                        -- end loop
END;                             -- end block
```

Reraising an Exception

At times, you might want to handle an exception locally and pass the exception to an enclosed block. The following example raises the exception `out_of_stock` in the sub-block and passes the exception handling to the enclosed block:

```
DECLARE
out_of_stock    exception;      -- declare exception
BEGIN     -- beginning of sub-block to check qty of order
IF qty_ordered > qty_on_hand THEN
RAISE out_of_stock;             -- raise the exception
END IF;
exception
```

8

```
-- for exception indicated that order_qty is invalid
when out_of_stock THEN
...
RAISE;                          -- reraise the current exception
...
END;
--  end of sub-block
exception
-- handle the exception differently than earlier.
when out_of_stock THEN
...
END;
```

Exception Scope Rules

You should be aware of the following guidelines with regard to the scope of an exception declaration:

- [ ] An exception cannot be declared twice in the same block, but the same exception can be declared in two different blocks.
- [ ] Exceptions are local to the block where they were declared and global to all of its sub-blocks. Enclosing blocks cannot reference exceptions that were declared in any of their sub-blocks.
- [ ] Global declarations can be redeclared at the local sub-block level. If this occurs, the local declaration takes precedence over the global declaration.

Propagate Exceptions

When an error is encountered, PL/SQL looks in the current block for the appropriate exception handler. If no handler is present, then PL/SQL propagates the error to the enclosing block. PL/SQL searches the enclosing block for the correct error handler. If no handler is found there, the error is continually propagated to the enclosing blocks until a handler is found. This process can continue until the host environment receives and handles the error. For example, if SQL*Plus received an unhandled error from a PL/SQL block, the way SQL*Plus handles this error is to display the error code and message on the user's screen.

Summary

You covered a lot of material in the chapter, including Oracle procedures and packages and error-handling capabilities. Procedures and packages offer the programmer powerful constructs for your PL/SQL blocks. The Oracle procedure is a concise and logically grouped set of statements to perform a specific task. A package is an encapsulated collection of related schema objects such as functions and procedures that achieve a common purpose. Runtime errors should be anticipated and planned for in your application, using exception-handling code to prevent the unwanted termination of your application.

Q&A

Q Do I have to use a package when I have only one function in my application?

A No. You do not have to use a package when you have only one function. I would suggest that you think seriously about the future growth of your application. If you think the application will grow and include additional functions and procedures, then I recommend that you start off using a package from the beginning.

Q Why do I need to write extra code to process errors detected by Oracle?

A If your code does not explicitly trap for any and all exceptions, your PL/SQL processing will halt when the error is detected.

Q Can I build my procedure prior to building my database?

A Not usually. Because of dependency issues, you might have to have the tables and views (or other schema objects) in place prior to compiling your procedure.

Q What if I don't know what error to anticipate from Oracle?

A Fortunately, Oracle provides you with the when others clause to handle this exception. This exception will trap all exceptions.

Workshop

The following workshop will test your understanding of Oracle procedures and packages and PL/SQL's capability to trap and handle processing exceptions. The answers to the quiz and exercises are provided in Appendix A, "Answers."

Quiz

1. What statement is used to recompile a procedure?
2. How do you invoke a procedure?
3. Name at least four predefined Oracle exception errors.
4. How do you call a module of a package?

Exercises

1. Write a package specification for the functions written in previous chapters. Additionally, include in the specification one or two of the procedures used in this chapter.

2. Write an exception-handling piece of code to trap the error of receiving more rows than you expected as well as an unknown error.

Day **9**

Using SQL: INSERT, SELECT, Advanced Declarations, and Tables

by Tom Luers

By definition, PL/SQL is SQL's procedural language extension. PL/SQL supports all of SQL's data manipulation commands (except for EXPLAIN PLAN), transaction control commands, functions, pseudocolumns, and operators. This chapter covers the usage of SQL's Data Manipulation Language (DML) commands within a PL/SQL block.

 *Data Manipulation Language* (DML) commands enable the user to query a database and to manipulate data in an existing database. The execution of a DML statement does not implicitly commit the current transaction. The user has an opportunity to roll back or save the transaction.

When a PL/SQL block executes a SQL DML command, the block passes the SQL command to the Oracle database for processing in its own SQL engine. Figure 9.1 illustrates this concept.

Figure 9.1.

*The Oracle PL/SQL
server engine.*

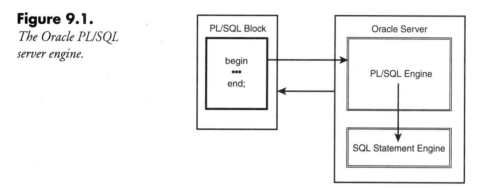

Because PL/SQL passes the DML statements to the RDBMS, the PL/SQL statements must conform to the required SQL syntax standards. This is one of the few times that you must be aware of the syntax differences between SQL and PL/SQL.

PL/SQL allows the use of SQL DML statements in order to provide an easy, safe, and flexible environment to manipulate data. In a simple program, SQL statements are processed one statement at a time, as diagrammed in Figure 9.2. If you have four separate SQL statements, Oracle would process these in four independent actions and return four different results. Through the use of PL/SQL, you can group these same SQL statements into a PL/SQL block and have them processed at one time, hence improving your overall performance.

Figure 9.2.

*SQL versus PL/SQL
code processing.*

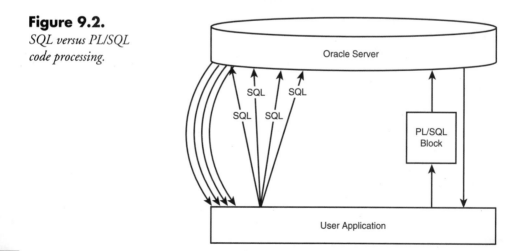

Types of SQL Statements

PL/SQL allows you to use four different DML commands: INSERT, DELETE, UPDATE, and SELECT. This chapter discusses each of these and their use within PL/SQL. The INSERT statement adds new data to the database. The DELETE command removes data from the database. The UPDATE command modifies existing data in the database, and the SELECT statement retrieves data from the database.

This chapter covers the four basic statements just described: INSERT, SELECT, UPDATE, and DELETE. This chapter does not teach the use or syntax of SQL itself. Only the most basic SQL statements and queries are included to illustrate the use of SQL within PL/SQL. Refer to the book *Teach Yourself SQL in 21 Days* for more in-depth knowledge of SQL queries.

Creating Some Oracle Tables

You now need to create several Oracle tables to use in the remainder of the book. In order to create these tables, you must have the CREATE TABLE system privilege. You will create three tables in this chapter. These are the employee table, department table, and emp_dept table. Figure 9.3 shows an Entity Relationship Diagram (ERD) for these three tables. This diagram also shows a physical layout of these tables.

Figure 9.3.

ERD and physical data model for the three tables.

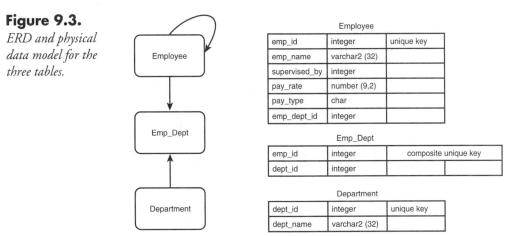

Employee

emp_id	integer	unique key
emp_name	varchar2 (32)	
supervised_by	integer	
pay_rate	number (9,2)	
pay_type	char	
emp_dept_id	integer	

Emp_Dept

emp_id	integer	composite unique key	
dept_id	integer		

Department

dept_id	integer	unique key
dept_name	varchar2 (32)	

The first table you need to create is the employee table. This table will hold information about the employees. Specifically, for each employee, it will hold the employee's name, supervisor's name, pay rate, pay type, and a key that indicates which department the employee belongs to.

The Syntax for the CREATE TABLE Command

```
CREATE TABLE table_name
(column_name column_datatype);
```

In this syntax, `table_name` is the name you assign to the table. `column_name` is the name of the column you assign, and `column_datatype` is the datatype for that column.

▲ Go ahead and execute the code shown in Listing 9.1 to create this table.

INPUT **Listing 9.1. Creating the employee table.**

```
CREATE TABLE employee
    (emp_id            INTEGER,
      emp_name        VARCHAR2(32),
      supervised_by     INTEGER,
      pay_rate            NUMBER(9,2),
      pay_type          CHAR,
      emp_dept_id              INTEGER);

ALTER TABLE employee
ADD CONSTRAINT pk_emp primary key (emp_id);
```

Take a look at some of the fields in the table you just created. The emp_id field will hold a unique numeric value that guarantees uniqueness across all rows of the table. For example, the emp_id field would be the only way to pick the correct row when you have two employees with the exact same name.

The supervised_by field will hold the value of the emp_id for that person's supervisors, as shown in the following example:

emp_id	emp_name	supervised_by	pay_rate	pay_type	emp_dept_id
1	Jack Richards	3	100.50	H	3
2	Melinda Williams	1	6.50	H	3
3	Jenny Catherines	5	2,000.00	S	3

You can see that Jenny is the supervisor of Jack. This is indicated by the supervised_by value of 3 in Jack's record. This 3 represents the emp_id of the person who is Jack's supervisor. In this case, it is Jenny.

The emp_dept_id is the ID number of the department where they all work.

The next table you will create is the department table. This table will contain information about the department in which the employees work. It will hold the department's ID, the department name, and the number of employees. Execute the code shown in Listing 9.2 to create this table.

INPUT   **Listing 9.2. Creating the department table.**

```
CREATE TABLE department
       (dept_id              INTEGER,
        dept_name      VARCHAR2(32));

ALTER TABLE department
ADD CONSTRAINT PRIMARY KEY (dept_id);
```

The final table you need to create is the emp_dept table. This table tells you which employees work in which departments. Execute the code shown in Listing 9.3 to create the emp_dept table.

INPUT   **Listing 9.3. Creating the emp_dept table.**

```
CREATE TABLE emp_dept
   (emp_id              INTEGER,
    dept_id              INTEGER,
    CONSTRAINT unq_1 unique (emp_id, dept_id));
```

Now that your base tables are created, go ahead and use them. First you will insert data into the tables, and then you will retrieve that same data.

The INSERT Statement

The INSERT command is used to add new rows to an existing Oracle table or view. In this case, you will only be inserting data into a table.

The Syntax for the INSERT Command

```
INSERT into table_name  [column_name]  values (values)
```

In this syntax, *table_name* is the name of the table into which you're inserting data. *column_name* is the name of the column being inserted into the table, and *values* is the data that will be placed in the column.

Try working through two examples to illustrate the usage of the INSERT command. You might want to refer back to Figure 9.3 to refresh your memory of the employee table layout.

The first example is

```
INSERT into employee values
    ( 1, ' Jessica Loraine', 2, 8.50, 'H', 3,
      2, ' Kurt Roberts', 5, 100.00, 'S', 3);
```

When this statement is executed, the table will have two rows in it and look like this:

emp_id	emp_name	supervised_by	pay_rate	pay_type	emp_dept_id
1	Jessica Loraine	2	8.50	H	3
2	Kurt Roberts	5	100.00	S	3

Note that there were no *column_name* references in the INSERT statement. The reason is that SQL will make a one-to-one match of the *column_name* to the data included in the INSERT statement. If you want, you can insert data into selected columns, as shown in the second example.

> **TIP**
>
> It is advisable to always include the column list to ensure clarity to others. The column list will come in handy whenever you have to debug your code.

Here's the second example:

```
INSERT into employee (emp_id, emp_name) values
        ( 1, ' Jessica Loraine',
          2, ' Kurt Roberts');
```

In the second example, you placed data only in the emp_id and emp_name columns. All other columns would be blank.

emp_id	emp_name	supervised_by	pay_rate	pay_type	emp_dept_id
1	Jessica Loraine				
2	Kurt Roberts				

Inserting Some Data

You will now insert data into the employee table for use in the remainder of the book. Type in the PL/SQL block shown in Listing 9.4, and then compile and execute it. When you run this block of code, it will ask you for an employee's name and related information and in turn insert this data into the employee table. Run this anonymous PL/SQL block multiple times in order to end up with roughly 10 employees' worth of data loaded. Your goal here is to input data that represents the typical organizational chart shown in Figure 9.4. You want data loaded for all levels of the org chart. While inserting data, feel free to use any names you like.

Figure 9.4.

Organization chart.

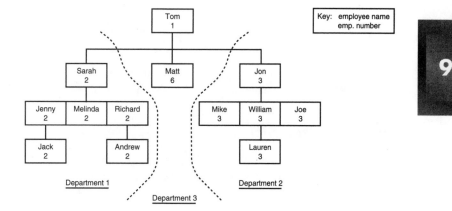

Listing 9.4 shows the PL/SQL anonymous block that you can run to insert the necessary data.

 Listing 9.4. Inserting records with PL/SQL code.

```
DECLARE              -- insert department data first
i_dept_id  INTEGER,
i_dept_name,
BEGIN
INSERT into department values
(&i_dept_id,'&dept_name');
END;

COMMIT;            -- save the department data

DECLARE            -- insert employee and emp_dept data
i_id   INTEGER;
e_id   INTEGER;
i_name  VARCHAR2(32);
i_super  INTEGER;
i_rate    NUMBER(9,2);
i_type   CHAR;
i_emp_dept INTEGER;
e_emp_dept INTEGER;
BEGIN
e_id:=&employee_id;
e_emp_dept:=&employee_department_id;
```

continues

Listing 9.4. continued

```
INSERT into employee values
(e_id, '&i_name',&i_super,&i_rate,'&i_type',e_emp_dept);
INSERT into emp_dept values (e_id,e_emp_dept);
END;

COMMIT;          -- save employee  and emp_dept datadata
```

ANALYSIS The code in Listing 9.4 is used to insert data first into the department table, then the employee table, and finally the emp_dept table.

Singleton SELECT Statement

The SELECT statement is one of the ways to get data out of the database. In order to use the SELECT statement, you must have SELECT system privileges. Depending on how you design and use the SELECT statement, you can retrieve a single (singleton) row or multiple rows of data from the database. Sometimes you'll want only a single row returned; otherwise, you want your PL/SQL block to handle the multiple rows without terminating. This chapter discusses methods of handling unexpected errors in your program in the section "Types of Exceptions."

The Syntax for the SELECT Statement

```
SELECT column_name
from table_name
WHERE condition
ORDER BY expression
```

In this syntax, `column_name` is the name of the column or columns from which you want data. `table_name` is the name of the table or tables in which the previous columns belong. The `condition` statement is used to specify the criteria to retrieve specific rows. The ORDER BY clause enables you to define the order in which to display the retrieved rows. For example, you might want to display the rows in alphabetical order or in numeric sequence. Both the WHERE and the ORDER BY clauses are optional.

Some SELECT Examples

The first example is a simple SELECT statement to retrieve all the rows from the employee table:

```
SELECT emp_id, emp_name, supervised_by, pay_rate, pay_type
from employee
ORDER BY emp_name
```

This statement will return all rows from the employee table sorted in ascending order by the employee name. Because this statement grabs all columns and rows from the table, you could use the wildcard * to achieve the same result:

```
SELECT * from employee ORDER BY emp_name
```

A more complex, but realistic, example would be

```
SELECT * from employee
WHERE pay_type = 'S'
ORDER BY pay_rate desc
```

This SELECT statement will return

☐ All columns from the table

☐ All rows from the table that have the pay_type equal to 'S'

The returned rows will be in pay_rate descending order.

Finally, Listing 9.5 is an example of a singleton SELECT. An assumption is made here that you only have one employee with the name of Jack Richards. You might want your program to indicate to you if you have multiple occurrences of a specific employee. The bottom line is that you don't want processing to halt if this happens.

INPUT   **Listing 9.5. Multiple-row SELECT command.**

```
DECLARE
v_emp_id        INTEGER;
BEGIN
SELECT emp_id
into v_emp_id
from employee
WHERE emp_name = 'Jack Richards';
exception
when too_many_rows THEN
emp_name:='TOO MANY EMPLOYEES FOUND';
END;
```

ANALYSIS   In this example, an exception is raised when more than one row is returned by the SELECT statement.

Types of Exceptions

Exceptions are errors that occur during runtime processing. These exceptions can arise due to different situations. Normally, PL/SQL processing will terminate as soon as it encounters an exception. Fortunately, PL/SQL gives you several tools to handle these exceptions so that processing does not terminate. After an exception is detected, processing is transferred to your handling routine within the PL/SQL block. Refer to Day 8, "Procedures, Packages, Errors, and Exceptions," for additional information about Oracle's exception-handling capabilities.

The following are the more commonly used predefined exceptions that you can trap in the exception-handling section of your PL/SQL block:

☐ no_data_found—Singleton SELECT statement returned no data.

☐ too_many_rows—Singleton SELECT statement returned more than one row of data.

☐ invalid_cursor—Illegal cursor operation occurred.

☐ value_error—Arithmetic, conversion, or truncation error occurred.

☐ when others—Used when no other exception is explicitly listed.

Listing 9.6 offers an enhancement to the code in Listing 9.5. In this example, I added another exception to handle the case when no rows are returned from the database.

INPUT

Listing 9.6. Multiple-row SELECT command with several exception-handling routines.

```
DECLARE
v_emp_id        INTEGER;
BEGIN
SELECT  emp_id
into v_emp_id
from employee
WHERE emp_name = 'Jack Richards';
exception
when no_data_found THEN
emp_name:='NO EMPLOYEE';
when too_many_rows THEN
emp_name:='TOO MANY EMPLOYEES FOUND';
END;
```

ANALYSIS

In the example in Listing 9.6, one of several exceptions can be raised. An exception is raised when no rows are returned by the SELECT statement as well as when more than one row is returned by the SELECT statement.

The UPDATE and DELETE Statements

The final two SQL DML statements to cover are the UPDATE and the DELETE statements. You can use these in any PL/SQL block as necessary. The purpose of these commands is synonymous with their names. The UPDATE command enables the user to change the values of an existing row. The DELETE command provides the means to remove or delete a row from a table.

The Syntax for the UPDATE Command

```
UPDATE table_name
set (column_name = value)
WHERE statement
```

In this syntax, `table_name` is the table containing the row you want to update, `column_name` is the column you want to update, and the WHERE statement identifies the row in the table to be identified.

The Syntax for the DELETE Command

```
DELETE from table_name
WHERE statement
```

In this syntax, `table_name` is the table containing the row to be deleted, and the WHERE statement identifies the row to be deleted.

Refer to the *Oracle SQL Language Reference Manual* for a more comprehensive syntax diagram for these last two commands.

Methods of Declaring Variables

As you learned in earlier chapters of this book, all PL/SQL variables must be declared in advance of using them. Declaration of variables is accomplished in the declaration portions of the PL/SQL block, function, package, or procedure. When a variable is defined, Oracle allocates memory to hold the variable. This section of this chapter covers several of PL/SQL's methods of declaring variables, including the following:

- ☐ Variables based on database columns
- ☐ Record variables (which can be based on tables or based on cursor definitions)
- ☐ Declarations at the package level

Variables Based on Database Columns

Oracle provides a means to declare a variable and define its datatype based on other variables, constants, or even table columns. You use the `%type` attribute in variable declarations to accomplish this task. As you recall, the employee table that you created earlier in this chapter in Listing 9.1 has the following structure:

```
employee:
    emp_id          INTEGER
    emp_name        VARCHAR2(32)
    supervised_by   INTEGER
    pay_rate        NUMBER(9,2)
    pay_type        CHAR
    emp_dept_id     INTEGER
```

The `%type` attribute enables you to define a variable based on a table column datatype. For example, in the following variable declarations, you see the `avg_rate` declared with the `%type` attribute based on the `pay_rate` column in the employee table. PL/SQL will treat this declaration as if you explicitly declared `avg_rate` as NUMBER(9,2).

```
avg_rate  employee.pay_rate%type
```

The following are a few more examples of the `%type` attribute, showing variables based on other variables and constants:

```
dept_id       INTEGER;
sub_dept_id   dept_id%type;  -- datatype based on a variable

area_id  dept_id%type := 9141; -- used with an initialization clause
```

PL/SQL allows you to use the `%type` attribute in a nesting variable declaration. The following example illustrates several variables defined on earlier `%type` declarations in a nesting fashion:

```
dept_sales     INTEGER;

area_sales     dept_sales%type;

group_sales     area_sales%type;
regional_sales  area_sales%type;

corporate_sales  regional_sales%type;
```

The `%type` attribute gives you several advantages. First, you base a declaration on a table column without having to know definitively what that column's datatype is. In really large applications and large databases (a database with over 500 objects), it does become hard to remember all the datatypes, especially if they change frequently. Second, as the datatypes of the item you based your declaration on do change, then your variables will automatically be changed as well. This can reduce maintenance of your application.

Record Variables

A *record* is a collection of individual fields that represents a row in a table. These fields are unique and each has its own values. The record as a whole does not have value.

By using records, you can group like data into one structure and then manipulate this structure as one entity or logical unit. This helps reduce coding and keeps the code easier to maintain and understand.

You declare a record in the declaration portion of a PL/SQL block, subprogram, or package. The following example declares a record named emp_sales:

```
TYPE emp_sales_rec is record        --record declaration
(emp_id        INTEGER,
emp_name       VARCHAR2(32),
commision_rate       employee.pay_rate%type);
```

After a record is declared, you can reference the record members directly by using dot notation. In the following example, the last field in the record emp_sales_rec is referenced:

```
IF emp_sales_rec.commision_rate > .05 THEN...
```

You can also pass a record type variable to a procedure, as in the following example:

```
procedure monthly_commissions (emp_sales_rec);
```

Oracle also allows you to assign expressions to a record, as shown in the following example:

```
emp_sale_rec.commission_rate := .01;
```

Record Variables Based on Tables

A record type variable based on a table means that each field in the record has the exact same name and datatype as the columns in the specified table. The %rowtype attribute is used to facilitate the declaration of a record based on a table.

The %rowtype is similar to the %type. The %type refers to only a single variable, whereas the %rowtype refers to an entire table row. The following example of the %rowtype attribute declares the record emp_rec, which can store an entire row from the employee table:

```
DECLARE
employee_name       employee.emp_name%type;
emp_rec             employee%rowtype;
```

As you did with other records, you use dot notation to reference a specific field. The following code examines the emp_name from the emp_rec just as if the code was interrogating the actual employee record:

```
IF emp_rec.emp_name like ' Madison% '  THEN...
```

As with other variables, you can assign a value to the record field directly, as shown following:

```
IF emp_rec.emp_name like 'Madison%'
THEN
emp_rec.pay_rate = 3000.00);
```

Records based on tables can also be used in a SELECT statement, as seen in the following example:

```
DECLARE
emp_rec     employee%rowtype;

BEGIN

SELECT *
into emp_rec
from employee
WHERE emp_name like 'Madison%';
```

Then you can reference any one of the fields of the emp_rec directly, like this:

```
IF emp_rec.pay_type is null THEN...
```

Record Variables Based on Cursor Definitions

Records that are based on an Oracle cursor draw their structure from the SELECT statement in the cursor. This type of record has the same number, name, and datatypes of columns as those in the cursor. The %rowtype attribute is used to declare the record that is based on a cursor. In the following example, the record named emp_rec is based on the cursor named get_emp_cur:

```
DECLARE

CURSOR get_emp_cur is          -- cursor declaration
SELECT emp_name, pay_rate
from employee
WHERE pay_type = 'H';

emp_rec   get_emp_cur%rowtype; -- record declaration
```

As you did with other Oracle records, you use dot notation to reference a specific field in the record, as shown following:

```
IF emp_rec.pay_rate > 3000 THEN ....
```

Declarations at the Package Level

Declaring a package has two parts: the package specification and the package body. The package body defines all the functions, procedures, and other constructs that are declared in the package specification. The package specification declares all variables, constants, cursors, procedures, and functions. This section reviews the declarations of variables in the package specification.

The package specification contains the declaration of all objects that will be used in the package body. The following are several examples of a package specification that declares a cursor, variable, constant, and record:

```
package emp_data is     -- package specification

pay_raise    constant real := 1.25;
high_rate    INTEGER;
CURSOR salary_cur (emp_id INTEGER, pay_rate NUMBER (9,2));
TYPE sal_rec is record (emp_name VARCHAR2(32), pay_rate NUMBER (9,2));
emp_rec  salary_cur%rowtype;

END emp_data;
```

One of the advantages of declaring items in a package is that they are global in nature and accessible by all. This means that any program in your application can use the variables, cursors, constants, and records declared in the package specification. You treat these items (except constants) as if they were declared locally, in that you can change their values as needed. This global nature of the data is only within a session and is not available across multiple sessions. This means, for example, that the variables running in one user's applications are not accessible to a different user's application unless the DBMS_PIPE package is used.

PL/SQL Tables

Like the PL/SQL record, the table is another composite datatype. PL/SQL tables are objects of type TABLE, and look similar to database tables but differ slightly. The following sections explore the PL/SQL table.

A PL/SQL table will have at least one column and one primary key. These two items remain unnamed. The column can have any datatype, whereas the primary key must be of the type BINARY_INTEGER. These tables are unconstrained in physical size and grow dynamically when rows are added. Hence, a row in a PL/SQL table does not exist until the primary key and single column are added to the table.

Declaring a PL/SQL Table

Declare the PL/SQL table in the declarative portion of your block, package, or other subprogram. The following declares a PL/SQL table called emp_table, which is based on the existing column emp_id in the employee table:

```
DECLARE
TYPE emp_table is table of employee.emp_id%type
INDEX BY BINARY_INTEGER;
```

You can also declare this as a not null table, as shown following:

```
DECLARE
TYPE emp_table is table of employee.emp_id%type not null
INDEX BY BINARY_INTEGER;
```

In both of the preceding examples, the clause INDEX BY BINARY_INTEGER is a mandatory feature of the PL/SQL table declaration. The INDEX BY clause is of the type BINARY_INTEGER, as this will lead to the fastest retrieval on the binary primary key.

Referencing Values in a PL/SQL Table

To reference a specific row in a PL/SQL table, you specify a primary key value using the array-like syntax. For example, to evaluate the twelfth employee from the emp_table (defined earlier), the statement would look like

```
IF emp_table(12) like 'Loretta%' THEN ....
```

Likewise, the following examples are valid references to PL/SQL tables, including using a table as a parameter:

```
building_floor_max_table(current_floor + 21);
part_num_cat (-150);

procedure calc_new_salaries (calc_salaries in emp_table);
```

Using a PL/SQL Table

PL/SQL allows you to manipulate the rows of a PL/SQL table, similar to a normal database table. You can insert, update, and delete rows in a PL/SQL table.

PL/SQL Table Insert

To insert rows into a PL/SQL table, you must use an iterative construct. As shown in the following example, to insert records into the guest_count_table, the WHILE statement is used. This PL/SQL block will insert the first ten thousand guests into the table:

```
DECLARE                      -- declare table type
TYPE guest_count_table
is table of VARCHAR2(55)
INDEX BY BINARY_INTEGER;

procedure find_10000_guest_table
(start_date  in date,
guest_count_out out guest_count_table)
is
guest_count BINARY_INTEGER := 0;
BEGIN
WHILE guest_count <= 10000           -- begin iterations
LOOP
guest_count = guest_count + 1;     -- guest (row) counter
/* the following inserts into the PL/SQL table */
guest_count_out (guest_count) := curr_guest_function;
END LOOP;
END find_10000_guest_table;
```

You can also directly assign a value into the PL/SQL table. The following line will insert a record into the emp_table:

```
emp_table(102) := 'Jacqueline Loraine';
```

Remember that the PL/SQL table is unconstrained and can contain virtually an unlimited number of rows. It is a good idea to manually track the current row count so that you can insert rows sequentially. This is easily done with a counter that you increment inside your loop. Likewise, the PL/SQL table function count is available to tell you how many rows are in the table. This function is covered in detail later in this chapter in the section "PL/SQL Table Functions."

PL/SQL Table Update

You update a PL/SQL table in a very similar way as you do for inserting data into a PL/SQL table. If you have already inserted a row number 102 in the emp_table, then you can update the same row with the following statement:

```
emp_table(102) := 'Jack Michaels';
```

This statement will update the contents of row 102 with the new value in the assignment statement.

PL/SQL Table Delete

Because the PL/SQL table is not stored in the database, the DELETE and DROP TABLE commands are limited in their effectiveness. PL/SQL does allow you to nullify and delete rows of a table, but you cannot drop a PL/SQL table.

The following command is an example of removing all the rows from a PL/SQL table using the Oracle DELETE built-in procedure:

```
emp_tab.DELETE;
```

The next example deletes the 2333rd record from the employee table:

```
emp_tab(2333);
```

This example deletes the first ten thousand guest records from the guest table:

```
guest_tab(0, 10000);
```

Likewise, the following statement will nullify the 100th record in the guest table:

```
guest_tab(100);
```

You can also assign an empty table to an existing table. This will make the existing table (one with rows) empty, as shown in the following example:

```
/* Statement will empty out the guest table   */

guest_tab := empty_tab;
```

Displaying the Contents of a PL/SQL Table

As with database tables, you will want to display the rows of a PL/SQL table. One of the easiest ways to view PL/SQL table rows is with the DBMS_OUTPUT public package. This package is supplied with your Oracle RDBMS.

The DBMS_OUTPUT package has a procedure named PUT LINE, which will output a single line of data to the output buffer. This buffer is usually your screen. The following example is a portion of code that you can include in your PL/SQL block to display the rows of a PL/SQL table. The code shown in Listing 9.7 will display the first 50 rows of the table.

INPUT

Listing 9.7. Using the DBMS_OUTPUT package to display the contents of a table.

```
1: BEGIN
2: for row_indicator in 1 .. 50
3: LOOP
4: dbms_output.put_line (emp_table (row_indicator);
5: END LOOP;
6: END;
```

ANALYSIS

In the example in Listing 9.7, several assumptions are made. First, I assumed that the table begins with row number one. Secondly, I assumed that the first 50 rows are sequentially numbered.

Both assumptions might not be true. You can adjust or customize your display block to suit your local needs.

PL/SQL Table Functions

PL/SQL provides a handful of useful built-in functions for use with PL/SQL tables. These functions are as follows:

☐ count—The count function returns the number of rows current in the PL/SQL table. The following line will return the number of rows in the employee table:

```
counter := emp_tab.count;
```

The specification for the function used in the preceding line is

```
FUNCTION count RETURN INTEGER;
```

☐ exists—This function returns the value of true if the specific row is present in the table. Otherwise, false is returned. The following example will evaluate to true if the guest table contains a third row:

```
IF guest_tab.exists(3) THEN...
```

The specification for the function used in the preceding line is

```
FUNCTION exists (index in INTEGER) RETURN boolean;
```

☐ first—This built-in function will return the value of the lowest index present in the PL/SQL table. The following will return the index value for the first row in the employee table:

```
first_row_value :=emp_tab.first;
```

The specification for the function used in the preceding line is

```
FUNCTION first RETURN INTEGER;
```

☐ last—This function will return the value of the last index in the PL/SQL table. The following example will return the value of the last index in the guest table:

```
last_row_value := guest_tab.last;
```

The specification for the function used in the preceding line is

```
FUNCTION last RETURN INTEGER;
```

☐ next—The next built-in function returns the value of the index that is the next largest index value. Take note of the syntax shown in the following example for the next built-in function:

```
next_index := guest_tab.next (current_index);
```

The specification for the function used in the preceding line is

```
FUNCTION next RETURN INTEGER;
```

☐ prior—The prior function will return the value of the index that is immediately prior to the current row. This is shown in the following example:

```
prior_index := guest_tab.prior (current_index);
```

The specification for the function used in the preceding line is

```
FUNCTION prior RETURN INTEGER;
```

Nested Tables

Oracle8 introduces a new collection type known as a nested table. A *nested table* is an item of the type TABLE and is similar to a single-dimension array that has no upper limit; that is, a nested table is unbounded. Data stored in a nested table is not stored in any particular order. However, when the data is retrieved into variables, the rows are ordered consecutively, based on their subscripts.

The Syntax for Declaring a Nested Table

```
TYPE type_name IS TABLE OF element_type
INDEX BY BINARY_INTEGER;
```

SYNTAX

In this syntax, *type_name* is the type specifier used later in the declaration. *element_type* is any valid PL/SQL datatype except for:

☐ BOOLEAN

☐ NCHAR

☐ NCLOB

☐ NVARCHAR2

☐ REF CURSOR

☐ TABLE

☐ VARRAY

▲ The INDEX BY clause is optional.

The following is an example in which the nested table is declared and used in an expression. You can use the nested table in all PL/SQL expressions. In this example, the nested table is named coworkers:

```
DECLARE
TYPE emp_table IS TABLE OF emp;
coworkers emp_table := emp_table
('Loretta','Robert','Stanton','Delores','Mary');
INDEX BY BINARY_INTEGER;
BEGIN
IF coworkers(i) = 'Timothy' THEN...
```

The following example illustrates the nesting of tables within PL/SQL. In this example, the department table will have a column named courses that contains all the courses offered by that department. The first part of the example creates an object type named courses:

```
CREATE TYPE courses AS OBJECT
(course_no    NUMBER(4),
title       VARCHAR2(100));
```

After this object type is created, you now create the table type called courselist:

```
CREATE TYPE courselist AS TABLE OF courses;
```

Finally, you create the table named department with a nested table column named courses:

```
CREATE TABLE department
(name       VARCHAR2(100),
professor    VARCHAR2(55),
courses    courselist)
NESTED TABLE courses STORE AS courses_table;
```

The following is an example of inserting data into the nested table named department. Note how the multiple courses are entered into the course column:

```
INSERT into department
values ('ENGLISH','Kathy Johns',
courselist (course(100,'Modern English'),
course(200,'Poetry'),
course(300,'Advanced Modern English')));
```

Likewise, you can perform a SELECT statement on the department table by executing the command shown in the following example:

```
SELECT course_no, title into var_course_no, var_title
from (SELECT courses from department
WHERE name = 'ENGLISH')
WHERE course_no = 200;
```

In this example, you select the English course with the course number 200 in the department table.

Summary

Today's lesson presents you with a quick overview of using SQL statements within a PL/SQL block. You learned how to insert and retrieve data from tables that you created and how to prepare for runtime errors. You also learned about PL/SQL variables—how to declare them; how to use them; and how to base them on other objects such as database tables, columns, constants, and even other variables. The %type attribute enables you to keep the variable declaration in synch with the datatypes in the database. PL/SQL tables are objects of type TABLE and look similar to database tables but differ slightly. These tables have one column and a binary primary index.

Q&A

Q What happens if my SQL statement fails inside the PL/SQL block?

A The processing of your PL/SQL block will terminate unless you have code in place to trap and handle the exception. PL/SQL allows for numerous predefined exceptions that make your coding easier.

Q What can a PL/SQL table do for me that a database table can't?

A A PL/SQL table provides several opportunities to the developer. The PL/SQL table is not bound to any size constraints, so as the rows are added, so grows the table. You don't have to ponder initial and incremental sizing issues. Many times a table is used as a working variable, so you do not want it to become an integral part of the schema.

Q What is a PL/SQL record?

A A PL/SQL record is a variable with the type record. It is a composite structure containing fields with its own datatypes. Records can help the developer by reducing the volume of code necessary. Records allow similar fields to be grouped and treated as one logical entity.

Workshop

The following workshop will test your comprehension of this chapter and give you an opportunity to practice what you have just learned. The answers to the quiz and exercises are provided in Appendix A, "Answers."

Quiz

1. Name some of the database objects that you can base a variable declaration on.
2. What is the variable attribute you use to base a variable on a table column?

3. Name several of the PL/SQL table built-in functions.

4. What are the four SQL DML statements permitted in a PL/SQL block?

Exercises

Evaluate each of the following three declarations and determine which ones are legal and which ones are not legal. Explain your answer for those that are not legal.

1. Legal or not legal:

```
DECLARE
emp_rec          emp_rec_type;
```

2. Legal or not legal:

```
DECLARE
emp_last_name            %type;
```

3. Legal or not legal:

```
DECLARE
TYPE    emp_table_type is table of VARCHAR2(55);
emp_dept_table    emp_table_type;
```

Day 10

Manipulating Data with Cursors, DELETE, and UPDATE

by Tom Luers

PL/SQL cursors provide a way for your program to select multiple rows of data from the database and then to process each row individually. Specifically, a *cursor* is a name assigned by Oracle to every SQL statement processed. This is done in order to provide Oracle a means to direct and control all phases of the SQL processing. This chapter discusses using cursors and how to define them.

What Is a Cursor?

NEW TERM Two kinds of *cursors* are used in Oracle: *implicit* and *explicit*. PL/SQL implicitly declares a cursor for every SQL statement used. It needs to do this in order to manage the processing of the SQL statement. Implicit cursors are declared by Oracle for each UPDATE, DELETE, and INSERT SQL command. Explicit cursors are declared and used by the user to process multiple rows returned by a SELECT statement. Explicitly defined cursors are constructs that enable the user to name an area of memory to hold a specific statement for access at a later time.

As you recall from earlier in this book, SELECT statements can return zero, one, or many rows of data. When a PL/SQL cursor query returns multiple rows of data, the resulting group of rows is called the *active set*. This active set is stored by Oracle in the explicitly defined and named cursor that you create. The Oracle cursor is a mechanism used to easily process multiple rows of data. Without cursors, the Oracle developer would have to explicitly fetch and manage each individual row that is selected by the cursor query.

Another feature of the cursor is that it contains a pointer that keeps track of the current row being accessed, which enables your program to process the rows one at a time. Figure 10.1 illustrates an Oracle cursor: It shows the active set, consisting of the rows returned by the cursor's SELECT statement, and the pointer indicating the latest row fetched from the active set.

Figure 10.1.

An Oracle multirow cursor.

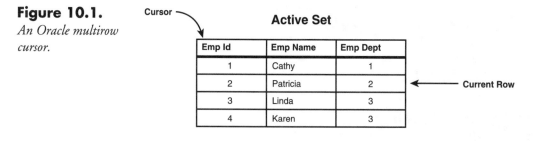

Explicit Cursors

Explicit cursors are defined by the programmer to process a multiple-row active set one record at a time. The following are the steps to using explicitly defined cursors within PL/SQL:

1. Declare the cursor.
2. Open the cursor.
3. Fetch data from the cursor.
4. Close the cursor.

Declaring a Cursor

The first step is to declare the cursor in order for PL/SQL to reference the returned data. This must be done in the declaration portion of your PL/SQL block. Declaring a cursor accomplishes two goals:

- ☐ It names the cursor.
- ☐ It associates a query with the cursor.

The name you assign to a cursor is an undeclared identifier, not a PL/SQL variable. You cannot assign values to a cursor name or use it in an expression. This name is used in the PL/SQL block to reference the cursor query.

The Syntax for Defining Cursors

```
DECLARE cursor_name
is
SELECT statement
```

In this syntax, *cursor_name* is the name you assign to the cursor. SELECT *statement* is the query that returns rows to the cursor active set.

In the following example, the cursor named c_names is defined with a SELECT statement that queries the employee table:

```
DECLARE c_names
  is
     SELECT emp_name from employee
   WHERE pay_type = 'S';
```

The only constraint that can limit the number of cursors is the availability of memory to manage the cursors. Oracle system administrators will use the OPEN_CURSOR parameter in the init.ora file to help manage this memory use.

Opening the Cursor

Opening the cursor activates the query and identifies the active set. When the OPEN command is executed, the cursor identifies only the rows that satisfy the query. The rows are not actually retrieved until the cursor fetch is issued. OPEN also initializes the cursor pointer to just before the first row of the active set.

The Syntax for the OPEN Command

```
OPEN cursor_name;
```

In this syntax, *cursor_name* is the name of the cursor that you have previously defined.

After the OPEN command is issued, the cursor will look like Figure 10.2, which shows that the active set has retrieved its data from the database. The cursor establishes its pointer at the very top of the the active set; the pointer is before the first row because the FETCH command has not been issued yet.

Figure 10.2.

View of the opened cursor.

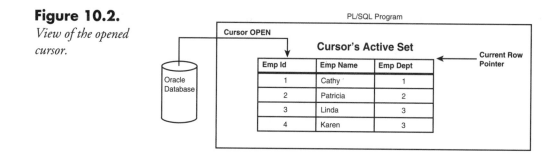

NOTE

After a cursor is opened, until the moment you close it, all fetched data in the active set will remain static. This means that the cursor will ignore all SQL DML commands (INSERT, UPDATE, DELETE, and SELECT) performed on that data after the cursor was opened. Hence, you should open the cursor only when you need it.

If you try to open a cursor that is already open, you receive the following error:

```
ORA-06511: PL/SQL: cursor already open
```

If this error occurs, check your logic or close the cursor earlier in the block and reopen it when needed. You can check the status of the cursor by using the cursor %isopen attribute. Later in the chapter, additional cursor attributes are covered in the section "Explicit Cursor Attributes." The %open attribute is used as demonstrated in the following example:

```
IF not employee%isopen
THEN
OPEN employee;
END IF;
```

Fetching Data in a Cursor

Getting data into the cursor is accomplished with the FETCH command. The FETCH command retrieves the rows in the active set one row at a time. The FETCH command is usually used in conjunction with some type of iterative process. The first FETCH statement sorts the active set as necessary. In the iterative processes, the cursor advances to the next row in the active set each time the FETCH command is executed. The FETCH command is the only means to navigate through the active set.

The Syntax for the FETCH Command

SYNTAX

```
FETCH cursor_name INTO record_list;
```

In this syntax, *cursor_name* is the name of the previously defined cursor from which you are now retrieving rows—one at a time. *record_list* is a list of variables that will receive the columns from the active set. The FETCH command places the results of the active set into these variables.

10

After a FETCH has been issued, the cursor will look like Figure 10.3, which shows that the results in the active set are fetched into the PL/SQL variables for use within that PL/SQL block. After each fetch, the cursor pointer moves to the next row in the active set.

Figure 10.3.

View of the opened cursor after the FETCH command is issued.

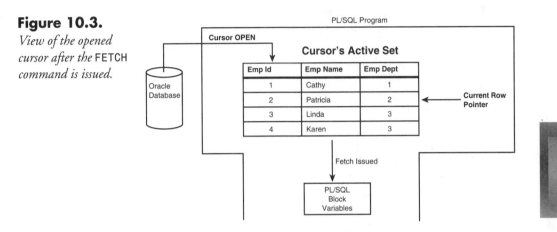

The *record list*, or variable list, is the PL/SQL structure that receives the fetched rows of data. For each column value retrieved by the cursor's query, there must be a corresponding variable in the INTO list. Additionally, their datatypes must be compatible. If you fetch into a record, the number of columns in the record must match the number of expressions in the select list in the cursor.

If you want to revisit a previously fetched row, you must close and reopen the cursor and then fetch each row in turn. If you want to change the active set, you must assign new values to the input variables in the cursor query and reopen the cursor. This re-creates the active set with the results of the revised query statement.

Closing the Cursor

The CLOSE statement closes or deactivates the previously opened cursor and makes the active set undefined. Oracle will implicitly close a cursor when the user's program or session is terminated. After the cursor is closed, you cannot perform any operation on it, or you will receive an invalid_cursor exception.

The Syntax for the CLOSE Command

```
CLOSE cursor_name;
```

In this syntax, cursor_name is the name of the previously opened cursor.

Explicit Cursor Attributes

Each cursor, whether it is explicitly or implicitly defined, carries with it attributes that provide useful data regarding the results of a multirow SELECT. The four cursor attributes are %isopen,

%found, %notfound, and %rowcount. These attributes can be used in any PL/SQL statement. Cursor attributes cannot be used against closed cursors; an invalid_cursor error will be issued if you attempt this.

The %isopen **Attribute**

The %isopen attribute indicates whether a cursor is open. If the named cursor is open, then this attribute equates to true; otherwise, it will be false. The following example uses the %isopen attribute to open a cursor if it is not already open:

```
IF c_names%isopen THEN
        process_data_procedure
ELSE
     OPEN  c_names;
END IF;
```

The %found **Attribute**

The %found attribute equates to true if the last FETCH statement affects one or more rows. Therefore, the %found attribute is the logical opposite of the %notfound attribute. The %found attribute equates to false when no rows are fetched. Like the %notfound, this attribute also equates to null prior to the first fetch.

The following example illustrates a practical use of the %found attribute:

```
LOOP
FETCH c_names INTO record_names;
IF c_names%found THEN
process_names_function;
ELSE
EXIT;
END IF;
END LOOP;
```

The %notfound **Attribute**

The %notfound attribute is useful in telling you whether a cursor has any rows left in it to be fetched. The %notfound attribute equates to false when there are rows remaining in the cursor. It will equate to true when there are no more rows remaining. After the fetching has started until and including the fetch on the last row, %notfound will be false. Prior to the first fetch, this attribute will equate to null. An error will be returned should you evaluate %notfound on a cursor that is not opened.

The following example illustrates a practical use of the %notfound attribute:

```
LOOP
 FETCH c_names INTO record_names
  EXIT when c_names%notfound
END LOOP;
```

The %rowcount **Attribute**

This attribute returns the number of rows fetched so far for the cursor. Prior to the first fetch, %rowcount is zero. There are many practical applications of the %rowcount attribute. The following example will perform a commit after the first 250 employees' salaries are processed:

```
LOOP
FETCH c_names INTO record_names
IF c_names%rowcount = 250
COMMIT
ELSE
EXIT;
END IF;
END LOOP;
```

Explicit Cursor Example

10

The following example illustrates the use of all four components of a PL/SQL cursor:

```
DECLARE

v_emp_name     VARCHAR2(32);
v_salary_rate    NUMBER(9,2);
v_payroll_total  NUMBER(9,2);
v_pay_type      CHAR;

CURSOR c_emp is                              -- cursor declaration
SELECT emp_name, pay_rate, pay_type from employee
WHERE emp_dept_id = 3;

BEGIN

OPEN c_emp;                                  -- opening cursor
LOOP
FETCH  c_emp INTO v_emp_name, v_salary_rate, v_pay_type;    -- FETCH command
EXIT when c_emp%notfound;

IF v_pay_type = 'S' THEN
v_payroll_total :=  (v_salary_rate *  1.25);
ELSE
v_payroll_total := (v_salary_rate * 40);
END IF;
INSERT INTO weekly_salary values (v_payroll_total);
END LOOP;

CLOSE c_emp;                                 -- closing cursor
END;
```

Automated Explicit Cursors

The previous section illustrates the basic mechanics of declaring and using cursors. In many programming situations, there is more than one way to code your logic. This also applies to PL/SQL cursors; there are opportunities to streamline or simplify the coding and usage of them. One such way is to place the cursor within a FOR loop. This is known as a CURSOR FOR loop. A CURSOR FOR loop will implicitly

☐ Declare the loop index

☐ Open the cursor

☐ Fetch the next row from the cursor for each loop iteration

☐ Close the cursor when all rows are processed or when the loop exits

CURSOR FOR loops are ideal when you want to loop through all records returned by the cursor. With CURSOR FOR loops, you should not declare the record that controls the loop. Likewise, you should not use CURSOR FOR loops when the cursor operations have to be handled manually. Listing 10.1 illustrates the use of CURSOR FOR loops.

INPUT   **Listing 10.1. Using CURSOR FOR loops.**

```
DECLARE
CURSOR c_employees is
      SELECT * from employees
      WHERE pay_type = 'H';

BEGIN                                      -- implicit cursor open
  FOR emp_record  in c_employees loop      -- implicit cursor fetch
      process_monthly_hourly_checks
 END LOOP;                                 -- implicit cursor close
 COMMIT;
END;
```

Implicit Cursors

As mentioned earlier in this chapter, Oracle creates and opens a cursor for every SQL statement that is not part of an explicitly declared cursor. The most recent implicit cursor can be referred to as the SQL cursor. You cannot use the OPEN, CLOSE, and FETCH commands with the implicit cursor. However, you can use the cursor attributes to access information about the most recently executed SQL statement through the SQL cursor.

In the following example, PL/SQL creates an implicit cursor to identify the set of rows that are affected by the UPDATE command:

```
UPDATE employee
set pay_rate=pay_rate*1.08
WHERE pay-type='S'
```

Implicit Cursor Attributes

Like explicit cursors, implicit cursors use attributes. The implicit cursor attributes are %isopen, %found, %notfound, and %rowcount. Because implicit cursors have no name, you must append SQL to the attributes. The implicit cursor contains information concerning the processing of the last SQL statement (INSERT, UPDATE, DELETE, and SELECT INTO) that was not associated with an explicit cursor. Implicit cursor attributes can be used only in PL/SQL statements and not in SQL statements. The following sections briefly describe each of these.

The %isopen Attribute

After the execution of the SQL statement, the associated SQL cursor is always closed automatically by Oracle. Hence the %isopen attribute always evaluates to false.

The %found Attribute

This attribute will equate to true if an INSERT, UPDATE, or DELETE affected one or more rows or a SELECT INTO returns one or more rows. Otherwise, it evaluates to false. %found will equate to null until a SQL DML statement is executed. The following is an example using the implicit %found attribute:

```
UPDATE employees
set pay_type = 'S'
WHERE name = 'Bernard' or name = 'Stanton';

IF sql%found THEN
     COMMIT;
ELSE
     employee_not_found_procedure;
END IF;
```

The %notfound Attribute

The %notfound attribute evaluates to true if the most recent SQL statement does not affect any rows. Otherwise, it will evaluate to false. The following example illustrates the implicit %notfound attribute:

```
UPDATE employees
set pay_type = 'S'
WHERE name = 'Bernard' or name = 'Stanton';

IF sql%notfound THEN
     employee_not_found_procedure;
ELSE
     COMMIT;
END IF;
```

10

Careful code design must be exercised when using the SELECT INTO statements. The %notfound attribute cannot be used immediately after the SELECT INTO statement when no records are retrieved. This is because the no_data_found exception will be raised before the %notfound attribute is set. The following example illustrates this point:

```
/* The exception %notfound used with no exception handler in place.*/
/*Hence, proper processing might be inappropriately missed.*/
BEGIN
SELECT pay_type INTO hold_type
from employee WHERE name = 'Catherine';
    IF SQL%notfound THEN                 -- processing may never reach here if
  employee_not_found_procedure;   -- the prior SELECT statement returns no rows
    END IF;
exceptions
        ...
END;
```

The following shows the same example, except with an exception handler in place:

```
/* The exception %notfound is used with exception handler in place.*/
/* Hence proper processing takes place.*/
BEGIN
SELECT pay_type INTO hold_type
from employee WHERE name = 'Catherine';    --processing goes to the exceptions
                                           -- area when no rows are returned.
when others THEN
    IF SQL%notfound THEN                      --not found logic is executed here
            employee_not_found_procedure;
    END IF;
END;
```

The %rowcount **Attribute**

This attribute equates to the total number of rows affected by the most recent SQL statement. An example of the %rowcount follows:

```
BEGIN
UPDATE employees
set pay_rate = pay_rate * 1.05
WHERE pay-type = 'S';
message('Total records updated are:'to_char(sql%rowcount));
END
```

Summary

Cursors are PL/SQL constructs that enable you to process, one row at a time, the results of a multirow query. Implicit cursors are created for each DML statement, whereas explicit cursors are created by users to process queries that return multiple rows. Furthermore, cursors improve code processing by reducing the need to parse code repeatedly.

Q&A

Q **When would you use an explicit cursor instead of an implicit cursor?**

A Explicit cursors must be declared and used when you want to process queries that return multiple rows and you want to handle these rows individually.

Q **What are the four steps to using an explicit cursor?**

A The four steps are

1. Declare the cursor.

2. Open the cursor.

3. Fetch the rows.

4. Close the cursor.

Q **Is there any way to expedite or simplify the steps to using a cursor?**

A Yes. The CURSOR FOR loop construct will cause Oracle to implicitly open, fetch, and close the cursor.

10

Workshop

The following workshop will test your understanding of PL/SQL cursors and their uses. The answers to the quiz and exercise can be found in Appendix A, "Answers."

Quiz

1. What are the cursor attributes and what is their purpose?

2. How many cursors can you use at a time?

3. Where is the cursor pointer when the cursor is first opened?

Exercise

Create a PL/SQL block that determines the top five highest-paid employees from your employee table. Be sure to incorporate the usage of the appropriate cursor attributes. Print these five employees to the screen.

Day 11

Writing Database Triggers

by Jonathan Gennick

Today's lesson discusses *database triggers*. A trigger is used to write procedural logic that is invoked in response to specific data manipulation events. Creative application of database triggers will enable you to accomplish many useful things that otherwise would be impossible. Examples of what you can do with triggers include replicating data, storing data redundantly to avoid frequent table joins, and enforcing complex business rules.

What Is a Trigger?

A trigger is a PL/SQL block that is associated with a table, stored in a database, and executed in response to a specific data manipulation event. Triggers can be executed, or *fired*, in response to the following events:

□ A row is inserted into a table.

□ A row in a table is updated.

□ A row in a table is deleted.

It is not possible to define a trigger to fire when a row is selected.

A trigger definition consists of these basic parts:

□ The event that fires the trigger

□ The database table on which the event must occur

□ An optional condition controlling when the trigger is executed

□ A PL/SQL block containing the code to be executed when the trigger is fired

A trigger is a database object, like a table or an index. When you define a trigger, it becomes part of the database and is always executed when the event for which it is defined occurs. It doesn't matter if the event is triggered by someone typing in a SQL statement using SQL*Plus, running a client/server program that updates the database, or running a utility like Oracle's SQL*Loader in order to bulk-load data. Because of this, triggers serve as a *choke point*, allowing you to perform critical validation or computations in response to database changes, no matter what the source.

An Example of a Trigger

Suppose for a moment that you wanted to be sure that all department names were stored using uppercase letters. Perhaps you are doing this to facilitate searching on that field. Listing 11.1 shows one way to do this with a trigger.

**INPUT/
OUTPUT**   **Listing 11.1. Example of a trigger.**

```
 1: CREATE OR REPLACE TRIGGER department_insert_update
 2:   BEFORE INSERT OR UPDATE ON department
 3:   FOR EACH ROW
 4: DECLARE
 5:   dup_flag   INTEGER;
 6: BEGIN
 7:   --Force all department names to uppercase.
 8: :NEW.dept_name := UPPER(:NEW.dept_name);
 9: END;
10: /
11: Trigger created.
```

ANALYSIS   Line 1 tells Oracle to create this trigger with the name department_insert_update and to replace any existing trigger of the same name if necessary. Line 2 says that it will be fired whenever a new row is inserted into the department table or whenever a department record is changed. In line 8 there is one line of code that uses the built-in UPPER function to force the department name to uppercase. Notice the reference to :NEW. This is the default alias for the new value of the record. The alias :OLD can be used to refer to the old value of a field, before an update takes effect. Line 3 tells Oracle to fire this trigger once for each row modified. If you were to issue an UPDATE statement to change the names of all departments in the table, this trigger would be fired for each one of those records.

To demonstrate the effect of this trigger, try issuing the input statements shown in Listing 11.2.

INPUT/OUTPUT **Listing 11.2. Testing the** department_insert_update **trigger.**

```
 1: INSERT INTO department (dept_id, dept_name) VALUES (10,'payroll');
 2: 1 row created.
 3: INSERT INTO department (dept_id, dept_name) VALUES (11,'Sewage');
 4: 1 row created.
 5: UPDATE department SET dept_name = 'Payroll' WHERE dept_id = 10;
 6: 1 row updated.
 7: SELECT dept_id, dept_name FROM department WHERE dept_id BETWEEN 10 AND 11;
 8:   DEPT_ID DEPT_NAME
 9:   -------- ------------------------------
10:        10 PAYROLL
11:        11 SEWAGE
```

ANALYSIS Note that the trigger has forced all department names to uppercase regardless of whether the name was the result of a new record inserted or an existing record that was updated.

Types of Triggers

Database triggers can be classified in two different ways: by when they fire in relation to the triggering SQL statement, and by whether or not they fire for each row affected by the triggering SQL statement. This results in four basic trigger types.

NEW TERM There are two choices for when a trigger fires in relation to a SQL statement, either before or after. *Before triggers* are executed before the triggering SQL statement. *After triggers* are executed following the triggering SQL statement.

NEW TERM A trigger is either a *row-level trigger* or a *statement-level trigger*. A row-level trigger executes once for each row affected by the triggering SQL statement, whereas a statement-level trigger is executed only once. Only row-level triggers have access to the data values in the affected records. Statement-level triggers do not. This is because SQL is a set-oriented language—SQL statements can affect many or even all rows in a table. Statement-level triggers are only fired once, so it would not be possible to resolve a column reference in such a trigger.

The possible combinations of the choices result in the four basic trigger types listed in Table 11.1.

Table 11.1. The four basic trigger types.

When Fired	Level	Description
Before	Statement	Executed once for the triggering SQL statement, before that statement is executed.
Before	Row	Executed once for each record affected by the triggering SQL statement, before the record in question is changed, deleted, or inserted.
After	Row	Executed once for each record affected by the triggering SQL statement, after the record in question has been changed, deleted, or inserted.
After	Statement	Executed once for the triggering SQL statement, after that statement has been executed.

Triggers execute in response to a SQL statement and can be defined for the INSERT, UPDATE, and DELETE statements. These are often referred to as *insert triggers*, *update triggers*, and *delete triggers*, respectively. Together with the four basic types from Table 11.1, this gives a total of 12 possible trigger types, which are listed in Table 11.2. Note that the SELECT statement is the only data manipulation statement for which no triggers can be defined.

Table 11.2. The 12 trigger types.

SQL Statement	When Fired	Level
INSERT	Before	Row
INSERT	After	Row
INSERT	Before	Statement
INSERT	After	Statement
UPDATE	Before	Row
UPDATE	After	Row
UPDATE	Before	Statement
UPDATE	After	Statement
DELETE	Before	Row
DELETE	After	Row
DELETE	Before	Statement
DELETE	After	Statement

Also note that one trigger can be defined to fire for more than one SQL statement. The example in Listing 11.1 shows a trigger that is both an insert trigger and an update trigger.

Because there are four possible trigger types that can be created for a specific SQL statement, it makes sense to ask about the execution order. Which trigger gets executed first? Which last? What if there are multiple triggers defined of the same type? Figure 11.1 shows the order of execution of the various trigger types in relation to each other and in relation to the triggering SQL statement.

Figure 11.1.

Trigger execution order.

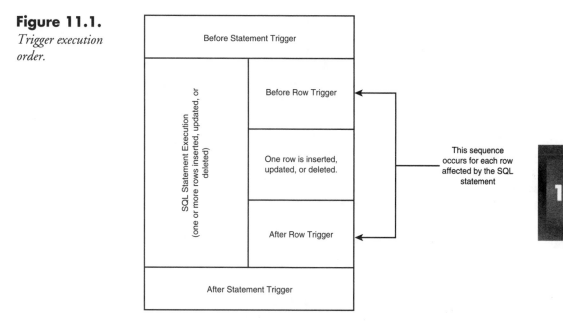

Triggers of the same type are executed in no particular order. If you write several triggers of the same type, for example three triggers that fire before a row is updated, you must ensure that the integrity of the database does not depend on the order of execution.

 TIP

If you have multiple triggers of the same type, and the execution order is important to you, you should rewrite those as one trigger.

Do	Don't

Do use before-update row-level triggers for complex business rule enforcement, security checking, and performing complex calculations. You want to do all these things before the row is inserted.

Do use after-update row-level triggers for data replication and logging of changes.

Don't use before triggers for data replication and change logging because an integrity constraint or another trigger could prevent the SQL statement from completing.

Don't use triggers to enforce referential integrity in cases where you can use a declarative constraint instead.

Do use statement-level before triggers to enforce security rules where the rule is not dependent on any values in the records being affected.

Syntax

The syntax used to define a database trigger is shown following. There are a number of optional and repeating clauses that cause the syntax explanation to look a bit cluttered, but don't be intimidated by them. The examples in the rest of this chapter make use of all the trigger features. Reading through these examples should give you a good feel for how the different variations in trigger definitions work and how you can use them.

The Syntax for Defining a Database Trigger

```
CREATE [OR REPLACE] TRIGGER trigger_name
  {BEFORE|AFTER} verb_list ON table_name
  [[REFERENCING correlation_names] FOR EACH ROW [WHEN (condition)]]
DECLARE
  declarations
BEGIN
  pl/sql_code
END;
/
```

In this syntax, the parameters are as follows:

- [ ] *trigger_name* is the name you want to give the trigger. By default, Oracle will create the trigger in your schema, but you can specify a specific schema by using the standard *schema_name.trigger_name* notation.

- [ ] *verb_list* identifies the SQL verbs that fire the trigger. The syntax of the *verb_list* is as follows:

  ```
  {INSERT|DELETE|UPDATE [OF column_list]} [OR verb_list]
  ```

In the preceding syntax, the parameters are

column_list   This is an optional, comma-delimited list of columns that controls when an update trigger is fired. If this list is present, the update trigger fires only when one of the columns listed is changed. Otherwise, if the column list is omitted, the trigger fires whenever any column in the table is changed.

verb_list   This is another iteration of the verb list. You can create a trigger that is fired by more than one SQL verb. See Listing 11.1 for an example of this.

☐ *table_name* is the table on which the trigger is defined. As with the trigger name, you can qualify this with a schema name; otherwise, the table is assumed to be in your schema.

☐ *correlation_names* allows you to specify correlation names other than the default of OLD and NEW. This is useful if the table on which the trigger is defined happens to be OLD or NEW and can also be helpful in making the trigger code self-documenting. The referencing clause looks like this:

```
{OLD AS old_alias¦NEW AS new_alias} [correlation_names]
```

In the preceding syntax, the parameters are

old_alias   This is a name you want to use when referring to the value of a field before the SQL verb executes.

new_alias   This is a name you want to use when referring to the value of a field after the SQL verb executes.

correlation_names   This is another iteration of the alias list. You can specify an alias for both old and new values.

☐ *condition* is an optional condition placed on the execution of the trigger. This can only be used on row-level triggers, and if *condition* is present, the trigger will only be fired when the condition is true. The condition can be any boolean expression, cannot contain any queries, and must use correlation names, in other words NEW and OLD, to refer to column values in the row being changed.

☐ *declarations* consists of any variable, record, or cursor declarations needed by this PL/SQL block.

☐ *pl/sql_code* is the PL/SQL code that gets executed when the trigger fires.

NEW TERM   The *correlation names* :OLD and :NEW deserve some extra explanation. It is common when writing a trigger to need to reference the values in the record being inserted, updated, or deleted. Further, in the case of an update, it is often necessary to access both the before and after values of a given field. The correlation names :OLD and :NEW are provided for this purpose. These function much like a PL/SQL record. :OLD contains the field values

11

before they are updated, and :NEW contains the field values after the update takes place. Use standard dot notation, in other words :OLD.*field_name*, to refer to the value of a particular field. You will see examples of this in several of the listings in this chapter.

NOTE
> Accessing both before and after versions of a record usually only makes sense in an update trigger. However, Oracle does allow you to reference both :OLD and :NEW in delete and insert triggers. In an insert trigger, the field values in :OLD are null and :NEW contains the data to be inserted. In a delete trigger, the situation is reversed. The field values in :OLD contain the data about to be deleted and the :NEW values are null.

Uses for Triggers

The possible uses for database triggers are varied and are limited only by your imagination. Some common uses are listed in the following:

- ☐ Enforcing business rules
- ☐ Maintaining referential integrity
- ☐ Enforcing security
- ☐ Maintaining a historical log of changes
- ☐ Generating column values, including primary key values
- ☐ Replicating data

The next few sections give examples of these uses.

Enforcing a Business Rule

Oracle provides a fine set of declarative options for enforcing referential integrity and business rules. The business world, however, is fast-paced and always changing. It is also full of exceptions, and some rules might be impossible to write as simple declarative statements. Triggers provide another option, allowing you to write code in support of even the most complex and convoluted rules.

Consider this rather simple business rule involving an employee's pay rate in the sample database:

> When an employee's pay type is changed from hourly to salary, or the reverse, his pay rate must also change.

Unlike many rules you might encounter in business, this actually makes sense! Simple as it is, though, it isn't possible to enforce at the database level without the use of a trigger. Now enhance this rule to include the following conditions:

If an employee is switching from salary to an hourly rate, the new yearly income, based on a 2000-hour year, must be within plus-or-minus 20 percent of his salary. The reverse condition applies to employees switching to a salary from an hourly rate.

Listing 11.3 shows one possible implementation of these rules using a before-update trigger on the employee table.

INPUT/OUTPUT **Listing 11.3. Trigger enforcing complex business rules.**

```
 1: CREATE OR REPLACE TRIGGER emp_pay_type_chg
 2: BEFORE UPDATE ON employee
 3: FOR EACH ROW WHEN (OLD.pay_type <> NEW.pay_type)
 4: DECLARE
 5:    new_yearly_rate        employee.pay_rate%TYPE;
 6:    old_yearly_rate        employee.pay_rate%TYPE;
 7:    allowed_variance_amt   employee.pay_rate%TYPE;
 8:    allowed_variance_pct   NUMBER(2,2) := .20;
 9:    hours_in_year          INTEGER := 2000;
10: BEGIN
11:    --Check to see if the pay rate has also been changed.
12: IF :OLD.pay_rate = :NEW.pay_rate THEN
13:       RAISE_APPLICATION_ERROR (-20000,
    ➥'The pay type changed and the pay rate did not.');
14: END IF;
15:
16:    --Check to verify that the new expected yearly rate is within
17:    --plus-or-minus 20% of the previous yearly rate.
18:    IF :OLD.pay_type = 'H' AND :NEW.pay_type = 'S' THEN
19: --the new salary must be + or - 20% of the old hourly rate * 2000 hours.
20: old_yearly_rate := ROUND(:OLD.pay_rate * hours_in_year,2);
21:       new_yearly_rate := :NEW.pay_rate;
22:       allowed_variance_amt := allowed_variance_pct * old_yearly_rate;
23:    IF ABS(new_yearly_rate - old_yearly_rate) > allowed_variance_amt THEN
24:          RAISE_APPLICATION_ERROR (-20000,'New salary is not within '
25:             ¦¦ TO_CHAR(allowed_variance_pct * 100) ¦¦ '% of the old rate.');
26:       END IF;
27:    ELSIF :OLD.pay_type = 'S' AND :NEW.pay_type = 'H' THEN
28: --the new hourly rate * 2000 hours must be + or - 20% of the old salary.
29: new_yearly_rate := ROUND(:NEW.pay_rate * hours_in_year,2);
30:       old_yearly_rate := :OLD.pay_rate;
31:       allowed_variance_amt := allowed_variance_pct
    ➥ * (old_yearly_rate * hours_in_year);
32: IF ABS(new_yearly_rate - old_yearly_rate) > allowed_variance_amt THEN
33:          RAISE_APPLICATION_ERROR (-20000,
    ➥'New project yearly rate is not within '
34: ¦¦ TO_CHAR(allowed_variance_pct * 100) ¦¦ '% of the old salary.');
35:       END IF;
```

11

continues

Listing 11.3. continued

```
36:    ELSE
37:       --Something is very wrong if we ever get here.
38:       RAISE_APPLICATION_ERROR(-20000,'Invalid combination of pay types: '
39:                               || :OLD.pay_type || ' ' || :NEW.pay_type);
40:    END IF;
41: END;
42: /
43: Trigger created.
```

ANALYSIS The trigger shown in Listing 11.3 is implemented as a before trigger (line 2) so that it can validate any changes to the employee record before they are actually saved in the database. The WHEN condition in line 3 causes this trigger to fire only when the pay type is changed. This trigger could be fired on every update, but that would decrease efficiency. Because the trigger validates changes to the pay_type field, it makes sense to fire it only when that particular field is changed.

> **NOTE** Be sure to notice that you need to precede the correlation names in the trigger body with a colon; in other words, use :OLD and :NEW. However, this is not the case in the WHEN clause.

The first, and easiest, test that this trigger performs is to verify that the pay_rate field has been changed (line 12). An error is raised (line 13) if the pay rate has not been changed. The next task is to check to be sure that the employee's new yearly income will be within 20 percent of its previous values. A value of 2000 hours (line 9) is used to compute the yearly wages for an hourly worker. Lines 18 through 26 check the new wage for an employee changing from an hourly rate to a yearly salary. If the new salary is not within 20 percent of what the employee had been making previously, then an error is raised (lines 24–25). The code in lines 27 through 35 makes a similar check for a salaried employee being switched to an hourly rate. Finally, the code in lines 37 through 39 is executed if the change is not one of these two cases, and an error is raised.

To test the trigger shown in Listing 11.3, try typing in the SQL INSERT and UPDATE statements shown in Listing 11.4.

INPUT/OUTPUT ## Listing 11.4. Testing the `pay_type_chg` trigger.

```
1: --Insert an employee record and try some updates that should fail.
2: --Then try an update that should succeed.
3: --Create an employee for testing.
4: INSERT INTO employee
5:    (emp_id, emp_name, pay_rate, pay_type)
```

```
 6:     VALUES (100,'Kazam el Shabar',100,'H');
 7: 1 row created.
 8: --Try updating to an invalid pay type.
 9: UPDATE employee
10:    SET pay_type = 'X',
11:        pay_rate = 200000
12:    WHERE emp_id = 100;
13: UPDATE employee
14: *
15: ERROR at line 1:
16: ORA-20000: Invalid combination of pay types: H X
17: ORA-06512: at "MY_READER.EMP_PAY_TYPE_CHG", line 34
18: ORA-04088: error during execution of trigger 'MY_READER.EMP_PAY_TYPE_CHG'
19: --Try an update where we only update the pay type and not the rate.
20: UPDATE employee
21:    SET pay_type = 'S'
22:    WHERE emp_id = 100;
23: UPDATE employee
24: *
25: ERROR at line 1:
26: ORA-20000: The pay type changed and the pay rate did not.
27: ORA-06512: at "MY_READER.EMP_PAY_TYPE_CHG", line 10
28: ORA-04088: error during execution of trigger 'MY_READER.EMP_PAY_TYPE_CHG'
29: --Update both type and rate, but the new  yearly rate is
30: --more than 20% greater or less than the previous rate.
31: UPDATE employee
32:    SET pay_type = 'S',
33:        pay_rate = 300000
34:    WHERE emp_id = 100;
35: UPDATE employee
36: *
37: ERROR at line 1:
38: ORA-20000: New salary is not within 20% of the old rate.
39: ORA-06512: at "MY_READER.EMP_PAY_TYPE_CHG", line 20
40: ORA-04088: error during execution of trigger 'MY_READER.EMP_PAY_TYPE_CHG'
41: --Update both type and rate, this time the new value is within range.
42: UPDATE employee
43:    SET pay_type = 'S',
44:        pay_rate = 240000
45:    WHERE emp_id = 100;
46: 1 row updated.
```

ANALYSIS The first statement, the INSERT statement, simply adds an employee record to the table for testing purposes. The first UPDATE statement tries to set the pay type code to 'X'. Because it is the pay type field that is changing, the pay_type_chg trigger fires and rejects the change because 'X' is an invalid code. The second UPDATE statement changes the pay type to salaried, but does not change the pay rate. This update is also rejected, this time because the rate has not also been changed. The business rule states that the new yearly pay must be within 20 percent of the previous value when an employee's pay type changes, and the next two examples deal with this. Using a value of 2000 hours in a year, and multiplying that by the employee's current rate of $100/hour, you get a total of $200,000 per year. Twenty percent of $200,000 is $40,000, so the valid range after changing the pay type would be $160,000–$240,000 inclusive. The third UPDATE statement attempts to change the employee's pay rate to a salary of $300,000. This is outside the valid range, so the update is rejected. The final update also changes the pay type to salaried, but at a rate of $240,000 per year. This is within the 20 percent range, so the trigger allows the update.

Maintaining Data Integrity

Another common use for triggers is to assist in maintaining the integrity of the data stored in the database. Suppose that you wanted to store a count of the number of employees in each department and that you wanted to store this count in the department table. You would first add an employee count field to the department table. To do so, enter and execute the input shown in Listing 11.5.

**INPUT/
OUTPUT**
Listing 11.5. Adding an employee count field to the department table.

```
ALTER TABLE department
   ADD (no_of_emps     NUMBER(38));
Table altered.
```

ANALYSIS   The ALTER TABLE command in Listing 11.5 adds one numeric field to the department table, which will be used to contain a current count of employees assigned to each department.

The department table in the sample database should now look like this:

```
SQL> describe department
 Name                             Null?    Type
 -----------------------------    -------- ----
 DEPT_ID                          NOT NULL NUMBER(38)
 DEPT_NAME                                 VARCHAR2(32)
 NO_OF_EMPS                                NUMBER(38)
```

The no_of_emps field is used to keep track of the number of employees in any given department. Think of how this employee count could be maintained. One possible solution would be to have any program that adds an employee, deletes an employee, or changes an employee's department assignment to update this value appropriately. This would work as long as the programs always worked correctly, and as long you never forgot that the no_of_emps value needed to be maintained. Unfortunately, as you add programmers to a project and as the number of programs that need to maintain this value increases, the likelihood of a mistake also increases. Wouldn't it be nice if there were one central point where you could code the logic to maintain the employee count for a department? Well, there is a way. Placing the code to maintain the employee count into a trigger gives you a central point of control and has the added benefit of reducing the burden on the programmers, who no longer must worry about this issue at all.

Writing the code to deal with this issue is a bit more complicated than the previous example regarding changes to an employee's pay type. To maintain the employee counts, you will need to write an insert trigger, an update trigger, and a delete trigger. Table 11.3 shows what each trigger will need to do.

Table 11.3. Triggers needed to maintain employee counts.

Trigger Type	What the Trigger Should Accomplish
Insert	When an employee is added, this trigger needs to increment the count for the appropriate department.
Update	When an employee's department is changed, this trigger needs to decrement the count for the previous department and increment the count for the new department.
Delete	When an employee is deleted, this trigger needs to decrement the count for the appropriate department.

 NOTE

These triggers will all be implemented as after triggers because you are only interested in adjusting the counts after a successful change. You could implement them as before triggers, but if subsequent validation caused a transaction to be rolled back, the work the triggers had done would also need to be rolled back, resulting in extra work for the database engine.

Listing 11.6 shows the code to create the three triggers needed to maintain employee counts for each department.

Listing 11.6. Triggers to maintain departmental employee counts.

```
 1: CREATE OR REPLACE TRIGGER emp_dept_ins
 2:   AFTER INSERT ON emp_dept
 3:   FOR EACH ROW
 4: BEGIN
 5:   --Increment the employee count for the department
 6:   --referenced by the record just inserted.
 7:   UPDATE department
 8:     SET no_of_emps = NVL(no_of_emps,0)+1
 9:   WHERE dept_id = :NEW.dept_id;
10: END;
11: /
```

continues

Listing 11.6. continued

```
12: Trigger created.
13:  CREATE OR REPLACE TRIGGER emp_dept_del
14:    AFTER DELETE ON emp_dept
15:    FOR EACH ROW
16: BEGIN
17:    --Decrement the employee count for the department
18:    --referenced by the record just deleted.
19:    UPDATE department
20:      SET no_of_emps = no_of_emps-1
21:     WHERE dept_id = :OLD.dept_id;
22: END;
23: /
24: Trigger created.
25: CREATE OR REPLACE TRIGGER emp_dept_upd
26:    AFTER UPDATE OF dept_id ON emp_dept
27:    FOR EACH ROW
28: BEGIN
29:    --Increment the employee count for the employee's new department
30:    UPDATE department
31:      SET no_of_emps = NVL(no_of_emps,0)+1
32:     WHERE dept_id = :NEW.dept_id;
33:
34:    --Decrement the employee count for the employee's
35:    --previous department.
36:    UPDATE department
37:      SET no_of_emps = no_of_emps - 1
38:     WHERE dept_id = :OLD.dept_id;
39: END;
40: /
41: Trigger created.
```

ANALYSIS The DDL, or data definition language, statements shown in Listing 11.6 create three triggers on the emp_dept table: one for inserts, one for updates, and one for deletes. Each trigger is very simple and just increments and/or decrements the employee counter for the department(s) affected by the operation that fired the trigger.

Now that you have created the triggers, one more task remains to be done. The triggers *maintain* the employee count; they do not initialize it to the correct value. You must initialize the counts yourself, which can be easily done by issuing the SQL statement shown in Listing 11.7.

INPUT/OUTPUT ### Listing 11.7. Initializing the departmental employee counts.

```
1: UPDATE department
2:   SET no_of_emps = (SELECT COUNT(*)
3:                        FROM emp_dept
4:                       WHERE emp_dept.dept_id = department.dept_id);
5: 3 rows updated.
6: COMMIT;
7: Commit complete.
```

ANALYSIS

NEW TERM

This UPDATE statement contains no WHERE clause, so it modifies all records in the department table. The *correlated subquery* (a correlated subquery is one that depends on a value in the main query, in this case the dept_id value) in lines 2 through 4 retrieves the total number of employees assigned to each department. This value is then assigned to the no_of_emps field for that department's record.

Now that you have created the necessary triggers and initialized the counters, you might just want to issue some queries to test your code. Listing 11.8 shows some examples of employee records being inserted, updated, and deleted, and also shows the effect on the no_of_emps field for the affected departments.

INPUT/ OUTPUT
Listing 11.8. Testing the employee count triggers.

```
1: --Create some departments.
2: INSERT INTO department (dept_id, dept_name, no_of_emps)
3:    VALUES (101,'Building Maintenance',0);
4: 1 row created.
5: INSERT INTO department (dept_id, dept_name, no_of_emps)
6:    VALUES (102,'Fleet Repair',0);
7: 1 row created.
8: --Insert some employees.
9: INSERT INTO employee (emp_id, emp_name, pay_rate, pay_type)
10:     VALUES (102,'Herman T Jugglehead',250000,'S');
11: 1 row created.
12: INSERT INTO employee (emp_id, emp_name, pay_rate, pay_type)
13:     VALUES (103,'Albert Foxtrot',23,'H');
14: 1 row created.
15: INSERT INTO employee (emp_id, emp_name, pay_rate, pay_type)
16:     VALUES (104,'Moncton Dequinder',19.95,'S');
17: 1 row created.
18: --Now, assign each employee to a department and then look at the counts.
19: INSERT INTO emp_dept (emp_id, dept_id) VALUES (102,101);
20: 1 row created.
21: INSERT INTO emp_dept (emp_id, dept_id) VALUES (103,101);
22: 1 row created.
23: INSERT INTO emp_dept (emp_id, dept_id) VALUES (104,102);
24: 1 row created.
25: SELECT * FROM department WHERE dept_id in (101,102);
26: DEPT_ID DEPT_NAME                       NO_OF_EMPS
27: ------- ----------------------------- ----------
28:     102 FLEET REPAIR                           1
29:     101 BUILDING MAINTENANCE                   2
30: --Delete one employee's department assignment and look again at the counts.
31: DELETE FROM emp_dept
32:   WHERE emp_id = 103 and dept_id = 101;
33: 1 row deleted.
34: SELECT * FROM department WHERE dept_id in (101,102);
35: DEPT_ID DEPT_NAME                       NO_OF_EMPS
36: ------- ----------------------------- ----------
37:     102 FLEET REPAIR                           1
38:     101 BUILDING MAINTENANCE                   1
```

continues

11

Listing 11.8. continued

```
39: --Reassign the other employee and take one last look at the counts.
40: UPDATE emp_dept
41:    SET dept_id = 101
42:  WHERE emp_id = 104 and dept_id = 102;
43: 1 row updated.
44: SELECT * FROM department WHERE dept_id in (101,102);
45:  DEPT_ID DEPT_NAME                      NO_OF_EMPS
46: -------- ------------------------------ ----------
47:      102 FLEET REPAIR                            0
48:      101 BUILDING MAINTENANCE                    2
49: COMMIT;
50: Commit complete.
```

The advantages of this set of triggers are twofold. They give you a central point of control for maintaining the number of employees in a department, and they relieve you from having to program and test this logic several places in your application.

Enforcing Security

You can use triggers to enhance database security and provide you with a finer level of control over database access than can be achieved simply by granting object privileges to users. Restricting access to a table based on the time of day, or the day of the week, would be a good example of this. Looking at the employee table in the sample database, you might consider it to be worthy of some extra security because it contains the pay rate and pay type fields, which directly affect an employee's pay. Because it would be highly unusual to change someone's pay rate outside of normal business hours, you might decide to disallow it entirely. Listing 11.9 shows a trigger that will only allow changes to the employee table to occur during business hours, and then only on weekdays.

INPUT/OUTPUT **Listing 11.9. A trigger restricting updates.**

```
 1: --This trigger allows changes to employee records
 2: --only on Mondays through Fridays, and only during
 3: --the hours of 8:00am to 5:00pm.
 4: CREATE OR REPLACE TRIGGER only_during_business_hours
 5:   BEFORE INSERT OR UPDATE OR DELETE ON employee
 6: BEGIN
 7:    IF  TO_NUMBER(TO_CHAR(SYSDATE,'hh24')) < 8 --nothing before 8:00am
 8:        OR TO_NUMBER(TO_CHAR(SYSDATE,'hh24')) >= 5
           ➥--changes must be made BEFORE 5:00pm
 9: OR TO_CHAR(SYSDATE,'dy') in ('sun','sat') THEN --nothing on weekends
10:        RAISE_APPLICATION_ERROR (-20000,
           ➥'Employee changes only allowed during business hours.');
11: END IF;
12: END;
13: /
14: Trigger created.
```

ANALYSIS The trigger shown in Listing 11.9 has been created as a table-level trigger. It fires once at the beginning of an insert, update, or delete, not for each row affected by the query. Because this restriction is based only on the time and day, and not on any values in the employee record, it makes sense to implement it at the table level.

Listing 11.10 shows the effects of attempting an update on the employee table outside of normal business hours.

INPUT/OUTPUT ## Listing 11.10. Testing the business hours restriction.

```
 1: --Establish what time it is.
 2: SELECT TO_CHAR(SYSDATE,'hh24:mm') FROM dual;
 3: TO_CHAR(SYSDATE,'HH24:MM')
 4: ------------------------
 5: 21:06
 6: UPDATE employee SET pay_rate = 500000 WHERE emp_id = 103;
 7: *
 8: ERROR at line 1:
 9: ORA-20000: Employee changes only allowed during business hours.
10: ORA-06512: at "MY_READER.ONLY_DURING_BUSINESS_HOURS", line 5
11: ORA-04088: error during execution of trigger
➥ 'MY_READER.ONLY_DURING_BUSINESS_HOURS'
```

ANALYSIS Notice that because the current time was 21:06 (lines 1–5), or 9:06 p.m. in normal time, the trigger rejected the update and an error message was returned (lines 7–11).

When you try this yourself, you might want to adjust the beginning and ending times of your trigger so you don't have to wait until after 5:00 p.m. to see it fire.

TIP

> To make it easier to run the remaining examples in this chapter, you might want to disable the time-of-day trigger. Otherwise, you will be limited to running the examples only during the hours specified by the trigger, in other words from 8:00 a.m. to 5:00 p.m. Do this by executing the following command from SQL*Plus:
>
> ```
> ALTER TRIGGER only_during_business_hours DISABLE;
> ```
>
> You will read more about the ALTER TRIGGER command later in this chapter in the section titled "Managing Triggers."

Maintaining History

The last example concerning triggers will involve using them to maintain a historical log of changes to a record. It is a common need, when developing a system, to come up with a way to track changes of certain critical data elements over time. One way to do this is to create a table with the date as part of the primary key and then program all the applications to log changes to it. Listing 11.11 shows the DDL to create such a table to track changes to an employee's pay rate over time. Type in the input and create the table as it will be used in the example to follow.

INPUT/OUTPUT **Listing 11.11. The employee pay history table.**

```
 1: CREATE TABLE emp_pay_history
 2:   (emp_pay_history_pk    INTEGER,
 3:    emp_id       INTEGER,
 4:    as_of        DATE,
 5:    emp_name     VARCHAR2(32),
 6:    pay_type     CHAR(1),
 7:    pay_rate     NUMBER(9,2),
 8:    constraint emp_pay_history_pk
 9:       primary key (emp_pay_history_pk)
10:   );
11: Table created.
12: CREATE sequence emp_pay_history_key
13:    start with 1
14:    increment by 1
15:    nocycle;
16: Sequence created.
```

ANALYSIS The table created by the preceding listing resembles the employee table but has two added fields. One additional field, named as_of (line 4), is of type DATE and represents the date and time an employee's pay was changed. The other additional field, named emp_pay_history_pk (line 2), is used as the table's primary key. To ensure uniqueness and to ensure that you can always add to the log, this primary key is populated from an Oracle sequence (lines 12–15). To make querying and reporting easier, the employee's name will also be saved with each record (line 5).

NOTE

> The date/time field as_of is not used as part of the primary key because it might not always be unique. Oracle only resolves a date/time value down to the second, and it is possible to make two changes to a record within a one-second window.

As you might have already guessed, there is a downside to having the applications maintain this table. The code would need to be replicated in several places, resulting in several possible points of failure. Furthermore, if you weren't developing a new system from scratch, you might already have several applications written and in production. Changing these would be costly. The solution? You guessed it—write some triggers.

Listing 11.12 shows a trigger that will maintain a chronological salary history for employees in the sample database.

INPUT/OUTPUT **Listing 11.12. Trigger to maintain employee pay history.**

```
 1: CREATE OR REPLACE TRIGGER maintain_pay_history
 2:   AFTER INSERT OR UPDATE OR DELETE ON employee
 3:   FOR EACH ROW
 4:   WHEN ((new.pay_rate <> old.pay_rate)
 5:     OR  (new.pay_rate IS NULL AND old.pay_rate IS NOT NULL)
 6:     OR  (new.pay_rate IS NOT NULL AND old.pay_rate IS NULL)
 7:     OR  (new.pay_type <> old.pay_type)
 8:     OR  (new.pay_type IS NULL AND old.pay_type IS NOT NULL)
 9:     OR  (new.pay_type IS NOT NULL AND old.pay_type IS NULL)
10:     )
11: DECLARE
12:   log_sequence_num    INTEGER;
13: BEGIN
14:   --Get the next value from the sequence. This can only
15:   --be done by using a SELECT statement.
16:   SELECT emp_pay_history_key.NEXTVAL INTO log_sequence_num FROM dual;
17:
18:   --Log this change in the history table
19:   INSERT INTO emp_pay_history
20:     (emp_pay_history_pk, emp_id, as_of, emp_name, pay_type, pay_rate)
21:     VALUES (log_sequence_num
22:             ,NVL(:NEW.emp_id,:OLD.emp_id), SYSDATE
23:             ,NVL(:NEW.emp_name,:OLD.emp_name)
24:             ,:NEW.pay_type, :NEW.pay_rate);
25: END;
26: /
27: Trigger created.
```

ANALYSIS This one trigger fires for inserts, updates, and deletes (line 2). The WHEN condition (lines 4–10) ensures that the trigger only fires in response to changes in the pay rate or pay type. It is rather long because either of those fields could be null; remember the three-valued logic issues from Day 4, "Writing PL/SQL Expressions." Notice in lines 22 and 23 that the NVL function is used on the emp_id and emp_name fields, and that if the new versions of these are null, the old versions are used. This is to accommodate deletes, because in a trigger the new values of a deleted record are null. However, even when deleting, the new values for pay rate and pay type are always logged (line 24). The SELECT statement in line 16, against the table dual, is used to grab the next available sequence number for use as a primary key.

Listing 11.13 shows an employee record being inserted, the pay rate being updated, and the employee record then being deleted. The history table is shown before and after so that you can see the effect of the trigger.

INPUT/OUTPUT **Listing 11.13. Pay rate history example.**

```
 1: SELECT * FROM emp_pay_history;
 2: no rows selected
 3: INSERT INTO employee
 4:    (emp_id, emp_name, pay_rate, pay_type)
 5:    VALUES (301,'Jerome Finkbeiner',2000,'H');
 6: 1 row created.
 7: UPDATE employee
 8:    SET pay_rate = 4000000,
 9:        pay_type = 'S'
10:  WHERE emp_id = 301;
11: 1 row updated.
12: DELETE FROM employee
13:    WHERE emp_id = 301;
14: 1 row deleted.
15: COLUMN as_of FORMAT a20
16: COLUMN emp_name FORMAT a20
17: SELECT  emp_pay_history_pk,
18:         emp_id,
19:         TO_CHAR(as_of,'dd-Mon-yyyy hh:mm pm') as_of,
20:         emp_name,
21:         pay_type,
22:         pay_rate
23:   FROM  emp_pay_history;
24: EMP_PAY_HISTORY_PK EMP_ID AS_OF                 EMP_NAME             P PAY_RATE
25: ------------------ ------ -------------------- -------------------- - --------
26: 7                     301 18-Jun-1997 06:06 pm Jerome Finkbeiner    H     2000
27: 8                     301 18-Jun-1997 06:06 pm Jerome Finkbeiner    S  4000000
28: 9                     301 18-Jun-1997 06:06 pm Jerome Finkbeiner
```

ANALYSIS You can see from lines 1 and 2 that the history table is initially empty. A new employee is then inserted (lines 3–5), his pay rate is changed from hourly to salaried (lines 7–10), and finally the employee is deleted (lines 12–13). The SELECT statement in line 17 displays the history table again, and this time it does have some data. There is one history record for each change made to Jerome Finkbeiner's pay rate. The last history record contains a null rate and type to reflect the fact that the employee record was deleted.

Managing Triggers

If you write database triggers, you need to be able to do several things in terms of managing the code:

☐ List triggers that already exist

☐ View code for triggers that already exist

☐ Enable and disable your triggers

If you are fortunate enough to have one of the new "workbench" type tools, such as Sylvain Faust's SQL-Programmer, these tasks become very easy. For the purposes of this book, however, we the authors assume that you are using SQL*Plus. Even if you do use other tools, it is still handy to know how to perform these functions using only SQL*Plus because it is pretty much ubiquitous in the Oracle world.

Listing Triggers

There is no specific SQL*Plus command to list the triggers defined in an Oracle database. To see a list of defined triggers, you must select the information you want to see from the USER_TRIGGERS view, which is shown in Listing 11.14.

INPUT/OUTPUT

Listing 11.14. The USER_TRIGGERS system view.

```
 1: DESCRIBE USER_TRIGGERS
 2:  Name                            Null?     Type
 3:  ------------------------------- --------  ----
 4:  TRIGGER_NAME                    NOT NULL  VARCHAR2(30)
 5:  TRIGGER_TYPE                              VARCHAR2(16)
 6:  TRIGGERING_EVENT                          VARCHAR2(26)
 7:  TABLE_OWNER                     NOT NULL  VARCHAR2(30)
 8:  TABLE_NAME                      NOT NULL  VARCHAR2(30)
 9:  REFERENCING_NAMES                         VARCHAR2(87)
10:  WHEN_CLAUSE                               VARCHAR2(2000)
11:  STATUS                                    VARCHAR2(8)
12:  DESCRIPTION                               VARCHAR2(2000)
13:  TRIGGER_BODY                              LONG
```

ANALYSIS

USER_TRIGGERS is a system view maintained by Oracle, and it gives you access to all triggers you own. The data contained in each of the columns should be fairly obvious from the column name. The DESCRIPTION column deserves some special mention because it contains the trigger name, triggering event, trigger type, and the referencing clause in a more usable format than the other columns. I will use the DESCRIPTION column in the next section to reconstruct the SQL CREATE TRIGGER statement.

For example, to see a list of triggers defined on the employee table, issue the SQL SELECT statement shown in Listing 11.15.

INPUT/OUTPUT

Listing 11.15. Listing all defined triggers.

```
1: SELECT trigger_name, triggering_event, trigger_type
2: FROM USER_TRIGGERS
3: WHERE table_name = 'EMPLOYEE'
4: ORDER BY trigger_name;
5: TRIGGER_NAME                TRIGGERING_EVENT             TRIGGER_TYPE
6: --------------------------- ---------------------------- ----------------
7: emp_pay_type_chg            UPDATE                       BEFORE EACH ROW
8: maintain_pay_history        INSERT OR UPDATE OR DELETE   AFTER EACH ROW
9: only_during_business_hours  INSERT OR UPDATE OR DELETE   BEFORE STATEMENT
```

ANALYSIS   There are three triggers defined on the employee table. These are, of course, the three you created while reading this chapter.

Viewing Trigger Code

The PL/SQL code for a trigger is stored in the TRIGGER_BODY column of the USER_TRIGGERS view. To see the PL/SQL code for a trigger, you could just select the TRIGGER_BODY column for the trigger in which you are interested. Usually, though, it will be more meaningful to see the DDL statement used to create the trigger. The SQL*Plus code in Listing 11.16 will rebuild the CREATE TRIGGER statement for any trigger you specify.

INPUT   **Listing 11.16. Commands to extract a trigger definition.**

```
 1: SET ECHO off
 2: SET MAXDATA 50000
 3: SET LONG 50000
 4: SET LONGCHUNKSIZE 1000
 5: SET PAGESIZE 0
 6: SET HEADING off
 7: SET VERIFY off
 8: ACCEPT trigger_name CHAR PROMPT 'What trigger do you want to see? '
 9: ACCEPT file_name CHAR PROMPT 'Enter the output filename: '
10: SET TERMOUT off
11: SET FEEDBACK off
12: COLUMN when_clause FORMAT a60 WORD_WRAPPED
13: SPOOL &file_name
14: SELECT 'CREATE OR REPLACE TRIGGER ' || description
15:    FROM USER_TRIGGERS
16:   WHERE trigger_name = UPPER('&Trigger_Name');
17: SELECT 'WHEN (' || when_clause || ')'  when_clause
18:    FROM USER_TRIGGERS
19:   WHERE trigger_name = UPPER('&Trigger_Name')
20:     AND when_clause IS NOT NULL;
21: SELECT trigger_body
22:    FROM USER_TRIGGERS
23:   WHERE trigger_name = UPPER('&Trigger_Name');
24: SELECT '/' FROM dual;
25: SPOOL off
26: SET TERMOUT on
27: SET FEEDBACK on
28: SET VERIFY on
29: SET HEADING on
30: SET PAGESIZE 24
```

ANALYSIS   In line 1, you disable the echoing of lines, which have been read from a command file to the display. Line 2 sets the maximum row length for a SQL query to 50,000 bytes. In line 3, you set the maximum size of a LONG column to be also 50,000 bytes. Lines 2 and 3 effectively limit you to retrieving triggers in which the combined length of the body and trigger specification is less than or equal to 50,000 bytes. You then set the page size to zero in line 5 in order to disable page headings, and you turn column headings off in line 6.

You don't want to clutter your reconstructed trigger with either type of heading. Line 7 tells SQL*Plus not to display statements to the terminal after substitutions have been made.

The two ACCEPT statements in lines 8–9 allow you to type in the name of the trigger that you want to retrieve and the filename in which you want to store the retrieved code. The trigger code will be retrieved to the file that you specify. The terminal output is disabled in line 10 so that you don't see the code on the screen as well. Turning feedback off keeps SQL*Plus from displaying lines telling you how many records were retrieved (line 11).

Only two commands are left before the trigger definition is retrieved. Line 12 formats the column containing the WHEN clause so that it will be a maximum of 60 characters wide. If you leave this out, the entire WHEN clause will print as one long line because the original line breaks are not preserved by Oracle when the trigger is stored. This is in contrast to the trigger body, for which Oracle does preserve the original formatting.

In line 13, the SQL*Plus SPOOL command directs output to a file, and the SELECT statements in lines 14–24 retrieve the various parts of the trigger. You turn off the file output with the SPOOL off command in line 25. In the last few lines, you return some of the session parameters to their defaults so that you will see column headings, page headings, and so on in subsequent queries.

Of course, you don't want to actually type all the commands shown in Listing 11.16 into SQL*Plus each time you want to see a trigger definition. Instead, build a file containing these commands. Be sure to save it with the .SQL extension. You can then use the SQL*Plus @ command to execute the file whenever you like. Listing 11.17 shows this command file being used to extract the definition of the maintain_pay_history trigger.

Listing 11.17. Extracting the definition for the
INPUT/
OUTPUT maintain_pay_history **trigger.**

```
1: @c:\a\list1416
2: What trigger do you want to see? maintain_pay_history
3: Enter the output filename: c:\a\list1418.sql
```

ANALYSIS Line 1 shows the command to execute the command file. Line 2 shows the user being prompted for a trigger name, and line 3 shows the prompt for an output filename. In this example, the DDL to re-create the maintain_pay_history trigger will be put in the file named C:\A\LIST1418.SQL. Listing 11.18 shows the contents of this file.

Listing 11.18. The extracted maintain_pay_history **trigger**
INPUT/
OUTPUT **definition.**

```
1: CREATE OR REPLACE TRIGGER maintain_pay_history
2:   AFTER INSERT OR UPDATE OR DELETE ON employee
```

continues

Listing 11.18. continued

```
 3:    FOR EACH ROW
 4:
 5:
 6: WHEN ((NEW.pay_rate <> OLD.pay_rate)      OR   (NEW.pay_rate
 7: IS NULL AND OLD.pay_rate IS NOT NULL)     OR   (NEW.pay_rate
 8: IS NOT NULL AND OLD.pay_rate IS NULL)     OR   (NEW.pay_type
 9: <> OLD.pay_type)     OR  (NEW.pay_type IS NULL AND
10: OLD.pay_type IS NOT NULL)    OR  (NEW.pay_type IS NOT NULL
11: AND OLD.pay_type IS NULL)          )
12:
13: DECLARE
14:    log_sequence_num     INTEGER;
15: BEGIN
16:    --Get the next value from the sequence. This can only
17:    --be done by using a SELECT statement.
18:    SELECT emp_pay_history_key.NEXTVAL INTO log_sequence_num FROM dual;
19:    --Log this change in the history table
20:    INSERT INTO emp_pay_history
21:      (emp_pay_history_pk, emp_id, as_of, emp_name, pay_type, pay_rate)
22:      VALUES (log_sequence_num
23:              ,NVL(:NEW.emp_id,:OLD.emp_id), SYSDATE
24:              ,NVL(:NEW.emp_name,:OLD.emp_name)
25:              ,:NEW.pay_type, :NEW.pay_rate);
26: END;
27:
28:
29: /
30: Trigger created.
```

ANALYSIS The WHEN clause in lines 6–11 won't be formatted exactly as you originally entered it. This is because Oracle stores it in a VARCHAR2 column as one long string. There are also a few extra blank lines in the listing, but the bottom line is that the code can be used to re-create the trigger.

TIP Consider saving the DDL you use to create a trigger in a file, which you can later edit and reexecute. You will find this easier than extracting the trigger definition from the database each time you need to change it.

Enabling and Disabling Triggers

Triggers can be temporarily disabled without having to go through the trouble of deleting and then re-creating them. This can be useful if you need to do some special processing such as loading data. The ALTER TRIGGER command is used to enable and disable triggers.

SYNTAX

The Syntax for the ALTER TRIGGER Command

```
ALTER TRIGGER name {ENABLED | DISABLED};
```

In this syntax, *name* is the name of the trigger you want to disable or enable.

Consider the `only_during_business_hours` trigger, which you created and which restricts update operations on the employee table to normal business hours on weekdays. This trigger could cause a problem if you wanted to do payroll processing during the evening. With the ALTER TRIGGER command, you can disable the trigger, run the payroll, and then reenable the trigger again. Listing 11.19 shows an example of this command being used. This listing assumes that the current time is outside the normal business hour range and that the `only_during_business_hours` trigger is currently enabled.

INPUT/OUTPUT **Listing 11.19. Disabling a trigger.**

```
 1:  UPDATE employee
 2:    SET pay_rate = 40
 3:  WHERE emp_id = 100;
 4: UPDATE employee
 5:       *
 6: ERROR at line 1:
 7: ORA-20000: Employee changes only allowed during business hours.
 8: ORA-06512: at "MY_READER.ONLY_DURING_BUSINESS_HOURS", line 5
 9: ORA-04088: error during execution of trigger
➥ 'MY_READER.ONLY_DURING_BUSINESS_HOURS'
10: ALTER TRIGGER only_during_business_hours DISABLE;
11: Trigger altered.
12: UPDATE employee
13:    SET pay_rate = 40
14:  WHERE emp_id = 100;
15: 1 row updated.
16: ALTER TRIGGER only_during_business_hours ENABLE;
17: Trigger altered.
```

ANALYSIS The first update failed because it was executed after business hours. After disabling the trigger (line 10), it was possible to reexecute the update, this time successfully. The command in line 16 reenables the trigger.

Trigger Limitations

When writing code for triggers, there are a few limitations you have to keep in mind. Here is a list of some things you cannot do with a trigger:

☐ Query or modify a *mutating table*

☐ Execute data definition language statements

☐ Execute COMMIT, ROLLBACK, or SAVEPOINT statements

NEW TERM A *mutating table* is one that is in the process of being changed while the trigger is executing. For example, executing an UPDATE statement on a table makes that table a mutating table for the duration of the UPDATE statement. Any triggers fired as a result of the update are not allowed to query or modify the table being changed.

NEW TERM Data definition language statements, such as a CREATE TABLE statement, cannot be executed from within a trigger, nor can they be executed from within any function or procedure that is called by a trigger.

Triggers are also not allowed to execute any sort of transaction control statement such as COMMIT or ROLLBACK. If you think about it, this limitation makes a lot of sense. You would quickly lose control of your transactions, and possibly compromise the integrity of your database, if COMMITs and ROLLBACKs were sprinkled throughout various triggers.

Triggers and Mutating Tables

The problem of a trigger needing to query the table that is being changed by the triggering statement is one that sooner or later vexes every trigger writer. Oracle does not allow row triggers to query the table being modified. Doing so gives rise to an error message that looks like this:

```
ORA-04091: table MY_READER.EMP_DEPT is mutating,
➥trigger/function may not see it
ORA-06512: at "MY_READER.ONLY_TWO_DEPARTMENTS", line 6
ORA-04088: error during execution of trigger
➥'MY_READER.ONLY_TWO_DEPARTMENTS'
```

Oracle refers to the table being changed as a *mutating table*.

Take a closer look at this issue. Suppose that you wanted to limit employees in the sample database to a maximum of two departments. The data model actually supports an infinite number of departments per employee; thus it is necessary to check each time you modify the emp_dept table to be sure that the two-department limit has not been exceeded. To do this, you might first think to write a trigger similar to the one shown in Listing 11.20.

INPUT/OUTPUT **Listing 11.20. A trigger to enforce the two-department limit.**

```
1: CREATE OR REPLACE TRIGGER only_two_departments
2:   BEFORE UPDATE OR INSERT ON emp_dept
3:   FOR EACH ROW
4: DECLARE
5:   dept_count   INTEGER;       --# of depts for this employee
6:   max_depts    INTEGER := 2; --max number of depts per employee.
7: BEGIN
8:   --Get the current number of departments for this employee.
9:   SELECT COUNT(*) INTO dept_count
10:     FROM emp_dept
11:    WHERE emp_id = :NEW.emp_id;
12:
```

```
13:    --On an update, when the old and new emp_id values are the same,
14:    --we do not need to recheck the count.
15:    IF :OLD.emp_id = :NEW.emp_id THEN
16:      RETURN;
17:    ELSE
18:      --if the employee already is at the max, don't allow him to
19:      --have another department.
20:      IF dept_count >= max_depts THEN
21:        RAISE_APPLICATION_ERROR (-20000,
➥'Employees are limited to a max of two departments.');
22: END IF;
23:    END IF;
24: END;
25: /
26: Trigger created.
```

ANALYSIS This trigger fires for each new record inserted into the emp_dept table, and it also fires for each updated record in the same table. In either case it checks to see if the employee in question already has been assigned to the maximum of two departments, and rejects any insert or update if that is the case. There is some special logic in lines 15 and 16 to account for the case where a department assignment is changed, but the employee ID is not changed.

The trigger shown in Listing 11.20 will almost work, but it will fail in certain cases. Listing 11.21 shows how the only_two_departments trigger functions when you insert and update data.

INPUT/OUTPUT **Listing 11.21. Testing the only_two_departments trigger.**

```
1: INSERT INTO employee
2:   (emp_id,emp_name) VALUES (401,'Harvey Wallbanger');
3: 1 row created.
4: INSERT INTO employee
5:   (emp_id,emp_name) VALUES (402,'Scarlet Tanninger');
6: 1 row created.
7: INSERT INTO department
8:   (dept_id, dept_name) VALUES (401,'Fermentation');
9: 1 row created.
10: INSERT INTO department
11:   (dept_id, dept_name) VALUES (402,'Distillation');
12: 1 row created.
13: INSERT INTO department
14:   (dept_id, dept_name) VALUES (403,'Bottling');
15: 1 row created.
16: INSERT INTO emp_dept
17:   (emp_id, dept_id) VALUES (401,401);
18: 1 row created.
19: INSERT INTO emp_dept
20:   (emp_id, dept_id) VALUES (401,402);
21: 1 row created.
```

continues

Listing 11.21. continued

```
22: INSERT INTO emp_dept
23:   (emp_id, dept_id) VALUES (402,402);
24: 1 row created.
25: INSERT INTO emp_dept
26:   (emp_id, dept_id) VALUES (402,403);
27: 1 row created.
28: INSERT INTO emp_dept
29:   (emp_id, dept_id) VALUES (401,403);
30: INSERT INTO emp_dept
31:             *
32: ERROR at line 1:
33: ORA-20000: Employees are limited to a max of two departments.
34: ORA-06512: at "MY_READER.ONLY_TWO_DEPARTMENTS", line 17
35: ORA-04088: error during execution of trigger
➥'MY_READER.ONLY_TWO_DEPARTMENTS'
36: UPDATE emp_dept
37:   SET dept_id = 403
38:   WHERE emp_id = 401 AND dept_id = 402;
39: UPDATE emp_dept
40:           *
41: ERROR at line 1:
42: ORA-04091: table MY_READER.EMP_DEPT is mutating,
➥trigger/function may not see it
43: ORA-06512: at "MY_READER.ONLY_TWO_DEPARTMENTS", line 6
44: ORA-04088: error during execution of trigger
➥'MY_READER.ONLY_TWO_DEPARTMENTS'
```

ANALYSIS The first five inserts in Listing 11.21 just set up some employee and department records for you to experiment with. The next four inserts assign each employee to two departments. So far, so good. However, the tenth INSERT statement (lines 28–29) attempts to assign employee number 401 to a third department. You can see that the trigger caught this and raised an error (lines 30–35), causing the insert to fail. The last statement (lines 36–38) is an update, and it gives rise to the "mutating" error (lines 39–44) because the trigger is querying the table being changed.

As you can see, this trigger will not serve the purpose of limiting each employee to a maximum of two departments. At this point, there are three options you can use to enforce this rule without redesigning the database:

- ☐ Enforce the rule in the application code.
- ☐ Take a different approach to the problem.
- ☐ Use a combination of table-level and row-level triggers, combined with a package, to enforce the rule at the database level.

Enforcing the rule at the application level is possible but requires that the code to enforce the rule be replicated in each program that updates the emp_dept table. Sometimes you can take an entirely different approach to the problem. For example, in this case you could choose not to allow updates to the emp_dept table at all. Any changes to an employee's department assignment would then be done by first deleting the old record and then inserting a new one. The third, and most complicated, approach is to code the validation in a table-level trigger while using a row-level trigger to build a list of newly inserted or modified records. This solution takes advantage of the fact that variables in an Oracle stored package persist throughout a database session. To implement this approach, you will need to write

☐ A table-level before trigger on emp_dept to initialize the list of records being inserted/updated.

☐ A row-level trigger on emp_dept to add the primary key of each new or updated record to the list.

☐ A table-level after trigger on emp_dept to loop through the list and check to be sure that none of the updates or inserts violates the maximum of two departments per employee.

☐ A package implementing procedures to add to the list, initialize the list, and retrieve from the list, and which will also contain the list itself.

Why will the approach just described work? It works because a row-level trigger cannot query a mutating table, but a table-level trigger can. By the time the table-level after trigger fires, all the changes have been made and the table is in a consistent state.

Listing 11.22 shows the emp_dept_procs package, which will be part of the solution to enforce the two-department rule. Listing 11.23 shows the DDL to create the triggers that will enforce this rule. Notice that the triggers in Listing 11.23 each call procedures that are part of the emp_dept_procs package, and that emp_dept_procs contains package-level variables that are used to maintain a list of records that have been inserted or modified.

INPUT/OUTPUT **Listing 11.22. The emp_dept_procs package.**

```
 1: CREATE OR REPLACE package emp_dept_procs AS
 2:   PROCEDURE init_list;
 3:   PROCEDURE add_to_list (emp_id IN emp_dept.emp_id%TYPE
 4:                         ,dept_id IN emp_dept.dept_id%TYPE);
 5:   FUNCTION get_count RETURN NUMBER;
 6:   PROCEDURE get_from_list (to_get IN BINARY_INTEGER
 7:                           ,emp_id OUT emp_dept.emp_id%TYPE
 8:                           ,dept_id OUT emp_dept.dept_id%TYPE);
 9: END emp_dept_procs;
10: /
11: Package created.
12: CREATE OR REPLACE package body emp_dept_procs AS
13:   --These variables persist throughout a session.
14:   listx  BINARY_INTEGER;  --current max index into the list.
15:
```

continues

Listing 11.22. continued

```
16:    --Declare a record containing the table's primary key.
17:    TYPE emp_dept_pk IS RECORD (
18:      emp_id  emp_dept.emp_id%TYPE,
19:      dept_id emp_dept.dept_id%TYPE);
20:
21:    --This defines a pl/sql table which will store a list of all records
22:    --"touched" by an insert or update statement.
23:    TYPE emp_dept_list_type IS TABLE OF emp_dept_pk
24:      INDEX BY BINARY_INTEGER;
25:
26:    --Declare the actual table which will contain our list.
27:    emp_dept_list  emp_dept_list_type;
28:
29: PROCEDURE init_list is
30: BEGIN
31:    --Initialize the list pointer to zero.
32:    listx := 0;
33: END;
34:
35: PROCEDURE add_to_list (emp_id IN emp_dept.emp_id%TYPE
36:                        ,dept_id IN emp_dept.dept_id%TYPE) IS
37: BEGIN
38:    --increment the list index and save the primary key values.
39:    listx := listx + 1;
40:    emp_dept_list(listx).emp_id := emp_id;
41:    emp_dept_list(listx).dept_id := dept_id;
42: END;
43:
44: FUNCTION get_count RETURN NUMBER IS
45: BEGIN
46:    --return the number of entries in the list.
47:    RETURN listx;
48: END;
49:
50: PROCEDURE get_from_list (to_get IN BINARY_INTEGER
51:                          ,emp_id OUT emp_dept.emp_id%TYPE
52:                          ,dept_id OUT emp_dept.dept_id%TYPE) IS
53: BEGIN
54:    emp_id := emp_dept_list(to_get).emp_id;
55:    dept_id := emp_dept_list(to_get).dept_id;
56: END;
57:
58: END emp_dept_procs;
59: /
60: Package body created.
```

ANALYSIS Lines 1–10 create the package header, which defines the procedures and functions from this package that are available to external objects, such as a trigger. Lines 17–19 define a record containing the primary key fields for the emp_dept table. This record in turn is used to define a PL/SQL table type (lines 23–24). Finally, in line 27, a PL/SQL table is declared. This is the table that will hold the list of records inserted or updated and that must be validated by the table-level after trigger.

INPUT/OUTPUT **Listing 11.23. Triggers to enforce the two-department limit.**

```
 1: DROP TRIGGER only_two_departments;
 2: Trigger dropped.
 3: CREATE OR REPLACE TRIGGER only_two_departments_1
 4:   BEFORE UPDATE OR INSERT ON emp_dept
 5: BEGIN
 6:   --Reset the list counter before starting any insert/update.
 7:   emp_dept_procs.init_list;
 8: END;
 9: /
10: Trigger created.
11: CREATE OR REPLACE TRIGGER only_two_departments_2
12:   BEFORE UPDATE OR INSERT ON emp_dept
13:   FOR EACH ROW
14: BEGIN
15:   --Add this record to the list of those changed.
16:   --Validation is done after the STATEMENT is finished.
17:   emp_dept_procs.add_to_list(:NEW.emp_id, :NEW.dept_id);
18: END;
19: /
20: Trigger created.
21: CREATE OR REPLACE TRIGGER only_two_departments_3
22:   AFTER UPDATE OR INSERT ON emp_dept
23: DECLARE
24:   check_emp_id     emp_dept.emp_id%TYPE;
25:   check_dept_id    emp_dept.dept_id%TYPE;
26:
27:   listx     BINARY_INTEGER;
28:   list_max  BINARY_INTEGER;
29:
30:   dept_count  NUMBER;
31: BEGIN
32:   --Get the number of records we "touched".
33:   list_max := emp_dept_procs.get_count;
34:
35:   --We need to check each record to see if we have
36:   --violated the "only two departments" rule.
37:   FOR listx IN 1..list_max loop
38:     --Get the primary key for the record we are checking.
39:     emp_dept_procs.get_from_list (listx, check_emp_id, check_dept_id);
40:
41:     --Get the number of departments for this employee.
42:     SELECT COUNT(*) INTO dept_count
43:       FROM emp_dept
44:      WHERE emp_id = check_emp_id;
45:
46:     --Does the employee in question have more than two departments?
47:     IF dept_count > 2 THEN
48:       RAISE_APPLICATION_ERROR(-20000,
         ➥'Employees are limited to a max of two departments.');
49: END IF;
50:   END LOOP;
51: END;
52: /
53: Trigger created.
```

11

ANALYSIS   Notice in line 1 that the previous trigger is dropped. Be sure to do this. The table-level before trigger in lines 3–9 is fired at the beginning of an INSERT or UPDATE statement. It calls a package procedure that initializes the list counter. The row-level trigger, named only_two_departments_2 (defined in lines 11–19), is fired for each row added or changed. This trigger adds the primary key of each record to the list maintained in the package-level PL/SQL table. The third trigger, defined in lines 21–52, is the one that does the actual validation work. It is fired after the INSERT or UPDATE statement is complete. It loops through each new or changed record and checks to be sure that each employee in question has a maximum of two department assignments.

Now that you have created these triggers and the emp_dept_procs package, you can execute the SQL statements shown in Listing 11.24 in order to demonstrate that it works.

**INPUT/
OUTPUT**

Listing 11.24. Testing the triggers and package that enforce the two-department rule.

```
1: INSERT INTO employee
2:    (emp_id,emp_name) VALUES (403,'Freddie Fisher');
3: 1 row created.
4: INSERT INTO employee
5:    (emp_id,emp_name) VALUES (404,'Charlie Tuna');
6: 1 row created.
7: INSERT INTO department
8:    (dept_id, dept_name) VALUES (404,'Scale Processing');
9: 1 row created.
10: INSERT INTO department
11:    (dept_id, dept_name) VALUES (405,'Gutting');
12: 1 row created.
13: INSERT INTO department
14:    (dept_id, dept_name) VALUES (406,'Unloading');
15: 1 row created.
16: INSERT INTO emp_dept
17:    (emp_id, dept_id) VALUES (403,404);
18: 1 row created.
19: INSERT INTO emp_dept
20:    (emp_id, dept_id) VALUES (403,405);
21: 1 row created.
22: INSERT INTO emp_dept
23:    (emp_id, dept_id) VALUES (404,405);
24: 1 row created.
25: INSERT INTO emp_dept
26:    (emp_id, dept_id) VALUES (404,406);
27: 1 row created.
28: INSERT INTO emp_dept
29:    (emp_id, dept_id) VALUES (403,406);
30: INSERT INTO emp_dept
31: *
32: ERROR at line 1:
33: ORA-20000: Employees are limited to a max of two departments.
34: ORA-06512: at "MY_READER.ONLY_TWO_DEPARTMENTS_3", line 21
35: ORA-04088: error during execution of trigger
➥'MY_READER.ONLY_TWO_DEPARTMENTS_3'
```

```
36: UPDATE emp_dept
37:   SET dept_id = 406
38:  WHERE emp_id = 403 AND dept_id = 405;
39: 1 row updated.
40: UPDATE emp_dept
41:    SET emp_id = 403
42:  WHERE emp_id = 404
43:    AND dept_id = 405;
44: UPDATE emp_dept
45:          *
46: ERROR at line 1:
47: ORA-20000: Employees are limited to a max of two departments.
48: ORA-06512: at "MY_READER.ONLY_TWO_DEPARTMENTS_3", line 21
49: ORA-04088: error during execution of trigger
➥ 'MY_READER.ONLY_TWO_DEPARTMENTS_3'
```

ANALYSIS The first five inserts (lines 1–15) put some sample employees and departments in place for testing purposes. The next four inserts (lines 16–27) assign each of the two employees just inserted to two departments. The tenth insert (lines 28–29) attempts to assign employee number 403 to a third department. This violates the two-department rule, causing the insert to fail (lines 30–35). There are two UPDATE statements. The first update (lines 36–38) is allowed because it only changes a department assignment for employee number 403. That employee still has exactly two departments. The second update (lines 40–43) fails because it is changing the emp_id field in a record from 404 to 403, resulting in 403 having more than two department assignments.

WARNING

> The solution shown in Listings 14.22 and 14.23 will work when triggers only need to query the mutating table. The problem gets more complex if you need to update those rows. Updating records in the mutating table from a trigger will fire off the very same set of triggers that will also try to use the very same package-level PL/SQL table to build a list of affected records, thus clobbering the data needed to validate the initial update.

Summary

This chapter has been complex, but it gave you the chance to see and experiment with triggers implementing several different types of functionality. To reiterate, some possible uses for triggers are to enforce business rules (Listing 11.3), generate column values (Listing 11.6), enhance security (Listing 11.9), and maintain a historical record (Listing 11.12). These are just the tip of the iceberg. The possibilities are limited only by your creativity and imagination. You have also learned about the mutating table error, the bane of many trigger writers, and should now have a good understanding of how to work around it.

Q&A

Q **If I am using a trigger to enforce a business rule or a referential integrity rule, does this do anything about the records that predate creation of the trigger?**

A No, it doesn't, and that's a good point to keep in mind. When you create a declarative constraint, you are really making a statement about the data that must always be true. You cannot create a constraint if data is present that violates that constraint. Triggers, on the other hand, affect only records that have been inserted, updated, or deleted after the trigger was created. For example, creating the triggers limiting an employee to only two-department assignments will do nothing about preexisting cases where an employee has more than two assignments.

Q **The inserts in Listing 11.21 (lines 16–27) did not generate a mutating table error message, yet they did query the table. Why is this?**

A Single-row inserts are an exception to the rule about querying the underlying table. However, if the insert is one that could possibly create more than one row, for example an `INSERT INTO emp_dept SELECT...`, the rule about not querying the mutating table still applies.

Q **What's the difference between a statement-level trigger and a row-level trigger?**

A A statement-level trigger is executed only once, either before or after the triggering SQL statement executes. It cannot refer to any values in the rows affected by the statement. A row-level trigger fires once for each row affected by the triggering SQL statement, and can reference the values for each of the rows.

Q **Why should I generally validate business rules in a before trigger rather than an after trigger?**

A It's potentially more efficient because you can prevent Oracle from doing the work involved in inserting, updating, or deleting a record. By validating in an after trigger, you are allowing Oracle to first update the table in question, update any indexes that might be affected by the change, and possibly fire off other triggers.

Q **The triggers in Listing 11.6 maintain employee counts for each department as records are inserted into, updated in, and deleted from the emp_dept table. What happens, however, if a department record is deleted and then reinserted? Won't the employee count be reset to zero in that case, making it incorrect?**

A Yes, this is absolutely true. Typically, in a production database, you would also have referential integrity constraints defined to prevent deletion of department records referenced by other tables.

Workshop

Use the following sections to test your comprehension of this chapter and put what you've learned into practice. You'll find the answers to the quiz and exercises in Appendix A, "Answers."

Quiz

1. Which data manipulation statements can support triggers?

2. What are the four basic parts of a trigger definition?

3. In a trigger, what are the correlation names :OLD and :NEW used for?

4. What is the name of the system view that can be used to retrieve trigger definitions?

5. What is a mutating table?

6. Name some possible uses for triggers.

Exercises

1. Write a set of triggers to maintain the emp_name and dept_name fields redundantly in the emp_dept relation, so that you do not have to join with the employee and department tables just to get a simple department listing.

2. Write the SQL statements necessary to populate the emp_name and dept_name fields for any existing emp_dept records.

11

Day 12

Using Cursors for Complex Processing

by Tom Luers

Today's lesson discusses using parameters to pass information into a cursor as well as using cursors as variables to other PL/SQL constructs such as procedures and functions. Using parameters to pass information provides the flexibility to reuse and modularize your cursor routines. This chapter covers using parameters with cursors as well as several other more advanced cursor topics.

Passing Parameters to Cursors

In PL/SQL, you can pass parameters into cursors just as you would for functions and procedures. For example, you can establish the value of a parameter depending on your logic and then pass this parameter into the cursor for processing. Cursors cannot pass parameters out of the cursors. These parameters allow your code to become more modular and maintainable. This lends itself to increased usability because you no longer have to hard-code values in the query statement.

Declaring Cursor Parameters

To declare cursor parameters, place the parameters in the cursor definition statement enclosed in parentheses. In Oracle, you can use as many parameters as you need.

The Syntax for Declaring a Cursor

```
CURSOR name (parameter_1 datatype, parameter_2 datatype...)
IS SELECT statement...
```

In this syntax, *name* is the name you assign to the cursor. *parameter_1* and *parameter_2* are the parameters that are passed into the cursor. The *datatypes* correspond to the parameters. Finally, SELECT *statement* is the statement that defines the cursor contents.

The following is an example of a cursor that is to receive two parameters. One of the parameters is used in the SELECT statement:

```
DECLARE
CURSOR emp_cur
(emp_nbr  number,  emp_name varchar2(32))
IS SELECT pay_rate FROM employee WHERE emp_id = emp_nbr;
                              -- parameter is used here
```

You can also initialize cursor parameters in the declaration statement. This is a very convenient method to pass default values to the cursor. Likewise, you can override these default values with different, explicitly defined values. The following example passes two different parameters to the cursor in a stock-purchasing scenario:

```
DECLARE
CURSOR stock_cur
(buy_price     number  default 23.50,
sell_price     number  default 38.33) IS SELECT ...
```

Using the preceding declaration, you can pass actual values to the two parameters in the OPEN cursor statement, thereby overriding the specified default values. The following example will cause the cursor to be declared with a buy_price of $24.25 and a sell_price of $44.67:

```
OPEN stock_cur (24.25, 44.67);
```

If you pass no values to the cursor in the OPEN statement, the default values take effect. Hence, the following two OPEN statements are equivalent:

```
OPEN stock_cur;
```

```
OPEN stock_cur (23.50,38.33);
```

Using Cursor Parameters

Carrying the stock-purchasing cursor example further, suppose that you want to see all the stocks that are in a particular category of stocks. Also, your desired category will change from time to time. The following declaration of the cursor would be helpful:

```
DECLARE
CURSOR stock_listing_cur  (stock_category  varchar2)  IS
SELECT stock_name, current_price from stocks
WHERE category = stock_category;

stock record  stock_listing_cur%rowtype;
```

This example allows you to specify any category of stock. You can use this cursor as shown in the next example. In an example like this, you can set the value of stock_type by using a substitution variable, Oracle Forms field, or other means:

```
DECLARE
CURSOR stock_listing_cur  (stock_category  varchar2)  IS
SELECT stock_name, current_price from stocks
WHERE category = stock_category;

stock record  stock_listing_cur%rowtype;

BEGIN
OPEN stock_listing_cur (:stock_type);     --use a bind variable set earlier
```

Scope of Cursor Parameters

Cursor parameters are visible only to that cursor. You cannot reference a cursor parameter outside the context of the cursor. If you try to refer to a cursor parameter outside the cursor, Oracle will return an error indicating that the variable is undefined.

Cursor Return Clause and Packages

As you learned on Day 9, "Using SQL: INSERT, SELECT, Advanced Declarations, and Tables," you can declare and use cursors inside packages. Oracle does allow you to place the cursor declaration in the package specification and the cursor body in the package body. This separation of declaration and body provides the developer some level of design and programming flexibility. The programmer can alter the cursor body without having to alter the specification. Or better yet, the programmer only needs to know what the cursor returns and not how it is accomplished. The following example illustrates the separation of the cursor body from its declaration.

The package specification is

```
CREATE PACKAGE  stock_purchase as
CURSOR stock_cur RETURN stock%rowtype;
END stock_purchase;
```

12

The package body is

```
CREATE PACKAGE BODY stock_purchase as
CURSOR stock_cur return stock%rowtype
SELECT stock_type, stock_name, curr_prics
FROM stocks
WHERE stock_type = :stock_type;
```

Note that in the preceding example, the return clause is used. The return clause is mandatory when you elect to separate the cursor components. This clause creates the bridge between the two just as if they appear together in a typical cursor construct.

Cursor Variables

As you recall from the previous chapter, the PL/SQL cursor is a named area in the database. The cursor variable, by definition, is a reference to that named area. A cursor variable is like a pointer that you would use in a programming language such as C. Cursor variables point to a query's work area in which the query's result set is stored. A cursor variable is also dynamic in nature because it is not tied to a specific query. Oracle retains this work area as long as a cursor pointer is pointing to it. You can use a cursor variable for any type-compatible query.

One of the most significant features of the cursor variable is that Oracle allows you to pass a cursor variable as an argument to a procedure or function call. The cursor variable cannot accept variables to itself.

Cursor variables can also be declared using programs such as Pro*C or OCI. After the cursor variable is declared there, you can pass it as a bind variable to your PL/SQL block. Likewise, these variables can be declared in other Oracle products such as Forms. Additionally, you can pass cursor variables back and forth between servers and applications through Oracle's remote procedure calls.

The Cursor Variable Declaration

To create a cursor variable, you must first create a referenced cursor type and then declare a cursor variable on that type.

The Syntax for Creating the Cursor Type

```
TYPE cursor_type_name IS REF CURSOR RETURN return_type;
```

In this syntax, REF stands for reference, cursor_type_name is the name of the type of cursor, and return_type is the data specification for the return cursor type. The return clause is optional.

Oracle makes a subtle distinction in cursor variables based upon whether or not a return clause is included in the cursor variable. If the return clause is present, then the cursor variable is known as a strong cursor variable. If the return clause is not present, the cursor variable is a weak cursor variable. Do not confuse the RETURN statement with the return clause, which specifies the datatype of the result value in a stored program.

12

The following example illustrates this declaration:

```
DECLARE
TYPE stocks_cur_type IS REF CURSOR RETURN stocks%rowtype;
                        -- strong cursor type creation
TYPE stocks_cur_price IS REF CURSOR;
                            -- weak cursor type creation

stocks_cur  stocks_cur_type;
      -- creation of cursor variable based on cursor type

BEGIN
...
END;
```

Remember, the cursor variable declaration does not create a cursor object, but rather a pointer to a cursor object. As such, you cannot substitute a cursor variable where a proper cursor is expected and required.

Cursor Usage with Cursor Variables

After the cursor variable is declared, you can use the variable in three different statements: OPEN...FOR, FETCH, and CLOSE. You can assign a value to it through the OPEN...FOR cursor statement.

The Syntax for the OPEN...FOR Cursor Statement

SYNTAX

```
OPEN cursor_name FOR select_statement
```

In this syntax, *cursor_name* is the name for the cursor, the cursor variable, or the host cursor variable, and *select_statement* is the appropriate SQL statement. This statement cannot use the FOR UPDATE clause.

The OPEN...FOR statement executes the multirow query associated with the declared cursor variable. The OPEN...FOR statement also identifies the result set, which consists of all rows that meet the query search criteria. Other OPEN...FOR statements can open the same cursor variable for different queries as needed. The following is an example of opening a cursor variable that is a bind variable:

```
BEGIN
OPEN :stocks_quote FOR SELECT * FROM stocks;
END;
```

After the cursor is opened, you can perform a typical FETCH using the cursor variable. The syntax for the FETCH statement using a cursor variable is the same as for a normal static cursor.

The Syntax for the FETCH Statement Using a Cursor Variable

SYNTAX

```
FETCH cursor_variable_name INTO record_name or variable_name
```

In this syntax, *cursor_variable_name* is the variable you declared in the local block, package specification, or host environment such as Pro*C, and *record_name* or *variable_name* is the object where the FETCH will place the data from the cursor.

12

PL/SQL will make sure the return type of the cursor variable is compatible with the INTO clause of the FETCH statement. For each column value returned by the query associated with the cursor variable, there must be a corresponding variable in the INTO clause. Also, the number of fields or variables must equal the number of column values.

The following example pulls together the concepts of declaring, opening, and fetching cursors:

```
DECLARE
TYPE stocks_cur_type IS REF cursor RETURN stocks%rowtype
stocks_cur    stocks_cur_type;

BEGIN
OPEN stocks_cur for
SELECT stock_name, stock_type, stock_quote from stocks;
FETCH stocks_cur INTO stocks_rec;
END;
```

After you are finished using the cursor variable in your logic, you need to close the variable. The syntax follows your normal cursor syntax as illustrated in the following:

```
CLOSE stocks_cur;
```

The following example illustrates the use of different INTO clauses on different fetches that happen to use the same cursor variable. Each of the fetches retrieves another row from the same result set:

```
BEGIN
...
FETCH stock_quote_cur INTO stock_rec1;
...
FETCH stock_quote_cur INTO stock_rec2:
...
END;
```

Cursor Variable Assignments

The cursor variable can be included in any assignment statement.

The Syntax for Cursor Variable Assignments

SYNTAX

assignment statement := cursor variable name

In this syntax, *cursor variable name* is a PL/SQL cursor variable that has been previously defined and is in the scope of the assignment statement. This can also be a host cursor variable name. The host cursor variable name is declared in a PL/SQL host environment such as Pro*C. This variable is passed into the assignment statement as a bind variable.

An example of the assignment statement using a cursor variable (bind variable) is

```
current_stock_price := :host_cur_stock_quote;
```

12

Cursor Variables as Arguments

As mentioned earlier, Oracle allows you to pass Oracle cursor variables as arguments to procedures and functions. When your parameter list contains a cursor variable, the mode of the parameter and the datatype must be specified. The datatype for the cursor variable used as an argument will be the REF cursor type.

The following example illustrates the use of the REF cursor syntax and the use of a cursor variable as a parameter:

```
DECLARE
TYPE cur_var_type IS REF CURSOR RETURN employee%rowtype;

PROCEDURE SELECT emp_query (cur_var_out  out cur_var_type) IS
BEGIN
...
END;
```

This example works well in local modules with a program. However, if you are creating a standalone procedure or function, then you must reference a pre-existing REF cursor type that exists in a package specification. As you recall from Day 8, "Procedures, Packages, Errors, and Exceptions," all variables declared in a package specification are global to the package body. Hence you can reference a cursor type using the standard package dot notation.

To use a cursor variable in a package, you must first declare the REF cursor type in the specification, as illustrated in the next example:

```
PACKAGE stocks
IS
TYPE cur_var_type IS REF CURSOR RETURN stocks%rowtype;
END package;
```

To use the cursor variable declared in the preceding example, simply reference the REF cursor type using the dot notation as shown following:

```
PROCEDURE obtain_stock_quotes (cur_var_out in stocks.cur_var_type) IS
BEGIN
...
END;
```

You can use the preceding notation for any of the function and procedure calls within that package.

The cursor variable is a true variable and global in nature to the package or local module. It does not reflect the state of the object but rather is the reference to the cursor object. To change the value of a cursor variable, you must change the cursor object to which the variable points.

The cursor variable argument can have one of three different modes. These modes are

- ☐ IN—The program can have read-only abilities with the parameter. In other words, the cursor argument is passed only to the procedure or function.

12

☐ OUT—The program can return values to the calling PL/SQL block.

☐ IN OUT—The program can read or write to the variable.

When you declare a cursor variable as a parameter of a procedure or function that fetches from the cursor variable, you must specify the IN or IN OUT mode. Likewise, if the procedure or function also opens the cursor variable, you must specify the IN OUT mode. Finally, the IN OUT mode must be used when you want the procedure or function to pass an open cursor back to the calling program.

The Current Row of Parameter and Cursors

The current row of a cursor always refers to the latest row retrieved by the FETCH statement. Oracle allows you to delete and update this current row. In order to delete or update the fetched row, the cursor must be declared using the FOR UPDATE clause and must be open. The following example illustrates the update of the current row for the employee cursor:

```
DECLARE
CURSOR emp_cur IS                            -- cursor declared for update
SELECT emp_name, pay_type, pay_rate
FROM employee
WHERE pay_rate > 5000.00
FOR UPDATE of pay_type;                          -- FOR UPDATE clause

emp_rec  emp_cur%rowtype;

BEGIN
OPEN emp_cur;                                    -- cursor is opened

LOOP
FETCH emp_cur INTO emp_rec;
UPDATE employee                                  -- updates current row
SET pay_type = 'H'
WHERE CURRENT OF emp_cur;
EXIT WHEN emp_cur%notfound;
END LOOP;
END;
```

Cursor Scoping

The scope of a cursor variable follows these rules:

☐ The cursor variable is available to the local module in which it is declared.

☐ The cursor variable is global in nature when declared in a package.

☐ The cursor variable can exist outside its original scope, as shown in Figure 12.1.

Figure 12.1.
Cursor variable scope.

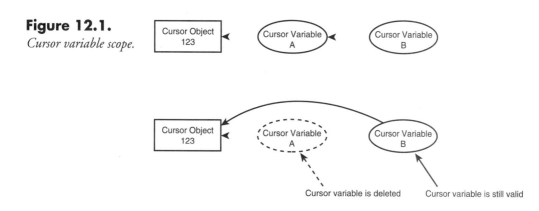

In the top of Figure 12.1, cursor variable B is assigned to cursor variable A. Cursor variable A is assigned to the cursor object 123. Both cursor variables are within the scope of cursor object 123. Cursor object 123 remains accessible to cursor variable B even when cursor variable A is deleted—as shown in the bottom half of Figure 12.1.

Remember that any variable, cursor or otherwise, is valid only in the scope of the loop. You cannot make any external reference to the cursor variable declared in a loop because it does not exist. Any cursor variable declared in an inner PL/SQL block is not accessible to the outer PL/SQL block. Likewise, you cannot refer to a cursor outside the declaring block unless the cursor is declared in a package specification.

Cursor Alias

As shown in Figure 12.1, you can have two cursor variables assigned to a single cursor object. Each of the variables is an alias to the cursor object. They both share the result set of the cursor object 123 query. Anything that one alias, or cursor variable, does that affects the cursor object will be seen immediately in the other cursor variable. This can be easily illustrated in the following cursor pseudocode:

```
PROCEDURE obtain_stock_quotes (stock_cv_1  in out  stock_cur_type,
                                   stock_cv_2 in out stock_cur_type);
stock_rec     stocks%rowtype;

BEGIN
OPEN stock_cv_1 FOR SELECT * FROM stocks;       -- open the cursor

stock_cv_2 := stock_cv_1;                       -- cursor variable assignment
FETCH stock_cv_1 INTO stock_rec;        -- fetch first record from cursor
FETCH stock_cv_2 INTO stock_rec;        -- fetch second record from cursor
FETCH stock_cv_2 INTO stock_rec;        -- fetch third record from cursor

CLOSE stock_cv_1;                       -- closes cursor for both aliases
```

12

Because the cursor is closed at this point, you *cannot* fetch from the cursor using either of the stock_cv_1 or stock_cv_2 variables. If you do attempt a fetch at this point, an error will occur stating that the cursor is closed.

Summary

This chapter presents you with several more applications and uses for cursors, including the concept of passing parameters into the cursor declaration. Cursor parameters allow your code to become more modular and maintainable. Likewise, you learned about declaring a cursor in a package specification, whereas the body of the cursors is in the cursor body. This gives the programmer an opportunity to know only the input and output return values of a cursor and not necessarily all the mechanics of exactly what the cursor is doing. The chapter also discusses the cursor variable. This cursor variable is like a pointer to a cursor. It is not a cursor itself but merely points to the same result set that the cursor created.

Q&A

Q Why should I use default values when I declare a cursor parameter?

A Defining default values for a cursor parameter gives the programmer two advantages. First, if no value is explicitly defined for the parameter, you know that processing will continue with a value you have set previously. Second, you can override or change the value of a parameter by passing the cursor a replacement value for the default value.

Q What is the purpose of declaring a cursor in the package specification and not in the package body?

A This makes programming cleaner in that the programmer will not have to handle the specification but only the cursor body. You can change the cursor body without having to alter the specification.

Q Cursor variables provide what advantages to the programmer?

A Included in the many advantages of cursor variables is the opportunity Oracle provides in that you can pass cursor variables as parameters to procedures and functions. Likewise, you can pass cursor variables from a host environment through Pro*C (or similar program) to your PL/SQL block.

Workshop

Use the following workshop to test your comprehension of this chapter and put what you've learned into practice. You'll find the answers to the quiz and exercise in Appendix A, "Answers."

Quiz

1. Name the different cursor variable parameter modes and their purposes.
2. What is the scope of a cursor parameter?

Exercise

Write a brief package declaration block and the beginning portion of the package body where you declare a cursor variable, and then use this variable in a procedure to open a cursor with a query.

12

Day 13

Using Oracle8 Objects for Object-Oriented Programming

by Jonathan Gennick

PL/SQL does objects! One of the exciting new features of the Oracle8 database is support for object-oriented programming. With Oracle8 and PL/SQL release 8.0, it is now possible to define object classes, instantiate objects, and save those objects in the database. The benefits to you are increased opportunities for abstraction and for writing reusable code. If you have Oracle8 available to you, read through this chapter carefully and take the time to fully understand how Oracle's new object-oriented features work, and how you can take advantage of them. If you don't yet have access to Oracle8, you will not be able to do any of the examples or exercises in this chapter. In that case, you might want to skim through it lightly now, in order to become familiar with the new features, and then revisit it later when you do have Oracle8 available.

A Quick Primer on Object-Oriented Programming

Let's begin by reviewing the basics of object-oriented programming (OOP). There is really no magic to object-oriented programming. It's simply a different way of organizing code and data within your programs, one that you can take advantage of in order to model your code to more closely match the real world. There are three pillars of good object-oriented design:

- ☐ Encapsulation
- ☐ Inheritance
- ☐ Polymorphism

Each of these is described in more detail in the following sections, using as examples some real-world objects that you interact with every day.

Encapsulation

NEW TERM   The term *encapsulation* refers to the fact that each object "takes care of itself." A well-designed object has a clear and well-defined interface that is used to manipulate the object. All the program code necessary to perform any function on the object is contained within the object definition itself. Thus an object is completely self-contained and can be "dropped in" anywhere you need it.

A classic, and often used, real-world example of objects is audio/video components. Say you are setting up a home theater. You drive down to the nearest appliance superstore and pick out whatever objects interest you, say a big-screen TV, an FM tuner, an amplifier, and some speakers. All these components have well-defined interfaces, and each contains whatever internal electronics and software are necessary to make them work. The FM tuner will tune in radio stations regardless of whether or not you plug it into the amplifier. The TV does not need any circuitry that might be present in the speakers. After integrating all these components, you might decide that you also want a subwoofer. Adding one is simple. You don't have to rebuild your stereo system. You just run back to the store, buy the desired component, come home, and plug it in.

It all sounds like nirvana, but there are some gotchas. In real life, interfaces are not always compatible and sometimes components have overlapping functionality. That amplifier, for example, might also have a built-in tuner, and how often have you had to buy an adapter to mate two incompatible connectors? Often it's easier to work with components that have all been built by the same manufacturer and that have been designed to work together. The same is true of object-oriented programming.

13

Inheritance

NEW TERM *Inheritance* refers to the fact that as programmers design new objects, they often build on objects that have been created previously. In other words, programmers can create new objects that *inherit* the functionality of previously created objects. Sometimes when you do this, you might choose to modify the inherited functionality, and almost certainly you will want to add new functionality. The telephone is a good example of this. Originally it was a very simple device. You picked up the phone, listened for a dial tone, and dialed a number using a rotary dial. When pushbutton phones came out, the original functionality was inherited, except for the dialing interface, which was replaced by buttons. Cordless phones inherited this functionality, added a radio to the implementation, and added an on/off switch to the handset interface so that the handset did not need to be returned to the cradle after each call.

One big advantage of inheritance in the programming world, which is not present in the physical world, is that you can change the definition of a software object and the change will propagate through all objects of that type, all objects inherited from those objects, and so forth. Think of changing the definition of a telephone to include pushbutton dialing and have all rotary phones in the world suddenly transform themselves. Of course that can't be done, but the software equivalent of it can be.

Polymorphism

NEW TERM *Polymorphism* enables different objects to have methods of the same name that accomplish similar tasks, but in different ways. Think back to your home entertainment system for a moment. Each of the components has an on button. The TV also has a remote with an on button. Each of these buttons can invoke different processes inside each piece of equipment. The remote, for example, has to send an infrared beam of light to the TV set when the on button is pushed. In spite of the fact that each on button invokes a different sequence of events, each button is still labeled "on." It would be quite inconvenient if this were not the case. Consistent naming frees your mind from having to remember specifically for each device how to turn it on. You quickly become conditioned to pushing the on button, or flipping a switch to on, no matter what device you are using. It becomes second nature.

Polymorphism enables your software objects to use method names that are consistent with the function being performed even though the way in which that function is implemented can differ from object to object.

Classes, Objects, Attributes, and Methods

NEW TERM The term *class* refers to the definition for an object. Like a blueprint for a house, it tells you everything you need to build an object, and it tells you what that object will look like when it is built. An `employee` class, for example, might be created to contain all attributes of an employee. Examples of employee attributes would be pay rate, name, address, and so on.

13

NEW TERM Many *objects* can be built from a class, just as one set of blueprints can be used to build numerous houses. If you were writing code to process employee records, you would use the `employee` class to *instantiate*, in other words to construct, an `employee` object for each employee record.

NEW TERM Objects consist of *attributes* and *methods*. An *attribute* can be anything you need to know about an object. Name, phone number, Social Security number, pay rate, and pay type are all good examples of attributes for an `employee` object. Attributes are implemented as variable declarations made within the object class definition.

NEW TERM *Methods* are the functions and procedures used to perform functions related to the object. Like attributes, methods are implemented as functions and procedures in the object class definition. Anything you want to do to an object should be implemented as a method. If you want to compare two objects, you should implement a compare method. If you want to copy an object, you should implement a copy method. An `employee` object class, for example, might contain a method to calculate an employee's yearly bonus based on pay type, longevity with the firm, and so on.

Advantages over Traditional Methods

Objects offer the opportunity for increased reliability because of their well-defined interfaces. Reuse is made easier because all necessary code and data are part of the object definition; thus object classes can easily be added to programs as new functionality is required. Because you can model real-world, business objects, as well as encapsulate and hide the details behind an object's functionality, you can program at a higher level of abstraction, minimizing the amount of detail you need to remember, which makes your job as a developer much easier.

How Oracle Implements Objects

Oracle8 implements several new constructs in support of object-oriented programming:

- [ ] The *object type*, with which you can define an object class
- [ ] *Object tables*, with which you can store your objects
- [ ] *Object views*, with which you can synthesize objects from your existing relational data

Oracle also implements an *object-relational* database. The underpinnings are still relational, and that underlying relational model has simply been extended to include support for new datatypes, which in this case happen to be object types. By doing this, Oracle has maintained compatibility with existing relational databases and provided a path for gradual migration to objects.

Object Types

NEW TERM
To use an object, first you need to define it. For this purpose Oracle8 introduces the *object type*. An *object type* is a database-level definition and is equivalent to the term *class* as used in object-oriented languages such as Java and C++. It contains both the code and data definitions for an object. Object types are also treated as datatypes and can be used in PL/SQL programs for declaring variables that will contain objects.

Object Tables

NEW TERM
Object tables are a special kind of table that you can create. These are based on an object definition and essentially map each attribute of an object to a column in the table.

Object Views

Object views are the object analog of a view on a table. A full discussion of object views is beyond the scope of this book, but your database administrator can use them to define pseudo-objects based on existing relational data. Like a relational view, object views are based on a SQL statement that retrieves the data for the object.

Defining an Object Type

You should now have a good overview of what object-oriented programming is and how Oracle handles objects. It's time to get down to some practical examples. To begin, define an object type for employee addresses. Listing 13.1 shows one possible implementation.

INPUT/ OUTPUT
Listing 13.1. Creating the `address` object type.

```
1: CREATE OR REPLACE TYPE address AS OBJECT (
2:    street_1       VARCHAR2(40),
3:    street_2       VARCHAR2(40),
4:    city           VARCHAR2(40),
5:    state_abbr     VARCHAR2(2),
6:    zip_code       VARCHAR2(5),
7:    phone_number   VARCHAR2(10),
8:    MEMBER PROCEDURE ChangeAddress (
9:      st_1 IN VARCHAR2, st_2 IN VARCHAR2, cty IN VARCHAR2,
10:     state IN VARCHAR2, zip IN VARCHAR2),
11:    MEMBER FUNCTION getStreet (line_no IN number) RETURN VARCHAR2,
12:    MEMBER FUNCTION getCity RETURN VARCHAR2,
13:    MEMBER FUNCTION getStateAbbr RETURN VARCHAR2,
14:    MEMBER FUNCTION getPostalCode RETURN VARCHAR2,
15:    MEMBER FUNCTION getPhone RETURN VARCHAR2,
16:    MEMBER PROCEDURE setPhone (newPhone IN VARCHAR2)
17: );

Type created.
```

13

continues

Listing 13.1. continued

```
 1: CREATE OR REPLACE TYPE BODY address AS
 2:   MEMBER PROCEDURE ChangeAddress (
 3:     st_1 IN VARCHAR2, st_2 IN VARCHAR2, cty IN VARCHAR2,
 4:     state IN VARCHAR2, zip IN VARCHAR2) IS
 5:   BEGIN
 6:     IF (st_1 IS NULL) OR (cty IS NULL) OR
        ➥(state IS NULL) OR (zip IS NULL)
 7:       OR (upper(state) NOT IN ('AK','AL','AR','AZ','CA','CO',
 8:                                'CT','DC','DE','FL','GA','HI',
 9:                                'IA','ID','IL','IN','KS','KY',
10:                                'LA','MA','MD','ME','MI','MN',
11:                                'MO','MS','MT','NC','ND','NE',
12:                                'NH','NJ','NM','NV','NY','OH',
13:                                'OK','OR','PA','RI','SC','SD',
14:                                'TN','TX','UT','VA','VT','WA'
15:                                'WI','WV','WY'))
16: OR (zip <> ltrim(to_char(to_number(zip),'09999'))) THEN
17:       RAISE_application_error(-20001,'The new Address is invalid.');
18:     ELSE
19:       street_1 := st_1;
20:       street_2 := st_2;
21:       city := cty;
22:       state_abbr := upper(state);
23:       zip_code := zip;
24:     END IF;
25:   END;
26:
27:   MEMBER FUNCTION getStreet (line_no IN number)
28:     RETURN VARCHAR2 IS
29:   BEGIN
30:     IF line_no = 1 THEN
31:       RETURN street_1;
32:     ELSIF line_no = 2 THEN
33:       RETURN street_2;
34:     ELSE
35:       RETURN ' ';      --send back a blank.
36:     END IF;
37:   END;
38:
39:   MEMBER FUNCTION getCity RETURN VARCHAR2 IS
40:   BEGIN
41:     RETURN city;
42:   END;
43:
44:   MEMBER FUNCTION getStateAbbr RETURN VARCHAR2 IS
45:   BEGIN
46:     RETURN state_abbr;
47:   END;
48:
49:   MEMBER FUNCTION getPostalCode RETURN VARCHAR2 IS
50:   BEGIN
51:     RETURN zip_code;
52:   END;
53:
```

```
54:    MEMBER FUNCTION getPhone RETURN VARCHAR2 IS
55:    BEGIN
56:      RETURN phone_number;
57:    END;
58:
59:    MEMBER PROCEDURE setPhone (newPhone IN VARCHAR2) IS
60:    BEGIN
61:      phone_number := newPhone;
62:    END;
63: END;
64: /

Type body created.
```

ANALYSIS   Notice that the form of an object type declaration closely resembles that of a package definition. Like packages, object types have both a specification and a body. The specification, shown in lines 1 through 17 of the first segment, lists the object's attributes and member functions. The object body, lines 1 through 64 of the second segment, contains the actual code for the methods.

The statements in Listing 13.1 show how to define an object type, or class if you prefer that term. The complete syntax for an object type definition is shown following.

The Syntax for Defining an Object Type

SYNTAX
```
CREATE TYPE type_name [IS | AS] OBJECT (
  attribute_name      datatype,
  attribute_name      datatype,
  ...
  MEMBER [function_specification | procedure_specification],
  MEMBER [function_specification | procedure_specification],
  ...
  [MAP | ORDER] MEMBER function_specification,
  pragma,
  pragma,
  ...
  );

CREATE TYPE BODY type_name [IS | AS]
  MEMBER [function_definition | procedure_definition];
  MEMBER [function_definition | procedure_definition];
  ...
  [MAP | ORDER] MEMBER function_definition;
END;
```

In this syntax, the parameters are as follows:

☐ type_name—The name of the object type that you are defining. This can be any name you choose, but it must conform to Oracle's naming rules. (The rules for objects are the same as for variables, tables, triggers, and so on.)

☐ attribute_name—Can be any name you choose, and must conform to the rules for naming variables. An object must have at least one attribute.

13

- [ ] *datatype*—Can be another object type, or an Oracle datatype. The following Oracle datatypes cannot be used here: LONG, LONG RAW, NCHAR, NCLOB, NVARCHAR2, and ROWID. PL/SQL-specific datatypes, such as BINARY_INTEGER and BOOLEAN, are also not allowed.

- [ ] *function_specification*—A PL/SQL function specification, the same as would appear in a package definition.

- [ ] *procedure_specification*—A PL/SQL procedure specification, the same as would appear in a package definition.

- [ ] *pragma*—Any pragmas, or compiler directives, such as those used to define exceptions or to tell Oracle whether or not a method modifies any database tables.

- [ ] *function_definition*—Contains the code for a function.

- [ ] *procedure_definition*—Contains the code for a procedure.

Objects must contain at least one attribute, and can contain as many as a thousand. Member functions and procedures are entirely optional, as are compiler directives (pragmas). The definition of a MAP function or an ORDER function is also optional, but if present, only one type can be used. MAP and ORDER functions are discussed later in this chapter in the section titled "Comparing Objects."

As mentioned earlier, an object type is a database-level definition. After an object type is defined in the database, it can be used to create object tables, to define table columns that are themselves objects, or to declare object variables in PL/SQL blocks.

Constructor Methods

NEW TERM   Each Oracle object type has a built-in *constructor* method that is used to create an instance of that type. This method is responsible for initializing all the object's attributes and for doing whatever internal housekeeping is necessary. You do not have to declare or define this method, and in fact you cannot—Oracle does it for you.

NOTE

> The inability to declare and define your own constructor methods represents a serious weakness in Oracle's current implementation of objects. Your flexibility is limited, and your control is limited as well because you have nowhere to write validation code, which can prevent an object from being created with an invalid combination of attribute values.

The constructor method always has the same name as the object type, and has as its arguments each of the object's attributes in the order in which you declared them. Thus the constructor method for the address object type would be

```
FUNCTION address (street_1 in VARCHAR2, street_2 in VARCHAR2,
                  city in VARCHAR2, state_abbr, zip_code,
                  phone_number) returns address
```

The constructor function always returns an object of the same type. In your code, you would reference address as a function, passing values for each argument, in order to create an object of the address type, for example

```
address_variable := address('101 Oak','','Detroit','MI',
    '48223','3135358886');
```

You will see more examples of this in the section titled "Instantiating and Using an Object." (See Listing 13.2.)

Accessor Methods

NEW TERM The term *accessor methods* is used to describe methods that are used to return an object's attributes. The implementation of address shown in Listing 13.1 contains five accessor methods:

- [ ] getStreet
- [ ] getCity
- [ ] getStateAbbr
- [ ] getPostalCode
- [ ] getPhone

In most cases, these simply return the attribute in question. The getStreet method does a bit more in that it will return a blank if an invalid street address line is requested. By convention, accessor method names typically begin with get.

At first glance, it might seem silly to use a function like getStreet when you could just as easily reference the street_1 and street_2 attributes directly. However, accessor methods provide extra insulation between the underlying implementation of your objects and your programs. Consider the implications if, for whatever reason, you decided to remove the street_2 attribute from the address object. What impact would that have on existing programs? None if they are using getStreet. One small change to that function, and your programs wouldn't know the difference.

13

WARNING

Most object-oriented languages allow you to force the use of accessor functions by letting you define attributes as "private," meaning that they cannot be accessed directly. Oracle does not yet do this, so even though the accessor functions exist, there is no way to be 100 percent sure that they are always used.

Mutator Methods

NEW TERM A *mutator method* is the opposite of an accessor method. It lets you set attribute values without referencing them directly. The advantages are the same as for accessor methods. Mutator methods simply provide an extra level of insulation between a program and an object's underlying implementation. By convention, mutator method names typically start with set.

The ChangeAddress method of your address object would be considered a mutator method. It could have been named setAddress to conform more closely to convention, but the name ChangeAddress was chosen because it is more descriptive of the real-world event for which this method exists.

Instantiating and Using an Object

After you have defined an object type, you probably want to do something with it. Using an object from within PL/SQL is not terribly difficult. You just have to follow these few simple steps:

1. Declare one or more variables in which the datatype is the object type you want to use.
2. Instantiate one or more of the objects.
3. Use your object's member methods to manipulate the objects.
4. Optionally, store your objects in the database.

This section discusses how to perform the first three of these four steps. There are two different approaches to storing objects, and those are discussed later in this chapter in the section titled "Storing and Retrieving Objects."

Listing 13.2 shows some fairly simple code that uses the address object defined earlier. Several variables of the address object type are declared, a few address objects are instantiated, their values are manipulated, and finally the objects' attributes are displayed for you to see.

INPUT/OUTPUT **Listing 13.2. Using the address object.**

```
1: --A PL/SQL block demonstrating the use of the address object.
2: SET SERVEROUTPUT ON
3: DECLARE
4:    address_1    address;
5:    address_2    address;
6:    address_3    address;
7: BEGIN
8:    --Instantiate a new address object named address_1,
9:    --and assign a copy of it to address_2.
10:   address_1 := address ('2700 Peerless Road','Apt 1',
```

13

```
11:                            'Cleveland','TN','37312','4235551212');
12:    address_2 := address_1;
13:
14:    --Change address #1
15:    address_1.ChangeAddress ('2800 Peermore Road','Apt 99',
16:                            'Detroit','MI','48823');
17:
18:    --Instantiate a second object.
19:    address_3 := address ('2700 Eaton Rapids Road','Lot 98',
20:                            'Lansing','MI','48911','5173943551');
21:
22:    --Now print out the attributes from each object.
23:    dbms_output.put_line('Attributes for address_1:');
24:    dbms_output.put_line(address_1.getStreet(1));
25:    dbms_output.put_line(address_1.getStreet(2));
26:    dbms_output.put_line(address_1.getCity
27:                            || ' ' || address_1.getStateAbbr
28:                            || ' ' || address_1.getPostalCode);
29:    dbms_output.put_line(address_1.getPhone);
30:
31:    dbms_output.put_line('------------------------');
32:    dbms_output.put_line('Attributes for address_2:');
33:    dbms_output.put_line(address_2.getStreet(1));
34:    dbms_output.put_line(address_2.getStreet(2));
35:    dbms_output.put_line(address_2.getCity
36:                            || ' ' || address_2.getStateAbbr
37:                            || ' ' || address_2.getPostalCode);
38:    dbms_output.put_line(address_2.getPhone);
39:
40:    dbms_output.put_line('------------------------');
41:    dbms_output.put_line('Attributes for address_3:');
42:    dbms_output.put_line(address_3.street_1);
43:    dbms_output.put_line(address_3.street_2);
44:    dbms_output.put_line(address_3.city
45:                            || ' ' || address_3.state_abbr
46:                            || ' ' || address_3.zip_code);
47:    dbms_output.put_line(address_3.phone_number);
48: END;
49: /
Attributes for address_1:
2800 Peermore Road
Apt 99
Detroit MI 48823
4235551212
------------------------
Attributes for address_2:
2700 Peerless Road
Apt 1
Cleveland TN 37312
4235551212
------------------------
Attributes for address_3:
2700 Eaton Rapids Road
Lot 98
Lansing MI 48911
5173943551

PL/SQL procedure successfully completed.
```

13

ANALYSIS Notice that in lines 4–6, three object variables are defined. They are of type `address` and will be used to contain `address` objects. When first created, these objects are considered to be null. Any calls to their member methods will result in an error, and any reference to their attributes will evaluate to null.

The first `address` object is instantiated in line 10. This is done by calling the constructor function for the `address` object and assigning the value returned to the object variable `address_1`. In line 12, a copy of this object is assigned to `address_2`. Then the value of `address_1` is changed. This is done with a call to the `ChangeAddress` method (lines 15–16), and is done in order to demonstrate that `address_1` and `address_2` are indeed separate objects. In line 19, a third `address` object is created.

The values of these three `address` objects are displayed by the code in lines 22–47. Notice that although the accessor methods are used to retrieve the attribute values from the first two objects, the attributes of the third object are accessed directly.

Storing and Retrieving Objects

NEW TERM There are two ways to store an object in an Oracle database. One is to store the object as a column within a table. This is the approach this chapter takes to storing the `address` objects. Each employee record will have one address associated with it. The other approach to storing objects involves the use of an *object table*. An *object table* is a relational table that has been defined to store a particular type of object. Each row in the table represents one object, and each column represents one attribute in the object.

Storing Objects as Table Columns

Oracle's object-relational model allows an object to be stored as a column in a database table. In order to do this, a column of the appropriate object type must first be added to the table in question. To create an address column in the employee table, you must first execute the DDL (Data Definition Language) statement shown in Listing 13.3.

INPUT/OUTPUT **Listing 13.3. Creating a column for the `address` object.**

```
1: ALTER TABLE employee
2:    ADD (
3:       home_address      address
4:    );
Table altered.
```

ANALYSIS The preceding statement simply adds a column, which is named `home_address`, to the employee table. The column type is given as `address`, which is a reference to the object type you defined earlier in this chapter. For any existing employee records, the object is considered to be null.

Now that an address column exists in the employee table, you can create some employee records and store each employee's address along with the other information. Listing 13.4 shows two different ways in which to do this.

INPUT/OUTPUT

Listing 13.4. Saving address objects with employee records.

```
1: INSERT INTO employee
2:   (emp_id, emp_name,pay_rate,pay_type,home_address)
3:   VALUES (597,'Matthew Higgenbottom',120000,'S',
4:           address('101 Maple','','Mio','MI','48640','5173943551'));
```

1 row created.

```
COMMIT;
```

Commit complete.

```
1: DECLARE
2:   emp_home_address     address;
3: BEGIN
4:   emp_home_address := address('911 Pearl','Apt 2','Lewiston',
                             ➥'MI','48645','5173363366');
5:   INSERT INTO employee
6:     (emp_id, emp_name,pay_rate,pay_type,home_address)
7:     VALUES (598, 'Raymond Gennick',55,'H',emp_home_address);
8:   COMMIT;
9: END;
10: /
```

PL/SQL procedure successfully completed.

```
1: SELECT emp_id, emp_name, home_address
2:   FROM employee
3:  WHERE home_address IS NOT null;
```

```
    EMP_ID EMP_NAME
---------- --------------------------------
HOME_ADDRESS(STREET_1, STREET_2, CITY, STATE_ABBR, ZIP_CODE, PHONE_NUMBER)
-------------------------------------------------------------------------------
       597 Matthew Higgenbottom
ADDRESS('101 Maple', NULL, 'Mio', 'MI', '48640', '5173943551')

       598 Raymond Gennick
ADDRESS('911 Pearl', 'Apt 2', 'Lewiston', 'MI', '48645', '5173363366')
```

13

ANALYSIS Lines 1–4 of the first segment show how a constructor method can be referenced from within a SQL statement. In fact, the statement in question was executed from within SQL*Plus, though it could just as well have been inside a PL/SQL block. Lines 1–10 of the third segment show a PL/SQL block that first instantiates an address object and then inserts that object into the employee table as part of an employee record. The emp_home_address variable is defined in line 2 of the third segment as being of type address. Then in line 4 of the third segment, the address constructor is used to instantiate a new address object, which is assigned to the emp_home_address variable. Finally, in lines 5–7 of the third segment, an INSERT statement is executed, saving the employee record. The emp_home_address variable is included in the values list and is stored as a part of the record.

The SELECT statement (lines 1–3 of the fourth segment) retrieves the address objects that you have just inserted into the database. Notice how SQL*Plus uses the address type constructor in the resulting output to indicate that the addresses are from an embedded object.

Retrieving and Updating Objects in a Table Column

As with inserting, you can retrieve and update an object that is stored in a column, just as you would any other column value. Listing 13.5 shows a PL/SQL block that retrieves the address for employee number 597, changes the phone number, and then updates the table to contain the new value of the object.

**INPUT/
OUTPUT** **Listing 13.5. Retrieving and updating the address object.**

```
 1: DECLARE
 2:    emp_addr      address;
 3: BEGIN
 4:    --Retrieve the object from the table
 5:    SELECT home_address INTO emp_addr
 6:      FROM employee
 7:     WHERE emp_id = 597;
 8:
 9:    --Use a mutator method to change the phone number.
10:    emp_addr.setPhone('3139830301');
11:
12:    UPDATE employee
13:       SET home_address = emp_addr
14:     WHERE emp_id = 597;
15:
16:    COMMIT;
17: END;
18: /

PL/SQL procedure successfully completed.

 1: SELECT emp_id, emp_name, home_address.phone_number home_phone
 2:    FROM employee
 3:   WHERE emp_id = 597;

   EMP_ID EMP_NAME                                 HOME_PHONE
--------- ------------------------------------ ----------
      597 Matthew Higgenbottom                     3139830301
```

ANALYSIS Lines 5–7 of the first segment retrieve the address object into the emp_addr variable for the employee whose phone number you want to change. In line 10 of the first segment, the setPhone method is used to update the phone number. At this point, only the object in memory has the updated phone number. Lines 12–14 of the first segment update the employee's record, storing the new value of the address object.

It is also possible to update an employee's phone number using only one update, rather than the three steps of retrieve, modify, and store shown in Listing 13.5. This can be accomplished by creating an entirely new address object and assigning it to the employee's home_address field. Listing 13.6 shows the phone number for employee number 598 being modified using this method.

INPUT/ OUTPUT **Listing 13.6. Updating an address object.**

```
 1: UPDATE employee
 2:    SET home_address  = address(home_address.street_1,
 3:                          home_address.street_2, home_address.city,
 4:                          home_address.state_abbr, home_address.zip_code,
 5:                          '5173433333')
 6:  WHERE emp_id = 598;

1 row updated.

COMMIT;

Commit complete.
```

ANALYSIS The SET clause of this UPDATE statement uses the information from the existing address object, plus a new phone number, to instantiate an entirely new address object. This is done in lines 2–5 by calling the object type's constructor and passing attributes of the original address as arguments. The home_address column is then set to the value of this new object.

Object Tables

NEW TERM Another way to store objects is in an *object table*. An *object table* is a relational table defined so that each column in the table matches one of the attributes of the object. Consequently each row of the table is used to store one instance of an object. In addition to the columns for the object's attributes, an object table also has an additional column that is used to contain an *object identifier*. This *object identifier* is an Oracle-generated value that uniquely identifies each object in the database.

Take a look at Listing 13.7. It defines a building type for the sample database and then creates an object table that can store instances of that type.

13

INPUT/
OUTPUT **Listing 13.7. The** building **object.**

```
1: CREATE OR REPLACE TYPE building AS OBJECT (
2:    BldgName          VARCHAR2(40),
3:    BldgAddress       address,
4:    BldgMgr           INTEGER,
5:    MEMBER PROCEDURE  ChangeMgr (NewMgr IN INTEGER),
6:    ORDER MEMBER FUNCTION Compare (OtherBuilding IN building)
7:        RETURN INTEGER
8:    );
```

Type created.

```
1: CREATE OR REPLACE TYPE BODY building AS
2:    MEMBER PROCEDURE  ChangeMgr(NewMgr IN INTEGER) IS
3:      BEGIN
4:        BldgMgr := NewMgr;
5:      END;
6:
7:    ORDER MEMBER FUNCTION Compare (OtherBuilding IN building)
8:    RETURN INTEGER IS
9:        BldgName1     VARCHAR2(40);
10:        BldgName2     building.BldgName%TYPE;
11:      BEGIN
12:        --Grab the two building names for comparison.
13:        --Make sure that we don't get messed up by leading/trailing
14:        --spaces or by case.
15:        BldgName1 := upper(ltrim(rtrim(BldgName)));
16:        BldgName2 := upper(ltrim(rtrim(OtherBuilding.BldgName)));
17:
18:        --Return the appropriate value to indicate the order of
19:        --this object vs OtherBuilding.
20:        IF BldgName1 = BldgName2 THEN
21:          RETURN 0;
22:        ELSIF BldgName1 < BldgName2 THEN
23:          RETURN -1;
24:        ELSE
25:          RETURN 1;
26:        END IF;
27:      END;
28: END;
29: /
```

Type body created.

CREATE TABLE buildings OF building;

Table created.

 ANALYSIS Lines 1–8 of the first segment contain the building object's type definition. As you can see, the building object has three attributes containing the building's name, the building's address, and the employee ID of the building manager. The second attribute is interesting because it itself is an object. Objects can be nested in this manner to any level.

13

The ORDER function, in line 6 of the first segment, enables you to compare two objects of type building for equality or to see which is greater. You decide what "equality" means when you write the function. The keyword ORDER tells Oracle which member function to call when doing comparisons. Comparing objects using order functions is described later in this chapter in the section titled "Comparing Objects."

Lines 1 through 29 of the second segment define the object body, which contains the definitions for the two member functions ChangeMgr and Compare.

The last command in the listing, shown in the third segment, is very important. This is a new form of the CREATE TABLE statement, which creates an object table for objects of type building. You will be using this table later in this chapter. Go ahead and look at the table's structure by typing this command:

```
describe buildings
```

When you use an object table to store your objects, they have visibility outside the table. Other objects can be linked to them, referencing them by their object identifiers. Another advantage of object tables is that they can also be queried just like any other relational tables. This gives you some flexibility and enables you to mix and match relational and object-oriented methods in your software development projects.

Storing Objects in an Object Table

You can insert information about buildings into the object table you just created by using a SQL INSERT statement. Instead of a values list containing separate values for each attribute, use the building object's constructor to create an object. This one object becomes the only value in the values list.

Type in the statements shown in Listing 13.8 in order to insert a few building objects. These will be used in later examples showing you how to update object tables and how to link objects in the database.

INPUT/OUTPUT   **Listing 13.8. Inserting some building objects.**

```
1: INSERT INTO buildings
2:    values (building('Victor Building',
3:            address('203 Washington Square',' ','Lansing',
            ➥'MI','48823',' '),
4:            597));

1 row created.

1: INSERT INTO buildings
2:    values (building('East Storage Shed',
3:            address('1400 Abbott Rd','','Lansing','MI','48823',''),
4:            598));
```

continues

Listing 13.8. continued

```
1 row created.

1: INSERT INTO buildings
2:    values (building('Headquarters Building',
3:             address('150 West Jefferson','','Detroit','MI','48226',''),
4:             599));

1 row created.

SELECT * from buildings;

BLDGNAME
----------------------------------------
BLDGADDRESS(STREET_1, STREET_2, CITY, STATE_ABBR, ZIP_CODE, PHONE_NUMBER)
-------------------------------------------------------------------------
   BLDGMGR
---------
Victor Building
ADDRESS('203 Washington Square', ' ', 'Lansing', 'MI', '48823', ' ')
     597

East Storage Shed
ADDRESS('1400 Abbott Rd', NULL, 'Lansing', 'MI', '48823', NULL)
     598

Headquarters Building
ADDRESS('150 West Jefferson', NULL, 'Detroit', 'MI', '48226', NULL)
     599

COMMIT;

Commit complete.
```

ANALYSIS   In each of the preceding inserts, the building constructor was called in order to instantiate a building object. Because one of the building attributes is an address object, the address constructor was also called to create that object. The SELECT statement at the end shows you that the building data was inserted properly.

NOTE   When inserting into an object table, it is not absolutely necessary to call the object constructor for that table, so in the preceding example the reference to the building constructor could have been omitted. Oracle knows what object type is stored in the table, and Oracle also allows you to treat the table as a regular relational table. However, the call to the address constructor cannot be omitted because the address object is an embedded object.

13

Retrieving and Updating Objects in an Object Table

When retrieving and updating data in an object table, you can choose to treat the table as a normal, relational table, and simply write conventional SELECT, UPDATE, and DELETE queries against it. For example, if you simply wanted to retrieve a list of building names, you could execute the query shown in Listing 13.9.

INPUT/OUTPUT **Listing 13.9. A simple SELECT against the building table.**

```
SELECT BldgName
  FROM buildings

ORDER BY BldgName;

BLDGNAME
-----------------------------------------
East Storage Shed
Headquarters Building
Victor Building
```

ANALYSIS   Notice that the query is simply a traditional, relational query against the buildings table. Even though buildings is a table of objects, you can still treat it like any other relational table.

Being able to execute a traditional, non–object-oriented query against an object table can be very handy if you have both object-oriented and non–object-oriented programs accessing the same database. A non–object-oriented program would simply treat the building table as if it were any other relational table. It's also worth noting that if you were doing a mass update, it would be more efficient to write one SQL UPDATE statement than it would be to write a PL/SQL loop to retrieve each object, update it, and save it again.

The VALUE Operator

As you move into object-oriented programming, you will want to retrieve building objects from the building table. With an embedded object, such as address, this was done by retrieving the object column into an object variable. Refer to Listing 13.5, line 5, for an example of this. However, the building object table has no column of type building. It simply has a column for each attribute. So what do you select in order to retrieve the building object? In order to retrieve building objects, you will need to use Oracle8's new VALUE operator. The VALUE operator takes a correlation variable as its argument and returns the value of the object stored in the selected row(s) of the table. Take a look at Listing 13.10, which retrieves all the building objects from the database.

13

INPUT/OUTPUT **Listing 13.10. Retrieving from an object table.**

```
 1: SET SERVEROUTPUT ON
 2: DECLARE
 3:   this_building    building;
 4:
 5:   CURSOR all_buildings IS
 6:     SELECT value (b) AS bldg
 7:       FROM buildings b
 8:      ORDER BY b.BldgName;
 9:
10: BEGIN
11:   FOR one_building IN all_buildings LOOP
12:     --Grab a copy of the building object.
13:     this_building := one_building.bldg;
14:     dbms_output.put_line(this_building.BldgName || ' is located in '
15:                      || this_building.BldgAddress.city
16:                      || ' ' || this_building.BldgAddress.state_abbr);
17:   END LOOP;
18:
19:   COMMIT;
20: END;
21: /
```

```
East Storage Shed is located in Lansing MI
Headquarters Building is located in Detroit MI
Victor Building is located in Lansing MI

PL/SQL procedure successfully completed.
```

ANALYSIS   In this example, a cursor was declared (lines 5–8) based on a SQL statement that would select building objects. Notice in line 6 that the result column is given the alias bldg. This makes it easy to reference the object retrieved by the cursor, and is used in line 13. The remainder of the code consists of a simple CURSOR FOR loop that retrieves each building object and displays each building's name and location. Notice in lines 15 and 16 how the dot notation is used to navigate from the building object, to the address object, and finally to the city name and state abbreviation.

Updating an Object Table

The SQL UPDATE statement is used to update object tables. There are two basic parts to an UPDATE statement. The first part contains the SET clause, and specifies which table and column you are updating. The second part contains the WHERE clause, and specifies the search condition used to identify the rows to update. Both of these now have object-oriented variations.

Consider the SET clause first. In order to update the building table, you could write an UPDATE statement that began like this:

```
UPDATE building
  SET BldgName = 'Some Name'
  ...
```

13

However, if you wanted to update an entire building object, you would want your UPDATE statement to look like this:

```
UPDATE building b
  SET b = building(...)
  ...
```

In the preceding code snippet, the building table has been given a correlation name of b. This correlation name is used to represent the object stored in each row of the table, and new building objects can be assigned to it. In the preceding example, the building constructor was used to generate a new building object.

In addition to setting the new values, there is also the question of the WHERE clause. A traditional WHERE clause for the building table might look like this:

```
WHERE BldgName = 'Victor Building'
```

In this case the building name is being used to identify the row to be changed. If you are writing a PL/SQL program, you have another option. You can use the object identifier to uniquely identify the row to be changed. This method makes use of the REF operator, which retrieves an object's unique identifier. Here is a short example:

```
UPDATE building b
...
WHERE REF(b) = SELECT REF(b2) FROM building b2
               WHERE BldgName = 'Victor Building'
```

This example is a bit contrived. Normally you would not use a subselect to retrieve the object identifier. If you were writing PL/SQL code, for example, you might already have the object identifier as a result of having retrieved that object. The use of the REF operator is described more fully in the next section, which is titled "Nesting and Sharing Objects."

The options you have just seen for updating can be mixed and matched, giving you at least four different ways to code UPDATE statements against an object table. The SQL statements in Listing 13.11 show two ways to update the buildings table.

INPUT/OUTPUT **Listing 13.11. Updating an object table.**

```
1: --For the first update, treat buildings as a traditional table.
2: UPDATE buildings
3:   SET BldgName = 'Software Research'
4:   WHERE BldgName = 'Headquarters Building';

1 row updated.

1: --This update calls the constructor in the SET clause.
2: UPDATE buildings b
3:   SET b = building(BldgName,BldgAddress,598)
4:  WHERE BldgName = 'Victor Building';
```

continues

Listing 13.11. continued

```
1 row updated.

COMMIT;

Commit complete.
```

ANALYSIS The first update, lines 1–4 of the first segment, treats the `building` object table as if it were a normal relational table. The second update, lines 1–4 of the second segment, is more interesting. It updates the entire `building` object and features a call to the building constructor in line 4. The first two arguments passed to the building constructor are actually attributes of the object being updated. The third argument of 598 represents a new building manager assignment. Especially notice in line 4 of the second segment that the correlation name of the table is used as the target of the SET clause. This tells Oracle8 that the entire `building` object is being updated.

Deleting Objects from an Object Table

Objects can be deleted from an object table through the use of the DELETE statement. The same issues apply to the WHERE clause of a DELETE statement as apply to the WHERE clause of an UPDATE statement. The WHERE clause of a DELETE can use the REF operator and an object identifier to delete a specific object, or it can specify conditions for one or more attributes of the object.

Nesting and Sharing Objects

Objects can be nested inside other objects. They can also be shared, or referenced, by one or more other objects. You have already seen two examples of nested objects. The `building` object, created in Listing 13.7, contains a nested `address` object. The employee table also contains an `address` object, added in Listing 13.3.

Dot Notation

NEW TERM When objects are nested, it is possible to navigate through the objects using standard *dot notation*. You already know that in a SQL statement, you can refer to a specific field using the following notation:

```
TableName.FieldName
```

The same notation can also be used to reference a specific object attribute, for example:

```
ObjectVarName.AttributeName
```

You have already seen examples of this in Listing 13.2, lines 24–29, 33–38, and 42–47. When you have objects that themselves contain objects, you can use this dot notation to navigate your way down to a specific attribute. That's because the nested object is itself an attribute of the containing object, and also contains attributes of its own. So if you had a building object and wanted to know what city the building was in, you could reference

```
BldgVar.BldgAddress.City
```

Listing 13.12 shows a brief example of using dot notation on a building object in order to print the city and state.

INPUT/OUTPUT **Listing 13.12. Using dot notation.**

```
 1: SET SERVEROUTPUT ON
 2: DECLARE
 3:   this_building      building;
 4: BEGIN
 5:   --Retrieve a building object so we can print the attribute values.
 6:   SELECT value(b) INTO this_building
 7:     FROM buildings b
 8:    WHERE BldgName = 'East Storage Shed';
 9:
10:   COMMIT;
11:
12:   dbms_output.put_line(this_building.BldgName
13:                      || ' ' || this_building.BldgAddress.city
14:                      || ' ' || this_building.BldgAddress.state_abbr);
15: END;
16: /

East Storage Shed Lansing MI

PL/SQL procedure successfully completed.
```

ANALYSIS Line 12 uses dot notation to reference the building name attribute, while lines 13 and 14 use it to navigate through the nested address object to get the city name and state abbreviation.

Object References

NEW TERM When you store an object as an attribute of another object, the nested object is said to have no *visibility* outside of the parent. This means that it exists only within the context of the parent object, and that same object cannot be referenced or made part of any other object. It makes sense to nest objects when you are dealing with something like a building address because each building has its own unique address, not shared with any other building.

13

Consider the case, though, where you want to specify the building in which an employee works. You could modify the employee table and add a column of type building, for example:

```
ALTER TABLE employee
  ADD (EmpBldg    building);
```

But this solution has a big problem. Each employee will have their own private building object. If you have 1,000 employees in a building, then there will be 1,000 separate building objects, one for each employee, all containing redundant information. Clearly there has to be another way to deal with this situation, and indeed there is. The solution is to store only a reference to a building object in each employee's record.

NEW TERM Each object stored in an object table is identified by a unique, system-generated, *object identifier*. It isn't necessary to know the precise nature of this identifier, and in fact Oracle does not document it. What's important is that given an object identifier, you can easily retrieve the object in question from the database.

As stated earlier, the solution to the problem of relating employees to buildings is to create a reference to the building object in each employee record. The REF keyword is used to do this, and Listing 13.13 shows how.

INPUT/ OUTPUT **Listing 13.13. Creating a reference to building.**

```
ALTER TABLE employee
  ADD (emp_bldg    REF building);

Table altered.
```

ANALYSIS As you can see, this listing adds one column of type REF building to the employee record. The use of the keyword REF tells Oracle that the column will contain only a reference to a building object and not the building object itself.

The REF and DEREF Operators

Oracle8 introduces two new SQL operators named REF and DEREF. The REF operator can be used in a SQL statement to return the object identifier for an object. The DEREF operator does just the opposite. It is used in a SQL statement to retrieve the actual object referenced by an object identifier. Doing this is referred to as *dereferencing* an object identifier.

The REF operator is used in Listing 13.14 to retrieve a reference to a specific building so that it can be stored in an employee's record. The DEREF operator is used in Listing 13.15 in order to retrieve an employee's building name and display it.

To demonstrate the use of the REF operator, Listing 13.14 shows a simple procedure that, given an employee number and a building name, will assign the employee to a building.

**INPUT/
OUTPUT** **Listing 13.14. Using the REF operator.**

```
 1: CREATE OR REPLACE PROCEDURE AssignEmpToBldg (
 2:    EmpNumIn IN employee.emp_id%TYPE,
 3:    BldgNameIn IN buildings.BldgName%TYPE
 4:    ) AS
 5: BEGIN
 6:    UPDATE employee
 7:      SET emp_bldg = (SELECT REF(b)
 8:                        FROM buildings B
 9:                        WHERE BldgName = BldgNameIn)
10:     WHERE emp_id = EmpNumIn;
11:
12:    --Raise an error if either the employee number or
13:    --building name is invalid.
14:    IF SQL%NOTFOUND THEN
15:      RAISE_application_error(-20000,'Employee ' || EmpNumIn
16:                           || ' could not be assigned to building '
17:                           || BldgNameIn);
18:    END IF;
19: END;
20: /
```

```
Procedure created.
```

```
 1: BEGIN
 2:    AssignEmpToBldg (598,'Victor Building');
 3:    AssignEmpToBldg (597,'East Storage Shed');
 4:    AssignEmpToBldg (599,'Software Research');
 5: END;
 6: /
```

```
PL/SQL procedure successfully completed.
```

ANALYSIS The first part of this listing contains the definition for the AssignEmpToBldg procedure. This procedure takes both an employee ID and a building name as arguments. An UPDATE statement (lines 6–10 of the first segment) uses the building name to retrieve the matching building object and stores a reference to that object in the employee table. The PL/SQL anonymous block in lines 1–6 of the second segment calls this procedure to make some building assignments.

To show the use of the DEREF operator, Listing 13.15 shows a simple function that retrieves the name of the building in which an employee works.

13

**INPUT/
OUTPUT**   **Listing 13.15. Using the DEREF operator.**

```
 1: CREATE OR REPLACE FUNCTION GetEmpBldgName (
 2:   EmpNumIn IN employee.emp_id%TYPE
 3:   ) RETURN VARCHAR2 AS
 4: TheBldg      building;
 5: BEGIN
 6:   --Select the building object reference from this employee's record.
 7:   SELECT DEREF(emp_bldg) INTO TheBldg
 8:     FROM employee
 9:    WHERE emp_id = EmpNumIn;
10:
11:   IF TheBldg IS NULL THEN
12:     RETURN 'No Building Assigned';
13:   ELSE
14:     RETURN TheBldg.BldgName;
15:   END IF;
16: END;
17: /

Function created.

 1: BEGIN
 2:   dbms_output.put_line(GetEmpBldgName(599));
 3:   dbms_output.put_line(GetEmpBldgName(598));
 4:   dbms_output.put_line(GetEmpBldgName(597));
 5: END;
 6: /

Software Research
Victor Building
East Storage Shed

PL/SQL procedure successfully completed.
```

ANALYSIS   The GetEmpBldgName function takes an employee ID as an argument and returns the
name of the building in which the employee works. The SELECT statement, in lines
7–9 of the first segment, retrieves the building information for the selected employee. It does
this by using the DEREF operator (line 7 of the first segment) to dereference the emp_bldg
pointer. The DEREF operator causes Oracle to automatically retrieve the referenced building
object from wherever it is stored, which in this case happens to be the building table.

NOTE   Notice that in Listing 13.15 you did not need to tell Oracle that the
building object you were retrieving was stored in the building table.
The object reference, used by the DEREF operator, contains all the
information necessary for Oracle to find the object. This is in contrast
to a relational join, in which you do need to specify the tables being
accessed.

The SELF **Parameter**

Each object method you write has a default first parameter named SELF. This SELF parameter, which is normally not specified in the method's declaration, is used to reference the attributes of the object being called. By default, any unqualified attribute reference in a member function or member procedure is automatically qualified by SELF. Listing 13.16 shows how the building object type definition would look if you explicitly defined and used the SELF parameter.

NOTE

In order to execute the code shown in Listing 13.16, you must first drop the building table and delete all references to building objects from the employee table. Because of that, you might not want to execute this listing.

If you do want to execute Listing 13.16, use these commands to eliminate any existing references to building objects:

DROP TABLE building;

UPDATE employee SET emp_bldg = null;

You can easily restore the information just deleted by re-executing the listings shown earlier in this chapter.

INPUT **Listing 13.16. Using the SELF parameter.**

```
 1: CREATE OR REPLACE TYPE building AS OBJECT (
 2:   BldgName          VARCHAR2(40),
 3:   BldgAddress       address,
 4:   BldgMgr           INTEGER,
 5:   MEMBER PROCEDURE  ChangeMgr (SELF IN OUT building,
 6:                               NewMgr IN INTEGER),
 7:   ORDER MEMBER FUNCTION Compare (SELF IN building,
 8:                                  OtherBuilding IN building)
 9:     RETURN INTEGER
10:   );
11:
12: CREATE OR REPLACE TYPE BODY building AS
13:   MEMBER PROCEDURE  ChangeMgr(SELF IN OUT building,
14:                              NewMgr IN INTEGER) IS
15:   BEGIN
16:     SELF.BldgMgr := NewMgr;
17:   END;
18:
19:   ORDER MEMBER FUNCTION Compare (SELF IN building,
20:                                  OtherBuilding IN building)
```

13

continues

Listing 13.16. continued

```
21:    RETURN INTEGER IS
22:        BldgName1        VARCHAR2(40);
23:        BldgName2        building.BldgName%TYPE;
24:    BEGIN
25:        --Grab the two building names for comparison.
26:        --Make sure that we don't get messed up by leading/trailing
27:        --spaces or by case.
28:        BldgName1 := upper(ltrim(rtrim(SELF.BldgName)));
29:        BldgName2 := upper(ltrim(rtrim(OtherBuilding.BldgName)));
30:
31:        --Return the appropriate value to indicate the order of
32:        --this object vs OtherBuilding.
33:        IF BldgName1 = BldgName2 THEN
34:            RETURN 0;
35:        ELSIF BldgName1 < BldgName2 THEN
36:            RETURN -1;
37:        ELSE
38:            RETURN 1;
39:        END IF;
40:    END;
41: END;
42: /
```

ANALYSIS   Notice that all the member method definitions now include SELF as the first parameter. All attribute references in the preceding listing are explicitly prefaced with "SELF." Oracle always treats any unqualified attribute references in member methods as if you had really written them this way.

The SELF parameter must always be the object type being defined. By default it is an input (IN) parameter for member functions and an input/output (IN OUT) parameter for member procedures. This is because functions usually return values without altering an object's attributes, whereas procedures frequently do alter an object's attributes.

Although you normally do not specify the SELF parameter, you might do so if you want to specify an input/output mode other than the default. For example, if you wanted a member function to be able to modify an object's attributes, you would explicitly define SELF as an IN OUT parameter.

Overloading

NEW TERM   The term *overloading* refers to the ability to have more than one function or procedure of the same name, but with a different number and types of parameters. This ability to *overload* function and procedure names is a key feature of object-oriented languages. It is what allows you to write a Compare function for several different object types. Being able to do this frees you from the burden of remembering a different comparison function name for each object type that you are using.

Overloading also enables you to provide additional flexibility to programmers using an object type. Consider the `building` object type defined in Listing 13.7. It has a method named `ChangeMgr`, which allows you to specify an employee who is the building manager for a building. This method takes one argument, the employee number. What if you also wanted the ability to specify the manager by name? One solution would be to write a method named `ChangeMgrName` to do this, but then you would have to constantly remember which method to call each time you wrote code to change a building manager. Worse, you might get confused about the naming convention and try writing a call to `ChangeMgrNo`, or perhaps to `ChangeMgrEmpNo`, neither of which exist. Instead you can simply declare another member function named `ChangeMgr`, but with a string argument instead of a number. This function would look up the employee by name, get the employee number, and store that number as an attribute. Oracle would know to call this new version of the method when you supplied a string argument, and would know to call the old version of the method when you supplied a numeric argument. The advantage to this is that when you are coding, you always call `ChangeMgr` whenever you need to specify a new building manager, regardless of whether you are specifying the new manager by name or number.

Comparing Objects

Are two objects equal? Is one "greater than" another? How do they compare? Sooner or later you will want to write code to answer these questions. Before you can do that, you must decide on the comparison semantics. What is it about two `building` objects, for example, that makes one "greater than" another? This is often not as simple a question as it might seem at first. When dealing with numbers, common convention dictates that the number with the larger value is "greater than" the other. But when dealing with buildings, what attribute do you consider? You could, for example, look at how high the building is. A taller building would be "greater than" a shorter building. Alternatively, you could look at the "footprint" of the building, basing your decision on the number of square feet of ground space that the building occupied. Another alternative would be to base the "greater than" decision on the total square footage of the building's floor space.

As you can see, even with a type as simple as the `building` type, there are many alternatives to look at when considering how comparisons should be done. The choice might ultimately become somewhat arbitrary based on how you intend to use the object.

To help you compare objects, Oracle allows you to declare two special member function types. These are identified by the keywords `MAP` and `ORDER`. A `MAP` function enables you to specify a single numeric value that is used when comparing two objects of the same type. The greater than/less than/equality decision is based on this value. An `ORDER` function enables you to write whatever code you want in order to compare two objects, the return value indicating equality or which of the two is greater.

13

NOTE

It is possible to write your own code to compare objects without defining a MAP or an ORDER method. When comparing building objects, for example, you could simply write:

```
IF BldgObj1.BldgName = BldgObj2.BldgName THEN ...
```

The disadvantages of this approach are that your comparison semantics are spread all through your code, they might not be consistent, and the intent of the comparison might not be obvious. From the preceding IF statement, it is not clear that you are inferring that two objects are equal because their names are the same. It might be that you are simply comparing the names.

Using the MAP and ORDER methods provides you with a way to store the comparison rules along with the object type, thus ensuring consistency wherever comparisons are made. The intent of your IF statements will then be clear. People will know that you are comparing two objects for equality when you write

```
IF BldgObj1 = BldgObj2 THEN ...
```

They'll also know that you are simply comparing two object attributes when you write

```
IF BldgObj1.BldgMgr = BldgObj2.BldgMgr THEN ...
```

The ORDER **Method**

You might have noticed back in Listing 13.7 that the keyword ORDER was used in front of one of the member functions for a building. The specification for that function looks like this:

```
ORDER MEMBER FUNCTION Compare (OtherBuilding IN building)
    RETURN INTEGER
```

The keyword ORDER tells Oracle that Compare is a specially written function that should be called whenever it is necessary to compare one building object with another. It takes one argument, which must be of the same type. In other words, because Compare is a method of the building object type, the argument to Compare must also be of the building object type.

Remember that every object method has a default first argument named SELF, and that the SELF argument represents the object whose method was called. An ORDER function is expected to compare SELF to its argument and return one of the values shown in Table 13.1.

Table 13.1. ORDER function return values.

Return Value	Meaning
-1	SELF is less than the argument.
0	SELF is equal to the argument.
1	SELF is greater than the argument.

After you have defined an ORDER function for an object type, you can then use any of the PL/SQL relational operators with objects of that type. Listing 13.17 instantiates some building objects and shows the result of some simple comparisons.

INPUT/
OUTPUT

Listing 13.17. Comparing objects with ORDER functions.

```
1: SET SERVEROUTPUT ON
2: DECLARE
3:   bldg_a       building;    --will be less than bldg_b
4:   bldg_b       building;
5:   bldg_b2      building;
6:   bldg_c       building;
7: BEGIN
8:   --First, create four building objects.
9:   bldg_a := building('A Building',null,null);
10:   bldg_b := building('Another Building',null,null);
11:   bldg_b2 := building('Another Building',null,null);
12:   bldg_c := building('Cosmotology Research Lab',null,null);
13:
14:   --Now compare the building objects and display the results;
15:   IF bldg_a < bldg_b THEN
16:     dbms_output.put_line('bldg_a < bldg_b');
17:   END IF;
18:
19:   --These two have the same name, so should be equal.
20:   IF bldg_b = bldg_b2 THEN
21:     dbms_output.put_line('bldg_b = bldg_b2');
22:   END IF;
23:
24:   IF bldg_c > bldg_b2 THEN
25:     dbms_output.put_line('bldg_c > bldg_b2');
26:   END IF;
27: END;
28: /

bldg_a < bldg_b
bldg_b = bldg_b2
bldg_c > bldg_b2

PL/SQL procedure successfully completed.
```

13

Lines 9–12 instantiate four new `building` objects. The remainder of the PL/SQL block compares these `building` objects against each other; see lines 15, 20, and 24. In each of these cases a relational operator is used to compare one `building` object to another. When executing these comparisons, Oracle automatically calls the `ORDER` method defined for this object type. The `ORDER` method then determines the result of the comparison.

The MAP Method

`MAP` functions provide an alternative way to specify comparison semantics for an object type. A `MAP` function enables you to compute a single scalar value, based on one or more of the object's attributes, which is then used to compare the object in question to other objects of the same type.

`MAP` functions have no parameter because their purpose is to return a value representing only the object whose `MAP` method was invoked. The result of a `MAP` function must be one of the following types:

- ☐ NUMBER
- ☐ DATE
- ☐ VARCHAR2

When comparing two objects with `MAP` methods defined, Oracle first calls the `MAP` function for each object and then compares the two results.

NOTE

> It is possible to write a `MAP` function for the `building` object type, which would return the building name for comparison purposes. This could be used instead of the `ORDER` function.

Limitations of Oracle's Implementation

Although the object features introduced in Oracle8 represent a significant step forward for Oracle, there are some limitations of which you should be aware. These limitations are listed following:

- ☐ Inheritance is not supported.
- ☐ Private attributes are not supported.
- ☐ There is no support for custom constructors.
- ☐ Object types must be declared at the database level and cannot be declared within a PL/SQL function or procedure.
- ☐ Certain datatypes cannot be used as attributes.
- ☐ Objects support a maximum of 1,000 attributes.

Some of these limitations are fairly significant. The lack of support for private attributes, for example, means that anyone using your objects is free to bypass whatever accessor and mutator methods you have defined. In more mature object-oriented languages, you can protect attributes, allowing them to be set only by member functions, which then contain code to validate the values being set. Another issue here is that you cannot separate implementation-specific attributes from those which you intend to be publicly referenced.

The inability to write your own constructor functions also serves to limit your opportunities to validate attribute values. Validation at object creation is impossible because the default constructors simply set the attributes to whatever values you supply. If you were dealing with an employee object, for example, you could easily instantiate it with a negative salary.

Inheritance is a key feature of any object-oriented language, and it is a feature that Oracle does not yet support. The other limitations are not as significant as the first three. The 1,000-attribute limit is probably not one you will often run up against. The datatype limitation is related to the fact that all object types must be declared at the database level, and although it might be convenient to be able to define object types local to a PL/SQL procedure, you wouldn't be able to store those objects permanently in the database.

Summary

The object-oriented features of Oracle8 described in this chapter represent a significant step forward in the effort to marry object and relational technologies, in the process providing Oracle developers with access to some of the same powerful object-oriented features enjoyed by developers using languages such as C++ and Java. Oracle now supports the definition and creation of objects, complete with methods and attributes. These objects can be stored in the database as attributes of other objects, columns in a table, or as rows in an object table. In addition, you can still access your data using standard, relational methods. This can ease your transition to object-oriented programming and lets you still use relational queries in cases where they are most efficient.

Q&A

13

Q Why is encapsulation so important?

A Encapsulation provides two benefits. It provides for reusability and lessens the amount of detail you need to remember about an object's implementation. When an object's functionality is exposed through a well-defined interface, you no longer have to worry about all the details behind that interface. You just call the methods and let the object do its work. Encapsulation also aids in reusability because all the necessary code is part of the object definition, making it easy to drop that definition into other programs.

Q **When I create objects based on an object type, is the code for all the methods replicated for each instance of the object?**

A No, the code for the member functions and procedures is not duplicated for each instance of an object type. The function and procedure code exists in one place; only the object's attributes are distinct. Oracle always passes the SELF parameter to each member function and procedure to ensure that the proper attributes are referenced. Usually this is done transparently to you, so conceptually it is easy to think of each object having its own code.

Q **What are accessor and mutator methods?**

A Accessor methods are member functions that exist primarily to enable you to retrieve specific attribute values from an object. Mutator methods are member procedures that enable you to set the value of a specific attribute or set of attributes. Using accessor and mutator methods helps insulate your code from changes to an object's underlying implementation.

Q **When should I use an object table to store objects, and when should I store objects as a single column in a table?**

A The answer to this depends on how you will use the objects in question. Generally, if an object has meaning only in the context of a parent object, you can store it as a column. Objects that stand alone and need to be referenced by several other objects must be stored in object tables.

Q **When do I need to worry about the SELF parameter?**

A Rarely. You only need to worry about the SELF parameter when you want to use an input/output mode different from the default. For example, the SELF parameter of a member function is by default input only. This means that by default a member function cannot change an object's attributes. To change this behavior and allow a member function to update an attribute, you would need to explicitly declare the SELF parameter as an IN OUT parameter.

Workshop

Use the following workshop to test your comprehension of this chapter and put what you've learned into practice. You'll find the answers to the quiz and exercises in Appendix A, "Answers."

Quiz

1. What is the difference between a class and an object?
2. What are the allowed return values for an ORDER function?

3. An object table has one column for each attribute of an object, plus one additional column. What is this additional column used for?

4. How is an object reference different from an object?

5. How many attributes must an object have? How many methods?

6. What datatypes are allowed for the return value of a MAP function?

Exercises

1. Write a stored function that creates and returns an object of type building. This function should accept as parameters the building's name, its address, and the manager's employee number. Have the function check the database before creating the new building object to be sure that another building with the same name does not already exist. If another building with the same name does exist, then the function should return null.

2. Modify the building object type definition to use a MAP function for comparisons instead of an ORDER function.

13

Day 14

Debugging Your Code and Preventing Errors

by Timothy Atwood

No matter how good a programmer you are, inevitably you will make some coding errors. These errors are composed of syntax and logic errors. Today's lesson demonstrates how to locate these bugs and how to reduce the number of coding mistakes you make. The topics today include

- ☐ Syntax errors
- ☐ Logic errors
- ☐ Debugging without tools
- ☐ Creating a debugging package
- ☐ Preventing errors
- ☐ Available add-on tools

Syntax Errors

The most common error is a *syntax error*. A syntax error simply means not following the guidelines of the programming language such as form, punctuation, and so on. When the PL/SQL code is compiled, it will generally point you in the area that needs correcting. However, this indication is not always perfect because the error could be from one or more lines above, which might be missing something as simple as a comma or a semicolon. The code in Listing 14.1 demonstrates syntax errors. The best way to debug syntax errors is through running the code and making the corrections until the code has compiled successfully. Simply look for the asterisk (*) where the compiler thinks the error occurred. In this section, you will attempt to debug this code, which is full of syntax errors.

TIP

Before you compile, or even after you compile and receive errors, it's a good idea to scan through the code to look for all possible syntax errors. In fact, sometimes if you type the code more slowly with proper formatting, you can Do It Right the First Time (DIRFT) and not waste time on debugging.

INPUT   **Listing 14.1. Practice correcting syntax errors.**

```
 1: DECALRE
 2:     v_MyChar VARCHAR2 := 'test';
 3:     v_NUMBER NUMBER;
 4:     Date DATE = SYSDATE;
 5:     v_counter INTEGER;
 6: NEGIN
 7:     DBMS_OUTPUT.PUT_LINE('This is a Test')
 8:     DBMS_OUT.PUTPUT_LINE("Of Syntax Error Debugging");
 9:     For v_COUNTER IN 1..5 LOOP
10:         DBMS_OUTPUT.PUTLINE('You are in loop: ¦¦ v_counter);
11:     END-LOOP;
12: END
 /
```

OUTPUT   When you execute the code in Listing 14.1, your output will look like the following:

```
DECALRE
*
ERROR at line 1:
ORA-01756: quoted string not properly terminated
```

14

ANALYSIS The Oracle error is looking for a proper string, which is a string encapsulated by single quotes. Even though it singled out the first line, is the first line a proper string, or is there a line without a beginning or end single quote? Remember, errors do not have to be located in the area the compiler suggests. In line 10, there is a string missing a single quote. Change the line to read

INPUT
```
DBMS_OUTPUT.PUTLINE('You are in loop: '¦¦ v_counter);
```

After you have corrected the changes, reexecute the code. Your next error is

OUTPUT
```
DECALRE
*
ERROR at line 1:
ORA-00900: invalid SQL statement
```

ANALYSIS Oracle, after checking for properly terminated strings, now starts checking top down. The first error is a misspelling of the keyword DECLARE in line 1. Make the change and reexecute the code. You will now receive many errors:

OUTPUT
```
Date DATE = SYSDATE;
          *
ERROR at line 4:
ORA-06550: line 4, column 15:
PLS-00103: Encountered the symbol "=" when expecting one of the
➥following:
:= . ( @ % ; not null range renames default
The symbol ":= was inserted before "=" to continue.
ORA-06550: line 8, column 5:
PLS-00103: Encountered the symbol "DBMS_OUT" when expecting
    one of the following:
:= ; not null default
The symbol ":=" was substituted for "DBMS_OUT" to continue.
ORA-06550: line 9, column 5:
PLS-00103: Encountered the symbol "FOR" when expecting
    one of the following:
begin function package pragma procedure subtype type use
<an identifier> <a double-quoted delimited-identifier> cursor
form
The symbol "begin" was subst
ORA-06550: line 11, column 8:
PLS-00103: Encountered the symbol "-" when expecting one of the
➥following:
loop
```

ANALYSIS Just changing one line now affects several other lines. The first error states that you are trying to compare one variable to another in a declaration area. In addition, you can correct two problems. You have defined a variable date of type DATE. You should never use keywords in variable names. Line 4 should read

```
v_Date DATE := SYSDATE;
```

14

Upon reexecution, your next set of errors is

OUTPUT

```
DBMS_OUT.PUTPUT_LINE("Of Syntax Error Debugging");
     *
ERROR at line 8:
ORA-06550: line 8, column 5:
PLS-00103: Encountered the symbol "DBMS_OUTPUT" when expecting
     one of the following:
:= ; not null default
The symbol ":=" was substituted for "DBMS_OUTPUT" to continue.
ORA-06550: line 9, column 5:
PLS-00103: Encountered the symbol "FOR" when expecting
     one of the following:
begin function package pragma procedure subtype type use
<an identifier> <a double-quoted delimited-identifier> cursor
form
The symbol "begin" was subst
ORA-06550: line 11, column 8:
PLS-00103: Encountered the symbol "-" when expecting one of the
⇒following:
loop
```

ANALYSIS Now you can narrow down the problems. In line 8, the program tries to assign a value to DBMS_OUTPUT.PUT_LINE because it still thinks it is in the declaration section. You need to make two corrections. Change NEGIN to BEGIN and change the double quotes in line 8 to single quotes, so the line now reads

```
DBMS_OUTPUT.PUT_LINE('Of Syntax Error Debugging');
```

Now, when you reexecute the code, the list of errors is

OUTPUT

```
DBMS_OUTPUT.PUT_LINE('Of Syntax Error Debugging');
     *
ERROR at line 8:
ORA-06550: line 8, column 5:
PLS-00103: Encountered the symbol "DBMS_OUTPUT" when expecting
     one of the following:
:= . ( % ;
The symbol ":=" was substituted for "DBMS_OUTPUT" to continue.
ORA-06550: line 11, column 8:
PLS-00103: Encountered the symbol "-" when expecting one of the
⇒following:
loop
```

ANALYSIS You still have an error on line 8. This is because the line above it is missing the semicolon. You can also fix the error on line 11. The END-LOOP statement should be END LOOP. Fix both errors (add the semicolon at the end of line 7, and remove the dash from END-LOOP), and reexecute the code.

```
DECLARE
*
ERROR at line 1:
ORA-06550: line 13, column 0:
PLS-00103: Encountered the symbol "END" when expecting
     one of the following:
; <an identifier> <a double-quoted delimited-identifier>
The symbol ";" was substituted for "END" to continue.
```

ANALYSIS Amazing—you are back to errors in the first line. In this case, the DECLARE statement does not have a matching END statement properly terminated. Change line 12 to read END;—you have missed the semicolon—and then reexecute the program.

```
v_MyChar VARCHAR2 := 'test';
                *
ERROR at line 2:
ORA-06550: line 2, column 14:
PLS-00215: String length constraints must be in range (1 .. 32767)
ORA-06550: line 2, column 14:
PL/SQL: Item ignored
ORA-06550: line 10, column 21:
PLS-00302: component 'PUTLINE' must be declared
ORA-06550: line 10, column 9:
PL/SQL: Statement ignored
```

ANALYSIS Now you have even more new errors. Notice that VARCHAR2 is missing how wide the string is? Also, PUTLINE should be PUT_LINE in line 10. Change the VARCHAR2 in line 2 to read VARCHAR2(20), change PUTLINE in line 10 to read PUT_LINE, and reexecute your code. Your output should now be

OUTPUT
```
This is a Test
Of Syntax Error Debugging
You are in loop: 1
You are in loop: 2
You are in loop: 3
You are in loop: 4
You are in loop: 5
```

The purpose of this example was to demonstrate the following:

☐ One syntax error fixed could lead to several new errors.

☐ The area of the error that Oracle flags might not necessarily be even near the location of the true error.

☐ Typing the data in properly saves a lot of time when testing your program.

☐ Syntax errors can be avoided!

For fun and learning, you might want to create a utility that searches the saved SQL file (using the UTLFILE package) and not only checks syntax, but also will fix some of the errors automatically, such as spelling keywords properly, adding missing keywords, adding missing punctuation, and so on.

Logic Errors

Unlike syntax errors, logic errors do not stop a program from compiling. After a program is compiled and tested to some extent, logic errors can still occur. Possible logic errors include

☐ Not using proper order of operations

☐ Wrong calculation used

14

☐ Loops that never terminate

☐ New data not handled by an exception

☐ Data entered out of range or incorrect datatype than originally expected

This list could easily be hundreds of pages; however, I think you get the idea. Logic errors are the hardest to debug. You will be examining debugging techniques later in this chapter when you create your DEBUG package! The main steps in debugging logic errors are to identify the problem, narrow the area where the problem exists, and if the error is not obvious, use debugging tools. The rest of this section reviews some samples of logic errors.

Order of Operations

For some reason, when people leave algebra class, the order of operations seems to be easily forgotten. Remember when students in class would ask if there are any real-world applications of math? Well, understanding the order of operations is critical not only in PL/SQL, but in every programming language, database, and spreadsheet package you might use. The order of operations simply states the order of precedence each operator is given. Table 14.1 covers just a few of the levels, with the top level being the highest priority order.

Table 14.1. Simple order of operations table.

Operator	Description
( )	Parentheses
*, /	Multiplication, division
+, -	Addition, subtraction

If two or more operators are on the same priority level, then the expression is evaluated from left to right. Take the following equation, which looks as if it should add two numbers and multiply 9 by the result:

5 + 3 * 9

Whenever I ask this question in the classroom, at least 25 percent of the class tells me the answer is 72. However, the order of operations tells you that multiplication should come first. In this case, 3 * 9 = 27, and when you add 5, the true answer is 32. What if you wanted to arrive at 72? Use parentheses around the expression you want to evaluate first.

Now (5 + 3) * 9 does = 72.

I find the order of operations to be a very common problem in areas of business, finance, statistics, and scientific application programming. This could have disastrous results, especially if your nuclear plant depends upon proper order of operations. The complete table can be found in the *Oracle Database Guide*. Study this guide, and even make a copy of it to keep near your desk.

Nonterminating Loops

Another common problem is loops that never terminate. As an example, take a look at the code in Listing 14.2.

INPUT **Listing 14.2. Example of an infinite loop.**

```
 1: DECLARE
 2:     v_MyNumber NUMBER := 0;
 3: BEGIN
 4:     LOOP
 5:         IF v_MyNumber = 7 THEN
 6:             EXIT;
 7:      END IF;
 8:     v_MyNumber := v_MyNumber + 2;
 9:     END LOOP;
10: END;
```

ANALYSIS As you can see, this loop will never exit because v_MyNumber will never evaluate to 7. These are just a few examples of logic errors. The next section goes into some debugging techniques.

The Nontool Approach

Oracle does not have any true built-in debugger packages. These can be acquired as additions from Oracle Forms, Oracle Developer/2000, or third-party applications. You could even create your own debugging package with pipes, UTLFILE, and so on, which you will do in the section "Using Tools to Help in Debugging a Program."

Setting Up a Test Environment

Although testing might seem like common sense, you would not believe how many major corporations either don't have test environments for all their applications or simply put code into production without thoroughly testing the code in a test environment. This problem occurred at one firm that used a program to calculate the raises for employees. The managers would enter a percentage such as .05. Unfortunately, the code took the current pay rate multiplied by the percentage of the raise and assigned this to the new value of the hourly rate. So people with a 5 percent raise on $10.00/hour now were making 50 cents per hour! The formula should have been pay _rate * (1+raise). Imagine being the IT manager trying to explain this "glitch" to your coworkers.

Unfortunately, this problem is more common than it might seem. Another case concerns code that works fine when initially placed in production, but it affects code in later production processes. Whenever possible, always set up a test environment and test extensively. The testing should not be done by the programmer, but by someone else who

14

has no knowledge and just tries to break the program. Users make the best beta-testers! If a test environment is not available, *back up the data before proceeding*. Also, make the changes at off-hours so as to not affect employees.

Setting Up Test Data

After you have set up your test environment, you need to test the code with sample data. One method to determine test data is to come up with a spreadsheet with a list of all possible values, or range of values, and then manually calculate the output. The whole purpose of programming is to work with the inputs, and output the *desired* results. Use test data that might not be used currently in the system, but could possibly be entered by the user, and so on. For example, if a program uses only positive numbers, enter a negative number as test data. The program should reject the entry—but only if this capability has been implemented. Furthermore, if you do not know the industry implicitly, seek help from your end users to provide you with test data. The final test would be to copy data in actual production, and see if you mirror the output.

Setting up test data and testing all possible outcomes is critical in debugging any application. A major insurance company had a programmer who sent only two examples through in a test environment, where the desired outcome was reached. Unfortunately, the code caused major problems in production that took two months to identify and an additional three months to fix; it has been two additional months and the data that was corrupted is still not fixed. Test everything from inputs to error handling and exceptions. The little extra time for more thorough testing will benefit you greatly down the road.

Narrowing Down the Location of a Bug

Suppose you do encounter a case in which outputs do not match the desired output. What steps do you take next? No matter what, you need to narrow down the search area, especially since large-scale applications have millions of lines of code. The steps I would take to troubleshoot for a logic error bug are as follows:

1. What is the overall process?
2. Where, when, and how frequently does the error occur?
3. What outputs are invalid?
4. What inputs and calculations make up those outputs?
5. What does work? (This question can help in determining the cause.)
6. Define the problem.
7. Use one of the many tools to trace your inputs, intermediate computations, and outputs.
8. If you're having a tough time, step away from the problem.

9. If you're having an extremely tough time, don't be afraid to ask for help. Software bugs have been discovered this way!

10. Document the solution.

What if the error is a syntax error in a new procedure you created and the compiler does not seem to pinpoint the true location of the error? What I do is to comment out a block of code until the procedure compiles. Then, I uncomment the area until I receive the same error, which usually identifies the problem rather quickly!

What Is the Overall Process?

Before you can troubleshoot, you should have some idea of the overall process and how it relates to the business. If you have no reinsurance knowledge, it will make troubleshooting that much more difficult. Even if you don't know the process, at least seeing the entire process should clarify and support your findings in troubleshooting.

Where, When, and How Frequently Does the Error Occur?

You should know where in the system the problem is occurring. What forms are involved? What data is involved? When does the problem occur? How frequently does this problem occur? Every time a user clicks the Send button? Every time a form is saved and the data is inserted into the table? Only when uniform #23 is inserted into the basketball database? All of these questions will help to determine the root problem.

What Outputs Are Invalid?

When attempting to define the problem, if it is not a systems crash but an error on output, attempt to define all outputs that are invalid. Such questions for a banking industry could be: Which accounts get a service fee when they are not supposed to? How much is the service fee? (You can use this information to see which variable references this value in a table.) How often does the error occur? What was the last transaction that occurred before the service fee? (Perhaps a trigger is causing the problem when updating the table.) What date does the error occur? (If the date is fixed, this will help to narrow down the problem area.) In reality, there should be no "random" problems ultimately even though the problems might initially seem random. You should eventually see a pattern evolve, which should lead you directly to the problem.

What Inputs and Calculations Make Up Those Outputs?

If you know a bank fee is accessed, you should now start a trace to which modules, programs, triggers, procedures, and so on are involved with processing a late fee. What tables do your inputs of a service fee come from? Knowing all possible locations can now help you trace the problem more effectively.

What Does Work?

The question "What does work?" might seem like an odd idea, but believe it or not, it is very effective. If you suspect that a procedure is bad because the data you pass to the procedure is not processing the data properly, check the other modules that access this procedure. If they all have the same problem, it is the module. If all of them process properly, and you pass the same number of parameters, maybe it is something in your module. If the range of values you pass is different than that of the other modules accessing the procedure, it could be an out-of-range error in the procedure.

Defining the Problem

Usually, this is the most difficult part. If you have worked your way through proper troubleshooting and the asking of questions, you should now be able to determine the root cause of the problem, and where to start your search to fix the problem. Most people try to define the problem first, and take away the symptoms with "workaround" coding rather than finding the true root cause, which could resurface at any time. It could even be something as simple as this: New values added to a lookup table are out of a valid range specified in the PL/SQL coding. Another possibility is that the new range goes to a default, which is not the proper path for the data to take.

Tracing Your Inputs, Intermediate Computations, and Outputs

You can use the DBMS_OUTPUT package to output the values of variables as the code executes, which will allow you to pinpoint the problems fairly quickly. You can also write a debugging package similar to the one in this book, which outputs text to a file for viewing. Sometimes you do not want data output to the screen because it moves too quickly, or you are using forms to access PL/SQL and want the user to take you through the problem. By outputting to a file, you can go back and examine the text until you find the problem. Tracing outputs will be discussed in greater detail in the section "Writing a Debugging Package."

Stepping Away from the Problem

Have you ever had the solution to the problem stare you in the face but you did not see it? All too often, we get so involved in trying to find and eliminate the bug that we get too frustrated and start to repeat steps that we have already eliminated. It usually helps to take a break and get away from the problem. I personally have deleted data files in a subdirectory accidentally when trying to fix a bug. The fingers are sometimes quicker than the mind! (Yes, I did have a backup!)

Don't Be Afraid to Ask for Help

If after examining the code, it appears that you have followed all punctuation and syntax, and you have a complete understanding of the function package, procedure, and so on, don't be afraid to ask another consultant or the product manufacturer for help. I worked at a company that was using a program that supposedly compiled with computing standards, until a repeating bug proved that the error was in how the program handled the standard, not an error in the coding. Sometimes an extra set of eyes can pinpoint the problem. In addition, you might learn some new tips and tricks to speed up development or troubleshooting the next time around.

Document the Solution

You should document the solution, on paper, in the program (if possible), and ideally in an Oracle database of troubleshooting solutions. This will help you if the problem reoccurs and you can't remember what you did to fix it. You are also on your way to building an expert system that might be of some value to other clients or end users. This is probably one of the most important processes you should complete after you have solved the problem. If you're too busy to document right after solving the problem, you may live to regret the decision if a similar error occurs, which uses more time trying to solve the problem again. Make the time!

Using Tools to Help in Debugging a Program

After you have narrowed down the problem to a set of modules, procedures, and so on, you can break out some troubleshooting tools. Two such tools demonstrated in this chapter are the creation of a debugging package and the use of DBMS_OUTPUT, both of which I use extensively.

TIP

If you get tired of typing DBMS_OUTPUT.PUT_LINE, you could always create a package or procedure, which will simply abbreviate the words DBMS_OUTPUT.PUT_LINE.

Writing a Debugging Package

You will create a debugging package called DEBUG that will allow you to

☐ Take the system date and time, comments, and the contents of a variable and write these to a file while the program executes. This format will be output as a comma-separated value file (CSV) to allow you to import it into a table for queries, or simply to view the file with a text editor.

☐ Reset the file (erase the file) to start a new debugging process.

Execute the first part of the DEBUG package in Listing 14.3, which defines the procedures available to the package.

INPUT **Listing 14.3. Defining the DEBUG package components.**

```
1: CREATE OR REPLACE PACKAGE DEBUG AS
2:     PROCEDURE OUT(p_Comments IN VARCHAR2, p_Variable IN VARCHAR2);
3: /* Procedure OUT is used to output a comment of your
4:    choice, along with the contents of the variable.  The
```

continues

14

Listing 14.3. continued

```
 5:     Procedure OUT statement defines the format of the function */
 6:        PROCEDURE Erase;
 7: /* Procedure Erase is used to erase the contents of the file.
 8:     Used to start a new debugging process.  Good idea to call
 9:     this function first.  */
10: END DEBUG; -- End Definition of package DEBUG
```

After you have executed the code, you should see on the screen

OUTPUT Package Created

If you do not see this message, review your code for syntax errors. You can now enter and
execute the final part of the DEBUG package from Listing 14.4.

Listing 14.4. Creating the actual DEBUG package
INPUT components.

```
 1: CREATE OR REPLACE PACKAGE BODY DEBUG AS
 2:     PROCEDURE OUT(p_Comments IN VARCHAR2,p_Variable IN VARCHAR2) IS
 3:         v_MyFHOUT UTL_FILE.FILE_TYPE; -- Declare File Handle
 4: BEGIN
 5: /* Use A to append all output being sent to the file */
 6:
 7:     v_MyFHOUT := UTL_FILE.FOPEN('c:\','debug.txt','a');
 8:
 9: /* This outputs the System Time and Date formatted in MM-DD-YY HH:MM:SS
10:     followed by any comments you want to output and the contents of the
11:     variables.  Notice each element is surrounded by quotation marks and
12:     separated by a comma to create a comma-separated value file */
13:
14:     UTL_FILE.PUT_LINE(v_MyFHOUT,'"'||
15:         TO_CHAR(SYSDATE,'mm-dd-yy HH:MM:SS AM')
16:           || '","Comment: ' || p_Comments ||
17:             '","Variable Contents: ' || p_Variable || '"');
18:
19: /* Close the file handle which points to debug.txt */
20:     UTL_FILE.FCLOSE(v_MyFHOUT);
21:
22: EXCEPTION
23: /* Create Exception to simply display error code and message */
24:     WHEN OTHERS THEN
25:         DBMS_OUTPUT.PUT_LINE
26:             ('ERROR ' || to_char(SQLCODE) || SQLERRM);
27:         NULL; -- Do Nothing
28:     END OUT; -- End Execution of Procedure OUT
29:
30:
31:     PROCEDURE Erase IS
32:         v_MyFH UTL_FILE.FILE_TYPE; -- Create File Handle
33:     BEGIN
```

14

```
34: /* Open file to overwrite current file contents.  Doing this
35:    erases the contents of the original file completely */
36:
37:       v_MyFH := UTL_FILE.FOPEN('c:\','debug.txt','w');
38:
39: -- Close the file handle which points to debug.txt
40:       UTL_FILE.FCLOSE(v_MyFH);
41:
42:       EXCEPTION
43: -- Create Exception to simply display error code and message
44:            WHEN OTHERS THEN
45:                DBMS_OUTPUT.PUT_LINE
46:                    ('ERROR ' || to_char(SQLCODE) || SQLERRM);
47:                NULL;
48:       END Erase; -- End Procedure Erase
49:
50: BEGIN
51:     Erase; -- Erase contents of the file
52:
53: END DEBUG; -- End procedure DEBUG
```

Again, after you have executed the code in Listing 14.4, your output should appear as

OUTPUT   Package body created.

You can now examine the components of the newly created DEBUG package.

The DEBUG.OUT Procedure

The DEBUG.OUT procedure enables you to print to a file called DEBUG.TXT the system date and time, a comment, such as where you are in the code and the name of the variable, and the contents of the variable. All the procedure does is accept two parameters: the comment specified by the end user, and the variable you are tracking. You then append to the file DEBUG.TXT—every time you hit the DEBUG.OUT statement—those three elements in a comma-separated value formula.

The Syntax for the DEBUG.OUT Procedure

SYNTAX

PROCEDURE OUT(p_Comments IN VARCHAR2,p_Variable IN VARCHAR2)

The parameter p_Comments is a string of type VARCHAR2, which will hold any comments you want to use to identify the location at the time of output to the file and the variable name. The p_Variable parameter is used to pass the actual variable, whose contents will be written to the DEBUG.TXT file.

One flaw with this process is that it does not identify where the variable information is coming from. You would simply add the comments such as: Mortgage Module Before Calculation or Add Qualified Mortgage Applicant Module.

14

A major benefit of going to a file instead of outputting to the screen is that you can run the program uninterrupted by screen outputs, and examine the file at your leisure. You can even build a package or start a trigger to a procedure to read this file into a database, which you can then query. The order output to the file is the order in which the code is executed.

The DEBUG.EMPTY Procedure

The DEBUG.EMPTY procedure simply erases the contents of the DEBUG.TXT file by opening a handle to the file in replace mode ('W') and then closing the file, which creates an empty file. The format for the procedure DEBUG.EMPTY is

```
PROCEDURE EMPTY;
```

Using DBMS_OUTPUT as a Debugging Tool

The DBMS_OUTPUT package is described in great detail on Day 18, "Writing to Files and the Display." This package will either pass information to a buffer that can be retrieved, or it can display information to the screen. When debugging a process, if I use DBMS_OUTPUT, I always output to the screen.

Because PL/SQL really has no output, previous chapters used the DBMS_OUTPUT.PUT_LINE procedure when they demonstrated constructing PL/SQL. However, in order to see any output to the screen, from SQL*Plus, you must type

INPUT   SET SERVEROUTPUT ON

To disable sending output to the screen, you would type at the SQL*Plus prompt

INPUT   SET SERVEROUTPUT OFF

If you do a lot of programming and application development in Oracle, I highly recommend that you add SET SERVEROUTPUT ON to your login script. This rest of this discussion centers on the DBMS_OUTPUT.PUT_LINE procedure.

The Syntax for the PUT_LINE Procedure

The format for this procedure is

```
PROCEDURE PUT_LINE(data_to_display IN VARCHAR2(DATE,NUMBER));
```

Because the function is overloaded, the data_to_display can be of type VARCHAR2, DATE, and NUMBER.

How is DBMS_OUTPUT utilized for debugging purposes? I use this extensively in small procedures in the development process, not just to debug, but also to monitor the values of variables as they enter and execute the procedure. By displaying the values to the screen with comments and knowing the outputs based upon your inputs, you will be able to narrow down, if not identify, the problem area.

You will now create a scenario with a logic error by first creating the function from Listing 14.5. Enter and execute this code to create the function RAISE.

INPUT ## Listing 14.5. Creating the RAISE function.

```
 1: CREATE OR REPLACE FUNCTION RAISE(
 2:            p_paylevel INTEGER, -- parameter for input of raise level
 3:            p_payrate NUMBER)   -- parameter for input of pay rate
 4: /* The purpose of this function is to calculate ANNUAL raises
 5:    for all of the hourly employees, based upon their raise level
 6:    values 1-4 and all others.  */
 7:    RETURN NUMBER IS
 8:    v_newrate NUMBER; -- New Hourly Rate After Raise
 9: BEGIN
10:     IF p_paylevel = 1 THEN
11:            v_newrate := p_payrate * 1.10; -- Promotion Raise
12:     ELSIF p_paylevel = 2 THEN
13:            v_newrate := p_payrate * 1.05; -- Exceeds Rate
14:     ELSIF p_paylevel = 3 THEN
15:            v_newrate := p_payrate * 1.04; -- Hi Meets Rate
16:     ELSIF p_paylevel = 4 THEN
17:            v_newrate := p_payrate * 1.03; -- Meets Rate
18:     ELSE
19:            v_newrate := p_payrate * 1.02; -- All Others
20:     END IF;
21:     RETURN v_newrate; -- Returns new paylevel rate to procedure
22: END RAISE;
```

ANALYSIS The purpose of the newly created function RAISE is to calculate the annual raises for hourly employees only based upon a raise level of 1–4, and all others. The new pay rate is then computed by taking the pay rate passed from the procedure multiplied by the percentage increase determined by the raise level, also passed from the function. You then return the new pay rate to the calling procedure.

Defining the Background

ABCDEF Corp. designs alphabet products for young children. Recently, they have begun to use consultants for applications development because they lack the knowledgeable resources. The Human Resources department has had no experience with consultants. To handle payroll, they enter the consultant's pay rate information into the hourly employee database. Each year, raises are given to all hourly employees but not to consultants, who do not receive raises because they are compensated by a generous hourly rate.

The Symptoms of the Problem

Raises have been processed last week. Consultants have been walking around with a funny smile and a gleam in their eyes. The payroll seems to be over the budget. Someone notices that the amount spent on consultants has increased substantially. An Oracle consultant is brought in to identify and fix the problem.

14

Narrowing the Problem

You know there is a payroll problem, and you know that it occurred after the last round of raises. You can now concentrate on the payroll modules. The next step is to find the source of data, which is the hourly payroll tables. The next step would be to take one of each type of data, in this case one of every type of raise level, which is 1 through 6. You would then write down the old pay rate and the new pay rate. After contacting Human Resources and having them verify the new pay rates from the initial inputs, you determine that levels 1–4 and 6 are calculating properly, but all level 5 rates are showing a raise when level 5 users should not be getting any raise. Further sampling of level 5 employees reveals that all level 5 employees are consultants who are getting raises when they shouldn't be getting any raise. No wonder they were so happy! You can now test the RAISE procedure with sample data, using DBMS_OUTPUT to track the variables.

Now you need to create the procedure that calls the function RAISE. You also need to track your variables with the DBMS_OUTPUT package. Enter and execute the code in Listing 14.6. Make sure you have typed from the SQL*Plus prompt SET SERVEROUTPUT ON, and press Enter to make sure all output is displayed to the screen.

INPUT **Listing 14.6. Calling the RAISE function.**

```
 1: DECLARE
 2:     v_paylevel INTEGER := 5; -- level for raise
 3:     v_payrate NUMBER := 55.25; -- hourly pay rate
 4:     v_newrate NUMBER ; -- new pay rate adjusted for raise
 5: BEGIN
 6:     DBMS_OUTPUT.PUT_LINE('Values before RAISE function: Payrate: ' ||
 7:     v_payrate || ' Raise Level: ' || v_paylevel || ' New Rate: ' ||
 8:     v_newrate);
 9: /* Calculate the new pay rate by calling the RAISE function */
10:     v_newrate := RAISE(v_paylevel,v_payrate);
11:     DBMS_OUTPUT.PUT_LINE('Values after RAISE function: Payrate: ' ||
12:     v_payrate || ' Raise Level: ' || v_paylevel || ' New Rate: ' ||
13:     v_newrate);
14: END;
```

In a normal environment, you would have an hourly employee table that you would access row by row with a cursor, and then insert the updated values back into the table. To keep things simple, you will assume that your one test case is one row from this table.

When you execute this code, your output should be

OUTPUT
```
Values before RAISE function: Payrate: 55.25 Raise Level: 5 New Rate:
Values after RAISE function: Payrate: 55.25 Raise Level: 5 New Rate:
➡56.355
```

ANALYSIS Right away, you know that the problem occurs in the function RAISE. One other item that you should note is this: What is the problem with New Rate? You should never have an uninitialized variable. To do so could cause problems at any point in time. I would correct this problem by assigning New Rate to the value of Pay Rate. This way, no one would ever potentially have a NULL or a 0 hourly pay rate. This will prevent bugs in the future.

You now need to look at the function RAISE. You have narrowed your search to the code in Listing 14.7.

INPUT   **Listing 14.7. The RAISE function.**

```
 1: CREATE OR REPLACE FUNCTION RAISE (
 2:           p_paylevel INTEGER, -- parameter for input of raise level
 3:           p_payrate NUMBER)   -- parameter for input of pay rate
 4: /* The purpose of this function is to calculate ANNUAL raises
 5:    for all of the hourly employees, based upon their raise level
 6:    values 1-4 and all others.  */
 7:    RETURN NUMBER IS
 8:    v_newrate NUMBER; -- New Hourly Rate After Raise
 9: BEGIN
10:    IF p_paylevel = 1 THEN
11:         v_newrate := p_payrate * 1.10; -- Promotion Raise
12:    ELSIF p_paylevel = 2 THEN
13:         v_newrate := p_payrate * 1.05; -- Exceeds Rate
14:    ELSIF p_paylevel = 3 THEN
15:         v_newrate := p_payrate * 1.04; -- Hi Meets Rate
16:    ELSIF p_paylevel = 4 THEN
17:         v_newrate := p_payrate * 1.03; -- Meets Rate
18:    ELSE
19:         v_newrate := p_payrate * 1.02; -- All Others
20:    END IF;
21:    RETURN v_newrate; -- Returns new paylevel rate to procedure
22: END RAISE;
```

ANALYSIS   At least the function is commented and formatted to make debugging easy. A quick glance at the comments, or an even quicker glance at the possible pay levels, shows that a level 5 is not defined, but falls into the category of all others, who get a 2 percent raise. Although Human Resources logically assumed that using the hourly table for consultants would be an easy nonprogramming fix, it has resulted in a problem almost one year later. The quick fix is just a matter of accounting for a level 5 as seen in Listing 14.8.

INPUT   **Listing 14.8. Creating the RAISE function.**

```
 1: CREATE OR REPLACE FUNCTION RAISE(
 2:           p_paylevel INTEGER, -- parameter for input of raise level
 3:           p_payrate NUMBER)   -- parameter for input of pay rate
 4: /* The purpose of this function is to calculate ANNUAL raises
 5:    for all of the hourly employees, based upon their raise level
 6:    values 1-4 and all others.  */
 7:
 8: /* On June 24, 1997, added feature to eliminate consultant raise,
```

14

continues

Listing 14.8. continued

```
 9:    which is pay level 5 */
10:
11:        RETURN NUMBER IS
12:        v_newrate NUMBER; -- New Hourly Rate After Raise
13: BEGIN
14:        IF p_paylevel = 1 THEN
15:            v_newrate := p_payrate * 1.10; -- Promotion Raise
16:        ELSIF p_paylevel = 2 THEN
17:            v_newrate := p_payrate * 1.05; -- Exceeds Rate
18:        ELSIF p_paylevel = 3 THEN
19:            v_newrate := p_payrate * 1.04; -- Hi Meets Rate
20:        ELSIF p_paylevel = 4 THEN
21:            v_newrate := p_payrate * 1.03; -- Meets Rate
22: ELSIF p_paylevel = 5 THEN
23:            v_newrate := p_payrate ; -- Consultants who get no raise
24:        ELSE
25:            v_newrate := p_payrate * 1.02; -- All Others
26:        END IF;
27:        RETURN v_newrate; -- Returns new paylevel rate to procedure
28: END RAISE;
```

ANALYSIS   Although the code in Listing 14.8 will do the trick, what if the problem reoccurs? At least you can document in the code the solution to the problem as seen in Listing 14.8. The reason I called this a quick fix is that it does not address long-term needs. The way to correct this long-term so that this error never occurs would be to create a table called raise_level. This would have the raise level INTEGER value along with the raise increase (or 0 if no raise to be given). On the hourly table, before the raises are calculated, I would reset all pay raise levels to no raise. I would then read in the new raise levels from a table where management has decided their employee's fate. This table can then be read in by using a cursor to update the new pay rates. I would also track the updated rates by using a pipe, which is discussed on Day 19, "Managing Database Jobs."

By using the nontool approach, you were able to narrow down the area significantly. After you identify the probable area, you can then use your tools to verify where the problem is and fix the problem. In this case you used DBMS_OUTPUT, but I would use DEBUG.OUT to output to a file to see what is going on from the function call in case other levels were affected because the test samples might have missed the one or two values that can cause a problem. You could read the data into a table and run a manual calculation compared to the new rate to see what is going on for all cases, and kick out a variance report.

Error Prevention and Planning for Debugging in the Future

If your code needs debugging in the future, you can plan to make it easier through the use of liberal commenting and properly formatted code. To reduce the probability for errors, you should approach the design phase by checking for all possible scenarios and outcomes. In addition, you should design your code in modules, not only to reduce the amount of code to sort through when a problem occurs, but to be able to reuse these modules from other programs or even other databases. Finally, you can purchase tools from Oracle or other third parties that will help you not only to write the code, but also to debug code when things go wrong.

Defining Requirements and Project Planning

The largest portion of an application should be defining the requirements of users. Not only does this require some knowledge of the business, but also all possible input and desired output scenarios should be covered. Someone knowledgeable in the industry should verify all calculations. What do you gain by sitting with the end users and verifying the application? You begin to understand the business and its needs, and you might be able to make suggestions that could aid in decision-making processes, reduce work time for manual processing, improve productivity, and so on. Not only that, it is easier to troubleshoot the system and identify problems before the application is placed in production. I can't stress enough how important understanding and planning for the application in the beginning are: They will save you a lot of time and aggravation at the tail end of the project.

There is one pitfall in obtaining user requirements, which I found out the hard way. Initially, I had coded an application that I felt met the user requirements for the Financial Department. When the end user was reviewing the application, when we discussed the outputs and how the calculations worked, I wound up redesigning the application to meet the new perceived needs. Unfortunately, due to a language barrier, I had the application coded correctly the first time, and the new changes implemented were wrong. Not only should you relay back to the end user what you perceive their requirements are; if possible, try to verify the process you are about to code with at least one other knowledgeable resource—if one exists! The next time I ran into a similar problem, by working with two resources, I was able to resolve any issues about what should be coded. The new application was able to recover balances never billed due to a prior misunderstanding of the process in existing legacy code.

Using a Modular Approach to Coding

When developing your applications, you should take a modular approach to make debugging easier, and also an added benefit of creating reusable code. For instance, in a payroll application, you could further divide this up into several procedures to

- ☐ Calculate gross wage
- ☐ Calculate FICA
- ☐ Calculate Federal withholdings
- ☐ Calculate state withholdings
- ☐ Take out for benefits such as flexible spending or insurance

14

If a problem occurs in net wages, you can easily narrow down which procedure(s) is broken and then fix the bug immediately. In addition, modules have a more important aspect: You can test the modules independent of one another.

TIP

When creating these modules, always use DBMS_OUTPUT or DEBUG.OUT to verify that all input and output variables are being passed properly and that the calculations are correct. Test with all possibilities including odd ranges of values, different datatypes, and so on to try to "break" the application. Better yet, get an end user to attempt to "break" the program.

Commenting Your Code

One of the greatest benefits you can provide for yourself and other Oracle developers is to liberally comment your code. Although you could provide documentation manuals, in practice, these manuals tend to get "misplaced" in almost every environment. Adding comments to your code will help whether you are trying to debug the application or you are simply modifying the application to meet new requirements.

Proper labeling of variables is also important. Poorly worded variables confuse the developer and waste valuable time trying to follow the logic of the program. Listing 14.9 reflects code that can be very confusing at a first glance.

INPUT   **Listing 14.9. Poorly commented code.**

```
 1: CREATE OR REPLACE FUNCTION RAISE(
 2:          p1 INTEGER,
 3:          p2 NUMBER)
 4:       RETURN NUMBER IS
 5:       p3 NUMBER;
 6: BEGIN
 7:       IF p1 = 1 THEN
 8:            p3 := p2 * 1.10;
 9:       ELSIF p1 = 2 THEN
10:            p3 := p2 * 1.05;
11:       ELSIF p1 = 3 THEN
12:            p3 := p2 * 1.04;
13:       ELSIF p1 = 4 THEN
14:            p3 := p2 * 1.03;
15: ELSIF p1 = 5 THEN
16:            p3 := p2 ;
17:       ELSE
18:            p3 := p2 * 1.02;
19:       END IF;
20:       RETURN p3;
21: END RAISE;
```

14

ANALYSIS On a first glance at this code, there are no comments, and very confusing variable names. In order to follow the code, you would have to first determine what p1, p2, and p3 are. You also do not know what the function raises: An hourly pay rate? The cost of benefits? Someone's GPA? The elevation of a building under construction?

"Raise" can mean almost anything to everyone, so a clarification is very important. If you review the same code in Listing 14.10, the comments easily clarify the function.

INPUT **Listing 14.10. Proper commenting and naming of variables.**

```
 1: CREATE OR REPLACE FUNCTION RAISE(
 2:          p_paylevel INTEGER, -- parameter for input of raise level
 3:          p_payrate NUMBER)   -- parameter for input of pay rate
 4: /* The purpose of this function is to calculate ANNUAL raises
 5:    for all of the hourly employees, based upon their raise level
 6:    values 1-4 and all others.  */
 7:
 8: /* On June 24, 1997, added feature to eliminate consultant raise,
 9:    which is pay level 5 */
10:
11:      RETURN NUMBER IS
12:      v_newrate NUMBER; -- New Hourly Rate After Raise
13: BEGIN
14:      IF p_paylevel = 1 THEN
15:          v_newrate := p_payrate * 1.10; -- Promotion Raise
16:      ELSIF p_paylevel = 2 THEN
17:          v_newrate := p_payrate * 1.05; -- Exceeds Rate
18:      ELSIF p_paylevel = 3 THEN
19:          v_newrate := p_payrate * 1.04; -- Hi Meets Rate
20:      ELSIF p_paylevel = 4 THEN
21:          v_newrate := p_payrate * 1.03; -- Meets Rate
22: ELSIF p_paylevel = 5 THEN
23:          v_newrate := p_payrate ; -- Consultants who get no raise
24:      ELSE
25:          v_newrate := p_payrate * 1.02; -- All Others
26:      END IF;
27:      RETURN v_newrate; -- Returns new paylevel rate to procedure
28: END RAISE;
```

ANALYSIS You now can follow the function, its purpose, what the variables are, and any modifications made at a later date. What a difference commenting and proper naming of variables makes!

Formatting Your Code

Another ounce of error prevention is the proper formatting of your code. Proper formatting includes the following guidelines:

☐ For each new block of code, indent five spaces.

☐ Use uppercase for keywords.

14

☐ Use upper- and lowercase for variable names.

☐ Precede variable names with a v_ for variable, p_ for parameters, and so on.

☐ Use one statement per line.

Proper Indentation of Five Spaces

Every time you use a new block of code, such as nesting loops, nesting IF statements, and so on, you should always indent five spaces to make the code more readable. Listing 14.11 shows poorly indented code.

INPUT **Listing 14.11. Code with no indentations.**

```
1: DECLARE
2: v_MyNumber NUMBER := 0;
3: BEGIN
4: LOOP
5: IF v_MyNumber = 7 THEN
6: EXIT;
7: v_MyNumber := v_MyNumber + 2;
8: END LOOP;
9: END;
```

ANALYSIS This code is very difficult to follow. At a glance, you cannot easily discern where the declarations begin and end, where the loop ends, or where the IF statement terminates.

If you reformat the code as shown in Listing 14.12, you can follow the program more easily. In fact, by reformatting the code, you can easily spot that the code contains an infinite loop. In addition, you can recognize that the code is missing an END IF statement.

INPUT **Listing 14.12. Proper indentation.**

```
 1: DECLARE
 2:     v_MyNumber NUMBER := 0; -- five spaces to set apart variable names
 3: BEGIN
 4:     LOOP -- five spaces to separate where procedure begins and ends
 5:         IF v_MyNumber = 7 THEN -- Five spaces for new block of code
 6:             EXIT;
 7:         END IF;
 8:     v_MyNumber := v_MyNumber + 2; -- Part of Loop Block
 9:     END LOOP;  -- Aligned under matching loop statement
10: END;
```

Using Uppercase for Keywords

Using uppercase for reserved words or functions helps to distinguish between regular code and Oracle-provided code. If a keyword is misspelled, you can easily spot the problem. The code in Listing 14.13 shows how unreadable code can become if keywords are not capitalized.

INPUT **Listing 14.13. Keywords not capitalized.**

```
1: declare
2:     v_MyNumber number := 0; -- five spaces to set apart variable names
3: begin
4:     loop -- five spaces to separate where procedure begins and ends
5:         if v_MyNumber = 7 then -- five spaces for new block of code
6:             exit;
7:     v_MyNumber := v_MyNumber + 2; -- Part of Loop Block
8:     end loop;  -- Aligned under matching loop statement
9: end;
```

ANALYSIS In the code in Listing 14.13, it is difficult to pick out the datatypes of the variables and what type of statements exist in this block of PL/SQL code.

Using Mixed Case for Variable Names

To identify code, output, keywords, or variable names, you can easily distinguish variable names by using mixed case. By using MyVariable, you can pick the variable name out faster than you could pick out myvariable or MYVARIABLE. Refer to Listing 14.14 for an example of poor formatting of variables.

Preceding Variable Names with v_ or p_

By preceding variables with a first letter and an underscore, you can quickly identify variables, and what type of variables you are coding. You would use v_ for regular variable names, p_ for parameters, and so on. Listing 14.14 shows both improper use of case and not preceding variable names with a letter followed by an underscore.

INPUT **Listing 14.14. Poor formatting of variables.**

```
1: DECLARE
2:     mynumber NUMBER := 0; -- five spaces to set apart variable names
3: BEGIN
4:     LOOP -- five spaces to separate where procedure begins and ends
5:         IF mynumber = 7 THEN -- Five spaces for new block of code
6:             EXIT;
7:     mynumber := mynumber + 2; -- Part of Loop Block
8:     END LOOP;  -- Aligned under matching loop statement
9: END;
```

Keeping One Statement per Line

Because the semicolon (;) is terminating, you could easily have multiple statements on one line. For instance, you could code

```
NULL;END LOOP;END;
```

The function, procedure, or other item would function properly. But you'll run into trouble if you try to troubleshoot this or comment out a statement that might be causing the error.

14

Summary

Today's lesson discussed the methodology of debugging an application. When debugging, you must deal with two kinds of errors—logic errors and syntax errors. Syntax errors are a result of improper formatting, missing punctuation, misspelled keywords, and so on. Logic errors do not cause your program to stop execution (usually); they allow the code to compile, but provide for the wrong type of processing. Other common problem areas that cause logic errors are improper order of operations when performing calculations and infinite loops. Oracle does not feature any built-in debugging package for trying to locate logic errors. You could purchase these tools, use DBMS_OUTPUT, use pipes, or create your own debugging package. Finally, proper commenting and formatting of code enables you to review and understand code much faster than no comments or no formatting.

Q&A

Q **What debugging packages does Oracle provide with its standard relational database package?**

A Currently, none are provided, although you can purchase tools from Oracle or other third-party support.

Q **What can I use to debug applications?**

A DBMS_OUTPUT and pipes are two methods of debugging. You can also create your own debugging package to track variables.

Q **If all operations are on the same level, how does Oracle know which calculations to process first?**

A If all calculations are at the same level, the order of evaluation is from left to right.

Q **What simple punctuation can easily override the natural order of operations?**

A Using parentheses (). Be careful when nesting parentheses.

Q **Are comments needed in your application if you have sufficient separate documentation?**

A Yes, absolutely. Documentation tends to get misplaced or never gets updated when a coding change is made. Document not only what each procedure, function, trigger, and so on is doing, but also document changes and updates as they occur.

Q **Must we really document solutions to problems?**

A Documenting solutions to problems helps you troubleshoot the same problem if it occurs in the future in the same application, a different application, and so on.

Q **Why does proper formatting help in debugging code?**

A Proper formatting allows you to view code quickly and assess what the code is doing. If you do not line up END IF statements in a multiple IF...THEN clause, it will be difficult to see when the first statement ends, the second ends, and so forth.

Workshop

The following workshop will give you the opportunity to test your knowledge of debugging code and to practice correcting errors. The answers to the quiz and exercises can be found in Appendix A, "Answers."

Quiz

1. True or False: Logic errors are easier to debug than syntax errors.
2. Missing a semicolon is what type of error?
3. Provide the answer to the calculation 6 + 4/2 = ?
4. True or False: Oracle comes with a built-in debugging package.
5. True or False: Proper planning reduces errors in the future.
6. True or False: Commenting code is a waste of time.
7. True or False: Formatting code is not necessary.

Exercises

1. Use the DEBUG package to troubleshoot the code in Listing 14.2.
2. Use the DBMS_OUTPUT package to troubleshoot the code in Listing 14.2.

14

WEEK 2

8

9

10

11

12

13

14

In Review

You have finished your second week of learning how to program in PL/SQL. The week started with you learning about stored procedures and packages on Day 8. These offer the programmer the advantages of encapsulation and grouping similar procedures and functions together in packages. You also learned how to plan for and react to certain runtime errors that can arise in your PL/SQL code. This includes how to write exception-handling routines to handle internal and user-defined PL/SQL processing errors.

The second week continued on Day 9 with you learning how to create and use two composite PL/SQL structures—the PL/SQL table and record. You also learned how to use INSERT and SELECT statements.

Next, on Day 10, you learned how to manipulate data with PL/SQL cursors. Cursors are wonderful constructs in that they enable you to process a multiple-row query result set, one row at a time. You were also presented with material that showed you how to pass arguments into cursors and how to use cursors as variables on Day 12.

On Day 11, you learned how to use triggers. These triggers are automatically executed based upon your predefined firing criteria. You were also introduced to the new objects contained in the Oracle8 release on Day 13.

Finally, the week ended with you learning how to prepare for errors and write error-handling routines to help prevent unwanted termination of the execution of your PL/SQL programs.

Week

3

At a Glance

At this point, you should have mastered the basics of Oracle, from functions to procedures to SQL*Plus. With this knowledge, you can now master the packages supplied by Oracle, which offer some additional advanced features. Each chapter guides you through a package or concept and demonstrates its topic through an actual example that you can try.

Where You Are Going

Day 15 covers advanced topics including features new to Oracle8, such as the DBMS_LOB package. You also learn how to implement recursion. Day 16 covers how to work with multiple users across multiple platforms by managing transactions and locks. On Day 17, you learn about the DBMS_SQL package. Continuing with packages, Day 18 covers the UTL_FILE and DBMS_OUTPUT packages for various methods of output. On Day 19 you are exposed to the DBMS_JOB package, which manages database jobs. You also see how sessions communicate with the DBMS_PIPE package. On Day 20, you learn how to manage alerts with the DBMS_ALERT package. Finally, the week ends with a discussion on how to interface Oracle to the Web using J/SQL on Day 21.

Day 15

Exploring Advanced Topics

by Timothy Atwood

Many new advanced features were added with the release of Oracle8. This chapter covers several of these features, including locators, large objects, and the DBMS_LOB package. In addition, you will learn how to create and implement recursive functions. Today's lesson focuses on the following topics:

- ☐ Writing recursive functions
- ☐ Defining large objects
- ☐ Using the DBMS_LOB package with external files
- ☐ Understanding locators
- ☐ Using the DBMS_LOB package with internal files

What Is Recursion?

Earlier in this book, you learned how to use Oracle's built-in functions, as well as how to create your own functions. Functions allow you to create reusable code, which is also easier to test and debug when broken into smaller components. In PL/SQL, functions can easily call other functions. A recursive function is one that calls itself until some exit condition occurs. One problem with coding recursion is making sure that the exit condition is met!

Practicing Recursion

As with any third-generation programming language, you have to code the functions as recursive because recursion is not already built into PL/SQL. The classic example of using recursion is to calculate the factorial of a number. To compute the factorial of the number, you would multiply the number by the number -1 (n*(n-1)) until n equals the value of 1. Table 15.1 shows factorial calculations for numbers 1 through 6. Factorial in math textbooks uses the punctuation !, so 3! means three factorial, which is 3 * 2 * 1 = 6.

Table 15.1. Factorial calculations.

Factorial	Calculation	Result
1!	1	1
2!	2 * 1	2
3!	3 * 2 * 1	6
4!	4 * 3 * 2 * 1	24
5!	5 * 4 * 3 * 2 * 1	120
6!	6 * 5 *4 * 3 * 2 * 1	720

Now try using recursion to calculate the factorial of an integer. First, you will need to create the function FACTORIAL by executing the code in Listing 15.1.

INPUT   **Listing 15.1. Creating the FACTORIAL recursive function.**

```
CREATE OR REPLACE FUNCTION Factorial(p_MyNum INTEGER)

/* Creates a recursive function that simply calculates
   the factorial of a number.  The function starts with
   the number and then calls the function with n-1,
   until n = 1 which returns a value of 1.  Without this
   statement, the function would never end.          */
```

15

```
        RETURN NUMBER AS
BEGIN -- Start of Factorial Function
    IF p_MyNum = 1 THEN -- Checking for last value to process of n-1
        RETURN 1;
    ELSE
        RETURN(p_MyNum * Factorial(p_MyNum-1)); -- Recursive
    END IF;
END; -- End of Factorial Function
```

After you execute the code in Listing 15.1, you should see the following output to the screen:

```
function created
```

This function FACTORIAL will continue to call itself until n-1, where n is the factorial processed, equals a value of one. After this value is reached, the return value is the running factorial multiplied by the value of calling the same function submitting the running factorial number less one. As you can see, this is a short function that is easy to read, but a little difficult to follow.

To see a demonstration of all factorial values from one to 10, first make sure that you have typed SET SERVEROUTPUT ON at the SQL*Plus prompt. Then execute the code in Listing 15.2.

INPUT

Listing 15.2. Testing the recursive function with an anonymous PL/SQL block.

```
DECLARE
    v_test NUMBER := 10;
    v_Counter INTEGER ; -- Counter for For Loop
BEGIN
    FOR v_Counter IN 1..v_test LOOP
        DBMS_OUTPUT.PUT_LINE('The factorial of ' ||
            v_Counter || ' is ' || factorial(v_Counter));
    END LOOP;
END;
```

Your output should look the same as the following:

OUTPUT

```
The factorial of 1 is 1
The factorial of 2 is 2
The factorial of 3 is 6
The factorial of 4 is 24
The factorial of 5 is 120
The factorial of 6 is 720
The factorial of 7 is 5040
The factorial of 8 is 40320
The factorial of 9 is 362880
The factorial of 10 is 3628800
```

Why Use Recursion?

When the need to call the function by itself does not occur more than 10 to 15 times, recursion provides an elegant solution to a problem. However, there are many reasons why you will probably never use recursion:

☐ All recursion problems can be solved by a different method, such as writing custom functions, using FOR loops, or using IF statements, all of which are discussed on Day 5, "Using Functions, IF Statements, and Loops." You could also use WHILE or LOOP statements, covered on Day 6, "Implementing Loops and GOTOs," instead of recursion.

☐ The more complex the calculation, or the more times the function calls itself, the slower the execution of the PL/SQL code.

☐ Recursion can be difficult for other programmers to follow.

Review of Large Object Datatypes

Oracle8 added four large object datatypes. These datatypes are summarized in Table 15.2. All these datatypes can store data up to 4 gigabytes. This is more than enough to accommodate such items as sound, pictures, and video in your databases. Of the available large object datatypes, three of them are internal to Oracle, and one is external. External refers to a physical file, for which Oracle stores the filename and file location. Internal objects store a *locator* in the large object column of the table, which points to the actual location of the data in the table.

Table 15.2. Large object datatypes.

Object	Location	Description
CLOB	Internal	Character Large Object—Holds up to 4 gigabytes of single-byte characters
NCLOB	Internal	National Character Large Object—Holds up to 4 gigabytes of single-byte characters or multibyte characters that conform to the national character set defined by the Oracle8 database
BLOB	Internal	Binary Large Object—Holds up to 4 gigabytes of "raw" binary data
BFILE	External	Binary File—Stored as a file accessible by the operating system, which Oracle can access and manipulate

Using External Files in Your Oracle8 Database

The BFILE datatype is a large binary object that is external to Oracle. External means that the file is accessible to the operating system and not stored within the Oracle database. The information required to access an external object is the directory object and the filename. Of course, you need to make sure that you have all the privileges associated with accessing the directories and files.

Creating the Directory Object

Before you can access outside files, you need to create a directory object. This object maps a name to a path specified in the CREATE statement. The directory object name can be up to 30 characters, and the filename can be up to 2000 characters maximum.

The Syntax for Creating a Directory Object

SYNTAX

CREATE (OR REPLACE) DIRECTORY *Directory_Name* AS *Path*

Directory_Name is the name of the directory object you are associating with the path. This directory name will be called by Oracle instead of specifying the actual path. *Path* is the physical path on the system of any secondary storage devices.

NOTE

> For the next several exercises, you will need to create a path called books somewhere on a hard drive to which you have access. Copy all the files from the books subdirectory from the CD-ROM into this subdirectory. You will have a total of nine files in the books subdirectory after the copy process has ended.

Before you can try several of the examples in this book, you will need to create a directory object called books. This object will hold the data and descriptions of future or current books required for purchase by your organization. To create the directory object, execute the code in Listing 15.3.

INPUT   **Listing 15.3. Creating the directory object books.**

```
CREATE OR REPLACE DIRECTORY books_Dir AS 'C:\BOOKS'
/
```

NOTE

> Change the last parameter of the path to correspond to the actual path specified by your operating system, such as /home/users/Atwood/books for UNIX users, to which you created and copied the nine files.

After you have executed the SQL statement, you should see output that states that the directory was created.

Limitations of BFILE

The BFILE datatype does not offer transactional support for COMMIT or ROLLBACK. Also, files are opened as read-only, so you can't write or alter these external files in any manner. Another problem that could occur is a "too many files open" error. In order to avoid this error, you need to edit the INIT.ORA file and change the statement SESSION_MAX_OPEN_FILES=20 to whatever value you require. Also keep in mind any operating system requirements. When you do open files, make sure that you close them; otherwise, they are tracked as opened files even when not in use, and you might get the message "too many files open" when you really are accessing under the limit. This mostly occurs when programs terminate abnormally, and there is nothing in place to close all files when the error occurs.

The DBMS_LOB Package with BFILE

The DBMS_LOB package provided by Oracle allows you to manipulate all types of large objects (LOBs). Because the BFILE datatype is the only external datatype, Oracle provides functions used solely for external LOBs. These are summarized in Table 15.3.

Table 15.3. Functions and procedures used with BFILE.

Function or Procedure	Accessed By	Description
BFILENAME	BFILE	Creates a pointer (locator) in the PL/SQL block, or in the table to the location of the file
COMPARE	All LOBs	Compares all or part of two LOBs
FILECLOSE	BFILE	Closes the file associated with the BFILE locator
FILECLOSEALL	BFILE	Closes all open BFILEs
FILEEXISTS	BFILE	Checks to see if the file exists where the locator says the file should be located

15

Function or Procedure	Accessed By	Description
FILEGETNAME	BFILE	Returns the directory object and path of the BFILE
FILEISOPEN	BFILE	Checks to see if the file is already open
GETLENGTH	All LOBs	Returns the actual length of the LOB
INSTR	All LOBs	Searches for matching patterns in a LOB with the string of characters specified
READ	All LOBs	Reads specific amount of a LOB into the buffer
SUBSTR	All LOBs	Returns part or all of the LOB specified by the parameters

The BFILENAME Function

When working with external files or inserting locators for BFILEs into a table, you will need to call the BFILENAME function, which creates the pointer (referred to as the locator in Oracle) to the external file.

The Syntax for the BFILENAME Function

```
FUNCTION BFILENAME(Directory_Object IN VARCHAR2,
                    Filename IN VARCHAR2);
RETURN BFILE_Locator;
```

When using this function, you pass the *Directory_Object*, which you have previously created. Again, this object stores the path of the file. The second parameter you will pass, *Filename*, is the actual name of the file. The function will then return a pointer (locator) to the file, so Oracle knows how to access the file. This value can be used in PL/SQL blocks, or it can be inserted into a table with a column of type BFILE.

NOTE If a file is deleted or moved and Oracle still has a locator pointing to where this file used to reside, Oracle will raise an error when attempting to open the file. Oracle does not automatically update or delete the locator if the file is erased or moved. Although this typically does not affect anonymous PL/SQL blocks, it does affect locators stored in a table.

The COMPARE **Function**

If you need to compare all or part of a LOB, you can use the COMPARE function. One useful purpose of this function is to check to see if you have two external files that are exactly identical. You could write a maintenance program to check for duplicate files and then remove the duplicate files because these large files can easily waste a lot of hard drive space.

The Syntax for the COMPARE **Function**

```
FUNCTION COMPARE(
                    Lob1 IN BFILE,
                    Lob2 IN BFILE,
                    Number_Bytes_to_Compare IN INTEGER,
                    Origin_Lob1    IN INTEGER := 1,
                    Origin_Lob2    IN INTEGER := 1)
RETURN Compare_Result_Integer;
```

Lob1 is the first LOB you are comparing to *Lob2*, the second LOB. *Number_Bytes_to_Compare* is the total number of bytes you want to compare from the first LOB to the second LOB. *Origin_Lob1* is the starting location in the file for where you want to compare. The value of 1 starts from the beginning of the LOB, or you could enter 100 to start comparing from the 100th byte. *Origin_Lob2* is the starting location of the second LOB you want to compare. The value returned will be 0 if the data is identical, non-zero if the data is not identical, or NULL if any of the parameters are invalid, such as an incorrect starting origin, comparing bytes past the end of the LOB, or any other invalid parameter.

The FILECLOSE **Procedure**

When you have finished reading a BFILE, you should always close the file not only to free up resources, but also so that you don't exceed the maximum number of allowable files that can be open. The FILECLOSE procedure closes a single file that is open.

The Syntax for the FILECLOSE **Function**

```
PROCEDURE FILECLOSE(BFILE_Locator);
```

The parameter *BFILE_Locator* is the BFILE locator assigned to the file from the BFILENAME function.

The FILECLOSEALL **Procedure**

If you are done processing all BFILEs and you want to end your session, you can use the procedure FILECLOSEALL to close every open BFILE. The format for the FILECLOSEALL procedure is as follows:

```
PROCEDURE FILECLOSEALL;
```

15

15

> **TIP** When writing error-handling routines, it is always a good idea to automatically code the FILECLOSEALL procedure to properly close all the files and free up resources.

The FILEEXISTS Function

As stated previously, Oracle does not know if a file has been moved, deleted, or changed in size. Therefore, it is always good coding practice to see if the file exists before performing any operations on the file. Oracle provides the function FILEEXISTS to see if the file is physically at the location specified by the directory object and the filename.

The Syntax for the Function FILEEXISTS

```
FUNCTION FILEEXISTS (BFILE_Locator)
    RETURN Status_Integer;
```

The parameter *BFILE_Locator* is the BFILE locator assigned to the file from the BFILENAME function. The function returns an INTEGER with a value of 1 if the file exists at that specific location, a value of 0 if the file does not exist, or a value of NULL if there is an operating system error, if you lack the privileges to access that file or path, or if the value of the locator is NULL.

The FILEGETNAME Procedure

Although you will probably never use FILEGETNAME in an anonymous block of PL/SQL because you will define the directory object and the filename, this is a useful procedure for BFILE locators stored in a table. The FILEGETNAME procedure returns the directory object and the filename associated with the locator. The directory object has a maximum size of 30 characters, and the filename has a maximum size of 2000 characters.

The Syntax for the FILEGETNAME Procedure

```
PROCEDURE FILEGETNAME(BFILE_Locator,
                      Directory_Object OUT VARCHAR2,
                      Filename OUT VARCHAR2);
```

The parameter *BFILE_Locator* is the BFILE locator assigned to the file from the BFILENAME function. *Directory_Object* is the directory object associated with the path created with the CREATE DIRECTORY command. The *Filename* parameter is the name of the file associated with the BFILE locator.

The FILEISOPEN Function

Before opening a BFILE, you should check to make sure that the file is not already opened by using the FILEISOPEN function.

The Syntax for the FILEISOPEN Function

```
FUNCTION FILEISOPEN (BFILE_Locator)
     RETURN Status_Integer;
```

The parameter *BFILE_Locator* is the BFILE locator assigned to the file from the BFILENAME function. The function returns an INTEGER with a value of 1 if the file is open or any other integer value if the file is closed. An exception is raised if the file doesn't exist, if you have insufficient privileges, or the directory does not exist.

The FILEOPEN Procedure

Before you can access an external file, you need to first open the file with the FILEOPEN procedure.

The Syntax for the FILEOPEN Procedure

```
PROCEDURE FILEOPEN(BFILE_Locator,
                      DBMS_LOB.FILE_READONLY);
```

The parameter *BFILE_Locator* is the BFILE locator assigned to the file from the BFILENAME function. The second parameter, DBMS_LOB.FILE_READONLY, is currently the only mode to open files.

The GETLENGTH Function

The GETLENGTH function returns the actual length of the objects in bytes.

The Syntax for the GETLENGTH Function

```
FUNCTION GETLENGTH (BFILE_Locator)
     RETURN Length_Integer;
```

The parameter *BFILE_Locator* is the BFILE locator assigned to the file from the BFILENAME function. The function returns an INTEGER of the length of the file, or NULL if the locator is NULL, if the file is not open, if there is an operating system error, or if you do not have the appropriate privileges to access the file.

The INSTR Function

The INSTR function allows you to match a pattern against the *n*th occurrence in the LOB starting from the offset specified.

The Syntax for the INSTR Function

```
FUNCTION INSTR(BFILE_Locator,
                   Pattern IN RAW,
                   Starting_Location IN INTEGER := 1,
                   Nth_Occurrence IN INTEGER := 1)
RETURN Status_Integer;
```

The parameter *BFILE_Locator* is the BFILE locator assigned to the file from the BFILENAME function. The *Pattern* of type RAW is the pattern you want to match. *Starting_Location* is

15

the position in the file where you want to start your search for a match. *Nth_Occurrence* is the *n*th time a match has been made. The function returns a value of 0 if the pattern is not found, it returns the offset from the start of the file where the match was found, or it returns a value of NULL if any of the parameters are NULL or invalid.

The READ Procedure

The READ procedure allows you to read part or all of a file into a buffer.

The Syntax for the READ Procedure

```
PROCEDURE READ(BFILE_Locator,
               Read_Amount IN BINARY_INTEGER,
               Starting_Location IN INTEGER,
               Buffer OUT RAW);
```

The parameter *BFILE_Locator* is the BFILE locator assigned to the file from the BFILENAME function. The second parameter, *Read_Amount*, is the number of bytes you will read from the file into the buffer. *Starting_Location* is the location you want to start reading from the file. For instance, you could read up to 32,768 bytes at a time from a file, then store these in a BLOB in the Oracle database, and change the starting location by 32,768 each time you read the file. *Buffer* is the location to store the contents of the file just read.

The VALUE_ERROR exception is raised if any of the parameters are NULL. The INVALID_ARGVAL exception is raised if any of the arguments are invalid. NO_DATA_FOUND is raised if you have reached the end of the file. If the file has not been opened, you will receive the UNOPENED_FILE exception.

The SUBSTR Function

The SUBSTR function allows you to extract a specified amount of bytes from a file.

The Syntax for the SUBSTR Function

```
FUNCTION SUBSTR(BFILE_Locator,
                Read_Amount IN BINARY_INTEGER,
                Starting_Location IN INTEGER := 1)
RETURN RAW;
```

The parameter *BFILE_Locator* is the BFILE locator assigned to the file from the BFILENAME function. *Read_Amount* is the number of bytes you want to extract from the file. *Starting_Location* is the position in the file where you want to start your extraction. The function will return a RAW value if successful.

Examples of BFILEs Using the DBMS_LOB Package

You can now test all these functions and procedures with an anonymous PL/SQL block in the next several examples. The functions and procedures common to internal and external LOBs, such as INSTR and SUBSTR, will be demonstrated later in this chapter in the section "Examples of Internal LOBs Using the DBMS_LOB Package."

Accessing BFILEs

This first example demonstrates how to open files, close files, and do some minor error checking. Before you run any of these examples, make sure you have entered SET SERVEROUTPUT ON at the SQL*Plus prompt so that you can see that the examples are working as they execute. Execute the code in Listing 15.4.

INPUT   **Listing 15.4. BFILE file operations.**

```
DECLARE

/* This Anonymous PL/SQL block will demonstrate how to
   open a BFILE, close the BFILE, and do some error checking
   with FILEEXISTS, FILEISOPEN, and retrieve the Directory
   Object and Path with GETFILENAME   */

   v_BOOKFILE BFILE; -- BFILE to access
   v_DIRNAME VARCHAR2(30); -- Holds Directory Object for FILEGETNAME
   v_LOCATION VARCHAR2(2000); -- Holds filename for FILEGETNAME
   v_FILEISOPEN INTEGER; -- Holds status to check if the file is open
   v_FILEEXISTS INTEGER; -- Holds status if the file actually exists

BEGIN
   v_BOOKFILE := BFILENAME('BOOKS_DIR','BOOK1.GIF'); -- Create Locator
   v_FILEISOPEN := DBMS_LOB.FILEISOPEN(v_BOOKFILE); -- Check if file open

   v_FILEEXISTS := DBMS_LOB.FILEEXISTS(v_BOOKFILE);

   IF v_FILEEXISTS = 1 THEN
        DBMS_OUTPUT.PUT_LINE('The file exists');
   ELSE
        DBMS_OUTPUT.PUT_LINE('The file cannot be found');
   END IF;

   IF v_FILEISOPEN = 1 THEN   --Determine actions if file is opened or not
        DBMS_OUTPUT.PUT_LINE('The file is open');
   ELSE
        DBMS_OUTPUT.PUT_LINE('Opening the file');
        DBMS_LOB.FILEOPEN(v_BOOKFILE);
   END IF;
   DBMS_LOB.FILEGETNAME(v_BOOKFILE,v_DIRNAME,v_LOCATION);
   DBMS_OUTPUT.PUT_LINE('The Directory Object is: ' || v_DIRNAME ||
        ' The File Name is: ' || v_LOCATION);
```

15

```
         DBMS_LOB.FILECLOSE(v_BOOKFILE); -- Close the BFILE

END;
```

After executing the code in Listing 15.4, your output will appear as

OUTPUT
```
The file exists
Opening the file
The Directory Object is: BOOKS_DIR The File Name is: BOOK1.GIF
```

ANALYSIS In the DECLARE section, a BFILE locator is defined as v_BOOKFILE. The v_DIRNAME and v_LOCATION variables hold the results of the FILEGETNAME function. The v_FILEISOPEN and v_FILEEXISTS variables hold the status if the file is open and if the file exists. The first step in the execution is to create the BFILE locator to the BOOKS_DIR path with a filename of BOOK1.GIF. Both v_FILEISOPEN and v_FILEEXISTS are assigned values to see if the file is open and if the file exists. Because the FILEOPEN procedure was not called, this value will be 0. If you have created the path and copied the files to the BOOKS directory, you should receive a value of 1, which states that the file does exist, and you should see output stating that the file exists.

Because the FILEOPEN procedure returned a value of 0, the file is not open. A message is then displayed, "Opening the file," and then the FILEOPEN procedure executes and opens the file for access from Oracle. Next, the FILEGETNAME procedure returns the directory object and the filename. Finally, the file is closed, and the execution ends.

Comparing Files

You can now practice comparing files and also getting the length of these files by executing the code in Listing 15.5.

INPUT **Listing 15.5. BFILE comparisons.**

```
DECLARE

/* The purpose of this anonymous PL/SQl block is to compare
   the contents of three files completely.  The size of the
   files is determined by the GETLENGTH function */

    v_FILE1 BFILE;
    v_FILE2 BFILE;
    v_FILE3 BFILE;
    v_GETLENGTH1 INTEGER; -- Hold length of the file
    v_GETLENGTH2 INTEGER; -- Hold length of the file
    v_GETLENGTH3 INTEGER; -- Hold length of the file
    v_COMPARELENGTH INTEGER; -- Holds smallest of two values
    v_COMPARERESULT INTEGER; -- Hold result of comparing files

BEGIN
```

continues

Listing 15.5. continued

```
    -- Create three locators for each of the files to compare

        v_FILE1 := BFILENAME('BOOKS_DIR','BOOK1.GIF');
        v_FILE2 := BFILENAME('BOOKS_DIR','BOOK2.GIF');
        v_FILE3 := BFILENAME('BOOKS_DIR','BOOK5.GIF');

    -- Open the files for access

        DBMS_LOB.FILEOPEN(v_FILE1);
        DBMS_LOB.FILEOPEN(v_FILE2);
        DBMS_LOB.FILEOPEN(v_FILE3);

        v_GETLENGTH1 := DBMS_LOB.GETLENGTH(v_FILE1);
        v_GETLENGTH2 := DBMS_LOB.GETLENGTH(v_FILE2);
        v_GETLENGTH3 := DBMS_LOB.GETLENGTH(v_FILE3);

    -- Compare 1st and 2nd File
        IF v_GETLENGTH1 < v_GETLENGTH2 THEN
            v_COMPARELENGTH := v_GETLENGTH1;
        ELSE
            v_COMPARELENGTH := v_GETLENGTH2;
        END IF;

        v_COMPARERESULT := DBMS_LOB.COMPARE(v_FILE1,v_FILE2,
            v_COMPARELENGTH,1,1);

        IF v_COMPARERESULT = 0 THEN
            DBMS_OUTPUT.PUT_LINE('Both Files Are Identical');
        ELSE
            DBMS_OUTPUT.PUT_LINE('Both Files Are Different');
        END IF;

    -- Compare 1st and 3rd file
        IF v_GETLENGTH1 < v_GETLENGTH3 THEN
            v_COMPARELENGTH := v_GETLENGTH1;
        ELSE
            v_COMPARELENGTH := v_GETLENGTH3;
        END IF;

        v_COMPARERESULT := DBMS_LOB.COMPARE(v_FILE1,v_FILE3,
            v_COMPARELENGTH,1,1);

        IF v_COMPARERESULT = 0 THEN
            DBMS_OUTPUT.PUT_LINE('Both Files Are Identical');
        ELSE
            DBMS_OUTPUT.PUT_LINE('Both Files Are Different');
        END IF;

        DBMS_LOB.FILECLOSEALL;

END;
```

After the code executes, your output should appear as

OUTPUT
```
Both Files Are Different
Both Files Are Identical
```

ANALYSIS Listing 15.5 first defines several variables for each of the three files to be compared. Three locators are defined as v_FILE1, v_FILE2, and v_FILE3. The file lengths of each of these files are stored in v_GETLENGTH1, v_GETLENGTH2, and v_GETLENGTH3. Both v_COMPARERESULT and v_COMPARELENGTH are used for storing the length of the files.

When the code starts to execute, the three locators are assigned values of three files. These three files are then opened, and the length is retrieved. The lengths of the first two files are compared. The smallest value is stored in v_COMPARELENGTH. If the length to compare was used for the larger file, an exception would be raised because you would attempt to compare the smaller file after the end of the file has been reached. The variable v_COMPARERESULT is assigned the result of comparing the first two files. These files are not identical, and the output correctly states this. The process is repeated for the first and third files, which are identical. The FILECLOSEALL procedure is executed to close all three files and free up the resources.

Working with Locators

Locators are stored in the large object column and point to the location of where the actual data is stored. It is important for you to understand what occurs at a transactional level when using Oracle locators. When copying LOBs from one row to the next, a new locator is created and the entire data is copied and stored from the source row. This is necessary because if you were to delete one row and you did not copy the entire contents to the new row, all the data of the LOB would be lost. When deleting internal LOBs, the locator and the contents of the LOB are both deleted. If you're deleting external BFILEs, the file remains but the locator is deleted. When adding internal LOBs to a table, you need to create the locator either by assigning data to the LOB column or using the function EMPTY_BLOB or EMPTY_CLOB. When adding a BFILE to the table, you would use BFILENAME to assign a locator to the column. The last issue applies to internal LOBs only. It is a good idea to lock the LOB when working with the LOB to prevent other users from accessing the LOB.

The DBMS_LOB Package with Internal LOBs

The DBMS_LOB package provided by Oracle allows you to manipulate all types of LOBs. Because the BFILE datatype is of type RAW, there are additional files to work with the database character set. Table 15.4 summarizes the functions and procedures that work with internal LOBs.

Table 15.4. Functions and procedures used with internal LOBs.

Function or Procedure	Accessed By	Description
APPEND	Internal LOBs	Appends one LOB to another LOB
COMPARE	All LOBs	Compares all or part of two LOBs
COPY	Internal LOBs	Copies a LOB from one row to another
EMPTY_BLOB	BLOB	Creates a locator in a BLOB column
EMPTY_CLOB	CLOB	Creates a locator in a CLOB column
ERASE	Internal LOBs	Erases all or part of an internal LOB
GETLENGTH	All LOBs	Returns the actual length of the LOB
INSTR	All LOBs	Searches for matching patterns in a LOB with the string of characters specified
READ	All LOBs	Reads specific amount of a LOB into the buffer
SUBSTR	All LOBs	Returns part or all of the LOB specified by the parameters
TRIM	Internal LOBs	Reduces a LOB to a length specified
WRITE	Internal LOBs	Writes data to a LOB

The APPEND Procedure

The APPEND procedure allows you to append one LOB to another LOB.

The Syntax for the APPEND Procedure for BLOBs and CLOBs

```
PROCEDURE APPEND(Dest_Locator IN OUT BLOB,
                Source_Locator  IN BLOB);


PROCEDURE APPEND(Dest_Locator IN OUT CLOB CHARACTER SET Set_Desired,
                Source_Locator  IN CLOB CHARACTER SET Dest_Locator%CHARSET);
```

Dest_Locator is the locator for the destination LOB that is appended by the source LOB identified by *Source_Locator*. When working with CLOBs, you can additionally specify the character set with the parameter *Set_Desired*.

The COMPARE Function

If you need to compare all or part of a LOB, you can use the COMPARE function.

15

The Syntax for the COMPARE Function for Both BLOBs and LOBs

```
FUNCTION COMPARE(
                Lob1 IN BLOB,
                Lob2 IN BLOB,
                Number_Bytes_to_Compare IN INTEGER,
                Origin_Lob1    IN INTEGER := 1,
                Origin_Lob2    IN INTEGER := 1)
RETURN Compare_Result_Integer;

FUNCTION COMPARE(
                Lob1 IN CLOB CHARACTER SET Set_Desired,
                Lob2 IN CLOB CHARACTER SET LOB1%CHARSET,,
                Number_Bytes_to_Compare IN INTEGER,
                Origin_Lob1    IN INTEGER := 1,
                Origin_Lob2    IN INTEGER := 1)
RETURN Compare_Result_Integer;
```

Lob1 is the first LOB you are comparing to *Lob2*, the second LOB. The *Set_Desired* parameter is the character set you want to use. If no character set is specified, the Oracle server's character set is used. *Number_Bytes_to_Compare* is the total number of bytes you want to compare from the first LOB to the second LOB. *Origin_Lob1* is the starting location in the LOB where you want to compare. The value of 1 starts from the beginning of the LOB, or you could enter 100 to start comparing from the 100th byte. *Origin_Lob2* is the starting location of the second LOB you want to compare. The value returned will either be 0 if the data is identical, non-zero if the data is not identical, or NULL if any of the parameters are invalid, such as an incorrect starting origin, comparing bytes past the end of the LOB, or any other invalid parameter.

The COPY Procedure

The COPY procedure allows you to copy all or part of a LOB from one row to another. The entire LOB is copied with a new locator entered into the table, which points to the copy of the original LOB.

The Syntax for the COPY Procedure

```
PROCEDURE COPY(Dest_Locator IN OUT BLOB,
               Source_Locator  IN BLOB,
               Amount IN OUT INTEGER,
               Dest_Start_Position IN INTEGER := 1,
               Source_Start_Position IN INTEGER := 1);


PROCEDURE APPEND(Dest_Locator IN OUT CLOB CHARACTER SET Set_Desired,
               Source_Locator  IN CLOB CHARACTER SET Dest_Locator%CHARSET,
               Amount IN OUT INTEGER,
               Dest_Start_Position IN INTEGER := 1,
               Source_Start_Position IN INTEGER := 1);
```

Dest_Locator is the locator for the destination LOB that is being copied. The *Set_Desired* parameter is the character set you want to use. If no character set is specified, the Oracle server's character set is used. *Source_Locator* is the locator of the source LOB being copied. *Amount* is how much of the LOB you intend to copy. *Dest_Start_Position* and *Source_Start_Position* are the locations in the LOB to copy from and copy to. A value of 1 indicates the starting position of the LOB.

The EMPTY_BLOB Function

To add a BLOB to a table, you need to assign a locator to the BLOB with the EMPTY_BLOB function.

The Syntax of the EMPTY_BLOB Function

```
FUNCTION EMPTY_BLOB();
    RETURN Locator;
```

Locator is the locator for the BLOB returned by the function.

The EMPTY_CLOB Function

To add a CLOB to a table, you need to assign a locator to the CLOB with the EMPTY_CLOB function.

The Syntax for the EMPTY_CLOB Function

```
FUNCTION EMPTY_CLOB();
    RETURN Locator;
```

This function returns a locator for the CLOB, defined in the syntax as *Locator*.

The ERASE Procedure

The ERASE procedure allows you to erase all or part of a LOB.

The Syntax for the ERASE Procedure

```
PROCEDURE ERASE(BLOB_Locator IN OUT BLOB,
                Amount IN OUT INTEGER,
                Start_Position IN INTEGER := 1);


PROCEDURE APPEND(CLOB_Locator IN OUT CLOB ,
                Amount IN OUT INTEGER,
                Start_Position IN INTEGER := 1);
```

BLOB/CLOB_Locator is the locator assigned to the LOB. *Amount* is how much of the LOB you want to erase. You could use the GETLENGTH function to return the length and specify this as the amount in order to erase the contents of the entire LOB. *Start_Position* is the starting position from which you want to erase part or all of the LOB. A value of 1 is the beginning of the LOB.

The GETLENGTH Function

The GETLENGTH function returns the actual length of the objects in bytes.

The Syntax for the GETLENGTH Function

```
FUNCTION GETLENGTH (BLOB_Locator)
    RETURN Length_Integer;

FUNCTION GETLENGTH (CLOB_Locator CHARACTER SET Set_Desired)
    RETURN Length_Integer;
```

The parameter *BLOB/CLOB_Locator* is the locator assigned to the LOB. The *Set_Desired* parameter is the Oracle character set you want to use. The function returns an INTEGER of the length of the LOB or NULL if the locator is NULL.

The INSTR Function

The INSTR function allows you to match a pattern against the *n*th occurrence in the LOB starting from the offset specified.

The Syntax for the INSTR Function

```
FUNCTION INSTR(BLOB_Locator,
               Pattern IN RAW,
               Starting_Location IN INTEGER := 1,
               Nth_Occurrence IN INTEGER := 1)
RETURN Status_Integer;

FUNCTION INSTR(CLOB_Locator CHARACTER SET Set_Desired,
               Pattern IN VARCHAR2 CHARACTER SET CLOB_Locator%CHARSET,
               Starting_Location IN INTEGER := 1,
               Nth_Occurrence IN INTEGER := 1)
RETURN Status_Integer;
```

The parameter *BLOB/CLOB_Locator* is the BFILE locator assigned to the LOB. The *Set_Desired* parameter is the character set you want to use. If not specified, the character set used for the Oracle database will be used. The *Pattern* of type RAW or VARCHAR2 is the pattern you want to match in the LOB. *Starting_Location* is the position in the LOB where you want to start your search for a match. *Nth_Occurrence* is the *n*th time a match has been made in the LOB. The function returns a value of 0 if the pattern is not found, it returns the offset from the start of the LOB where the match was found, or it returns a value of NULL if any of the parameters are NULL or invalid.

The READ Procedure

The READ procedure allows you to read part or all of a LOB into a buffer.

The Syntax for the READ Procedure

```
PROCEDURE READ(BLOB_Locator,
               Read_Amount IN BINARY_INTEGER,
               Starting_Location IN INTEGER,
               Buffer OUT RAW);

PROCEDURE READ(CLOB_Locator CHARACTER SET Set_Desired,
               Read_Amount IN BINARY_INTEGER,
               Starting_Location IN INTEGER,
               Buffer OUT VARCHAR2 CHARACTER SET CLOB_Locator%CHARSET);
```

The parameter *BLOB/CLOB_Locator* is the locator assigned to the LOB. The *Set_Desired* parameter is the character set you want to use. If no character set is specified, the Oracle server's character set is used. The second parameter, *Read_Amount*, is the number of bytes you will read from the LOB into the buffer. The *Buffer* parameter stores the data from the READ procedure. *Starting_Location* is the location you want to start reading from the LOB. The VALUE_ERROR exception is raised if any of the parameters are NULL. The INVALID_ARGVAL exception is raised if any of the arguments are invalid. NO_DATA_FOUND is raised if you have reached the end of the LOB.

The SUBSTR Function

The SUBSTR function allows you to extract a specified amount of bytes from a LOB.

The Syntax for the SUBSTR Function

```
FUNCTION SUBSTR(BLOB_Locator,
                Read_Amount IN BINARY_INTEGER,
                Starting_Location IN INTEGER := 1)
RETURN RAW;

FUNCTION SUBSTR(CLOB_Locator CHARACTER SET Set_Desired,
                Read_Amount IN BINARY_INTEGER,
                Starting_Location IN INTEGER := 1)
RETURN VARCHAR2 CHARACTER SET CLOB_Locator%CHARSET;
```

The parameter *BLOB/CLOB_Locator* is the locator assigned to the LOB. The *Set_Desired* parameter is the character set you want to use. If no character set is specified, the Oracle server's character set is used. *Read_Amount* is the number of bytes you want to extract from the LOB. *Starting_Location* is the position in the LOB where you want to start your extraction. The function will return a RAW value if successful for a BLOB or VARCHAR2 for a CLOB.

The TRIM Procedure

The TRIM procedure allows you to reduce the LOB to the length specified.

The Syntax for the TRIM Procedure

```
PROCEDURE TRIM(BLOB_Locator,New_Length IN INTEGER);

PROCEDURE TRIM(CLOB_Locator,New_Length IN INTEGER);
```

The parameter *BLOB/CLOB_Locator* is the locator assigned to the LOB. The variable *New_Length* is the new length desired for the LOB.

The WRITE Procedure

If you can read a LOB, you should be able to write to a LOB. The WRITE procedure allows you to write to a LOB.

The Syntax for the WRITE Procedure

```
PROCEDURE WRITE(BLOB_Locator,
               Amount IN OUT INTEGER,
               Starting_Position IN INTEGER,
               Buffer IN RAW);

PROCEDURE WRITE(CLOB_Locator CHARACTER SET Set_Desired,
               Amount IN OUT INTEGER,
               Starting_Position IN INTEGER,
               Buffer IN VARCHAR2 CHARACTER SET CLOB_Locator%CHARSET);
```

The parameter *BLOB/CLOB_Locator* is the locator assigned to the LOB. The *Set_Desired* parameter is the character set you want to use. If no character set is specified, the Oracle server's character set is used. The variable *Amount* is how many bytes to write to the LOB. *Starting_Position* is the position you want to write in the LOB. The *Buffer* parameter is the buffer of the data to write to the LOB.

Examples of Internal LOBs Using the DBMS_LOB Package

You can now test all these functions and procedures using an anonymous PL/SQL block in the next several examples for internal LOBs.

Creating the Table

Before you can work with LOBs, you first need to create and populate a table. Before you run any of these examples, make sure that you have entered SET SERVEROUTPUT ON at the SQL*Plus prompt so that you can see that the examples are working as they execute. Execute the code in Listing 15.6 to create the table called LOBS.

INPUT   **Listing 15.6. Internal LOB table creation.**

```
CREATE TABLE LOBS(
    lob_index INTEGER,
    CLOB_Locator CLOB)
/
```

After the code has completed execution, your output should say Table Created. You just created a table with two columns. The first column, lob_index, will store an integer value that will be used to identify the LOB. The second column is where the locator is stored for the CLOB datatype.

Adding Data to the Table

You can now add data of type CLOB to the table. Execute the code in Listing 15.7 to populate the LOBS table with some preliminary data.

INPUT **Listing 15.7. Populating the CLOB table.**

```
INSERT INTO LOBS VALUES(1,'Teach Yourself Oracle8 in 21 Days')
/
INSERT INTO LOBS VALUES(2,'Oracle Data Warehousing Unleashed')
/
INSERT INTO LOBS VALUES(3,'Teach Yourself Database Development with
    Oracle in 21 Days')
/
INSERT INTO LOBS VALUES(4,'Oracle Unleashed 2E')
/
INSERT INTO LOBS VALUES(5,EMPTY_CLOB())
/
INSERT INTO LOBS VALUES(6,'EMPTY_CLOB())
/
```

The last two items initialize a locator with no data. To verify that the LOBS table was populated, at the SQL prompt, enter

```
SELECT * FROM LOBS;
```

OUTPUT Your output should be

```
LOB_INDEX CLOB_LOCATOR
--------- ----------------------------------------------------------------
        1 Teach Yourself Oracle8 in 21 Days
        2 Oracle Data Warehousing Unleashed
        3 Teach Yourself Database Development with Oracle in 21 Days
        4 Oracle Unleashed 2E
        5
        6
```

Populating the LOBS Table with the COPY Procedure

Listing 15.8 contains an example with internal LOBs, which uses the procedure COPY to copy two rows where no data exists.

INPUT **Listing 15.8. Copying internal LOBs.**

```
DECLARE
    Source_Lob   CLOB;
    Dest_Lob    CLOB;
    Copy_Amount INTEGER;
BEGIN
    SELECT CLOB_LOCATOR into Dest_LOB
        FROM LOBS
        WHERE LOB_INDEX = 5 FOR UPDATE; -- FOR UPDATE locks the ROW
    SELECT CLOB_LOCATOR into Source_LOB
        FROM LOBS
        WHERE LOB_INDEX = 1;
    Copy_Amount := DBMS_LOB.GETLENGTH(Source_Lob);
    DBMS_LOB.COPY(Dest_LOB, Source_LOB,Copy_Amount);
    COMMIT;
```

```
-- Start second copy process
   SELECT CLOB_LOCATOR into Dest_LOB
       FROM LOBS
       WHERE LOB_INDEX = 6 FOR UPDATE;
   SELECT CLOB_LOCATOR into Source_LOB
       FROM LOBS
       WHERE LOB_INDEX = 2;
   Copy_Amount := DBMS_LOB.GETLENGTH(Source_Lob);
   DBMS_LOB.COPY(Dest_LOB, Source_LOB,Copy_Amount);
   COMMIT;
END;
```

To verify that the COPY procedure worked, at the SQL prompt type

```
SELECT * FROM LOBS;
```

OUTPUT
Your output should be

```
LOB_INDEX CLOB_LOCATOR
--------- ------------------------------------------------------------------
        1 Teach Yourself Oracle8 in 21 Days
        2 Oracle Data Warehousing Unleashed
        3 Teach Yourself Database Development with Oracle in 21 Days
        4 Oracle Unleashed 2E
        5 Teach Yourself Oracle8 in 21 Days
        6 Oracle Data Warehousing Unleashed
```

ANALYSIS
Two LOBs are defined as type CLOB, which will store the locator for the source and destination LOBs. The Copy_Amount variable will store how much of the Source_Lob is to be copied. In this case, you assign this value to the length of the Source_Lob by using the GETLENGTH function. The locators are then read into the Source_Lob and Dest_Lob. The COPY procedure then copies from the source to the destination LOB, and then COMMIT commits the transaction.

Manipulating Internal LOBs with APPEND and WRITE

Now, you can practice appending from one LOB to another, and even writing to a LOB. Execute the code in Listing 15.9.

INPUT **Listing 15.9. Appending and writing to LOBs.**

```
DECLARE
/* This appends the contents of Row 1 to the contents of Row 5.
   In addition, it writes text at the end of the values in
   Row 6.  */

   Source_Lob   CLOB;
   Dest_Lob   CLOB;
   Write_Amount INTEGER := 10;
   Writing_Position INTEGER ;
```

continues

Listing 15.9. continued

```
     Buffer VARCHAR2(10) := 'Added Text';
BEGIN
-- Append from Row 1 to Row 5
   SELECT CLOB_LOCATOR into Dest_LOB
        FROM LOBS
        WHERE LOB_INDEX = 5 FOR UPDATE; -- Locks Row for Update
   SELECT CLOB_LOCATOR into Source_LOB
        FROM LOBS
        WHERE LOB_INDEX = 1;
   DBMS_LOB.APPEND(Dest_LOB, Source_LOB);
   COMMIT;
-- Write to a LOB
   SELECT CLOB_LOCATOR into Source_LOB
        FROM LOBS
        WHERE LOB_INDEX = 6 FOR UPDATE;   -- Locks Row for Update

   Writing_Position := DBMS_LOB.GETLENGTH(Source_Lob) + 1;
   DBMS_LOB.WRITE(Source_LOB,Write_Amount,Writing_Position,Buffer);
   COMMIT;
END;
```

To verify that the WRITE and APPEND procedures worked, at the SQL prompt type

```
SELECT * FROM LOBS;
```

OUTPUT   Your output should be

```
LOB_INDEX CLOB_LOCATOR
--------- ------------------------------------------------------------
        1 Teach Yourself Oracle8 in 21 Days
        2 Oracle Data Warehousing Unleashed
        3 Teach Yourself Database Development with Oracle in 21 Days
        4 Oracle Unleashed 2E
        5 Teach Yourself Oracle8 in 21 DaysTe
          ach Yourself Oracl
          e8 in 21 Days
        6 Oracle Data Warehousing UnleashedAdded Text
```

ANALYSIS   As you can see from the output, you appended row 1 to row 5, and you also added text to row 6. For the purposes of the APPEND procedure, two variables of type CLOB are created for the source and destination location. For the WRITE procedure, three additional variables are created to hold how much data to write stored in Write_Amount, where to start writing in the CLOB stored in Writing_Position, and the text to write to the CLOB stored in the Buffer variable. The procedure then copies the source and destination locators into the corresponding variables and then calls the APPEND procedure. The transaction is then committed.

The second part of the procedure selects the row where text will be added, locks the row for updating, assigns the starting position to the length of the contents + 1 (so no data is overwritten), and then calls the WRITE procedure. This transaction is then committed.

Analyzing the Contents of an Internal LOB

In the next exercise, you analyze the contents of an internal LOB. You will work with the functions INSTR and SUBSTR. Execute the code in Listing 15.10. Make sure that you have entered SET SERVEROUTPUT ON at the SQL*Plus prompt so that you can see output as the program executes.

INPUT **Listing 15.10. Extracting and matching data inside CLOBs.**

```
DECLARE
/* This PL/SQL block finds patterns in a CLOB.  It also
   extracts part of the data from a CLOB with SUBSTR */

    Source_Lob    CLOB;
    v_Pattern VARCHAR2(6) := 'Oracle';
    v_Starting_Location INTEGER := 1;
    v_Nth_Occurrence INTEGER := 1;
    v_Position INTEGER ;
    v_Extract_Amount INTEGER;
    v_Buffer VARCHAR2(100) ;
BEGIN
-- Search for 1st Occurrence of Oracle in Row 5
    SELECT CLOB_LOCATOR into Source_LOB
        FROM LOBS
        WHERE LOB_INDEX = 5;
    v_Position := DBMS_LOB.INSTR(Source_LOB,v_Pattern,
        v_Starting_Location,v_Nth_Occurrence);
    DBMS_OUTPUT.PUT_LINE('The first occurrence starts at position: '
        ¦¦ v_Position);

-- Search for 2nd Occurrence of Oracle in Row 5

    v_Nth_Occurrence := 2;

    SELECT CLOB_LOCATOR into Source_LOB
        FROM LOBS
        WHERE LOB_INDEX = 5;
    v_Position := DBMS_LOB.INSTR(Source_LOB,v_Pattern,
        v_Starting_Location,v_Nth_Occurrence);
    DBMS_OUTPUT.PUT_LINE('The second occurrence starts at position: '
        ¦¦ v_Position);

-- Extract part of the data from a CLOB
    SELECT CLOB_LOCATOR into Source_LOB
        FROM LOBS
        WHERE LOB_INDEX = 6;
    v_Buffer := DBMS_LOB.SUBSTR(Source_LOB,11,v_Starting_Location);
    DBMS_OUTPUT.PUT_LINE('The substring extracted is: '  ¦¦ v_Buffer);

END;
```

OUTPUT Your output should be

```
The first occurrence starts at position: 16
The second occurrence starts at position: 50
The substring extracted is: Oracle Data
```

ANALYSIS The procedure begins by selecting the data from row 5 and reading the locator into the Source_Lob variable. Using the INSTR function, the pattern 'Oracle', assigned to the v_Pattern variable, is searched for the first occurrence, specified by the v_Nth_Occurrence variable. The starting location is defaulted to the first position in the CLOB, stored in the v_Starting_Location variable. The process is repeated except that you are now searching for the second occurrence of 'Oracle' in the CLOB.

The last part of the procedure extracts 11 characters from row 6 and stores this in v_Buffer, which is then displayed to the screen.

Using TRIM and ERASE to Edit CLOBs

The last exercise will demonstrate the TRIM and ERASE procedures. Execute the code in Listing 15.11.

INPUT   **Listing 15.11. Reducing data in CLOBs.**

```
DECLARE
/* This erases the data in Row 6, and trims the data in
   row 5 to one occurrence of the book title. */

    Source_Lob    CLOB;
    Erase_Amount INTEGER;
    Trim_Amount INTEGER;

BEGIN
-- Erase the data completely in Row 6

    SELECT CLOB_LOCATOR into Source_LOB
        FROM LOBS
        WHERE LOB_INDEX = 6 FOR UPDATE; -- Locks Row for Update
    Erase_Amount :=DBMS_LOB.GETLENGTH(Source_LOB);
    DBMS_LOB.ERASE(Source_LOB,Erase_Amount,1);

--Reduce Data in Row 5 to one instance of Book Title
    SELECT CLOB_LOCATOR into Source_LOB
        FROM LOBS
        WHERE LOB_INDEX = 5 FOR UPDATE;

    TRIM_AMOUNT := DBMS_LOB.GETLENGTH(Source_LOB) / 2;
    DBMS_LOB.TRIM(Source_LOB, TRIM_AMOUNT);
    COMMIT;

END;
```

15

15

To verify that the ERASE and TRIM procedures worked, at the SQL prompt type

```
SELECT * FROM LOBS;
```

OUTPUT Your output should be

```
LOB_INDEX CLOB_LOCATOR
--------- -------------------------------------------------------------
        1 Teach Yourself Oracle8 in 21 Days
        2 Oracle Data Warehousing Unleashed
        3 Teach Yourself Database Development with Oracle in 21 Days
        4 Oracle Unleashed 2E
        5 Teach Yourself Oracle8 in 21 Days
        6
```

ANALYSIS Three variables are declared: Source_Lob holds the locator for the CLOBs you will alter. The variable Erase_Amount will hold the number of bytes to erase from row 6. The Trim_Amount will store the number of bytes that should remain in row 5. The procedure starts by reading the locator for the CLOB into the variable Source_Lob. Erase_Amount is assigned the value of the length of the data in row 6 by using the GETLENGTH function. The ERASE procedure is called and passes the CLOB locator, the total bytes to erase, and the starting position for erasing the data, which is hard-coded to a value of 1 in this example.

The second half of the block will reduce the data in row 5 by half. The locator for the CLOB in row 5 is read into the variable Source_Lob. The Amount of data to remain is calculated by taking the total length of the data by using the GETLENGTH function and dividing this value by 2. The TRIM procedure is called, passing the locator and the amount of bytes to remain. The transactions are then committed.

Summary

In this lesson, you learned about recursion. Recursion is a method in which a function continuously calls itself until some exit condition occurs. One of the problems with using recursion is that possible logic errors could cause an infinite loop. Although recursion code is short and brief, it is rarely used because it is hard to follow and causes poor execution when the number of calls to the function increases. All problems that can be solved with recursion can also be solved using a different approach.

You also learned how Oracle handles large objects, referred to as LOBs. The two types of LOBs are internal and external LOBs. External LOBs, called BFILEs, are files accessible to the operating system, rather than data stored in a table. Oracle stores a pointer to the location of the file in a table, which contains the path and filename of the file. The path is defined by the CREATE DIRECTORY SQL statement. If the locator is not updated and the file is moved or deleted, an exception is raised. Internal LOBs can also be binary, character, multicharacter, and fixed width. These have full transactional support and can be committed or rolled back. When you copy an internal LOB, all data is copied and a new locator is entered into the table. LOBs can have a maximum size of 4 gigabytes, or the size of an unsigned long integer.

Q&A

Q What is recursion?

A Recursion is a method in which a function calls itself until some exit condition occurs.

Q When should I use recursion?

A Use recursion when there would be a small number of iterations, no more than 10 to 15.

Q What is the difference between an external and an internal large object?

A Internal large objects are stored within the Oracle database. External large objects are stored and maintained by the operating system.

Q What possible uses are there for large objects?

A You can easily store and track pictures, large text files, and sound files, which can then be used by front-end systems to display or play back the data.

Q How are paths accessed by Oracle?

A A path is defined as a directory object by using the SQL statement CREATE DIRECTORY.

Workshop

You will now have a chance to practice your knowledge of recursion and the DBMS_LOB package. The answers to the quiz and exercise can be found in Appendix A, "Answers."

Quiz

1. Could you use recursion to generate an organizational chart as long as you had the ID of your immediate boss coded in your employee record?

2. Should you use recursion as much as possible?

3. What is the largest size of a large object?

4. Can you write to external files?

5. When copying LOBs from one row to another, is only a new locator copied?

Exercise

Rewrite the code in Listing 15.1, but as a loop instead of a recursive function. Provide the result of 6 factorial (6!).

Day **16**

Managing Transactions and Locks

by Tom Luers

In today's lesson you will learn about transactions and the benefits you can gain by controlling them. Managing transactions provides the user of the Oracle server, application developer, or database administrator the capability of guaranteeing data consistency and data concurrency. Data consistency provides the user a consistent view of data, which consists of data committed by other users as well as changes made by the user. Data concurrency provides the user access to data concurrently used by many other users. Without transactions coordinating data concurrency and data consistency, the user of the server would experience inconsistent data reads, lost updates, and nonrepeatable reads.

Types of Transactions

A *transaction* is a logical unit of work that is composed of one or more Data Manipulation Language (DML) or Data Definition Language (DDL) statements. For every transaction in Oracle, one of two situations occurs. If the statements in a transaction complete normally, then the effects of the transaction are made permanent in the database. This is called *committing* the transaction. The other situation occurs when any one of the statements is unable to complete for whatever reason. In this case, the effects of the transaction are removed from the database and the transaction ends. This removal of the effects of a transaction is called *rolling back* the transaction.

Oracle provides two general types of transactions: *read-only* and *read-write* transactions. The read-only transaction specifies that the queried data and all queries within the same transaction will not be affected by any other transactions that take place in the database. In other words, any subsequent query can only read changes committed prior to the beginning of the current transaction. The read-write transaction guarantees that data returned by a query is consistent with respect to the time the query began.

The read-only transaction enforces transaction-level read consistency. This type of transaction can only contain queries and cannot contain any DML statements. In this situation, only data committed prior to the start of the transaction is available to the query. Thus, a query can be executed multiple times and return the same results each time.

The read-write transaction provides for statement-level read consistency. This type of transaction will never see any of the changes made by transactions that commit during the course of a query execution.

Starting a Transaction

The transaction begins with the first SQL statement being executed and ends when the effects of the transaction are saved or backed out. The SET TRANSACTION command also will initiate a transaction.

The SET TRANSACTION command is an integral part of transaction management. This command performs one of these operations on the current transaction:

☐ Establishes the transaction as either a read-only or a read-write transaction.

☐ Assigns the current read-write transaction to a specified rollback segment.

The Syntax for the SET TRANSACTION **Command**

SYNTAX

```
SET TRANSACTION parameter
```

In this syntax, *parameter* will be one of the following values:

☐ READ ONLY—Establishes transaction-level read consistency.

☐ READ WRITE—Establishes statement-level read consistency.

☐ USE ROLLBACK SEGMENT—Defines the appropriate rollback segment to be used.

16

The read-only transaction is the default mode of all transactions. With this mode, you will not have a rollback segment assigned. Additionally, you cannot perform an INSERT, a DELETE, an UPDATE, or a SELECT FOR UPDATE clause command during this transaction. The read-write transaction mode provides no restrictions on the DML statements allowed in the transaction.

The SET TRANSACTION command allows you to explicitly assign a particular rollback segment to the read-write transaction. This rollback segment is used to undo any changes made by the current transaction should a rollback be executed. If you do not specify a rollback segment, Oracle will assign one to the transaction.

The following example of the SET TRANSACTION command would allow the user to run this script every weekend without worrying about any other users who might be modifying data:

```
COMMIT;
SET TRANSACTION read only;
execute_weekend_packages;
COMMIT;
```

Ending a Transaction

Ending a transaction will either save the changes made by the transaction or will back out all changes. Saving all pending changes to the database is known as committing the transaction. Backing out is accomplished through the ROLLBACK statement or when there is abnormal termination in the transaction. The ROLLBACK statement is discussed further in the next section, "Canceling a Transaction."

Committing occurs when the user either explicitly or implicitly saves the transaction changes to the database permanently. Until you perform a commit, the following principles characterize the state of your transaction:

☐ Data Manipulation Language operations only affect the database buffer. Because the changes have only affected the buffer, these changes can be backed out.

☐ A rollback segment buffer is created in the server.

☐ The owner of the transaction can view the effects of the transaction with the SELECT statement.

☐ Other users of the database cannot see the effects of the transaction.

☐ The affected rows are locked and other users cannot change the data within the affected rows.

After the commit is executed, the following occurs:

1. Locks held on the affected rows are released.

2. The transaction is marked as complete.

3. The internal transaction table of the server generates a system change number, assigns this number to the transaction, and saves them both in the table.

Use the COMMIT statement to explicitly make permanent the changes from a transaction. The following example shows a simple transaction being executed with a commit being issued after the transaction is executed:

```
SQL>INSERT INTO TABLE raw_material VALUES
SQL>(part_id, part_name)
SQL>VALUES (s_raw_mat.nextval, "18g Copper Wire")
1 row created
SQL> COMMIT;
Commit completed
```

You can use the COMMENT clause with the COMMIT statement to place a text string in the data dictionary along with the transaction ID. You can view this information in the dba_2pc_pending data dictionary view. Usually you will use this view to obtain additional information about a transaction that has a questionable status in a distributed environment.

To make an explicit commit, you must have the force transaction system privilege. To manually commit a distributed transaction that was originated by another user, you must have the force any transaction system privilege.

Oracle performs an implicit commit before and after every Data Definition Language command.

Canceling a Transaction

Rolling back a transaction means to undo any change that the current transaction has made. The ROLLBACK command will undo the entire transaction. To execute a rollback of the entire transaction, issue the ROLLBACK command. The following example illustrates the use of the ROLLBACK command to undo the effects of the UPDATE command:

```
UPDATE TABLE employee
set pay_rate = pay_rate * 1.25
WHERE pay_type = 'S';
ROLLBACK;
```

Alternatively, you can roll back a portion of a transaction with the ROLLBACK TO SAVEPOINT command. Savepoints are discussed later in this chapter in the section titled "Savepoints."

When you roll back an entire transaction, the following occurs:

1. All changes made by the current transaction are undone using the corresponding rollback segment.
2. All locks on the rows caused by the transaction are released.
3. The transaction is ended.

When you roll back a transaction to a savepoint, the following occurs:

☐ Only the SQL statements executed after the last savepoint are rolled back.

☐ The specified savepoint in the ROLLBACK command is preserved, but all other savepoints after that savepoint are removed from the database.

☐ All locks established since the specified savepoint are released.

☐ The transaction is still active and can continue.

No privileges are required to roll back your own transaction. Oracle requires that you have the force transaction system privilege to roll back any in-doubt distributed transaction owned by you. If the distributed transaction is owned by someone else, then you are required to have the force any transaction system privilege.

Oracle will perform an implicit rollback if a severe failure occurs with the host computer or in the application program.

Two-Phase Commit

Oracle manages the commits and rollbacks of distributed transactions and maintains data integrity for all the distributed databases participating in the distributed transaction. Oracle performs these tasks by a mechanism known as *two-phase commit*.

In a nondistributed environment, all transactions are either committed or rolled back as a unit. However, in a distributed environment, commits and rollbacks of a distributed transaction must be coordinated over a network so that all the participating databases either commit or roll back the transaction. This must hold true even if the network fails during the distributed transaction. The two-phase commit guarantees that the nodes participating in the transaction either commit or roll back the transaction, thus maintaining complete data integrity of the global database.

All implicit DML operations performed by integrity constraints, remote procedure calls, and triggers are protected by Oracle's two-phase commit.

Savepoints

A savepoint is like a bookmark in the transaction. You explicitly place this bookmark for reference at a later time. Savepoints are used to break a large transaction up into smaller pieces. This allows you to roll back your work to intermediate points in the transaction rather than rolling back the entire transaction. For example, if you are performing a large number of updates and an error occurs, you only have to roll back to the last savepoint; therefore, you would not need to reprocess every statement.

The following code creates the savepoint named `master_credit`:

```
SAVEPOINT master_credit
```

Savepoint names must be unique within a given transaction. If you create a second savepoint named the same as an earlier savepoint, the previous savepoint is erased.

The following is an example of rolling back a transaction to the `employee_1` savepoint:

```
INSERT INTO employee VALUES
(6,'Tom Bluekers',3,1000.00,'S');
SAVEPOINT employee_1;
INSERT INTO employee VALUES
(7,'Catherine Ann',2,2000.00,'S');
ROLLBACK TO SAVEPOINT employee_1;
```

In this example, the insertion of the employee Catherine Ann is removed from the transaction. At the point of the rollback to the savepoint, the insertion of Tom Bluekers is the pending data in the current transaction.

Locking

Oracle automatically locks a row on behalf of a transaction to prevent other transactions from acquiring a lock on the same row. You don't want simultaneous row manipulations by two separate transactions. Data locks prevent destructive interference of simultaneous conflicting DDL and DML statements. For example, Oracle prevents a table from being dropped if there are uncommitted transactions on that table. These data locks are automatically released when the transaction completes by a commit or rollback. The next two sections examine two types of data locks: table and row.

Table Locking

DML operations can obtain data locks for specific rows and for specific tables. These locks occur to protect the data in the table when the table is being accessed concurrently by multiple users.

A transaction acquires a table lock when a table is modified by the following DML statements: INSERT, UPDATE, DELETE, SELECT with the UPDATE option, and LOCK TABLE. The table lock is specifically in place to ensure that the current transaction has access to the data and to prevent any conflicting DDL operations that might happen.

An important note to consider is that placing a table lock prevents other transactions from acquiring a lock (row or table) on the same table.

The table lock can be executed in five different modes:

☐ row share—This table lock is the least restrictive of the table locks. This lock allows for other concurrent transactions to query, insert, update, delete, and lock rows in the same table. The row share table lock will not allow exclusive write access to the same table.

☐ row exclusive—This lock occurs when several rows in a table have been updated. This lock still allows other transactions to query, insert, update, delete, or lock rows in the same table. The row exclusive lock will not prevent any manual locking or exclusive reads and writes on the same table.

☐ share lock—The share lock table lock allows for other transactions only to query and lock specific rows. This lock prevents all updates, inserts, and deletes from the same table.

☐ share row exclusive—This table lock is only accomplished through the lock table with the share row exclusive parameter. This lock will only permit queries and SELECT FOR UPDATE statements.

☐ exclusive—This lock allows the transaction write access to a table. This lock means that other transactions can only query the table.

Implicit data locking occurs automatically for all SQL statements, so users of the database do not have to explicitly lock any rows. By default, Oracle locks resources at the lowest level possible.

In a multiuser database, locks have two different levels:

☐ exclusive—This prohibits the sharing of the associated resource. The first transaction that acquires the resource is the only transaction that can alter the resource until the lock is released.

☐ share—This lock allows the associated resource to be shared, depending on the operations involved. Several transactions can acquire share locks on the same resource. share locks provide a higher degree of data concurrency than exclusive locks.

16

Row Locking

Row locks are acquired automatically by the transactions when a row is modified by the following commands: INSERT, DELETE, UPDATE, and SELECT with the FOR UPDATE clause.

The following example of the SELECT command places a row lock on the employee table:

```
SELECT emp_id, pay_rate
FROM employee
WHERE pay_type = 'H'
FOR UPDATE;
```

These row locks stay in effect until the transaction is completed or rolled back. The row lock is always exclusive, which prohibits other transactions from modifying the same row. When the row lock is issued, a corresponding table lock is also issued to prevent any conflicting DDL statements from taking effect.

Other Locks

Oracle provides a variety of other "minor" locks. I call them minor not because of their importance, but because from a user's perspective, you don't usually interact with them directly.

The *dictionary lock* is used to protect the database objects from changing during a transaction. This lock is automatically acquired by Oracle when a DDL statement requires it. Like the locks mentioned in the previous section, the dictionary lock can be either exclusive or shared.

Internal locks protect the internal components of the database and memory. These components are inaccessible by end users. For example, locks can be placed on log files, control files, data dictionary cache files, and archive files.

Distributed locks ensure data consistency across multiple instances. Oracle automatically creates these locks as needed.

Monitoring Locks

Oracle provides several ways to monitor which locks are in place within the database. For example, examining the V$LOCK database view will list information about a lock, such as the system ID of the process holding the lock and type of lock held. Additionally, the DBA_DDL_LOCKS, DBA_DML_LOCKS, and DBA_LOCKS tables display similar data about locks.

Likewise, you can use the Oracle tool SQL*DBA. In SQL*DBA, the Lock Monitor screen gives similar information from the V$LOCK database view.

Summary

Transactions are logical groups of SQL statements that begin when the statements are executed and end with either a commit or rollback. Transactions provide database users the guarantee of data concurrency and data consistency. This guarantee holds true for distributed and nondistributed databases.

Q&A

Q Why do DML statements need to be committed?

A Committing a transaction accomplishes several things: The transaction is ended, which in turn releases any locks that the transaction might have created.

Q Do I have to roll back an entire transaction if something does not process completely?

A The rollback can be issued to remove all effects of the current transaction. Additionally, you can roll back to an intermediate point in the transaction known as a savepoint.

Q What are the two types of transactions?

A The two main types of transactions are read-only and read-write.

Workshop

Use the following workshop to test your comprehension of this chapter and put what you've learned into practice. You'll find the answers to the quiz and exercise in Appendix A, "Answers."

Quiz

1. How is a transaction ended?
2. What is the difference between row locking and table locking?
3. What is the purpose of a savepoint?

Exercise

Write a PL/SQL block that establishes a savepoint, inserts a single record into the employee table, commits the data if the new record does not replicate an existing record, or rolls back the data if the new record insert fails.

Day 17

Generating Dynamic SQL

by Timothy Atwood

The DBMS_SQL package is a powerful package, and the most difficult to understand. This package allows you to execute non-query DDL and DML statements, SQL queries, and anonymous blocks of PL/SQL from within PL/SQL.

Why are you not allowed to execute these items from within PL/SQL? The problem occurs when executing code in a SQL environment. A typical SQL query always opens a cursor and then parses the SQL for any errors. Any variables are then bound to the session. In regular PL/SQL, before the code is executed, it is parsed for errors. For example, if you were trying to create a table without using dynamic SQL, the PL/SQL code would check the code and then attempt to validate that all tables are present and all values are valid before executing the PL/SQL block. Because the table does not exist yet, the PL/SQL code will raise an error and never execute because the table could not be bound. PL/SQL was designed to bind all variables first, in order to allow for faster execution. DBMS_SQL circumvents this limitation by allowing you to literally create and execute SQL code dynamically. If you use this powerful feature, your users can execute different queries from the same table based upon variables instead of fixed SQL.

Today's lesson discusses the following topics:

☐ Steps for using DBMS_SQL

☐ Using non-query DDL and DML statements

☐ Executing queries with DBMS_SQL

☐ Executing PL/SQL with DBMS_SQL

NOTE

In order to work with the DBMS_SQL package, you must have Oracle7 or later, the package must be installed, and you must have all the appropriate privileges such as DROP TABLE, CREATE TABLE, and so on. Oracle does provide backward compatibility for version 6.

Steps for Using DBMS_SQL

The following steps give you an overview of what is required for coding non-query DDL and DML statements, executing SQL queries, and executing anonymous blocks:

1. Open the cursor with OPEN_CURSOR.

2. Parse the SQL statement with PARSE.

3. Bind any variables with BIND_VARIABLE.

4. If using SELECT statements, you must define the output columns by using DEFINE_COLUMN.

5. Execute the SQL statement with EXECUTE.

6. Use FETCH_ROWS to fetch rows from the cursor. You can also use EXECUTE_AND_FETCH to achieve the same goal in only one step.

7. Use VARIABLE_VALUE to retrieve values, which can change upon the execution of dynamic SQL.

8. If fetching rows, then you must use COLUMN_VALUE to retrieve data from the cursor and store it into a local variable.

9. When all processing is finished, you must close the cursor using CLOSE_CURSOR.

Three Types of Statements Processed with DBMS_SQL

As stated earlier, the three types of statements that can be processed by the DBMS_SQL package are non-query DDL and DML statements, SQL queries, and anonymous blocks of PL/SQL. Based upon the steps required for processing these types of statements, this section examines each type of statement in much greater detail.

Using the DBMS_SQL Package with Non-Query DDL and DML Statements

DDL (Data Definition Language) and DML (Data Manipulation Language) allow you to use CREATE, DROP, INSERT, UPDATE, DELETE, and so forth in your PL/SQL code. The following steps are required:

1. Open the cursor.
2. Parse the statement.
3. Bind input variables (if required).
4. Execute the statement.
5. Close the cursor.

Opening a Cursor for Non-Query DDL and DML Statements

Whenever you execute SQL or PL/SQL, a cursor is opened transparently. When creating dynamic SQL, you must specify every step, including opening the cursor by using OPEN_CURSOR. The syntax for the OPEN_CURSOR function is as follows:

```
FUNCTION OPEN_CURSOR RETURN INTEGER;
```

The OPEN_CURSOR function returns an integer, which is the cursor ID. The cursor ID will be retained for use until the cursor is closed. As you can see, leaving a cursor open without closing the cursor using CLOSE_CURSOR wastes valuable resources. You can now perform as many statements as desired by referencing the cursor ID returned.

Parsing Statements for Non-Query DDL and DML Statements

After the cursor is opened, the statements are parsed to check for syntax errors. Normally, a procedure would show all errors before it could be run successfully. You now run the risk of syntax errors during production runtime, so you must check for all possible errors and trap user mistakes.

The Syntax for the PARSE Procedure

```
PROCEDURE PARSE(cursor_id IN INTEGER,
                      statement_to_parse IN VARCHAR2,
                      version IN VARCHAR2);
```

cursor_id is the cursor assigned by the OPEN_CURSOR statement. *statement_to_parse* is the SQL statement you want to parse. The last parameter, *version*, is the version type.

The following versions are allowed:

☐ NATIVE—Native handling for the server

☐ V6—Handling for Oracle version 6.*x*

☐ V7—Handling for Oracle version 7.*x*

☐ V8—Handling for Oracle version 8.*x*

The version can be expressed as DBMS_SQL.NATIVE, DBMS_SQL.V8, and so on.

NOTE

> Oracle6 databases can only be accessed by the DBMS_SQL package through a database link.

Binding Variables for Non-Query DDL and DML Statements

Binding enables you to bind a specific variable to a placeholder, which is identified by a colon. Because you can bind all types of PL/SQL variables, the overloaded BIND_VARIABLE procedure can handle many datatypes.

The Syntax for Binding Variables

The syntax for the NUMBER datatype is

```
PROCEDURE BIND_VARIABLE(cursor_id IN INTEGER,
                          placeholder_name IN VARCHAR2,
                          value IN NUMBER);
```

The two syntaxes for type VARCHAR2 are

```
PROCEDURE BIND_VARIABLE(cursor_id IN INTEGER,
                          placeholder_name IN VARCHAR2,
                          value IN VARCHAR2);
```

and

```
PROCEDURE BIND_VARIABLE(cursor_id IN INTEGER,
                          placeholder_name IN VARCHAR2,
                          value IN VARCHAR2,
                          out_value_size IN INTEGER);
```

The two syntaxes for type CHAR2 are

```
PROCEDURE BIND_VARIABLE(cursor_id IN INTEGER,
                        placeholder_name IN VARCHAR2,
                        value IN CHAR2);
```

and

```
PROCEDURE BIND_VARIABLE(cursor_id IN INTEGER,
                        placeholder_name IN VARCHAR2,
                        value IN CHAR2,
                        out_value_size IN INTEGER);
```

The syntax for the DATE datatype is

```
PROCEDURE BIND_VARIABLE(cursor_id IN INTEGER,
                        placeholder_name IN VARCHAR2,
                        value IN DATE);
```

The two syntaxes for type RAW are

```
PROCEDURE BIND_VARIABLE(cursor_id IN INTEGER,
                        placeholder_name IN VARCHAR2,
                        value IN RAW);
```

and

```
PROCEDURE BIND_VARIABLE(cursor_id IN INTEGER,
                        placeholder_name IN VARCHAR2,
                        value IN RAW,
                        out_value_size IN INTEGER);
```

The syntax for ROWID is

```
PROCEDURE BIND_VARIABLE(cursor_id IN INTEGER,
                        placeholder_name IN VARCHAR2,
                        value IN ROWID);
```

Finally, there is support for MLSLABEL in Trusted Oracle with

```
PROCEDURE BIND_VARIABLE(cursor_id IN INTEGER,
                        placeholder_name IN VARCHAR2,
                        value IN MLSLABEL);
```

As you can see, there is support for almost any conceivable datatype.

cursor_id is the ID returned from OPEN_CURSOR. placeholder_name is the name of the variable preceded by a colon. value is the value to be bound (assigned) to the placeholder variable name. For any of the procedures with out_value_size, this is the output size expressed in bytes for those datatypes.

Executing Statements for Non-Query DDL and DML Statements

After you have bound variables, if required, you are ready to execute the DDL or DML statements with the function EXECUTE.

The Syntax for the EXECUTE Function

```
FUNCTION EXECUTE (cursor_id IN INTEGER) RETURN INTEGER;
```

cursor_id is the cursor assigned by the OPEN_CURSOR statement. The function also returns an integer that is valid only for DML statements, which returns the number of rows processed. The applicable DML statements are INSERT, UPDATE, and DELETE. This value should be ignored for all other purposes.

Closing the Cursor for Non-Query DDL and DML Statements

After all processing has been completed, you should close the cursor with the CLOSE_CURSOR procedure to free up those resources.

The Syntax for the CLOSE_CURSOR Procedure

```
PROCEDURE CLOSE_CURSOR (cursor_id IN OUT INTEGER);
```

cursor_id is the cursor assigned by the OPEN_CURSOR statement. After the call has been complete, the value of *cursor_id* is set to NULL.

Using DDL to Create a Table

You'll start the review of dynamic SQL by creating a table from within SQL. Although this example is still "fixed," it would be easy to modify the example in the form of a stored function or procedure to allow a user to create any type of table. Enter and then execute the code in Listing 17.1.

INPUT   **Listing 17.1. Creating the table called MyTable.**

```
 1: DECLARE
 2: /* The purpose of this PL/SQL block is to create a table
 3:    called MyTable, which has two columns of type INTEGER and
 4:    the second column of type VARCHAR2(50).  This uses the
 5:    DBMS_SQL package to execute DDL statements */
 6:
 7:      v_CursorID  NUMBER; -- Variable assigned to value from OPEN_CURSOR
 8:      v_CreateTableString  VARCHAR2(500); -- SQL stored as string to create
        ➥table
 9:      v_NUMRows  INTEGER; -- Number of rows processed - of no use
10:
11: BEGIN
12:      v_CursorID := DBMS_SQL.OPEN_CURSOR; -- Get the Cursor ID
13:      v_CreateTableString := 'CREATE TABLE MyTable(
14:          MyRow INTEGER,
15:          MyDesc VARCHAR2(50))'; -- Write SQL code to create table
16:
17:      DBMS_SQL.PARSE(v_CursorID,v_CreateTableString,DBMS_SQL.V7);
18:          /* Perform syntax error checking */
19:      v_NumRows := DBMS_SQL.EXECUTE(v_CursorID);
20:          /* Execute the SQL code  */
21:
```

```
22: EXCEPTION
23:     WHEN OTHERS THEN
24:         IF SQLCODE != -955 THEN -- 955 is error that table exists
25:             RAISE; -- raise if some other unknown error
26:         ELSE
27:             DBMS_OUTPUT.PUT_LINE('Table Already Exists!');
28:         END IF;
29:     DBMS_SQL.CLOSE_CURSOR(v_CursorID); -- Close the cursor
30: END; -- End PL/SQL block
```

OUTPUT After you have executed the block, you should see

```
PL/SQL procedure successfully completed.
```

ANALYSIS You have just created a table called MyTable. The code in Listing 17.1 sets up three variables:

☐ v_CursorID—Holds the cursor ID returned by the call to OPEN_CURSOR. This variable is set up in line 7.

☐ v_CreateTableString—Holds the SQL code required to create the table. This variable is set up in line 8.

NOTE It's very important that the SQL code used to create the table, or any SQL code used with the DBMS_SQL package, should not end with a semicolon.

☐ v_NUMRows—Holds the number of rows processed, which is meaningless with the DDL statements, but required by PL/SQL to hold the return value. This variable is set up in line 9.

Next, in line 12, v_CursorID is assigned the cursor ID supplied by OPEN_CURSOR. In line 13, the v_CreateTableString is assigned the necessary SQL code to create the table. Again, it is very important that the SQL code you will execute should not end in a semicolon! The statement is parsed for syntax errors in line 17. No variables need to be bound in this PL/SQL code. The dynamic SQL statement is then executed in line 19, and the cursor is then closed.

If the table already exists, I do not want this procedure to automatically delete the table. I have seen valid production tables get deleted this way. Instead, if the error 955 occurs, which means that the table exists, the program displays the message that the table exists. This exception-handling routine is in lines 22 through 28. After making sure to enter SET SERVEROUTPUT ON, go ahead and execute the code in Listing 17.1 again. You will then see the message that the table already exists. In the exception area, if any other error occurs, I want the error to be raised for you to view because this error would be truly unknown.

Using DML to Add Records to the Table

Now that you have created a table with DDL statements, you can add some records with DML statements. You can finally see how many rows were processed. You will add a total of five records; the fifth record will not need binding because it takes the default values of the previous bind, which effectively duplicates the fourth record. Go ahead and execute the code in Listing 17.2.

INPUT   **Listing 17.2. Using INSERT to add records.**

```
 1: DECLARE
 2: /* The purpose of this PL/SQL block is to demonstrate the use
 3:    of DML statements by adding a total of four records. This will
 4:    illustrate the use of binding variables and the multiple use
 5:    of accessing the Cursor ID */
 6:
 7:     v_CursorID  NUMBER; -- Variable assigned to value from OPEN_CURSOR
 8:     v_InsertRecords  VARCHAR2(500); -- SQL stored as string to insert
        ➥records
 9:     v_NUMRows  INTEGER; -- Number of rows processed - of no use
10:
11: BEGIN
12:     v_CursorID := DBMS_SQL.OPEN_CURSOR; -- Get the Cursor ID
13:     v_InsertRecords := 'INSERT INTO MyTable(MyRow,MyDesc)
14:          VALUES (:mynum,:mytext)'; -- Write SQL to insert records
15:
16: /*  Define and Insert the First Record */
17:
18:     DBMS_SQL.PARSE(v_CursorID,v_InsertRecords,DBMS_SQL.V7);
19:          /* Perform syntax error checking */
20:     DBMS_SQL.BIND_VARIABLE(v_CursorID, ':mynum',1);
21:     DBMS_SQL.BIND_VARIABLE(v_CursorID, ':mytext','One');
22:     v_NumRows := DBMS_SQL.EXECUTE(v_CursorID);
23:          /* Execute the SQL code  */
24:     DBMS_OUTPUT.PUT_LINE('The number of records just processed is: '
25:          || v_NUMRows);
26:
27: /*  Define and Insert the Second Record */
28:
29:     DBMS_SQL.BIND_VARIABLE(v_CursorID, ':mynum',2);
30:     DBMS_SQL.BIND_VARIABLE(v_CursorID, ':mytext','Two');
31:     v_NumRows := DBMS_SQL.EXECUTE(v_CursorID);
32:          /* Execute the SQL code  */
33:     DBMS_OUTPUT.PUT_LINE('The number of records just processed is: '
34:          || v_NUMRows);
35:
36: /*  Define and Insert the Third Record */
37:
38:     DBMS_SQL.BIND_VARIABLE(v_CursorID, ':mynum',3);
39:     DBMS_SQL.BIND_VARIABLE(v_CursorID, ':mytext','Three');
40:     v_NumRows := DBMS_SQL.EXECUTE(v_CursorID);
41:          /* Execute the SQL code  */
```

```
42:        DBMS_OUTPUT.PUT_LINE('The number of records just processed is: '
43:             || v_NUMRows);
44:
45: /*  Define and Insert the Fourth Record */
46:
47:        DBMS_SQL.BIND_VARIABLE(v_CursorID, ':mynum',4);
48:        DBMS_SQL.BIND_VARIABLE(v_CursorID, ':mytext','Four');
49:        v_NumRows := DBMS_SQL.EXECUTE(v_CursorID);
50:            /* Execute the SQL code  */
51:        DBMS_OUTPUT.PUT_LINE('The number of records just processed is: '
52:             || v_NUMRows);
53:
54: /* Duplicate the Fourth Entry! */
55:
56:        v_NumRows := DBMS_SQL.EXECUTE(v_CursorID);
57:            /* Execute the SQL code  */
58:        DBMS_OUTPUT.PUT_LINE('The number of records just processed is: '
59:             || v_NUMRows);
60:
61: EXCEPTION
62:     WHEN OTHERS THEN
63:                 RAISE; -- raise if some other unknown error
64:
65:        DBMS_SQL.CLOSE_CURSOR(v_CursorID); -- Close the cursor
66:        COMMIT;
67: END; -- End PL/SQL block
```

After you have executed the block, you should see

OUTPUT
```
The number of records just processed is: 1
The number of records just processed is: 1
The number of records just processed is: 1
The number of records just processed is: 1
The number of records just processed is: 1
```

ANALYSIS You have just inserted five complete records, duplicating the fourth record!

Now review the steps for DML statements. In line 12, you first open the cursor with OPEN_CURSOR. You then assign the value of v_InsertRecords to the SQL required to insert the records in line 13. You will notice the placeholder variables as identified by the colon in front of the placeholder names in line 14. Your next step is to parse the statement for syntax error checking, as shown in line 18. After parsing the statement, you need to bind the placeholder variables as in lines 20 through 21. You are ready to execute the statement in line 22 and finally close the cursor in line 65 after all records are inserted. This identical process is repeated four more times to add four more records. Again, if you were to create a stored function or procedure, you should be able to pass as the parameter simply the record to insert, which could be variable names, for true dynamic SQL! Creating this type of function demonstrates the practicality of dynamic SQL with the DBMS_SQL package.

Using the DBMS_SQL Package with Queries

This section demonstrates how to execute queries with the DBMS_SQL package. The processing method is very similar to DDL and DML processing. The following steps are required:

1. Open the cursor.
2. Parse the statement.
3. Bind input variables (if required).
4. Define the output variables.
5. Execute the statement.
6. Fetch the rows.
7. Store the results from fetching the rows into PL/SQL variables.
8. Close the cursor.

Opening a Cursor for Executing Queries

This is identical to DDL and DML processing. Whenever you execute SQL or PL/SQL, a cursor is opened transparently. When creating dynamic SQL, you must specify every step, including opening the cursor by using OPEN_CURSOR. The syntax for the OPEN_CURSOR function is as follows:

```
FUNCTION OPEN_CURSOR RETURN INTEGER;
```

The OPEN_CURSOR function returns an integer, which is the cursor ID. The cursor ID will be retained for use until the cursor is closed. As you can see, leaving a cursor open without closing the cursor using CLOSE_CURSOR wastes valuable resources. You can now perform as many statements as desired by referencing the cursor ID returned.

Parsing Statements for Queries

Parsing is again almost identical to DDL and DML statements. Both have the same syntax and requirement that no semicolon should appear at the end of the SQL code. However, additional requirements when executing queries are

☐ The SELECT statement can't be embedded in PL/SQL. There should be only one SELECT statement.

☐ The query should not contain an INTO statement. You can work around this through the use of DEFINE_COLUMNS and COLUMN_VALUES.

The Syntax for the PARSE Procedure

```
PROCEDURE PARSE(cursor_id IN INTEGER,
                       statement_to_parse IN VARCHAR2,
                       version IN VARCHAR2);
```

cursor_id is the cursor assigned by the OPEN_CURSOR statement. *statement_to_parse* is the SQL statement you want to parse. The last parameter, *version*, is the version type.

SYNTAX

17

The following versions are allowed:

- ☐ NATIVE—Native handling for the server
- ☐ V6—Handling for Oracle version 6.*x*
- ☐ V7—Handling for Oracle version 7.*x*
- ☐ V8—Handling for Oracle version 8.*x*

The version can be expressed as DBMS_SQL.NATIVE, DBMS_SQL.V8, and so on.

NOTE

Oracle6 databases can only be accessed by the DBMS_SQL package through a database link.

17

Binding Variables for Queries

There is no difference between binding variables for queries and binding variables for DDL and DML statements. *Binding* enables you to bind a specific variable to a placeholder, which is identified by a colon. Because you can bind all types of PL/SQL variables, the overloaded BIND_VARIABLE procedure can handle many datatypes.

The Syntax for Binding Variables

SYNTAX

The syntax for the NUMBER datatype is

```
PROCEDURE BIND_VARIABLE(cursor_id IN INTEGER,
                        placeholder_name IN VARCHAR2,
                        value IN NUMBER);
```

The two syntaxes for type VARCHAR2 are

```
PROCEDURE BIND_VARIABLE(cursor_id IN INTEGER,
                        placeholder_name IN VARCHAR2,
                        value IN VARCHAR2);
```

and

```
PROCEDURE BIND_VARIABLE(cursor_id IN INTEGER,
                        placeholder_name IN VARCHAR2,
                        value IN VARCHAR2,
                        out_value_size IN INTEGER);
```

The two syntaxes for type CHAR2 are

```
PROCEDURE BIND_VARIABLE(cursor_id IN INTEGER,
                        placeholder_name IN VARCHAR2,
                        value IN CHAR2);
```

and

```
PROCEDURE BIND_VARIABLE(cursor_id IN INTEGER,
                        placeholder_name IN VARCHAR2,
                        value IN CHAR2,
                        out_value_size IN INTEGER);
```

The syntax for the DATE datatype is

```
PROCEDURE BIND_VARIABLE(cursor_id IN INTEGER,
                       placeholder_name IN VARCHAR2,
                       value IN DATE);
```

The two syntaxes for type RAW are

```
PROCEDURE BIND_VARIABLE(cursor_id IN INTEGER,
                       placeholder_name IN VARCHAR2,
                       value IN RAW);
```

and

```
PROCEDURE BIND_VARIABLE(cursor_id IN INTEGER,
                       placeholder_name IN VARCHAR2,
                       value IN RAW,
                       out_value_size IN INTEGER);
```

The syntax for ROWID is

```
PROCEDURE BIND_VARIABLE(cursor_id IN INTEGER,
                       placeholder_name IN VARCHAR2,
                       value IN ROWID);
```

Finally, there is support for MLSLABEL in Trusted Oracle with

```
PROCEDURE BIND_VARIABLE(cursor_id IN INTEGER,
                       placeholder_name IN VARCHAR2,
                       value IN MLSLABEL);
```

As you can see, there is support for almost any conceivable datatype.

cursor_id is the ID returned from OPEN_CURSOR. placeholder_name is the name of the variable preceded by a colon. value is the value to be bound (assigned) to the placeholder variable name. For any of the procedures with out_value_size, this is the output size expressed in bytes for those datatypes.

Defining the Output Variables for Queries

The difference in processing of DML and DDL statements compared to queries occurs at this point. The DML and DDL statements would simply execute, and then the cursor would be closed. However, you are now writing a query with output. You have to define everything to the DBMS_SQL package including output, which uses the DEFINE_COLUMN procedure. You first have to declare variables identical in column datatypes and lengths. You can then call DEFINE_COLUMN to specify the column order and the variable used for output. Because you can define several datatypes, the procedure DEFINE_COLUMN is overloaded.

The Syntax for Defining Output Variables

The syntax for NUMBER is

```
PROCEDURE DEFINE_COLUMN (cursor_id IN INTEGER,
                         column_order IN INTEGER,
                         column_name IN NUMBER);
```

The syntax for VARCHAR2 is

```
PROCEDURE DEFINE_COLUMN (cursor_id IN INTEGER,
                                column_order IN INTEGER,
                                column_name IN VARCHAR2,
                                column_size IN INTEGER);
```

The syntax for CHAR is

```
PROCEDURE DEFINE_COLUMN (cursor_id IN INTEGER,
                                column_order IN INTEGER,
                                column_name IN CHAR,
                                column_size IN INTEGER);
```

The syntax for DATE is

```
PROCEDURE DEFINE_COLUMN (cursor_id IN INTEGER,
                                column_order IN INTEGER,
                                column_name IN DATE);
```

The syntax for RAW is

```
PROCEDURE DEFINE_COLUMN (cursor_id IN INTEGER,
                                column_order IN INTEGER,
                                column_name IN RAW,
                                column_size IN INTEGER);
```

The syntax for ROWID is

```
PROCEDURE DEFINE_COLUMN (cursor_id IN INTEGER,
                                column_order IN INTEGER,
                                column_name IN ROWID);
```

The syntax for MLSLABEL in Trusted Oracle is

```
PROCEDURE DEFINE_COLUMN (cursor_id IN INTEGER,
                                column_order IN INTEGER,
                                column_name IN MLSLABEL);
```

cursor_id is the cursor assigned by the OPEN_CURSOR statement. column_order is the order of the columns, starting from position 1. column_name is the variable defined in the declaration that is associated with the column in the table. The optional column_size allows you to specify the size of the column; otherwise, the default is the length of the variable name.

Executing Statements for Queries

The execute procedure is identical to DDL and DML statements. After you have defined the columns, you are ready to execute the query with the function EXECUTE.

The Syntax for the EXECUTE Function

```
FUNCTION EXECUTE (cursor_id IN INTEGER) RETURN INTEGER;
```

The cursor_id is the cursor assigned by the OPEN_CURSOR statement. The function also returns an integer that is valid only for DML statements, which returns the number of rows processed. The applicable DML statements are INSERT, UPDATE, and DELETE. This value should be ignored for all other purposes.

Fetching the Rows into the Buffer with Queries

After the query is executed, you need to store the results into the buffer by using FETCH_ROWS. This function returns the number of rows stored into the buffer. You can then error-check or process based upon %FOUND or %NOTFOUND.

The Syntax for the FETCH_ROWS Function

```
FUNCTION FETCH_ROWS (cursor_id IN INTEGER) RETURN INTEGER;
```

Using EXECUTE_AND_FETCH to Retrieve the First Set of Rows

Instead of first running EXECUTE and then executing FETCH_ROWS, you can do the initial execution and fetching in one step with the use of the function EXECUTE_AND_FETCH.

The Syntax for the EXECUTE_AND_FETCH Function

```
FUNCTION EXECUTE_AND_FETCH (cursor_id IN INTEGER,
                               total_rows IN BOOLEAN DEFAULT FALSE)
     RETURN INTEGER;
```

The only difference is the added parameter *total_rows*. The value returns true if more than one row has been fetched. You can still process all these rows with no problem.

Using COLUMN_VALUE to Read the Results into PL/SQL Variables

You now need to read the data from the buffer into variables, which you can then process with the use of the procedure COLUMN_VALUE. Because the procedure is overloaded, it can handle the various datatypes.

The Syntax for the COLUMN_VALUE Procedure

The syntaxes of the two possible calls for type NUMBER are

```
PROCEDURE COLUMN_VALUE (cursor_id IN INTEGER,
                            column_order IN INTEGER,
                            column_variable OUT NUMBER);
```

and

```
PROCEDURE COLUMN_VALUE (cursor_id IN INTEGER,
                            column_order IN INTEGER,
                            column_variable OUT NUMBER,
                            column_error OUT NUMBER,
                            actual_length OUT INTEGER);
```

The formats for VARCHAR2 are

```
PROCEDURE COLUMN_VALUE (cursor_id IN INTEGER,
                            column_order IN INTEGER,
                            column_variable OUT VARCHAR2);
```

and

```
PROCEDURE COLUMN_VALUE (cursor_id IN INTEGER,
                        column_order IN INTEGER,
                        column_variable OUT VARCHAR2,
                        column_error OUT NUMBER,
                        actual_length OUT INTEGER);
```

The formats for CHAR are

```
PROCEDURE COLUMN_VALUE (cursor_id IN INTEGER,
                        column_order IN INTEGER,
                        column_variable OUT CHAR);
```

and

```
PROCEDURE COLUMN_VALUE (cursor_id IN INTEGER,
                        column_order IN INTEGER,
                        column_variable OUT CHAR,
                        column_error OUT NUMBER,
                        actual_length OUT INTEGER);
```

The formats for DATE are

```
PROCEDURE COLUMN_VALUE (cursor_id IN INTEGER,
                        column_order IN INTEGER,
                        column_variable OUT DATE);
```

and

```
PROCEDURE COLUMN_VALUE (cursor_id IN INTEGER,
                        column_order IN INTEGER,
                        column_variable OUT DATE,
                        column_error OUT NUMBER,
                        actual_length OUT INTEGER);
```

The formats for RAW are

```
PROCEDURE COLUMN_VALUE (cursor_id IN INTEGER,
                        column_order IN INTEGER,
                        column_variable OUT RAW);
```

and

```
PROCEDURE COLUMN_VALUE (cursor_id IN INTEGER,
                        column_order IN INTEGER,
                        column_variable OUT RAW,
                        column_error OUT NUMBER,
                        actual_length OUT INTEGER);
```

The formats for ROWID are

```
PROCEDURE COLUMN_VALUE (cursor_id IN INTEGER,
                        column_order IN INTEGER,
                        column_variable OUT ROWID);
```

and

```
PROCEDURE COLUMN_VALUE (cursor_id IN INTEGER,
                        column_order IN INTEGER,
                        column_variable OUT ROWID,
                        column_error OUT NUMBER,
                        actual_length OUT INTEGER) ;
```

17

The formats for MLSLABEL in Trusted Oracle are

```
PROCEDURE COLUMN_VALUE (cursor_id IN INTEGER,
                               column_order IN INTEGER,
                               column_variable OUT MLSLABEL) ;
```

and

```
PROCEDURE COLUMN_VALUE (cursor_id IN INTEGER,
                               column_order IN INTEGER,
                               column_variable OUT MLSLABEL,
                               column_error OUT NUMBER,
                               actual_length OUT INTEGER) ;
```

Again, *cursor_id* is the ID assigned by OPEN_CURSOR. *column_order* is the order of the columns. *column_variable* is the variable you declared to represent the column. Optionally, *column_error* enables you to determine which column caused an error. The value is set to zero if the column has no error, such as truncating a value, and so on. *actual_length* is the length of the variable in the buffer before it is placed into the associated PL/SQL variable. This parameter is useful only if trying to determine which columns are truncating values and how to handle the errors.

Closing the Cursor for Queries

You can now finally close the cursor with CLOSE_CURSOR, which is the same format as DML and DDL statements. After all processing has been completed, you should close the cursor with the CLOSE_CURSOR procedure to free up those resources.

The Syntax for the CLOSE_CURSOR Procedure

```
PROCEDURE CLOSE_CURSOR (cursor_id IN OUT INTEGER);
```

cursor_id is the cursor assigned by the OPEN_CURSOR statement. After the call has been complete, the value of the *cursor_id* is set to NULL.

Using Queries with the DBMS_SQL Package

This section demonstrates using queries inside PL/SQL through the DBMS_SQL package. You will simply display the values you inserted into the table to the screen. Execute the code in Listing 17.3 to verify that you added the records. Make sure that you have entered SET SERVEROUTPUT ON at the SQL*Plus prompt.

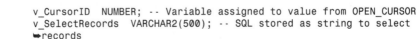

INPUT   **Listing 17.3. Using SELECT to verify inserted records.**

```
1: DECLARE
2: /* The purpose of this PL/SQL block is to demonstrate
3:     executing queries within PL/SQL through the use of the
4:     DBMS_SQL package.  We will simply display the output to
5:     screen with the DBMS_OUTPUT package */
6:
7:     v_CursorID  NUMBER; -- Variable assigned to value from OPEN_CURSOR
8:     v_SelectRecords  VARCHAR2(500); -- SQL stored as string to select
     ➥records
```

```
 9:        v_NUMRows  INTEGER; -- Number of rows processed - of no use
10:        v_MyNum INTEGER;
11:        v_MyText VARCHAR2(50);
12:
13: BEGIN
14:        v_CursorID := DBMS_SQL.OPEN_CURSOR; -- Get the Cursor ID
15:        v_SelectRecords := 'SELECT * from MyTable'; -- SQL to view records
16:
17:
18:        DBMS_SQL.PARSE(v_CursorID,v_SelectRecords,DBMS_SQL.V7);
19:            /* Perform syntax error checking */
20:
21:        DBMS_SQL.DEFINE_COLUMN(v_CursorID,1,v_MyNum);
22:        DBMS_SQL.DEFINE_COLUMN(v_CursorID,2,v_MyText,50);
23:
24:        v_NumRows := DBMS_SQL.EXECUTE(v_CursorID);
25:            /* Execute the SQL code  */
26: LOOP
27:        IF DBMS_SQL.FETCH_ROWS(v_CursorID) = 0 THEN
28:            EXIT;
29:        END IF;
30:
31:        DBMS_SQL.COLUMN_VALUE(v_CursorId,1,v_MyNum);
32:        DBMS_SQL.COLUMN_VALUE(v_CursorId,2,v_MyText);
33:
34:        DBMS_OUTPUT.PUT_LINE(v_MyNum ¦¦ ' ' ¦¦ v_MyText);
35:
36: END LOOP;
37:
38: EXCEPTION
39:        WHEN OTHERS THEN
40:                RAISE; -- raise if some other unknown error
41:
42:        DBMS_SQL.CLOSE_CURSOR(v_CursorID); -- Close the cursor
43:
44: END; -- End PL/SQL block
```

After you have executed the block, you should see

OUTPUT
```
1 One
2 Two
3 Three
4 Four
4 Four
```

ANALYSIS It takes some work, but you should have been able to print a SELECT query to the screen. First, you open the cursor with OPEN_CURSOR in line 14. Then, v_SelectRecords is assigned the string for the SQL query to select all records from MyTable in line 15. The SQL statement is then parsed in line 18. No variables need binding in this example, but if you were inserting values into a table, you could have used binding. In lines 21 and 22, you then define the two output variables of v_MyNum and v_MyText, which are the two columns created from Listing 17.1. The query is then executed with DBMS_SQL.EXECUTE in line 24. In line 26, you then enter a loop that will fetch the rows and then display to the screen with

COLUMN_VALUE. The EXIT condition in line 28 occurs when no more rows are found, which is a value of 0. Finally, the cursor is properly closed in line 42.

Using the DBMS_SQL Package with Anonymous PL/SQL Blocks

This section demonstrates how to execute anonymous PL/SQL blocks with the DBMS_SQL package. The processing method is very similar to processing queries and executing DDL or DML statements. The following steps are required:

1. Open the cursor.
2. Parse the statement.
3. Bind input variables (if required).
4. Execute the statement.
5. Retrieve the results into variables.
6. Close the cursor.

Opening a Cursor for Anonymous Blocks

This is identical to DDL and DML processing. Whenever you execute SQL or PL/SQL, a cursor is opened transparently. When creating dynamic SQL, you must specify every step, including opening the cursor by using OPEN_CURSOR. The syntax for the OPEN_CURSOR function is as follows:

```
FUNCTION OPEN_CURSOR RETURN INTEGER;
```

The OPEN_CURSOR function returns an integer, which is the cursor ID. The cursor ID will be retained for use until the cursor is closed. As you can see, leaving a cursor open without closing the cursor using CLOSE_CURSOR wastes valuable resources. You can now perform as many statements as desired by referencing the cursor ID returned.

Parsing Anonymous Blocks

This is identical to DDL and DML processing with one exception. Here, you need to use proper punctuation including the semicolon. You would never use the semicolon in queries or DDL or DML statements.

Binding Variables for Anonymous Blocks

This is identical to DDL and DML processing. Binding enables you to bind a specific variable to a placeholder, which is identified by a colon. Because you can bind all types of PL/SQL variables, the overloaded BIND_VARIABLE procedure can handle many datatypes.

The Syntax for Binding Variables

SYNTAX

The syntax for the NUMBER datatype is

```
PROCEDURE BIND_VARIABLE(cursor_id IN INTEGER,
                        placeholder_name IN VARCHAR2,
                        value IN NUMBER);
```

The two syntaxes for type VARCHAR2 are

```
PROCEDURE BIND_VARIABLE(cursor_id IN INTEGER,
                        placeholder_name IN VARCHAR2,
                        value IN VARCHAR2);
```

and

```
PROCEDURE BIND_VARIABLE(cursor_id IN INTEGER,
                        placeholder_name IN VARCHAR2,
                        value IN VARCHAR2,
                        out_value_size IN INTEGER);
```

The two syntaxes for type CHAR2 are

```
PROCEDURE BIND_VARIABLE(cursor_id IN INTEGER,
                        placeholder_name IN VARCHAR2,
                        value IN CHAR2);
```

and

```
PROCEDURE BIND_VARIABLE(cursor_id IN INTEGER,
                        placeholder_name IN VARCHAR2,
                        value IN CHAR2,
                        out_value_size IN INTEGER);
```

The syntax for the DATE datatype is

```
PROCEDURE BIND_VARIABLE(cursor_id IN INTEGER,
                        placeholder_name IN VARCHAR2,
                        value IN DATE);
```

The two syntaxes for type RAW are

```
PROCEDURE BIND_VARIABLE(cursor_id IN INTEGER,
                        placeholder_name IN VARCHAR2,
                        value IN RAW);
```

and

```
PROCEDURE BIND_VARIABLE(cursor_id IN INTEGER,
                        placeholder_name IN VARCHAR2,
                        value IN RAW,
                        out_value_size IN INTEGER);
```

The syntax for ROWID is

```
PROCEDURE BIND_VARIABLE(cursor_id IN INTEGER,
                        placeholder_name IN VARCHAR2,
                        value IN ROWID);
```

17

Finally, there is support for MLSLABEL in Trusted Oracle with

```
PROCEDURE BIND_VARIABLE(cursor_id IN INTEGER,
                        placeholder_name IN VARCHAR2,
                        value IN MLSLABEL);
```

cursor_id is the ID returned from OPEN_CURSOR. *placeholder_name* is the name of the variable preceded by a colon. *value* is the value to be bound (assigned) to the placeholder variable name. For any of the procedures with *out_value_size*, this is the output size expressed in bytes for those datatypes.

Executing Anonymous Blocks

This is identical to DDL and DML processing. After you have bound variables, if required, you are ready to execute the anonymous block with the function EXECUTE.

The Syntax for the EXECUTE Function

```
FUNCTION EXECUTE (cursor_id IN INTEGER) RETURN INTEGER;
```

cursor_id is the cursor assigned by the OPEN_CURSOR statement. The function also returns an integer that is valid only for DML statements, which returns the number of rows processed. The applicable DML statements are INSERT, UPDATE, and DELETE. This value should be ignored for all other purposes.

Retrieving Values with Anonymous Blocks

The only other variation from queries or DML and DDL statements is the need to retrieve the values of the variables from the buffer. To retrieve the variables, you will use the VARIABLE_VALUE procedure. When the EXECUTE function executes, it stores the values into the buffer. The VARIABLE_VALUE procedure will retrieve these values into PL/SQL variables. This overloaded procedure has various syntaxes for various datatypes.

The Syntax for the VARIABLE_VALUE Procedure

The syntax for NUMBER is

```
PROCEDURE VARIABLE_VALUE(cursor_id IN INTEGER
                         placeholder_name IN VARCHAR2,
                         output_variable OUT NUMBER);
```

The syntax for VARCHAR2 is

```
PROCEDURE VARIABLE_VALUE(cursor_id IN INTEGER
                         placeholder_name IN VARCHAR2,
                         output_variable OUT VARCHAR2);
```

The syntax for CHAR is

```
PROCEDURE VARIABLE_VALUE(cursor_id IN INTEGER
                         placeholder_name IN VARCHAR2,
                         output_variable OUT CHAR);
```

The syntax for DATE is

```
PROCEDURE VARIABLE_VALUE(cursor_id IN INTEGER
                        placeholder_name IN VARCHAR2,
                        output_variable OUT DATE);
```

The syntax for RAW is

```
PROCEDURE VARIABLE_VALUE(cursor_id IN INTEGER
                        placeholder_name IN VARCHAR2,
                        output_variable OUT RAW);
```

The syntax for ROWID is

```
PROCEDURE VARIABLE_VALUE(cursor_id IN INTEGER
                        placeholder_name IN VARCHAR2,
                        output_variable OUT ROWID);
```

The syntax for MLSLABEL in Trusted Oracle is

```
PROCEDURE VARIABLE_VALUE(cursor_id IN INTEGER
                        placeholder_name IN VARCHAR2,
                        output_variable OUT MLSLABEL);
```

cursor_id is the cursor ID returned from OPEN_CURSOR. *placeholder_name* is the name of the placeholder. Don't forget to identify these by the preceding colon encapsulated with single quotes. *output_variable* is the PL/SQL variable to hold the output retrieved from the buffer.

Closing the Cursor for Anonymous Blocks

This is identical to DDL and DML processing. After all processing has been completed, you should close the cursor with the CLOSE_CURSOR procedure to free up those resources.

The Syntax for the CLOSE_CURSOR Procedure

```
PROCEDURE CLOSE_CURSOR (cursor_id IN OUT INTEGER);
```

cursor_id is the cursor assigned by the OPEN_CURSOR statement. After the call has been complete, the value of *cursor_id* is set to NULL.

Using Anonymous PL/SQL Blocks with the DBMS_SQL Package

This section demonstrates using anonymous PL/SQL blocks through the DBMS_SQL package. You will simply display the values you inserted into the table to the screen with values equal to 2. Execute the code in Listing 17.4 to display these values to the screen. Make sure that you have entered SET SERVEROUTPUT ON at the SQL*Plus prompt.

INPUT   **Listing 17.4. Using anonymous blocks.**

```
 1: DECLARE
 2: /* This procedure calls an anonymous block which performs a
 3:    query to look up the description for the row id value = 2.
 4:    This demonstrates the use of an anonymous PL/SQL block
 5:    within PL/SQL   */
 6:
 7:     v_CursorID  NUMBER; -- Variable assigned to value from OPEN_CURSOR
 8:     v_MatchRecord  VARCHAR2(500); -- SQL stored as string to select one
        ➥record
 9:     v_NUMRows  INTEGER; -- Number of rows processed - of no use
10:     v_MyNum INTEGER;
11:     v_MyText VARCHAR2(50);
12:
13: BEGIN
14:     v_CursorID := DBMS_SQL.OPEN_CURSOR; -- Get the Cursor ID
15:     v_MatchRecord := 'BEGIN -- Start of Anonymous PL/SQL Block
16:                         SELECT MyRow,MyDesc
17:                           INTO :MyRow, :MyText FROM MyTable
18:                          WHERE MyRow = 2; -- Notice has ending semicolon
19:                       END;'; -- End of Anonymous PL/SQL Block
20:
21:     DBMS_SQL.PARSE(v_CursorID,v_MatchRecord,DBMS_SQL.V7);
22:         /* Perform syntax error checking */
23:
24:     DBMS_SQL.BIND_VARIABLE(v_CursorID, ':MyRow',v_MyNum);
25:     DBMS_SQL.BIND_VARIABLE(v_CursorID, ':MyText',v_MyText,50);
26:
27:     v_NumRows := DBMS_SQL.EXECUTE(v_CursorID);
28:         /* Execute the SQL code  */
29:
30:
31:     DBMS_SQL.VARIABLE_VALUE(v_CursorId,':MyRow',v_MyNum);
32:     DBMS_SQL.VARIABLE_VALUE(v_CursorId,':MyText',v_MyText);
33:     /* Defines variables to hold output */
34:
35:     DBMS_OUTPUT.PUT_LINE(v_MyNum || ' ' || v_MyText);
36:
37:
38: EXCEPTION
39:     WHEN OTHERS THEN
40:             RAISE; -- raise if some other unknown error
41:
42:     DBMS_SQL.CLOSE_CURSOR(v_CursorID); -- Close the cursor
43:
44: END; -- End PL/SQL block
```

After you have executed the block, you should see

OUTPUT   2 Two

ANALYSIS The order is to first use OPEN_CURSOR in line 14 to retrieve an assigned cursor ID. You then assign the anonymous PL/SQL block to a variable called v_MatchRecord in line 15. This string codes the PL/SQL block with proper syntax. Before, in the examples of queries and DDL and DML statements, you had to remove the semicolon. You can see that now the block of SQL statements in lines 16 to 18 ends in a semicolon. You then call DBMS_SQL.PARSE in line 21 to check for syntax errors. After binding the appropriate variables in lines 24 and 25, you execute the anonymous PL/SQL block in line 27. You then retrieve from the buffer the values and store them into the variables using DBMS_SQL.VARIABLE_VALUE in lines 31 and 32. The output is displayed in line 35 with DBMS_OUTPUT.PUT_LINE. Finally, after the entire process has completed, in line 42 you close the cursor with CLOSE_CURSOR.

Now you can experiment to show how the buffer truly operates. You will change the code from Listing 17.4 to select values from MyRow = 4. See Listing 17.5 for the change and then execute.

17

INPUT **Listing 17.5. Errors with anonymous blocks.**

```
 1: DECLARE
 2: /* This procedure calls an anonymous block which performs a
 3:    query to look up the description for the row id value = 4.
 4:    This demonstrates the use of an anonymous PL/SQL block
 5:    within PL/SQL  */
 6:
 7:     v_CursorID  NUMBER; -- Variable assigned to value from OPEN_CURSOR
 8:     v_MatchRecord  VARCHAR2(500); -- SQL stored as string to select one
          ➥record
 9:     v_NUMRows  INTEGER; -- Number of rows processed - of no use
10:     v_MyNum INTEGER;
11:     v_MyText VARCHAR2(50);
12:
13: BEGIN
14:     v_CursorID := DBMS_SQL.OPEN_CURSOR; -- Get the Cursor ID
15:     v_MatchRecord := 'BEGIN -- Start of Anonymous PL/SQL Block
16:                         SELECT MyRow,MyDesc
17:                             INTO :MyRow, :MyText FROM MyTable
18:                             WHERE MyRow = 4; -- Notice has ending semicolon
19:                       END;'; -- End of Anonymous PL/SQL Block
20:
21:     DBMS_SQL.PARSE(v_CursorID,v_MatchRecord,DBMS_SQL.V7);
22:         /* Perform syntax error checking */
23:
24:     DBMS_SQL.BIND_VARIABLE(v_CursorID, ':MyRow',v_MyNum);
25:     DBMS_SQL.BIND_VARIABLE(v_CursorID, ':MyText',v_MyText,50);
26:
27:     v_NumRows := DBMS_SQL.EXECUTE(v_CursorID);
28:         /* Execute the SQL code  */
29:
30:
```

continues

Listing 17.5. continued

```
31:          DBMS_SQL.VARIABLE_VALUE(v_CursorId,':MyRow',v_MyNum);
32:          DBMS_SQL.VARIABLE_VALUE(v_CursorId,':MyText',v_MyText);
33:          /* Defines variables to hold output */
34:
35:          DBMS_OUTPUT.PUT_LINE(v_MyNum ¦¦ ' ' ¦¦ v_MyText);
36:
37:
38: EXCEPTION
39:      WHEN OTHERS THEN
40:                RAISE; -- raise if some other unknown error
41:
42:          DBMS_SQL.CLOSE_CURSOR(v_CursorID); -- Close the cursor
43:
44: END; -- End PL/SQL block
```

When you execute the code, your output will appear as

OUTPUT
```
ORA-01422: exact fetch returns more than requested number of rows
ORA-06512: at line 30
```

ANALYSIS Why did you receive the error? When using anonymous blocks, the buffer will only hold one row of data. If you recall, you have two records with a value of 4, which are selected by the SQL statements in lines 16 to 18. Because you can't use FETCH_ROWS, but can only return one row, the error occurs. This is the primary difference between queries and anonymous blocks.

Error Handling

In addition to exceptions, there are many other ways to handle errors with the DBMS_SQL package. You can check to see if the cursor is open with IS_OPEN. You can also check to see information provided by the DBMS_SQL package concerning the last set of rows retrieved with the FETCH_ROWS function with the functions LAST_ROW_COUNT and LAST_ROW_ID. Other functions that provide information on errors are LAST_ERROR_POSITION and LAST_SQL_FUNCTION_CODE.

IS_OPEN

The IS_OPEN function enables you to see if a cursor is open. Some possible uses for this are to check for an open cursor, and if still open, close the cursor. You can also use this to reopen a closed cursor.

The Syntax for the IS_OPEN Function

```
FUNCTION IS_OPEN(cursor_id IN INTEGER) RETURN BOOLEAN;
```

The cursor_id parameter is the cursor ID assigned from calling the OPEN_CURSOR function. If the cursor is open, it returns true; otherwise, if the cursor is closed, it passes the value false.

LAST_ROW_COUNT

The LAST_ROW_COUNT function passes the total number of rows fetched from the cursor to date. This should be called immediately after FETCH_ROWS to receive accurate results. The syntax for the LAST_ROW_COUNT function is as follows:

```
FUNCTION LAST_ROW_COUNT RETURN INTEGER;
```

If the call is made before FETCH_ROWS, you will receive a value of zero.

LAST_ROW_ID

The LAST_ROW_ID function returns the ROWID of the last row processed. Again, this should be called immediately after FETCH_ROWS for it to be of any usefulness. The syntax for the LAST_ROW_ID function is as follows:

```
FUNCTION LAST_ROW_ID RETURN ROWID;
```

Testing LAST_ROW_ID and LAST_ROW_COUNT

Enter and execute the code in Listing 17.6 to test these two functions. Make sure that you have entered SET SERVEROUTPUT ON at the SQL*Plus prompt.

INPUT **Listing 17.6. Checking the progress of fetched rows.**

```
 1: DECLARE
 2: /* The purpose of this PL/SQL block is to demonstrate
 3:    executing queries within PL/SQL through the use of the
 4:    DBMS_SQL package.  We will simply display the output to
 5:    screen with the DBMS_OUTPUT package.  We also demonstrate
 6:    the use of tracking the progress of fetching rows*/
 7:
 8:     v_CursorID  NUMBER; -- Variable assigned to value from OPEN_CURSOR
 9:     v_SelectRecords  VARCHAR2(500); -- SQL stored as string to select
        ➥records
10:     v_NUMRows  INTEGER; -- Number of rows processed - of no use
11:     v_MyNum INTEGER;
12:     v_MyText VARCHAR2(50);
13:     v_MyROWID ROWID;
14:     v_TotRow INTEGER;
15:
16: BEGIN
17:     v_CursorID := DBMS_SQL.OPEN_CURSOR; -- Get the Cursor ID
18:     v_SelectRecords := 'SELECT * from MyTable'; -- SQL to view records
19:
20:
21:     DBMS_SQL.PARSE(v_CursorID,v_SelectRecords,DBMS_SQL.V7);
22:         /* Perform syntax error checking */
23:
24:
25:     DBMS_SQL.DEFINE_COLUMN(v_CursorID,1,v_MyNum);
26:     DBMS_SQL.DEFINE_COLUMN(v_CursorID,2,v_MyText,50);
27:
```

continues

17

Listing 17.6. continued

```
28:        v_NumRows := DBMS_SQL.EXECUTE(v_CursorID);
29:            /* Execute the SQL code  */
30: LOOP
31:        IF DBMS_SQL.FETCH_ROWS(v_CursorID) = 0 THEN
32:            EXIT;
33:        END IF;
34:
35: /*   The next four rows are used for seeing the progress for
36:      fetching rows  */
37:
38:        v_TOTROW := DBMS_SQL.LAST_ROW_COUNT;
39:        v_MyROWID := DBMS_SQL.LAST_ROW_ID;
40:        DBMS_OUTPUT.PUT_LINE('The last row count is: ' ||
41:            v_TOTROW || ' The last ROWID is: ' || v_MyROWID);
42:
43:        DBMS_SQL.COLUMN_VALUE(v_CursorId,1,v_MyNum);
44:        DBMS_SQL.COLUMN_VALUE(v_CursorId,2,v_MyText);
45:
46:        DBMS_OUTPUT.PUT_LINE(v_MyNum || ' ' || v_MyText);
47:
48: END LOOP;
49:
50: EXCEPTION
51:     WHEN OTHERS THEN
52:             RAISE; -- raise if some other unknown error
53:
54:        DBMS_SQL.CLOSE_CURSOR(v_CursorID); -- Close the cursor
55:
56: END; -- End PL/SQL block
```

Your output should be

OUTPUT
```
The last row count is: 1 The last ROWID is: 000000DF.0004.0002
1 One
The last row count is: 2 The last ROWID is: 000000DF.0004.0002
2 Two
The last row count is: 3 The last ROWID is: 000000DF.0004.0002
3 Three
The last row count is: 4 The last ROWID is: 000000DF.0004.0002
4 Four
The last row count is: 5 The last ROWID is: 000000DF.0004.0002
4 Four
```

ANALYSIS   The LAST_ROW_ID is the same for all the entries because the buffer was able to hold all the fetched rows from lines 30 to 48. The inception-to-date count for tracking total rows fetched also worked as stated.

LAST_ERROR_POSITION

The LAST_ERROR_POSITION function returns the location in the SQL statement where the error occurred. This is only used if PARSE was unsuccessful. The syntax for the LAST_ERROR_POSITION function is as follows:

17

```
FUNCTION LAST_ERROR_POSITION RETURN INTEGER;
```

LAST_SQL_FUNCTION_CODE

The LAST_SQL_FUNCTION_CODE function returns the SQL function code associated with the SQL statement. You can find a list of these function codes in the *Oracle7 Server Application Developer's Guide*.

The syntax for the LAST_SQL_FUNCTION_CODE function is as follows:

```
FUNCTION LAST_SQL_FUNCTION_CODE RETURN INTEGER;
```

Fetching Long Data

In a table, a long column can hold up to 2 gigabytes of data. The maximum storage in a PL/SQL LONG type variable is 32,768 bytes. The difficulty lies in how to retrieve 2 gigabytes' worth of data into a single 32,768-byte field. Because you can't possibly fit the whole 2 gigabytes' worth into a 32KB field, the only solution is to break up the field into smaller 32KB size components and then retrieve them in the same order. You can do this by using the procedures DEFINE_COLUMN_LONG and COLUMN_VALUE_LONG. By the way, it would take up to 63 loops to retrieve up to 2 gigabytes in 32KB increments.

DEFINE_COLUMN_LONG

This procedure is almost identical in use to DEFINE_COLUMN described earlier in the chapter. The purpose of DEFINE_COLUMN was to associate a variable name with a column of a table.

The Syntax for the DEFINE_COLUMN_LONG Procedure

```
PROCEDURE DEFINE_COLUMN_LONG(cursor_id IN INTEGER,
                                position IN INTEGER);
```

cursor_id is the cursor ID supplied by OPEN_CURSOR. *position* is the relative position in the row that you are trying to define. If this column were the first field in the row, it would be position 1. If there were two columns, the first one 4 bytes long, this would be position 5.

COLUMN_VALUE_LONG

After the data is in the buffer, you need to retrieve it into a local variable. For LONG variables, you would use COLUMN_VALUE_LONG.

The Syntax for the COLUMN_VALUE_LONG Procedure

```
PROCEDURE COLUMN_VALUE_LONG(cursor_id IN INTEGER,
                                position IN INTEGER,
                                length IN INTEGER,
                                offset IN INTEGER,
                                variable_out OUT VARCHAR2,
                                length_value OUT INTEGER);
```

cursor_id is the cursor ID supplied by OPEN_CURSOR. *position* is the starting position of the column in the row. If the column were the first field in the row, it would start at position 1. *length* is how much of the segment you are trying to retrieve, expressed in bytes. *offset* is used for the current location in the actual LONG field. This value starts at 0. If you were retrieving lengths in increments of 1000 bytes, the first offset would be 0, the next offset would be 1000, then 2000, and so on. The variable in which you want to store the output retrieved from the buffer is the *variable_out* parameter. Finally, *length_value* is how much data was actually retrieved in bytes. If *length_value* is less than the *length* you wanted to retrieve, you have come to the end of the data for the LONG field.

Summary

Today's lesson covered the DBMS_SQL package provided by Oracle. Before you can use this package, you must make sure that the package has been installed and that you have the appropriate privileges. Using this package, you can execute DDL statements, which allow you to create, drop, and alter items, and DML statements, which allow you to update, delete, and insert rows. You can also run queries from within PL/SQL and dynamically change these queries to suit a particular condition.

This package also provides a way to execute anonymous blocks from PL/SQL. The DBMS_SQL package provides additional error checking and the ability to store and retrieve LONG data up to 2 gigabytes to and from the buffer.

Q&A

Q What three types of statements can the DBMS_SQL package process?

A The DBMS_SQL process allows for the dynamic processing of SQL for non-query DDL and DML statements, SQL queries, and anonymous blocks of PL/SQL from within PL/SQL.

Q What is the one of the main differences between an anonymous PL/SQL block and a query using the DBMS_SQL package when retrieving data?

A With queries, you can use FETCH_ROWS to bring back multiple rows, whereas anonymous blocks can retrieve only one row. Attempting to store more than one row in the buffer will result in an error.

Q Should queries end with the appropriate punctuation of a semicolon?

A When using queries from within PL/SQL, you should not end the query with a semicolon.

Q What are the general steps in using any of the operations?

A You need to open a cursor, parse the statements to be executed at runtime, bind any variables if necessary, define columns if using SELECT statements, execute the query, retrieve the data from the buffer into variables, and finally close the cursor.

Q How can you determine if the last operation was a success?

A In addition to using exceptions, you can use the LAST_SQL_FUNCTION_CODE function to verify that the operation performed successfully, based upon the return code.

Workshop

You can now review your knowledge of the DBMS_SQL package, starting with a quiz, followed by some challenging exercises. You will practice writing queries, DML and DDL statements, and anonymous blocks with the DBMS_SQL package. You can find the answers in Appendix A, "Answers."

Quiz

1. For DML and DDL statements, and also for queries, what punctuation must not occur at the end of the query?
2. For anonymous blocks, is all punctuation required?
3. What is the largest size a PL/SQL variable can hold in kilobytes?
4. Why is processing queries and SQL with the DBMS_SQL package considered dynamic?

Exercises

1. Write a SQL query to show all records and all fields to the screen where the value of MyRow is greater than or equal to 2.
2. Write a SQL query to delete all records with MyRow equal to 4.
3. Write the DML code to update the record where MyRow is equal to 1. Change the description to say It Worked.
4. Write the DDL code required to drop the table called MyTable.

Day **18**

Writing to Files and the Display

by Timothy Atwood

By default, Oracle does not have any functional input and output processes when using PL/SQL. However, Oracle provides several packages that perform input and output. Today's lesson discusses the following packages:

☐ The UTL_FILE package

☐ The TEXT_IO package

☐ The DBMS_OUTPUT package

UTL_FILE Definition

The UTL_FILE package is a very powerful and flexible package that enables you to work with files on both the client side and server side; you can work with files on different operating systems. This can be a scary proposition on the server side unless proper security is in place. You can specify the only directories that can be written to by the UTL_FILE package with the `utl_file_dir` parameter located in the INIT.ORA Oracle initialization file. If you do not have this line in your initialization file, add the statement `utl_file_dir = directory_name`, where `directory_name` is the directory location where the files are stored.

You could then limit access to a `temp` directory on the server (assuming Personal Oracle) by specifying

 INPUT
```
utl_file_dir = c:\temp
```

NOTE

> If the operating system is case sensitive, then the subdirectories must be assigned with the same case as the actual directory. (`/tmp` is different in UNIX than `/Tmp`.)

In addition, if you want to give write permission to all directories, you would simply specify

 INPUT
```
utl_file_dir = *
```

NOTE

> Be careful with permissions granted to directories. They can overwrite operating system permissions, thereby giving access to users who normally wouldn't be able to access files in those directories.

When an Oracle user creates a file, all rights and permissions to the file are assigned to the user. If other users need access to those files, it is up to the security administrator to change the permissions on the files.

File Input

The UTL_FILE package enables you to read into Oracle files located on the server or on the client. You could easily convert ASCII to EBCDIC files between the client and the server, utilizing some of the Oracle functions you learned on Day 7, "Using Oracle's Built-in Functions," and in Appendix B, "Oracle Functions Reference." Other possibilities include

☐ Reading in files output from any application in text mode (ASCII or EBCDIC)

☐ Reading files from any operating system

☐ Reading files created by a scanner with OCR capabilities

☐ Inserting this data into a table or just viewing the data

As you can see, this gives you tremendous flexibility when exchanging files between platforms, applications, and so on with Oracle. The process to read in a file is

1. Assign a file handle to the file. This creates a pointer to the file to provide information to the operating system such as whether the file is in use, and where the user is currently located in the file for reading and writing operations.

2. Declare a string of type VARCHAR2 to act as a buffer for reading in the file one line at a time.

3. Use FOPEN to open the file in read mode, as specified by the parameter R.

4. Use GET_LINE to read in data from the file into your declared buffer of type VARCHAR2, one line at a time.

5. Close the file and release the file handle by using FCLOSE.

The next few sections examine the details of reading a file into Oracle.

Declaring a File Handle

When you open a file with the UTL_FILE package, a file handle is returned with a datatype of UTL_FILE.FILE_TYPE.

The Syntax for Creating a File Handle

The format to create the file handle is

```
DECLARE
    v_READFILE UTL_FILE.FILE_TYPE;
BEGIN
```

The FILE_TYPE is a PL/SQL record, which contains the necessary information about the file you are attempting to read or write including the filename, file location, method of accessing the file, and so on.

Using FOPEN to Open a File

FOPEN opens a file for reading or writing only. Table 18.1 provides a listing of possible exceptions raised from the function call. You cannot perform both operations on the same file simultaneously.

18

The Syntax for the FOPEN Function

FOPEN is defined as

```
FUNCTION FOPEN(location IN VARCHAR2,
                       filename IN VARCHAR2,
                       openmode IN VARCHAR2)
RETURN UTL_FILE.FILE_TYPE;
```

The first parameter *location* is a VARCHAR2 string, which holds the location (path) of the file. This can be restricted by utl_file_dir as mentioned earlier in this chapter. The second parameter, *filename*, is the actual filename itself. The third parameter, *openmode*, defines how you will access the file.

You can access the file as

- ☐ R—Read-only access.
- ☐ W—If the file does not exist, the file is created; otherwise, all information in the original file is deleted and replaced with the new contents you are writing.
- ☐ A—Allows you to append text to a file instead of overwriting the file with the parameter W. If the file does not exist, it will be created.

For file input, you will use only mode 'R'. The function then returns the file handle of type UTL_FILE.FILE_HANDLE for subsequent use.

Table 18.1. Exceptions raised by FOPEN.

Error Raised	Description of Error
UTL_FILE.INVALID_PATH	Directory path or filename specified is invalid, or the file is not accessible.
UTL_FILE.INVALID_MODE	Invalid mode specified. Raised if using any other characters except R, W, and A.
UTL_FILE.INVALID_OPERATION	Due to lack of permissions for access to the file. Contact the DBA for access rights.
UTL_FILE.INTERNAL_ERROR	Error internal to the system.

Using IS_OPEN to Test If a File Is Open

As part of error control, before you attempt to open a file, you can test to see if the file is already open by using IS_OPEN. You can also test to make sure a file is open before you attempt to close the file.

The Syntax for the IS_OPEN Function

SYNTAX

The format for the function IS_OPEN is

```
FUNCTION IS_OPEN(file_handle IN UTL_FILE.FILE_TYPE)
    RETURN BOOLEAN;
```

If the file is open, the value true is returned; otherwise, false is returned. file_handle is the file handle returned by FOPEN.

Using GET_LINE for File Input

When performing file input, in order to read data from the file into the buffer, you'll use the GET_LINE function. The maximum input length is 1022 bytes.

NOTE

When the line is read into the buffer, the function does not pass the newline character (\n for all you C programmers out there). If you are reading in a fixed-length record where the data is 60 characters, you will not have to worry about the carriage return/line feed characters. Your buffer in this case would have to be only 60 characters. If you do need to add a newline character, you can use the NEW_LINE procedure as discussed later in the chapter in the section "File Output."

18

The Syntax for the GET_LINE Function

The format for the function GET_LINE is

SYNTAX

```
PROCEDURE GET_LINE(file_handle IN UTL_FILE.FILE_TYPE,
    buffer OUT VARCHAR2);
```

The first parameter, file_handle, is the file handle returned from the FOPEN function. The second parameter, buffer, is the buffer of type VARCHAR2. Possible errors that could arise are shown in Table 18.2.

Table 18.2. Exceptions raised by GET_LINE.

Error Raised	Description of Error
UTL_FILE.INVALID_FILEHANDLE	Not a valid file handle.
UTL_FILE.INVALID_OPERATION	File not opened for reading ('R' mode), or problems with file permissions.
UTL_FILE.VALUE_ERROR	Buffer not long enough to hold input from file up to the newline character.
UTL_FILE.NO_DATA_FOUND	End of file has been reached.

continues

Table 18.2. continued

Error Raised	Description of Error
UTL_FILE.INTERNAL_ERROR	Error internal to the system.
UTL_FILE.READ_ERROR	Operating system error occurred while reading from the file.

File Output

Because you can input files, you should be able to output files. As you will see, this is a great method for importing and exporting files from one application, operating system, and so on to another. It works well in mixed IBM, UNIX, and PC shops. The steps to output to a file are as follows:

1. Assign a file handle to the file. This creates a pointer to the file to provide information to the operating system such as whether the file is in use, and where the user is currently located in the file for reading and writing operations.
2. Use FOPEN to open the file to replace or append text. FOPEN returns the file handle associated with the open file.
3. Use PUT, PUTF, PUT_LINE, NEW_LINE, or FFLUSH to write to the file.
4. Close the file and release the file handle by using FCLOSE.

The next few sections look at the detailed process of writing to a file into Oracle.

Opening a File for Output

You will open the file in the same manner for output as you did for input. The only difference is that the mode of operations will be REPLACE ('W') or APPEND ('A').

The Syntax for Opening a File for Output

The syntax again is

```
FUNCTION FOPEN(location IN VARCHAR2,
               filename IN VARCHAR2,
               openmode IN VARCHAR2)
RETURN UTL_FILE.FILE_TYPE;
```

All the same exceptions apply to opening the file for writing as they did for reading from a file.

TIP   If you are experiencing user data exceptions when calling this function, there are two possibilities. One is that the Oracle product has been corrupted and needs to be reinstalled. The second is a possible problem in Windows NT or UNIX, where the filename specified also has to include the path. Try both of these if you get an error message with `SYS:UTL_FILE` on lines 82 and 120.

Using `IS_OPEN` to Test If a File Is Open When Writing to a File

You should test to make sure the file is open before writing to the file. This can be accomplished through properly handling the raised exceptions.

The Syntax for Testing to Make Sure a File Is Open

The syntax is still the same for both reading and writing to files:

```
FUNCTION IS_OPEN(file_handle IN UTL_FILE.FILE_TYPE)
    RETURN BOOLEAN;
```

If the file is open, the value `true` is returned; otherwise, `false` is returned. `file_handle` is the file handle returned by `FOPEN`.

Using `PUT` to Write to the Output File

The `PUT` procedure outputs the string to the output file. This assumes that the file has been opened for writing.

The Syntax for the `PUT` Procedure

The format for the `PUT` procedure is

```
PROCEDURE PUT(file_handle IN UTL_FILE.FILE_TYPE,
    buffer IN VARCHAR2);
```

The `file_handle` parameter is the file handle returned from `FOPEN`. The `buffer` parameter is the output to the file. The maximum length of the buffer is 1023. Table 18.3 lists possible exceptions and their meanings.

Table 18.3. Exceptions raised by `PUT`, `PUT_LINE`, `PUTF`, and `FFLUSH`.

Error Raised	Description of Error
UTL_FILE.INVALID_FILEHANDLE	Not a valid file handle
UTL_FILE.INVALID_OPERATION	Attempting to write to a file without the proper permissions or not specifying 'W' or 'A' for output mode
UTL_FILE.WRITE_ERROR	Error caused by the operating system when attempting to write to a file, such as disk full error
UTL_FILE.INTERNAL_ERROR	Error internal to the system

18

NOTE

> Similar to the GET_LINE procedure, PUT does not output a newline character. You can use the NEW_LINE procedure to write out the newline character for your specific operating system, which is discussed in the following section.

Using the NEW_LINE Procedure

The NEW_LINE procedure outputs one or more newline characters in the format specified by the operating system. For instance, ASCII is '0D0A' and EBCDIC is '0D25' for the newline character. This procedure would be used to add a newline character in conjunction with the PUT statement.

The Syntax for the NEW_LINE Procedure

```
PROCEDURE NEW_LINE(file_handle IN UTL_FILE.FILE_TYPE,
    no_newline_output IN NATURAL :=1);
```

The *file_handle* parameter is the file handle returned from FOPEN. *no_newline_output* is the total number of newline characters you want to write to the file. The default is one newline character if not specified. The same exceptions are raised as with PUT, so you can refer to Table 18.3 for a brief review.

TIP

> To simplify writing output to a file, which requires a newline character, you could easily create a function called WRITE_LINE, which will then output using PUT, and then call the NEW_LINE procedure. This works great for features such as double spacing. The other trick is to simply use PUT_LINE (if only one newline character per line) or PUTF (most flexible, combination of PUT, PUT_LINE, NEW_LINE and then some), which supports the NEW_LINE procedure.

Using the PUT_LINE Procedure

The PUT_LINE procedure outputs a string to a file, followed by the platform-specific newline character. Basically it combines PUT and NEW_LINE into one procedure. Again, it is assumed that the file has been opened before you attempt to write to the file.

The Syntax for the PUT_LINE Procedure

```
PROCEDURE PUT_LINE(file_handle IN UTL_FILE.FILE_TYPE,
    buffer IN VARCHAR2);
```

The *file_handle* parameter is the file handle returned from FOPEN. *buffer* is your output string, which will be terminated by the newline character associated with the operating system. The same exceptions are raised as with PUT, so you can refer to Table 18.3 for a brief review.

18

Using the PUTF **Procedure**

The PUTF procedure is the most flexible for output to a file. This procedure operates similarly to the printf() function in C. You can output text and up to five sets of special string data, represented by '%s'. In addition, you can have as many newline characters as required, represented by the '\n'.

The Syntax for the PUTF **Procedure**

```
PROCEDURE PUTF(file_handle IN UTL_FILE.FILE_TYPE,
    formatted_line IN VARCHAR2,
    <string_item1 IN VARCHAR2 DEFAULT NULL,
    <string_item2 IN VARCHAR2 DEFAULT NULL,
    <string_item3 IN VARCHAR2 DEFAULT NULL,
    <string_item4 IN VARCHAR2 DEFAULT NULL,
    <string_item5 IN VARCHAR2 DEFAULT NULL,);
```

The *file_handle* parameter is the file handle returned from FOPEN. *formatted_line* is simply the line of text, which can optionally contain up to five '%s' for special strings of characters, and optionally as many newline characters ('\n') as desired (up to a maximum of 1023 bytes).

> **TIP**
>
> If you need to output more than five arguments, just call the PUTF statement as many times in a row as necessary.

18

Comparison of PUT, PUTF, **and** PUT_LINE

Listing 18.1 shows the PL/SQL code that will output to a file the same exact text using the three different output procedures. Even though all three procedures accomplish the same exact output to the file, you will be able to see the different methods of using these procedures.

> **NOTE**
>
> Make sure that you have entered SET SERVEROUTPUT ON at the SQL*Plus prompt so that you can view output to the screen with several of these listings.

INPUT **Listing 18.1. Writing to a file with** PUT, PUTF, **and** PUT_LINE.

```
1: DECLARE
2: -- Create a file handle of type UTL_FILE.FILE_TYPE
3:     v_MyFileHandle UTL_FILE.FILE_TYPE;
4: -- User defined variables to output
5:     v_FirstName VARCHAR2(15) := 'Thomas';
6:     v_LastName VARCHAR2(20) := 'Jefferson';
7:     v_Occupation VARCHAR2(15) := 'President';
```

continues

Listing 18.1. continued

```
 8: BEGIN
 9: -- Open the file to write.
10:     v_MyFileHandle := UTL_FILE.FOPEN('c:\','myout.txt','w');
11: -- Example of Using PUT
12:     UTL_FILE.PUT(v_MyFileHandle,'First Name: ' || v_FirstName
13:             || ' Last Name: ' || v_LastName
14:             || ' Occupation: ' || v_Occupation);
15:     UTL_FILE.NEW_LINE(v_MyFileHandle,1);
16: -- Repeat but with PUT_LINE
17:     UTL_FILE.PUT_LINE(v_MyFileHandle,'First Name: ' || v_FirstName
18:             || ' Last Name: ' || v_LastName
19:             || ' Occupation: ' || v_Occupation);
20: -- Repeat with PUTF
21:     UTL_FILE.PUTF(v_MyFileHandle,'%s' || v_FirstName ||
22:             ' %s' || v_LastName || ' %s' || v_Occupation || '\n',
23:         'First Name: ',
24:         'Last Name: ',
25:         'Occupation: ');
26: -- Close the file handle which points to myout.txt
27:     UTL_FILE.FCLOSE(v_MyFileHandle);
28: EXCEPTION
29: -- Create Exception to simply display error code and message
30:     WHEN OTHERS THEN
31:         DBMS_OUTPUT.PUT_LINE
32:             ('ERROR ' || to_char(SQLCODE) || SQLERRM);
33:         NULL;
34: END;
```

OUTPUT   Your output should appear similar to the following:

```
First Name: Thomas Last Name: Jefferson Occupation: President
First Name: Thomas Last Name: Jefferson Occupation: President
First Name: Thomas Last Name: Jefferson Occupation: President
```

The first PUT statement in line 12 is followed by NEW_LINE in line 15, which is identical to PUT_LINE in line 17, which adds the newline character at the end of the line. Finally, PUTF in line 21 demonstrates using strings (up to five per call) and using '\n' in line 22 to output the newline character.

Using FFLUSH to Clear the Buffer

When you use any of the PUT commands, the data is stored in the UTL_FILE package's buffer until it is full, and then the buffer writes to the file. If you need to flush the contents of the buffer and write to disk immediately, Oracle provides the FFLUSH procedure.

The Syntax for the FFLUSH Procedure

The format for the procedure FFLUSH is

```
PROCEDURE FFLUSH(file_handle IN UTL_FILE.FILE_TYPE);
```

The file_handle parameter is the file handle returned from FOPEN. Refer to Table 18.3 for a list of possible exceptions raised by FFLUSH.

SYNTAX

Closing Files

When you have completed reading or writing from a file, you should close the file in order to flush the buffer and then free up resources in Oracle (that is, file handles, and so on). There are two methods to close files: FCLOSE and FCLOSE_ALL.

Using FCLOSE to Close Files

The FCLOSE procedure flushes the buffer (if not empty) and then closes one file specified by the file handle of UTL_FILE.FILE_TYPE.

The Syntax for the FLCLOSE Function

The syntax for FCLOSE is

```
PROCEDURE FCLOSE(file_handle IN UTL_FILE.FILE_TYPE);
```

The file_handle parameter is the file handle returned from FOPEN. Refer to Table 18.4 for a list of possible exceptions raised by FCLOSE.

Table 18.4. Exceptions raised by FCLOSE and FCLOSE_ALL.

Error Raised	Description of Error
UTL_FILE.INVALID_FILEHANDLE	Not a valid file handle
UTL_FILE.WRITE_ERROR	Error caused by the operating system when attempting to write to a file, such as disk full error
UTL_FILE.INTERNAL_ERROR	Error internal to the system

Using FCLOSE_ALL to Close All Files

The FCLOSE_ALL procedure flushes the buffer (if not empty) and then closes all open files. The format of the FCLOSE_ALL procedure is as follows:

```
PROCEDURE FCLOSEALL;
```

Refer to Table 18.4 for a list of possible exceptions raised by FCLOSEALL. You should use FCLOSE_ALL only in emergencies, such as an exception handler to properly close all files for any error that can occur. Improperly closed files can lead to corruption. Always use FCLOSE instead of FCLOSE_ALL for normal file handling.

NOTE

Oracle closes all files, but does not mark them as closed. Therefore, IS_OPEN will return a boolean value of true. However, you still need to use FOPEN to read from or write to the files.

Examples Utilizing the UTL_FILE Package

You will now see some practical uses of the UTL_FILE package. The first example will demonstrate data conversion from one character set to another.

Converting Text Files from ASCII to EBCDIC

You can easily incorporate the CONVERT function with the UTL_FILE package to convert from ASCII to EBCDIC (or any other character set for that matter) as long as the source file is pure text and does not contain any binary data. The ASCII character set is typically used on all computers except IBM mainframes, which use the EBCDIC character set. Before you run the code in Listing 18.2, use a text editor to create a file called ASCII.TXT that contains the words THIS IS A TEST.

INPUT **Listing 18.2. Converting from ASCII to EBCDIC.**

```
 1: DECLARE
 2: -- Create a file handle of type UTL_FILE.FILE_TYPE to read in a file
 3:     v_INFileHandle UTL_FILE.FILE_TYPE;
 4: -- Create a file handle of type UTL_FILE.FILE_TYPE to output a file
 5:     v_OUTFileHandle UTL_FILE.FILE_TYPE;
 6: -- User defined variable for buffer
 7:     v_MyBuffer VARCHAR2(1022);
 8: SET SERVEROUTPUT ON
 9: BEGIN
10: -- Open the files to read and write.
11:     v_INFileHandle := UTL_FILE.FOPEN('c:\','ascii.txt','r');
12:     v_OUTFileHandle := UTL_FILE.FOPEN('c:\','ebcdic.txt','w');
13: -- Loop until the entire file is read in and converted
14: LOOP
15:     BEGIN
16: -- Read in One Line
17:     UTL_FILE.GET_LINE(v_INFileHandle,v_MyBuffer);
18: --Output one line as EBCDIC
19:     DBMS_OUTPUT.PUT_LINE(v_MyBuffer);
20:     UTL_FILE.PUT_LINE(v_OUTFileHandle,
21:         convert(v_MyBuffer,'WE8EBCDIC500'));
22:
23:     EXCEPTION
24:         WHEN NO_DATA_FOUND THEN
25:             EXIT;
26:
27:     END;
28: END LOOP;
29:
30: -- Close the file handles to the input and output file.
31:     UTL_FILE.FCLOSE(v_INFileHandle);
32:     UTL_FILE.FCLOSE(v_OUTFileHandle);
33: EXCEPTION
34: -- Create Exception to simply display error code and message
35:     WHEN OTHERS THEN
```

```
36:                   DBMS_OUTPUT.PUT_LINE
37:                       ('ERROR ' || to_char(SQLCODE) || SQLERRM);
38:                   NULL;
39: END;
```

ANALYSIS The program begins by assigning a file handle to the ASCII input file in line 3 and a file handle to the converted EBCDIC file in line 5. In line 14, you use a LOOP to continue reading the file until the exception NO_DATA_FOUND is raised, which simply means that there is no more data to read from the file. The body of the loop gets one line at a time and then outputs one line at a time converted to EBCDIC. Again, you can convert to any character set. Refer to Appendix B for the CONVERT function. If any other errors occur, the exception handler will print out the code and the meaning of the error message. You might want to add code that could state invalid operation, disk read error, disk write error, and so on in the exception section.

Reading a File into a Table

You will now practice reading a file of former presidents and inserting the data into a table. The first step is to create the table for importing. Execute the code in Listing 18.3.

INPUT **Listing 18.3. Creating the table.**

```
1: CREATE TABLE PRES
2:     (SSNO VARCHAR2(9) CONSTRAINT PK_PRES PRIMARY KEY,
3:      FNAME VARCHAR2(15),
4:      LNAME VARCHAR2(20))
5: /
```

ANALYSIS Now you need to create a file called PRES.TXT for import into the table just created in Listing 18.3. Use any text editor to create the file in Listing 18.4. The first 9 digits are the Social Security number, the next 15 characters are the first name, and the last 20 characters are the last name. This is a fixed-block file, meaning that all columns line up and all fields are the same width, blank-filled if necessary.

INPUT **Listing 18.4. Sample text file to import.**

```
001010111George         Washington
005124745Thomas         Jefferson
223445726Richard        Nixon
378112475Jimmy          Carter
541129744Abraham        Lincoln
587145961John           Kennedy
665474112Theodore       Roosevelt
725139511George         Bush
998211247Ronald         Reagan
```

18

You can now execute the code in Listing 18.5 to import this file. If you are on a Windows/
DOS platform, copy the file into the root directory of drive C and then execute the code. If
you are on a UNIX or mainframe platform, you will need to specify the path where you have
created the text files, such as /home/ for your path.

INPUT **Listing 18.5. Using UTL_FILE to import data.**

```
 1: DECLARE
 2: -- Create a file handle of type UTL_FILE.FILE_TYPE to read in a file
 3:        v_INFileHandle UTL_FILE.FILE_TYPE;
 4: -- User defined variable for buffer
 5:        v_MyBuffer VARCHAR2(1022);
 6: -- Begin variables to hold fields you are importing
 7:        v_SSNO VARCHAR2(9);
 8:        v_FirstName VARCHAR2(15);
 9:        v_LastName VARCHAR2(20);
10: BEGIN
11: -- Open the files to read and import.
12:        v_INFileHandle := UTL_FILE.FOPEN('c:\','pres.txt','r');
13: LOOP
14:        BEGIN
15: -- Read in One Line
16:        UTL_FILE.GET_LINE(v_INFileHandle,v_MyBuffer);
17: -- Parse Data and assign to variables
18: -- Use RTRIM to remove any blank spaces
19:        v_SSNO := RTRIM(SUBSTR(v_MyBuffer,1,9));
20:        v_FirstName := RTRIM(SUBSTR(v_MyBuffer,10,15));
21:        v_LastName := RTRIM(SUBSTR(v_MyBuffer,25,20));
22: -- Insert Data into the Table
23: INSERT INTO PRES(SSNO,FNAME,LNAME)
24:        VALUES(v_SSNO,v_FirstName,v_LastName);
25: -- Check for end of file
26:        EXCEPTION
27:             WHEN NO_DATA_FOUND THEN
28:                    EXIT;
29:        END;
30: END LOOP;
31:
32: -- Close the file handle which points to pres.txt
33:        UTL_FILE.FCLOSE(v_INFileHandle);
34: Commit the additions
35: COMMIT;
36: EXCEPTION
37: -- Create Exception to simply display error code and message
38:        WHEN OTHERS THEN
39:             DBMS_OUTPUT.PUT_LINE
40:                  ('ERROR ' ¦¦ to_char(SQLCODE) ¦¦ SQLERRM);
41:             NULL;
42: END;
43: /
```

18

After the code has been entered and executed, you can verify that everything went successfully by typing in

INPUT   `SELECT * from PRES;`

The output should be

OUTPUT

```
SNO         FNAME            LNAME
---------   ---------------  --------------------
001010111   George           Washington
005124745   Thomas           Jefferson
223445726   Richard          Nixon
378112475   Jimmy            Carter
541129744   Abraham          Lincoln
587145961   John             Kennedy
665474112   Theodore         Roosevelt
725139511   George           Bush
998211247   Ronald           Reagan

9 rows selected.
```

Exporting a File as a Comma-Separated Value (CSV)

You can now export the file you just imported in the Comma-Separated Value format, which can be read by almost every application in the world. A CSV format simply places quotes around text fields; number fields typically do not have quotes, and a comma separates each field. You will export the table, which you created in the previous example, by entering and executing the code in Listing 18.6.

18

INPUT   **Listing 18.6. Exporting the table.**

```
 1: DECLARE
 2: -- Variables to write out to text file called presexp.csv
 3:     v_SSNO        pres.ssno%TYPE;
 4:     v_FirstName   pres.fname%TYPE;
 5:     v_LastName    pres.lname%TYPE;
 6: --Declare filehandle
 7:     v_MYFileHandle UTL_FILE.FILE_TYPE;
 8: -- Cursor declaration to fetch data from table, row by row
 9: CURSOR c_PRES IS
10:     SELECT * from PRES;
11: BEGIN
12: -- Open File for writing
13:     v_MYFileHandle := UTL_FILE.FOPEN('c:\','presexp.csv','w');
14: -- Open the cursor
15:     OPEN c_PRES;
16:     LOOP
17: -- Get each row, one at a time
18:         FETCH c_PRES INTO v_SSNO,v_FirstName,v_LastName;
19: -- Output as CSV file
20:         EXIT WHEN c_PRES%NOTFOUND;
```

continues

Listing 18.6. continued

```
21:              UTL_FILE.PUT_LINE(v_MYFileHandle,'"' || v_SSNO || '","'
22:                   || v_FirstName || '","' || v_LastName || '"');
23:       END LOOP;
24: -- Close Cursor
25:       CLOSE c_PRES;
26: -- Close CSV file
27:       UTL_FILE.FCLOSE(v_MYFileHandle);
28: END;
29: /
```

After you have executed the code in Listing 18.6, your output should be identical to the following:

```
"001010111","George","Washington"
"005124745","Thomas","Jefferson"
"223445726","Richard","Nixon"
"378112475","Jimmy","Carter"
"541129744","Abraham","Lincoln"
"587145961","John","Kennedy"
"665474112","Theodore","Roosevelt"
"725139511","George","Bush"
"998211247","Ronald","Reagan"
```

As you learned on Day 10, "Manipulating Data with Cursors, DELETE, and UPDATE," you use an explicit cursor to read in the entire table, one row at a time. After the loop executes, you can then use the UTL_FILE package to output using PUT_LINE the data from the table in CSV format.

TIP

Be careful when working with cursors. The placement of the output statement had to occur after the check to see if there are any more rows in the table. If you placed it before the EXIT statement, the last row would be written out twice. I encourage you to experiment by moving the UTL_FILE.PUT_LINE statement before the EXIT statement to see logic errors that frequently occur in any programming environment.

TEXT_IO

The TEXT_IO package is available only by purchasing Oracle Developer/2000. This package is not as sophisticated as UTL_FILE because it lacks the named exceptions provided by the UTL_FILE package, and it is missing such modules as FFLUSH and FCLOSE_ALL. It is my recommendation that you stick with the UTL_FILE package when working with file input and output.

18

The DBMS_OUTPUT Package

Several of the previous chapters used the DBMS_OUTPUT package already to demonstrate PL/SQL when there was no apparent output. I use this package extensively as a debugging tool in my PL/SQL, similar to using printf statements in C to see the value of variables as the code executes. This package enables you to store information into a buffer and then to retrieve this information. The buffer can contain lines of 255 characters up to the size of the buffer. As you saw in earlier chapters, using PUT or PUT_LINE will send the output to screen if GET_LINE or GET_LINES is not used.

Enabling the DBMS_OUTPUT Package

There are two methods to enable the DBMS_OUTPUT package. The first method utilizes SQL*Plus, which you saw in earlier chapters.

The code line used to enable is

```
SET SERVEROUTPUT ON
```

You can increase the buffer size in SQL*Plus by adding the following:

```
SET SERVEROUTPUT ON SIZE 1000000
```

The maximum size of the buffer is 1,000,000 bytes. The default size is only 20,000 bytes, so it is usually a good idea to increase it to the maximum of 1,000,000 bytes.

You can also enable output through PL/SQL by using the ENABLE statement, as in the following procedure:

```
DBMS_OUTPUT.ENABLE;
```

If you want to control the buffer size, the command would now be

```
DBMS_OUTPUT.ENABLE (1000000);
```

Disabling the DBMS_OUTPUT Package

After you are finished with the DBMS_OUTPUT package, you can disable it through SQL*Plus or PL/SQL by entering the following code line:

```
SET SERVEROUTPUT OFF
```

When using PL/SQL with the DBMS_OUTPUT package instead of SQL, you would use

```
DBMS_OUTPUT.DISABLE;
```

All output will now be disabled completely after executing the preceding statements.

18

Using PUT with the DBMS_OUTPUT Package

The PUT procedure works similarly to the UTL_FILE package. This procedure enables you to place up to a maximum of 255 characters into the buffer. The datatypes can be NUMBER, DATE, and VARCHAR2. This does not add a newline character, so it will not output to screen until you call the procedure NEW_LINE or use PUT_LINE, as long as you do not exceed 255 characters. The syntax for PUT is

```
PROCEDURE PUT(data_to_display);
```

The NEW_LINE Procedure

Similar to the ULT_FILE package, NEW_LINE generates the operating specific newline character. Generally, NEW_LINE is used in conjunction with PUT. The syntax for NEW_LINE is

```
PROCEDURE NEW_LINE;
```

Working with PUT_LINE

PUT_LINE works the same as PUT, except that it adds the newline character at the end so output is printed immediately.

The Syntax for the PUT_LINE Procedure

```
PROCEDURE PUT_LINE(data_to_display);
```

The data_to_display can be of type VARCHAR2, DATE, and NUMBER.

| TIP | Although the buffer can hold only 255 characters maximum, you can output more than 255 characters by using format commands such as TO_CHAR with numbers and dates. |

Testing PUT, NEW_LINE, and PUT_LINE

In this section, you will test three of the procedures by enabling from within SQL*Plus and also from within PL/SQL.

Enabling with SQL*Plus

To enable the DBMS_OUTPUT package, at the prompt type in

```
SET SERVEROUTPUT ON
```

After you press Enter, the output package will be enabled. Now enter and execute the code in Listing 18.7.

18

Listing 18.7. Using DBMS_OUTPUT with PUT, NEW_LINE, and PUT_LINE.

```
 1: DECLARE
 2: --Counter for the For Loop
 3:      v_Counter NUMBER;
 4: BEGIN
 5:      FOR v_Counter IN 1..5 LOOP
 6: -- This will cause two of each number to appear on same line as
 7: -- PUT_LINE will flush PUT with it
 8:          DBMS_OUTPUT.PUT(v_Counter);
 9:          DBMS_OUTPUT.PUT_LINE(v_Counter);
10:      END LOOP;
11: --Demonstrate PUT with NEW_LINE
12:      DBMS_OUTPUT.PUT_LINE('We will now test with a newline character');
13:      FOR v_Counter IN 1..5 LOOP
14:          DBMS_OUTPUT.PUT(v_Counter);
15:          DBMS_OUTPUT.NEW_LINE;
16:      END LOOP;
17: END;
```

OUTPUT

Your output should appear as

```
11
22
33
44
55
We will now test with a newline character
1
2
3
4
5
```

ANALYSIS Because NEW_LINE is not called after the PUT statement in line 8 in the first FOR loop (beginning in line 5), no output occurred until PUT_LINE was called, because PUT_LINE includes the NEW_LINE character. This is why you doubled the numbers on the output for the first FOR loop. The second loop, starting in line 13, is identical to the first loop, except it adds NEW_LINE in line 15 after PUT in line 14. You can now display one set of numbers for the counter in the FOR loop. It still would be easier to use PUT_LINE instead of PUT and NEW_LINE. You can now disable the output by typing

INPUT   SET SERVEROUTPUT OFF

If you want, go ahead and re-execute the code in Listing 18.7, and you will notice that output is no longer shown on the screen.

Enabling with PL/SQL

The next examples will demonstrate the same process completely within PL/SQL. Go ahead and execute the code in Listing 18.8.

INPUT

Listing 18.8. Using DBMS_OUTPUT with PUT, NEW_LINE, and PUT_LINE with the PL/SQL ENABLE procedure.

```
 1: DECLARE
 2: --Counter for the For Loop
 3:     v_Counter NUMBER;
 4: BEGIN
 5:     DBMS_OUTPUT.ENABLE;
 6:     FOR v_Counter IN 1..5 LOOP
 7: -- This will cause two of each number to appear on same line
 8: -- as PUT_LINE will flush PUT with it
 9:         DBMS_OUTPUT.PUT(v_Counter);
10:         DBMS_OUTPUT.PUT_LINE(v_Counter);
11:     END LOOP;
12: --Demonstrate PUT with NEW_LINE
13:     DBMS_OUTPUT.PUT_LINE('We will now test with a newline character');
14:     FOR v_Counter IN 1..5 LOOP
15:         DBMS_OUTPUT.PUT(v_Counter);
16:         DBMS_OUTPUT.NEW_LINE;
17:     END LOOP;
18: END;
```

ANALYSIS Your output will still be identical to the output generated from Listing 18.7. By now, you can see how great the DBMS_OUTPUT package can be as a debugging tool. You can finally see alternative ways to gain access to the data by using GET_LINE or GET_LINES.

GET_LINE and the DBMS_OUTPUT Package

The GET_LINE procedure allows you to retrieve only one line from the buffer up to a maximum of 255 characters. A line is defined as all characters up to the newline character. The format for GET_LINE is

```
PROCEDURE GET_LINE(single_line OUT VARCHAR2, status OUT INTEGER);
```

If GET_LINE is successful reading a single line, a value of 1 is returned for a status; otherwise, a value of 0 is returned if false. You can test GET_LINE by executing the code in Listing 18.9.

INPUT ### Listing 18.9. An example using GET_LINE.

```
1: DECLARE
2:     v_Counter NUMBER;
3:     v_HoldBuffer VARCHAR2(255);
4:     v_HoldStatus INTEGER;
```

```
 5: BEGIN
 6:      DBMS_OUTPUT.ENABLE;
 7:      FOR v_Counter IN 1..5 LOOP
 8:           DBMS_OUTPUT.PUT(v_Counter);
 9:           DBMS_OUTPUT.PUT_LINE(v_Counter);
10:      END LOOP;
11:      DBMS_OUTPUT.PUT_LINE('We will now test with a newline character');
12:      FOR v_Counter IN 1..5 LOOP
13:           DBMS_OUTPUT.PUT(v_Counter);
14:           DBMS_OUTPUT.NEW_LINE;
15:      END LOOP;
16:      DBMS_OUTPUT.GET_LINE(v_HoldBuffer,v_HoldStatus);
17:      DBMS_OUTPUT.PUT_LINE(v_HoldBuffer);
18: END;
```

OUTPUT

Your output will appear as only

11

ANALYSIS

Why did only the first line appear instead of all the output lines from Listing 18.7 or Listing 18.8? Earlier, I stated that all output would be sent to the screen as long as GET_LINE or GET_LINES had not been used. Now because you are using GET_LINE in line 16, all output is suppressed from the screen. GET_LINE went to the buffer and extracted the first line with a value of 11, which was the result of the first FOR loop. You could only output the line with a subsequent PUT_LINE statement in line 17 displaying the data in the variable v_HoldBuffer, which was returned from the GET_LINE call.

Using GET_LINES

Although GET_LINE retrieves only one line, you can use GET_LINES to retrieve more than one line. You can read more than one line because GET_LINES reads the buffer into a PL/SQL table, which will be defined in the DECLARE section as a type CHARARR.

The Syntax for the GET_LINES Procedure

The syntax for GET_LINES is

```
PROCEDURE GET_LINES(line(s) OUT CHARARR,
    no_lines_retrieve IN OUT  INTEGER);
```

The Syntax for the CHARARR Datatype

The format for the datatype of CHARARR is

```
TYPE CHARARR IS TABLE OF VARCHAR2(255) INDEX BY BINARY_INTEGER;
```

When the call is made, the number of rows to retrieve is stored in the array, starting with row zero. If you ask for more lines than there actually are, only the number of available lines are read into the table. Again, GET_LINES, like GET_LINE, defines a line as all characters up to the newline character. You can now practice GET_LINES by executing the code in Listing 18.10.

INPUT   **Listing 18.10. Using** `GET_LINES` **in place of** `GET_LINE`.

```
 1: DECLARE
 2:     v_Counter NUMBER;
 3:     v_HoldBuffer DBMS_OUTPUT.CHARARR;
 4:     v_HoldLines INTEGER := 11;
 5: BEGIN
 6:     DBMS_OUTPUT.ENABLE;
 7:     FOR v_Counter IN 1..5 LOOP
 8:         DBMS_OUTPUT.PUT(v_Counter);
 9:         DBMS_OUTPUT.PUT_LINE(v_Counter);
10:     END LOOP;
11:     DBMS_OUTPUT.PUT_LINE('We will now test with a newline character');
12:     FOR v_Counter IN 1..5 LOOP
13:         DBMS_OUTPUT.PUT(v_Counter);
14:         DBMS_OUTPUT.NEW_LINE;
15:     END LOOP;
16:     DBMS_OUTPUT.GET_LINES(v_HoldBuffer,v_HoldLines);
17:     FOR v_Counter IN 1..v_HoldLines LOOP
18:         DBMS_OUTPUT.PUT_LINE(v_HoldBuffer(v_Counter));
19:     END LOOP;
20: END;
```

ANALYSIS   Your output will look identical to the output generated from Listing 18.7 and Listing 18.8. One of the interesting things you should note is how to display or access the information from `GET_LINES`. If you remember, the datatype `CHARARR` is really an array table. To access it, you simply access the variable assigned to the table and specify the location in the array. In this case, this was `v_Counter`. You could simply think of this as `v_HoldBuffer(1)` ... `v_HoldBuffer(11)`.

One useful feature of `GET_LINES` is that you can use it as another means to enter data into a table. However, the source for the buffer called by `PUT` or `PUT_LINES` could easily copy from one table to another using a cursor instead, and only use `PUT_LINE` to display the information as it is copied from one table to the next. As with any procedural language, there are many ways to accomplish the same goal!

Exceptions Raised from the DBMS_OUTPUT Package

There are two exceptions that you have to worry about when using the DBMS_OUTPUT package. These are described in Table 18.5, along with the actions required to fix the problem.

Table 18.5. Exceptions raised by DBMS_OUTPUT.

Error Code	Error Description	Corrective Action
ORU-10027	Buffer overflow	Increase buffer size to at least 1,000,000 bytes.
ORU-10028	Line length overflow, limit of 255 characters per line	Make sure that all calls made to PUT and PUT_LINE are under 255 characters.

Now that you know the exceptions, you can trap errors as they occur.

Summary

Today you discovered two methods of output from Oracle. The UTL_FILE package enables you to read and write files for input and output. You can then export the data in any format desired or import from practically any application's output. The DBMS_OUTPUT package, which you used before without much in-depth discussion, enables you to output information to the screen to use primarily as a debugging tool with your PL/SQL code. If you use any version of GET, all output to the screen is suppressed, unless you use PUT_LINE with the variable assigned to the values returned from GET_LINE or GET_LINES. In most cases, you will rarely use GET_LINE or GET_LINES. Instead, PUT_LINE should be sufficient for most of your debugging needs.

Q&A

Q When working with UTL_FILE, can you access a file for reading and writing simultaneously?

A No. You can choose only one method of operations on a file. If you attempt to write to a file that is read-only, an exception will be raised.

Q What is one major purpose of the UTL_FILE package?

A It provides a slick way to import and export data from one application to another, even allowing you to do the proper character conversions.

Q What is one problem with not using FCLOSE?

A If you are writing a small amount of data to the buffer, if the procedure ends before the buffer fills, the data will not be written. This will lead to data missing from files as well as probable file corruption. You need to flush the buffer either with FFLUSH or FCLOSE, which is the proper way to flush the buffer, and then close the file.

18

Q What is the difference between the UTL_FILE package and the DBMS_OUTPUT package?

A The UTL_FILE package allows you to work with reading and writing files, whereas DBMS_OUTPUT is concerned with displaying data from variables to the screen for debugging purposes.

Q What happens if I try to store more than 255 characters in a line of the buffer?

A An exception is raised. Refer to Table 18.5 for definitions of the errors.

Q How do you display output with the DBMS_OUTPUT package?

A If using SQL*Plus, simply use SET SERVEROUTPUT ON. If using PL/SQL, then use DBMS_OUTPUT.ENABLE. It is a good idea in any login script to automatically enable the output package.

Workshop

In the following workshop, you will first be quizzed on your understanding of how file input and output works. Then you will practice file input and output using the UTL_FILE and DBMS_OUTPUT packages in the exercises. You can find the answers in Appendix A, "Answers."

Quiz

1. What is the difference between PUT and PUT_LINE with the UTL_FILE package or even the DBMS_OUTPUT package?
2. What is the maximum number of bytes that can be read into a buffer when using UTL_FILE?
3. What is the maximum number of bytes that can be output to a file when using UTL_FILE?
4. When using FCLOSE_ALL, what boolean value will be returned by testing to see if the file is open using IS_OPEN?
5. What suppresses output from PUT or PUT_LINE when using the DBMS_OUTPUT package?
6. What is the maximum number of characters allowed in a buffer line when using DBMS_OUTPUT?
7. What is the maximum number of characters that can possibly be allocated to the buffer when using DBMS_OUTPUT?

Exercises

1. From the code in Listing 18.6, output the data in a fixed block format. The output should be SSNO with a length of 11 bytes formatted as ###-##-####, FirstName at 20 bytes, and LastName at 30 bytes. Remember, VARCHAR2 data does not pad spaces to the right. You could either use a character function to fill the data with spaces or assign the variables to type CHAR before outputting the data. Name the output file PRESFIX.TXT.

2. From Exercise 1, add DBMS_OUTPUT.PUT_LINE to display the lines to the screen as they are output to the file.

18

Day 19

Managing Database Jobs

by Timothy Atwood

As with any production system, Oracle provides a way to handle jobs with the DBMS_JOB package. This package enables you to schedule jobs immediately, or schedule jobs at a precise time and day, which could be monthly, weekly, and so on. This lesson also discusses how to communicate between multiple processes. Today's lesson focuses on

- ☐ The DBMS_JOB package
- ☐ Running a job in the background
- ☐ Running a job immediately
- ☐ Viewing jobs
- ☐ Removing a job
- ☐ Altering a job

☐ Importing and exporting jobs
☐ Working with broken jobs
☐ Using pipes
☐ Public versus private pipes
☐ Using pipe messages

The DBMS_JOB Package

The DBMS_JOB package enables you to submit jobs to a job queue. From the job queue, you can schedule these jobs to execute immediately, or you can specify when to run the jobs and how often to run the jobs. In addition, you can find information on currently executing jobs, broken jobs, the scheduling of jobs, and other pieces of job information. The DBMS_JOB package requires PL/SQL 2.2 or higher. You also need the appropriate privileges to access the DBMS_JOB package.

Background Processes

Instead of utilizing a lot of resources by running the same multiple programs for each user to schedule or run a job, Oracle provides SNP background processes. These processes share common functions and code, which allows them to monitor Oracle processes for possible parallel execution. One key feature of SNP (Snapshot Refresh Process) is that if a job fails, it does not bring down the database as other processes would. In addition, SNP processes monitor jobs at user-specified time intervals, start any jobs that need to be executed, and then wait for the next time interval. You could liken this to grocers monitoring for expired food in the freezer or refrigerator. At night after close (specific time interval), the background process looks for jobs to execute (employees scan for expired food), and if found (expired food found), the job executes (food is discarded), and the process waits to repeat the process again (employees go home and will repeat the same process tomorrow).

Oracle provides up to 10 SNP processes identified as SNP0 through SNP9. The three parameters defined in the INIT.ORA file are listed in Table 19.1.

Table 19.1. SNP parameters.

Parameter	Value Range	Default Value	Description
JOB_QUEUE_PROCESSES	0–10	0	Determines the number of background processes to start for each instance.

Parameter	Value Range	Default Value	Description
JOB_QUEUE_ INTERVAL	1–3600 (seconds)	60	The interval, in seconds, in which the SNP process searches for jobs to execute.
JOB_QUEUE_KEEP_ CONNECTIONS	true, false	false	If true, all database connections are kept open until the job completes. Otherwise, connections are opened and closed as needed.

Each job uses one process; therefore, you cannot have one job executing across multiple processes.

NOTE

If the JOB_QUEUE_PROCESSES parameter is set to 0 (the default), no jobs will execute. Make sure that you have defined this in your INIT.ORA configuration file. I always set this value to 10, which on today's systems, does not greatly affect performance.

Execution of Jobs

There are two methods of job execution—timed by submitting to a job queue, or immediate execution. This section focuses first on submitting jobs on a timed basis to a job queue through the use of the SUBMIT procedure or the ISUBMIT procedure.

Submitting Jobs to the Job Queue with SUBMIT

SUBMIT is used to submit jobs to the job queue.

The Syntax for the SUBMIT Procedure

The format for SUBMIT is

```
PROCEDURE SUBMIT(job_number OUT BINARY_INTEGER,
    job_to_submit IN VARCHAR2,
    next_run IN DATE DEFAULT SYSDATE,
    interval IN VARCHAR2 DEFAULT NULL,
    job_parsing IN BOOLEAN DEFAULT false);
```

SYNTAX

You can review the parameters for SUBMIT in Table 19.2.

Table 19.2. Parameters for SUBMIT.

Parameter	Description
job_number	Job number assigned to the process. The job number will remain the same for as long as the job exists. Only one job number can be assigned to a process.
job_to_submit	This is the PL/SQL code to submit.
next_run	The date when the job will next run.
interval	The time when the job will next run.
job_parsing	If this parameter is set to false, Oracle will parse the job, making sure that all objects exist. If the objects do not yet exist, such as tables that you will create later, set the value to true. The job will then be parsed upon execution, and if the tables still do not exist, it will become a broken job.

Examples of Using SUBMIT

Take a look at some sample listings for submitting jobs. The first listing, Listing 19.1, is a basic submittal of a procedure HELLO. This procedure is a stored procedure, which does not include any arguments.

WARNING

> Listing 19.1 is only a sample procedure and won't execute.

INPUT **Listing 19.1. A simple procedure with SUBMIT.**

```
1: DECLARE
2:      v_JobNum   BINARY_INTEGER;
3: BEGIN
4:      DBMS_JOB.SUBMIT(v_JobNum,'HELLO;',SYSDATE,
5:          'SYSDATE + (1/(24*60*60))');
6: END;
```

ANALYSIS First, the program declares a variable of type BINARY_INTEGER in line 2 to hold the value of the job number assigned to the job. Then it submits the job in line 4 by passing the job number assigned, the PL/SQL code to execute (HELLO), the next date to execute (system date), and the interval (system date executing every minute). You can compute this by multiplying 24 hours in the day by 60 minutes/hour by 60 seconds/minute and then taking the inverse.

The next example calls a stored procedure, which passes three parameters with values of maintenance, 1000, and Friday and will always occur every Friday night at 10:00 p.m. This procedure will launch several jobs for maintenance and then back up the system. Review this procedure in Listing 19.2.

INPUT **Listing 19.2. A more complex approach using SUBMIT.**

```
1: DECLARE
2:      v_JobNum   BINARY_INTEGER;
3: BEGIN
4:      DBMS_JOB.SUBMIT(v_JobNum,'WEEKLY(''maintenance'',1000,
5:          ''Friday'');',SYSDATE,
6:          'NEXT_DAY(TRUNC(SYSDATE),''FRIDAY'') + 22/24');
7: END;
```

 ANALYSIS This process submits a stored procedure called WEEKLY in line 4, which requires three parameters.

NOTE A requirement for the DBMS_JOB package is that all parameters that regularly require a single quote must have two single quotes around each string (see lines 4 and 5). When the string is parsed, one set of single quotes is removed and then sent to the process for handling.

Another different parameter is the interval specified in line 6. These settings guarantee that the job will always run on Friday at precisely 22/24, or 10:00 p.m.

NOTE You could not realistically use SYSDATE + 7 when executing the initial job on Friday to run every Friday. The way SNP processes work is that if the system or network goes down, when the system is brought back up, any jobs that should have executed and didn't will then be processed. So if the network went down on the weekend, the first occurrence would be Monday, and the job would execute every subsequent Monday until the next disturbance occurs.

Submitting Jobs to the Job Queue with ISUBMIT

With SUBMIT, the job number is assigned automatically by Oracle, which keeps track of the last job number assigned and increments this number by one. However, what if you want to assign a specific job number to a process? You can safely do this with ISUBMIT, as long as the job number has not been used!

The Syntax for the ISUBMIT Procedure

The format for ISUBMIT is almost identical to that for SUBMIT:

```
PROCEDURE ISUBMIT(job_number_specified OUT BINARY_INTEGER,
    job_to_submit IN VARCHAR2,
    next_run IN DATE DEFAULT SYSDATE,
    interval IN VARCHAR2 DEFAULT NULL,
    job_parsing IN BOOLEAN DEFAULT false);
```

The only difference is that you specify the job number when calling ISUBMIT. See Listing 19.3 for an example of ISUBMIT.

INPUT   **Listing 19.3. Working with ISUBMIT.**

```
1: BEGIN
2:      DBMS_JOB.ISUBMIT(110,'HELLO;',SYSDATE,'SYSDATE + (1/(24*60*60))');
3: END;
```

ANALYSIS   In this example, the job number is hard-coded to 110 in line 2. You can also set this parameter to a variable for use in manipulation with PL/SQL code, as shown in Listing 19.4.

INPUT   **Listing 19.4. Using ISUBMIT with variables.**

```
1: DECLARE
2:      v_jobnum BINARY_INTEGER := 109;
3: BEGIN
4:      DBMS_JOB.ISUBMIT(v_jobnum,'HELLO;',SYSDATE,
5:          'SYSDATE + (1/(24*60*60))');
6: END;
```

ANALYSIS   The only difference here is declaring the variable v_jobnum, assigning to it a value of 109 in line 2, and then passing this parameter with ISUBMIT in line 4.

Using RUN to Execute Jobs Immediately

You can execute jobs immediately after they have been sent to the job queue by using the RUN procedure.

The Syntax for the RUN Procedure

The format for RUN is

```
PROCEDURE RUN(job_number_specified IN BINARY_INTEGER);
```

19

In order to process this, you must know the job number assigned to the job you want to execute. When the process executes, the next date for the job is reset. The time interval will occur after the run date and time when the job was executed. Again, if you had initially run the job on Friday with a SYSDATE + 7 time interval and you expect the job to run every Friday, and if you now immediately execute this job on Thursday, the job will run every Thursday. Listing 19.5 shows the original submission of the job, and Listing 19.6 shows an example of using RUN.

INPUT

Listing 19.5. Using DBMS_OUTPUT to see the job number assigned.

```
1: DECLARE
2:      v_jobnum BINARY_INTEGER;
3: BEGIN
4:      DBMS_JOB.SUBMIT(v_jobnum,'HELLO;',SYSDATE,
5:           'SYSDATE + (1/(24*60*60))');
6:      DBMS_OUTPUT.ENABLE;
7:      DBMS_OUTPUT.PUT_LINE('Your Job Number assigned is: ' ¦¦ v_jobnum);
8: END;
```

The two lines added allow you to see what job number is assigned to the process you just submitted for execution. In this case, the sample output is

OUTPUT `Your Job Number assigned is: 13`

You can now run the job from Listing 19.6.

INPUT

Listing 19.6. Using RUN to execute the job in the queue immediately.

```
1: BEGIN
2:      DBMS_JOB.RUN(13);
3: END;
```

The code in Listing 19.6 will immediately execute job 13.

The Job Environment

When you submit a job, the following variables are stored within Oracle:

☐ The current user.

☐ The user submitting or altering the job.

19

☐ Current job schemas, such as the job number assigned, and so on. This is reviewed in the section "Viewing Jobs."

☐ MAC privileges (optional).

In addition, the NLS parameters stored in Oracle include

☐ NLS_LANGUAGE

☐ NLS_CURRENCY

☐ NLS_ISO_CURRENCY

☐ NLS_NUMERIC_CHARACTERS

☐ NLS_DATE_FORMAT

☐ NLS_DATE_LANGUAGE

☐ NLS_SORT

When the job is executed, the NLS parameters are restored. You can change these characteristics with the ALTER procedure discussed later in this chapter in the section "Altering a Job."

The Job Owner

As soon as a job is submitted, Oracle records and assigns ownership of the job to the user who submitted the job. Only the owner can change the job, execute the job upon demand, and remove the job from the queue.

The Job Numbers

As previously discussed, Oracle assigns the next sequential job number from the stored value SYS.JOBSEQ. This job number can't be changed or assigned to a different process until the job is removed. You can always specify your own job number with ISUBMIT, but if the job number already exists, your job will not execute. The error you will receive if you attempt to use the same job number is

OUTPUT
```
ERROR at line 1:
ORA-00001: unique constraint (SYS.I_JOB_JOB) violated
ORA-06512: at "SYS.DBMS_JOB", line 105
ORA-06512: at line 2
```

The Job Definition

The job definition is the identifier of the PL/SQL code to execute. This is usually, but not always, a stored procedure. Any parameters that must have the single quote with normal PL/SQL parameters must now be enclosed by two single quotes; otherwise, when Oracle removes the single quotes when processing the job, you will get an invalid parameter. Table 19.3 lists some additional special parameters recognized by Oracle.

Table 19.3. Special job definition parameters.

Parameter	Mode	Description
job	IN	The current job number.
next_date	IN/OUT	The next date for the job to execute. If not specified, the default is SYSDATE.
broken	IN/OUT	Job status: The IN value is always false, and the OUT value is true if broken and false if not.

Some examples of the job definition when submitting a job are

```
'HELLO;'
'paycheck(''FRIDAY'',SYSDATE);'
'sample(''String1'',100,20,''String2'');'
'final_try(''good'',next_date_broken);'
'dbms_job.remove(job);'
```

Viewing Jobs

To view any information about jobs, you can use queries. The three views that display information about jobs in the job queue are shown in Table 19.4.

Table 19.4. Data dictionary views for jobs.

View	Description
DBA_JOBS	Shows all jobs in the database.
DBA_JOBS_RUNNING	Shows all jobs currently running.
USER_JOBS	Shows all jobs owned by the user. PRIV_USER = your user ID.

The view for USER_JOBS and DBA_JOBS has the same structure. At any point in time, you could type

INPUT   `SELECT * from USER_JOBS;`

The preceding command enables you to view all the possible columns. See Table 19.5 for some of the possible columns and meanings.

NOTE

> You will most likely have to reduce your array size by typing SET ARRAYSIZE 10 in order for all the columns to appear on the screen without getting a size/memory error.

Table 19.5. Columns used in views DBA_JOBS and DBA_USERS.

Column Name	Description
JOB	Job number
LOG_USER	User associated with the job
PRIV_USER	User who submitted and owns the job
LAST_DATE	Date of last successful execution
LAST_SEC	Time of last successful execution
THIS_DATE	Date started of currently executing job
THIS_SEC	Time started of currently executing job
NEXT_DATE	Next date job is to be scheduled
NEXT_SEC	Next time job is scheduled
TOTAL_TIME	Total time it took to execute the job, in seconds
BROKEN	Shows Y if the job is broken
WHAT	The WHAT parameter supplied with SUBMIT or ISUBMIT
INTERVAL	Time interval between jobs
FAILURES	Number of times job has started and failed since last successful completion

To see all the available columns (and all jobs currently running), you would type

INPUT   `SELECT * from DBA_JOBS_RUNNING;`

The available columns and descriptions are shown in Table 19.6.

Table 19.6. Columns used in view DBA_JOBS_RUNNING.

Column Name	Description
JOB	Job number
SID	Lists the process executing the job
LAST_DATE	Date of last successful execution

 19

Column Name	Description
LAST_SEC	Time of last successful execution
THIS_SEC	Time started of currently executing job
FAILURES	Number of times job has started and failed since last successful completion

Samples for Viewing Jobs

This section gives some more examples of how to view jobs. The first example in Listing 19.7 will display all the jobs that are currently executing.

INPUT **Listing 19.7. Viewing executing jobs.**

```
SELECT SID,JOB,THIS_SEC,FAILURES from DBA_JOBS_RUNNING;
```

If you want to view information on jobs that you own, use the code in Listing 19.8 to view the process name, job number, and the next date the job will execute.

INPUT **Listing 19.8. Viewing your own jobs.**

```
SELECT JOB,WHAT,NEXT_DATE,FAILURES,BROKEN from USER_JOBS;
```

Job Management

So far, you have focused on creating and viewing jobs. Now, you will learn about a major responsibility of a systems administrator—performing job management. Job management can include removing a job, altering a job, importing and exporting jobs from one database to another, and even fixing broken jobs. You might also need to manage how long a job runs; if a job is taking too long, you might have to review the procedure and either fine-tune it or delegate this task to another Oracle expert.

Removing a Job

If you can submit jobs, you should be able to remove them. Oracle provides the REMOVE procedure, which enables you to remove only jobs that you own.

19

The Syntax for the REMOVE Procedure

The format for the procedure REMOVE is

```
PROCEDURE REMOVE(job_number IN BINARY_INTEGER);
```

NOTE

> You cannot remove a job if the job has started executing. You will have to wait for the job to complete before removing it from the job queue.

Listing 19.9 shows an example of removing a job assigned the number 109.

INPUT **Listing 19.9. Removing a job.**

```
1: BEGIN
2:      DBMS_JOBS.REMOVE(109);
3: END;
```

ANALYSIS After you execute the code, if the job isn't running, job 109 will be removed permanently from the job queue.

Altering a Job

After a job has been submitted, you can change its parameters with the CHANGE procedure. If you want to alter specific parameters of the job, you would use WHAT, NEXT_DATE, or INTERVAL. Again, you can only change jobs that you own; otherwise there would be utter chaos!

The Syntax for Changing Job Parameters

Several possible formats can be used to change job parameters. The first uses the CHANGE procedure:

```
PROCEDURE CHANGE(job_number IN BINARY_INTEGER,
                 process_name IN VARCHAR2,
                 next_run IN DATE,
                 interval IN VARCHAR2 );
```

The second option uses the WHAT procedure:

```
PROCEDURE WHAT(job_number in BINARY_INTEGER,
                 process_name IN VARCHAR2);
```

The third option uses the NEXT_DATE procedure:

```
PROCEDURE NEXT_DATE(job_number IN BINARY_INTEGER,
                         next_run IN DATE);
```

The fourth option uses the INTERVAL procedure:

```
PROCEDURE INTERVAL(job_number IN BINARY_INTEGER,
                        interval IN VARCHAR2 );
```

The procedure CHANGE alters all the job parameters, whereas WHAT, NEXT_DATE, and INTERVAL alter only those specific parameters.

Importing and Exporting Jobs

A nice feature that is provided in the DBMS_JOB package is the ability to import and export jobs from one database to another. However, the job number assigned from the source database will become the job number in the destination database. This is a problem only if the destination database already has a job with the same job number. If there is a conflict with job numbers, simply resubmit the job in the source database with ISUBMIT and assign it a job number not used in the destination database, export the job, and delete the extra job in the source database.

The Syntax for the USER_EXPORT Procedure

The format for USER_EXPORT is

```
PROCEDURE USER_EXPORT(job_number IN BINARY_INTEGER,
                        Destination_database OUT VARCHAR2);
```

Handling Broken Jobs

A broken job is a job that has failed to execute 16 times in a row. Oracle marks this job with a flag in the BROKEN column and stores the value true in the column. The only way this job will execute is if you

- ☐ Use DBMS_JOB.RUN to execute the job.
- ☐ Change the flag in the BROKEN column to a status of fixed, where BROKEN is equal to false.

The section "Using RUN to Execute Jobs Immediately" has already covered how to run a job.

The Syntax for the BROKEN Procedure

To mark a job as fixed with the BROKEN procedure, the syntax is

```
PROCEDURE BROKEN(job_number IN BINARY_INTEGER,
                        broken_status IN BOOLEAN,
                        next_date IN DATE DEFAULT SYSDATE);
```

19

Listing 19.10 shows how to start a broken job running.

INPUT **Listing 19.10. Starting a broken job.**

```
1: BEGIN
2:      DBMS_JOBS.BROKEN(109,false,SYSDATE + 7);
3: END;
```

ANALYSIS This job will now execute in one week. You could also mark a valid job as broken by the code in Listing 19.11.

INPUT **Listing 19.11. Creating a broken job.**

```
1: BEGIN
2:      DBMS_JOBS.BROKEN(109,true);
3: END;
```

Hands-On Practice in Job Management

You will now run through a long exercise to demonstrate some of the concepts learned today. You will practice creating a few procedures, submitting the jobs, immediately executing the jobs, viewing jobs, altering a job, and removing a job.

Creating Procedures to Submit as Jobs

Before you can really get started, go ahead and enter and then execute the three procedures in Listings 19.12 through 19.14. After creating these procedures, you will be able to submit them as jobs to test the DBMS_JOB package. The procedure in Listing 19.12 displays "Hello World!" to the screen. Listing 19.13 writes "Hello World!" to a file and adds the current system time and date when the procedure executes. Listing 19.14 accesses the same file as Listing 19.13, adds "Hello Again for the Second Time!," and adds the current system time and date when the procedure executes.

INPUT **Listing 19.12. Displaying "Hello World!" to the screen.**

```
1: CREATE OR REPLACE PROCEDURE HELLO AS
2: BEGIN
3:      DBMS_OUTPUT.PUT_LINE('Hello World! ' ||
4:          TO_CHAR(SYSDATE,'MM-DD-YY HH:MI:SS AM'));
5: END;
```

19

INPUT ## Listing 19.13. Writing "Hello World!" to a file.

```
 1: CREATE OR REPLACE PROCEDURE HELLOFLE IS
 2:
 3: --DECLARE
 4: -- Create a file handle of type UTL_FILE.FILE_TYPE
 5:     v_MyFileHandle UTL_FILE.FILE_TYPE;
 6: BEGIN
 7: -- Open the file to write.
 8:     v_MyFileHandle := UTL_FILE.FOPEN('C:\','HELLO.TXT','a');
 9:     UTL_FILE.PUT_LINE(v_MyFileHandle,
10:         'Hello World! ' || TO_CHAR(SYSDATE,'MM-DD-YY HH:MI:SS AM'));
11:
12: -- Close the file handle which points to myout.txt
13:     UTL_FILE.FCLOSE(v_MyFileHandle);
14: EXCEPTION
15: -- Create Exception to simply display error code and message
16:     WHEN OTHERS THEN
17:         DBMS_OUTPUT.PUT_LINE
18:             ('ERROR ' || TO_CHAR(SQLCODE) || SQLERRM);
19:         NULL;
20: END;
```

INPUT ## Listing 19.14. Another process accessing the same file.

```
 1: CREATE OR REPLACE PROCEDURE SHAREFLE IS
 2:
 3: --DECLARE
 4: -- Create a file handle of type UTL_FILE.FILE_TYPE
 5:     v_MyFileHandle UTL_FILE.FILE_TYPE;
 6: BEGIN
 7: -- Open the file to write.
 8:     v_MyFileHandle := UTL_FILE.FOPEN('C:\','HELLO.TXT','a');
 9:     UTL_FILE.PUT_LINE(v_MyFileHandle,
10:         'Hello Again for the Second Time! ' ||
11:             TO_CHAR(SYSDATE,'MM-DD-YY HH:MI:SS AM'));
12: -- Close the file handle which points to myout.txt
13:     UTL_FILE.FCLOSE(v_MyFileHandle);
14: EXCEPTION
15: -- Create Exception to simply display error code and message
16:     WHEN OTHERS THEN
17:         DBMS_OUTPUT.PUT_LINE
18:             ('ERROR ' || TO_CHAR(SQLCODE) || SQLERRM);
19:         NULL;
20: END;
```

19

WARNING

Make sure that utl_file_dir = *; is in the INIT.ORA file; otherwise, you will get a USER_EXCEPTION error.

Submitting All Jobs to the Job Queue

You can submit all three jobs at once to the job queue with the code in Listing 19.15.

INPUT **Listing 19.15. Submitting all three jobs at once.**

```
 1: DECLARE
 2:      v_jobnum BINARY_INTEGER;
 3: BEGIN
 4:      DBMS_JOB.SUBMIT(v_JobNum,'HELLO;',SYSDATE,
 5:          'SYSDATE + (1/(24*60*60))');
 6:      DBMS_OUTPUT.ENABLE;
 7:      DBMS_OUTPUT.PUT_LINE('Your Job Number assigned to hello is: '
 8:          ||v_jobnum);
 9:      DBMS_JOB.SUBMIT(v_JobNum,'hellofle;',SYSDATE,
10:          'SYSDATE + (1/(24*60*60))');
11:      DBMS_OUTPUT.PUT_LINE('Your Job Number assigned to hellofle is: '
12:          ||v_jobnum);
13:      DBMS_JOB.ISUBMIT(109,'sharefle;',SYSDATE,'SYSDATE +
14:          (1/(24*60*60))');
15:      DBMS_OUTPUT.PUT_LINE('Your Job Number assigned to
16:          sharefle is: 109');
17: END;
```

OUTPUT The output should look similar to

```
Your Job Number assigned to hello is: 24
Your Job Number assigned to hellofle is: 25
Your Job Number assigned to sharefle is: 109
```

Running All Three Jobs Immediately

Because I have no patience, let's submit all three jobs immediately in Listing 19.16. Before you execute the code, make sure that you have typed SET SERVEROUTPUT ON and pressed Enter at the SQL*Plus prompt.

INPUT **Listing 19.16. Submitting all three jobs at once.**

```
1: BEGIN
2: --Make sure you enter the job numbers assigned for the first two jobs
3:      DBMS_JOB.RUN(24);
4:      DBMS_JOB.RUN(25);
5:      DBMS_JOB.RUN(109);
6: END;
```

OUTPUT Your output should look similar to

```
Hello World! 06-22-97 09:37:42 PM
```

Viewing Information About the Jobs

You can now view information about your jobs. Type the code in Listing 19.17.

INPUT **Listing 19.17. Viewing information on your jobs.**

```
SELECT JOB,WHAT,LAST_SEC,INTERVAL from USER_JOBS;
```

OUTPUT Your output should look similar to

```
JOB
--------
WHAT
--------------------------------
LAST_SEC
--------
INTERVAL
--------------------------------
        24
HELLO;
21:57:43
SYSDATE + (1/(24*60*60))

        25
hellofle;
21:57:43
SYSDATE + (1/(24*60*60))

       109
sharefle;
21:57:43
SYSDATE + (1/(24*60*60))
```

Altering the Job Running the Procedure HELLO

Listing 19.18 demonstrates modifying the Hello file to execute from once every minute to once per week from the current date. Remember, as background processes, you will not see "Hello World!" on the screen, but the job is still running and can be verified by running a query against USER_JOBS.

INPUT **Listing 19.18. Altering the HELLO process to run once per week.**

```
1: BEGIN
2: -- Enter your job number assigned!
3:     DBMS_JOB.INTERVAL(24,'SYSDATE + 7');
4: END;
```

19

You can now see if the modification truly was successful by executing the query from Listing 19.17. Your output should look similar to

OUTPUT
```
JOB
--------
WHAT
-----------------------------
LAST_SEC
--------
INTERVAL
-----------------------------
        24
HELLO;
21:57:43
SYSDATE + 7

        25
hellofle;
21:57:43
SYSDATE + (1/(24*60*60))

       109
sharefle;
21:57:43
SYSDATE + (1/(24*60*60))
```

ANALYSIS Notice that the Hello file's time interval reflects SYSDATE + 7! You have successfully altered the interval.

Removing the Hello Job

Listing 19.19 demonstrates removing the Hello job.

INPUT ### Listing 19.19. Removing the Hello job from the queue.

```
1: BEGIN
2: -- Enter your job number assigned!
3:     DBMS_JOB.REMOVE(24);
4: END;
```

To verify it, execute the code in Listing 19.20.

INPUT ### Listing 19.20. Verifying the job removal.

```
SELECT JOB from USER_JOBS;
```

OUTPUT Your output should look similar to

```
JOB
--------
        25
       109
```

ANALYSIS Notice that you now have only two jobs. By the way, if you look at the file `C:\HELLO.TXT`, it should look similar to

OUTPUT
```
Hello World! 06-22-97 09:37:42 PM
Hello Again for the Second Time! 06-22-97 09:37:42 PM
Hello World! 06-22-97 09:38:35 PM
Hello Again for the Second Time! 06-22-97 09:38:35 PM
Hello World! 06-22-97 09:38:36 PM
Hello Again for the Second Time! 06-22-97 09:38:36 PM
Hello World! 06-22-97 09:39:36 PM
Hello Again for the Second Time! 06-22-97 09:39:36 PM
Hello World! 06-22-97 09:39:37 PM
Hello Again for the Second Time! 06-22-97 09:39:37 PM
Hello World! 06-22-97 09:40:38 PM
Hello Again for the Second Time! 06-22-97 09:40:38 PM
Hello World! 06-22-97 09:40:38 PM
Hello Again for the Second Time! 06-22-97 09:40:38 PM
Hello World! 06-22-97 09:41:38 PM
Hello Again for the Second Time! 06-22-97 09:41:38 PM
Hello World! 06-22-97 09:41:38 PM
Hello Again for the Second Time! 06-22-97 09:41:38 PM
Hello World! 06-22-97 09:42:39 PM
Hello Again for the Second Time! 06-22-97 09:42:39 PM
Hello World! 06-22-97 09:42:39 PM
Hello Again for the Second Time! 06-22-97 09:42:39 PM
Hello World! 06-22-97 09:43:40 PM
Hello Again for the Second Time! 06-22-97 09:43:40 PM
Hello World! 06-22-97 09:43:40 PM
Hello Again for the Second Time! 06-22-97 09:43:40 PM
Hello World! 06-22-97 09:44:40 PM
```

Your output might be a lot longer, depending on when you view this file. Notice that the two procedures HELLOFLE and SHAREFLE are appending to HELLO.TXT the phrase and the date and time every minute.

The DBMS_PIPE Package

The DBMS_PIPE package enables you to communicate between multiple sessions in the same database instance. You communicate by sending and receiving messages over the pipe. When you send a message, this is referred to as a *writer*. When you receive a message, this is referred to as a *reader*. Each pipe can have one or more writers and one or more readers. Pipes can be accessed by anyone who has access to the database instance, has access to the pipe, and can execute PL/SQL code.

One key feature of pipes is that they are asynchronous. You can access a pipe without having to use COMMIT. In addition, the ROLLBACK command does not work with pipes. This fact allows you to use pipes as a powerful debugging tool, as well as using pipes as an audit trail.

19

NOTE

If you receive error messages when trying to work with pipes, this means one of two things. Either you do not have access to the DBMS_PIPE package, or the package has not been installed. If you need access, contact the system administrator who should then grant you permissions to the EXECUTE ANY PROCEDURE privilege. For Personal Oracle 95 users, to install the package, you must sign as SYS, with the password CHANGE_ON_INSTALL, and then execute @c:\ORAWIN95\RDBS73\ADMIN\CATPROC.SQL.

Public Versus Private Pipes

In PL/SQL version 2.2, private pipes were added. All earlier versions supported public pipes, which could be accessed by anyone in the database instance as long as the name of the pipe was known by the user and the user had EXECUTE access to DBMS_PIPE. Now you can create private pipes, which can be accessed only by

☐ DBAs

☐ The creator of the pipe

☐ Any stored procedure created by the owner

You would use private pipes in cases such as running three modules of a job simultaneously that need to share data without being interrupted. Another possibility is to use the private pipes as an audit trail or debugging tool. Public pipes would be used for projects to which everyone needs access.

Steps in Using Pipes

The following steps demonstrate the order in which pipes operate:

☐ If you are creating a private pipe, you first issue the CREATE_PIPE function.

☐ Whether the pipe is public or private, you send the data you want to transmit to a pipe to the message buffer by issuing the PACK_MESSAGE procedure. You are limited to 4096 bytes in the message buffer area.

☐ Before the buffer is overfilled, you should then issue the SEND_MESSAGE function to send the data to the pipe. If you are creating a public pipe, SEND_MESSAGE will create the pipe by default.

☐ When you are ready to receive data, you first call the RECEIVE_MESSAGE function. Each time the function is called, it will read the first unread message in the pipe, and dump it into the message buffer. Every time you want to extract the next message, you need to call RECEIVE_MESSAGE. If you need to know the datatype, because it could vary, you call the function NEXT_ITEM_TYPE.

☐ You can now use UNPACK_MESSAGE to interpret the message.

Of course, at any time, multiple sessions can be writing to the same pipe, and multiple sessions can be reading from the same pipe. A great application use, especially for multiple processor servers, would be an application for student registration. Two or more terminals can use the same form to send data to the same pipe concerning registration of students. The pipe can be read by multiple sessions to then process the records as each one comes across the pipe to process the records much faster. In return, you can send triggers, which can also use pipes if the enrollment gets too large.

By default, pipes will retain the information for up to 1,000 days. The constant is defined in Oracle as

```
Maxwait CONSTANT INTEGER := 86400000;
```

The constant is expressed in seconds, so 60 seconds/minute * 60 minutes/hour * 24 hours/ day * 1000 days = 8,640,000 seconds. Of course, you could change the default to increase or decrease the time the pipe will retain the data.

When naming a pipe, there are some naming conventions you should follow. You should never begin a pipe name with ORA$, which is reserved for use by Oracle. The pipe name can be up to 128 characters. Also, you should make sure that the pipe name is always unique. When in doubt, assign the name of the pipe to an Oracle-defined name by using the function UNIQUE_SESSION_NAME.

You can change the pipe size from the default of 8192 bytes. You still have to deal with a 4096-byte limitation on the message buffer.

Table 19.7 lists all functions and procedures used with the DBMS_PIPE package.

Table 19.7. DBMS_PIPE functions and procedures.

Name	Type	Description
CREATE_PIPE	Function	Primarily used to create a private pipe, but can be used to create a public pipe.
NEXT_ITEM_TYPE	Function	Extracts the datatype of the next item in the message buffer. Used primarily with unpacking the message received.
PACK_MESSAGE	Procedure	Sends data to the message buffer to eventually be sent to the pipe.
PURGE	Procedure	Removes all data from the pipe.
RECEIVE_MESSAGE	Function	Receives message from pipe and writes to message buffer.
REMOVE_PIPE	Function	Deletes the pipe from memory.

continues

19

Table 19.7. continued

Name	Type	Description
RESET_BUFFER	Procedure	Clears the data from the message buffer.
SEND_MESSAGE	Function	Sends all data from the message buffer to the pipe specified. If the pipe does not exist, it is created as a public pipe.
UNIQUE_SESSION_NAME	Function	Returns unique session name.
UNPACK_MESSAGE	Procedure	Retrieves the next item from the message buffer.

The Functions and Procedures of DBMS_PIPE

This section discusses the functions and procedures in more detail, including the syntax and another complete hands-on example for passing data back and forth between pipes.

The CREATE_PIPE Function

As stated earlier, you primarily need the CREATE_PIPE function to create private pipes.

The Syntax for the CREATE_PIPE Function

The syntax for the CREATE_PIPE function is

```
FUNCTION CREATE_PIPE(name_of_pipe IN VARCHAR2,
                     pipesize IN INTEGER DEFAULT 8192,
                     private IN BOOLEAN DEFAULT true);
RETURN INTEGER; -- Status on pipe creation
```

name_of_pipe is the name you will assign to the pipe. The next parameter is pipesize, which is the maximum size of the pipe. The default is 8192 bytes, which can be changed to the size desired. The private parameter simply states whether the pipe is private or public based upon the BOOLEAN value passed. The value should be false for public and true for private. Remember, by calling SEND_MESSAGE, you do not have to use CREATE_PIPE to create a public pipe!

An example of creating a private pipe is simply

```
v_status := DBMS_PIPE.CREATE_PIPE('mypipe');
```

You just created a pipe with a maximum size of 8192 bytes, which is also private (default of true). Remember, this is a function with a return type of status.

To create the public pipe, the code would look similar to

```
v_status := DBMS_PIPE.CREATE_PIPE('itpublic',8192,false);
```

You now have a public pipe called itpublic with a size of 8192 bytes.

If the return value (this example uses the variable v_status) is zero, the pipe was successfully created. If the user does not have access rights to create a pipe, or the pipe name exists, the ORA-23322 exception is raised.

The PACK_MESSAGE Procedure

After a pipe is created (or will be created with SEND_MESSAGE for public pipes), you can send data to the message buffer for later transmittal to the pipe using the PACK_MESSAGE procedure. Because the function is overloaded, you can send a datatype of VARCHAR2, DATE, or NUMBER.

The Syntax for the PACK_MESSAGE Procedure

The format for PACK_MESSAGE is

```
PROCEDURE PACK_MESSAGE(data IN VARCHAR2);
PROCEDURE PACK_MESSAGE(data IN DATE);
PROCEDURE PACK_MESSAGE(data IN NUMBER);
```

data is the data that you are sending to the buffer. Remember that the buffer has only 4096 bytes available for use. If you go over this limitation, you will receive the following error:

OUTPUT
```
ORA-06558 buffer in DBMS_PIPE package is full.
No more items allowed.
```

Using the SEND_MESSAGE Function

Before you overflow your message buffer, you should send the data to the pipe with the SEND_MESSAGE function. This function moves the data in the message buffer to the pipe specified from the function call.

The Syntax for the SEND_MESSAGE Function

The format for the function SEND_MESSAGE is

```
FUNCTION SEND_MESSAGE(name_of_pipe IN VARCHAR2,
                      timeout IN INTEGER DEFAULT maxwait,
                      pipesize IN INTEGER DEFAULT 8192);
RETURN INTEGER;
```

name_of_pipe is the name of the pipe already in existence, whether private or public. If no pipe of this name exists, Oracle will create one upon successful execution of SEND_MESSAGE. timeout is how long it will attempt to place the message in the pipe, in seconds. The default is 1000 days. Finally, because you can create a public pipe on execution, you should be able to control the size of the pipe.

The SEND_MESSAGE values are listed in Table 19.8.

Table 19.8. Return values from SEND_MESSAGE.

Return Code	Meaning
0	The message was sent successfully.
1	The maximum wait time has been exceeded while waiting for some room to clear from the pipe from the RECEIVE_MESSAGE function.
3	The message being sent was interrupted.

19

You should use these return codes for proper error checking and error handling.

Using the RECEIVE_MESSAGE Function

The RECEIVE_MESSAGE function moves a message from the pipe to the message buffer. Then the datatype can be identified with NEXT_ITEM_TYPE, or you could use UNPACK_MESSAGE to read the message buffer and use in your process.

The Syntax for the RECEIVE_MESSAGE Function

The format for RECEIVE_MESSAGE is

```
FUNCTION RECEIVE_MESSAGE(name_of_pipe IN VARCHAR2,
                    timeout IN INTEGER DEFAULT maxwait);
RETURN INTEGER;
```

name_of_pipe is the name of the pipe already in existence. *timeout* is how long it will attempt to read the next line from the pipe if there are no current messages in the pipe. The possible return codes are listed in Table 19.9.

Table 19.9. Return values from RECEIVE_MESSAGE.

Return Code	Meaning
0	The message was received successfully.
1	The maximum wait time has been exceeded while waiting for a message to be sent to the pipe.
2	The message in the pipe is too big for the message buffer. This should never occur because both SEND_MESSAGE and RECEIVE_MESSAGE buffers are limited to the same length of 4096 bytes.
3	The message being received was interrupted.

The UNPACK_MESSAGE Procedure

After you have received a message in the buffer, you need to move the message from the buffer into a variable. This is done through the use of the UNPACK_MESSAGE procedure. As with the PACK_MESSAGE procedure, the UNPACK_MESSAGE procedure is overloaded, and can accept such datatypes as VARCHAR2, DATE, and NUMBER.

The Syntax for the UNPACK_MESSAGE Procedure

The syntax of the procedure is

```
PROCEDURE UNPACK_MESSAGE(data OUT VARCHAR2);
PROCEDURE UNPACK_MESSAGE(data OUT DATE);
PROCEDURE UNPACK_MESSAGE(data OUT NUMBER);
```

data is the data that you are receiving from the message buffer. You can receive two possible errors when trying to unpack the message, which are

```
ORA-06556 the pipe is empty, cannot fulfill the UNPACK_MESSAGE request
ORA-06559 wrong datatype requested, datatype, actual datatype is datatype
```

Both can be handled through error message handlers. The first error occurs when you try to read the message buffer, which is empty. The second error message says that the datatype that you are requesting is a different datatype than the one stored in the pipe. You would most likely not have this problem if the datatype in the pipe is always the same, but if it can vary, you would use the NEXT_ITEM_TYPE function to determine the datatype of the next item in the buffer before you retrieve it.

The format for NEXT_ITEM_TYPE function is

```
FUNCTION NEXT_ITEM_TYPE RETURN INTEGER;
```

There are no parameters required to send to the function. It returns a value of the datatype, which is listed in Table 19.10.

Table 19.10. Return datatype definitions from NEXT_ITEM_TYPE.

Return Code	Description
0	No more items
6	NUMBER
9	VARCHAR2
11	ROWID
12	DATE
13	RAW

You can use the NEXT_ITEM_TYPE function for exception handling for no data in the pipe, as well as for determining the type of data being passed to you from the message buffer. This can easily be implemented with a series of IF...ELSIF statements.

The REMOVE_PIPE Function

After you no longer need a pipe, you can either wait for the system to eventually delete the pipe, or you can use the REMOVE_PIPE function.

The Syntax for the REMOVE_PIPE Function

The syntax for the function is

```
FUNCTION REMOVE_PIPE(name_of_pipe IN VARCHAR2);
RETURN INTEGER; -- Status on pipe deletion
```

The return value is 0 whether the pipe exists or not. The only exception you will receive is ORA-23322, which means that you don't have access to remove the pipe. When a pipe is removed, all messages stored in the pipe are also deleted.

An Example of Using Pipes

This section demonstrates the use of pipes by creating both a public and a private pipe and then extracting the data from both pipes and displaying it to the screen.

Creating Public and Private Pipes

To create the public and private pipes, enter and execute the code in Listing 19.21. Before you execute the code, make sure that you type SET SERVEROUTPUT ON to see output from the DBMS_OUTPUT package.

INPUT   **Listing 19.21. Creating pipes.**

```
 1: DECLARE
 2:      v_statpipe1 integer; -- Status for private pipe
 3:      v_statpipe2 integer; -- Status for public pipe created on-the-fly
 4:      v_pubchar VARCHAR2(100) := 'This is a text string';
 5:      v_pubdate DATE := SYSDATE;
 6:      v_pubnum NUMBER := 109;
 7: BEGIN
 8: -- Creates Private Pipe
 9:      v_statpipe1 := DBMS_PIPE.CREATE_PIPE('myprivatepipe');
10: -- If the pipe was successfully created
11:      IF (v_statpipe1 = 0) THEN
12:          DBMS_PIPE.PACK_MESSAGE('privateline1');
13:          DBMS_PIPE.PACK_MESSAGE('privateline2');
14: -- Send Message Buffer to Private Pipe
15:          v_statpipe1 := DBMS_PIPE.SEND_MESSAGE('myprivatepipe');
16:      END IF;
17:
18:      DBMS_PIPE.PACK_MESSAGE(v_pubchar); -- sends datatype VARCHAR2
19:      DBMS_PIPE.PACK_MESSAGE(v_pubdate); -- sends datatype DATE
20:      DBMS_PIPE.PACK_MESSAGE(v_pubnum);  -- sends datatype NUMBER
21: --Creates public pipe and sends message buffer to the pipe
22:      v_statpipe2 := DBMS_PIPE.SEND_MESSAGE('mypublicpipe');
23: --Check status of both pipes to make sure they're 0 (created properly)
24:      DBMS_OUTPUT.PUT_LINE('The Status of your Private Pipe is: ' ||
25:          v_statpipe1 );
26:      DBMS_OUTPUT.PUT_LINE('The Status of your Public Pipe is: ' ||
27:          v_statpipe2 );
28:
29: END;
```

After the code has executed, if you have all permissions to the DBMS_PIPE package, then you should see the following output:

```
The Status of your Private Pipe is: 0
The Status of your Public Pipe is: 0
```

In this example, the program first creates a private pipe called myprivatepipe in line 9. It then sends two messages of type VARCHAR2 to the message buffer and then uses SEND_MESSAGE in line 15 to output the buffer to the pipe. The only error checking done here is to make sure that the private pipe is created properly in line 11. Ideally, you should check for overflows of the message buffer and whether the data was sent to the pipe (pipe not full, and so on).

The program then sends more data to the message buffer of type VARCHAR2, DATE, and NUMBER in lines 18 through 20, and upon execution of SEND_MESSAGE in line 22, it creates the public pipe mypublicpipe. The DBMS_OUTPUT package will then display the status of the newly created pipes in lines 24 through 27.

Reading Data from the Pipes

You can now prepare to read data from both pipes. Enter and execute the code in Listing 19.22. Again, make sure that you have typed SET SERVEROUTPUT ON for proof that the pipes worked.

Listing 19.22. Reading data from the private and public pipe.

```
 1: DECLARE
 2:     v_statpipe1 integer; -- status of private pipe
 3:     v_statpipe2 integer; -- status of public pipe
 4:     v_holdtype INTEGER; -- holds status of next item type
 5:     v_holdchar VARCHAR2(100);
 6:     v_holddate DATE;
 7:     v_holdnum NUMBER;
 8: BEGIN
 9: -- start procedure of getting message from private pipe
10:     v_statpipe1 := DBMS_PIPE.RECEIVE_MESSAGE('myprivatepipe',15);
11:     DBMS_PIPE.UNPACK_MESSAGE(v_holdchar);
12:     DBMS_OUTPUT.PUT_LINE(v_holdchar);--display 1st datatype from msg
13:     DBMS_PIPE.UNPACK_MESSAGE(v_holdchar);
14:     DBMS_OUTPUT.PUT_LINE(v_holdchar);--display 2nd datatype from msg
15:
16: -- start procedure of getting message from public pipe
17:     v_statpipe2 := DBMS_PIPE.RECEIVE_MESSAGE('mypublicpipe',10);
18:     LOOP
19:         v_holdtype := DBMS_PIPE.NEXT_ITEM_TYPE;
20:         IF v_holdtype = 0 THEN EXIT;
21:         ELSIF v_holdtype = 6 THEN
22:             DBMS_PIPE.UNPACK_MESSAGE(v_holdnum);
23:         ELSIF v_holdtype = 9 THEN
24:             DBMS_PIPE.UNPACK_MESSAGE(v_holdchar);
25:         ELSIF v_holdtype = 12 THEN
26:             DBMS_PIPE.UNPACK_MESSAGE(v_holddate);
27:         END IF;
```

19

continues

Listing 19.22. continued

```
28:      END LOOP;
29: -- display all three types of data
30:      DBMS_OUTPUT.PUT_LINE(v_holdchar || ' ' || v_holddate || ' '
31:         || v_holdnum);
32: END;
```

If the code executed with no errors, then your output will look similar to

```
privateline1
privateline2
This is a text string 24-JUN-97 109
```

ANALYSIS This example shows how you can write different code that performs the same function. Because you know that the private pipe has only two lines in the message buffer, you can use two UNPACK_MESSAGE statements in a row to retrieve the information. Because only one variable is holding the data, you use DBMS_OUTPUT to display the information to the screen before it is overwritten.

You can now retrieve the information from the public pipe. However, I am assuming that you do not know what datatype is in the message buffer or how many items are in the buffer. (I do make an assumption improperly when displaying the final results with DBMS_OUTPUT because I display only one of each datatype because I sent to the pipe one of each datatype. Proper coding would correct this.) You first read the message from the pipe and store this into the message buffer. You then execute a continuous loop until no more data is found in the pipe (NEXT_ITEM_TYPE = 0). I use IF...ELSIF to assign the appropriate datatype to the appropriate variable—no guesswork here.

☐ If the return type is 6, it is of type NUMBER.

☐ If the return type is 9, it is of type VARCHAR2.

☐ If the return type is 12, it is of type DATE.

☐ If the return type is 0, EXIT because no more data!

The loop ends and prints to screen the three datatypes initially sent on the CREATE procedure.

NOTE One more point I would like to make is the use of parameters with both RECEIVE_MESSAGE statements. I wait 10 to 15 seconds for a response before I give up. I would not want to tie up resources for the default of 1000 days!

Removing the Pipe

You can free up resources by removing the pipes. Enter and execute the code in Listing 19.23.

INPUT **Listing 19.23. Removing both pipes.**

```
 1: DECLARE
 2:     v_stat NUMBER ;
 3: BEGIN
 4:     v_stat := dbms_pipe.remove_pipe('myprivatepipe');
 5:     DBMS_OUTPUT.PUT_LINE('The status for removing the
 6:         private pipe is: ' ¦¦ v_stat);
 7:     v_stat := dbms_pipe.remove_pipe('mypublicpipe');
 8:     DBMS_OUTPUT.PUT_LINE('The status for removing the
 9:         public pipe is: '¦¦ v_stat);
10: END;
```

Your output should look similar to

OUTPUT
```
The status for removing the private pipe is: 0
The status for removing the public pipe is: 0
```

Other Pipe Functions and Procedures

Several other functions and procedures are available for use with the DBMS_PIPE package. These functions and procedures include PACK_MESSAGE_RAW, UNPACK_MESSAGE_RAW, PACK_MESSAGE_ROW_ID, UNPACK_MESSAGE_ROW_ID, RESET_BUFFER, PURGE, and UNIQUE_SESSION_NAME.

PACK_MESSAGE_RAW

When writing data to the message buffer, there was no provision to handle RAW data. The PACK_MESSAGE_RAW function enables you to process RAW data.

The Syntax for the PACK_MESSAGE_RAW Procedure

The format for the procedure is

```
PROCEDURE PACK_MESSAGE_RAW(data IN VARCHAR2);
```

You still have the limitation of 4096 bytes for the message buffer size; therefore, you cannot use the LONG RAW datatype.

UNPACK_MESSAGE_RAW

Because you can send the RAW datatype, in order to decode the RAW datatype from the message buffer, you will use UNPACK_MESSAGE_RAW.

The Syntax for the UNPACK_MESSAGE_RAW Procedure

The syntax for the procedure is

```
PROCEDURE UNPACK_MESSAGE_RAW(data OUT VARCHAR2);
```

PACK_MESSAGE_ROWID

You can send the ROWID datatype to the message buffer, which is ultimately sent to the pipe by using the PACK_MESSAGE_ROWID procedure.

The Syntax for the PACK_MESSAGE_ROWID Procedure

The syntax of the procedure is

```
PROCEDURE PACK_MESSAGE_ROWID(data IN VARCHAR2);
```

Again, don't forget the 4096-byte message buffer limitation.

UNPACK_MESSAGE_ROWID

In order to decode the information from the pipe, you would use the UNPACK_MESSAGE_ROWID procedure.

The Syntax for the UNPACK_MESSAGE_ROWID Procedure

The format for the UNPACK_MESSAGE_ROWID procedure is

```
PROCEDURE UNPACK_MESSAGE_ROWID(data OUT VARCHAR2);
```

RESET_BUFFER

If you ever need to clear the message buffer, such as when an exception is raised, you can do so with the RESET_BUFFER procedure. The format of the RESET_BUFFER procedure is as follows:

```
PROCEDURE RESET_BUFFER;
```

PURGE

PURGE enables you to remove all data in the pipe specified, which is useful if you need to clear the pipes before processing data to the pipes. It's also useful if an error occurs and you need to reset the pipes.

The Syntax for the PURGE Procedure

The format for the procedure is

```
PROCEDURE PURGE(name_of_pipe IN VARCHAR2);
```

UNIQUE_SESSION_NAME

If you are worried that the name of a pipe could exist, you could always assign the name of the pipe to the function UNIQUE_SESSION_NAME, which will provide a name for the pipe that is not used in Oracle. The format for the UNIQUE_SESSION_NAME function is as follows:

```
FUNCTION UNIQUE_SESSION_NAME RETURN VARCHAR2;
```

The function will return a unique name, which can be assigned to the name of the pipe with a length up to 30 bytes.

Other Uses for Pipes

Although you can use pipes for parallel processing in multiple processor environments, use pipes for an audit trail, or just use pipes to debug processes, you can also use third-generation languages to communicate with database procedures through pipes.

You can refer to the *Oracle Server Applications Guide* in the documentation for some examples of C code communicating with Oracle pipes.

Summary

Today you learned how to work with the DBMS_JOB package in Oracle. This package handles all jobs by using background processes to check for jobs to execute at a specific interval, which are placed in job queues. In order to submit a job for processing, you must still submit the job to the queue first. After a job is submitted, the owner can only change the parameters. The owner can also fix any of his broken jobs as well as remove only his own jobs from the queue. You can also import and export jobs from one database to the next. Always remember that the job number is unique, and any attempt to use the same job number will result in a failure of the job to execute.

Q&A

Q Can jobs be executed immediately without being sent to the job queue?

A No. All jobs must be submitted to a job queue, and then you can use DBMS_JOB.RUN to execute the job immediately. The job will then return to executing at its scheduled time interval.

Q What is the difference between SUBMIT and ISUBMIT?

A ISUBMIT enables you to assign your job numbers, provided that the job number is not being used in the system.

Q Which parameters can be altered in the job?

A All the parameters can be altered in a job. You can use CHANGE to alter all of them immediately or use specific procedures such as WHAT, NEXT_DATE, or INTERVAL.

19

Q Who can remove or alter a job?

A Only the owner of the job can alter or remove the job.

Q What can be done about a broken job?

A You could either use RUN to execute the job immediately or use the BROKEN procedure to reschedule the job. If needed, you could also delete the job with REMOVE.

Q When submitting a job, what punctuation should be used around regular procedure parameters?

A Any parameters that normally are surrounded by a single quote (') must be surrounded by two single quotes (''); otherwise, the job will never execute.

Q What are the steps to send data to the pipe?

A Create the pipe (if private), then send the data to the message buffer with PACK_MESSAGE, and then finally, send the message buffer to the pipe with SEND_MESSAGE.

Q What are the steps to receive data from the pipe?

A Retrieve the message from the pipe into the message buffer with RETRIEVE_MESSAGE. Then you would use UNPACK_MESSAGE to retrieve all data from the message you just received.

Workshop

You can now test your knowledge of the DBMS_JOB and DBMS_PIPE packages, starting with a quick quiz. You can then practice with several short exercises. You can find the answers in Appendix A, "Answers."

Quiz

1. If the server goes down for two days (Monday to Tuesday), and a job with an execution of SYSDATE + 7 was supposed to run when the server went down (Tuesday), will the job always run on the original day of the week (run every Tuesday)?

2. Why must you use two single quotes around parameters specified in SUBMIT that used to take only one set of single quotes?

3. Can you alter someone else's job?

4. Is there any way to assign your own job number to a job?

5. What interval would you use to run a procedure every hour on the hour starting from the current date?

6. If you send a message to a full pipe, how long will you wait before you abort the process?

7. What is the maximum length of the message buffer?

Exercises

1. Write the code to submit a procedure called PAYDAY, where the parameters are FRIDAY, Bi_Monthly, and 6. The job should always execute at 4 a.m. on Saturday.

2. Write the code to view the JOB, last second run, and WHAT from USER_JOBS.

3. Write the code to submit job 200 once per day starting from SYSDATE for the procedure EASY, which has no parameters.

4. Write the code to alter job 200 to execute once per week for the interval (SYSDATE + 7).

5. Write the code to remove job 200.

6. From Listing 19.22, add the ELSIF procedures to handle RAW and ROWID datatypes.

7. From Listing 19.22, all data read into the public pipe should be inserted into a table called PIPETAB with the following schema: MyString VARCHAR2, MyDate DATE, and MyNum NUMBER. Make sure that you run the CREATE_PIPE procedure from Listing 19.21 so that you have data in the pipes for placing in the table.

19

Day 20

Alerting Other Procedures: The DBMS_ALERT Package

by Timothy Atwood

As the name suggests, alerts can be used to warn you or alert you for informational purposes. The DBMS_ALERT package is typically a one-way asynchronous communication, which is triggered when a transaction commits. Unless a transaction commits, no information will be sent to the alert. Because alerts are used for one-way communication, they have limited usage. Some examples of how you could use alerts are as follows: If you work for an insurance company, you can be alerted to natural disasters so that your team of experts can immediately be dispatched to aid the survivors. You can be alerted if a trigger fails, which could cause database corruption. You can implement a system to trap errors using alerts; however, this case would be better handled with exception handlers in the PL/SQL code.

Today's lesson discusses the following:

- [ ] How to send an alert
- [ ] Registering the alert
- [ ] Waiting for a specific alert
- [ ] Waiting for any alert
- [ ] Removing an alert
- [ ] Polling and events
- [ ] Alerts versus pipes
- [ ] Walkthrough example of an alert

 NOTE

> Because the DBMS_ALERT package uses COMMIT, this package cannot be used in Oracle Forms.

Because the DBMS_ALERT package is transaction-based, any ROLLBACK will remove any waiting alerts affected. The order for setting up an alert is

- [ ] Use REGISTER to record your interest in a particular alert.
- [ ] Issue the WAITONE procedure to wait for a specific alert.
- [ ] Issue the WAITANY procedure to wait for any of your registered alerts.
- [ ] Use SIGNAL when the condition for the alert is met and the transaction has been committed.

 NOTE

> In order to work with the DBMS_ALERT package, you must have the package installed, and you must have EXECUTE permission to the package.

Using SIGNAL to Issue an Alert

When you want to send an alert, you need to use the SIGNAL procedure.

The Syntax for the SIGNAL Procedure

```
PROCEDURE SIGNAL(alert_name IN VARCHAR2,
                 message_sent IN VARCHAR2);
```

alert_name can be a maximum of 30 characters, and it is not case-sensitive. In addition, the name must not start with ORA$, because this is reserved for use with Oracle. *message_sent* can be up to 1800 characters, which allows for a generous concatenation of text, variable names, and so on.

After the alert is sent, Oracle changes the state of the alert from not signaled to a state of signaled. This information is recorded in the DBMS_ALERT_INFO data dictionary. Because there is only one record for each alert, any other sessions attempting to send an alert will be blocked until the alert has been received.

If no sessions have registered the alert, the alert will remain signaled until the session has registered the alert. If multiple sessions have registered for the alert, after the alert has been signaled, all sessions will receive the alert, and then the alert will return to the nonsignaled state.

Registering for an Alert

Before you can even search for an alert, you must register the alert or alerts you want to monitor, which adds you to the master registration list. This is done through the use of the REGISTER procedure.

The Syntax for the REGISTER Procedure

```
PROCEDURE REGISTER(alert_name IN VARCHAR2);
```

In this syntax, *alert_name* is the name of the alert to monitor. You can monitor as many alerts as you are registered for. You can remove yourself from the master registration list through the use of the REMOVE or REMOVEALL procedures.

 NOTE

Simply registering an alert does not block the session from executing; rather, it simply records an interest in the alert. Only the WAITONE and WAITANY commands can block the session from executing. Although you can benefit from registering for all possible alerts and then checking for the alert later in a procedure at any time, you are still using valuable resources to monitor the registration. Use REGISTER only when necessary!

20

Waiting for a Specific Alert

If you want to monitor one alert, you can accomplish this through the WAITONE procedure.

The Syntax for the WAITONE Procedure

```
PROCEDURE WAITONE(alert_name IN VARCHAR2,
                  alert_message OUT VARCHAR2,
                  alert_status OUT INTEGER,
                  timeout IN NUMBER DEFAULT maxwait);
```

Again, alert_name is the name of the alert you are monitoring. alert_message is the message that you will receive when the alert has been signaled. The alert_status parameter has two possible values: 0 if the alert was signaled before the timeout or 1 if the timeout has occurred before any alert has been received. timeout is how long you will wait (in seconds) for the alert before the procedure continues executing if no alert was received. As you might recall, the default for maxwait is 1000 days.

> **TIP** When testing a DBMS_ALERT procedure, it is a good idea to make maxwait no longer than five minutes—otherwise, you could be at the keyboard for 1000 days!

If the alert_name specified has not been registered, you will receive an error message:

```
ORA-20000, ORU-10024:  there are no alerts registered.
```

Waiting for Any Registered Alert

The WAITANY procedure allows you to constantly monitor for any alert for which you have registered.

The Syntax for the WAITANY Procedure

```
PROCEDURE WAITANY(alert_name OUT VARCHAR2,
                  alert_message OUT VARCHAR2,
                  alert_status OUT INTEGER,
                  timeout IN NUMBER DEFAULT maxwait);
```

alert_name is an OUT parameter of type VARCHAR2, instead of type IN VARCHAR2. Instead of specifying alert_name as an input, you now receive the alert_name of the first registered alert that was sent. alert_message is the message that you will receive when the specific alert is signaled. The alert_status parameter has two possible values: 0 if any alert was signaled before the timeout or 1 if the timeout has occurred before any alert has been received. timeout is how long you will wait (in seconds) for the alert before the procedure continues executing. Again, the default for maxwait is 1000 days. You will also receive the same error message as WAITONE if you do not register the alert before trying to wait for an alert.

Removing One Alert

To remove only one specific alert from the registration list, use the REMOVE procedure.

The Syntax for the REMOVE Procedure

```
PROCEDURE REMOVE(alert_name IN VARCHAR2);
```

alert_name is the alert you want to remove from the registration list. After you no longer need to wait for an alert, you should use REMOVE to remove the registration instead of using up valuable resources. Whether you wait for an alert or not, once registered, the alert will try to signal all procedures that are registered. Not only does the system waste resources attempting to send an alert to what it believes will be a waiting process, but it also takes longer for the system to process through the registration list.

Removing All Alerts

You can remove all registered alerts by placing a call to the procedure REMOVEALL. The format for the REMOVEALL procedure is as follows:

```
PROCEDURE REMOVEALL;
```

After the procedure is executed, all registered alerts are deleted.

Polling Versus Events with the SET_DEFAULTS Procedure

As an Oracle event occurs, it is picked up in the system and processed. You will see this in the walkthrough example of the DBMS_ALERT package using the WAITONE procedure. The WAITONE procedure waits for the specific event to occur, and either alerts you when the alert occurs or eventually times out. On the other hand, there are situations that will require polling, or specifically searching for an alert:

☐ When shared instances of a database could issue an alert, you need to poll for an alert for any of the shared instances.

☐ When using the WAITANY procedure. The WAITANY procedure goes into a looping poll mode to search for any alerts signaled for registered alerts. When WAITANY goes into a sleep mode after polling for alerts, if three alerts are signaled during this sleep period, WAITANY will pick up only the most recent signaled alert. The default poll starts at one second and increases exponentially to 30 seconds.

Because two possibilities—using shared instances or using WAITANY for any alert to be signaled—could result in missed alerts, you can change the polling time in seconds using SET_DEFAULTS.

SYNTAX

The Syntax for the SET_DEFAULTS Procedure

```
PROCEDURE SET_DEFAULTS(polling_interval IN NUMBER);
```

You simply specify the interval between polling expressed in seconds. The default interval for this procedure is five seconds.

Alerts Versus Pipes

By now, you should see many similarities and differences between pipes and alerts. The similarities can be summarized as follows:

- [ ] Both use asynchronous communication.
- [ ] Both send messages between sessions of the same instance.
- [ ] Both can signal the execution of a C program.
- [ ] Both are PL/SQL packages.

The differences between alerts and pipes are

- [ ] The DBMS_ALERT package uses COMMIT, whereas DBMS_PIPE does not. Because alerts are transaction-based and use commits, a ROLLBACK can remove any waiting alert that has not been received. With pipes, after the message has been sent out, there is no recalling of the message.
- [ ] Alerts are generally used for one-way communication, whereas pipes are usually used for two-way communications.
- [ ] The DBMS_ALERT package not only allows multiple sessions to wait for an alert, but also all sessions will receive the alert after it has been signaled. This is similar to broadcasting a message in networking. If more than one session is waiting for a message from the pipe, only one of the sessions will receive the message and then clear the pipe when using the DBMS_PIPE package.
- [ ] Alerts can only send a string of characters, whereas pipes can send STRING, DATE, and NUMBER datatypes.

A Demonstration of the DBMS_ALERT Package

The best way to understand alerts is to try using the DBMS_ALERT package. Your goal is to solve a security problem. It has been noted that some employees have gained access to the payroll database and have had some fun changing around pay rates. The IS director empowered you to devise an alert, which will be constantly monitored by security, to detect whether anything in the payroll database is changed.

In order for you to meet this goal, you have decided to create a copy of the payroll database, along with who changed what data at what time. In addition, because human resources can legitimately change data in the database, you need to add a Verified field, which security will change to Y for Yes after the change has been approved. You will have to create the following:

☐ A backup database called security, which will hold the old and new values, the user who changed the information, the date the user changed the information, and whether the information has been verified.

☐ A trigger based upon the insert, update, or delete performed on a row, which will then issue an alert.

☐ A program to monitor for the security alert.

Creating the Backup Database

As with any type of an audit trail, you will create a database that will hold a copy of the old and new information, the date, time, and user who changed the data, and whether the data was verified by security. To create the database, enter and execute the code in Listing 20.1.

INPUT   **Listing 20.1. Creating the backup security database.**

```
CREATE TABLE security(
/*This database holds the original and new data archived from
  the payroll database to look for any violations of pay rate,
  name changes, and so on by internal employees or external hackers */

/*  Store the original values */
    OLD_Emp_Id INTEGER,
    OLD_Emp_Name VARCHAR2(32),
    OLD_Supervised_By INTEGER,
    OLD_Pay_Rate NUMBER(9,2),
    OLD_Pay_Type CHAR,
    OLD_Emp_Dept_Id INTEGER,
/* Store the changed values */
    NEW_Emp_Id INTEGER,
    NEW_Emp_Name VARCHAR2(32),
    NEW_Supervised_By INTEGER,
    NEW_Pay_Rate NUMBER(9,2),
    NEW_Pay_Type CHAR,
    NEW_Emp_Dept_Id INTEGER,
/* Flag to retain status if security has verified the change (Y/N)*/
    Verified CHAR(1),
/* Store Date and who made the changes */
    Changed_By VARCHAR2(8),
    Time_Changed DATE)
/
```

20

This is based on the original table called employee, which you created on Day 9, "Using SQL: INSERT, SELECT, Advanced Declarations, and Tables." After you execute the code, the following message should appear at the prompt:

OUTPUT   Table Created

You can now create the trigger that will occur whenever anyone alters the employee table.

Creating the Trigger to Signal an Alert

You can now create the trigger that will signal an alert when any changes have been made to the employee table. Enter and execute the code in Listing 20.2.

INPUT   **Listing 20.2. Creating the trigger to signal the alert.**

```
CREATE or REPLACE TRIGGER security

/* This trigger package will send an alert called emp_change when
   a row has been inserted, deleted, or updated. It will also send
   a message with the old Employee ID, the New Employee ID, the old
   Pay Rate and the new Pay Rate   */

BEFORE INSERT OR UPDATE OR DELETE ON employee
FOR EACH ROW
BEGIN

/* Send the Alert emp_change with the old and new values from the
   row being updated, changed, or deleted. Notice the use of :OLD
   for the contents of the original data and :NEW for the contents
   of the new data   */

    DBMS_ALERT.SIGNAL('emp_change','NOTICE:  OLD ID: ' ¦¦ :OLD.emp_id
         ¦¦ ' NEW ID: ' ¦¦ :NEW.emp_id ¦¦ ' OLD Pay Rate: '
         ¦¦ :OLD.pay_rate ¦¦ ' NEW Pay Rate:  ' ¦¦ :NEW.pay_rate);

/* Insert all of the values into the security table */
    INSERT INTO security
        (OLD_emp_id,OLD_emp_name,OLD_supervised_by,
         OLD_pay_rate,OLD_pay_type,OLD_emp_dept_id,
         NEW_emp_id,NEW_emp_name,NEW_supervised_by,
         NEW_pay_rate,NEW_pay_type,NEW_emp_dept_id,
         verified,changed_by,time_changed)
    VALUES
        (:OLD.emp_id,:OLD.emp_name,:OLD.supervised_by,
         :OLD.pay_rate,:OLD.pay_type,:OLD.emp_dept_id,
         :NEW.emp_id,:NEW.emp_name,:NEW.supervised_by,
         :NEW.pay_rate,:NEW.pay_type,:NEW.emp_dept_id,
         'N',USER,SYSDATE);

END security; -- End of the Trigger Security
```

20

ANALYSIS Because you are looking at values being altered in a row, you base the trigger on FOR EACH ROW only when the values of the row have been inserted, updated, or deleted from the table employee. If any of those conditions occur, an alert is signaled called emp_change, which passes the following in the message:

☐ The original employee ID

☐ The new employee ID

☐ The original employee pay rate

☐ The new employee pay rate

All of these are concatenated into a VARCHAR2 string using the concatenation operator (¦¦). This is well under the message limit of 1800 characters.

The trigger then performs an INSERT on the security table to add all the original data, the new data, who changed the data, the date the data was changed, and finally whether the data has been verified by security. At any point in time you could run a query against this table for Security.Verified = 'N' when no one has been watching the screen waiting for this to occur.

Waiting for the Alert

The next step is to wait for an alert, and then finally cause an alert to happen. Because you are going to practice inserting, deleting, and updating, I recommend that *before* you do anything, you enter the code in Listings 20.3 through 20.6. Listing 20.3 registers the alert and then waits for the alert. The other three listings practice, in order, an insert, an update, and then a delete. Again, at the SQL*Plus prompt, type SET SERVEROUTPUT ON and press Enter to see output to the screen.

INPUT **Listing 20.3. Registering and waiting for an alert.**

```
DECLARE
    message VARCHAR2(1800); -- Display Incoming Message from Alert
    status INTEGER; -- Holds Status 0 if success, 1 if timed out
BEGIN
    DBMS_ALERT.REGISTER('emp_change'); -- Registers for Alert emp_change
    DBMS_ALERT.WAITONE('emp_change',message,status,60); -- Wait for alert
    DBMS_OUTPUT.PUT_LINE(message);  -- Display Message
    DBMS_ALERT.REMOVE('emp_change'); -- Remove Registration for Alert
END;
```

ANALYSIS You first create two variables, one called message to hold the message sent by the alert, and the other called status to hold the status of the procedure WAITONE. You begin by registering for the alert emp_change. You then wait for the alert for 60 seconds. For these examples, I recommend that you set this to a value of 600 to wait for the alert. This gives you enough time to execute this procedure in one window, and you can then execute the insert,

20

update, and delete in another window. If the alert is signaled before your time limit expires, the DBMS_OUTPUT package displays the message to the screen. Then remove the alert from the registration. This wait time will change, depending upon the circumstance.

Using INSERT to Signal the Alert

You can practice inserting a record into the employee database. This will require two open sessions. In the first session, execute the code in Listing 20.3. Make sure that you have first typed SET SERVEROUTPUT ON and hit Enter. Before you execute the code, make sure that you have changed the time to wait to 600 seconds if you need the time to enter the SQL code in Listing 20.4.

INPUT **Listing 20.4. Inserting a record to trigger an alert.**

```
INSERT INTO employee
    (emp_id, emp_name,supervised_by,pay_rate,pay_type,emp_dept_id)
    VALUES(9109,'Benjamin Franklin',209,20.50,'H',10);
COMMIT;
```

Without the final COMMIT statement, the alert would never trigger. When you execute the code from Listing 20.4, on the screen where you perform the insert, your output should be

```
1 row created
```

After the COMMIT has been executed, you should see

```
Commit complete
```

On the other screen that is monitoring the alert, your output should look like

```
NOTICE:  OLD ID:  NEW ID: 9109 OLD Pay Rate:  NEW Pay Rate:  20.5

PL/SQL procedure successfully completed.
```

If the procedure ends without output, make sure that you have entered SET SERVEROUTPUT ON. The other possibility is that the INSERT command did not complete before the time to wait for the alert elapsed.

Because this is a new record, as would be expected, there is no data in the OLD values.

Using UPDATE to Signal the Alert

With your two sessions still open, execute in one of the SQL*Plus screens the code in Listing 20.3. On the other screen, execute the code in Listing 20.5 to practice updating a record. Before you execute the code from Listing 20.3, make sure that you have changed the time to wait to 600 seconds if you need the time to enter the SQL code in Listing 20.5.

INPUT **Listing 20.5. Updating a record to trigger an alert.**

```
UPDATE employee
   SET pay_rate = 75
   WHERE emp_id = 9109;
COMMIT;
```

When you execute the code in Listing 20.5, on the screen where you perform the update, your output should be

```
1 row updated
```

After the COMMIT has been executed, you should see

```
Commit complete
```

On the other screen that is monitoring the alert, your output should look like

```
NOTICE:  OLD ID: 9109 NEW ID: 9109 OLD Pay Rate: 20.5 NEW Pay Rate:  75
PL/SQL procedure successfully completed.
```

If the procedure ends without output, make sure that you have entered SET SERVEROUTPUT ON. The other possibility is that the UPDATE command did not complete before the time to wait for the alert elapsed or you forgot to commit the transaction.

Look at this! You now have someone going from $20.50 per hour to $75.00 per hour. This is reminiscent of the movie *Superman III*, in which Richard Pryor gives himself a huge raise after breaking into the payroll computer. This definitely bears investigation!

Using DELETE to Signal the Alert

With your two sessions still open, execute in one of the SQL*Plus screens the code in Listing 20.3. On the other screen, execute the code in Listing 20.6 to practice deleting a record. Before you execute the code from Listing 20.3, make sure that you have changed the time to wait to 600 seconds if you need the time to enter the SQL code in Listing 20.6.

INPUT **Listing 20.6. Deleting a record to trigger an alert.**

```
DELETE from employee
   WHERE emp_id = 9109;
COMMIT;
```

20

When you execute the code in Listing 20.6, on the screen where you perform the delete, your output should be

```
1 row deleted
```

After the COMMIT has been executed, you should see

```
Commit complete
```

On the other screen that is monitoring the alert, your output should look like

```
NOTICE: OLD ID: 9109 NEW ID: OLD Pay Rate: 75 NEW Pay Rate:
PL/SQL procedure successfully completed.
```

If the procedure ends without output, make sure that you have entered SET SERVEROUTPUT ON. The other possibility is that the UPDATE command did not complete before the time to wait for the alert elapsed or you forgot to commit the transaction.

Security finally escorted the person who manipulated the payroll database out the door to the police waiting outside. Human resources then deleted this person from their system. There are no NEW values since you deleted this record! You can now run a query against the security database to show that the trigger did indeed work and place the data into the table security.

Viewing the Results of the Trigger in the security Database

To see the three rows in the security database, execute the following code line:

```
SELECT * from security;
```

When you execute this code line, your output should look like

```
OLD_EMP_ID OLD_EMP_NAME         SUPERVISED_BY OLD_PAY_RATE O OLD_EMP_DEPT_ID
---------- -----------------    ------------- ------------ - ---------------
NEW_EMP_ID NEW_EMP_NAME         SUPERVISED_BY NEW_PAY_RATE N NEW_EMP_DEPT_ID V
---------- -----------------    ------------- ------------ - --------------- -
CHANGED_ TIME_CHANGED
-------- ----------
      9109 Benjamin Franklin 209                    20.5 H              10
      9109 Benjamin Franklin 209                      75 H              10 N

SCOTT    29-JUN-97

      9109 Benjamin Franklin 209                      75 H              10 N

SCOTT    29-JUN-97

      9109 Benjamin Franklin 209                    20.5 H              10 N
SCOTT    29-JUN-97
```

Summary

Today you discovered how the DBMS_ALERT package works in Oracle. In order to receive an alert, you must first register the alert. You can then wait for one specific alert with WAITONE or poll for any registered alert with WAITANY. The procedure will be blocked until the wait time has expired, which returns a status of 1, or an alert is signaled, which returns a status of 0. Alerts are asynchronous, and can generally only communicate one way. A message can be sent with the alert up to 1800 bytes as one huge VARCHAR2 string.

Q&A

Q What is required to check for an alert?

A You must first register the alert and then use WAITONE or WAITANY to wait for the alert to occur.

Q What is the difference between WAITONE and WAITANY?

A WAITONE waits for one specific alert to occur as an event, whereas WAITANY polls for all alerts that are registered to that session.

Q Do you need to remove the alert after the session ends?

A This is highly recommended to clean up the registration table of alerts and also to recover resources used by the alert process.

Q Why use alerts instead of pipes?

A Alerts offer you the ability to broadcast a message to all sessions monitoring the alert. The DBMS_PIPE package will only send the message to the first session that reads the pipe. In addition, pipes do not offer ROLLBACK to remove the message waiting for pickup.

Q Why should you change the polling interval when using WAITANY?

A If you do not create a short polling interval, when WAITANY awakes and goes to poll, it will receive only the most recent alert, ignoring any that might have occurred while the process was in sleep mode.

20

Workshop

Use the following workshop to test your comprehension of this chapter and put what you've learned into practice. You'll find the answers to the quiz and exercises in Appendix A, "Answers."

Quiz

1. What is the maximum length of an alert name?

2. What is the maximum length of the message?

3. What datatype is the message sent as?

4. If 20 sessions are monitoring for an alert and the alert is sent, how many of those sessions receive the signaled alert?

5. Alerts require a(n) _____ because you are dealing more on a transactional level, whereas pipes do not.

Exercises

1. Change the code in Listing 20.3 to wait for any alert, and also register for two more alerts called `'my_test'` and `'extra_alert'`. Store the name of the alert that is signaled in a variable entitled `alert_name` of type `VARCHAR2(30)`. After the alert has been handled, remove all registered alerts.

2. Write a loop that will continually execute until the value of `FIRE` equals `1`, which will then trigger the alert called `'a_fire'`, which will pass the message `'A Fire has Broken Out'`.

Day 21

Implementing J/SQL for Web Applications

by Tom Luers

In the world of the Internet, there will be times when you need to design and build an application that uses a Web browser to access information inside an Oracle database. With the advent of Java and multimedia technologies, you can now use your browser with these new tools in your Internet/database applications. It seems as though every day new products hit the marketplace that claim they can integrate your browser and the Internet with an Oracle database. Some claims are true while others offer only a partial solution.

Today provides an overview of the Internet browser/Oracle database junction. This chapter is intended to make you aware of the Internet's ability to access data within the Oracle database. Specifically, the primary focus of this chapter will be an overview of J/SQL.

J/SQL

J/SQL (Java/Structured Query Language) provides the integration of SQL statements inside a Java program. This means that a J/SQL program is simply a Java source program with embedded SQL statements. J/SQL was developed by Oracle as the open specification for a precompiled, embedded SQL interface to Java. It is much like embedding SQL code into other languages like PRO*COBOL or PRO*C. In fact, the SQL in J/SQL looks and behaves exactly the same way as it does inside PL/SQL. J/SQL will open the door for Java to become the enterprise language choice for all MIS organizations. Java access to the Oracle relational database is vital to the future of building robust applications that combine Java's power and ease of use with the functionality of the database.

The J/SQL processor consists of a precompiler written in Java and several Java classes that implement J/SQL's runtime support. A developer will write J/SQL source code and then pass it through the J/SQL precompiler to produce Java source code with standard JDBC calls. This processing flow is illustrated in Figure 21.1. JDBC (Java Database Connectivity) is discussed briefly later in this section and in more detail later in the chapter in the section "JDBC."

Figure 21.1.

Overview of J/SQL processing.

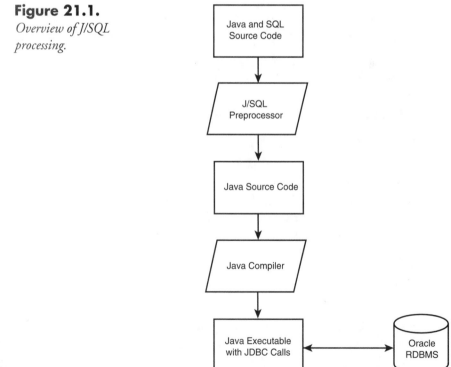

21

As shown in Figure 21.1, the Java compiler will do the necessary checks for the argument number and types of arguments. This will make sure that the arguments pass cleanly from the SQL statements and the Java programs. J/SQL automatically maps SQL types to Java types, making it easier to pass information between the Java application and the Oracle database.

J/SQL takes full advantage of its own precompiler's many features. For example, the J/SQL precompiler will check the SQL source code's syntax and optimize the code for performance. This precompiler, or preprocessor, receives as input either a file of J/SQL classes that are SQL statements using J/SQL parameter syntax, or a file of Java source code with SQL statements embedded within it. In either situation, the precompiler generates Java classes source code as its output. J/SQL programs can include queries, Data Manipulation Language (DML) statements, Data Definition Language (DDL) statements, transaction controls, and calls to stored programs.

Oracle has promoted J/SQL as an open standard for embedding SQL within Java. This makes J/SQL code very portable and open to any SQL-compliant database. Additionally, the J/SQL syntax is the same across all platforms and architectures, so programs written in J/SQL can be partitioned across the application architecture. J/SQL programs can be run on the client, the server, or even the middle tier. J/SQL is built on JDBC so that it can be used to write programs to access any data server that is JDBC compliant.

J/SQL can also be stored in the database just like PL/SQL. This enables programmers to extend the functionality of the server with their user-defined stored programs. Furthermore, PL/SQL and Java can call each other seamlessly, which adds to J/SQL's capabilities because the J/SQL preprocessor will treat PL/SQL code as a J/SQL clause and will present it to the Java compiler and programs as standard Java classes and objects.

J/SQL Coding Standards

J/SQL is very class structured and a strongly typed object-oriented programming language. This section summarizes its current methods and classes. However, Oracle makes no commitment to maintain future compatibility with J/SQL's current features and those of later versions, and this version of J/SQL is not final.

Interface Methods

The first method to discuss is using a static cursor. A cursor defines methods available to all J/SQL cursor objects that correspond to the result set obtained by the execution of a statement.

21

The Syntax for the Cursor Interface

SYNTAX

```
SQL.cursor ( public identifier ( jsql-column-list ) )
```

In this syntax, the parameters are as follows:

- ☐ SQL.cursor—The reserved J/SQL cursor declaration syntax.
- ☐ *public*—Defines the Java class as public.
- ☐ *identifier*—The name for this class.
- ☐ *jsql-column-list*—Specifies the names of the columns of any JDBC result set the cursor can receive. The cursor has a public accessor method for each of these names that returns the value of the named column of the cursor's current row.

The following is an example of a J/SQL cursor:

```
SQL.cursor
(
  SalesCursor
  (
    int item_number,
    String item_name,
    java.sql.Date sales_date,
    double cost,
    Integer sales_rep_number,
    String sales_rep_name
  )
)
```

The comma-separated terms appearing in parentheses after the class name serve two purposes: They correspond to column names in the result sets that can occupy SalesCursor objects, and they become the names of accessor methods for the corresponding data. The correspondence between the terms and column names is usually case insensitive, but the correspondence between the terms and method names is case sensitive.

In some cases, it is desirable to immediately release a cursor's database and JDBC resources instead of waiting for this to happen when the database is automatically closed; the CLOSE() method provides this immediate release.

The NEXT() method will move the cursor to the next row. The getrownum() method obtains the row number for the current row.

The second interface method is outholder. This public holder interface for objects should be treated as an out parameter when used in J/SQL operations.

J/SQL Classes

The common J/SQL classes are as follows:

- ☐ oracle.jsql.AsciiStream—An InputStream-derived class whose bytes should be interpreted as ASCII characters.

- [ ] `oracle.jsql.BinaryStream`—An `InputStream`-derived class whose bytes should be interpreted as binary.
- [ ] `oracle.jsql.BooleanInOut`—A holder class used to pass an argument of type `BOOLEAN` as an in-out parameter to a J/SQL operation.
- [ ] `oracle.jsql.byteArrayInOut`—A holder class used to pass an argument of type `byte[]` as an in-out parameter to a J/SQL operation.
- [ ] `oracle.jsql.DateInOut`—A holder class used to pass an argument of type `java.sql.Date` as an in-out parameter to a J/SQL operation.
- [ ] `oracle.jsql.DateOut`—A holder class used to pass an argument of type `java.sql.Date` as an out parameter to a J/SQL operation.
- [ ] `oracle.jsql.ExecStatus`—`ExecStatus` defines the status of the last successfully executed `SQL.exec()` operation on a particular instance of `JSQLContext`.
- [ ] `oracle.jsql.IntegerInOut`—A holder class used to pass an argument of type `Integer` as an in-out parameter to a J/SQL operation.
- [ ] `oracle.jsql.JSQLContext`—`JSQLContext` manages a set of SQL operations performed during a session with a specific database. `JSQLContext` implements the JDBC connection interface, and as such it can be used as an entry point for performing dynamic SQL operations in the same way you would use any other JDBC connection.
- [ ] `oracle.jsql.JSQLException ()`—A constructor without an associated error message.
- [ ] `oracle.jsql.JSQLException (string)`—A constructor with an associated error message.
- [ ] `oracle.jsql.ObjectInOut`—A holder class used to pass an argument of type `Object` as an in-out parameter to a J/SQL operation.
- [ ] `oracle.jsql.StreamWrapper`—This class wraps a particular instance of `InputStream`. It also extends the `InputStream` class by providing direct call-throughs to the wrapped `InputStream` instance for all methods.
- [ ] `oracle.jsql.StringInOut`—A holder class used to pass an argument of type `String` as an in-out parameter to a J/SQL operation.
- [ ] `oracle.jsql.TimeInOut`—A holder class used to pass an argument of type `java.sql.Time` as an in-out parameter to a J/SQL operation.
- [ ] `oracle.jsql.TimestampInOut`—A holder class used to pass an argument of type `java.sql.Timestamp` as an in-out parameter to a J/SQL operation.
- [ ] `oracle.jsql.UnicodeStream`—An `InputStream`-derived class whose bytes should be interpreted as Unicode. When passing `InputStream` as an input parameter to a `SQL.exec()` operation, you must specify both the length of `InputStream` and the way to interpret its bytes.

21

JDBC

As mentioned earlier, JDBC provides the standard interface between Java and the database. At this point, I would like to take a brief minute and discuss JDBC.

JDBC (Java Database Connectivity) is a standard relational database access interface. It's somewhat analogous to Microsoft's ODBC (Open Database Connectivity) in that JDBC is driver based and database independent. JDBC is widely supported by third-party tool vendors and many popular databases. As such, JDBC will remain the main database access mechanism for Java for the near future.

JDBC requires an operating system driver to access the relational database. Several company vendors provide generic JDBC-ODBC bridge drivers that allow any ODBC driver to be used with JDBC. With these bridge drivers, the JDBC API acts as a wrapper for the underlying ODBC calls. To use the drivers, place JDBC calls within your Java source code.

Unfortunately, being driver based is also the main disadvantage of JDBC. JDBC requires the drivers to be installed on the same platform as the JDBC application, which means that Java and the drivers must be installed with the Internet browser. This adds to the complexity of the overall application architecture. This is a limitation you must endure to have the Java-relational database connectivity. Another limitation of JDBC is that it provides access to the standard SQL types only and does not support the Oracle-specific types such as ROWID.

Even though JDBC has these few limitations, it does offer the following benefits:

- ☐ Oracle supports the entire JDBC standards. Some RDBMSs support only a partial JDBC standard.
- ☐ Oracle's JDBC drivers are portable to several other environments.
- ☐ Oracle has designed a special version of JDBC that is stored inside the Oracle database. This dramatically improves access performance.

PL/SQL Versus Java

PL/SQL and Java have many similarities and common strengths that make them both outstanding programming languages. Likewise, they have some differences that are attributable to their purposes and origins. PL/SQL and Java compare and contrast as follows:

- ☐ One of PL/SQL's main strengths is its ability to manipulate data. Structures such as cursors, loops, and arrays offer an advantage over Java.
- ☐ Both Java and PL/SQL allow SQL to be embedded within them for standard data access routines. PL/SQL allows native SQL code within it while Java source code requires J/SQL or a similar language to incorporate SQL.

□ PL/SQL is very integrated and operates almost seamlessly with the Oracle database. To access Oracle through Java, you need to use J/SQL or some other means.

□ PL/SQL and Java both have the capability to process data locally, without regard for execution location and networking aspects.

□ Java enables you to take advantage of several object orientation (OO) features such as classes and inheritance. PL/SQL doesn't support these two OO features. However, both languages incorporate OO encapsulation—PL/SQL through packages and Java through classes.

□ Java tends to be more "wordy" than PL/SQL. In other words, Java requires more definitions and lacks the capability to use logical pointers.

The World Wide Web and SQL

Over the past several years, the primary user interface to the Internet and the World Wide Web (WWW) has been the browser. Internet browsers from companies such as Oracle, Microsoft, and Netscape primarily access Web pages, which are written in Hypertext Markup Language (HTML) and Java.

You learned earlier in this chapter that Java and J/SQL can be integrated to give Java access to an RDBMS. J/SQL opens the door and allows Web pages that use Java to access Oracle databases. This RDBMS access from a Web browser is the architecture of the future. In fact, it has already begun. Internet applications such as E-COMMERCE (Electronic Commerce) would not be possible without this Web-page-to-database connectivity. E-COMMERCE is the applications that allow you to perform sales and purchasing activities over the Internet. Figure 21.2 illustrates typical scenarios for the processing of SQL statements through a Web page or a Web server.

At this point, I want to share with you several options, other than J/SQL and JDBC, that enable you to have Java-to-RDBMS connectivity. Although I prefer and recommend J/SQL, it's important and reasonable for me to review alternatives with you:

□ Oracle provides a Java cartridge that includes classes for calling stored procedures directly from a Java application. This is accomplished by Oracle using class wrappers around the PL/SQL packages, functions, and procedures.

□ One vendor, WebLogic Inc., offers APIs for database access from Java. These APIs are classes that treat Oracle tables as arrays and records to automatically generate the necessary DML statements.

□ Various vendors offer their own, nonstandard interfaces that use JDBC, ODBC, or their own proprietary database drivers. Exercise some caution here to ensure driver compatibility. For information about JDBC interfaces and drivers, check out the site at `http://splash.javasoft.com/jdbc`.

21

Figure 21.2.

SQL processing through the Internet.

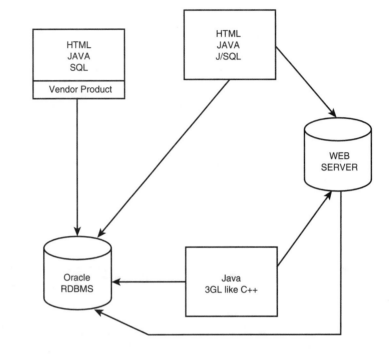

☐ You can also write your own code with Java. This Java code tends to be nonportable and might not operate or download exactly as a pure Java class.

☐ Sybase offers a tool called Web*SQL that allows you to insert SQL statements directly into your HTML statements. The HTML statements are executed against a Web server and then gain access to the Oracle database. The database inquiries are executed every time the Web page is called.

Summary

The Internet is providing many opportunities for developers to create enterprisewide applications that access the Oracle relational database. Until recently, such database access from the Internet has not been possible. Through tools such as J/SQL and JDBC, this connectivity between the two has been made possible.

Java is the engine that enables the World Wide Web and the Internet to access data on the relational database. Tools such as J/SQL and Web*SQL have evolved so that you can now embed SQL statements directly in your Java source code. These tools interpret the SQL code into Java code, making for a portable and standard application.

Q&A

Q **Is it possible to access an Oracle database through the Internet?**

A Yes. There are several ways to access an Oracle database from the Internet, such as embedding SQL statements inside your Java code through J/SQL, using JDBC drivers, or using alternatives such as programming languages like C and vendor-specific packages.

Q **What is J/SQL?**

A J/SQL is a language that embeds SQL in Java with no compatibility issues. J/SQL allows you to access the Oracle database directly from Java.

Q **Why should I use J/SQL instead of Pro*C?**

A Choosing to develop with one language over another is really a personal preference. I recommend J/SQL because it is specifically developed to take advantage of Java's power as an Internet application language.

Workshop

Use the following workshop to test your comprehension of this chapter and put what you've learned into practice. You'll find the answers to the quiz in Appendix A, "Answers."

Quiz

1. List several of the options available to access the Oracle database through Java.
2. What are the differences between PL/SQL and Java?
3. What role does JDBC play in Internet-to-database connectivity?

21

WEEK 3

In Review

Day 15

On Day 15, you learned some advanced topics such as managing large objects new to Oracle8 with the DBMS_LOB package. You also learned how to implement recursive functions in Oracle.

Day 16

On Day 16, you learned how to manage transactions by locking a record as it is processed, which prevents another user from accessing the record and thus prevents data corruption. You also learned how to restore the database to the old data with the ROLLBACK procedure. You learned what a savepoint is when working with COMMIT and ROLLBACK. You looked at optimum ways to lock data from users, sometimes using a row lock and sometimes using a table lock.

Day 17

On Day 17, you worked with the DBMS_SQL package. This package offers the capability to create dynamic SQL from within PL/SQL. It also allows you to use DDL from within PL/SQL.

Day 18

On Day 18, you were able to write and read files with the UTL_FILE package, which is an excellent way to import and export data in any format for any application. In addition, you learned how to output information to the screen with the DBMS_OUTPUT package, which is used primarily for debugging purposes.

Day 19

On Day 19, you learned how to handle the communications between sessions with the DBMS_PIPE package. Some unique features regarding pipes are that they can handle almost any datatype, they are not affected by a rollback, and they communicate asynchronously. In addition, you learned how to manage jobs with the DBMS_JOB package. You should be able to run any job on demand, schedule a future job, or fix a broken job.

Day 20

On Day 20, you learned how to alert someone with the DBMS_ALERT package. Although this package is similar to the DBMS_PIPE package, this is a transaction-based process that uses COMMIT. Communications typically occur one way, and the message sent is of type VARCHAR2. The major advantage of using alerts is that an alert can be broadcasted and thus received by all sessions monitoring that alert. So if an alert is used for an emergency, for example, many people can be notified immediately to evacuate the building!

Day 21

On Day 21, you learned how to implement J/SQL with Oracle for Web-based access to the database. As electronic commerce proliferates, it will become more and more important for you to understand database connectivity with Web pages.

APPENDIX

A

Answers

This appendix provides the answers to the quiz and exercise sections at the end of each chapter.

Day 1

Quiz

1. What tells SQL*Plus to send your PL/SQL code to the Oracle database for execution?

A Typing the slash character (/) on a line by itself immediately following the end of the PL/SQL block.

2. What is the fundamental basis of all PL/SQL code?

A The PL/SQL block.

3. List an advantage of pushing program logic up to the server level.

A There are at least two advantages:

- [ ] It gives a central point of control.
- [ ] Intermediate data does not have to be brought down to the client.

4. Name three Oracle products that use PL/SQL.

A There are several that execute PL/SQL:

- [ ] Developer/2000
- [ ] Oracle Forms
- [ ] Oracle Reports
- [ ] The Oracle database itself
- [ ] Procedure Builder

And several that recognize it:

- [ ] SQL*Plus
- [ ] SQL*DBA
- [ ] Server Manager

5. What command tells SQL*Plus to display PL/SQL output?

A SET SERVEROUTPUT ON

6. Name at least two options for managing your PL/SQL source code.

A The three options described in the chapter are as follows:

- [ ] Cut and paste from Notepad.
- [ ] Execute a text file using the SQL*Plus @ command.
- [ ] Use the SQL*Plus EDIT command.

Exercises

1. If you didn't encounter any errors when compiling your first function, try putting some in on purpose. Then try out the SHOW ERRORS command.

A I'll leave the task of generating errors up to you.

2. Try each of the three ways mentioned in the chapter for managing your source code. Become familiar with the SQL*Plus EDIT command. Try using the @ command or the START command to execute your PL/SQL code from a text file.

A You should be able to type any PL/SQL block into SQL*Plus, execute it, and then use the EDIT command to bring up Notepad so that you can change it.

As for executing a PL/SQL block from a file, one possible solution is to create a file with these lines and call it test.sql:

```
SET SERVEROUTPUT ON
BEGIN
  dbms_output.put_line('Hello there!');
END;
/
```

You can then execute the file from SQL*Plus using the command

```
@test
```

You may need to specify the full path, for example:

```
@c:\test
```

Day 2

Quiz

1. Name several PL/SQL development tools.

A SQL*Plus, Developer/2000 Forms, Developer/2000 Reports, Developer/2000 Graphs, and Oracle Call Interfaces.

2. What is a bind variable?

A A bind variable is a variable that is created outside PL/SQL but referenced within a PL/SQL block.

3. What is a substitution variable?

A A substitution variable is a user-defined variable. This variable is preceded by an ampersand (&) when it is defined.

Exercise

Write a simple piece of code outline that uses substitution variables and bind variables.

A The following is a simple illustration (code outline) of using bind variables and substitution variables in the same PL/SQL block:

```
DECLARE

v_Emp_name   varchar2(35);
v_emp_no     number(3);
...
BEGIN
...
v_emp_name := &emp_name;           -- substitution variable
SELECT emp_no into v_emp_no from emp
where emp_name = :v_emp_name;       -- bind variable
...
end;
```

Day 3

Quiz

1. What are three benefits of using functions and procedures?

A Procedures and functions hide complexity, promote modularity, and allow for reuse of code.

2. What values can a variable declared as NUMBER(6,2) hold? What will be the maximum value?

A A declaration of NUMBER(6,2) allows you to store values such as 1234.56, −2333.99, and so on. The maximum value you can store is 9999.99.

3. What values can a variable declared as NUMBER(2,2) hold? Where will rounding occur?

A A declaration of NUMBER(2,2) allows you to store values such as 0.01, 0.02, up through 0.99. All values will be rounded to the nearest hundredth.

4. What is the maximum length of a VARCHAR2 variable in PL/SQL? In the Oracle database?

A The maximum length of a VARCHAR2 in PL/SQL is 32767 bytes. In an Oracle database, version 8 or later, the maximum length is 4000 bytes. Prior to version 8 the maximum length was 2000 bytes.

5. What can you do to ignore the time portion of a DATE variable?

A The TRUNC() function can be used to truncate a date so that it no longer contains a time element.

6. When comparing a VARCHAR2 and a CHAR variable, how can you eliminate any trailing spaces?

A The RTRIM() function can be used to eliminate trailing spaces from both CHAR and VARCHAR2 strings.

Exercises

1. Try writing an anonymous block that declares a variable and displays its value. Then add a nested block that declares a variable of the same name and displays its value. What happens and why?

A Here is one solution:

```
--Remember to execute:SET SERVEROUTPUT ON
DECLARE
  state_name  VARCHAR2(30);

BEGIN
  state_name := 'Michigan';

  --Now code a nested block which declares and prints
  --a variable of the same name.
  DECLARE
    state_name  VARCHAR2(30);
  begin
    state_name := 'Tennessee';
    DBMS_OUTPUT.PUT_LINE(state_name);
  END;

  --Now print the state_name variable's value in the outer block.
  DBMS_OUTPUT.PUT_LINE (state_name);
END;
/

Tennessee
Michigan

PL/SQL procedure successfully completed.
```

The inner block will print the value assigned to state_name within that block. However, the value of state_name in the outer block is undisturbed because the scope of the inner block's state_name declaration is limited to that block.

2. Write a function that computes a person's age in years. Hint: To get started on this, look at Listing 3.3.

A Here is a PL/SQL block containing a function named age_as_of, which is one possible solution to the exercise of coding an age calculation function:

```
--Remember to execute: SET SERVEROUTPUT ON
DECLARE
  age   BINARY_INTEGER;

  birth_date    DATE := TO_DATE('11-15-1961','mm-dd-yyyy');
  current_date  DATE;

  FUNCTION age_as_of (birth_date IN DATE, as_of_date IN DATE)
  RETURN POSITIVE IS
    as_of_year  NATURAL;     --a year of 00 is valid.
    as_of_month POSITIVE;
    as_of_day   POSITIVE;

    birth_year    NATURAL;   --a year of 00 is valid.
    birth_month   POSITIVE;
    birth_day     POSITIVE;

    age   POSITIVE;
```

```
BEGIN
  --Get the various parts of the dates needed to determine age.
  as_of_year := TO_NUMBER(TO_CHAR(as_of_date,'yyyy'));
  as_of_month := TO_NUMBER(TO_CHAR(as_of_date,'mm'));
  as_of_day := TO_NUMBER(TO_CHAR(as_of_date,'dd'));

  birth_year := TO_NUMBER(TO_CHAR(birth_date,'yyyy'));
  birth_month := TO_NUMBER(TO_CHAR(birth_date,'mm'));
  birth_day := TO_NUMBER(TO_CHAR(birth_date,'dd'));

  --Now make the actual computation.
  IF as_of_month > birth_month THEN
    age := as_of_year - birth_year;
  ELSIF (as_of_month = birth_month) and (as_of_day >= birth_day) THEN
    age := as_of_year - birth_year;
  ELSE
    age := as_of_year - birth_year - 1;
  END IF;

  RETURN age;
END;
BEGIN
  --Let's test each of the cases that the age
  --function needs to consider.
  DBMS_OUTPUT.PUT_LINE('Age as of 11-13-1997');
  current_date := TO_DATE('11-13-1997','mm-dd-yyyy');
  age := age_as_of (birth_date, current_date);
  DBMS_OUTPUT.PUT_LINE(age);

  DBMS_OUTPUT.PUT_LINE('Age as of 11-15-1997');
  current_date := to_date('11-15-1997','mm-dd-yyyy');
  age := age_as_of (birth_date, current_date);
  DBMS_OUTPUT.PUT_LINE(age);

  DBMS_OUTPUT.PUT_LINE('Age as of 12-13-1997');
  current_date := to_date('12-13-1997','mm-dd-yyyy');
  age := age_as_of (birth_date, current_date);
  DBMS_OUTPUT.PUT_LINE(age);

  DBMS_OUTPUT.PUT_LINE('Age as of 5-13-1997');
  current_date := TO_DATE('5-13-1997','mm-dd-yyyy');
  age := age_as_of (birth_date, current_date);
  DBMS_OUTPUT.PUT_LINE(age);

END;
/
Age as of 11-13-1997
35
Age as of 11-15-1997
36
Age as of 12-13-1997
36
Age as of 5-13-1997
35

PL/SQL procedure successfully completed.
```

Day 4

Quiz

1. What is the difference between a unary operator and a binary operator?

A A unary operator works on only one value. An example is the negation operator, which is often used to write negative numbers. Binary operators work on two values. Examples are the addition and multiplication operators.

2. What are the results of each of the following expressions?

    a. `(5-4)-(3-1)`

    b. `4*2**3-2`

    c. `4*2**(3-2)`

    d. `4=4 AND 5=6 OR 3=3`

A The expressions evaluate as follows:

    a. `(5-4)-(3-1)` evaluates to `-1`.

    b. `4*2**3-2` evaluates to `30`.

    c. `4*2**(3-2)` evaluates to `8`.

    d. `4=4 AND 5=6 OR 3=3` evaluates to `true`.

3. Using the `NOT` operator, write equivalent expressions for each of the following:

    a. `A <> B`

    b. `A < B`

    c. `(A <= B) AND (B <= C)`

A a. `NOT (A = B)`

  b. `NOT (A >= B)`

  c. `NOT ((B < A) OR (B > C))`

4. Match the patterns and strings shown following. Hint: Not every string or pattern has a match, and one pattern matches more than one string.

    `'123-45-6789' '___-__-____'`

    `'Boom' 'John%'`

    `'Johnson' '_oo_'`

    `'517-555-1212'`

    `'Broom'`

    `'Jonson'`

    `'Johnston'`

A `'John%'` matches `'Johnson'` and `'Johnston'`. `'_oo_'` matches `'Boom'`. `'___-__-____'` matches `'123-45-6789'`. The remaining strings and patterns don't match at all.

5. When does PL/SQL not pad strings with spaces, in order to make them of equal length, when doing comparisons?

A Any time a VARCHAR2 string is involved.

Exercise

Write a function to compute wages based on an hourly rate and the number of hours worked. Have it use a minimum wage of $5 per hour if the rate is unknown. Have it also use the minimum wage if the rate is too low.

A Here is one solution:

```
--Remember to execute: SET SERVEROUTPUT ON
DECLARE
FUNCTION wage_calculate (
  hours_worked IN NUMBER,
  hourly_rate IN NUMBER) RETURN NUMBER IS
hourly_rate_to_use  NUMBER;
minimum_wage  NUMBER := 5;
BEGIN
  IF (hourly_rate IS NULL) OR (hourly_rate < minimum_wage) THEN
    hourly_rate_to_use := minimum_wage;
  ELSE
    hourly_rate_to_use := hourly_rate;
  END IF;
  RETURN hours_worked * hourly_rate_to_use;
END;
BEGIN
  DBMS_OUTPUT.PUT_LINE(wage_calculate(40,10));
  DBMS_OUTPUT.PUT_LINE(wage_calculate(40,2));
  DBMS_OUTPUT.PUT_LINE(wage_calculate(40,NULL));
END;
/

400
200
200
PL/SQL procedure successfully completed.
```

Day 5

Quiz

1. What parts of the function are required for coding?

A The required parts of the function are the function keyword and name, the RETURN statement and type, and a BEGIN and an END statement with the function name occurring at the end of the END statement.

2. If a function takes parameters, is it always necessary to pass these parameters from the calling statement?

A It is not always necessary to pass values, even if the function allows for this. To compensate, make sure that you have a DEFAULT for the parameter if nothing is passed.

3. If an error occurs and you haven't coded an EXCEPTION statement, what is returned from the function?

A The function will error out with no value returned.

4. Is there a way to return more than one value from a function?

A You can return more than one parameter by using the optional MODE of OUT or IN OUT. However, this is not a recommended programming practice.

5. If you code an IF...ELSE statement, and you do not have any conditions to execute if the statement is false, how would you code the ELSE statement?

A After the ELSE statement, code a NULL;.

6. What are some of the common pitfalls in coding IF statements?

A Some common errors are forgetting to put a space between END and IF; forgetting the semicolon after the END IF; missing an END IF statement, especially if nested IFs are used; and finally, misspelling ELSIF as ELSEIF.

7. How can I determine what is wrong with my code when it compiles?

A From your command prompt, type the words SHOW ERRORS and then troubleshoot. Remember, a program can compile and still be incorrect due to logic errors.

8. When coding a loop in reverse, how must the beginning and ending values be coded?

A Even though you are adding the REVERSE keyword, the starting and ending values must still be coded from lowest value to highest value.

Exercises

1. Rewrite the Grade example from Listing 5.11 as a stored function that passes the parameter of the score and returns a value of a grade letter.

A Here's one solution:

```
CREATE OR REPLACE FUNCTION mygrade(p_score NUMBER)
    RETURN CHAR IS
BEGIN
IF p_Score >= 90 THEN
    RETURN 'A';
ELSIF p_Score >= 80 THEN
    RETURN 'B';
ELSIF p_Score >= 70 THEN
    RETURN 'C';
ELSIF p_Score >= 60 THEN
    RETURN 'D';
ELSE
    RETURN 'E';
```

```
END IF;
END;
```

2. Rewrite the Grade example from Listing 5.11 and use between for the ranges. Make sure that there is no overlapping of ranges.

A Here's one solution:

```
DECLARE
v_Score Number := 85; --Percentage
v_LetterGrade Char(1);
BEGIN
IF v_Score between 90 and 100 THEN
        v_LetterGrade := 'A';
ELSIF v_Score between 80 and 89 THEN
        v_LetterGrade := 'B';
ELSIF v_Score between 70 and 79 THEN
        v_LetterGrade := 'C';
ELSIF v_Score between 60 and 69 THEN
        v_LetterGrade := 'D';
ELSE
        v_LetterGrade := 'E';
END IF;
        DBMS_OUTPUT.PUT_LINE('Your Letter Grade is: ' ¦¦ v_LetterGrade);
END;
/
```

3. Write a loop that increments by a value of 3 and then multiplies a counter by the returned value of the function mypi. The range should be from 1 to 9. Output the values with DBMS_OUTPUT. Make sure that you have entered SET SERVEROUTPUT ON to see the output.

A Here's one solution:

```
BEGIN
        FOR v_loopcounter IN 1..9 LOOP
            IF MOD(v_loopcounter,3) = 0 THEN
                DBMS_OUTPUT.PUT_LINE('The counter * pi is ' ¦¦
                        v_loopcounter * mypi );
            END IF; -- End execution of statements for even counter
        END LOOP;
END;
```

4. Write a loop to calculate a factorial. For example, 6! is 6 * 5 * 4 * 3 * 2 * 1. Allow the high boundary to be a variable that can change. Use an initial value of 3 for testing.

A Here's one solution:

```
DECLARE
        v_factorial NUMBER := 1;
BEGIN
        FOR v_loopcounter IN REVERSE 1..4 LOOP
          v_factorial := v_factorial * v_loopcounter;
            DBMS_OUTPUT.PUT_LINE('Your factorial value is now ' ¦¦
                v_factorial);
        END LOOP;
END;
```

Day 6

Quiz

1. True or False: The label name must be within the same PL/SQL block of code as the GOTO statement calling the label name.

A True. This is one of many reasons why you probably will never need to use the GOTO statement.

2. When should GOTO be used?

A The GOTO statement is typically used in emergency situations that require you to respond immediately. It could be something as simple as a server going down, or as complex as an incoming nuclear warhead. Other than that, it is not good coding practice to use the GOTO statement.

3. WHILE loops must end with a(n) _____ statement.

A END LOOP;

4. Can you potentially write a WHILE loop that never ends?

A Yes. As long as the condition never evaluates to true, the same code will repeat over and over again.

5. What statement(s) allow you to abort the processing of a loop?

A The EXIT and EXIT WHEN statements allow you to break out of the execution of a loop.

6. In order to change execution of nested loops, you can use the EXIT and EXIT WHEN statement in conjunction with _____.

A Label names for loops

7. Must you have EXIT or EXIT WHEN as part of a simple LOOP?

A This is not required as part of the syntax. However, you should make it mandatory as part of good programming practice instead of having infinite loops!

8. Does Oracle have a REPEAT...UNTIL loop?

A No. You can simulate this by using a simple LOOP with the EXIT or EXIT WHEN statement.

9. In a simple LOOP, where is the best location for the EXIT or EXIT WHEN statements to appear?

A These statements should appear at the beginning or at the end of the LOOP body to avoid potential logic errors.

Exercises

1. Create an example using GOTO that checks some variable for a value of 10 and then branches off to a NULL statement.

A Here is one solution:

```
DECLARE
    v_GOTOVARIABLE NUMBER := 0;
BEGIN
    v_GOTOVARIABLE := 10;
    IF v_GOTOVARIABLE = 10 THEN
        GOTO nullstatement;
    ELSE
        NULL;
    END IF;
<<nullstatement>>
    NULL;
END;
/
```

2. Create a WHILE loop to calculate a factorial. For example, 6! is 6 * 5 * 4 * 3 * 2 * 1. Use an initial value of 4! for testing. Make sure to issue the command SET SERVEROUTPUT ON and use DBMS_OUTPUT.

A Here is one solution:

```
DECLARE
    v_factorial NUMBER := 1;
    v_factorial_counter NUMBER := 4;
BEGIN
    WHILE v_factorial_counter != 1 LOOP
        v_factorial := v_factorial * v_factorial_counter;
        DBMS_OUTPUT.PUT_LINE('Your factorial value is now '
            || v_factorial);
        v_factorial_counter := v_factorial_counter - 1;
    END LOOP;
END;
/
```

3. Create the same factorial calculation as Exercise 2, but use a simple LOOP statement instead.

A Here is one solution:

```
DECLARE
    v_factorial NUMBER := 1;
    v_factorial_counter NUMBER := 4;
BEGIN
    LOOP
        v_factorial := v_factorial * v_factorial_counter;
        DBMS_OUTPUT.PUT_LINE('Your factorial value is now '
            || v_factorial);
        v_factorial_counter := v_factorial_counter - 1;
        EXIT WHEN v_factorial_counter = 1;
    END LOOP;
END;
/
```

A

Day 7

Quiz

1. True or False: All functions are accessible from within PL/SQL.

A False. There are many SQL-only commands, which perform calculations on rows, such as AVG, MIN, MAX, and so on.

2. What function would I use to combine two strings together?

A You would use the CONCAT function; however, you can still fall back on ¦¦ to concatenate strings.

3. What function would convert '11/28/97' to an Oracle DATE?

A The TO_DATE function gives you this flexibility.

4. In a VARCHAR2 string, each string can be a variable length. What function would you use to determine the length so that you can search through the entire string?

A By using the LENGTH function, you can determine the actual length of VARCHAR2. If the value is NULL, NULL is returned. If you are using type CHAR, it will include the padded spaces in the count.

5. How do you get rid of padded spaces to the right of a string in Oracle?

A By using RTRIM and specifying the space as a character, you can trim any padded spaces in a string.

6. To determine the remainder, you would use the _____ function.

A MOD

7. To determine how many months a customer is delinquent, you can use the _____ function.

A MONTHS_BETWEEN

8. The TRUNC and ROUND functions can be used with what datatypes?

A Both NUMBER and DATE include the ROUND and TRUNC functions.

Exercises

1. Create a PL/SQL block that reads in the month of a date and displays the month in a Roman numeral format. Use a date of 06/11/67. This will allow you to practice the TO_CHAR function. When printing the Roman numeral equivalent, use LTRIM to remove spaces padded to the left of the Roman numeral. If you are really ambitious, on your own you could create the same RM type function by using IF...THEN...ELSE statements for practice from Day 5, "Using Functions, IF Statements, and Loops." Remember, practice helps to solidify your knowledge through repetition and understanding.

A Here is one solution:

```
DECLARE
      v_Hold_Month Number;
BEGIN
      v_Hold_Month := TO_NUMBER(TO_CHAR(TO_DATE('11-JUN-67'),'MM'));
      DBMS_OUTPUT.PUT_LINE(v_Hold_Month);
      DBMS_OUTPUT.PUT_LINE('Converted to Roman Numeral ' ||
            LTRIM(TO_CHAR(v_Hold_Month,'RM'),' '));
END;
/
```

Your output will be

```
6
Converted to Roman Numeral VI
```

2. Use the TRUNC function on the SYSDATE to round to the nearest century.

A The answer is

```
SELECT TO_CHAR(TRUNC(SYSDATE,'CC'),'MM/DD/YYYY HH:MI:SS AM')
      "Today's Date and Time"
  from DUAL
```

The output will be similar to

```
Today's Date and Time
------------------------
01/01/1900 12:00:00 AM
```

3. Use CONCAT to link two strings together. Repeat the same line by using || instead of CONCAT.

A Here is one solution:

```
DECLARE
      v_String1 VARCHAR2(60) := CONCAT('Connect String1 to',
                                        ' String2');
      v_String2 VARCHAR2(60) := 'Connect String1 to' || ' String2';
BEGIN
      DBMS_OUTPUT.PUT_LINE(v_String1);
      DBMS_OUTPUT.PUT_LINE(v_String2);
END;
/
```

Your output will look similar to

```
Connect String1 to String2
Connect String1 to String2
```

4. Calculate the number of days between 01/01/97 to 03/31/97. Remember to use the TRUNC function to eliminate the TIME dependency.

A The answer is

```
SELECT TRUNC(TO_DATE('03/31/97','MM/DD/YY')) -
      TRUNC(TO_DATE('01/01/97','MM/DD/YY')) "Days_Subtracted"
      from DUAL;
```

Your output will be
```
Days_Subtracted
- - - - - - - - - - - - - -
             89
```

5. Convert the CHARACTER string '06/11/67' to a date, and subtract from 06/11/97 to see how old your author is (and holding).

A The answer is
```
SELECT (TO_DATE('06/11/97','MM/DD/YY') -
    TO_DATE('06/11/67','MM/DD/YY'))/365 "Years Old"
    from DUAL;
```

Your output will be
```
Years Old
- - - - - - - - - -
30.021918
```

6. Calculate how many months are between 05/15/97 to 08/22/97.

A The answer is
```
SELECT MONTHS_BETWEEN('22-AUG-97','15-MAY-97') "Fractional"
    from DUAL;
```

Your output will be
```
Fractional
- - - - - - - - - -
 3.2258065
```

7. Round the SYSDATE to the nearest century.

A The answer is
```
SELECT TO_CHAR(ROUND(SYSDATE,'CC'),'MM/DD/YYYY HH:MI:SS AM')
    "Today's Date and Time"
  from DUAL;
```

Your output will be similar to
```
Today's Date and Time
- - - - - - - - - - - - - - - - - - - - - - -
01/01/2000 12:00:00 AM
```

8. Calculate the time in Newfoundland from Central Standard Time from 02/22/97, 05:00 a.m.

A Here is one solution:
```
SELECT TO_CHAR(NEW_TIME(TO_DATE('02-22-97 05:00:00 AM',
        'MM-DD-YY HH:MI:SS AM'),
        'CST','NST'), 'DD-MON-YY HH:MI:SS AM')
            "Central to Newfoundland"
    from DUAL;
```

Your output will be

```
Central to Newfoundland
..........................
22-FEB-97 07:30:00 AM
```

9. From Listing 7.22, subtract one month and explain the answer.

A Several possible answers are

```
SELECT ADD_MONTHS(TO_DATE('31-MAR-97'),-1) from DUAL;
SELECT ADD_MONTHS(TO_DATE('31-MAR-97'),-1.5) from DUAL;
SELECT ADD_MONTHS(-1,TO_DATE('31-MAR-97')) from DUAL;
```

The output, of course, is the end of February because February has fewer than 30 days:

```
ADD_MONTH
..........
28-FEB-97
```

10. Calculate the number of days until Christmas from the last day of the month of today's date! (We don't get paid until the end of the month!)

A Here is one solution:

```
SELECT LAST_DAY(SYSDATE) "Last_Day",
        TO_DATE('25-DEC-97') - LAST_DAY(SYSDATE) "Shopping Days"
    from DUAL;
```

The output will be similar to

```
Last_Day  Shopping Days
..........  .............
30-JUN-97     177.67266
```

Day 8

Quiz

1. What statement is used to recompile a procedure?

A The CREATE OR REPLACE PROCEDURE command is used to recompile a procedure.

2. How do you invoke a procedure?

A You use the execute command if you want to explicitly and manually call a procedure. From within a package or other PL/SQL construct, you simply list the procedure name in the code, and the call to it is made automatically.

3. Name at least four predefined Oracle exception errors.

A There are many Oracle predefined exceptions including: no_data_found, too_many_rows, invalid_cursor, value_error, invalid_number, zero_divide, cursor_already_open, login_denied, and others.

4. How do you call a module of a package?

A To call a specific procedure within a package, you use dot notation as shown in the following example:

```
package_name.procedure_name
```

Exercises

1. Write a package specification for the functions written in previous chapters. Additionally, include in the specification one or two of the procedures used in this chapter.

A Package specifications contain public declarations of the name of the package and its functions and procedures. The following is an example and might differ slightly from your answer:

```
CREATE PACKAGE day_8_package_spec as
-- package name declaration
FUNCTION  inv_count (qty number, part_nbr varchar2(25))
-- function declaration
return number;
PROCEDURE pay_salary (emp_id number);
-- procedure declaration
PROCEDURE hire_employee (emp_name, pay_date number, pay_type char));
--procedure declaration
END day_8_package_spec;
```

2. Write an exception-handling piece of code to trap the error of receiving more rows than you expected as well as an unknown error.

A One possible way to write this exception handler is

```
exception
WHEN too_many_rows THEN
    ...             -- code to be executed when a SELECT returns
                    -- too many rows
END;
WHEN others THEN
    ...             -- code to be executed when an exception is
                    -- encountered which is not the too_many_rows
END;
```

Day 9

Quiz

1. Name some of the database objects that you can base a variable declaration on.

A PL/SQL variables can be based on database table columns, other variables, constants, and cursors.

2. What is the variable attribute you use to base a variable on a table column?

A The %type variable attribute enables you to base a variable on a specific database table column.

3. Name several of the PL/SQL table built-in functions.

A The following built-ins can be used with the PL/SQL table: DELETE, first, last, next, prior, and count.

4. What are the four SQL DML statements permitted in a PL/SQL block?

A The four DML statements that are supported within a PL/SQL block are INSERT, DELETE, UPDATE, and SELECT.

Exercises

Evaluate each of the following three declarations and determine which ones are legal and which ones are not legal. Explain your answer for those that are not legal.

1. Legal or not legal:

```
DECLARE
emp_rec          emp_rec_type;
```

A This is not a legal declaration because emp_rec_type must be declared prior to this declaration. A proper declaration would be

```
DECLARE
TYPE emp_rec_type IS record
      (id        INTEGER,
        name     VARCHAR2(35));
emp_rec          emp_rec_type;
```

2. Legal or not legal:

```
DECLARE
emp_last_name          %type;
```

A This is not a legal declaration. The proper declaration would have to include a table and column reference such as

```
emp_last_name          emp.l_name%type;
```

3. Legal or not legal:

```
DECLARE
TYPE   emp_table_type is table of VARCHAR2(55);
emp_dept_table   emp_table_type;
```

A This declaration is not legal because the INDEX BY clause is missing. This declaration should look like

```
DECLARE
TYPE   emp_table_type is table of VARCHAR2(55)
INDEX BY BINARY_INTEGER;
emp_dept_table   emp_table_type;
```

Day 10

Quiz

1. What are the cursor attributes and what is their purpose?

A The implicit and explicit cursors each have four attributes, which provide useful information about the cursor. The attributes are `%isopen`, `%found`, `%notfound`, and `%rowcount`.

2. How many cursors can you use at a time?

A There is no predefined limit to the number of cursors a session can have. The only constraint that can limit the number of cursors is the availability of memory to manage the cursors. Also, there is a systemwide limit of cursors, which is defined by the `OPEN_CURSOR` parameter.

3. Where is the cursor pointer when the cursor is first opened?

A When the cursor is opened, the cursor pointer is pointing to immediately prior to the first row.

Exercise

Create a PL/SQL block that determines the top five highest-paid employees from your employee table. Be sure to incorporate the usage of the appropriate cursor attributes. Print these five employees to the screen.

A This exercise can be solved in several different ways. Your solution can include exception handling as well as other methods of processing the data. I have chosen the following method as my solution:

```
DECLARE
c_emp_name              VARCHAR2(32);
c_sal                   NUMBER(9,2);

CURSOR  emp_cursor is                          -- cursor declaration
SELECT emp_name, pay_type
from employee
ORDER BY pay_rate desc;      -- key to getting top 5 highest-paid employees

BEGIN

OPEN emp_cursor;
FETCH emp_cursor
INTO c_emp_name, c_sal;    --fetch into variables for later use
WHILE emp_cursor%rowcount<=5 and           -- only fetch top 5 employees
    emp_cursor%found                        -- be sure there is data
LOOP
DBMS_OUTPUT (c_emp_name || ' is paid ' || c_sal );
                        -- prints results to screen
FETCH emp_cursor INTO c_emp_name, c_sal;
END LOOP;
CLOSE emp_cursor;                              -- closes the cursor
END;
```

Day 11

Quiz

1. Which data manipulation statements can support triggers?

A INSERT, UPDATE, and DELETE.

2. What are the four basic parts of a trigger definition?

A The event that fires the trigger, the database table on which the trigger is defined, the optional WHEN clause, and the PL/SQL block containing the code to be executed.

3. In a trigger, what are the correlation names :OLD and :NEW used for?

A :OLD is used to refer to the values in a row before it is changed. :NEW is used to refer to the values after the row is changed.

4. What is the name of the system view that can be used to retrieve trigger definitions?

A The USER_TRIGGERS view shows all triggers you own. In addition, you might want to look at the ALL_TRIGGERS view and the DBA_TRIGGERS view. The ALL_TRIGGERS view adds triggers that others own but which are defined on your tables. If you have database administrator privileges, the DBA_TRIGGERS view lists all triggers defined in the database.

5. What is a mutating table?

A A mutating table is one that is in the process of being modified by the SQL statement which fired a trigger. Because the table is being changed it is not in a consistent state, and Oracle does not allow queries against it.

6. Name some possible uses for triggers.

A Some possible uses for triggers are enforcing a business rule, enforcing security, logging changes, replication of data, and calculation of column values.

Exercises

1. Write a set of triggers to maintain the emp_name and dept_name fields redundantly in the emp_dept relation, so that you do not have to join with the employee and department tables just to get a simple department listing.

A Here is one solution:

```
CREATE OR REPLACE TRIGGER emp_dept_names
   BEFORE INSERT OR UPDATE OF emp_id, dept_id ON emp_dept
   FOR EACH ROW
DECLARE
   redundant_dept_name        department.dept_name%TYPE;
   redundant_emp_name         employee.emp_name%TYPE;
BEGIN
   --Get the employee's name
```

A

```
BEGIN
  SELECT emp_name INTO redundant_emp_name
    FROM employee
   WHERE employee.emp_id = :NEW.emp_id;
EXCEPTION
  --the employee record may not exist.
  WHEN OTHERS THEN
    redundant_emp_name := '';
END;

  --Get the department name
BEGIN
  SELECT dept_name INTO redundant_dept_name
    FROM department
   WHERE department.dept_id = :NEW.dept_id;
EXCEPTION
  --the department record may not exist.
  WHEN OTHERS THEN
    redundant_dept_name := '';
END;

  --Store the employee and department names in the emp_dept record.
  :NEW.dept_name := redundant_dept_name;
  :NEW.emp_name := redundant_emp_name;
END;
/
Trigger created.
CREATE OR REPLACE TRIGGER department_emp_dept
  AFTER UPDATE OF dept_name ON department
  FOR EACH ROW
BEGIN
  UPDATE emp_dept
    SET emp_dept.dept_name = :NEW.dept_name
  WHERE emp_dept.dept_id = :NEW.dept_id;
END;
/
Trigger created.
CREATE OR REPLACE TRIGGER employee_emp_dept
  AFTER UPDATE OF emp_name ON employee
  FOR EACH ROW
BEGIN
  UPDATE emp_dept
    SET emp_dept.emp_name = :NEW.emp_name
  WHERE emp_dept.emp_id = :NEW.emp_id;
END;
/
Trigger created.
```

ANALYSIS The first trigger, emp_dept_name, handles inserts and updates on the emp_dept table itself. Whenever a new record is inserted or an existing record updated, the current employee and department names are retrieved from their respective tables and stored with the emp_dept record. The second trigger, department_emp_dept, ensures that any changes to a department's name are propagated to all the related records in the emp_dept table. The third trigger does the same thing for changes to employee names.

Writing these triggers almost leads to a mutation problem. Recall the emp_dept_upd trigger shown in Listing 11.6. It is defined to fire only when the dept_id field is updated; in other words it is defined as AFTER UPDATE OF dept_id ON emp_dept. Removing the words OF dept_id would cause the trigger to fire whenever an emp_dept record was changed. In that case a change to a department name would fire department_emp_dept, which would issue an update against the emp_dept table. That would in turn fire the emp_dept_upd trigger, which would issue an update against the department table, which would be mutating because the SQL statement that started all this was an update against that table.

2. Write the SQL statements necessary to populate the emp_name and dept_name fields for any existing emp_dept records.

A This could be done as either one or two updates. Here is a solution done with one UPDATE statement:

```
UPDATE emp_dept ed
  SET emp_name = (SELECT emp_name
                    FROM employee e
                   WHERE e.emp_id = ed.emp_id),
      dept_name = (SELECT dept_name
                     FROM department d
                    WHERE d.dept_id = ed.dept_id);
```

Day 12

Quiz

1. Name the different cursor variable parameter modes and their purposes.

A The cursor variable argument can have one of three different modes. These modes are

- [ ] IN—The program can have read-only abilities with the parameter. In other words, the cursor argument is passed only to the procedure or function.

- [ ] OUT—The program can return values to the calling PL/SQL block.

- [ ] IN OUT—The program can read or write to the variable.

2. What is the scope of a cursor parameter?

A The cursor parameter is used to pass information into a cursor just as you would pass a parameter into a function or procedure. This can make your code more modular and maintainable. Likewise, you can establish initial or default values for these parameters to make your coding more simplistic.

Exercise

Write a brief package declaration block and the beginning portion of the package body where you declare a cursor variable, and then use this variable in a procedure to open a cursor with a query.

A Like many programming designs, your answer can vary slightly from the following. The idea is for you to get practice declaring cursor variables and parameters in the package specification and body.

```
/* Package Specification  */
CREATE PACKAGE stock_quotes as
TYPE stock_cur_type IS REF cursor;
PROCEDURE get_quotes (stock_cv in out stock_cur_type);
END stock_quotes;

/* Package Body        */

CREATE PACKAGE BODY stock_quotes as
PROCEDURE get_quotes (stock_cv in out stock_cur_type) IS
SELECT * from stocks;
...
END get_quotes;

END stock_quotes;
```

Day 13

Quiz

1. What is the difference between a class and an object?

A A class, or object type as it is called by Oracle, serves as the blueprint for one or more objects. It is just a design, and you might compare it to a table definition. An object, on the other hand, represents an instance of a class. You can create many objects of a given type, just as you can create many records in a table.

2. What are the allowed return values for an ORDER function?

A The allowed return values for an ORDER function are 0, -1, and 1. A 0 value means that the two objects being compared are equal. A value of -1 means that the object whose method was called is less than the other object. A value of 1 means that the object whose method was called is greater than the other object.

3. An object table has one column for each attribute of an object, plus one additional column. What is this additional column used for?

A The extra column in an object table is used to store the *object identifier,* which uniquely identifies that object in the database. It is an Oracle-generated value, and is automatically assigned to each object when it is first stored in the table.

4. How is an object reference different from an object?

A An object reference functions much like a pointer in a language such as C. It is used to store a reference from one object to another. It is only a pointer, and in order to access the referenced object, you must use that pointer in a query to retrieve the specified object.

5. How many attributes must an object have? How many methods?

A Objects must have at least one attribute. They do not, however, have to have any methods at all.

6. What datatypes are allowed for the return value of a MAP function?

A A MAP function can only return values of type NUMBER, VARCHAR2, or DATE.

Exercises

1. Write a stored function that creates and returns an object of type building. This function should accept as parameters the building's name, its address, and the manager's employee number. Have the function check the database before creating the new building object to be sure that another building with the same name does not already exist. If another building with the same name does exist, then the function should return null.

A Here is one solution:

```
 1: CREATE OR REPLACE FUNCTION CreateBuilding (
 2:    --This is an example of how you can work around the
 3:    --fact that you can't write your own "constructor" for
 4:    --the building object. This stored function serves
 5:    --as a psuedo-constructor. Note however, that Oracle can't
 6:    --force you to call this.
 7:    inBldgName        VARCHAR2,
 8:    inBldgStreet      VARCHAR2,
 9:    inBldgCity        VARCHAR2,
10:    inBldgStateAbbr   VARCHAR2,
11:    inBldgZip         VARCHAR2,
12:    inBldgMgr         employee.emp_id%TYPE
13:    ) RETURN building AS
14: TheNewBldg    building;
15: NoFlag        integer;
16: BEGIN
17:    --Check to see if this building already exists in the database.
18:      SELECT count(*) INTO NoFlag
19:        FROM buildings
20:       WHERE BldgName = inBldgName;
21:
22:      IF NoFlag > 0 THEN
23:        RETURN null;
24:      END IF;
25:
26:    --Check to see if the manager employee ID is valid.
27:      SELECT count(*) INTO NoFlag
28:        FROM employee
29:       WHERE emp_id = inBldgMgr;
30:
31:      IF NoFlag = 0 THEN
32:         RETURN null;
33:      END IF;
34:
35:    --All validation checks have been passed, create the new
36:    --building object.
37:    TheNewBldg := building (inBldgName
```

```
38:                             ,address (inBldgStreet
39:                                      ,'' --no second addr line
40:                                      ,inBldgCity
41:                                      ,inBldgStateAbbr
42:                                      ,inBldgZip
43:                                      ,'') --no phone number
44:                             ,inBldgMgr);
45:
46:     RETURN TheNewBldg;
47: END;
48: /
```

Function created.

```
 1: SET SERVEROUTPUT ON
 2: DECLARE
 3:   a_building    building;
 4: BEGIN
 5:     --This will succeed
 6:     a_building := CreateBuilding('The Red Barn',
 7:                                  '101 Pasture Lane',
 8:                                  'Mio','MI','48826',599);
 9:     dbms_output.put_line('Created: ' || a_building.BldgName);
10:
11:     --This will fail because the building exists.
12:     a_building := CreateBuilding('East Storage Shed',
13:                                  '101 Pasture Lane',
14:                                  'Mio','MI','48826',599);
15:     dbms_output.put_line('Created: ' ||
➥nvl(a_building.BldgName,'Nothing'));
16:
17:     --This will fail because the manager does not exist.
18:     a_building := CreateBuilding('The Blue Barn',
19:                                  '101 Pasture Lane',
20:                                  'Mio','MI','48826',999);
21:     dbms_output.put_line('Created: ' ||
➥nvl(a_building.BldgName,'Nothing'));
22:
23: END;
24: /
```

Created: The Red Barn
Created: Nothing
Created: Nothing

PL/SQL procedure successfully completed.

ANALYSIS   The CreateBuilding function takes five arguments: a building name, street address, city, state abbreviation, and manager ID. It returns an object of type building. The SELECT statement in lines 18–20 of the first segment first checks to see if a building with the same name already exists. Then the SELECT statement in lines 27–29 of the first segment checks to be sure that the manager ID is a valid employee ID. If everything checks out, the building constructor is called in lines 37–44 of the first segment to actually create the building object, which is then returned to the calling program (see line 46 of the first segment).

The PL/SQL block at the end of the listing shows the results of three attempts to create building objects. The first succeeds. The second fails because a building with the same name already exists. The third also fails, but this time because the building manager ID does not represent a valid employee ID.

2. Modify the building object type definition to use a MAP function for comparisons instead of an ORDER function.

A Here is one solution:

INPUT/OUTPUT

```
1: CREATE OR REPLACE TYPE building AS OBJECT (
2:    BldgName          VARCHAR2(40),
3:    BldgAddress       address,
4:    BldgMgr           INTEGER,
5:    MEMBER PROCEDURE  ChangeMgr (NewMgr IN INTEGER),
6:    MAP MEMBER FUNCTION Compare
7:        RETURN VARCHAR2
8:    );
```

Type created.

```
1: CREATE OR REPLACE TYPE BODY building AS
2:    MEMBER PROCEDURE  ChangeMgr(NewMgr IN INTEGER) IS
3:       BEGIN
4:          BldgMgr := NewMgr;
5:       END;
6:
7:    MAP MEMBER FUNCTION Compare
8:    RETURN VARCHAR2 IS
9:       BEGIN
10:          RETURN BldgName;
11:       END;
12: END;
13: /
```

Type body created.

ANALYSIS

This version of the building object is much the same as the one you first created in Listing 13.7, except that it has a MAP function defined instead of an ORDER function. This MAP function, declared in lines 6–7 of the first segment and defined in lines 7–11 of the second segment, simply returns the building name. When comparing objects of type building, Oracle will call this function and base the comparison on the values returned.

Day 14

Quiz

1. True or False: Logic errors are easier to debug than syntax errors.

A False. You might not even know logic errors exist until years later.

2. Missing a semicolon is what type of error?

A   A logic error.

3. Provide the answer to the calculation 6 + 4/2 = ?

A   8. You perform the division calculation first and then add the result to 6.

4. True or False: Oracle comes with a built-in debugging package.

A   False. You can create one, purchase one, use pipes, or use the DBMS_OUT package.

5. True or False: Proper planning reduces errors in the future.

A   True. Proper planning helps you to improve the application and do it right the first time.

6. True or False: Commenting code is a waste of time.

A   False. Comments improve readability of code and clarify the intent of the application programmer.

7. True or False: Formatting code is not necessary.

A   False. Without proper formatting techniques, the code is hard to read and even harder to follow.

Exercises

1. Use the DEBUG package to troubleshoot the code in Listing 14.2.

A   One possible answer is

```
DECLARE
    v_MyNumber NUMBER := 0;
BEGIN
    DEBUG.ERASE;
    LOOP
        IF v_MyNumber = 7 THEN
            EXIT;
        END IF;
    v_MyNumber := v_MyNumber + 2;
        DEBUG.OUT('v_MyNumber',v_MyNumber);
    END LOOP;
END;
```

2. Use the DBMS_OUTPUT package to troubleshoot the code in Listing 14.2.

A   One possible answer is

```
SET SERVEROUTPUT ON

DECLARE
    v_MyNumber NUMBER := 0;
BEGIN
    LOOP
        IF v_MyNumber = 7 THEN
            EXIT;
```

```
        END IF;
      v_MyNumber := v_MyNumber + 2;
          DBMS_OUTPUT.PUT_LINE('The valye of v_MyNumber is: ' ¦¦ v_MyNumber);
      END LOOP;
  END;
```

Day 15

Quiz

1. Could you use recursion to generate an organizational chart as long as you had the ID of your immediate boss coded in your employee record?

A Yes, but a large organizational chart will make for slower execution time than an alternative method.

2. Should you use recursion as much as possible?

A No. In fact, you will probably rarely use recursion.

3. What is the largest size of a large object?

A Four gigabytes.

4. Can you write to external files?

A Currently, you can only read from external files.

5. When copying LOBs from one row to another, is only a new locator copied?

A Not only is the newly created locator copied, but the entire LOB from the row is copied as well. If you have some 4-gigabyte objects, this table can eat up storage space fast!

Exercise

Rewrite the code in Listing 15.1, but as a loop instead of a recursive function. Provide the result of 6 factorial (6!).

A One possible answer is

```
DECLARE
    v_MyNum NUMBER := 6;
    v_Factorial NUMBER := 1;
BEGIN
    LOOP
        IF v_MyNum = 0 THEN
            EXIT;
        ELSE
            v_Factorial := v_Factorial * v_MyNum;
        END IF;
        v_MyNum := v_MyNum - 1;
    END LOOP;
    DBMS_OUTPUT.PUT_LINE('The factorial is:  ' ¦¦ v_Factorial);
END;
```

Your output will look similar to

```
The factorial is:   720
```

Day 16

Quiz

1. How is a transaction ended?

A A transaction is ended when it is committed or when it is rolled back.

2. What is the difference between row locking and table locking?

A To summarize, row locks are enabled when a specific row is being modified by a DML statement. Likewise, a table lock is acquired either explicitly or implicitly when either a row or a table is being modified. Refer to the section in this chapter regarding locks, "Locking."

3. What is the purpose of a savepoint?

A Savepoints are like bookmarks within a transaction; they facilitate the rollback of a transaction to some intermediate point. This intermediate point is defined by the placement of the savepoint.

Exercise

Write a PL/SQL block that establishes a savepoint, inserts a single record into the employee table, commits the data if the new record does not replicate an existing record, or rolls back the data if the new record insert fails.

A Here is one solution:

```
SAVEPOINT exercise;            -- use this to roll back to
INSERT INTO employee VALUES (1, 'Loraine Williams',2,4000.00,'S');
COMMIT;      -- saves the data if insert was successful
             -- this is not executed if there is an exception
EXCEPTION
WHEN DUP_VAL_ON_INDEX THEN   -- exception handler
ROLLBACK;                    -- back out data from insert
```

Day 17

Quiz

1. For DML and DDL statements, and also for queries, what punctuation must not occur at the end of the query?

A You must not end queries, DDL statements, or DML statements with a semicolon.

2. For anonymous blocks, is all punctuation required?

A Anonymous blocks require all punctuation.

3. What is the largest size a PL/SQL variable can hold in kilobytes?

A The largest value a PL/SQL variable can hold is 32KB.

4. Why is processing queries and SQL with the DBMS_SQL package considered dynamic?

A Unlike fixed queries, these queries are created during runtime operations and executed in real time, thus making them dynamic.

Exercises

1. Write a SQL query to show all records and all fields to the screen where the value of MyRow is greater than or equal to 2.

A One possible answer is

```
DECLARE
/* The purpose of this PL/SQL block is to demonstrate
   executing queries within PL/SQL through the use of the
   DBMS_SQL package.  We will simply display the output to
   screen with the DBMS_OUTPUT package */

    v_CursorID  NUMBER; -- Variable assigned to value from OPEN_CURSOR
    v_SelectRecords  VARCHAR2(500); -- SQL stored as string to select
                                    ➥records
    v_NUMRows  INTEGER; -- Number of rows processed - of no use
    v_MyNum INTEGER;
    v_MyText VARCHAR2(50);

BEGIN
    v_CursorID := DBMS_SQL.OPEN_CURSOR; -- Get the Cursor ID
    v_SelectRecords := 'SELECT * from MyTable
        WHERE MyRow >= 2'; -- SQL to view records


    DBMS_SQL.PARSE(v_CursorID,v_SelectRecords,DBMS_SQL.V7);
        /* Perform syntax error checking */

/*    DBMS_SQL.BIND_VARIABLE(v_CursorID, ':mynum',1);
    DBMS_SQL.BIND_VARIABLE(v_CursorID, ':mytext','One'); */

    DBMS_SQL.DEFINE_COLUMN(v_CursorID,1,v_MyNum);
    DBMS_SQL.DEFINE_COLUMN(v_CursorID,2,v_MyText,50);

    v_NumRows := DBMS_SQL.EXECUTE(v_CursorID);
        /* Execute the SQL code  */
LOOP
    IF DBMS_SQL.FETCH_ROWS(v_CursorID) = 0 THEN
        EXIT;
    END IF;

    DBMS_SQL.COLUMN_VALUE(v_CursorId,1,v_MyNum);
    DBMS_SQL.COLUMN_VALUE(v_CursorId,2,v_MyText);

    DBMS_OUTPUT.PUT_LINE(v_MyNum || ' ' || v_MyText);

END LOOP;
```

```
EXCEPTION
     WHEN OTHERS THEN
                 RAISE; -- raise if some other unknown error

     DBMS_SQL.CLOSE_CURSOR(v_CursorID); -- Close the cursor

END; -- End PL/SQL block
```

Your output should appear as follows:

```
2 Two
3 Three
4 Four
4 Four
```

2. Write a SQL query to delete all records with MyRow equal to 4.

A Here's one solution:

```
DECLARE
/* The purpose of this PL/SQL block is to demonstrate the use
   of DML statements by deleting two records where MyRow
   has a value of 4 */

     v_CursorID  NUMBER; -- Variable assigned to value from OPEN_CURSOR
     v_DeleteRecords  VARCHAR2(500); -- SQL stored as string to insert
                                ➥records
     v_NUMRows  INTEGER; -- Number of rows processed - of no use

BEGIN
     v_CursorID := DBMS_SQL.OPEN_CURSOR; -- Get the Cursor ID
     v_DeleteRecords := 'DELETE FROM MyTable
             where MyRow = :mynum';

/*  Update the record */

     DBMS_SQL.PARSE(v_CursorID,v_DeleteRecords,DBMS_SQL.V7);
         /* Perform syntax error checking */
     DBMS_SQL.BIND_VARIABLE(v_CursorID, ':mynum',4);
      v_NumRows := DBMS_SQL.EXECUTE(v_CursorID);
         /* Execute the SQL code  */
     DBMS_OUTPUT.PUT_LINE('The number of records just processed is: '
         || v_NUMRows);


EXCEPTION
     WHEN OTHERS THEN
                 RAISE; -- raise if some other unknown error

     DBMS_SQL.CLOSE_CURSOR(v_CursorID); -- Close the cursor
     COMMIT;
END; -- End PL/SQL block
```

Your data should look like:

```
MYROW MYDESC
----- --------------------------------------------------
    1 One
    2 Two
    3 Three
```

3. Write the DML code to update the record where MyRow is equal to 1. Change the description to say It Worked.

A One possible answer is

```
DECLARE
/* The purpose of this PL/SQL block is to demonstrate the use
    of DML statements by updating one records where MyRow
    has a value of 1 */

    v_CursorID  NUMBER; -- Variable assigned to value from OPEN_CURSOR
    v_UpdateRecords  VARCHAR2(500); -- SQL stored as string to insert
                                        ➥records
    v_NUMRows  INTEGER; -- Number of rows processed - of no use

BEGIN
    v_CursorID := DBMS_SQL.OPEN_CURSOR; -- Get the Cursor ID
    v_UpdateRecords := 'UPDATE MyTable
        Set MyDesc = :mytext
            where MyRow = :mynum';

/*  Update the record */

    DBMS_SQL.PARSE(v_CursorID,v_UpdateRecords,DBMS_SQL.V7);
        /* Perform syntax error checking */
    DBMS_SQL.BIND_VARIABLE(v_CursorID, ':mynum',1);
    DBMS_SQL.BIND_VARIABLE(v_CursorID, ':mytext','It Worked');
    v_NumRows := DBMS_SQL.EXECUTE(v_CursorID);
        /* Execute the SQL code  */
    DBMS_OUTPUT.PUT_LINE('The number of records just processed is: '
        ¦¦ v_NUMRows);


EXCEPTION
    WHEN OTHERS THEN
                RAISE; -- raise if some other unknown error

    DBMS_SQL.CLOSE_CURSOR(v_CursorID); -- Close the cursor
    COMMIT;
END; -- End PL/SQL block
```

Your data should look like:

```
MYROW MYDESC
----- --------------------------------------------------
    1 It Worked
    2 Two
    3 Three
```

4. Write the DDL code required to drop the table called MyTable.

A One possible answer is

```
DECLARE
/* The purpose of this PL/SQL block is to delete a table
    called MyTable, which has two columns of type INTEGER and
    the second column of type VARCHAR2(50).  This uses the
    DBMS_SQL package to execute DDL statements */
```

```
        v_CursorID   NUMBER; -- Variable assigned to value from OPEN_CURSOR
        v_CreateTableString   VARCHAR2(500); -- SQL stored as string to drop
                                        ➥table
        v_NUMRows   INTEGER; -- Number of rows processed - of no use

     BEGIN
        v_CursorID := DBMS_SQL.OPEN_CURSOR; -- Get the Cursor ID
        v_CreateTableString := 'DROP TABLE MyTable'; -- Write SQL code to drop
                                                ➥table

        DBMS_SQL.PARSE(v_CursorID,v_CreateTableString,DBMS_SQL.V7);
            /* Perform syntax error checking */
        v_NumRows := DBMS_SQL.EXECUTE(v_CursorID);
            /* Execute the SQL code  */

     EXCEPTION
        WHEN OTHERS THEN
            RAISE; -- raise if some other unknown error

        DBMS_SQL.CLOSE_CURSOR(v_CursorID); -- Close the cursor
     END; -- End PL/SQL block
```

Day 18

Quiz

1. What is the difference between PUT and PUT_LINE with the UTL_FILE package or even the DBMS_OUTPUT package?

A PUT_LINE adds a newline character after each line written to the file, whereas PUT does not write out the newline character. You would have to use the NEW_LINE statement with PUT in order for PUT to behave identically to PUT_LINE.

2. What is the maximum number of bytes that can be read into a buffer when using UTL_FILE?

A 1022 bytes.

3. What is the maximum number of bytes that can be output to a file when using UTL_FILE?

A 1023 bytes.

4. When using FCLOSE_ALL, what boolean value will be returned by testing to see if the file is open using IS_OPEN?

A Even though the files are truly closed, the files are not marked as closed, so IS_OPEN will return a value of true.

5. What suppresses output from PUT or PUT_LINE when using the DBMS_OUTPUT package?

A Either GET_LINE or GET_LINES will cause any form of PUT not to default to the screen.

6. What is the maximum number of characters allowed in a buffer line when using DBMS_OUTPUT?

A 255 characters—any more will raise an error.

7. What is the maximum number of characters that can possibly be allocated to the buffer when using DBMS_OUTPUT?

A 1,000,000 total characters. If the buffer limit is exceeded, an error is raised.

Exercises

1. From the code in Listing 18.6, output the data in a fixed block format. The output should be SSNO with a length of 11 bytes formatted as ###-##-####, FirstName at 20 bytes, and LastName at 30 bytes. Remember, VARCHAR2 data does not pad spaces to the right. You could either use a character function to fill the data with spaces or assign the variables to type CHAR before outputting the data. Name the output file PRESFIX.TXT.

A One possible answer is

```
DECLARE
-- Variables to write out to text file called presexp.csv
    v_SSNO      pres.ssno%TYPE;
    v_FirstName CHAR(20);
    v_LastName  CHAR(30);
--Declare filehandle
    v_MYFileHandle UTL_FILE.FILE_TYPE;
-- Cursor declaration to fetch data from table, row by row
CURSOR c_PRES IS
    SELECT * from PRES;
BEGIN
-- Open File for writing
    v_MYFileHandle := UTL_FILE.FOPEN('c:\','presfix.txt','w');
-- Open the cursor
    OPEN c_PRES;
    LOOP
-- Get each row, one at a time
        FETCH c_PRES INTO v_SSNO,v_FirstName,v_LastName;
-- Output as FIXED BLOCK file
        EXIT WHEN c_PRES%NOTFOUND;
        UTL_FILE.PUT_LINE(v_MYFileHandle, SUBSTR(v_SSNO,1,3) || '-'
            || SUBSTR(v_SSNO,4,2) || '-' || SUBSTR(v_SSNO,6,4)
            || v_FirstName || v_LastName);
    END LOOP;
-- Close Cursor
    CLOSE c_PRES;
-- Close CSV file
    UTL_FILE.FCLOSE(v_MYFileHandle);
END;
```

Your file should look like:

```
001-01-0111George              Washington
005-12-4745Thomas              Jefferson
```

```
223-44-5726Richard              Nixon
378-11-2475Jimmy                Carter
541-12-9744Abraham              Lincoln
587-14-5961John                 Kennedy
665-47-4112Theodore             Roosevelt
725-13-9511George               Bush
998-21-1247Ronald               Reagan
```

2. From Exercise 1, add DBMS_OUTPUT.PUT_LINE to display the lines to the screen as they are output to the file.

A One possible answer is

```
DECLARE
-- Variables to write out to text file called presexp.csv
    v_SSNO          pres.ssno%TYPE;
    v_FirstName     CHAR(20);
    v_LastName      CHAR(30);
--Declare filehandle
    v_MYFileHandle UTL_FILE.FILE_TYPE;
-- Cursor declaration to fetch data from table, row by row
CURSOR c_PRES IS
    SELECT * from PRES;
BEGIN
-- Open File for writing
    v_MYFileHandle := UTL_FILE.FOPEN('c:\','presfix.csv','w');
-- Open the cursor
    OPEN c_PRES;
    LOOP
-- Get each row, one at a time
        FETCH c_PRES INTO v_SSNO,v_FirstName,v_LastName;
-- Output as FIXED BLOCK file
        EXIT WHEN c_PRES%NOTFOUND;
        UTL_FILE.PUT_LINE(v_MYFileHandle, SUBSTR(v_SSNO,1,3) || '-'
            || SUBSTR(v_SSNO,4,2) || '-' || SUBSTR(v_SSNO,6,4)
            || v_FirstName || v_LastName);
        DBMS_OUTPUT.PUT_LINE(v_SSNO || v_FirstName || v_LastName);
    END LOOP;
-- Close Cursor
    CLOSE c_PRES;
-- Close CSV file
    UTL_FILE.FCLOSE(v_MYFileHandle);
END;
```

The output will be similar to:

```
001010111George                 Washington
005124745Thomas                 Jefferson
223445726Richard                Nixon
378112475Jimmy                  Carter
541129744Abraham                Lincoln
587145961John                   Kennedy
665474112Theodore               Roosevelt
725139511George                 Bush
998211247Ronald                 Reagan
```

Day 19

Quiz

1. If the server goes down for two days (Monday to Tuesday), and a job with an execution of SYSDATE + 7 was supposed to run when the server went down (Tuesday), will the job always run on the original day of the week (run every Tuesday)?

A No, because the new SYSDATE is assigned when the server is restored (Wednesday). The job will now be running every Wednesday until the job is altered, removed, or another problem occurs.

2. Why must you use two single quotes around parameters specified in SUBMIT that used to take only one set of single quotes?

A When Oracle parses the data and removes the quotes, any part that does not have two sets of single quotes and is a string parameter will be stripped down to no single quotes and thus cause the job to fail.

3. Can you alter someone else's job?

A Only if you know his or her login and password and sign on as that person. In other words...no!

4. Is there any way to assign your own job number to a job?

A Use ISUBMIT.

5. What interval would you use to run a procedure every hour on the hour starting from the current date?

A SYSDATE + 1/24.

6. If you send a message to a full pipe, how long will you wait before you abort the process?

A The default of maxwait is 1000 days! A more typical approach is to set the wait period for up to 60 seconds.

7. What is the maximum length of the message buffer?

A A maximum of 4096 bytes can be held in the message buffer before an overflow message will be displayed.

Exercises

1. Write the code to submit a procedure called PAYDAY, where the parameters are FRIDAY, Bi_Monthly, and 6. The job should always execute at 4 a.m. on Saturday.

A One possible answer is

```
DECLARE
    v_JobNum  BINARY_INTEGER;
```

```
BEGIN
    DBMS_JOB.SUBMIT(v_JobNum,'PAYDAY(''FRIDAY'',''BI_Monthly,6);',SYSDATE,
        'NEXT_DAY(TRUNC(SYSDATE),''SATURDAY'') + 4/24');
END;
```

2. Write the code to view the JOB, last second run, and WHAT from USER_JOBS.

A One possible answer is

```
SELECT JOB,LAST_SEC,WHAT from USER_JOBS;
```

3. Write the code to submit job 200 once per day starting from SYSDATE for the procedure EASY, which has no parameters.

A One possible answer is

```
DECLARE
BEGIN
    DBMS_JOB.ISUBMIT(200,'EASY;',SYSDATE,'SYSDATE + 1');
END;
```

4. Write the code to alter job 200 to execute once per week for the interval (SYSDATE + 7).

A One possible answer is

```
BEGIN
    DBMS_JOB.INTERVAL(200,'SYSDATE+7');
END;
```

5. Write the code to remove job 200.

A One possible answer is

```
BEGIN
    DBMS_JOB.REMOVE(200);
END;
```

6. From Listing 19.22, add the ELSIF procedures to handle RAW and ROWID datatypes.

A One possible answer is

```
DECLARE
    v_statpipe1 integer; -- status of private pipe
    v_statpipe2 integer; -- status of public pipe
    v_holdtype INTEGER; -- holds status of next item type
    v_holdchar VARCHAR2(100);
    v_holddate DATE;
    v_holdnum NUMBER;
    v_holdraw RAW(4000);
    v_holdrowid ROWID;
BEGIN
-- start procedure of getting message from private pipe
    v_statpipe1 := DBMS_PIPE.RECEIVE_MESSAGE('myprivatepipe',15);
    DBMS_PIPE.UNPACK_MESSAGE(v_holdchar);
    DBMS_OUTPUT.PUT_LINE(v_holdchar);
        -- display first datatype from message
    DBMS_PIPE.UNPACK_MESSAGE(v_holdchar);
    DBMS_OUTPUT.PUT_LINE(v_holdchar);
        -- display second datatype from message
```

```
-- start procedure of getting message from public pipe
    v_statpipe2 := DBMS_PIPE.RECEIVE_MESSAGE('mypublicpipe',10);
    LOOP
        v_holdtype := DBMS_PIPE.NEXT_ITEM_TYPE;
        IF v_holdtype = 0 THEN EXIT;
        ELSIF v_holdtype = 6 THEN
            DBMS_PIPE.UNPACK_MESSAGE(v_holdnum);
        ELSIF v_holdtype = 9 THEN
            DBMS_PIPE.UNPACK_MESSAGE(v_holdchar);
        ELSIF v_holdtype = 12 THEN
            DBMS_PIPE.UNPACK_MESSAGE(v_holddate);
        ELSIF v_holdtype = 11 THEN
            DBMS_PIPE.UNPACK_MESSAGE_ROWID(v_holdrowid);
        ELSIF v_holdtype = 23 THEN
            DBMS_PIPE.UNPACK_MESSAGE_RAW(v_holdraw);
        END IF;
    END LOOP;
-- display all three types of data
    DBMS_OUTPUT.PUT_LINE(v_holdchar || ' ' ||
            v_holddate || ' ' || v_holdnum);
END;
```

7. From Listing 19.22, all data read into the public pipe should be inserted into a table called PIPETAB with the following schema: `MyString VARCHAR2`, `MyDate DATE`, and `MyNum NUMBER`. Make sure that you run the `CREATE_PIPE` procedure from Listing 19.21 so that you have data in the pipes for placing in the table.

A You would first create the table PIPETAB with

```
CREATE TABLE PIPETAB (
    MyString VARCHAR2(100),
    MyDate DATE,
    MyNumber NUMBER)
/
```

You would then read the pipe with the following:

```
DECLARE
    v_statpipe2 integer; -- status of public pipe
    v_holdtype INTEGER; -- holds status of next item type
    v_holdchar VARCHAR2(100);
    v_holddate DATE;
    v_holdnum NUMBER;
    v_holdraw RAW(4000);
    v_holdrowid ROWID;
BEGIN

-- start procedure of getting message from public pipe
    v_statpipe2 := DBMS_PIPE.RECEIVE_MESSAGE('mypublicpipe',10);
    LOOP
        v_holdtype := DBMS_PIPE.NEXT_ITEM_TYPE;
        IF v_holdtype = 0 THEN EXIT;
        ELSIF v_holdtype = 6 THEN
            DBMS_PIPE.UNPACK_MESSAGE(v_holdnum);
        ELSIF v_holdtype = 9 THEN
            DBMS_PIPE.UNPACK_MESSAGE(v_holdchar);
        ELSIF v_holdtype = 12 THEN
```

```
            DBMS_PIPE.UNPACK_MESSAGE(v_holddate);
        ELSIF v_holdtype = 11 THEN
            DBMS_PIPE.UNPACK_MESSAGE_ROWID(v_holdrowid);
        ELSIF v_holdtype = 23 THEN
            DBMS_PIPE.UNPACK_MESSAGE_RAW(v_holdraw);
        END IF;
    END LOOP;
-- display all three types of data
    DBMS_OUTPUT.PUT_LINE(v_holdchar || ' ' || v_holddate
        || ' ' || v_holdnum);
-- Insert Three Data Elements into the table
INSERT INTO PIPETAB(MyString,MyDate,MyNumber)
    VALUES(v_holdchar,v_holddate,v_holdnum);
COMMIT;

END;
```

You can verify this by typing `SELECT * from PIPETAB;`.

Day 20

Quiz

1. What is the maximum length of an alert name?

A 30 characters. It cannot begin with ORA$, which is reserved by Oracle.

2. What is the maximum length of the message?

A 1800 bytes.

3. What datatype is the message sent as?

A Only a string type `VARCHAR2(1800)` is passed and received.

4. If 20 sessions are monitoring for an alert and the alert is sent, how many of those sessions receive the signaled alert?

A Unlike pipes, all 20 sessions will receive the alert.

5. Alerts require a(n) _____ because you are dealing more on a transactional level, whereas pipes do not.

A Commit

Exercises

1. Change the code in Listing 20.3 to wait for any alert, and also register for two more alerts called `'my_test'` and `'extra_alert'`. Store the name of the alert that is signaled in a variable entitled `alert_name` of type `VARCHAR2(30)`. After the alert has been handled, remove all registered alerts.

A One possible answer is

```
DECLARE
    message VARCHAR2(1800); -- Display Incoming Message from Alert
    alert_name VARCHAR2(30); -- Hold name of alert which was received
    status INTEGER; -- Holds Status 0 if success, 1 if timed out
```

```
BEGIN
    DBMS_ALERT.REGISTER('emp_change'); -- Registers for Alert emp_change
    DBMS_ALERT.REGISTER('my_test'); -- Registers for Alert my_test
    DBMS_ALERT.REGISTER('extra_alert'); -- Registers for Alert extra_alert
    DBMS_ALERT.WAITANY(alert_name,message,status,600); -- Wait for alert
    DBMS_OUTPUT.PUT_LINE(message); -- Display Message
    DBMS_ALERT.REMOVEALL; -- Remove Registration for Alert
END;
```

2. Write a loop that will continually execute until the value of FIRE equals 1, which will then trigger the alert called 'a_fire', which will pass the message 'A Fire has Broken Out'.

A One possible answer is

```
DECLARE
    IS_FIRE INTEGER := 0;
BEGIN
    LOOP
        IF IS_FIRE = 1 THEN
            DBMS_ALERT.SIGNAL('a_fire','A Fire has Broken Out');
            EXIT;
        END IF;
        CHECKFIRE; -- procedure called to check for fire
    END LOOP;
END;
```

Day 21

Quiz

1. List several of the options available to access the Oracle database through Java.

A Java can access a relational database through the use of J/SQL or JDBC. J/SQL is the integration of SQL code within Java. JDBC is a driver-based approach to accessing the database from Java.

2. What are the differences between PL/SQL and Java?

A There are several differences between PL/SQL and Java. To summarize them, I would say that Java lacks the data manipulation capabilities that PL/SQL provides. PL/SQL does not take full advantage of some common object-oriented features such as classes and inheritance. The differences between PL/SQL and Java are important to know because they will guide you to choosing the appropriate language for your application.

3. What role does JDBC play in Internet-to-database connectivity?

A JDBC allows Java applications to have data access from your Oracle database. JDBC uses a driver-based approach to database connectivity, which is very similar to the ODBC approach.

APPENDIX

B

Oracle Functions Reference

by Timothy Atwood

This appendix consists of descriptions and examples of Oracle functions. The categories include character functions, number functions, date functions, conversion functions, miscellaneous functions, and grouping functions. I describe each function and the situations in which it would be used, and I show the syntax and one or more examples of each function.

NOTE   All the samples in this appendix are the results from an IBM PC. Answers will vary depending upon the character set. In addition, with any of the functions that use dual-byte character systems, the output is reflected as a dual-byte character system as well, not a single-byte system such as IBM PC ASCII.

Character Functions

The first set of functions deal exclusively with manipulating character datatypes. These various powerful functions allow you to manipulate a character string down to the individual character.

ASCII

Description: Returns the decimal equivalent of a single ASCII character. If a string is passed, only the first character is translated. This function translates whatever character set is in use, such as EBCDIC, ASCII, and all the variants, from the appropriate lookup table.

Syntax

```
ASCII(character to translate)
```

Where Used: PL/SQL and SQL statements

Samples

```
SELECT ASCII('T') from DUAL;

ASCII('T')
----------
        84

SELECT ASCII('Tim') from DUAL;

ASCII('TIM')
-----------
         84

SELECT ASCII('t') from DUAL;

ASCII('T')
----------
       116
```

CHR

Description: Returns the corresponding character represented by the decimal number passed in this function. The decimal equivalent must be passed in an integer format. This function is the inverse of ASCII, and the character returned depends upon the character set of the operating system.

TIP

You could use either the ASCII or the CHR function to determine which character set is in use, so proper conversion can take place if you're downloading data from the database.

Syntax

```
CHR(decimal number)
```

Where Used: PL/SQL and SQL statements

Samples

```
SELECT CHR(84) from DUAL;

C
-
T

SELECT CHR(65) from DUAL;

C
-
A

SELECT CHR(181) from DUAL;

C
-
μ
```

CONCAT

Description: Joins two character strings into one—concatenates the two strings. The second string passed is appended to the first string. As in the examples throughout the book, I still prefer to use the | | operator over this function. Both achieve the same result, but | | uses fewer keystrokes, and the intent is easier to spot.

Syntax

```
CONCAT(string1,string2)
```

Where Used: PL/SQL and SQL statements

TIP When concatenating strings, don't forget the space when appending strings; otherwise, words will run together.

Sample

```
SELECT CONCAT('The quick brown fox ', 'jumped over the lazy dog') "Concat",
        'The quick brown fox ','jumped over the lazy dog' "¦¦ Operator"
    from DUAL;

Concat                                           'THEQUICKBROWNFOX'    ¦¦ Operator
-------------------------------------------------  --------------------  --------
The quick brown fox jumped over the lazy dog The quick brown
 fox  jumped over the lazy dog
```

INITCAP

Description: Capitalizes the first letter only for each word in a string of characters, and the remaining characters in the word are converted, if necessary, to lowercase. Nonalphabetic characters, such as a space, numbers, and punctuation, remain unchanged.

Syntax

INITCAP(*input_string*)

Where Used: PL/SQL and SQL statements

Sample

```
SELECT INITCAP('NOW is the tImE for AlL GOOd peoplE to come to
    the AID of Their Country')
        "Quote of the Day"
    from DUAL;

Quote of the Day
----------------------------------------------------------------------------
Now Is The Time For All Good People To Come To The Aid Of Their Country
```

INSTR

Description: Finds the nth occurrence of a string in a substring, starting from the starting position specified. This function is case sensitive, so 'the', 'The', and 'tHe' are three different strings and will not match. If *string2* is not found in *string1*, either because it does not exist or because the starting position or nth occurrence is out of range, the function returns a value of 0. By default, the starting position and nth occurrence are both set equal to 1. If the starting position is positive, the scan occurs from left to right.

Syntax

INSTR(*string1_compared*,*string2_to_compare*,<*starting_position*>,
    <*the_nth_occurrence*>)

Where Used: PL/SQL and SQL statements

Samples

```
SELECT INSTR('Now is the time for Tim to get his act together','tim')
        "INSTR_TEST"
    from DUAL;
```

```
INSTR_TEST
----------
        12
```

```
SELECT INSTR('Now is the time for Tim to get his act together','tim',1,2)
        "INSTR_TEST"
    from DUAL;
```

```
INSTR_TEST
----------
         0
```

NOTE The second occurrence can't be found because the match is case sensitive.

You can always guarantee a match by the following listed code:

```
SELECT INSTR(UPPER('Now is the time for Tim to get his act
    together'),UPPER('tim'),1,2)
        "INSTR_TEST"
    from DUAL;
```

```
INSTR_TEST
----------
        21
```

```
SELECT INSTR('Now is the time for Tim to get his act together','tim',-1)
        "INSTR_TEST"
    from DUAL;
```

```
INSTR_TEST
----------
        12
```

```
SELECT INSTR('Now is the time for Tim to get his act together','tim',16)
        "INSTR_TEST"
    from DUAL;
```

```
INSTR_TEST
----------
         0
```

INSTRB

Description: Performs the same function as INSTR, except that the starting position, the nth occurrence, and the return values are all expressed in bytes. For single-byte character systems (one byte per character), INSTRB will return the same results as INSTR. For double-byte systems, you will get a different response.

Syntax

```
INSTRB(string1_compared,string2_to_compare,<starting_position>,
    <the_nth_occurrence>)
```

Where Used: PL/SQL and SQL statements

Samples

```
SELECT INSTRB('Now is the time for Tim to get his act together','tim')
        "INSTR_TEST"
    from DUAL;

INSTR_TEST
----------
        23
```

LENGTH

Description: Returns the length of a string, including padding for datatype CHAR. If the input string has a value of NULL, NULL is returned.

Syntax

```
LENGTH(input_string)
```

Where Used: PL/SQL and SQL statements

Sample

```
SET SERVEROUTPUT ON
DECLARE
    v_PASS CHAR(12) := 'GREAT';
BEGIN
    IF LENGTH(v_PASS) > 10 THEN
        DBMS_OUTPUT.PUT_LINE('The length including the padding is '
            || LENGTH(v_PASS));
    END IF;
    IF LENGTH(RTRIM(v_PASS,' ')) <= 5 THEN
        DBMS_OUTPUT.PUT_LINE('Password too short.  Your length is:    '
            || LENGTH(RTRIM(v_PASS,' ')));
    END IF;
END;/

The length including the padding is 12
Password too short.  Your length is:   5
```

The preceding sample uses a function discussed later in this chapter called RTRIM, which is used in this case to trim the padded spaces of type CHAR. You can easily mix and match functions to allow for your desired complexity.

LENGTHB

Description: This function is identical to the LENGTH function except that it returns the length of the string in bytes. If a single-byte-per-character operating system is being used, both LENGTH and LENGTHB will return the same value. If a double-byte system is used, it will double the answer.

Syntax

LENGTHB(*input_string*)

Where Used: PL/SQL and SQL statements

Sample

NOTE

The following example assumes a double-byte character system.

```
SELECT LENGTHB('This is a test if double byte') "Double_Byte"
    from DUAL;

Double_Byte
-----------
         58
```

LOWER

Description: Returns all characters in a string in lowercase. Nonalphabetic characters, such as punctuation and numbers, are unaffected by this function. This function returns the same datatype as sent in the input string; therefore, type VARCHAR2 returns VARCHAR2 and CHAR returns CHAR.

Syntax

LOWER(*input_string*)

Where Used: PL/SQL and SQL statements

Sample

```
SELECT LOWER('THIS IS a Test OF tHe LoWER Function') "Lower Function"
    from DUAL;

Lower Function
-----------------------------------
this is a test of the lower function
```

LPAD

Description: Pads a string of characters, starting from the left, up to the maximum of the length specified, with any character. If no character is selected, the single space is used for default, similar to the RPAD function.

TIP You can use this function in combination with REPLACE to reformat and display numbers in a new format. For instance, you could remove the $ from $10000 with REPLACE and add padding with zeros and a length of 10 to make the number appear as a numeric entry 0000010000.

Syntax

LPAD(*input_string*,*total_string_length*,<*character_to_pad*>)

Where Used: PL/SQL and SQL statements

Samples

```
SELECT LPAD('Test default character',25) "Default Pad"
     from DUAL;

Default Pad
- - - - - - - - - - - - - - - - - - - - - - - -
   Test default character

SELECT LPAD('New Pad Character',25,'@') "Default Pad"
     from DUAL;

Default Pad
- - - - - - - - - - - - - - - - - - - - - - - -
@@@@@@@@New Pad Character

SELECT LPAD('New Pad Character',15,'@') "Default Pad"
     from DUAL;

Default Pad
- - - - - - - - - - - - - - -
New Pad Charact
```

LTRIM

Description: Allows you to remove characters that you specify from the beginning of a string until the first occurrence in the string that does not contain those characters, and then the function returns the remaining characters in the string. This function is useful to remove spaces, all numbers (the string set you would specify is '0123456789'), words, or whatever else is required. If the string of characters to remove is not specified, the default is a single blank.

Syntax

LTRIM(*input_string*,*characters_to_remove*)

Where Used: PL/SQL and SQL statements

Samples

```
SELECT LTRIM('     You will remove leading spaces')
    "Space Removal as Default"
    from DUAL;

Space Removal as Default
----------------------------
You will remove leading spaces

SELECT LTRIM('56911Row ID','0123456789') "Remove Numbers"
    from DUAL;

Remove
------
Row ID

SELECT LTRIM('AMPMStops Here before removing AM here','AMP')
     "Remove Letters"
    from DUAL;

Remove Letters
----------------------------------
Stops Here before removing AM here
```

NLS_INITCAP

Description: Works the same as INITCAP to return the first letter capitalized and the remaining in lowercase, except that it has an added NLS parameter to change the sort sequence based upon the language. If the NLS_SORT parameter is not used, the function operates the same as INITCAP. Refer to *Oracle7 Server SQL Reference* for all available NLS parameters.

Syntax

```
NLS_INITCAP('Input String',<'NLS_SORT=parameter'>)
```

Where Used: PL/SQL and SQL statements

Sample

```
SELECT NLS_INITCAP('This is a test of a nls_initcap with ijsland',
    'NLS_SORT=xDutch')
    from DUAL;

NLS_INITCAP('THISISATESTOFANLS_INITCAPWITHIJ
---------------------------------------------
This Is A Test Of A Nls_Initcap With IJsland
```

NLS_LOWER

Description: Operates in the same manner as the function LOWER, except that NLS_LOWER has an optional NLS_SORT parameter to specify the language and characters returned. All characters are returned in lowercase and all nonalphabetic characters are unaffected. If no NLS_SORT parameter is used, this function operates identically to the function LOWER. Refer to *Oracle7 Server SQL Reference* for all available NLS parameters.

Syntax

```
NLS_LOWER('Input String',<'NLS_SORT=parameter'>)
```

Where Used: PL/SQL and SQL statements

Sample

```
SELECT NLS_LOWER('This is a test OF a nls_LOWER with IJSLAND',
    'NLS_SORT=XDUTCH')
    from DUAL;

NLS_LOWER('THISISATESTOFANLS_LOWERWITHIJS
----------------------------------------
this is a test of a nls_lower with ijsland
```

NLS_UPPER

Description: Operates in the same manner as the function UPPER, except you have an optional NLS_SORT parameter to specify the language and characters returned. All characters are returned in uppercase and all nonalphabetic characters are unaffected. If no NLS_SORT parameter is used, this function operates identically to the function UPPER. Refer to *Oracle7 Server SQL Reference* for all available NLS parameters.

Syntax

```
NLS_UPPER('Input String',<'NLS_SORT=parameter'>)
```

Where Used: PL/SQL and SQL statements

Sample

```
SELECT NLS_UPPER('This is a test OF a nls_uppER with ijslanD',
    'NLS_SORT=XDutch')
    from DUAL;

NLS_UPPER('THISISATESTOFANLS_UPPERWITHIJSL
----------------------------------------
THIS IS A TEST OF A NLS_UPPER WITH IJSLAND
```

NLSSORT

Description: Returns the input string in bytes to reflect the methodology used by Oracle to sort the string sequence. All character values are converted into bytes and sorted by the optional NLSSORT parameter. If no NLSSORT parameter is specified, the default sort sequence is used. Refer to *Oracle7 Server SQL Reference* for all available NLS parameters.

Syntax

```
NLSSORT('Input String',<'NLSSORT=parameter'>)
```

Where Used: PL/SQL and SQL statements

Samples

```
SELECT NLSSORT('This returns bytes')
    from DUAL;

NLSSORT('THISRETURNSBYTES')
------------------------------------
54686973207265747572 6E7320627974657300
```

You can pick out the representation of ASCII characters. Each space has a value of 32.

REPLACE

Description: Allows you to replace characters or NULL using a search string from an input string. If no replacement characters are specified, the search string characters are evaluated to NULL and removed from the input string. This function is case sensitive, so 'tim', 'Tim', and 'tIm' are three different meanings and search strings. This function is useful to help you get rid of unwanted punctuation. For instance, if you are pulling data from a CHAR or VARCHAR2 field that contains a single quote ('), this would cause errors because you would have an unbalanced set of quotes. This function is also great for search-and-replace missions such as changing the name of a company that has been sold. Also, if you wanted to change all occurrences of Corporation to Corp, you could specify the search string as 'oration', with no replace value. Don't forget that you can always nest the REPLACE function for complex changes.

Syntax

```
REPLACE('Input String',search_string,<replacement_string>)
```

Where Used: PL/SQL and SQL statements

Samples

```
SELECT REPLACE('This is a test of that','th')
    from DUAL;

REPLACE('THISISATEST
--------------------
This is a test of at
```

This function is case sensitive, but you can change that by converting all characters to UPPER or LOWER. See the function INSTR for an example of handling a case-sensitive function.

```
SELECT REPLACE('You are proud affiliates of NBC Corp.','NBC','MSNBC')
    from DUAL;

REPLACE('WEAREPROUDAFFILIATESOFNBCCORP
--------------------------------------
You are proud affiliates of MSNBC Corp.

SELECT REPLACE('You will remove it''s apostrophe','''')
    from DUAL;

REPLACE('WEWILLREMOVEIT''SAPO
----------------------------
You will remove its apostrophe
```

RPAD

Description: Pads a string of characters at the end of a string up to the length specified, with any character or characters. If no character is selected, the single space is used for default, similar to the LPAD function.

Syntax

```
RPAD(input_string,total_string_length,<character_to_pad>)
```

Where Used: PL/SQL and SQL statements

Samples

```
SELECT RPAD('Test default character',25) "Default Pad"
    from DUAL;

Default Pad
-------------------------
Test default character

SELECT RPAD('New Pad Character',25,'@') "Default Pad"
    from DUAL;

Default Pad
-------------------------
New Pad Character@@@@@@@@

SELECT RPAD('New Pad Character',15,'@') "Default Pad"
    from DUAL;

Default Pad
---------------
New Pad Charact
```

RTRIM

Description: Allows you to remove characters that you specify from the end of a string until the first occurrence in the string that does not contain those characters, and then the function returns the remaining characters in the string. This function is useful to remove spaces, all numbers (the string set you would specify is '0123456789'), words, or whatever else is required. If the string of characters to remove is not specified, the default is a single blank.

Syntax

```
RTRIM(input_string,characters_to_remove)
```

Where Used: PL/SQL and SQL statements

Samples

```
SELECT RTRIM('  You will remove ending spaces  ')
     "Space Removal as Default"
     from DUAL;

Space Removal as Default
------------------------------
  You will remove ending spaces

SELECT RTRIM('DYZ355683864','0123456789') "Remove Numbers"
     from DUAL;

Rem
---
DYZ

SELECT RTRIM('The time is now 10:00 PM','AMP') "Remove Letters"
     from DUAL;

Remove Letters
--------------------
The time is now 10:00
```

SOUNDEX

Description: Returns the phonetic representation of a string of characters. You can thus compare based on how the word is pronounced, not how the word is spelled. The following rules apply:

☐ SOUNDEX is not case sensitive.

☐ The first five consonants are used to generate the return value, so beammeupscottynow is the same as beammeupscot.

☐ The return value always begins with the first letter in the string.

☐ All vowels are ignored when computing the return value to match unless the vowel is the first letter in the string.

Donald Knuth, in the *Art of Computer Programming*, defined the algorithm for the SOUNDEX function. The algorithm is as follows:

☐ Keep the first letter of the string and remove all vowel occurrences a, e, h, i, o, u, w, and y.

☐ Assign numbers to the remaining letters:

1. b,f,p,v

2. c,g,j,k,q,s,x,z

3. d,t

4. l

5. m,n

6. r

☐ If two or more numbers are in sequence, remove all but the first number.

☐ Return the first four bytes padded with 0.

This function enables you to perform searches without knowing the spelling, similar to the LIKE operator in many different languages. You could search for 'Cathy' and find 'Cathy', 'Kathy', 'Kathi', 'Cathi', and so on if you did not know how *Cathy* was spelled.

Syntax

SOUNDEX(*input_string*)

Where Used: PL/SQL and SQL statements

Sample

```
SET SERVEROUTPUT ON
DECLARE
    v_String1  VARCHAR2(12) := 'their';
    v_String2  VARCHAR2(12) := 'ThERe';
BEGIN
    IF SOUNDEX(v_String1) = SOUNDEX(v_String2) THEN
        DBMS_OUTPUT.PUT_LINE('You have a match!!!!!');
    ELSE
        DBMS_OUTPUT.PUT_LINE('You do not have a match!!!!!');
    END IF;
    DBMS_OUTPUT.PUT_LINE('The phonetic value of their is ' ||
        SOUNDEX(v_String1));
    DBMS_OUTPUT.PUT_LINE('The phonetic value of ThERe is ' ||
        SOUNDEX(v_String1));
END;
/

The phonetic value of their is T600
The phonetic value of ThERe is T600
```

SUBSTR

Description: Extracts a string from within a string by specifying the starting position and total length of the string to extract. The following rules apply:

- ☐ If the total length is not specified, the entire string is used.
- ☐ If the starting position or total length is passed as real numbers (contains fractions), the value is automatically truncated to an integer before processing.
- ☐ If the total length is less than 1, NULL is returned.
- ☐ If the starting position is positive, start counting from the left to arrive at the starting position.
- ☐ If the starting position is negative, start counting from the right to arrive at the starting position.

Syntax

SUBSTR(*input_string*,*starting_position*,*<number_of_characters_to_extract>*)

Where Used: PL/SQL and SQL statements

TIP	By combining SUBSTR with INSTR to find the location of a set of characters, you can dynamically extract words. The length can be computed dynamically also by using the LENGTH function.

Samples

```
SELECT SUBSTR('You will extract Tim from here starting from left',17,3)
    "Extract_Example"
    from DUAL;

Ext
---
Tim

SELECT SUBSTR('You will extract Tim from here starting from right',-33,3)
    "Extract_Example"
    from DUAL;

Ext
---
Tim
```

The next query uses variables to determine the starting point and the length to extract:

```
SELECT SUBSTR('You will extract Tim from here starting from left',INSTR
    ('You will extract Tim from here starting from left','Tim')
```

```
,LENGTH('Tim')) "Extract_Example"
    from DUAL;

Ext
---
Tim
```

SUBSTRB

Description: Operates the same as SUBSTR except that the starting position and length are expressed in bytes. If you are in a single-byte-per-character system, this operates identically to the function SUBSTR.

Syntax

```
SUBSTRB(input_string,starting_position,<number_of_characters_to_extract>)
```

Where Used: PL/SQL and SQL statements

 TIP If you combine SUBSTRB with INSTR to find the location of a set of characters, you can dynamically extract words. The length can be computed dynamically also by using the LENGTH function.

Sample

```
SELECT SUBSTR('You will extract Tim from here starting from left',33,6)
    "Extract_Example"
    from DUAL;

Ext
---
Tim
```

TRANSLATE

Description: Allows you to replace all occurrences of each character in *from_string* with the characters from *to_string*. If *from_string* is shorter than *to_string*, *to_string* will truncate. When using this function, there are no optional parameters. If *to_string* is NULL, the function returns a value of NULL. This function is case sensitive.

Syntax

```
TRANSLATE(input_string,from_string,to_string)
```

Where Used: PL/SQL and SQL statements

Sample

```
SELECT TRANSLATE('This is a test of that','th','newstring')
    from DUAL;

TRANSLATE('THISISATEST
--------------------
Teis is a nesn of nean
```

UPPER

Description: Returns all characters in a string in uppercase. Nonalphabetic characters, such as punctuation and numbers, are unaffected by this function. This function returns the same datatype as sent in the input string; therefore, type VARCHAR2 returns VARCHAR2 and CHAR returns CHAR.

Syntax

```
UPPER(input_string)
```

Where Used: PL/SQL and SQL statements

Sample

```
SELECT UPPER('THIS IS a Test OF tHe Upper Function for the 1st time')
     "Upper Function"
     from DUAL;

Upper Function
----------------------------------------------------
THIS IS A TEST OF THE UPPER FUNCTION FOR THE 1ST TIME
```

Number Functions

The number functions are accurate to 36 decimal places. These functions manipulate number datatypes.

ABS

Description: Returns the absolute value of any number passed. If the number passed is negative or positive, the absolute value always returns the number as positive.

Syntax

```
ABS(input_number)
```

Where Used: PL/SQL and SQL statements

Sample

```
SELECT ABS(-2.345),ABS(19.99) from DUAL;

ABS(-2.345) ABS(19.99)
----------- ----------
2.345       19.99
```

ACOS

Description: Returns the arc cosine in radians of any number passed to the function. The input range is from −1 to 1, and the output range is 0 to pi.

Syntax

`ACOS(input_number)`

Where Used: PL/SQL and SQL statements

Sample

`SELECT ACOS(-.33), ACOS(1) from DUAL;`

```
ACOS(-.33)   ACOS(1)
----------   -------
 1.9070999         0
```

ASIN

Description: Returns the arc sine in radians of any number passed to the function. The input range is from −1 to 1, and the output range is −pi/2 to pi/2.

Syntax

`ASIN(input_number)`

Where Used: PL/SQL and SQL statements

Sample

`SELECT ASIN(-.33), ASIN(1) from DUAL;`

```
ASIN(-.33)    ASIN(1)
----------  ---------
 -.3363036  1.5707963
```

ATAN

Description: Returns the arc tangent in radians of any number passed to the function. The input range is infinity, meaning unbounded at both ends, and the output range is −pi/2 to pi/2.

Syntax

`ATAN(input_number)`

Where Used: PL/SQL and SQL statements

Sample

`SELECT ATAN(-10.33), ATAN(1),ATAN(25)  from DUAL;`

```
ATAN(-10.33)    ATAN(1)   ATAN(25)
------------  ---------  ---------
  -1.474292  .78539816  1.5308176
```

ATAN2

Description: Returns the arc tangent in radians of the two numbers (y/x) passed to the function. The input range is infinity, meaning unbounded at both ends, and the output range is −pi to pi.

Syntax

`ATAN2(input_number_y,input_number_x)`

Where Used: PL/SQL and SQL statements

Sample

`SELECT ATAN2(-10.33,5), ATAN2(1,5),ATAN2(25,25)  from DUAL;`

```
ATAN2(-10.33,5) ATAN2(1,5) ATAN2(25,25)
--------------- ---------- -----------
     -1.120008  .19739556    .78539816
```

CEIL

Description: Returns the value representing the smallest integer that is greater than or equal to the *input_number*.

Syntax

`CEIL(input_number)`

Where Used: PL/SQL and SQL statements

Sample

`SELECT CEIL(9),CEIL(9.6),CEIL(-12),CEIL(-12.3) from DUAL;`

```
CEIL(9) CEIL(9.6) CEIL(-12) CEIL(-12.3)
------- --------- --------- -----------
      9        10       -12         -12
```

COS

Description: Returns the cosine of any number passed as an angle in radians to the function.

Syntax

`COS(input_number)`

Where Used: PL/SQL and SQL statements

Sample

`SELECT COS(0), COS(-30),COS(180),COS(-265),COS(360) from DUAL;`

```
COS(0)  COS(-30)  COS(180) COS(-265)  COS(360)
------  --------- --------- --------- ---------
     1 .15425145 -.5984601 .44804667 -.2836911
```

COSH

Description: Returns the hyperbolic cosine of any number passed to the function.

Syntax

`COSH(input_number)`

Where Used: PL/SQL and SQL statements

Sample

```
SELECT COSH(0), COSH(-30),COSH(180),COSH(-265),COSH(360/22.3) from DUAL;

COSH(0) COSH(-30) COSH(180) COSH(-265) COSH(360/22.3)
------- --------- --------- ---------- --------------
      1 5.343E+12 7.447E+77  6.12E+114      5128637.4
```

EXP

Description: Returns e raised to the nth power, where $e = 2.71828183\ldots$.

Syntax

```
EXP(nth_power)
```

Where Used: PL/SQL and SQL statements

Sample

```
SELECT EXP(0),EXP(1),EXP(-.55),COSH(-3),COSH(10/5) from DUAL;

EXP(0)     EXP(1) EXP(-.55)  COSH(-3) COSH(10/5)
------ ---------- --------- --------- ----------
     1 2.7182818 .57694981 10.067662  3.7621957
```

FLOOR

Description: Returns the value representing the largest integer that is less than or equal to the *input_number*.

Syntax

```
FLOOR(input_number)
```

Where Used: PL/SQL and SQL statements

Sample

```
SELECT FLOOR(9),FLOOR(9.6),FLOOR(-12),FLOOR(-12.3) from DUAL;

FLOOR(9) FLOOR(9.6) FLOOR(-12) FLOOR(-12.3)
-------- ---------- ---------- ------------
       9          9        -12          -13
```

LN

Description: Returns the natural logarithm of some *input_number* that is greater than 0.

Syntax

```
LN(input_number)
```

Where Used: PL/SQL and SQL statements

Sample

```
SELECT LN(9),LN(0.22),LN(1) from DUAL;

LN(9)      LN(0.22)       LN(1)
---------- ---------- ----------
2.1972246 -1.514128          0
```

LOG

Description: Returns the logarithm of some *input_number* calculated upon the *input_base*. The base must be a positive value greater than 1, and *input_number* must be a positive number greater than 0.

Syntax

```
LOG(input_base, input_number)
```

Where Used: PL/SQL and SQL statements

Sample

```
SELECT LOG(10,5),LOG(10,0.33),LOG(10,2),LOG(16,2),LOG(2,2) from DUAL;

LOG(10,5) LOG(10,0.33) LOG(10,2) LOG(16,2)   LOG(2,2)
---------- ------------ ---------- ---------- ----------
   .69897    -.4814861    .30103       .25          1
```

MOD

Description: Returns the remainder of *input_x* divided by *input_y*. The function returns 0 if there is no remainder. MOD is useful to write a function to see if a number is a prime number, or a function to determine the divisors of a number.

Syntax

```
MOD(input_x,input_y)
```

Where Used: PL/SQL and SQL statements

Sample

```
SELECT MOD(9,3),MOD(9,2),MOD(-3,4) from DUAL;

MOD(9,3)   MOD(9,2) MOD(-3,4)
---------- ---------- ----------
       0          1         -3
```

NOTE

This function operates differently than the classic version of MOD only when using negative numbers. To see the difference and how to use the classic MOD, execute the following samples.

Syntax

```
input_x - input_y  * FLOOR(input_x/input_y)
```

Sample

```
SELECT MOD(-3,4) "Oracle MOD", -3 - 4*FLOOR(-3/4)  from DUAL;

Oracle MOD -3-4*FLOOR(-3/4)
---------- ----------------
       -3                 1
```

NOTE

> Do not put parentheses around *input_x - input_y* or you will get a wrong answer!

POWER

Description: Returns a number (*input_x*), raised to the power of a number (*input_y*). *input_x* and *input_y* can be any number, except that if *input_x* is negative, *input_y* must be an integer.

Syntax

```
POWER(input_x,input_y)
```

Where Used: PL/SQL and SQL statements

Sample

```
SELECT POWER(2,3),POWER(9,1.2),POWER(-3,4) from DUAL;

POWER(2,3) POWER(9,1.2) POWER(-3,4)
---------- ------------ -----------
         8     13.96661          81
```

ROUND

Description: Rounds the *input_x* number to the number of places specified. If the number of places specified is positive, it rounds to the right of the decimal. If the number of places specified is negative, it rounds to the left of the decimal. If no places are specified, the default is 0, which rounds to the nearest integer.

Syntax

```
ROUND(input_x,<places_to_round>)
```

Where Used: PL/SQL and SQL statements

Sample

```
SELECT ROUND(99.26723), ROUND(99.26723,-1), ROUND(99.26723,2),
    ROUND(99.26723,4)
    from DUAL;

ROUND(99.26723) ROUND(99.26723,-1) ROUND(99.26723,2) ROUND(99.26723,4)
--------------- ------------------ ----------------- ----------------
             99                100             99.27          99.2672
```

SIGN

Description: Used to check the sign of a number. The rules of the function are

☐ If the number is negative, a value of -1 is returned.

☐ If the number is zero, a value of 0 is returned.

☐ If the number is positive, a value of 1 is returned.

> **TIP**   You could easily test if a number is positive with an IF statement such as: IF (SIGN(x)) THEN... or to continuously loop until a 0 or negative number is entered.

Syntax

SIGN(*input_number*)

Where Used: PL/SQL and SQL statements

Sample

```
SELECT SIGN(-44.54),SIGN(0),SIGN(9.22) from DUAL;

SIGN(-44.54)   SIGN(0) SIGN(9.22)
------------ --------- ----------
          -1         0          1
```

SIN

Description: Returns the sine of any number, which is passed as an angle in radians, to the function.

Syntax

SIN(*input_number*)

Where Used: PL/SQL and SQL statements

Sample

```
SELECT SIN(0), SIN(-30),SIN(180),SIN(-265),SIN(360) from DUAL;

SIN(0)  SIN(-30) SIN(180) SIN(-265)  SIN(360)
------ --------- --------- --------- ---------
     0 .98803162 -.8011526 -.8940102 .95891572
```

SINH

Description: Returns the hyperbolic sine of any number passed to the function.

Syntax

```
SINH(input_number)
```

Where Used: PL/SQL and SQL statements

Sample

```
SELECT SINH(0), SINH(-30),SINH(180),SINH(-265),SINH(360/22.3) from DUAL;

SINH(0) SINH(-30) SINH(180) SINH(-265) SINH(360/22.3)
------- --------- --------- ---------- --------------
      0 -5.34E+12 7.447E+77  -6.1E+114      5128637.4
```

SQRT

Description: Returns the square root of `input_number`. `input_number` can't be negative, so imaginary numbers are out of the question.

Syntax

```
SQRT(input_number)
```

Where Used: PL/SQL and SQL statements

Sample

```
SELECT SQRT(9),SQRT(1.22),SQRT(25) from DUAL;

SQRT(9) SQRT(1.22)  SQRT(25)
------- ---------- ---------
      3  1.1045361         5
```

TAN

Description: Returns the tangent of any number, which is passed as an angle in radians, to the function.

Syntax

```
TAN(input_number)
```

Where Used: PL/SQL and SQL statements

Sample

```
SELECT TAN(0), TAN(-30),TAN(180),TAN(-265),TAN(360) from DUAL;

TAN(0)   TAN(-30)  TAN(180) TAN(-265)  TAN(360)
------ --------- --------- --------- ---------
     0 6.4053312 1.3386902 -1.995351  -3.38014
```

TANH

Description: Returns the hyperbolic tangent of any number passed to the function.

Syntax

TANH(*input_number*)

Where Used: PL/SQL and SQL statements

Sample

```
SELECT TANH(0), TANH(-30),TANH(180),TANH(-265),TANH(360/22.3) from DUAL;

TANH(0) TANH(-30) TANH(180) TANH(-265) TANH(360/22.3)
------- --------- --------- ---------- --------------
      0        -1         1         -1              1
```

TRUNC

Description: Truncates the *input_x* number to the number of places specified. If the number of places specified is positive, it truncates to the right of the decimal. If the number of places specified is negative, it truncates to the left of the decimal. If no places are specified, the default is 0, which truncates to the integer.

Syntax

TRUNC(*input_x*,*<places_to_truncate>*)

Where Used: PL/SQL and SQL statements

Sample

```
SELECT TRUNC(99.26723), TRUNC(99.26723,-1), TRUNC(99.26723,2),
    TRUNC(99.26723,4)
    from DUAL;

TRUNC(99.26723) TRUNC(99.26723,-1) TRUNC(99.26723,2) TRUNC(99.26723,4)
--------------- ------------------ ----------------- -----------------
             99                 90             99.26           99.2672
```

Date Functions

The DATE datatypes can be controlled by the functions below. You can perform almost any type of computation on both date and time.

ADD_MONTHS

Description: This function adds or subtracts months from a date. Because the function is overloaded, you can specify the parameters in any order. If *months_to_add* is positive, it will add months into the future. If the *months_to_add* number is negative, it will subtract months from the *date_passed*. You can specify *months_to_add* as a fraction, but Oracle completely ignores the fraction. You can go down to the day level by using other Oracle functions.

Another caution is that Oracle will return the same day in the resulting calculation unless the last day in one month (for example March 31st) is greater than the last day of the resulting month (for example April 30th). Your result would not be April 31 or even May 1, but the actual last day of the month, which in this case is April 30. Again, if you are really concerned about not adding exactly 31 days, you can use other Oracle functions to achieve your goal.

Syntax

The syntax can be expressed in two ways:

ADD_MONTHS(*date_passed*,*months_to_add*)

or

ADD_MONTHS(*months_to_add*, *date_passed*)

Where Used: PL/SQL and SQL statements

Samples

All three of the following statements will produce the same result:

```
SELECT ADD_MONTHS(SYSDATE,2) from DUAL;
SELECT ADD_MONTHS(2,SYSDATE) from DUAL;
SELECT ADD_MONTHS(SYSDATE,2.654) from DUAL;

Output:  (assuming the date is 06/02/97)
ADD_MONTH
---------
02-AUG-97
```

LAST_DAY

Description: This function provides you with the last day of the given month. A useful purpose would be to determine how many days are left in the given month.

Syntax

LAST_DAY(*input_date_passed*)

Where Used: PL/SQL and SQL statements

Samples

```
SELECT TO_CHAR(LAST_DAY('30-JUN-97'),'MM/DD/YYYY HH:MM:SS AM') "Last_Day"
 from DUAL;

Last_Day
-----------------------
06/30/1997 12:06:00 AM

Calculating the Days of Summer in June
```

```
SELECT LAST_DAY('20-JUN-97') "Last_Day",
        LAST_DAY('20-JUN-97') - TO_DATE('20-JUN-97') "Days_Summer"
    from DUAL;

Last_Day  Days_Summer
--------- -----------
30-JUN-97          10
```

MONTHS_BETWEEN

Description: Returns the number of months between two given dates. If the day is the same in both months, you will get an integer value returned. If the day is different, you will get a fractional result based upon a 31-day month. If the second date is prior to the first date, the result will be negative.

Syntax

MONTHS_BETWEEN(*input_date1*,*input_date2*)

Where Used: PL/SQL and SQL statements

Samples

```
SELECT MONTHS_BETWEEN('25-DEC-97','02-JUN-97') "Fractional",
        MONTHS_BETWEEN('02-FEB-97','02-JUN-97') "Integer"
    from DUAL;

Fractional  Integer
----------  -------
 6.7419355       -4
```

NEW_TIME

Description: Have you ever wondered what time it is in Germany? Would the phone call be waking the person up in the middle of the night? The NEW_TIME function enables you to find out the time in a time zone by simply passing the date and time of the first zone, and specifying the second zone. See Table B.1 for valid time zones.

Syntax

NEW_TIME(*input_date_and_time*,*time_zone1*,*time_zone2*)

Where Used: PL/SQL and SQL statements

Samples

```
SELECT TO_CHAR(NEW_TIME(TO_DATE('060297 01:00:00 AM',
        'MMDDYY HH:MI:SS AM'),
        'CDT','PDT'), 'DD-MON-YY HH:MI:SS AM') "Central to Pacific"
    from DUAL;

Central to Pacific
--------------------
01-JUN-97 11:00:00 PM
```

TIP

> Remember, minutes are expressed as MI, not MM. This is a common mistake!

Table B.1. Time zone table.

Time Zone Abbreviation Passed	Time Zone Description
AST	Atlantic Standard Time
ADT	Atlantic Daylight Savings Time
BST	Bering Standard Time
BDT	Bering Daylight Savings Time
CST	Central Standard Time
CDT	Central Daylight Savings Time
EST	Eastern Standard Time
EDT	Eastern Daylight Savings Time
GMT	Greenwich Mean Time (Date Line!)
HST	Alaska-Hawaii Standard Time
HDT	Alaska-Hawaii Daylight Savings Time
MST	Mountain Standard Time
MDT	Mountain Daylight Savings Time
NST	Newfoundland Standard Time
PST	Pacific Standard Time
PDT	Pacific Daylight Savings Time
YST	Yukon Standard Time
YDT	Yukon Daylight Savings Time

NEXT_DAY

Description: Returns the next date in the week for the day of the week specified after the input date. The time returned is the time specified by the input date when called.

Syntax

```
NEXT_DAY(input_date_passed,day_name)
```

Where Used: PL/SQL and SQL statements

Samples

```
SELECT TO_CHAR(NEXT_DAY(SYSDATE,'Monday'),'MM/DD/YYYY HH:MM:SS AM')
      "Next_Day"
 from DUAL;

Output for the SYSDATE of June 3rd, 1997:
Next_Day
--------------------
06/09/1997 07:06:38 AM


SELECT TO_CHAR(NEXT_DAY('31-AUG-97','Monday'),'MM/DD/YYYY HH:MM:SS AM')
      "Next_Day"
 from DUAL;

Next_Day
--------------------
09/01/1997 12:00:00 AM
```

ROUND

Description: ROUND is very similar to the TRUNC function. In fact, it uses the same format mask as the TRUNC function. The format masks appear in Table B.2. This function allows you to round up or down based upon the format mask. The default mask when specifying a DATE value is DD. Some useful purposes for this function are

☐ Rounding to the nearest minute for billing cellular-based calls

☐ Rounding to the closest month to determine a pay period

Syntax

```
ROUND(input_date_and_time_or_number,rounding_specification)
```

Where Used: PL/SQL and SQL statements

Samples

```
SELECT TO_CHAR(ROUND(TO_DATE('060297 01:00:35 AM',
         'MMDDYY HH:MI:SS AM'),
         'MI'), 'DD-MON-YY HH:MI:SS AM') "Rounded to nearest Minute"
     from DUAL;

Rounded to nearest Minute
-------------------------
02-JUN-97 01:01:00 AM  10
```

Table B.2. Format mask table for rounding and truncating with dates.

Mask Options	Method of Rounding or Truncating Used
CC, SCC	Rounds or truncates to the century
YYYY, SYYYY, YEAR, SYEAR, YYY, YY, Y	Truncates to the year, or rounds up to the next year after July 1st
IYYY, IYY, IY, I	ISO year
Q	Truncates to the quarter or rounds up to the nearest quarter on or after the sixteenth day of the second month of the quarter
MM, MON, MONTH, RM	Truncates the month or rounds up to the next month on or after the sixteenth day
DD, DDD, J	Truncates or rounds to the day
WW	Same day of the week as the first day of the year
IW	Same day of the week as the first day of the ISO year
W	Same day of the week as the first day of the month
Day, Dy, D	Truncates or rounds to the first day of the week
HH24, HH12, HH	Truncates to the hour, or rounds up to the next hour on or after 30 minutes
MI	Truncates to the minute or rounds up on or after 30 seconds

SYSDATE

Description: Returns the current date and time in the Oracle server. Note the distinction that it is the server's, not the client's, date and time that is being returned.

Syntax

SYSDATE

Where Used: PL/SQL and SQL statements

Samples

```
SELECT SYSDATE from DUAL;

SYSDATE
---------
01-JUN-97

SELECT TO_CHAR(SYSDATE,'MM/DD/YYYY HH:MM:SS AM')
    "Today's Date and Time" from DUAL;

Today's Date and Time
------------------------------
06/01/1997 11:06:21 PM
```

TRUNC

Description: The TRUNC function is useful for returning a truncated DATE or TIME to a specified mask. For instance, you can truncate to the nearest day, month, quarter, century, and so on. The main use of TRUNC is to simply eliminate the time from the SYSDATE by setting all time values for all dates to 12:00 a.m. Refer to Table B.2 for the format masks to truncate dates and times.

Syntax

```
TRUNC(date_passed,truncate mask)
```

Where Used: PL/SQL and SQL statements

Sample

This example removes the time from the date:

```
SELECT TO_CHAR(TRUNC(SYSDATE),'MM/DD/YYYY HH:MM:SS AM')
    "Today's Date and Time"
    from DUAL;

Today's Date and Time
----------------------
06/01/1997 12:00:00 AM
```

Conversion Functions

Oracle provides several functions for converting datatypes, character sets, and tables.

CHARTOROWID

Description: Converts CHAR or VARCHAR2 from the external format provided by Oracle to its internal binary format.

Syntax

```
CHARTOROWID(string_row_format)
```

Where Used: PL/SQL and SQL statements

Sample

```
SELECT name FROM employees
    WHERE ROWID = CHARTOROWID('0000001C.0001.0002');
```

```
Name:
- - - - -
Atwood
```

CONVERT

Description: Used to convert from one character set to another character set. The source character set is optional, and if not specified, defaults to the standard character set used by the database. See Table B.3 for valid character sets.

Syntax

```
CONVERT(input_string,destination_character_set,<source_character_set>)
```

Where Used: PL/SQL and SQL statements

Sample

The default is IBM PC ASCII for the following samples:

```
SELECT CONVERT('This was ASCII, now EBCDIC','WE8EBCDIC500','WE8PC850')
    from DUAL;
```

```
CONVERT('THISWASASCII,NOWE
- - - - - - - - - - - - - - - - - - - - - - - - - -
âˆ‰¢@¦ ¢@ÁâÃÉÉk@·-¦@ÅÂÂÄÉÂ
```

You should expect weird characters to be output because EBCDIC uses a whole different decimal numbering scheme than ASCII.

Table B.3. Character sets.

Character Set	Description
US7ASCII	U.S. ASCII 7-bit character set
WE8DEC	DEC Western Europe 8-bit character set
WE8HP	Hewlett-Packard Western Europe 8-bit character set
F7DEC	DEC French 7-bit character set
WEBCDIC500	IBM Western Europe EBCDIC character set
WEPC850	Western Europe PC character set
WE8ISO8895P1	Western Europe ISO 8895-1 character set

HEXTORAW

Description: Converts hex string values to internal raw values. The hex values must be two bytes for each character.

Syntax

```
HEXTORAW(input_string,destination_character_set,<source_character_set>)
```

Where Used: PL/SQL and SQL statements

Sample

```
SELECT HEXTORAW('1a2b1c') from DUAL;

HEXTOR
------
1A2B1C
```

RAWTOHEX

Description: Converts an internal RAW number to a string of characters in hexadecimal format.

Syntax

```
RAWTOHEX(raw_value)
```

Where Used: PL/SQL and SQL statements

Sample

```
SELECT RAWTOHEX('1a2b1c') from DUAL;

RAWTOHEX('1A
------------
316132623163
```

ROWIDTOCHAR

Description: Converts row_id into its external 18-character string format.

Syntax

```
ROWIDTOCHAR(row_id)
```

Where Used: PL/SQL and SQL statements

Sample

```
SELECT ROWIDTOCHAR(ROWID) from DUAL;

ROWIDTOCHAR(ROWID)
------------------
00000342.0000.0001
```

Remember that the DUAL table has only one row and is used for DUMMY data and queries.

TO_CHAR **(with Dates)**

Description: Converts Oracle DATE values into a VARCHAR2 character string, thus allowing for you to format the date in any way imaginable. The format masks are shown in Table B.4 at the end of the TO_DATE function. The NLS parameters enable you to specify the language to output to the screen by using NLS_DATE_LANGUAGE = 'language_desired'.

Syntax

```
TO_CHAR(Date_Value,format_mask,<NLS_Parameters>
```

Where Used: PL/SQL and SQL statements

Samples

```
SELECT TO_CHAR(SYSDATE,'MONTH DDTH YYYY') "Today" from DUAL;

Birthday
-------------------
JUNE      03RD 1997

SET SERVEROUTPUT ON

DECLARE
    v_Convert_Date DATE := TO_DATE('06112067BC','MMDDYYYYBC');
    v_Hold_Date VARCHAR2(100);
BEGIN
    v_Hold_Date := TO_CHAR(v_Convert_Date,'MMDDSYYYY');
    DBMS_OUTPUT.PUT_LINE('The converted date is: ' ¦¦ v_Hold_Date);
END;
/

The converted date is: 0611-2067

SELECT TO_CHAR(SYSDATE,'MONTH DD YY','NLS_DATE_LANGUAGE=german')
       "German Date" from DUAL;

German Date
-------------------
JUNI      04 97
```

TO_CHAR **(with Labels)**

Description: Converts MLSLABEL label to a VARCHAR2 character string. This function is relevant only when using Trusted Oracle. If no format is specified, the default label format is used.

Syntax

```
TO_CHAR(label,<format_mask>
```

Where Used: PL/SQL and SQL statements in a Trusted Oracle database

Samples

See the *Trusted Oracle7 Server Administrator's Guide* for many examples and a more in-depth explanation.

TO_CHAR (with Numbers)

Description: Converts any number into a VARCHAR2 character string. Again, this will allow you to improve on your output of NUMBER data. You can format this in many ways; see Table B.5 in the section "TO_NUMBER" for the applicable format masks.

Syntax

```
TO_CHAR(number,format_mask,NLS_Parameters)
```

The available NLS parameters are

☐ NLS_NUMERIC_CHARACTERS—Specifies characters to use for group separators and the decimal point.

☐ NLS_CURRENCY—Specifies the local currency.

☐ NLS_ISO_CURRENCY—Character(s) to represent the ISO currency symbol.

Where Used: PL/SQL and SQL statements

Samples

```
SET SERVEROUTPUT ON

DECLARE
     v_Convert_Number NUMBER := 90210;
     v_Hold_Char VARCHAR2(21) ;
BEGIN
     v_Hold_Char := TO_CHAR(v_Convert_Number,'0000000000');
     DBMS_OUTPUT.PUT_LINE('The employee ID is: ' ¦¦ v_Hold_Char);
END;
/

The employee ID is:   0000090210
```

TO_DATE

Description: Converts a character string (CHAR or VARCHAR2), as denoted by the apostrophes (') surrounding the character string, to an actual DATE value. The optional NLS_DATE_LANGUAGE parameter enables you to specify the language to output to screen.

Syntax

```
TO_DATE(character_string,format,<NLS_DATE_LANGUAGE>)
```

There are some limitations to the TO_DATE function:

- ☐ You can pass no more than 220 characters into the function for conversion.
- ☐ You are limited to the format masks listed in Table B.4.
- ☐ You can't mix and match formats such as specifying 24-hour time and also requesting AM/PM because you want either 24-hour time or 12-hour time, not both.
- ☐ You can't specify the same element twice in the conversion, such as YYYY-MM-MMM-DD. The MM and MMM are duplicate elements. The function will have problems attempting to decode the intent and will always cause an error.

Where Used: PL/SQL and SQL statements

Samples

```
SELECT TO_DATE('061167','MMDDYY') "Birthday" from DUAL;

Birthday
---------
11-JUN-67


SELECT TO_DATE('January 15','MONTH DD') "Sample" from DUAL;

Sample
---------
15-JAN-97


SET SERVEROUTPUT ON

DECLARE
    v_Convert_Date DATE;
BEGIN
    v_Convert_Date := TO_DATE('061167','MMDDYY');
    DBMS_OUTPUT.PUT_LINE('The converted date is: ' || v_Convert_Date);
END;
/

The converted date is: 11-JUN-67


SET SERVEROUTPUT ON

DECLARE
    v_Convert_Date DATE;
BEGIN
    v_Convert_Date := TO_DATE('061167','MMDDYY') + 10;
    DBMS_OUTPUT.PUT_LINE('The converted date is: ' || v_Convert_Date);
END;
/

The converted date is: 21-JUN-67
```

Table B.4. DATE **format masks.**

Format Element	Description
BC, B.C.	BC indicator, which can be used with or without the periods.
AD, A.D.	AD indicator, which can be used with or without the periods.
CC, SCC	Century code. Returns negative value if using BC with SCC format.
SYYYY, YYYY	Four-digit year. Returns negative value if using BC with SYYYY format.
IYYY	Four-digit ISO year.
Y,YYY	Four-digit year with a comma inserted.
YYY, YY, Y	The last three, two, or one digit of the year. The default is the current century.
IYY, IY, I	The last three, two, or one digit of the ISO year. The default is the current century.
YEAR, SYEAR	Returns the year spelled out. SYEAR returns a negative value if using BC dates.
RR	Last two digits of year in prior or future centuries.
Q	Quarter of the year, values 1 to 4.
MM	The month number from 01 to 12—Jan=01, Feb=02, and so on.
MONTH	The month name always allocated to nine characters, right-padded with blanks.
MON	The month name abbreviated to three characters.
RM	Roman numeral representation of the month, values I to XII.
WW	The week in the year, values 1 to 53.
IW	The ISO week in the year, values 1 to 52 or 1 to 53.
W	The week in the month, values 1 to 5. Week 1 begins on the first day of the month.
D	The day of the week, values 1 to 7.
DD	The day of the month, values 1 to 31.
DDD	The day of the year, values 1 to 366.
DAY	The name of the day spelled out, always occupying nine characters, right space padded.
DY	Abbreviated name of the day to two characters.
J	Julian day counted since January 1, 4712 BC.
HH, HH12	The hour of the day, values 1 to 12.

continues

Table B.4. continued

Format Element	Description
HH24	The hour of the day, values 0 to 23.
MI	The minute of the hour, values 0 to 59.
SS	The second of the minute, values 0 to 59.
SSSS	How many seconds past midnight, values 0 to 86399 (60 minutes/ hr * 60 seconds/minute * 24 hours = 86400 seconds).
AM, A.M.	The ante meridiem indicator for morning, with or without the periods.
PM, P.M.	The post meridiem indicator for evening, with or without the periods.
Punctuation	All punctuation passed through to maximum of 220 characters.
Text	All text passed through to a maximum of 220 characters.
TH	Suffix to convert numbers to ordinal format, so 1 would be 1st, 2 would be 2nd, and so on. Always returns value in English language only.
SP	Converts a number to its spelled format, so 109 becomes one hundred nine. Always returns value in English language only.
SPTH	Spells out numbers converted to ordinal format, so 1 would be FIRST, 2 would be SECOND, and so on. Always returns value in English language only.
FX	Uses exact pattern matching between data element and the format.
FM	Fill Mode: Toggles suppression of blanks in output from conversion.

TO_LABEL

Description: Allows you to convert a CHAR or VARCHAR2 string into an MLSLABEL. If the format is not specified, the default format is used.

Syntax

TO_LABEL(*string*,*<format_mask>*)

Where Used: PL/SQL and SQL statements in a Trusted Oracle database

Sample

See the *Trusted Oracle7 Server Administrator's Guide* for many examples and a more in-depth explanation.

TO_MULTI_BYTE

Description: Converts a single-byte character string to its multibyte counterpart. This function is only applicable to a database with both single- and multibyte character sets.

Syntax

```
TO_MULTI_BYTE(string)
```

Where Used: PL/SQL and SQL statements

Sample

```
SELECT TO_MULTI_BYTE('Now Multibyte!') from DUAL;

TO_MULTI_BYTE('
--------------
Now Multibyte!
```

TO_NUMBER

Description: This function is very similar to the TO_DATE function. This function converts a character string of type CHAR or VARCHAR2 into a number, usually to perform calculations on the number. As with TO_DATE, the format mask is very important for a proper conversion. The format masks appear at the end of this function in Table B.5.

Syntax

```
TO_NUMBER(character_string,format,<NLS_Params>)
```

The optional NLS parameters are

- ☐ NLS_NUMERIC_CHARACTERS—Specifies characters to use for group separators and the decimal point.
- ☐ NLS_CURRENCY—Specifies the local currency.
- ☐ NLS_ISO_CURRENCY—Characters to represent the ISO currency symbol.

Where Used: PL/SQL and SQL statements

Samples

```
SET SERVEROUTPUT ON

DECLARE
    v_Convert_Number VARCHAR2(20) := '1997';
    v_Hold_Number NUMBER ;
BEGIN
    v_Hold_Number := TO_NUMBER(v_Convert_Number,'9999');
    DBMS_OUTPUT.PUT_LINE('The converted number is: ' || v_Hold_Number);
    DBMS_OUTPUT.PUT_LINE('The converted number plus 10 is: ' ||
        (v_Hold_Number+10));
END;
/
```

B

```
The converted number is: 1997
The converted number plus 10 is: 2007

SET SERVEROUTPUT ON

DECLARE
    v_Convert_Number VARCHAR2(20) := '$119,252.75';
    v_Hold_Number NUMBER ;
BEGIN
    v_Hold_Number := TO_NUMBER(v_Convert_Number,'$999,999,999.99');
    DBMS_OUTPUT.PUT_LINE('The converted number is: ' || v_Hold_Number);
    DBMS_OUTPUT.PUT_LINE('Your commission at 6% is: ' || (v_Hold_Number*.06));
END;
/
```

```
The converted number is: 119252.75
Your commission at 6% is: 7155.165
```

```
SET SERVEROUTPUT ON

DECLARE
    v_Convert_Number VARCHAR2(20) := '33.33';
    v_Hold_Number NUMBER ;
BEGIN
    v_Hold_Number := TO_NUMBER(v_Convert_Number,'999.999999');
    DBMS_OUTPUT.PUT_LINE('The converted number is: ' || v_Hold_Number);
    DBMS_OUTPUT.PUT_LINE('Your decimal equivalent is: ' ||
        (v_Hold_Number/100));
END;
/
```

```
The converted number is: 33.33
Your decimal equivalent is: .3333
```

Table B.5 describes the format masks available for use with number elements.

Table B.5. Number format elements.

Format Mask	Example	Description
9	9999	Each nine is considered a significant digit. Any leading zeros are treated as blanks.
0	09999 or 99990	By adding the 0 as a prefix or suffix to the number, all leading or trailing zeros are treated and displayed as zeros instead of drawing a blank (pun intended). Think of this display type as NUMERIC values, such as 00109.
$	$9999	Prefix of currency symbol printed in the first position.

Format Mask	Example	Description
B	B9999	Returns any portion of the integer as blanks if the integer is 0. This will override the leading zeros by using a 0 for the format.
MI	9999MI	Automatically adds a space at the end to hold either a minus sign if the value is negative or a placeholder space if the value is positive.
S	S9999 or 9999S	Displays a leading or trailing sign of + if the value is positive, and a leading or trailing sign of - if the value is negative.
PR	9999PR	If the value is negative, angle brackets <> are placed around the number; if the number is positive, place-holder spaces are used.
D	99D99	Decimal point location. The nines on both sides reflect the maximum number of digits allowed.
G	9G999G999	Specifies a group separator such as a comma.
C	C99	Returns the ISO currency symbol in the specified position.
L	L9999	Specifies the location of the local currency symbol (such as $).
,	9,999,999	Places comma in specified position, regardless of the group separator.
.	99.99	Specifies location of decimal point, regardless of the decimal separator.
V	999V99	Returns the number multiplied to the $10n$ power, where n is the number of nines after the V.
EEEE	9.99EEEE	Returns the value in scientific notation.
RM, rm	RM, rm	Returns the value as upper- or lowercase Roman numerals.
FM	FM9,999.99	Fill Mode: Removes leading and trailing blanks.

After the format mask are several possible NLS parameters:

☐ NLS_NUMERIC_CHARACTERS—Specifies characters to use for group separators and the decimal point.

☐ NLS_CURRENCY—Specifies the local currency.

☐ NLS_ISO_CURRENCY—Characters to represent the ISO currency symbol.

TO_SINGLE_BYTE

Description: Converts all multibyte characters in a string to their single-byte counterparts. If the database is single-byte, this has no effect, and the output of this function is the same as the string passed as input.

Syntax

```
TO_SINGLE_BYTE(string)
```

Where Used: PL/SQL and SQL statements

Sample

```
SELECT TO_SINGLE_BYTE('Now Single-Byte!') from DUAL;

TO_SINGLE_BYTE('
--------------
Now Single-Byte!
```

Grouping Functions

The next set of functions is for use by SQL only. These functions are primarily used for computations on groups of records.

AVG

Description: Calculates the average of a column's values. The average is calculated by adding up all rows selected and dividing this result by the count of the number of rows.

Syntax

```
AVG(<DISTINCT or ALL>column_to_average)
```

The two methods to access rows are as follows:

- [ ] DISTINCT—Selects unique values from the population selected by the query.
- [ ] ALL—Selects all rows from the population selected by the query.

Where Used: SQL queries and GROUP BY clauses

Sample

The sample is a query against the standard Oracle sample database:

```
SELECT AVG(LOSAL),AVG(HISAL) from salgrade;

AVG(LOSAL) AVG(HISAL)
---------- ----------
1660.8     3519.8
```

COUNT

Description: Counts the number of rows selected by the query. If you pass COUNT(*), you will select all rows in the table.

Syntax

```
COUNT(<DISTINCT or ALL> column_to_count)
```

The two methods to access rows are as follows:

☐ DISTINCT—Selects unique values from the population selected by the query.

☐ ALL—Selects all rows from the population selected by the query.

Where Used: SQL queries and GROUP BY clauses

Samples

The samples are queries against the standard Oracle sample database:

```
SELECT COUNT(*) from EMP;

COUNT(*)
---------
      14

SELECT deptno,count(deptno) from EMP
GROUP BY deptno;

DEPTNO COUNT(DEPTNO)
------ -------------
    10             3
    20             5
6
```

GLB

Description: Used in Trusted Oracle only to locate the greatest lower bound of a label.

Syntax

```
GLB(<DISTINCT or ALL> label)
```

The two methods to access rows are as follows:

☐ DISTINCT—Selects unique values from the population selected by the query.

☐ ALL—Selects all rows from the population selected by the query.

Where Used: SQL queries and GROUP BY clauses in Trusted Oracle only

Samples

Refer to the *Trusted Oracle7 Server Administrator's Guide* for examples and information on Trusted Oracle.

B

LUB

Description: Used in Trusted Oracle only to locate the least upper bound of a label.

Syntax

```
LUB(<DISTINCT or ALL> label)
```

The two methods to access rows are as follows:

☐ DISTINCT—Selects unique values from the population selected by the query.

☐ ALL—Selects all rows from the population selected by the query.

Where Used: SQL queries and GROUP BY clauses in Trusted Oracle only

Sample

Refer to the *Trusted Oracle7 Server Administrator's Guide* for examples and information on Trusted Oracle.

MAX

Description: Locates the largest value (maximum) in the column of a population of records selected by the query. DISTINCT and ALL always provide the same answer.

Syntax

```
MAX(<DISTINCT or ALL> column_to_search)
```

The two methods to access rows are as follows:

☐ DISTINCT—Selects unique values from the population selected by the query.

☐ ALL—Selects all rows from the population selected by the query.

Where Used: SQL queries and GROUP BY clauses

Sample

The sample is a query against the standard Oracle sample database:

```
SELECT MAX(SAL) from EMP;

MAX(SAL)
--------
    5000
```

MIN

Description: Locates the smallest value (minimum) in the column of a population of records selected by the query. DISTINCT and ALL always provide the same answer.

Syntax

```
MIN(<DISTINCT or ALL> column_to_search)
```

The two methods to access rows are as follows:

- [ ] DISTINCT—Selects unique values from the population selected by the query.
- [ ] ALL—Selects all rows from the population selected by the query.

Where Used: SQL queries and GROUP BY clauses

Sample

The sample is a query against the standard Oracle sample database:

```
SELECT MIN(SAL) from EMP;

MIN(SAL)
---------
     800
```

STDDEV

Description: Calculates the standard deviation of the values in a column selected by the query, which is simply the square root of the variance.

Syntax

```
STDDEV(<DISTINCT or ALL> column_to_calculate_STD)
```

The two methods to access rows are as follows:

- [ ] DISTINCT—Selects unique values from the population selected by the query.
- [ ] ALL—Selects all rows from the population selected by the query.

Where Used: SQL queries and GROUP BY clauses

Sample

The sample is a query against the standard Oracle sample database:

```
SELECT STDDEV(SAL) from emp;

STDDEV(SAL)
-----------
  1182.5032
```

SUM

Description: Adds up all the values in a column of the population of records selected by the query.

Syntax

```
SUM(<DISTINCT or ALL> column_to_add)
```

The two methods to access rows are as follows:

- ☐ DISTINCT—Selects unique values from the population selected by the query.
- ☐ ALL—Selects all rows from the population selected by the query.

Where Used: SQL queries and GROUP BY clauses

Samples

The samples are queries against the standard Oracle sample database:

```
SELECT SUM(SAL) from EMP;

SUM(SAL)
--------
   29025

SELECT deptno,SUM(SAL) from emp
    GROUP BY deptno;

DEPTNO   SUM(SAL)
------   --------
    10       8750
    20      10875
    30       9400
```

VARIANCE

Description: Calculates the variance of the values in a column selected by the query.

Syntax

```
VARIANCE(<DISTINCT or ALL> column_to_calculate_Variance)
```

The two methods to access rows are as follows:

- ☐ DISTINCT—Selects unique values from the population selected by the query.
- ☐ ALL—Selects all rows from the population selected by the query.

Where Used: SQL queries and GROUP BY clauses

Sample

The sample is a query against the standard Oracle sample database:

```
SELECT VARIANCE(SAL) from emp;

VARIANCE(SAL)
-------------
    1398313.9
```

Miscellaneous Functions

Oracle provides several other miscellaneous functions that can be used from within PL/SQL.

BFILENAME

Description: Similar to the C language, this function returns a pointer to the physical path and location of where a LOB (large object) binary file is stored. This file is not stored within an Oracle table but is stored as a file accessible by the operating system. You can store the locators in the Oracle table, which are the pointers to the physical file on the system. You must create a directory object that stores the binary file's system path. This function is available only in Oracle8.

Syntax

```
BFILENAME('directory_object','filename')
```

Where Used: PL/SQL and SQL statements

Sample

This sample first creates a directory object called MYPATH. Type the CREATE DIRECTORY statement at the SQL*Plus prompt and hit Enter. Next, enter the code, which assigns a locator to the filename PLUS40.EXE, which is stored in the path c:\orant\bin.

```
CREATE DIRECTORY MYPATH AS 'C:\ORANT\BIN'

DECLARE

/* This Anonymous PL/SQL block will demonstrate how to
   create a locator with the BFILENAME function, and
   then test to see if the file exists.  You can change
   the name of the file or path to suit your platform */

    v_MYFILE BFILE; -- BFILE to access
    v_FILEEXISTS INTEGER; -- Holds status if the file actually exists

BEGIN
    v_MYFILE := BFILENAME('MYPATH','PLUS40.EXE'); -- Create locator
    v_FILEEXISTS := DBMS_LOB.FILEEXISTS(v_MYFILE);

    IF v_FILEEXISTS = 1 THEN
            DBMS_OUTPUT.PUT_LINE('The file exists');
    ELSE
            DBMS_OUTPUT.PUT_LINE('The file cannot be found');
    END IF;

END;

The file exists
```

DECODE

Description: Enables you to perform an IF...THEN...ELSE type comparison from a list of values. Each comparison value is compared against *main_value*. If all the comparisons return the value of *false*, then the default value is used; otherwise, the first true comparison returns the value associated with the comparison.

Syntax

```
DECODE(main_value,comparison1,value1,
                  comparison2,value2, ...
                  default)
```

Where Used: SQL queries only

Sample

The sample is a query against the standard Oracle sample database. The DECODE function compares the value 3000 to every occurrence of 3000 in the salary column, or 3000 in the commission column, and returns the value 3000 if there is a match or a value of 0 (default value) if there is no match.

```
SELECT
DECODE(3000,sal,3000,comm,3000,0) from emp

DECODE(3000,SAL,3000,COMM,3000,0)
---------------------------------
                                0
                                0
                                0
                                0
                                0
                                0
                                0
                             3000
                                0
                                0
                                0
                             3000
                                0
```

DUMP

Description: Provides a dump of values in a string VARCHAR2 to see the representation in many different formats. This function returns the datatype code, length, and representation in the *number_format* specified. The default *number_format* is decimal.

Syntax

```
DUMP(column,<number_format>,<start_position>,<length>)
```

The optional number format can be specified as follows:

Number Format	Description
8	Octal
10	Decimal
16	Hexadecimal
17	Single characters

The return datatype codes are as follows:

Datatype Code	Description
1	VARCHAR2
2	NUMBER
8	LONG
12	DATE
23	RAW
24	LONG RAW
69	ROWID
96	CHAR
106	MLSLABEL

Where Used: SQL queries only

Sample

The sample is a query against the standard Oracle sample database:

```
SELECT JOB,DUMP(JOB) from EMP;

JOB        DUMP(JOB)
--------   ----------------------------------------------
CLERK      Typ=1 Len=5: 67,76,69,82,75

SALESMAN   Typ=1 Len=8: 83,65,76,69,83,77,65,78

SALESMAN   Typ=1 Len=8: 83,65,76,69,83,77,65,78

MANAGER    Typ=1 Len=7: 77,65,78,65,71,69,82

SALESMAN   Typ=1 Len=8: 83,65,76,69,83,77,65,78

MANAGER    Typ=1 Len=7: 77,65,78,65,71,69,82

MANAGER    Typ=1 Len=7: 77,65,78,65,71,69,82

ANALYST    Typ=1 Len=7: 65,78,65,76,89,83,84

PRESIDENT  Typ=1 Len=9: 80,82,69,83,73,68,69,78,84
```

B

```
SALESMAN  Typ=1 Len=8: 83,65,76,69,83,77,65,78

CLERK     Typ=1 Len=5: 67,76,69,82,75

CLERK     Typ=1 Len=5: 67,76,69,82,75

ANALYST   Typ=1 Len=7: 65,78,65,76,89,83,84

CLERK     Typ=1 Len=5: 67,76,69,82,75
```

All of these are Type 1, which represents the datatype VARCHAR2. The length and decimal representation are displayed. The decimal representation is based on an IBM PC or compatible ASCII table.

EMPTY_BLOB

Description: Initializes a BLOB variable or column that stores a locator pointing to the data stored in the table. This function is available only in Oracle8.

Syntax

EMPTY_BLOB()

Where Used: PL/SQL and SQL statements

Sample

This example shows how to add a locator to the table. You first need to execute the command at the SQL*Plus prompt to create the table. Then enter and execute the code to add a BLOB and CLOB locator to the table.

```
CREATE TABLE MYLOBTABLE(
  blobloc BLOB,
  clobloc CLOB)
/

INSERT INTO MYLOBTABLE VALUES(EMPTY_BLOB(),EMPTY_CLOB())
/

1 row created.
```

EMPTY_CLOB

Description: Initializes a CLOB variable or column that stores a locator pointing to the data stored in the table. This function is available only in Oracle version 8.

Syntax

EMPTY_CLOB()

Where Used: PL/SQL and SQL statements

Sample

This example shows how to add a locator to the table. You first need to execute the command at the SQL*Plus prompt to create the table. Then enter and execute the code to add a BLOB and CLOB locator to the table. You don't need to create the table if the table already exists from completing the exercise with the EMPTY_BLOB function.

```
CREATE TABLE MYLOBTABLE(
  blobloc BLOB,
  clobloc CLOB)
/

INSERT INTO MYLOBTABLE VALUES(EMPTY_BLOB(),EMPTY_CLOB())
/

1 row created.
```

GREATEST

Description: Selects the greatest value from a list. All items are compared and converted to the same datatype as the first value in the list.

Syntax

```
GREATEST(expression_or_value1,<value_or_expression2>,...)
```

Where Used: PL/SQL and SQL statements

Sample

```
SELECT SAL,GREATEST(sal,2000) from emp;

SAL       GREATEST(SAL,2000)
--------- ------------------
      800               2000
     1600               2000
     1250               2000
     2975               2975
     1250               2000
     2850               2850
     2450               2450
     3000               3000
     5000               5000
     1500               2000
     1100               2000
      950               2000
     3000               3000
2000
```

This query lets you see who has a salary of 2000 or greater. In the second column, the GREATEST function either uses 2000 or the value in the column SAL if this value is greater than 2000. You can make the comparison between the two columns to verify that this function worked.

GREATEST_LB

Description: Selects from a list of labels the greatest lower bound. All values compared must be of datatype MLSLABEL or RAW MLSLABEL in order to execute properly.

Syntax

```
GREATEST_LB(label1,<label2>,...)
```

Where Used: SQL query in Trusted Oracle only

Samples

Refer to the *Trusted Oracle7 Server Administrator's Guide* for further details and examples.

LEAST

Description: Selects the smallest value from a list. All items are compared and converted to the same datatype as the first value in the list.

Syntax

```
LEAST(expression_or_value1, <value_or_expression2>,...)
```

Where Used: PL/SQL and SQL statements

Sample

The sample is a query against the standard Oracle sample database:

```
SELECT sal,LEAST(sal,2000) from emp;

SAL        LEAST(SAL,2000)
--------   ---------------
     800              800
    1600             1600
    1250             1250
    2975             2000
    1250             1250
    2850             2000
    2450             2000
    3000             2000
    5000             2000
    1500             1500
    1100             1100
     950              950
    3000             2000
    1300             1300
```

LEAST_LB

Description: Selects from a list of labels the least lower bound. All values compared must be of datatype MLSLABEL or RAW MLSLABEL in order to execute properly.

Syntax

```
LEAST_LB(label1,<label2>,...)
```

Where Used: SQL query in Trusted Oracle only

Samples

Refer to the *Trusted Oracle7 Server Administrator's Guide* for further details and examples.

NLS_CHARSET_ID

Description: Returns the NLS character set ID number associated with the NLS character set name, which must be passed in uppercase. For the `character_set_name` parameter, you can use CHAR_CS to obtain the server's database character set ID number or NCHAR_CS to return the server's national character set ID number. Refer to the *Oracle8 Server Reference Manual* for a list of over one hundred available character sets. This function is available only in Oracle version 8.

Syntax

```
NLS_CHARSET_ID(character_set_name)
```

Where Used: PL/SQL and SQL statements

Sample

This example shows the server's character set ID and national character set ID. Make sure that you have typed SET SERVEROUTPUT ON at the SQL*Plus prompt to see these values output to the screen.

```
DECLARE
     v_HOLDCHARSETID Number;  -- Holds Character Set ID
     v_HOLDNCHARSETID Number; -- Holds National Char Set ID
BEGIN
/*Calls the function NLS_CHARSET twice - The first time
  returns the server's character set ID, and the second
  time returns the server's national character set ID */
     v_HOLDCHARSETID := NLS_CHARSET_ID('CHAR_CS');
     v_HOLDNCHARSETID := NLS_CHARSET_ID('NCHAR_CS');
-- Outputs the two values to screen
DBMS_OUTPUT.PUT_LINE('The server's character set ID is: '
     || v_HOLDCHARSETID);
DBMS_OUTPUT.PUT_LINE('The server's national character set ID is: '
     || v_HOLDNCHARSETID);
END;

The server's character set ID is: 31
The server's national character set ID is: 31
```

NLS_CHARSET_NAME

Description: Returns the NLS character set name associated with the NLS character set ID passed to the function. Refer to the *Oracle8 Server Reference Manual* for a list of over one hundred available character sets. This function is available only in Oracle version 8.

Syntax

```
NLS_CHARSET_NAME(character_set_id)
```

Where Used: PL/SQL and SQL statements

Sample

This sample passes several NLS character set IDs to the NLS_CHARSET_NAME function and displays the corresponding NLS character set names associated with the ID.

```
DECLARE
    v_CHARNAME1 VARCHAR2(60);  -- Holds 1st character set name
    v_CHARNAME2 VARCHAR2(60);  -- Holds 2nd character set name
    v_CHARNAME3 VARCHAR2(60);  -- Holds 3rd character set name

BEGIN
/*Calls the function NLS_CHARSET_NAME three times with
  three different character set ID numbers */
    v_CHARNAME1 := NLS_CHARSET_NAME(174);
    v_CHARNAME2 := NLS_CHARSET_NAME(835);
    v_CHARNAME3 := NLS_CHARSET_NAME(11);
-- Outputs the three values to screen
DBMS_OUTPUT.PUT_LINE('Character Set 174 is: '
    || v_CHARNAME1);
DBMS_OUTPUT.PUT_LINE('Character Set 835 is: '
    || v_CHARNAME2);
DBMS_OUTPUT.PUT_LINE('Character Set 11 is: '
    || v_CHARNAME3);

END;

Character Set 174 is: EL8MSWIN1253
Character Set 835 is: JA16EBCDIC930
Character Set 11 is: D7DEC
```

NVL

Description: Allows you to compare to values in the function. If the first value is NULL, the second value is returned; otherwise, the first value is returned. This function is useful to check for NULL values. If the first value is NULL, you can simply return a default value from *Expression2*.

Syntax

```
NVL(Expression1,Expression2)
```

Where Used: PL/SQL and SQL statements

Sample

```
SELECT NVL('Tim',NULL) "Example1",NVL(NULL,'Expression2')
       "Example2",NVL(NULL,NULL) "Example3"
    from DUAL;

Exa Example2     E
--- ----------- -
Tim Expression2
```

SQLCODE

Description: Used primarily in the handling of errors. This function returns the error code based upon the current error. Refer to "Oracle7 Server Messages" in *Oracle7 Server SQL Reference* for a complete listing of error codes and their meanings.

Syntax

```
SQLCODE
```

Where Used: PL/SQL and SQL statements

Sample

```
CREATE OR REPLACE FUNCTION emptype (paytype CHAR)
    RETURN VARCHAR2 IS
BEGIN
    IF paytype = 'H' THEN
        RETURN 'Hourly';
    ELSIF paytype = 'S' THEN
        RETURN 'Salaried';
    ELSIF paytype = 'E' THEN
        RETURN 'Executive';
    ELSE
        RETURN 'Invalid Type';
    END IF;
EXCEPTION
    WHEN OTHERS THEN
        DBMS_OUTPUT.PUT_LINE('Your Error Code is ' || SQLCODE);
        DBMS_OUTPUT.PUT_LINE('The Errror Code Means ' ||
            SQLERRM(SQLCODE));
END emptype;
```

SQLERRM

Description: Used primarily in the handling of errors. This function returns the error message associated with the error code. You can also create your own error codes and messages. Refer to "Oracle7 Server Messages" in *Oracle7 Server SQL Reference* for a complete listing of error codes and their meanings.

Syntax

```
SQLERRM(Error_Code)
```

Where Used: PL/SQL and SQL statements

Sample

```
BEGIN
    DBMS_OUTPUT.PUT_LINE('Error message 100 means ' || SQLERRM(100));
    DBMS_OUTPUT.PUT_LINE('Error message 0 means ' || SQLERRM(0));
    DBMS_OUTPUT.PUT_LINE('Error message -1 means ' || SQLERRM(-1));
    DBMS_OUTPUT.PUT_LINE('Error message 10 means ' || SQLERRM(10));
    DBMS_OUTPUT.PUT_LINE('Error message -54 means ' || SQLERRM(-54));
    DBMS_OUTPUT.PUT_LINE('Error message -6502 means ' || SQLERRM(-6502));
    DBMS_OUTPUT.PUT_LINE('Error message -1012 means ' || SQLERRM(-1012));
END;
```

```
Error message 100 means ORA-01403: no data found
Error message 0 means ORA-0000: normal, successful completion
Error message -1 means ORA-00001: unique constraint (.) violated
Error message 10 means ORA-65526:
    Message 65526 not found;  product=RDBMS73; facility=ORA
Error message -54 means ORA-00054:
    resource busy and acquire with NOWAIT specified
Error message -6502 means ORA-06502: PL/SQL: numeric or value error
Error message -1012 means ORA-01012: not logged on
```

UID

Description: Returns the unique number associated with the user ID of the current database user.

Syntax

```
UID
```

Where Used: PL/SQL and SQL statements

Sample

```
SELECT UID from DUAL;
```

```
UID
---------
        8
```

USER

Description: Returns the username in the VARCHAR2 datatype of the current user. Similar to a WHOAMI command.

Syntax

```
USER
```

Where Used: PL/SQL and SQL statements

Sample

```
SELECT USER from DUAL;

USER
-----
SCOTT
```

USERENV

Description: Returns the information about the environment of the database logged into by the user. This function returns a VARCHAR2 value based upon the environment option desired (see Table B.6).

Syntax

```
USERENV(environment_option)
```

Table B.6. Environment options for USERENV.

Environment Option	Description of Returned Value
OSDBA	Returns true if the user has the OSDBA role enabled; otherwise, returns false.
LABEL	Returns the current session label. Valid only in Trusted Oracle. Refer to *Trusted Oracle7 Server Administrator's Guide* for more details.
LANGUAGE	Returns both the language and character set currently used in the session.
TERMINAL	Returns the value of the operating system environment.
SESSIONID	If the AUDIT_TRAIL initialization is set to true, returns the audit session identifier.
ENTRYID	If the AUDIT_TRAIL initialization is set to true, returns the available auditing entry identifier.

Where Used: PL/SQL and SQL statements

Samples

```
SELECT USERENV('TERMINAL'),USERENV('LANGUAGE') from DUAL;

USERENV('TERMINA USERENV('LANGUAGE')
---------------- ------------------------------
Windows 95 PC    AMERICAN_AMERICA.WE8ISO8859P1
```

B

VSIZE

Description: Returns number of bytes of the internal representation of the value. If the value is NULL, then NULL is returned.

Syntax

VSIZE(*Column_Name*/*Value*)

Where Used: PL/SQL and SQL statements

Samples

```
SELECT VSIZE(100),VSIZE('TIM'),VSIZE(100.3232) from DUAL;

VSIZE(100) VSIZE('TIM') VSIZE(100.3232)
---------- ------------ ---------------
         2            3               5
```

```
SELECT ENAME,VSIZE(ENAME) from EMP;

ENAME      VSIZE(ENAME)
---------- ------------
SMITH                 5
ALLEN                 5
WARD                  4
JONES                 5
MARTIN                6
BLAKE                 5
CLARK                 5
SCOTT                 5
KING                  4
TURNER                6
ADAMS                 5
JAMES                 5
FORD                  4
MILLER                6
```

INDEX

Symbols

A

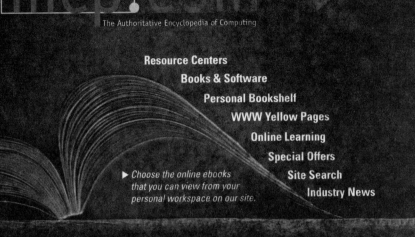

Sams Teach Yourself SQL in 21 Days, Second Edition

—Morgan, Perkins, Stephens, and Plew

Fully updated and revised to include coverage of PL/SQL and Transact-SQL, this easy-to-understand guide teaches users everything they need to know from database concepts and processes to implementing security and constructing and optimizing queries.

Q&A sections, step-by-step instructions, and review sections make learning easy and fun.

Shows how to create tables, modify data, incorporate security features, and tune the database for optimum performance. Emphasizes common database concepts, including SQL functions and queries.

Price: $39.99 USA/$56.95 CAN
ISBN: 0-672-31110-0

User Level: New–Casual
624 pages

Windows NT Troubleshooting and Configuration

—Robert Reinstein, et al.

Written for system administrators, this book details how to use Windows NT with the other components of the BackOffice suite. It includes coverage of NT design, system management, Registry modification and management, troubleshooting, Internet support, and security issues.

Teaches how to use NT with BackOffice and as a Web server with Internet Information Server and Microsoft's other Internet tools. Contains a complete troubleshooting section outlining known problems and their solutions.

The CD-ROM contains scripts and source code from the book.

Covers Windows NT 4 and BackOffice.

Price: $59.99 USA/$84.95 CAN
ISBN: 0-672-30941-6

User Level: Accomplished–Expert
1,200 pages

Sams Teach Yourself Windows NT Workstation 4 in 24 Hours

—Martin Kenley, et al.

This beginner-level book shows readers how to use the Windows 95–like environment of Windows NT Workstation. Many corporations might be migrating soon to this powerful new crash-proof Windows operating system. This book shows end users, not system administrators, the differences between Windows 3.1 and Windows NT Workstation 4.

Readers learn how to install, configure, and use Windows NT Workstation 4. They also learn how to customize the desktop, create shortcuts, and conduct peer-to-peer networking.

Covers Windows NT Workstation 4.

Price: $19.99 USA/$28.95 CAN
ISBN: 0-672-31011-2

User Level: New–Casual
486 pages

Windows NT 4 Administrator's Survival Guide

—Rick Sant'Angelo

This is the one and only survival guide an NT network administrator needs. Written by best-selling author Rick Sant'Angelo, this concise, easy-to-use guide provides all the information users need to successfully implement and maintain a Windows NT 4 Server.

This book is full of tips and notes from the author on improving performance and saving money when implementing a Windows NT Server. It serves as a reference guide to third-party products, programming logon scripts, technical terms, and commonly used NT utilities.

The CD-ROM includes demos of Windows NT applications, utilities, and source code from the book.

Covers Windows NT version 4.

Price: $49.99 USA/$70.95 CAN
ISBN: 0-672-31008-2

User Level: Accomplished–Expert
900 pages

Add to Your Sams Library Today with the Best Books for Programming, Operating Systems, and New Technologies

The easiest way to order is to pick up the phone and call

1-800-428-5331

between 9:00 a.m. and 5:00 p.m. EST.

For fastest service please have your credit card available.

ISBN	Quantity	Description of Item	Unit Cost	Total Cost
0-672-31110-0		Sams Teach Yourself SQL in 21 Days, Second Edition	$39.99	
0-672-30941-6		Windows NT Troubleshooting and Configuration (Book/CD-ROM)	$59.99	
0-672-31011-2		Sams Teach Yourself Windows NT Workstation 4 in 24 Hours	$19.99	
0-672-31008-2		Windows NT 4 Administrator's Survival Guide (Book/CD-ROM)	$49.99	
		Shipping and handling: See information below.		
		TOTAL		

Shipping and handling: $4.00 for the first book and $1.75 for each additional book. If you need to have it immediately, we can ship your order to you in 24 hours for an additional charge of approximately $18.00, and you will receive your order overnight or in two days. Overseas shipping and handling adds $2.00 per book. Prices subject to change. Call for availability and pricing information on latest editions.

201 W. 103rd Street, Indianapolis, Indiana 46290

1-800-428-5331 — Orders   1-800-835-3202 — Fax   1-800-858-7674 — Customer Service

Book ISBN 0-672-31123-2

What's on the CD-ROM

The companion CD-ROM contains all the authors' source code, examples from the book, and many third-party software products.

Windows 3.1 and Windows NT 3.5.1 Installation Instructions

1. Insert the CD-ROM into your CD-ROM drive.
2. From File Manager or Program Manager, choose File | Run.
3. Type `<drive>\SETUP.EXE` and press Enter, where `<drive>` corresponds to the drive letter of your CD-ROM. For example, if your CD-ROM is drive D:, type `D:\SETUP.EXE` and press Enter.
4. The installation creates a program named TY PLSQL. This group will contain icons to browse the CD-ROM.

Windows 95 and Windows NT 4 Installation Instructions

1. Insert the CD-ROM into your CD-ROM drive.
2. From the Windows 95 desktop, double-click the My Computer icon.
3. Double-click the icon representing your CD-ROM drive.
4. Double-click the icon titled SETUP.EXE to run the installation program.
5. The installation creates a program group named TY PLSQL. This group will contain icons to browse the CD-ROM.

NOTE

> If Windows 95 is installed on your computer and you have the AutoPlay feature enabled, the SETUP.EXE program starts automatically whenever you insert the disc into your CD-ROM drive.